The Correspondence of the Kings of Ur

Mesopotamian Civilizations

The Correspondence of the Kings of Ur

An Epistolary History of an Ancient Mesopotamian Kingdom

Piotr Michalowski

Winona Lake, Indiana
Eisenbrauns
2011

Library of Congress Cataloging-in-Publication Data

The correspondence of the kings of Ur : an epistolary history of an ancient Mesopotamian
    kingdom / [edited by] Piotr Michalowski.
      p.   cm. — (Mesopotamian civilizations ; 15)
   Includes bibliographical references and indexes.
   ISBN 978-1-57506-194-8 (hardback : alk. paper)
   1. Sumerian letters—Translations into English.   2. Ur (Extinct city)—Kings and
rulers.   3. Ur (Extinct city)—History—Sources.   I. Michalowski, Piotr, 1948–
   PJ3882.C67   2011
   899′.956008—dc22

                                         2011015402

Contents

Contents

Foreword

My work on the royal letters of the Ur III kings began many years ago as a doctoral dissertation at Yale University under the direction of W. W. Hallo. Soon after I began work on my thesis, I visited the Oriental Institute of the University of Chicago to examine the pertinent cuneiform documents that were in their care. Advised by a friend to pay my respects to the great master, A. Leo Oppenheim, I knocked on the frame of his open door and was granted an audience. After a minor exchange of pleasantries, Prof. Oppenheim asked me what I was doing at the Institute; when I told him that I was editing the Sumerian literary correspondence, he looked into my eyes and stated dismissively: "This is work for an experienced scholar, not for a beginner." This was hardly what I wanted to hear at the time, and I left in a somewhat depressed mood. I eventually finished my dissertation, and by that time I had come to appreciate the wisdom of his prescient, if troubling statement, but I never saw him again and was unable to acknowledge his advice.

Oppenheim was right, of course, and once I finished my dissertation I never wanted to touch the topic again; I was tired of the subject, the material seemed too difficult, and I could not imagine doing it justice. In addition, personal and political affairs prevented me from traveling abroad for a time, and thus I could not collate many of the sources. Over the years, colleagues would remind me of the obligation I had taken on and implored me to publish my editions of the royal letters; periodically, I returned to the subject, only to be sidetracked by other interests and obligations. In 2005, I was able to visit the Museum of the Ancient Orient in Istanbul to photograph all the relevant tablets in that collection, and this opportunity spurred me on to make a serious attempt to finish this book. The final product bears little resemblance to my original dissertation and I therefore decided to rename it, to distinguish it from the unpublished "Royal Correspondence of Ur" (RCU), which has, in photocopy, often been cited in the literature. As I send this out into the world, I still hear Oppenheim's words in my head and worry that they may continue to apply to this difficult material, the only large body of Sumerian literary prose that we possess at present.

This book is divided into two parts: an analytical section, and one that contains the text editions. For practical reasons, I have used different citation conventions for each: in the first part, scholarly works are referred to according to the social science format, but in the commentaries to the text editions, which will only be

used by philologists, I use standard familiar Assyriological abbreviations as listed by
the Cuneiform Digital Library Initiative (CDLI) and used in the Database of Neo-
Sumerian Texts (BDTNS). Within the narrative, CKU items are cited according to
the abbreviations assigned to them in the letter list, in tandem with their consecutive number; thus, the first letter, Aradmu to Šulgi 1, is referred to as Aršl (1). The
new labeling and numbering replaces the system used for the letters decades ago in
RCU as well as the names used in ETCSL and elsewhere, and therefore a concordance between the RCU and CKU is provided on p. 246. The manuscript of this
book was finished in the fall of 2009; I have updated it, within reason, in the proof
stage, but much of the text has remained the same.

Because it has taken so long to bring this research project to a close, I am indebted to many people and to numerous institutions for support, information, scholarly materials, and generosity of spirit. First, I must thank my teachers at Yale, J. J.
Finkelstein, Harry H. Hoffner, Richard Ellis, and above all, William W. Hallo, who
asked me to take on this topic, generously mentored me, and directed my thesis. I
could never have completed the work without fellowship support from the National
Endowment for the Humanities and from the University of Michigan. I am also be-
holden to the Committee on Mesopotamian Civilization of the American Schools
of Oriental Research for allocating funds from the Nies Trust to cover editorial work
on this volume.

I am grateful to many museums for permission to collate as well as make public
unpublished cuneiform tablets and to the people in these collections who facilitated
my work and provided assistance and hospitality: The Museum of the Ancient Ori-
ent in Istanbul (Asuman Dönmez, Veysel Donbaz, Fatma Yıldız), the Louvre (Béatrice André-Salvini), The British Museum (Irving Finkel, Jon Taylor, Christopher
Walker), De Liagre Böhl Collection of Leiden University (T. J. H. Krispijn), Frau
Professor Hilprecht Collection-Jena (Manfred Krebernik), the Jonathan and Janette
Rosen tablet collection at Cornell University (David I. Owen), the Babylonian
Section of the University Museum, Philadelphia (Steve Tinney, Åke W. Sjöberg,
Erle Leichty), the Yale Babylonian Collection (W. W. Hallo, Ulla Kasten, Benja-
min R. Foster), the Ashmolean Museum (Roger Moorey, Kathrine Wodehouse, Jack
Green), the Oriental Institute Museum (John A. Brinkman, Walter Farber), the
Tehran Museum (Mohammad R. Kargar), the Phoebe A. Hearst Museum of Anthro-
pology, University of California, Berkeley (Ann Kilmer, Leslie Freund, Alicja Egbert,
Niek Veldhuis), the Schøyen Collection, Oslo (Martin Schøyen), the Andrews Uni-
versity Archaeological Museum (Constance Gane), and the Cotsen Collection (Ivy
Trent, Lloyd E. Cotsen).

Tablets from the British Museum are published with permission of the Trustees
of the British Museum. The Uruk tablet is published with the permission of Dr.
Margarete van Ess, Deutsches Archäologisches Institut - Orient-Abteilung, Uruk-
Archiv. Photographs of texts from the Louvre Museum are published with permission
of Dr. Béatrice André-Salvini, Conservateur general, Directeur du department des
Antiquités Orientales, Musée du Louvre. Tablets from the Yale Babylonian Collec-

tion are published by permission of Prof. Benjamin R. Foster, Curator of the Yale Babylonian Collection. Tablets from the Babylonian Section of the University Museum, Philadelphia are published with permission of Prof. Steve Tinney, Associate Curator-in-Charge of the Babylonian Section. Tablets from Jena are published with the permission of Prof. Dr. Manfred Krebernik, Curator of the Frau Professor Hilprecht Collection of Babylonian Antiquities, Friedrich Schiller University, Jena. Texts from the Tablet Collection of the Oriental Institute, Chicago are published with the permission of Prof. Walter Farber, Curator. The copy and photograph of the Isin tablet is published by permission of Prof. Dr. Claus Wilcke and Prof. Dr. Berthold Hrouda. Photographs of tablets from the Phoebe A. Hearst Museum of Anthropology, Berkeley, are published with permission of the Phoebe A. Hearst Museum of Anthropology and the Regents of the University of California. The photographs of tablets from the Cotsen Collection are published with the permission of the UCLA Library Special Collections; photography courtesy Lloyd Cotsen. Photographs from the Schøyen Collection are published by permission of the Schøyen Collection, Oslo and London. The Cornell University, Carl A. Kroch Library tablet is published by permission of Prof. David I. Owen, Curator of Tablet Collections. The photograph of the tablet from the De Liagre Böhl Collection is published by permission of its owner The Netherlands Institute for The Near East (NINO), Leiden, The Netherlands. Photographs of tablets from the Istanbul Archaeology Museums (İstanbul Arkeoloji Müzesi) are published with the permission of the Director Zeynep Kızıltan and the assistance of Asuman Dönmez, director of the Archive of Documents with Cuneiform Inscriptions (Çiviyazılı Belgeler Arşivi). The photograph of the tablet in the Tehran National Museum is published with the permission of Mrs. Zahra Jafarmohammadi, now the Ex-Curator of Central Treasury of the National Museum of Iran. All photographs published herein are subject to copyright and cannot be reproduced without permission of the owners of the objects and of the photographers.

Many other friends and colleagues have helped me in his undertaking over the years, providing advice, support, information, photographs, hand copies, and good fellowship; I thank them all: Robert Mc. Adams, Jeremy Black, Harold Borkin, Nicole Brisch, Miguel Civil, Jerrold S. Cooper, Parsa Daneshmand, Daniel A. Foxvog, Alhena Gadotti, Andrew George, N. Ilgi Gercek, Alexandra Kleinerman, Renee Gallery Kovacs, M. Ghelichkhan, Lisa Kinney-Bajwa, Manfred Krebernik, Marie-Christine Ludwig, Peter Machinist, M. Malyeri, Catherine Mittermayer, Manuel Molina, Andreas Müller-Karpe, Jeremy Peterson, Eleanor Robson, Aaron Shaffer, Marcel Sigrist, Steve Tinney, Piotr Steinkeller, Matthew W. Stolper, Margarete van Ess, Konrad Volk, Claus Wilcke, Henry T. Wright, Norman Yoffee, Richard L. Zettler, and others.

I am profoundly indebted to Jerry Cooper for his friendship and help over the years but, more specifically, for his firm and insightful editorial hand. He was kind enough to accept this manuscript for publication, encourage its completion, and his comments on the draft made me rethink many faulty assumptions. I am equally indebted to Wolfgang Heimpel, who also served as a reader of the book and offered much important learned advice. Robert McAdams, Henry T. Wright, and Norman Yoffee read some chapters and offered valuable comments, for which I am most grateful; Wright's wise insights have been particularly helpful. I thank Laura Culbertson and Gina Konstantopoulos for reference checking, helping with indexes, and other editorial assistance. I am indebted to Kay Clahassey of the University of Michigan Museum of Anthropology for her artistry in preparing the maps. I must also express my full gratitude to Billie Jean Collins for years of friendship, collaboration, and collegiality; her copyediting, indexing and academic skills very much helped make this book possible. Many thanks are due to Jim Eisenbraun for agreeing to publish this work, for his excellent editorial assistance, for his diligence, and for his patience in seeing it through to press. I am also indebted to all the other members of his publishing company for first-rate professional work.

Most of all, I must thank my wife Deanna Relyea for her love and patience, my small but intense family, and the grandkids, Levi, Josephine, Jamisen, Nicholas, Charlie, and Jeremy for making it all worthwhile.

Abbreviations

A	tablets in the collections of the Oriental Institute, University of Chicago
Aa	lexical series á A = *nâqu*
AAICAP	*Archives administratives et inscriptions cunéiformes: Ashmolean Museum, Bodleian Collection, Oxford*, by J-P. Grégoire. Paris: Paul Geuthner, 1996.
AbB	Altbabylonische Briefe in Umschrift und Übersetzung
AEM	*Archives épistolaires de Mari*
AfO	*Archiv für Orientforschung*
AHw	*Akkadisches Handwörterbuch*, by W. von Soden. 3 vols. Wiesbaden, Harrassowitz, 1959–1981.
AJSL	*American Journal of Semitic Languages and Literatures*
Ali, SL	*Sumerian Letters: Two Collections from the Old Babylonian Schools*, by F. A. Ali. Ph.D. Dissertation, University of Pennsylvania, 1964.
Alster, *Proverbs*	*Proverbs of Ancient Sumer: The World's Earliest Proverb Collections*, by B. Alster. Bethesda, MD: CDL, 1997.
Alster, *Wisdom*	*The Wisdom of Ancient Sumer*, by B. Alster. Bethesda, MD: CDL, 2005.
Amorites	*The Amorites of the Ur III Period*, by G. Buccellati. Naples: Istituto Orientale di Napoli, 1966.
ANL	*Ancillary Nippur Letters*
ANN	tablets in the collections of the Ashmolean Museum, Oxford (formerly Ashm.)
AnOr	*Analecta Orientalia*
AnSt	*Anatolian Studies*
Antagal	lexical series antagal = *šaqû*
AO	tablets in the collections of the Musée du Louvre
AoF	*Altorientalische Forschungen*
AOAT	Alter Orient und Altes Testament
AOS	American Oriental Series
ARA	*Annual Reviews of Anthropology*
ARES	Archivi reali di Ebla. Studi
ARM	Archives royales de Mari
ARMT	*Archives royales de Mari, traduction*. Paris, 1950–
Arnaud, *Emar VI*	*Recherches au pays d'Aštata: Emar 6/1–4. Textes sumériens et accadiens*, by Daniel Arnaud. Paris: Éditions Recherche sur les Civilisations, 1986.

ArOr	*Archiv Orientalní*
ARRIM	*Annual Review of the Royal Inscriptions of Mesopotamia Project*
AS	Assyriological Studies
ASJ	*Acta Sumerologica*
Attinger, *Eléments*	*Eléments de linguistique sumérienne: la construction de du$_{11}$/e/di "dire,"* by P. Attinger. Fribourg: Editions universitaires / Göttingen: Vandenhoeck & Ruprecht, 1993.
AUCT	Andrews University Cuneiform Texts
AUCT 1	*Neo-Sumerian Account Texts in the Horn Archaeological Museum*, by M. Sigrist. Andrews University Cuneiform Texts 1, Berrien Springs: Andrews University Press, 1984.
AUCT 2	*Neo-Sumerian Account Texts in the Horn Archaeological Museum*, by M. Sigrist. Andrews University Cuneiform Texts 2, Berrien Springs: Andrews University Press, 1988.
AuOr	*Aula Orientalis*
AUWE	Ausgrabungen in Uruk-Warka. Endberichte / Deutsches Archäologisches Institut, Abteilung Baghdad. Mainz: von Zabern, 1987–
Babyl	*Babyloniaca*
BaM	*Baghdader Mitteilungen*
BBVO	Berliner Beiträge zum Vorderen Orient
BCT 1	*Catalogue of Cuneiform Tablets in Birmingham City Museum 1*, by P. J. Watson. Warminster: Philip & Aries, 1986.
BCT 2	*Catalogue of Cuneiform Tablets in Birmingham City Museum 2*, by P. J. Watson. Warminster: Philip & Aries, 1993.
BDTNS	Base de Datos de Textos Neosumerios. Online: http://bdtns.filol.csic.es
BE	The Babylonian Expedition of the University of Pennsylvania
BibMes	Bibliotheca Mesopotamica
BIN	Babylonian Inscriptions in the Collection of J. B. Nies
BiOr	*Bibliotheca Orientalis*
BM	tablets in the collections of the British Museum
BMAC	Bactria-Margiana Archaeological Complex
BOAM	*Bulletin of the Ancient Orient Museum*
BPOA	Biblioteca del Proximo Oriente Antiguo
BSA	*Bulletin on Sumerian Agriculture*
BSOAS	*Bulletin of the School of Oriental and African Studies*
CAD	*The Assyrian Dictionary of the University of Chicago*
Cavigneaux, *Uruk*	*Uruk, Altbabylonische Texte aus dem Planquadrat Pe XVI-4/5, nach Kopien von Adam Falkenstein*, by A. Cavigneaux. AUWE 23. Mainz: von Zabern, 1996.
CBS	tablets in the collections of the University Museum of the University of Pennsylvania, Philadelphia (Catalog of the Babylonian Section)
CDLB	*Cuneiform Digital Library Bulletin*. Online: http://cdli.ucla.edu/pubs/cdlb.html

CDLI	Cuneiform Digital Library Initiative
CDLJ	*Cuneiform Digital Library Journal.* Online: http://cdli.ucla.edu/pubs/cdlj.html
CH	Code of Hammurabi
Charpin, *Archives*	*Archives familiales et propriété privée en Babylonie ancienne: étude des documents de "Tell Sifr,"* by D. Charpin. Geneva, Librairie Droz, 1980.
Charpin, *Lire*	*Lire et écrire à Babylone*, by D. Charpin. Paris: Presses Universitaires de France, 2008.
Charpin, OBO 160/4	*Die altbabylonische Zeit*, by D. Charpin, D. O. Edzard, and M. Stol. OBO 160/4. Fribourg: Academic Press; Göttingen: Vandenhoeck & Ruprecht, 2004.
CHEU	*Contribution à l'histoire économique d'Umma*, by G. Conteau. Bibliothèque de l'école des Hautes Études, sciences philologiques et historiques 119. Paris 1915.
Civil, Forerunners	The Forerunners of *Marû* and *Ḫamṭu* in Old Babylonian. Pp. 63–71 in *Riches Hidden in Secret Places: Ancient Near Eastern Studies in Memory of Thorkild Jacobsen*, ed. T. Abusch. Winona Lake, IN: Eisenbrauns, 2002.
Civil, *Instructions*	*The Farmer's Instructions: A Sumerian Agricultural Manual*, by M. Civil. Sabadell: AUSA, 1994.
CKU	*Correspondence of the Kings of Ur*
CM	Cuneiform Monographs
CM 33	*Cuneiform Inscriptions in the Collection of the Bible Lands Museum Jerusalem: The Old Babylonian Inscriptions*, edited by J. Goodnick Westenholz and A. Westenholz. CM 33. Leiden: Brill, 2006.
Cooper, *Agade*	*The Curse of Agade*, by J. S. Cooper. Baltimore: Johns Hopkins University Press, 1983.
Cooper, Death	Apodotic Death and the Historicity of "Historical" Omens. Pp. 99–105 in *Death in Mesopotamia*, ed. Bendt Alster. Mesopotamia 8. Copenhagen: Akademisk Forlag.
Cornell	tablets in the collections of the Jonathan and Janette Rosen tablet collection at Cornell University
Cotsen	tablets in the collections of the Cotsen Collection (now at UCLA)
Crozer	tablets in the collections of the Crozer Theological Seminary (dispersed)
CST	*Catalogue of Sumerian Tablets in the John Rylands Library*, by T. Fish. Manchester, The Manchester University Press, and the Librarian, the John Rylands Library, 1932.
CT	Cuneiform Texts from Babylonian Tablets in the British Museum
CTMMA	Cuneiform Texts in the Metropolitan Museum of Art
CUSAS	Cornell University Studies in Assyriology and Sumerology
DAS	*Documents administratifs sumériens, provenant du site de Tello et conservés au Musée du Louvre*, by B. Lafont. Paris, Éditions Recherche sur les Civilizations, 1985.

DP — *Documents présargoniques*, by M. F. Allotte de la Fuÿe. Paris: E. Leroux, 1908–1920.

Ea — lexical series ea A = *nâqu*

ECTJ — *Early Cuneiform Texts in Jena: Pre-Sargonic and Sargonic Documents from Nippur and Fara in the Hilprecht-Sammlung vorderasiatischer Altertümer, Institut fur Altertumswissenschaften der Friedrich-Schiller-Universität, Jena*, by A. Westenholz. Det Kongelige Danske Videnskabernes Selskab Historisk-Filosofiske Skrifter 7, 3. Copenhagen: Munksgaard, 1995.

ED — Early Dynastic

Edzard, *Grammar* — *Sumerian Grammar*, by D. O. Edzard. HdO 1/71. Leiden: Brill, 2003.

ETCSL — Electronic Text Corpus of Sumerian Literature. Online: http://www-etcsl.orient.ox.ac.uk

FAOS — Freiburger altorientalische Studien

FAOS 15/2 — *Altsumerische Verwaltungstexte aus Lagas, Teil 2*, Die altsumerischen Wirtschaftsurkunden aus amerikanischen Sammlungen, by G. Selz. 2 vols. FAOS 15/2. Stuttgart: Steiner, 1992.

FAOS 19 — *Die sumerischen und akkadischen Briefe des III. Jahrtausends aus der Zeit vor der III. Dynastie von Ur*, by B. Kienast and K. Volk, FAOS 19. Stuttgart: Steiner, 1995

FS Adams — *Festschrift in Honor of Robert McCormick Adams*, ed. E. Stone. Los Angeles: Cotsen Institute of Archaeology.

Fs. Baumgartner — *Hebräische Wortforschung: Festschrift zum 80. Geburtstag von Walter Baumgartner*, ed. B. Hartmann. Leiden, Brill, 1967.

FS Biggs — *Studies Presented to Robert D. Biggs, June 4, 2000*, ed. M. T. Roth, W. Farber, M. W. Stolper, and P. von Bechtolsheim. Chicago: The Oriental Institute of the University of Chicago, 2007.

FS Civil — *Velles Paraules: Ancient Near Eastern Studies in Honor of Miguel Civil on the Occasion of His Sixty-fifth Birthday*, ed. P. Michalowski, P. Steinkeller, E. C. Stone, and R. L. Zettler. Barcelona: Editorial AUSA, 1991.

FS Hallo — *The Tablet and the Scroll: Near Eastern Studies in Honor of William W. Hallo*, ed. M. E. Cohen et al. Bethesda, MD: CDL, 1993.

FS Houwink ten Cate — *Ancient Near Eastern Studies Presented to Philo H. J. Houwink ten Cate on the Occasion of His 65th Birthday*, edited by T. P. J. van den Hout and J. de Roos. Leiden: Nederlands Instituut voor het Nabije Oosten, 1995.

FS Kienast — *Festschrift für Burkhart Kienast zu seinem 70. Geburtstage dargebracht von Freunden, Schülern und Kollegen*, ed., G. J. Selz. AOAT 274. Münster: Ugarit-Verlag, 2003.

FS Kraus — *Zikir Šumim: Assyriological Studies Presented to F. R. Kraus*, edited by G. van Driel. Leiden: Brill, 1982.

FS Lambert — *Wisdom, Gods and Literature: Studies in Assyriology in Honour of W. G. Lambert*, ed. A. R. George and I. L. Finkel. Winona Lake, IN: Eisenbrauns, 2000.

FS Leichty	*If a Man Builds a Joyful House: Assyriological Studies in Honor of Erle Verdun Leichty*, ed. Ann K. Guinan, et al. Leiden: Brill, 2006.
FS Oppenheim	*Studies Presented to A. Leo Oppenheim, June 7, 1964*. Chicago: The Oriental Institute, 1964.
FS Reiner	*Language, Literature, and History: Philological and Historical Studies Presented to Erica Reiner*, ed. F. Rochberg-Halton. AOS 67. New Haven: American Oriental Society, 1987.
FS Renger	*Munuscula Mesopotamica: Festschrift für Johannes Renger*, ed. B. Böck, E. Cancik-Kirschbaum, and T. Richter. AOAT 267. Münster: Ugarit Verlag, 1999.
FS Sjöberg	*DUMU E$_2$-DUB-BA-A: Studies in Honor of Åke W. Sjöberg*, ed. H. Behrens, D. Loding, and M. T. Roth. Philadelphia: University Museum, 1989.
Fs. Veenhof	*Veenhof Anniversary Volume: Studies Presented to Klaas R. Veenhof on the Occasion of his Sixty-fifth Birthday*, ed. W. H. van Soldt et al. Leiden, Nederlands Instituut voor het Nabije Oosten, 2001.
FS Wilcke	*Literatur, Politik und Recht in Mesopotamien: Festschrift für Claus Wilcke*, ed. W. Sallaberger, K. Volk and A. Zgoll. OBC 14. Wiesbaden: Harrassowitz, 2003.
FTS	fat-tailed sheep
HANES	History of the Ancient Near East Studies
HANES 5	*Akkad. The First World Empire: Structure, Ideology, Traditions*, ed. M. Liverani. HANES 5. Padova: Sargon 1993.
HdO	Handbuch der Orientalistik
Hg	Lexical series HAR.gud = *imru* = *ballu*
Hh	Lexical series HAR.ra = *ḫubullu*
HJAS	*Harvard Journal of Asiatic Studies*
HLC	*Haverford Library Collection of Cuneiform Tablets or Documents from the Temple Archives of Telloh*, by G. Barton. Philadelphia: John C. Winston, 1905–14.
HMA	tablets in the collections of the Phoebe A. Hearst Museum of Anthropology, University of California at Berkeley
HS	tablets in the collections of the Frau Professor Hilprecht-Collection of Babylonian Antiquities, Jena
HSAO	Heidelberger Studien zum Alten Orient
HSAO 1	*Heidelberger Studien zum Alten Orient. Adam Falkenstein zum (60. Geburtstag) 17. Sept. 1966*, edited by D. O. Edzard. HSAO 1. Wiesbaden: Harrassowitz, 1967.
HSM	tablets in the collections of the Harvard Semitic Museum
HSS	Harvard Semitic Studies
HTR	*Harvard Theological Review*
HUCA	*Hebrew Union College Annual*
IB	tablets excavated at Ishan Bahriyat (Isin), in the collections of the Iraq Museum in Baghdad
IM	tablets in the collections of the Iraq Museum in Baghdad
ISET	*Istanbul Arkeoloji Müzelerinde bulunan Sumer edebî tablet ve parçaları*

ISET 1   *Istanbul Arkeoloji Müzelerinde bulunan Sumer edebî tablet ve parçaları – I (Sumerian Literary Tablets and Fragments in the Archaeological Museum of Istanbul – I)*, by Muazzez Çığ and Hatice Kızılyay. ISET 1. Ankara: Türk Tarih Kurumu Basımevi, 1969.

ISET 2   *Istanbul Arkeoloji Müzelerinde bulunan Sumer edebî tablet ve parçaları – II (Sumerian Literary Tablets and Fragments in the Archaeological Museum of Istanbul – II)*, by Samuel Noah Kramer. ISET 2. Ankara: Türk Tarih Kurumu Basımevi, 1976.

IT   Inanna Temple (Nippur)

ITT   Inventaire des tablettes de Tello conservées au Musée Impérial Ottoman

JA   *Journal Asiatique*

Jacobsen Memorial   *Sumerological Studies in Honor of Thorkild Jacobsen on His Seventieth Birthday June 7, 1974*, ed. S. J. Lieberman. AS 20. Chicago: The Oriental Institute, 1976.

Jaques, *Vocabulaire*   *Le vocabulaire des sentiments dans les textes sumériens. Recherche sur le lexique sumérien et akkadien*, by M. Jaques. AOAT 332. Münster, Ugarit-Verlag, 2006.

JAOS   *Journal of the American Oriental Society*

JAR   *Journal of Anthropological Research*

JCS   *Journal of Cuneiform Studies*

JCSSup   *Journal of Cuneiform Studies* Supplements Series

JEOL   *Jaarbericht Ex Oriente Lux*

JESHO   *Journal of the Economic and Social History of the Orient*

Jeyes, OBE   *Old Babylonian Extispicy: Omen Texts in the British Museum*, by U. Jeyes. Istanbul: Nederlands Historisch-Archaeologisch Institut te Istanbul, 1989.

JFA   *Journal of Field Archaeology*

JHS   *Journal of Hellenic Studies*

JMS   *Journal of Magan Studie*

JNES   *Journal of Near Eastern Studies*

JSS   *Journal of Semitic Studies*

JWP   *Journal of World Prehistory*

Karahashi, *Verbs*   *Sumerian Compound Verbs with Body-Part Terms*, by F. Karahashi. Ph.D. Dissertation, The University of Chicago, 2000.

Koch-Westenholz, BLO   *Babylonian Liver Omens: The Chapters Manzāzu, Padānu and Pān Tākalti of the Babylonian Extispicy Series Mainly from Assurbanipal's Library*, by U. Koch-Westenholz. Copenhagen: Museum Tusculanum Press, 2000.

Kramer, *The Sumerians*   *The Sumerians: Their History, Culture, and Character*, by S. N. Kramer. Chicago, University of Chicago Press, 1963.

Krecher, SKLy   *Sumerische Kultlyrik*, by Joachim Krecher. Wiesbaden: Harrassowitz, 1966.

Kutscher, Brockmon 1   *The Brockmon Tablets at the University of Haifa: Royal Inscriptions*, by Raphael Kutscher. Haifa: Haifa University Press, 1989.

Lafont, *Documents*	*Documents administratifs sumériens provenant du site de Tello et conservés au Musée du Louvre,* by B. Lafont. Paris: Éditions Recherche sur les Civilisations, 1985.
Lambert and Millard, *Atra-ḫasīs*	*Atra-ḫasīs: The Babylonian Story of the Flood,* by W. G. Lambert and A. R. Millard, Oxford: Claredon, 1969; repr., Winona Lake, IN: Eisenbrauns, 1999.
LAPO	Littératures anciennes du Proche-Orient
LAPO 16–18	*Les documents épistolaires du palais de Mari,* by Jean Marie Durand. LAPO 16–18. Paris: Cerf, 1997–.
MAD	Materials for the Assyrian Dictionary
MAOG	*Mitteilungen der Altorientalischen Gesellschaft*
M.A.R.I.	*MARI, Annales de Recherches Interdisciplinaires*
MC	Mesopotamian Civilizations
MCS	Manchester Cuneiform Studies
MDAI	*Mitteilungen des Deutschen Archäologischen Instituts*
MDP	Mémoires de la Délégation en Perse
Mélanges Birot	*Miscellanea Babylonica. Mélanges offerts à Maurice Birot,* ed. J.-M. Durand and J.-R. Kupper. Paris: Éditions Recherche sur les Civilisations, 1985.
Michalowski, LEM	*Letters from Early Mesopotamia,* by Piotr Michalowski. Atlanta, GA: Scholars Press, 1993.
Michalowski, Royal Letters	Royal Letters of the Ur III Kings, by P. Michalowski. Pp. 75–80 in *The Ancient Near East,* ed. M. Chavalas. Blackwell's Sourcebooks in Ancient History. Oxford: Blackwell.
Mittermayer, aBZL	*Altbabylonische Zeichenliste der sumerisch-literarischen Texte,* by C. Mittermayer. Fribourg: Academic Press; Göttingen: Vandenhoeck & Ruprecht, 2006.
MM	tablets in the collections of the Abbey of Montserrat
MS	tablets in the collections of the Schøyen Collection, Oslo
MSL	Materialien zum sumerischen Lexikon/Materials for the Sumerian Lexicon
MVN	Materiali per il vocabulario neosumerico
N	tablets in the collections of the University Museum of the University of Pennsylvania, Philadelphia (Nippur)
N.A.B.U.	*Nouvelles Assyriologiques Bréves et Utilitaires*
NATN	*Neo-Sumerian Archival Texts Primarily from Nippur,* by D. I. Owen. Winona Lake, IN: Eisenbrauns, 1982.
NBGT	Neo-Babylonian Grammatical Texts
Ni.	tablets excavated at Nippur, in the collections of the Archaeological Museum of Istanbul
Nigga	lexical series niggur = *makkūru*
Nik. 2	*Dokumenty khozaistvennoij otčetnosti drevneijšeij epokhi Chaldei iz sobrania N.P. Lichačeva čast' II: Epokha dinastii Agade i epokha dinastii Ura,* by M. V. Nikol'ski. Drevnosti Vostochnya 5. Moscow: Tipografija G. Lissnera, 1915.
Nisaba	Nisaba. Studi Assiriologici Messinesi

NRVN   *Neusumerische Rechts- und Verwaltungsurkunden aus Nippur*, I, by
              M. Çığ and H. Kızilyay. Ankara: Türk Tarih Kurumu Basımevi,
              1965.
NSGU II   *Die Neusumeriche Gerichtsurkunden II*, by Adam Falkenstein.
              Bayerische Akademie der Wissenschaften (München) Kommission
              zur Erschliessung von Keilschrifttexten, Bayerische Akademie der
              Wissenschaften (München) Philosophisch-Historische Klasse.
              München: Bayerische Akademie der Wissenschaften, 1956.
NT   field numbers of tablets excavated at Nippur by the Oriental
              Institute and other institutions
NYPL   *Les tablettes cuneiformes de l'époque d'Ur de la New York Public
              Library*, by H. Sauren. Louvain-la-Neuve: Université catholique de
              Louvain, Institut orientaliste, 1978.
OB   Old Babylonian
OBC   Orientalia Biblica et Christiana
OBGT   Old Babylonian Grammatical Texts
OBO   Orbis Biblicus et Orientalis
OBTR   *Old Babylonian Texts from Tell al Rimah*, by S. Dalley, C. Walker,
              and J. D. Hawkins. London: British School of Archaeology in Iraq,
              1976.
OECT   Oxford Editions of Cuneiform Texts
OECT 5   *Sumerian Literary Texts in the Ashmolean Museum*, by O. R. Gurney
              and S. N. Kramer. OECT 5. Oxford: Clarendon, 1976.
OIP   Oriental Institute Publications
OIS   Oriental Institute Seminars
OLP   *Orientalia Lovaniensia Periodica*
OLZ   *Orientalistische Literaturzeitung*
Ontario 1   *The Administration at Drehem*, by M. Sigrist. Neo-Sumerian Texts
              from the Royal Ontario Museum 1. Bethesda, MD: CDL Press,
              1995.
OPBF   Occasional Publications of the Babylonian Fund
OrNS   *Orientalia, Nova Series*
OrAn   *Oriens Antiquus*
OrSP   *Orientalia, Series Prior*
OSP   Old Sumerian and Old Akkadian Texts in Philadelphia
OSP1   *Old Sumerian and Old Akkadian Texts in Philadelphia Chiefly
              from Nippur. Part One: Literary and Lexical Texts and the Earliest
              Administrative Documents from Nippur*, by A. Westenholz. OSP 1.
              BibMes 1. Malibu: Undena, 1975.
OSP 2   *Old Sumerian and Old Akkadian Texts in Philadelphia, Part Two: The
              'Akkadian' Texts, and the Enlilmaba Texts, and the Onion Archive*,
              by A. Westenholz. OSP 2. Carsten Niebuhr Institute Publications
              3, Copenhagen: The Carsten Niebuhr Institute for Ancient Near
              Eastern Studies, 1987.
PBS   Publications of the Babylonian Section, the University Museum,
              Philadelphia

PDT 1	*Die Puzriš-Dagan-Texte der Istanbuler Archäologischen Museen Teil I: Nrr. 1–725*, by M. Çığ, H. Kızilyay, and A. Salonen. Helsinki: Soumalaisen kirjallisuuden kirpajaino Oy, 1954.
PDT 2	*Die Puzriš-Dagan-Texte der Istanbuler Archäologischen Museen II: Nr. 726–1379*, by F. Yıldız and T. Gomi. Freiburger Altorientalische Studien 16. Stuttgart: Franz Steiner, 1988.
PH	private house
PIHANS	Publications de l'Institut historique-archéologique néerlandais de Stamboul
Potts, *Civilization*	*Mesopotamian Civilization: The Material Foundations*, by D. T. Potts. Ithaca, Cornell University Press, 1997.
PPAC 1	*Sargonic Inscriptions from Adab*, by Y. Zhi. Chanchun, Institute for the Study of Ancient Civilizations, 1989.
PRAK	*Premières recherches archéologiques à Kich*, by H. de Genouillac. Paris: Champion, 1924–1925.
Princeton 1	*Tablettes du Princeton Theological Seminary: Époque d'Ur III*, by M. Sigrist. Occasional Publications of the Samuel Noah Kramer Fund 10. Philadelphia: The Samuel Noah Kramer Fund, 1990.
Princeton 2	*Tablets from the Princeton Theological Seminary. Ur III Period. Part 2*, by M. Sigrist. Occasional Publications of the Samuel Noah Kramer Fund 18, Philadelphia: The Samuel Noah Kramer Fund, 2008.
PSD	Pennsylvania Sumerian Dictionary Project. Online: http://psd .museum.upenn.edu/epsd/nepsd-frame.html
RA	*Revue d'assyriologie et d'archéologie orientale*
RCU	*The Royal Correspondence of Ur*, by Piotr Michalowski. Ph.D. Dissertation, Yale University.
Rev. Sem.	*Revue Semitique*
RGTC	Répertoire Géographique des Textes Cunéiformes
RIME	Royal Inscriptions of Mesopotamia, Early Period
RLA	*Reallexikon der Assyriologie*
Robson, *Mathematics*	*Mesopotamian Mathematics 2100-1600 BC: Technical Constants in Bureaucracy and Education*, by E. Robson. Oxford, Oxford University Press, 1999.
Robson, Metrology	More than Metrology: Mathematics Education in an Old Babylonian Scribal School, by E. Robson. Pp. 325–66 in *Under One Sky: Mathematics and Astronomy in the Ancient Near East*, ed. J. M. Steele and A. Imhausen. Münster, Ugarit-Verlag, 2002.
Rochester	*Documents from Tablet Collections in Rochester, New York*, by M. Sigrist. Bethesda: CDL, 1991.
RT	*Recueil de travaux relatifs à la philologie et à l'archéologie égyptiennes et assyriennes*
RTC	*Recueil de tablettes chaldéennes*, by F. Thureau-Dangin. Paris: E. Leroux, 1903.
Sallaberger, *Kalendar*	*Der kultische Kalender der Ur III-Zeit*, by W. Sallaberger. Berlin, de Gruyter, 1993.
SANTAG	SANTAG. Arbeiten und Untersuchungen zur Keilschriftkunde

SAOC   Studies in Ancient Oriental Civilization
SAT 1   *Texts from the British Museum*, by M. Sigrist. Sumerian Archival
                        Texts 1. Bethesda: CDL, 1993.
SAT 2   *Texts from the Yale Babylonian Collections*, by M. Sigrist. Sumerian
                        Archival Texts 2. Bethesda: CDL, 2000.
SAT 3   *Texts from the Yale Babylonian Collections II*, by M. Sigrist. Sumerian
                        Archival Texts 3, Bethesda: CDL, 2000.
SCIAMVS   *Sources and Commentaries in Exact Sciences*
SEEJ   *Slavonic and East European Journal*
SEL   *Studi Epigrafici e Linguistici sul Vicino Oriente Antico*
SEpM   *Sumerian Epistolary Miscellany*
SET   *Sumerian Economic Texts from the Third Ur Dynasty. A Catalogue and
                        Discussion of Documents from Various Collections*, by T. B. Jones and
                        N. Snyder. Minneapolis: University of Minnesota, 1961.
Si.   field numbers of tablets excavated at Sippar, in the collections of
                        the Archaeological Museum of Istanbul
Sjöberg, *Nanna-Suen*   *Der Mondgott Nanna-Suen in der sumerischen Überlieferung*, by Å. W.
                        Sjöberg. Stockholm: Almquist & Wiksell, 1960.
SLFN   *Sumerian Literary Fragments from Nippur*, by J. W. Heimerdinger.
                        Occasional Publications of the Babylonian Fund 4. Philadelphia:
                        The University Museum, 1979.
SCT   *Smith College Tablets: 110 Cuneiform Texts Selected from the College
                        Collection*, by C. H. Gordon. Smith College Studies in History 38.
                        Northampton: Smith College, 1952.
SMM   tablets in the collections of the Science Museum, University of
                        Minnesota
SNAT   *Selected Neo-Sumerian Administrative Texts from the British Museum*,
                        by T. Gomi. Abiko: The Research Institute, Chuo-Gakuin
                        University, 1990.
Starr, *Rituals of the Diviner*   *The Rituals of the Diviner*, by I. Starr. Malibu, 1983.
Steinkeller, *Sale Documents*   *Sale Documents of the Ur III Period*, by Piotr Steinkeller.
                        Stuttgart: Steiner, 1989.
Stol, OBO 160/4   Wirtschaft und Gesselschaft in Altbabylonischer Zeit, by
                        M. Stol. Pp. 643–975 in *Mesopotamien. Die altbabylonische Zeit*,
                        by D. Charpin, D. O. Edzard, and M Stol. OBO 160/4. Friburg:
                        Academic Press; Göttingen: Vandenhoeck & Ruprecht, 2004.
STVC   *Sumerian Texts of Varied Contents*, by Edward Chiera. OIP 16.
                        Chicago: The University of Chicago Press, 1934.
Sullivan, *Sumerian and Akkadian Sentence Structure*   *Sumerian and Akkadian Sentence
                        Structure in Old Babylonian Literary Bilingual Texts*, by B. B. Sullivan.
                        Ph. D. Dissertation, Hebrew Union College, 1979.
SumRecDreh   *Sumerian Records from Drehem*, by W. M. Nesbit. Columbia
                        University Oriental Studies 8. New York: Columbia University
                        Press, 1914.
Susa   field numbers of tablets excavated at Susa

ŠA   *Šumer et Akkad. Contribution à l'histoire de la civilisation dans la Basse-Mésopotamie*, by C-F. Jean. Paris: Paul Geuthner, 1923.

TAPS   Transactions of the American Philosophical Society

TCL   Textes cunéiformes, Musées du Louvre

TCS   Texts from Cuneiform Sources

TCS 3   *The Collection of the Sumerian Temple Hymns*, by Å. W. Sjöberg and E. Bergmann. TCS 3. Locust Valley, NY: Augustin, 1969.

TCTI 1   *Tablettes cunéiformes de Tello au Musée d'Istanbul: datant de l'époque de la IIIe Dynastie d'Ur*. Tome I. ITT II/1, 617-1038, by B. Lafont and F. Yıldız. PIHANS 65. Leiden, Nederlands Instituut voor het Nabije Oosten, 1989.

TCTI 2   *Tablettes cunéiformes de Tello au Musée d'Istanbul, datant de l'époque de la IIIe Dynastie d'Ur*. Tome II. ITT II/1, 2544–2819, 3158–4342, 4708–4714, by Bertrand Lafont and Fatma Yıldız. PIHANS 77. Leiden, Nederlands Instituut voor het Nabije Oosten, 1996.

TÉL   *Tablettes économiques de Lagash (époque d'Ur III)*, by C. Virolleaud. Cahiers de la Société asiatique 19. Paris: Société asiatique, 1968.

TIM   Texts in the Iraq Museum

Tinney, *Nippur Lament*   *The Nippur Lament: Royal Rhetoric and Divine Legitimation in the Reign of Išme-Dagan of Isin (1953–1935 B.C.)*, by S. Tinney. Occasional Publications of the Samuel Noah Kramer Fund 16. Philadelphia: The University of Pennsylvania Museum, 1996.

TLB   Tabulae Cuneiformes a F. M. Th. De Liagre Böhl collectae

TLB 3   *Sumerian Archival Texts*, by W. W. Hallo. TLB 3. Leiden, Nederlands Instituut voor het Nabije Oosten, 1963.

TMHNF   Texte und Materialien der Frau Professor Hilprecht Collection, Neue Folge

Torino 1   *Testi cuneiformi neo-sumerici da Drehem. N. 0001–0412*, by A. Archi and F. Pomponio. Catalogo del Museo Egizio di Torino 7. Milan, Istituto Editoriale Universitario, 1990.

Torino 2   *Testi Cuneiformi neo-Sumerici da Umma. NN. 0413-0723*, by A. Archi and F. Pomponio. Catalogo del Museo Egizio di Torino 8. Turin: Ministero per i bent culturali e ambientali, 1995.

Trouvaille   *La trouvaille de Dréhem. Étude avec un choix de textes de Constantinople et Bruxelles*, by H. de Génouillac. Paris: Paul Geuthner, 1911.

TRU   *Les temps des rois d'Ur. Recherches sur la société antique d'après des textes nouveaux*, by L. Legrain. Bibliothèque de l'École des Hautes Études 199. Paris, Champion, 1912.

TSA   *Tablettes sumériennes archaïques. Matériaux pour servir à l'histoire de la société sumérienne*, by H. de Génouillac. Paris: Paul Geuthner, 1909.

TSDU   *Textes sumériens de la IIIe dynastie d'Ur*, by H. Limet. Documents du Proche Orient Ancien: Epigraphie 1. Brussels: Musées Royaux d'Art et d'Histoire, 1976.

TUAT   Texte aus der Umwelt des Alten Testaments

TUT   *Tempelurkunden aus Telloh*, by G. A. Reisner. Berlin, Spemann, 1901.

Tutub   *Die Texte der Akkad-Zeit, 1. Das Dijala-Gebiet: Tutub*, by W. Sommerfeld. IMGULA 3/1. Münster: Rhema, 1999.

U.   field numbers of tablets excavated at Ur

UCP   University of California Publications in Semitic Philology

UDT   *Ur Dynasty Tablets*, by J. B. Nies. AB 25. Leipzig: Hinrichs, 1920.

UET   Ur Excavations, Texts

UF   *Ugarit-Forschungen*

ULC   *Uruk Letter Catalog*

UM   tablets in the collections of the University Museum of the University of Pennsylvania, Philadelphia

USFS   *Une saison de fouilles à Sippar*, by V. Scheil. Cairo: Imprimerie de l'Institut français d'archéologie orientale, 1902.

UTI 4   *Die Umma-Texte aus den Archaologischen Museen zu Istanbul 4*, by T. Gomi and F. Yıldız. Bethesda, MD: CDL, 1997.

UTI 5   *Die Umma-Texte aus den Archaologischen Museen zu Istanbul 5*, by T. Gomi and F. Yıldız. Bethesda, MD: CDL, 2000.

UTI 6   *Die Umma-Texte aus den Archaologischen Museen zu Istanbul 6*, by T. Gomi and F. Yıldız. Bethesda, MD: CDL, 2001.

VDI   *Vestnik Drevneij Istorii*

Veldhuis, *Elementary Education*   *Elementary Education at Nippur: The Lists of Trees and Wooden Objects*, by N. C. Veldhuis. Ph.D. Dissertation, University of Groningen, 1997.

VN   *Votivnyija nadpisi sumeriijskih praviteleij*, by V. K. Šileiijko. St. Petersburg: Tip. M. A. Aleksandrova, 1915.

VO   *Vicino Oriente*

VS   Vorderasiatische Schriftdenkmäler der (Königlichen) Museen zu Berlin

W   field numbers of tablets excavated at Uruk (Warka)

Wasserman, *Style and Form*   *Style and Form in Old Babylonian Literary Texts*, by N. Wasserman. Leiden, Styx, 2003.

Wilcke, *Early Ancient Near Eastern Law*   *Early Ancient Near Eastern Law: A History of its Beginnings: The Early Dynastic and Sargonic Periods*, by C. Wilcke. Winona Lake, Eisenbrauns, 2007.

Wilcke, *Kollationen*   *Kollationen zu den sumerischen literarischen Texten aus Nippur in der Hilprecht-Sammlung Jena*, by Claus Wilcke. Berlin: Akademie Verlag, 1976.

Wilcke, *Lugalbandaepos*   *Das Lugalbandaepos*, by C. Wilcke. Wiesbaden: Harrassowitz, 1969.

Wilson, *Education*   *Education in the Earliest Schools: Cuneiform Manuscripts in the Cotsen Collection*, by M. Wilson. Los Angeles: Cotsen Occasional Press, 2008.

WMAH	*Wirtschaftsurkunden aus der Zeit der III. Dynastie von Ur im Besitz des Musée d'Art et d'Histoire in Genf,* by Herbert Sauren. Istituto orientale di Napoli. Pubblicazioni del seminario di semitistica. Ricerche, 6. Napoli : Istituto orientale, 1969.
WO	*Die Welt des Orients*
w/n	without number
WF	*Wirtschaftstexte aus Fara,* by Anton Deimel. WVDOG 45. Berlin, J. C. Hinrichs'sche Buchhandlung, 1924.
WVDOG	Wissenschaftliche Veröffentlichungen der Deutschen Orient-Gesellschaft
WZKM	*Wiener Zeitschrift für die Kunde des Morgenlandes*
YBC	tablets in the collections of the Yale Babylonian Collection, Yale University Library
YBT	Yale Babylonian Texts
YN	Year Name
YOS	Yale Oriental Series
YOSR	Yale Oriental Series, Researches
ZVO	*Zapiski Vostočnago Otdelenija Russkago Archeologičeskago Obščestva, Petersburg*

Part 1

The Royal Correspondence
of the Ur III Kings in
Literary and Historical Perspective

Chapter 1

Introduction

This book is about the Sumerian-language letters of the kings of the Third Dynasty of Ur (2112–2004 B.C.), texts known to us through the medium of school exercises left behind by young elite students who were learning to read and write in eighteenth-century Mesopotamia. The main part of the monograph consists of editions of all twenty-four items of this literary correspondence; in the pages that follow, I will provide background material and analysis that will facilitate the further study of these intriguing letters. The preserved copies may be Old Babylonian, but the setting of these compositions—real, imaginary, or a mixture of both—lies in the time when all of Babylonia was ruled by a highly centralized territorial state with the capital located at the city of Ur.[1]

This short century of Ur's hegemony was only the second time that anyone had managed to bring the disparate city-states of southern Mesopotamia under one banner, about a hundred years or so after the collapse of the previous experiment of this kind under the kings of the Sargonic Dynasty. The founder of the new state, Ur-Namma (2112–2095 B.C.) and his long-lived son and successor Šulgi (2094–2047 B.C.), took great pains to create a unified polity in a political landscape dominated by regionalism and local autonomy.[2] Following in some ways the patterns established by the Sargonic rulers, the new dynasty consolidated power, in theory at least, in the person of the charismatic supreme monarch, transcended local traditions without completely suppressing them by means of cooption as well as coercion, developed an elaborate road and water transport system, and created a new training system for bureaucrats. They also imposed centralization by partly standardizing the official mechanisms of communication and control—namely, weight measures, calendars, and the writing system itself. This allowed for increased monitoring capacity or, at

---

1. For a comprehensive overview of all things Ur III, with extensive bibliography, see Sallaberger 1999.

2. When citing ancient personal and geographical names, I have used conventional renditions and not etymological or phonological approximations, eschewing length marks, etc.; after all, to paraphrase Charpin and Ziegler (2003: vi), this is a book about epistolary history, not about onomastics.

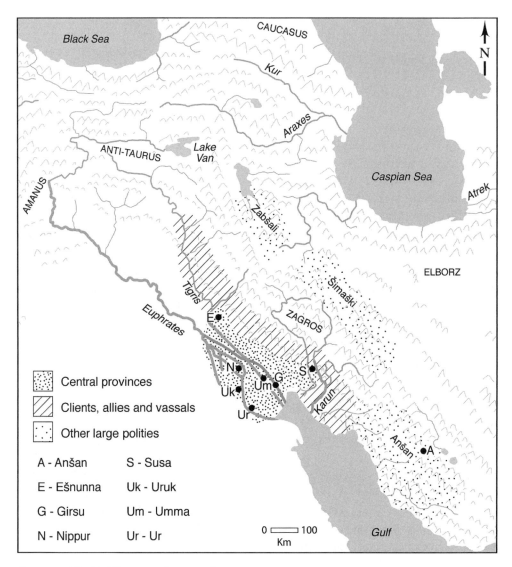

Figure 1. The Ur III state at the time of maximum expansion.

least, a potential for such activity, a factor that some modern scholars consider essential for the development of bureaucracy (e.g., Kiser and Cai 2003: 512).

At the same time, these kings and their commanders conducted an incessant series of skirmishes and raids, as well as outright major wars, on their northeastern and
southeastern border areas, fighting on the frontier as well as deep in enemy territory.
One can observe certain patterns in all of this martial excess: the search for booty,
preemptive strikes against raiders, or the defense of trade and communication routes
to areas that were sources of prestige goods, but much of it also seems haphazard and

pointless, even taking into account the poor state of our knowledge. In the end, all they achieved was the consolidation of powerful new rival polities in the east and this, coupled with an exhaustion of resources and military power, brought about the collapse of the Ur III experiment.

For most Assyriologists, Ur III studies are synonymous with research on archival documents. The study of ideological matters, of official self-representation, and of state-integrating strategies, has lagged behind the abundant research on socioeconomic matters and has been split between different disciplines. Art historians have focused on contemporary Ur III materials such as seals, while literary specialists have looked at royal hymnography and epic texts, which are attested primarily in later, altered versions. The letters that are the subject of this work belong together with these literary compositions, all of which were incorporated into the various school curricula of Mesopotamia sometime after the fall of Ur. Since we cannot establish definitively when most of the later poetic and prose texts about Ur-Namma and his successors were originally composed, it is difficult to know which of them belong together, which provide evidence of contemporary royal legitimization and self-representational strategies, and which were composed or radically altered in Old Babylonian times and are thus part of a later portrait of the earlier age.

Legitimation and legitimacy are often invoked to explain the ideological messages of Mesopotamian writings. These concepts, with their Weberian overtones, have rarely been systematically debated within Sumerology, and one suspects that they are often used in a vague manner as a substitute for intuitive notions concerning propaganda and acceptance of central authority. There are, of course, many views on the theoretical aspects of these issues; here it will be useful to cite a recent statement by Rodney Barker (2001: 30), who writes:

> [Self-legitimation] is an activity, which can be observed and which comprises all those actions which rulers, but not only rulers, take to insist on or demonstrate, as much to themselves as to others, that they are justified in the pattern of actions that they follow. Self-legitimation is an inherent and characterizing activity of government, just as worship is one of the characterizing activities of religion or singing one of the characterizing features of choral music.

In this formulation, self-legitimation is an inherent characteristic that helps to define the very essence of royal rule (or any other type of rule, for that matter), one that simply has to be taken for granted as an essential attribute of kingship. In any given society and historical formation, one must investigate the tools used by the monarch as well as the intended audience for such display. Most important for our purposes is the observation that the self-justification of personal rule is usually concerned with legitimating the ruling individual, not the corporate state. This is useful, because we have very little information on the structural fabric of early Mesopotamian states on elite levels; it is difficult enough to determine who the elites were and what their relationships to the crown were. Equally important, we cannot investigate the continuity or lack of continuity of social and economic structures between specific formations such as the Sargonic and Ur III polities. There is no doubt that certain le-gitimating strategies of earlier rulers were adopted and transformed by dynasties that were to follow, but we cannot at this time say anything about the carry-over of elite strata between these states, and thus the continuity of the audience is a moot point.

There is still much to be learned about early Mesopotamian kingship, but there can be little doubt that the ideological and representational aspects of supreme rule changed radically with the rise of larger territorial states—specifically, with the ad-vent of the Sargonic and Ur III dynasties. Sargon (2334–2279 B.C.), the first king of Agade, had to create new ways of controlling and representing power in a manner that subjugated and subordinated various smaller political units with long traditions of independent rule, and these mechanisms were eventually refashioned by his suc-cessors, most notably by his grandson Naram-Sin (2254–2218 B.C.).[3] When, a cen-tury or so after the collapse of Akkad, Ur-Namma founded a new territorial state, he had only that single precedent to work with, and he had to rework the ideological foundations of centralized rule anew into a manner that was right for the times. Although the details of his conception still elude us, it seems that his project was successful in the short term, since we cannot detect any large-scale opposition to the central government for the three or more generations that he and his first three suc-cessors occupied the throne.

The person of the king, in Sargonic as well as in Ur III times, was represented in a manner that meant to portray the monarch as the focal axis of the state and of the universe as well. For city dwellers and visitors, the visible signs of royal authority per-meated daily experience. The Ur III kings virtually remodeled the urban landscapes of their realms. Although we have only limited archeological confirmation of these activities, the votive texts, year-names, and monumental inscriptions document ex-tensive building and rebuilding work throughout the land. The organizational and fiscal efforts were considerable, to say the least. During his eighteen-year reign, Ur-Namma initiated and perhaps even completed work on at least four massive stepped temples (ziggurats) in the most important cities of his realm: Ur, Eridu, Uruk, Nip-pur, and possibly Larsa.[4] These massive works required immense labor and invest-ment resources, not to mention logistical support. The ziggurats dominated the inter-nal and external view of the cities, drawing the gaze to the ceremonial center and to the royal patronage that made these structures possible. And this royal patronage of select cities resulted in major expansion. Thus, we know that "the city of Nippur had been much smaller until Ur III times, when it had expanded greatly. Subsequently, it shrank in size and presumably population, growing to its full size in only two other periods (Kassite and early Neo-Babylonian)" (Gibson 1998–99). In the countryside, the vigorous work on major canal networks likewise affected the rural landscape. On a smaller scale, royal public messages were encoded on monuments, of which only

3. See the essays in Liverani ed., 1993.
4. Sauvage 1998: 45 with n. 4. On Ur-Namma's work on the Ekur in Nippur, see Frayne 1997: 17.

one significant example, the Ur-Namma stele from the ceremonial center of Ur, survives (Canby 2001). And on an even smaller scale, the relationships between the crown and elites were visually rendered on cylinder seals and on the surfaces that carried their impressions.

The scribes of the land, who in their youth had to memorize and copy various texts extolling the magnificence of their prince, were not exempt from daily reminders of royal accomplishments, as they had to copy the same year-name countless times daily for twelve months or more. But in the surviving sources the most vivid examples of royal self-representation come from the hymnography (Hallo 1963b). The Old Babylonian corpus of such texts, selectively preserved, rewritten, modernized, and perhaps even archaized, now comprises more than forty compositions, although the exact number very much depends on various opinions about generic adscription. Just how much is lost to us at present can be gauged from the Ur III Yale catalog of unknown origins published by William W. Hallo (1963a), which contains forty-two incipits, of which only one, the ubiquitous hymn *Šulgi* A, can be identified with certainty.[5] The rhetoric and contents of these hymns is well known; suffice it to say that most of the central themes that run thorough all of Ur III royal literature are designed to place the figure of the king in the center of the universe and to link him with the maintenance of order in the state as well as in the universe at large. Divine birth, divine care and nurture, mythological foundation in the time of Uruk heroes, as well as extraordinary and all-encompassing personal abilities—martial, sexual, linguistic, and intellectual—all locate the individual of the king at a central locus where both state and cosmos achieve immanent harmony and order. Analogies to this are not hard to find. Consider the following statement by Sarit Helman (1989: 126–27):

> The Javanese concept of order assumed the immanency of the sacred in the world. Thus, it lacked the perception of a separateness and consequent tension between the mundane and the cosmic realm. The immanency of the sacred in the world and its very embeddedness in the center of society implied that there were no criteria beyond those of the center in which the performance of institutions could be evaluated. Therefore, any instability, any event which destabilized the socio-political order and the smooth functioning of nature, was interpreted in catastrophic terms, as driving both society and the cosmos into chaos.

This description could easily be applied to the central ideas of early Mesopotamian political world order as represented in Sumerian royal literature: in hymns, city laments, and in the Gilgamesh stories, which in their original formulation articulated the foundation myth of the family of Ur-Namma. It may also reveal the ideological fragility of the state and help us understand why it was so easily toppled. Nevertheless, one must be careful not to over-interpret the evidence, reducing all literary analysis to politics and ideology. I am by no means espousing such reductionism: I

---

5. Line 42, dumu an-na, may perhaps be the Baba hymn of "Luma" (CT 36 39–40).

concentrate on these issues as they are pertinent to the discussion at hand and by no means renounce poetics. A few examples will illustrate some of the more salient points.

An exceptional pair of examples can be found in two texts that in a sense bracket the literary portrait of Ur-Namma. The first is *Ur-Namma Hymn B*, which provides divine sanction for his rule at Ur, and the second is his *Hymn A*, written after his death, which attempts to deal with his untimely demise. The latter is unique, and its poetic depiction of the death and burial of the king serves as the best example of Ur III concepts of the temporal embeddedness of the sacred in the political center of the state. The premature, violent death of the ruler could only signal divine displeasure and must have precipitated an ideological crisis that threatened to undermine the fragile fabric of the new state, which was only eighteen years old and in which local ideas of independence far outweighed the burden of imposed state authority. The unusual nature of this event and of the text that commemorated it becomes particularly vivid when we observe that, with very few exceptions, the death of kings appears to have been a taboo subject in early Mesopotamian literature. The Ur-Namma text aside, there are only two other compositions that touch on this subject—namely, a cultic text that lists the burial places of early kings (Jacobsen 1963: 476–77 n. 8) and an incompletely preserved Akkadian-language text that is concerned with the death of Naram-Sin (J. Westenholz 1997: 203–20). Anecdotes about unusual royal deaths appear sporadically in the omen literature (Glassner 1997: 101–5), but this is undoubtedly a separate tradition that belongs to a different semantic space.

We often assume that the Old Babylonian school life of older royal hymns is a secondary development: that is to say, we assume that they were originally written for specific occasions and were only secondarily and quite selectively inscribed into the school curriculum after undergoing various degrees of orthographic, grammatical, and even thematic modernization. This may indeed be the case with some texts, but there is actually no evidence to support this view as far as the vast majority of royal hymns are concerned. To the contrary, a number of such poems written in the name of Šulgi and his latter-day admirers specifically refer to the glorification of the king in the eduba'a, that is in the place where the literary arts were taught in Ur III and Old Babylonian times (Sjöberg 1975a; George 2005).

The meaning of the word eduba'a remains elusive. As is well known, there is a strong disjuncture between archaeological evidence that strongly suggests schooling was done in private and institutional settings and the literary depictions of more-formally organized schoolhouses. For the Ur III period, the only school texts we have come from the Inana temple in Nippur (Rubio, in press). What did Šulgi have in mind when he stated that he had established centers of learning? Adam Falkenstein (1953) was certain that the crown controlled schooling, but this interpretation has not been in favor of late. I suggest that in a sense Falkenstein was right, namely, that there were royal academies where poems were composed and elements of the curriculum were established, although these were probably quite separate from the private houses where instruction of a few schoolboys at a time actually took place. It is possible, although one cannot prove this at present, that some of this compositional and redactional activity took place in places designated as é-g̃eštu₂-ᵈnidaba, the "establishments of Nidaba's wisdom." The term eduba'a may have been antiquated by Old Babylonian times, referring back to Ur III and early Isin reality (George 2005: 7).[6] In this context, royal self-representation addressed the schoolmasters, to use a somewhat anachronistic term, as well as their pupils, the future bureaucrats and elite scribes of the land.

These were the places from which knowledge emanated to those who taught in the large institutions and in their own houses. The masters of the eduba'a adapted various existing compositions for pedagogic uses and composed hymns in honor of rulers for the use of other teachers and of their students. One might also speculate that these were the places where the Ur III writing reform, as well as the whole-sale revision of the contents of the curriculum, took place. Although contemporary evidence is still sparse, it appears that sometime under Ur-Namma and Šulgi the masters of the academies wiped the literary slate clean and discarded all but a few of the old compositions that went back to Early Dynastic times. They kept most of the lexical teaching tools but discarded old narratives, replacing them with materials written in honor of the contemporary ruling house—royal hymns, stories about their Uruk ancestors, and so on. Once again, I suggest that the literary texts had a circumscribed social role—that is, they were addressed to the literate minority and to select schoolchildren.[7]

The Ur III state has often been described as a patrimonial state, a distinctive form of rule typified by segmentation of sovereignty between rulers and corporate elites (Garfinkle 2008). If we continue to view the house of Ur through a patrimonial lens, then the identification and description of such corporate groups is absolutely necessary for any meaningful analysis. Certainly, we can speak of a few powerful families such as the well-known dynasty of grand viziers, discussed in chap. 3, the hereditary governors of Umma (Dahl 2007), the house of Ur-Meme at the Inana temple in Nippur (Hallo 1972; Zettler 1984), or the clan of the cantor Dada (Michalowski 2006b). Our knowledge of these groups is suggestive, but it is hardly adequate for a broad-ranged analysis.

Current knowledge sheds little light on the origins and formation of the Ur III state. We simply have no way of establishing the degree of force or co-option that was required to bring together various local power centers that rose to promise in the wake of the Akkad collapse and to subject them to a new central authority. Here the distinction made by social scientists between consent—understood as behav-

6. Various etymologies of é-dub-ba-a have been proposed, but none of them have found general acceptance. The Akkadian translation *bīt ṭuppi* points to the simplest solution—that it indeed does mean "house of tablets" and that the additional final -a is there to distinguish it from é-kišib₃(DUB)-ba, "storehouse."

7. There is evidence that suggests, however, that the study of literature was only available to elite schoolchildren and that the majority of Old Babylonian scribes-to-be learned to read and write by means of basic exercises only; see Michalowski 2011.

ioral acceptance and legitimization, perceived as normative assent—is particularly important (Della Fave 1986: 477). To what extent did the various strata of society, including the important elites, simply consent to the rise of a new center, what was the degree of coercion, and how was the legitimating process used to arrive at normative assent? Were the existing elites co-opted and integrated into the power structure of the new state or was it dominated by a few families from Uruk and Ur? We know that during the Akkad period local elites were dominated by officials sent from the center, and it appears that similar methods may have been used by Ur-Namma and his successor, but the fact remains that, while data on civilian and military governors grows, we actually know very little about most of them, especially about their origins and corporate allegiances.

One of the most powerful methods of vertical social integration in this period was the familial expansion of the patrimonial state. Multiple royal wives resulted in a multitude of children. When one considers that the Drehem texts alone provide us with the names of almost a hundred princes and princesses during a period that spans no more than two generations, the issue is thrown into particularly sharp relief. A hundred children means many more mothers than are currently known; more important, these children could potentially have at least a hundred spouses, and even if we subtract a dozen or two who became unmarried priestesses, the number is still imposing (Sigrist 1992: 361 n. 41). One of the best-known uses of royal children is for international alliances by means of dynastic marriages; the Ur III kings managed to create such bonds with most of the bordering and outlying polities, including Mari, Hamazi, Simanum, Bašime, Marhaši, Zabšali, Simanum, and Anšan, as well as others, including possibly Nineveh. These marriages did not always have the desired effect, and not all hostilities were averted. More important, they did not prevent a number of these polities from taking part in the wars that ended the Ur III state.

These dynastic marriages have received much attention, but other familial alliances may have been more significant for internal integration and for the dominance of the royal family. The evidence is incomplete, but there are good reasons to believe that the top echelons of state organizations, including the military, were occupied either by members of the extended royal family or by men who had married into the family of Ur-Namma. Princely generals aside, prominent examples include Arad-Nanna, the grand chancellor, whose wife was a daughter of Šulgi, and Babati, the queen's brother, who was perhaps as important during the reign of his nephew Šu-Sin. The Garšana archive offers a unique picture of a strategic rural estate run by a princess and her spouse (Owen and Mayr 2007). Royal children who did not marry into other elite families—within and without the state—became high priests and priestesses; in one sense, they were betrothed to divinities, thus extending royal familial control over central religious institutions.

The manner in which the rulers represented themselves to these corporate elites is only partially recoverable. In addition to the visual manifestations of power described above, we have to take into account the pomp and circumstance of public ceremony, the constant banquets, royal progresses, and ceremonial events during which kings affirmed their power, status, and charisma, constantly defining their place in the world to their elite subjects, their large extended family, as well as to themselves. These were the primary loci of self-representation, and literature, so dear to many of us, had only a minor role in this game.

In the works of our time, the short century when Sumer and Babylonia were ruled by the house of Ur-Namma is uniformly described as a marvelous time of great architectural, military, literary, and of scholarly achievements, albeit one that, for some, was also a period when the heavy hand of a strongly centralized government oppressed various strata of the population. Until recently, the period was often described as a "Neo-Sumerian Renaissance," and even though most now think that it was neither "neo" nor a "renaissance" of anything and although opinion is more divided on the matter of its "Sumerianness" and what that might have actually entailed, the descriptive term is not completely dead in some circles.[8] Much of this requires reexamination for the simple reason that the manner in which we often describe that period is in essence not much more than a paraphrase of ancient sources, in concert with the self-representation strategies of the monarchs of Ur. The propagandistic language of the royal hymns, particularly those of Šulgi, and the hyperbolic touting of accomplishments in year-names have survived the ages and have had their desired effect on an audience that the ancient authors could not have even imagined. One has to admit to an admiration of their efforts.

Šulgi is remembered as a semidivine polyglot who could outrun and outfight any opponent, whose strategic and martial efforts created a world-class empire, and whose organizational, legal, and bureaucratic imagination reinvented ancient statecraft, while his second successor Šu-Sin lives on in the Assyriological imagination as a gentle but charismatic lover (*Šu-Sin Hymn B* 1–8):

> Youth of my heart, my beloved man;
> Your allure is sweetness, sweet as syrup.
> Lover of my heart, my beloved man;
> Your allure is sweetness itself, sweet as syrup.
> You have captivated me, I will come to you on my own,
> I will snatch you, o youth, right into the bedchamber!
> You have captivated me, I will come to you on my own,
> I will snatch you, o youth, right into the bedchamber!

But his scribes also wanted the world to obey him out of fear, anticipating what A. T. Olmstead (1918) so felicitously described as the "calculated frightfulness" of the Assyrian kings. An Old Babylonian copy of an inscription placed on an illustrated stele with representations of scenes from a victory over the highland land of Zabšali contains these words:

> (Šu-Sin) killed both the strong and the weak, heads of the just and wicked he piled up like (heaps) of grain, corpses of their people he piled up like sheaves. . . . their

---

8. For a critique of the term "neo-Sumerian renaissance," see Becker 1985.

established cities and villages he turned into (empty) tells, destroyed their walls, blinded all the young men of the cities he had conquered, and made them serve in the orchards of Enlil, Ninlil, and in the orchards of all the great gods; he donated all the women of the cities he had conquered to the weaving establishments of Enlil, Ninlil, and of the great gods."[9]

These seemingly contradictory portraits of a Sumerian sovereign are, of course, hardly unique as far as tyrants are concerned. And yet the word "tyrant" is scarcely, if ever, used in describing ancient Mesopotamian kings. Instead, they are usually portrayed, in the manner of their own propaganda, as heroic and patriotic, bringing together quarrelling smaller political units for the common good. From the modern nationalistic worldview, nation-states, especially one's own, are superior, and the bigger the better; but it is questionable if the projection into the past of such feelings results in good history-writing. In the study of early Mesopotamia, we invariably favor periods of centralization of authority, if for no other reason than that such times provide more ample documentation. But this sort of centralization is the anomaly rather than the norm; in the third and early-second millennia, it accounts for 250 years or so at the most. We may celebrate the various civil accomplishments of the famous kings associated with these times—namely, Sargon, Naram-Sin, Šulgi, or Hammurabi—but we should also remember the piles of corpses and shattered lives that they left in their wake. I. M. Diakonoff (1969) famously dismissed the glorious vision of Ur, charging that it was a highly despotic state, and although his opinion is often cited without approval, his insights may prove to be much more prescient than is often assumed. And yet one has to also look at all of this from a different angle and ask if the members of the Ur-Namma dynasty actually dominated their realm to such a degree, or rather if "the Ur III state was centralized only in the sense that the crown was the locus for the direction of resources from throughout the state," as Steven Garfinkle asserts (2008: 60).

These states were not only ephemeral, but, as Norman Yoffee (1995) keeps reminding us, relatively small affairs, even if they are sometimes described as "empires." The Ur III polity was undoubtedly more compact and less expansive than the Old Akkadian kingdom, but we must keep in mind that it lasted only a few decades longer than the one-person "empires" of Puzur-Inšušinak or Šamši-Addu, which may have been equal or even territorially more extensive in size.[10] Likewise, one must be cautious not to overestimate the military power of Ur and the intensity of war at the time. To be sure, some of the expeditions mounted by Ur-Namma's successors were serious military offensives that drove deep into the highlands of Iran, but the Orwellian year-names—the main source of our knowledge of most of these events—treat all battles, border skirmishes, and low-intensity warfare on the frontier quite equally and describe them all as "destructions" of the enemy. The well-known case

9. Šu-Sin E3/2.1.4.3 iii 16–21, iv 11–31 (Frayne 1997: 303–4).

10. For a discussion of the Ur III state as much smaller and much less militarily effective than is assumed by some modern scholars, see Michalowski 2009a.

of the highland city of Simurum serves as the best illustration of the futility of some of the martial successes proclaimed in the year-names: Šulgi claimed victory or, more literally, the destruction of Simurum, nine times, and yet it still caused problems for his successors.

This is, broadly sketched, the ideological and political background against which we have to judge the stories that the Ur III royal correspondence purports to narrate. As Old Babylonian literary pieces, they contribute to the manner in which Mesopotamians looked at their past, but it is not at all clear if they can be used to illuminate the issues that have been highlighted in the preceding paragraphs. Much of this depends, as already noted, not only on when the texts were included in the loosely structured school system but also on the date of composition of each individual member of the royal letter collection. One author, in the context of defending the "authenticity" of the letters, writes provocatively: "I defy anyone to write the history of that period without its *Royal Correspondence* and other literary sources" (Hallo 2006: 100). I hope my teacher will forgive me, but on the preceding pages, I have, quite briefly to be sure, attempted to do just that. But the proper response to this challenge must take into account many factors associated with the Sumerian language school curricula and on how one confronts the information found in the correspondence with the data of Ur III archival and historical records. In the chapters that follow, I will address a range of literary, archival, philological, historical, and historiographic issues associated with the interpretation of the letters. Because these epistles straddle, in an often-messy manner, the borders between history and fiction, reality and make-believe, as well as between literature and everyday writing, my own approach will be equally discursive, mirroring to a degree the structural idiosyncrasies of this group of texts. I begin with an analysis of the place of the *Correspondence of the Kings of Ur* in its most immediate setting: the Old Babylonian school tradition.

Chapter 2

Sumerian Literary Letters

Letters came late in the history of cuneiform writing. The earliest examples known to us have been found not in Mesopotamia but in Syria, in the third-millennium archives of Tell Mardikh, and are written in Eblaite, the Semitic archival language of the area (Fronzaroli 2003). It is hardly surprising that letters were not composed before Early Dynastic times, because until then the cuneiform writing system was not suitable for such expression. The five earliest Sumerian letters from Mesopotamia itself were discovered in the city of Girsu and probably date to the time of Urukagina, around 2390 B.C. (Kienast and Volk 1995: 25–35). Another Early Dynastic text of this type of unknown provenience may come from roughly the same time (Kienast and Volk 1995: 36).

Letter-writing in Sumerian and Akkadian came into its own during the Sargonic period. More than a hundred texts of this type have been recovered to date, and they were found in almost every place that has yielded cuneiform tablets from this period, from Susa in Iran to Tell Brak in Syria, from the Diyala region as well as from both northern and southern Babylonia (Kienast and Volk 1995: 37–198). There is even an example of a training letter from this time (Foster 1982a, 1982b). The vast majority of Sumerian letters come from the time of the Third Dynasty of Ur, even if they are possibly to be counted as a different form of written expression than the standard letter. Most of them are relatively simple orders or reports, and few of them ever achieved the complexity that we find in Akkadian-language epistles (Sollberger 1966; Michalowski 1993). The generic epistolary of these texts differs contextually from what we think of as "letters"; they may be ascribed to the genre on formal grounds but from a pragmatic point of view they are artifacts of a different sort.

Individual letters, described in Western classical literature as part of a conversation between absent friends, are elements in a complex semiotic interchange and are usually part of a theoretically endless epistolary chain. One can see this in the literary ordering of the *Correspondence of the Kings of Ur* (CKU) and in the political letters of the *Sumerian Epistolary Miscellany* (SEpM) (nos. 2–5), which tend to be transmitted in pairs; that is, a letter to a king followed by an answer. The aptly named letter-orders are not intended to elicit an epistolary response; they require an action that may or may not be recorded in writing. When it is, the form is a receipt,

14

not another letter, and therefore they are to be thought of more properly as part of the textual universe of the administrative recording archives. The letter-order is a demand for an action and once the recipient fulfilled the order the original letter was enveloped with clay, and the new surface became the vehicle for a receipt. D. I. Owen published a rare preserved example of this sort of letter-order (1972; for another fragmentary one, see *CUSAS* 3 1037):

Tablet (Letter-Order)	Envelope (Receipt)
1. hé-sa₆-ra	1. 1 (ĝéš) 3 (u) 5 (aš) še gur lugal
2. ù-na-a-dug₄	2. ki DIĜIR-ba-ni šabra-ta
3. 1 (ĝéš) 3 (u) 5 (aš) še gur	3. šu-ᵈIM kuš₇
4. šà é ᵈšára-ka	4. šu ba-ti
5. šu-ᵈIM-ra	5. šà é ᵈšára-ka
6. hé-na-ab-šúm-mu	seal:
7. na-mi-gur-re	šu-ᵈIM, kuš₇ lugal, dumu ga-mi-lum

"Tell Hesa to give 95 kor of grain to Šu-Adad in the temple of Šara, and not to argue (about it)."

"The animal-trainer Šu-Adad received 95 kor of grain from the administrator Ilum-bani, in the temple of Šara." Seal: "Šu-Adad, royal animal-trainer, son of Gamilum."

In this case, someone ordered Hesa to arrange for the transfer of grain to the royal animal-trainer Šu-Adad. The name of the person who made the request is now lost, as it would have been certified by the seal impression on the original envelope that Hesa, or his representative, had cracked open to reveal the message. Hesa then in turn gave an order to Ilum-bani, who took care of the matter, disbursing the grain to Šu-Adad; a new envelope was created around the original letter-order, and this served as the surface for the receipt of the transaction, which was certified by the seal of the recipient. The inclusion of both the order and the receipt thus provides the "clay trail" for the transaction.

As one can see in this example, Ur III letter-orders do not as a rule include the full letter-address formula, as the sender of the message is rarely mentioned in the body of the letter but is identified by his or her seal impression rolled either on the tablet or on the envelope. The recipient in the process of reading destroyed the envelopes, and therefore these texts were not meant to be permanent records of any kind. This is a pattern that will be continued in letter-orders from later periods, as, for example, in the often unaddressed messages of this type known from the Late Old Babylonian period (Finkelstein 1972: 4–6), although by Late Babylonian times missives of this type include the names of both senders and recipients (MacGinnis 1995).

As things stand today, there is only one text from those times that can be considered a true narrative epistle. The letter was first published by D. I. Owen (1980) and has largely been ignored, although H. Neumann (2006: 17–19) has recently contributed to its understanding. The text is extremely difficult and will profit from further study; it is presented here in full to show just how different it is, in tone and in language, from both the Ur III letter-orders and from the Old Babylonian school letters written in Sumerian (MVN 11 168 [HSM 7192]):[1]

1. [ki]-ˈáŋˈ-ra
2. ˈùˈ-na-a-dug$_4$
3. a-na-aš-àm
4. tur-tur-e-ne-ke$_4$-eš
5. inim-sig-ŋu$_{10}$ íb-bé
6. 60 (diš) ninda šu-ùr-ra 2(bán) zíd
7. kuš-a-ŋá-lá-šè ha-mu-ní-kéš
8. é-a še ì-ŋál-la-àm munus-ra la-ba-an-kéš
9. é-kišib$_3$-ba-ka-na a-tu-da nu-me-a nu-un-ku$_4$-re-en$_6$
10. níŋ-gur$_{11}$ me-en$_8$-ŋál-la-ni ŋá-e íb-bi-bi-re[2]
11. é-a-na 1(u) 1(diš) bappir$_2$ ì-ŋál-àm im-ta-è šà-gal é-a-šè ì-zi
12. še apin-lá-a nam-érin-e ba-ab-de$_6$
13. é-a še na-me nu-ŋál
14. a-šà-ga-ke$_4$-eš lú-^{d}nanna-ra
15. in-na-dug$_4$ ga-ra-ab-šúm-bi ma-an-dug$_4$
16. tukum-bi a-šà šu-na nu-um-šúm
17. ki na-me-a apin-lá ga-ba-ab-dab$_5$
18. gu$_4$-du-ke$_4$-eš lú-ús ŋá-ar ha-mu-ši-in-gi$_4$-gi$_4$
19. še é-a nu-mu-da-ŋál
20. še šu ha-ma-ab-tak$_4$-tak$_4$
21. a-ma-ru-kam hé-em-du
22. igi-du$_8$-e lú-kíŋ-gi$_4$-a ^{d}šára ba-an-ši-DU ma-an-dug$_4$
23. na-àm-mu-dab$_5$ hé-em-du

[1–2]Say to Kiaŋa: [3–5]Why am I being maligned about the children/servants, [6–7]even though I bound up sixty half-loafs of bread and two ban of flour in leather sacks (for provisions for each of them)? [8]There is grain in the household but none was bound up (in sacks as provisions) for the woman. [9]She would not allow me to enter into the storehouse without Atu's permission. [10]Would I squander the property that belongs to him?

[11]The eleven beer-breads that were in his house have been taken out; they have been distributed as food for the household. [12]The troops/workers took away the seed grain, [13]and (now) there is no grain whatsoever in the household.

1. Collated on photographs kindly provided by James A. Armstrong. The translation is admittedly tenuous, and many lines could be rendered differently. I am grateful to Wolfgang Heimpel for helping me with the understanding of this letter, even if we do not agree on all points.

2. Read perhaps níŋ-gur$_{11}$-me-en$_8$ ⟨níŋ⟩-ŋál-la-ni ŋá-e íb-bi-bi-re, and translate, perhaps, as "That is my/your property, I would only squander it if it belonged to him/her!"

[14-15]I spoke to Lu-Nanna about the field, and he gave me his word that he would give it to me. [16]If he does not entrust it to me, [17]then I will have to take (lease of a field) somewhere else, [18]and then he should send me a drover[3] in the matter of the oxen. [19]There is no grain in the household, [20]and therefore he should dispatch grain to me. [21]Please—let him come!

[22]He (Lu-Nanna?) told me: "The *dike worker*[4] took along the messenger of the (temple of) Šara." [23]He must not be detained—let him come!

The exceptional nature of this piece is striking, but it may be that it represents the kind of letter one might find in a private archive, and therefore it is possible that when more such non-official tablet collections are recovered we will have a different picture of Ur III epistolarity. Indeed, it is difficult to imagine that a text of this sort could be unique; the extensive use of letters among entrepreneurs and state officials in Old Assyrian and Old Babylonian times, some of whom could undoubtedly read and write, could not have been completely unprecedented. While direct evidence is admittedly extremely limited at the present time, the numerous references to the circulation of messengers in Ur III times lead one to suspect that many of them may have carried letter tablets. By analogy, it is interesting to note that in India there is no direct evidence for early letter writing, and yet circumstantial evidence suggests that there probably was a vigorous culture of international epistolary exchange already in the third century B.C.E. during the reign of Aśoka (Hinüber 2010).

The lack of proper epistolary materials from the Ur III period makes it difficult to assess the elaborate Sumerian letters, some supposedly written during that period, that were copied in the Babylonian schools of the eighteenth century when the language was long dead and ordinary epistles were composed in Akkadian. These are the letters that we consider to be "literary" simply because they were part of the school curriculum and were written in the ductus reserved for such texts. Indeed, although they are therefore considered "literary," they are often not treated as true "literature" and are thought to be found objects, somehow inferior to epic, myths, or hymns. But a generic value judgment of this sort ignores cultural realities and perpetuates assumptions about textual authority that can hardly be substantiated from a theoretical or practical point of view.

The matter of letters as literature has been the subject of much debate. In the words of one author, "since the seventeenth century, 'letters' have been made to serve (as) 'literature,' that is letters have been made to serve the law of literary genre" (Benstock 1985: 257). This implies a definition in which the law of genre is a dominant force, an arbitrator of the social and epistemological status of texts as literature. Although this type of generic imperialism has surfaced often in literary studies, in theories as varied as those of Northrop Frye or Mikhail Bakhtin, to name but two oft-cited authors, the immediate impetus for the statement cited above was

---

3. Assuming lú-ús = *rēdû*.

4. I provisionally assume that igi-du₈ is the Umma equivalent of a-igi-du₈ "dike/canal worker" (*sēkiru*), commonly attested in Girsu.

the notorious *Carte Postale* of Jacques Derrida (1980), which dominated much late-twentieth-century discussion of both epistolarity and genre. The epistles of the *Carte* assembled together achieve the form of a love letter (Benstock 1985: 258), and this has led many to debate the sexual aspects of the exchange of letters, desire, the body, and the role of the feminine in Western letters. From the point of view of literary reception, genre is above all a matter of model and tradition, and for European readers, the erotic and gendered aspects of epistolarity reach at least as far back as Ovid's *Epistulae Heroidum* (de Jean 1989: 60; Cherewatuk 1993: 31 with n. 18).

Such a long continuous tradition of reading and misreading creates its own laws and values, and therefore much of this discussion is historicist and culture specific; whatever its intrinsic interest might be, it remains to be seen if it has much to offer to the student of Mesopotamian writings. The same can be said, of course, about any invocation of the matter of genre, but the issue is particularly delicate when the epistolary genre is in focus. The letter has figured prominently in Western speculations about literature and writing: since Greek times, letters have been at the center of debates about genre and literature, truth and fiction, as well as gender and power (Altman 1982). This makes sense in the Western environment, but one can question just how relevant all of this is to writings from different places and different times.

Letters loomed large in the debate about mimesis, truth, and the ontological status of literature itself because the literary form mirrored epistolary exchanges from everyday life. The chaining of letters, or rather the seriation of epistolary exchanges, has reappeared at various times in ancient Greece as well as in much later epochs in the West, in a manner that has been seen as leading to a new genre, the novel. Indeed, this is precisely why epistolarity has been so important in speculations about genre. The rise of the epistolary novel, as well as those of the non-qualified garden variety, has been linked to epistolarity and feminine discourse; genre and gender have been engaged in this discussion, leading to the problem of power and authority and the problem of the law of genre (e.g., Cherewatuk and Wiethaus 1993). These Western debates are rooted in a variety of culture-specific hermeneutics and have centered on specific bodies of epistolary texts that were often self-consciously composed by authors well versed in the rhetorical and generic debates of their time.

Are the laws of genre universal, or do they only rule over the intellectual descendants of Aristotle? More important, can one in any way link the debates over the rise of the epistolary novel in ancient Greece or latter-day England with developments that took place thousands of years ago in Mesopotamia? To answer these questions, one would have to investigate synchronic and diachronic aspects of ancient systems of categorization of discourse, but such an undertaking would undoubtedly be hampered by the lack of any written native critical tradition, the uneven synchronic and diachronic distribution of texts, as well as the incomplete recovery of cuneiform documents. I have argued in a very different context (1999a: 89) that "generic qualities were essential properties of Mesopotamian discourse, qualities that surfaced in the way in which texts spoke to each other, in the way that they were transformed, and in the way that they lived out their existence in the flow of literary traditions . . . they found their expression not in external labels and *taxa* but in the poetics of a complex written world."

To the scribes of second-millennium Babylonia, the letter was emblematic, and its complicated history may have some bearing on the native perception of the form. The only old story that we have concerning the origin of writing is embedded in the long poem that we call *Enmerkar and the Lord of Aratta*, and it deals, as chance would have it, with the origin of the letter. The Borgesian paradox of this episode is worth mentioning here because it sheds light on the native perceptions of epistolarity, power, and corporate identity. I will limit my remarks to pertinent facts, since Hermann Vanstiphout (1983, 1989) has already written well about this matter. The setting is a contest between a Sumerian city, Uruk, and its barbarian double, a mythical place called Aratta, somewhere deep in a fantasy image of some area of present-day Iran. The rulers of the two cities exchange riddles, and this requires that a messenger travel with lightning speed across the mountain ranges that separate the two, carrying in his brain ever-longer messages. To ease his burden, the Sumerian king invents cuneiform writing on the spot and sends his rival a letter, which the latter cannot, of course, read. I cite the pertinent passage according to Catherine Mittermayer's new edition (2009: 144–45), which she graciously put at my disposal before publication (*Enmerkar and the Lord of Aratta* 500–506):

> du_{11}-ga-ni-àm šà-bi su-su-a-àm
> kíǧ-gi_4-a inim ì-dugud šu nu-mu-un-da-an-gi_4-gi_4
> bar kíǧ-gi_4-a inim ì-dugud šu nu-mu-un-da-an-gi_4-gi_4-da-kam
> en kul-aba_4^{ki}-a-ke_4 im-e šu bí-in-ra inim $kišib_3$-gin_7 bí-in-gub
> u_4-bi-ta inim im-ma gub-bu nu-ub-ta-ǧál-la
> ì-ne-šè ^{d}utu u_4-ne-a ur_5 hé-en-na-nam-ma-àm
> en kul-aba_4^{ki}-a-ke_4 in[im im-ma b]í-in-gub ur_5 hé-en-na-nam-ma

This was his message but its meaning was lost;
The words were too difficult for the messenger, so he could not repeat (them);
Because the words were too difficult for the messenger, so he could not repeat (them),
The king of Kulaba applied his hand to clay and stamped the message as if with a seal.
Before that time no one had ever written down words on a tablet,
But now, under the sun of this very day, indeed it was so!
The king of Kulaba wrote down words on a tablet, indeed it was so!

The messenger takes the tablet with him and once again tackles the long road to Aratta; he presents himself before the local ruler, and then the narrator informs us that (*Enmerkar and the Lord of Aratta* 537–541; Mittermayer 2009: 146–47):

> en $aratta^{ki}$-ke_4 kíǧ-gi_4-a
> im šu $niǧin_2$-na-ni šu ba-ši-in-ti
> en $aratta^{ki}$-ke_4 im-ma igi i-ni-in-bar

inim du$_{11}$-ga gag-àm saĝ-ki mi-rí-da-àm[5]
en aratta^{ki}-ke$_4$ im šu-niĝin$_2$-na-ni igi im-bar-bar-re

The king of Aratta received
The tablet *on which all was recorded for him*;
The king of Aratta looked at the tablet,
The spoken words seemed like nails , . . .
The king of Aratta continued to look at the tablet *on which all was recorded for
    him.*

The symbolism of this episode is self-evident, but it also includes a critical absurdity.
It is obvious that a letter is useless unless it has a recipient, but one never doubts, in
correspondence, that the addressee can read or, in Mesopotamia, that the messenger
who carries it can read it to him or her. Here is a new twist on or, perhaps better, a
blind anticipation of the purloined letter, for the message of this particular epistle
lies not in its content, which is irrelevant, but in its form. The letter is in plain
sight but cannot be understood. The medium is truly the message—for once the
cliché fits—since the surface message of the letter is gibberish to the illiterate king
of Aratta. There is an underlying epistemological as well as epistolary theory here,
one that comes close to the way in which letters have been theorized in the West.
Consider the words of Claudio Guillén from his excellent essay on the Renaissance
letter (1986: 78):

> In the history of our civilization letters have signified a crucial passage between
> orality to writing itself—or a practical interaction between the two. As écriture,
> it begins to involve the writer in a silent, creative process if self-distancing and
> self-modeling, leading perhaps, as in autobiography, to fresh knowledge or even to
> fiction.

I will pick up some of these strands below. For now, one can simply note that the real
message of the newly invented Sumerian letter is clear: it heralds the superiority of
literate Mesopotamian civilization, much to the despair of the highland king, who
must recognize the inferiority of his own culture, which had no writing and no letters. This is the obvious ideological import of this story for a modern reader versed
in contemporary theory, but it is not necessarily the only or the best interpretation.

For the scribes who taught the Sumerian poem in school, as well as for their pupils, this passage may have carried additional meanings, as they would recognize their
own power as writers and readers for nobles and kings, many of whom were illiterate
and needed them for access to written communication. Nor can this story be dis-
associated from the similar etiological tale of the origin of clay envelopes for letters,

---

5. The reading of this line follows Keetman 2010: 73 ("Die gesprochen Worte waren Pflöcke
waren (wie) eine zornig geruhzelte Stirn"). Mittermeyer 2009: 146 reads the first half of the line
as u$_4$-ba du$_{11}$-ga-ni ("Damals war [dies Enmerkaras] Forderung, es war eine wütende Willen-
säusserung"). This is not the place to discuss the difficult second half of the line.

which, similar to the story recounted above, was embedded in a tale about another pair of ancient kings, Ur-Zababa of Kish and the future ruler of Agade named Sargon (*Sargon and Ur-Zababa* 53–56).[6]

u_4-bi-ta im-ma ˹gub-bu hé-ğál˺ im ˹si-si˺-ge ba-ra-ğál-la-àm
lugal ur-^{d}za-ba$_4$-ba$_4$ ˹šar-ru-um-ki-in ˹diğir-re-e˺-ne šu-du$_{11}$-ga-ar
im-ma gub-bu níğ ní ba-ug$_7$-a-ta
ṭu-up-pa iš-ṭù-ur-šu ša šu-mu-ut ra-ma-ni-[šu]
unug^{ki}-ga lugal-zà-ge$_4$-e-si šu ba-ni-ib-tag$_4$-tag$_4$

In those days, writing on tablets already existed but the enveloping of tablets
    did not exist,
So King Ur-Zababa, for Sargon, the creature of the gods,
Wrote a tablet that could cause his (i.e., Sargon's) own death,
And dispatched it to Lugalzagesi in Uruk.

Here the envelope is invented in order to hide the contents of the epistle from the eyes of the messenger, since the letter contained instructions for the recipient to murder the carrier. Thus, a letter can kill, transgressing the separations imposed by mimesis; écriture becomes potential deed, and fiction is subordinated to the murderer's dagger. It is important to observe that these two passages concerning the origins of writing tablets and hiding their content with an envelope have to do with letters and not any other form of written communication. We cannot determine the date at which these two pieces of literature were first composed, but it seems that it is not accidental we have them from the very same time that letters become literature—that is, when the genre is extended and reformulated by inserting it into the inscribed world in which focus is brought upon the very mechanisms of language and discourse.

I will now move on to a brief survey of Sumerian literary correspondence. This survey is limited in scope: it serves only as introduction to the main topic of this book, the royal letters of the Ur III kings. The matter is dealt with in more detail by Brisch (2007) and Kleinerman (2011).

The Number of Letters

At present, there are more than 73 texts that have been qualified as Sumerian literary letters, although some of them are known only by name from "literary catalogs." In the rather confusing modern classification currently in use, the largest number, 24, belong to the CKU, 17 to the SEpM (now fully edited in Kleinerman 2011),

6. There is a clear intertextual relationship between the Sargon story and the Enmerkar passage, as the metaphor of applying a seal to the invented letter anticipates the discovery of the envelope, which is the normal vehicle for such impressions; but this is a complex matter that lies outside of the topic of this discussion.

as well as more-or-less 35 other miscellaneous private and royal letters, letters to gods, and letters of petition, including four or more compositions from the *Royal Correspondence of Larsa* (RCL; Brisch 2007: 75–89).[7] The imprecise figures given here reflect the uncertainty about the attribution of fragments, redactional differences, as well as other philological problems that cannot be addressed here. The SEpM was formerly designated as Collection B (Ali 1964), but this is something of a misnomer, because there is no "Collection A." Three of the most-commonly-copied letters of the CKU were included together by one Nippur scribe on a single tablet, but there is no evidence that this constituted a regular "collection."[8]

Geographical and Temporal Distribution

Copies of letters have been found at almost all sites that have Old Babylonian Sumerian-language instructional texts: at Nippur, Ur, Isin, Uruk, Kish, Sippar, Meturan, Mari, and Susa. The CKU letters are found in all of these places except Meturan and Mari.[9]

With only a few exceptions, the Sumerian-language epistolary texts are known from Old Babylonian copies that testify to their use in scribal instruction during this period. As such, they were used at a somewhat advanced level of the curriculum. The few examples of letter extracts used for elementary instruction come from Sippar and Susa, where round tablets with Sumerian epistolary phraseology were found.[10] Only a handful of these letters survived the Middle Babylonian revision of education. An expanded bilingual version of letter SEpM 22 was widely copied during the second and first millennia; it has been found in a Neo-Babylonian version from Babylon and Ur, as well as on earlier tablets from Assur, Ugarit, Boghazköy, and Assur (Civil 2000: 109–16). A Middle Babylonian tablet found at Susa contains two CKU letters in syllabic Sumerian with Akkadian translations.[11] Only one Sumerian literary letter

---

7. Kleinerman (2009: vii) refers to seventeen of these letters as the *Ancillary Nippur, Ur, and Uruk Correspondence* (ACL, AukC, AUrC); she now uses the term *Additional Nippur Letters* (ANL) in her revised publication (Kleinerman 2011, with editions). Brisch 2007: 87 is undoubtedly correct in her suspicions that RCL "is perhaps a misnomer;" the label is retained here only for the sake of convenience.

8. 3 N-T 311, compilation tablet Nd (p. 54, below). See Michalowski 2006d: 152.

9. The only letter tablet found at Meturan is H 184 C, which had the *Letter of Ninšatapada to Rim-Sin* on one side and the *Letter of Sin-šamuḫ to Enki* on the other (Brisch 2007: 82); a tablet with part of SEpM was found at Mari, but nothing from the CKU has been identified up to the present time. See Cavigneaux and Colonna d'Istria 2009: 52; the "extrait de la correspondence littéraire" mentioned there contains SEpM (personal communication, Antoine Cavigneaux; now included in the edition of Kleinerman [2011]).

10. Susa: *MDP* 27 87, 88; Sippar: *USFS* 134 (Si. 420). Currently, only two other round epistolary exercises are known: *BIN* 2 53 (SEpM7), of unknown origin, and CBS 4078, from Nippur (*Letter of Sin-iddinam to Utu*; Hallo 1982: 97, source N3 in Brisch 2007: 170).

11. *MDP* 57 no. 1 (compilation tablet Su1, pp. 56–56 below).

has been found in the Assurbanipal libraries, namely, the *Letter of Sin-iddinam to Utu*. Finally, one should mention a curious Neo-Babylonian fragment that contains what seems to have been a Šulgi letter, copied or forged in a script imitating an archaic Ur III hand (Neumann 1992a).[12]

Original Date of Composition

Letters by definition mention people by name and, thus, together with royal hymns, are among the few Old Babylonian Sumerian literary texts that proclaim their historical context, spurious or real. The royal letters and letters of petition of the Ur III, Isin, and Larsa kings constitute a large percentage of the total. Many of the private letters and letters of petition appear to have originated in the Ur III period or were made to look as if they did. The letter SEpM 21 is addressed from Inim-Inana to Enlil-massu. Toward the end of the missive there is an invocation to the former professors for wisdom. They are named Lugal-šu, Nabi-Enlil, and Enlil-alsa.[13] The latter appears as a witness in SEpM 14, which is not a letter at all but a public announcement of the loss of a seal of a merchant by the name of Ur-dun. The name of an Ur III governor of Nippur from the time of Amar-Sin is also mentioned as a witness, providing a date and locale—spurious or real—for many of the letters in SEpM. These names also gave opportunity for a form of intertextual bleeding and generic play. The schoolmaster of Nippur (um-mi-a nibru^{ki}), Enlil-alsa, also appears in these letters under the name Zuzu, a nickname that meant "teacher," "wise one," perhaps even "know-it-all" (Hallo 1977: 57). One of the elementary schoolbooks from this period was a list of simple personal names, verbs, and other elements, listed in a form maximized for memorization, presently known as *Silbenalphabet A*. During the late Old Babylonian period, a second and third column were added, providing esoteric as well as playful etymological and other comments and games in the form of explanations and simple associations. One section reads (Sollberger 1965: 23, ll. 39–41)

ì-zu	dub-sar	^{d}alamuš
a-zu	šà-tam	^{d}aš-n[a-an]
zu-zu	um-mi-a	^{d}h[a-ià]

The verbal forms derived from Sumerian zu, "to know," are associated in the second column with various professional names such as dub-sar, "scribe," šà-tam, "administrator, auditor," and um-mi-a, "scholar, schoolmaster." The third column contains divine names: I have no idea why the first is here; the goddess of grain, Ašnan would presumably have something to do with the "auditor," and Haja was the husband of Nidaba, the patroness of writing, so there can be little mystery as to what he is do-

---

12. For general surveys of the literary letters, see Hallo 1968, 1981; and Michalowski 1981.
13. On some of these issues, see Hallo 1977.

ing here. The associations of this passage clearly hark back to the entries in SEpM, which the author had to suffer through during his school days, leading up to the association of zu-zu with um-mi-a, just as in the letters where the former is a nickname for Enlil-alsa.[14]

Native Designation

The standard Old Babylonian Sumerian word for "letter" was ù-na-(a)-dug₄ or ù-ne-(e)-dug₄, borrowed into Akkadian as *unnedukkum*, a frozen verbal form taken literally from the opening formula of letters (Brisch 2007: 31). The word is used in Sumerian to refer to all letters, even the simplest letter-orders, and is attested from Ur III times on, although in texts from this period á-ág-gá was used as well (Sallaberger 2003). One occurrence of the word suggests that in the north, during Old Babylonian times at least, it was also used as a designation for literary epistles; if not as a Sumerian word, then at least as a logographic writing for Akkadian *unnedukkum*. This usage is found only in an Akkadian language literary catalog of unknown provenience, most probably from the north, which includes the line (M. Cohen 1976: 132, l. 25):[15]

ꜛu ù.neꜜ.e.dug₄ ꜛšaꜜ ᵈšul-gi (= *ešer unnedukki ša šulgi*), "ten Šulgi letters"

A different term is encountered in the subscript on a large tablet of unknown provenience that contains the four letters of the Ibbi-Sin and Išbi-Erra correspondence (A 7475). These texts are summarized as limmu₄ lugal-ĝu₁₀-ra, literally, "four 'to-my-kings'." Here a scribe took a different part of the salutation, the one from letters addressed to kings and gods, and created a term for "royal letter." In the Ebla archives, the Semitic word for "letter," whatever it may have been, remains hidden behind the logogram níĝ.mul (Sallaberger 2003). In the CKU, two terms for "letter" are used: im-sar-ra and ù-na-a-dug₄.[16]

Letters are not present in the two lists of incipits that are thought to enumerate the central texts of the Old Babylonian curriculum of Nippur (Kramer 1942). The two Old Babylonian catalogs that do include letters have no known parallels. The first has already been mentioned above (M. Cohen 1976: 131–33). This text, of unknown origin, lists a variety of Sumerian and Akkadian compositions, including, in lines 25–27:[17]

---

14. A more detailed examination of the Nippur connections of SEpM is provided in Michalowski 1976: 19–27 and more comprehensively in Kleinerman 2011: 102–3.

15. See n. 17 below. The term "literary catalog" must arouse some suspicion and, therefore, I use it here only as a convenient label, fully aware that the lists of this type served a variety of purposes: some simply recorded tablets at hand, but the purpose of most of them unknown; see, in general, J. Krecher (1976–1980).

16. See the commentary to ŠAr1: 31 (2).

17. See above; I collated this text many years ago and was able to do so again on photographs kindly provided by Constance Gane of the Andrews University Archaeological Museum.

ᵘu ù.neˀ.e.dug₄ ˹ša˺ ᵈšul-gi (= *ešer unnedukki ša šulgi*)

[ᵈen].zu lugal ud-sar mah ù-na-a-dug₄

[*su-mu-l*]*a-el* lugal-ğu₁₀-ra ù-na-a-dug₄

If my restorations are correct, two otherwise unattested missives follow the unidentifiable ten items of the Šulgi correspondence—namely, a letter of petition to the moon god Nanna, and a letter to King Sumu-la-el of Babylon (1880–1845 B.C.). One should note that this catalog also includes compositions that were part of the central Nippur curriculum, such as *Šulgi Hymn A*, *Lipit-Eštar Hymn A*, *Inana and Ebih*, and the *Farmer's Instructions*.

More informative is a unique list of letter incipits discovered in the city of Uruk. Unfortunately, it is difficult to reconstruct the complete list, which consists of letters as well as two compositions, the *Tumal Inscription* and *An Axe for Nergal* (Behrens 1988), which were often included in various letter collections, including certain redactions of the SEpM. Although this catalog has been edited twice (van Dijk 1989; Cavigneaux 1996: 57–59), its importance for our discussion requires a full transliteration here, collated from photographs.[18] Note that of the 27 preserved entries, only three cannot presently be identified (these are marked by an asterisk):[19]

[1. lugal-ğu₁₀-ra]

[2. árad-ğu₁₀-ra]

[3. lugal-ğu₁₀-ra]

  4. šu-ᵈen.zu ˹šar-ru-um-ba-niˀ˺-[ra]

  5. šar-ru-um-ba-˹ni-ra˺

  6. i-bi-ᵈen.zu lugal-˹ğu₁₀˺

  7. i-bi-˹ᵈen.zu˺ [x x] x x [. . .]

  8. puzur₄-ᵈšul-g[i P]A.TE.⟨SI⟩ k[a-zal-luᵏⁱ]

  9. ᵈnanna ˹dumu sağ ᵈen-líl˺-lá

10. ᵈen-˹ki enˀ z[agˀ-dibʲ x] x x [. . .]

11. lugal-ğu₁₀-ra [x x x x] x [. . .]

12. ˹pisağ-dub-ba˺ x x [. . .]

13. ˹ᵈutu˺ lugal-ğu₁₀-˹úrˀ˺ [d]i-ku₅ mah an ki

14. ᵈen-išib-bára-ge₄-˹si˺

15. ᵈen-líl-mas-˹su-ra˺

16. ˹šeš˺-ğu₁₀-˹ne˺-ra

The tablet has deteriorated somewhat since Mark Cohen copied it. The readings offered here differ somewhat from the original edition (see already Michalowski 1991).

18. Courtesy of Irmgard Wagner. The original is in Baghdad; a scan of the photograph is included on the disk that accompanies this book.

19. The top of the tablet is broken, but the scribe marked every tenth line on the left side, although this is not indicated in the published hand-copy. The first preserved notation is on line 7, so the first preserved line is actually line 4 of the tablet; the second notation is 20 on the left edge before line 20. The scribe also marked lines 13′, 27′, and 28′ with a PAP sign on the left side; such notations are attested on other tablets, but their meaning escapes us at present.

·

17. ⌜lú-di⌝ du ⌜ama-ğu₁₀-ra⌝[20]
18. ᴵsu-mi-a-tar
19. ᵈamurrum dumu an-na
20. ᴵnibru^(ki)-ta-lú
21. ᵈinin-an-dùl-du₁₀-ga-ra
22. ᵈnin-tin-ug₅-ga agrig zi é-[kur-ra]
23. ᴵur-ᵈnanna-ra
24. ᴵi-la-ak-nu-i-id
25. ᴵbur-ᵈen.zu lugal-ğu₁₀
26. ᴵᵈen-líl-mas-su inim du₁₀ ad-gi₄ s[a₆ . . .]
27. lugal-x-me-ra
28. énsi sağa-ra
29. šakkana-e-ne
30. lugal-nisağ-ğ[á ...]

20. This is what I see on the photographs, and it agrees with the reading of van Dijk (1989: 444, 445) and with his identification of this as the *Letter of Monkey to Mother* (SEpM 16); Cavigneaux (1996: 58) prefers kur-⌜šè⌝ DU-⌜DU-ğu₁₀-ra⌝.

21. Attested at Uruk; see n. 23 below.

22. In view of the context, this should be the first item of SEpM, which could be either AbŠ1 (4) or ArŠ3 (7); both begin lugal-ğu₁₀-ra ù-na-a-dug₄, and both can open the collection.

23. Without collation of the original, one cannot be sure of anything, but perhaps this is a version of the letter *ISET* 1 121 [179] (Ni. 9710). This fragmentary tablet may perhaps be restored as: [pisağ-dub]-⌜ba⌝-a ğárza a-na-me-a-⌜aš⌝, [ù]-na-⌜dug₄⌝, [ᵈen.z]u-mu-ba-al-lí-⌜iṭ⌝ ⌜na-ab-bé⌝-[a] (rest broken). Or, it might reference ŠuLuŠa1 (200; see p. 414 below).

18. *Letter of Iddatum to Sumutara*   ANL 3
19. *Letter of Etel-pi-Damu to Amurrum*
20. SEpM 10
21. *Letter of Lu-Ninurta to Inin-andul-duga*   ANL 6
22. SEpM 19
23. *Letter to Ur-Nanna*   *
24. SEpM 17
25. *Letter to King Bur-Sin*   *
26. SEpM 18
27. SEpM 13
28. SEpM 12
29. SEpM 11
30. SEpM 20

If the listing of these entries is any indication of the order in which they were used in school, someone in Uruk had a repertoire that was similar to what was generally used in Nippur, albeit with a few additions and perhaps some omissions. Only three literary letter-tablets were actually found in Uruk: an otherwise unattested bilingual letter of petition to Nanna, equivalent to line 9 of the catalog; two identical tablets with the first eight lines of SEpM 6, which is not in the catalog; as well as a compilation tablet that had at least one letter to Šulgi, which may have been the first entry of this list, preceded by SEpM 2, which is not mentioned in the catalog.[24] Indeed, based on the distribution of letters, as reconstructed below, it is more than likely that the missing three lines contained incipits of the Šulgi correspondence—more precisely, of the items ArŠ1 (1), ŠAr1 (2), and ArŠ2 (2); and the beginning of the text has been restored—hypothetically, to be sure—in accordance with this assumption. It is possible that all or most of SEpM and ANL were also utilized in Uruk education, with the addition of *Sin-šamuḫ to Enki, Etel-pi-Damu to Amurrum, Letter of Petition to Nanna*, as well as the two otherwise unknown items from the list addressed to Ur-Nanna (23) and to the Isin ruler Bur-Sin (25). None of these letters are presently attested in Nippur.

The inferences one can draw from these facts are sketchy at best. At least some Old Babylonian schoolteachers appear to have thought of Sumerian letters as a separate category and on occasion listed them together in catalogs in association with a few other miscellaneous compositions. They do not appear to have been used at the earliest levels of instruction, since they are not, as a rule, written on round tablets or on other types of preliminary exercise tablets. They were clearly not models for practical letter-writing, since contemporary correspondence was conducted exclusively in the Babylonian language. The authors of Sumerian literary epistles anticipated

24. Cavigneaux (1996: no. 143; compilation tablet Uka). This fragment is unidentified but it contains at least SEpM 2, the *Letter of Sin-tillati to Iddin-Dagan*, and ŠAr1 (1, source Uk1). Another unidentified literary fragment in the volume is no. 148, which can now be identified as a manuscript of *Nidaba Hymn C* (both tablets collated from photographs).

classical theorists and kept their narratives to one theme; Akkadian letters often introduced second and even third issues, sometimes introduced by the adverb *šanitam*, "on another matter." Akkadian model school-letters do exist (Michalowski 1983a), and one wonders if students studied equivalent Sumerian models in earlier times, when the language was still used for practical epistolary exchanges.

Formal Structure

In a pioneering overview of Sumerian literary epistolography, W. W. Hallo (1968) proposed a formal distinction between "letters" and "letter-prayers." This nomenclature has remained with us to this day. For formal reasons, to avoid ritual connotations and in order to stress the generic similarity between the Sumerian and the Akkadian examples, such as the much later elaborate pleas addressed by the exorcist Urad-Gula to King Assurbanipal (Parpola 1987), it might be better to use the term "letter of petition" rather than "letter-prayer." There are specific formal differences between these two types of epistle, but the major distinguishing feature is the opposition between poetry and prose. Although literary letters are certainly characterized by some use of poetic language, they were essentially prose texts, while letter-prayers used all the devices of Sumerian "verse," including construction by means of written lines, figurative and marked literary language, as well as assonance and parallelism. Letters shared certain formal and semantic features: they used a limited set of opening and closure formulas; they were dialogic, and thus often came in pairs; they named names; they purported to come from the past; and they were written in prose.[25] The letter-prayers/letters of petition had similar features except that they were unidirectional and written as poetry.

As a general rule, this distinction has much to recommend it—but the distinction is not so simple. Many years ago, I analyzed the poetic characteristics of one poetic epistle, the *Letter of Ursaga to a King* (SEpM 6; Michalowski 1976: 12–16). I will not repeat that exercise here but I will paraphrase something I wrote many years later in a volume on Mesopotamian poetic language (Michalowski 1996: 148–49).

Synonymous parallelism is one of the defining characteristics of Sumerian poetry. It is therefore disturbing to encounter it in a letter that one would normally consider to be prose. The opening lines of the first letter of CKU read (ArŠ1: 1–5):

lugal-ğu$_{10}$-ra ù-na-a-dug$_4$
^{l}árad-mu árad-zu na-ab-bé-a
kur su-bir$_4$^{ki}-šè har-ra-an kaskal si sá-sá-e-ra
gun ma-da-zu ge-en-ge-né-dè
a-rá ma-da zu-zu-dè

25. On the formal organization of letters and letter-prayers, as well as on the literary nature of both, see Brisch 2007: 31–33.

Speak to my king,
saying (the words) of Aradmu, your servant:
(You commanded me),
while I was on an expedition to Subir,
to firmly secure the taxes on the frontier territory,
to thoroughly investigate the state of (this) frontier . . .

Someone who is convinced of a strict distinction between poetry and prose might not expect the synonymous word-pair in the third line. One could see in this a lexicalization of the compound and leave it at that, were it not for the obvious highlighting of syntagmatic elements in lines 3–5. These lines are organized as lines of text; they are perceived as visually distinct and heard or recited in parallelistic fashion. Line 3 includes a synonymous pair in which the first element har-ra-an is a loan from Akkadian *ḫarranum*, while the second is the normal Sumerian word for "road, highway." Sumerian texts use both words independently, but the use of synonymous parallelism appears to be a poetic device. This kind of pairing is not unique to Sumerian: examples can be found in languages as diverse as Georgian, Tok Pisin, Provençal, Middle English, Thai, or Hindi. Characteristically, such pairs, which are often lexicalized in poetic contexts, always begin with the loan, followed by the native word (Boeder 1991).

The nonfinite verbal forms at the end of each line unite all three, and the reduplicated roots at the end of lines 4 and 5, as well as the repetition of ma-da, "land, frontier," a loan from Semitic and a partial synonym of kur in the previous line, echo, in a sense, the relationship between har-ra-an and kaskal, loanword and native term, in line 3. All of this creates a complex system of parallelism and repetition that is characteristic of Sumerian poetic language. One does not expect such things in a prose letter. We perceive literature as a distinct form of language and action. In the words of Peter Steiner (1982: 508):

> But unlike other written forms, literary discourse is especially vulnerable because it is impersonal. Personal written communication benefits from the mutual acquaintance between the communicants since this helps in bringing their respective semantic contexts together. . . . But literary communication appears through an institutionalized channel and undergoes editing, grammatical and typographical standardization and commercial dissemination.

This is an enlightening perspective because we are dealing with epistolary communication, normally the opposite of "literary discourse," and yet we appear to be in the realm of poetic language. In our case the institutionalized channel is the school environment, in which letters were no longer bounded by the immediate contexts of communication. They became literary texts, no different contextually than hymns, epics, and other literary poems inherited from earlier times. Thus, even documents could become art, either by simple appropriation or by extensive reworking.

When Hallo (1968) distinguished letters from letter-prayers, his approach was strictly evolutionary generic, and he considered the letter-prayer as an example of a larger category of "individual prayer." More important, the letter-prayer was for him the precursor to the eršahunga, a form of prayer used in rituals down to the first millennium. Subsequently, Old Babylonian eršahungas contemporary with the most-developed examples of the letter of petition came to light (Michalowski 1987; Maul 1988: 8–16), and therefore we can no longer posit any direct "evolutionary" relationship between the two forms. The letters of petition and the eršahungas not only overlap in time but also have more formal differences than similarities; they also fulfilled different rhetorical functions. In the present context, one recalls the oft-quoted statement by E. D. Hirsch (1967: 98) that "every disagreement about an interpretation is usually a disagreement about genre."

From a formal point of view, the main differences between the letter and the letter prayer are prosodic and structural. The former was written in prose and the latter in poetry. Moreover, the letter was usually organized in the following manner:

RECIPIENT-ra ù-na-a-dug₄	To RECIPIENT speak:
ADRESSOR-e na-ab-bé-a	saying (the words) of:
ARGUMENT	
SALUTATION	
CLOSING FORMULAS	

In CKU, the closing formulas, which can sometimes be expanded with an additional phrase (+), are:

A. Letters to kings conclude lugal-ĝu₁₀ hé-en-zu, "now my king is informed (about all this)." This is a calque from Akkadian (*annītam*) *bēlī lu idī*, which is sometimes used as the last element in Old Babylonian letters to royalty.[26]

B. Letters from kings conclude a-ma-ru-kam, "it is urgent," "please." This literally means, "it is a flood"; M. Civil (1994: 179–80) explains this as having originated from a shout of warning that was meant to alert those downstream of a coming flood wave. This formula, which is already found many times in Ur III letter-orders and in the letter presented above on pp. 15–16, is also used in SEpM 12, 15, 16, and 17, none of which is addressed to a royal.

C. Additionally, five letters addressed to Šulgi end with the formula níĝ lugal ab-be-na-(ĝu₁₀) (ga-ab-ak), "whatever my king orders me, I will do" (ArŠ2: 14: 14 [7], ArŠ5: 13 [9], ArŠ6: r 8′ [10], UdŠ1: 20 [11], AmŠ1: 12 [16]), another calque from Akkadian *ša bēlī iqabbû lūpuš*.[27] In the first two of these letters, this is included before formula A.

---

26. E.g., ARM 26 27: 46; ARM 27 1: 4; 72: 37.

27. On this Akkadian construction, see Buccellati 1972: 13. Note also *ša qabē bēlīja lūpuš*, "whatever my king might decide, I will do," e.g., ARM 28 129 r. 1′–2′; 138: 30 (also discussed by Buccellati).

The typical letter of petition is structurally more complex: a string of poetic epithets, sometimes covering many lines, anticipates the name of the RECIPIENT, whose name may be followed by further epithets. Then comes the verb ù-na-a-dug$_4$, "speak," which can be followed by more epithets of the RECIPIENT and by the verb ù-na-dè-dah, "and furthermore." Then comes the argument of the letter—the very petition itself—followed by a formulaic plea (Hallo 1968: 76–77; Brisch 2007: 32). [28]

Sumerian letters are narratives embedded in a frame that consists of an introductory formula and a series of optional endings. The opening formula has been the subject of some debate, and there are contradictory grammatical and pragmatic interpretations of the evidence. The Old Babylonian literary letters use a formula that begins to crystallize in Sargonic times but is formalized, with some variation, during the Ur III period. The basic outline of this development was described by Sollberger (1966: 2–3) and his outline remains valid to this day. In its classic form, the formula reads:

> RECIPIENT-ra ù-na-(a)-dug$_4$
> ADDRESSOR na-ab-bé-a

Most scholars have interpreted the first verb as formally "prospective" but functionally imperative, corresponding to Akkadian *qibīma*. Thus, the exhortation is to the carrier or other reciter of the letter, who is to read it aloud to the recipient, who would most probably be illiterate. Civil (2008a: 11–12) takes a different view; for him, the "prospective" refers to the speech situation, that is, not to the letter or message itself but to the traditional greetings and salutations that messenger must offer before actually reading aloud the text of the letter. In his rendition, the opening formula should be translated: "After you address PN$_1$, (you will say) 'this is what PN$_2$ says'." This makes pragmatic sense, but there is evidence to support the older interpretation, which links the formulas in the two languages.

The first argument is diachronic. The oldest Sumerian letters—the five from Early Dynastic III Girsu and one of unknown origin—all use the formula PN$_1$ na-e-a, PN$_2$-ra du$_{11}$-ga-na, "(This) is what PN$_1$ says, speak it to PN$_2$," with the second verb in the imperative (Kienast and Volk 1995: 25–36). In the Sargonic period, the imperative is replaced with the prospective ù-na-dug$_4$. At the same time, some letters have a new version of the formula in which the order of the constituents is interchanged—that is, the classic order that will become standard in Ur III times and later. Without listing minor variations, the development of all of this can be summarized thus:

> PN$_1$ na-e-a, PN$_2$-ra du$_{11}$-ga-na > PN1 na-e-a, PN2-ra ù-na-(a)-dug$_4$
> → PN$_2$-ra ù-na-(a)-dug$_4$, PN$_1$ na-ab-bé-a

---

28. Lexical texts preserve an invocation for a third part, ù-na-dè-peš, "say for the third time," but this is rare in actual letters (Brisch 2007: 32).

As I have already noted above, the Ur III letter-orders are functionally and structurally different. The few texts that include the names of both correspondents have varying orders of constituents:

> PN_1-ra ù-na-a-dug_4, PN_2-e na-ab-bé-a: *TCS* 1 7; *AOAT* 274 246 4
> PN_2-e na-ab-bé-a, PN_1-ra ù-na-a-dug_4: *TCS* 1 1; *BiOr* 15 78; *BiOr* 26
>   173; Michalowski, *LEM*, 182; *AuOr* 17–18 228 40

As a result, one can observe that the standardization of the opening formula of Sumerian-language letters is first encountered in Old Babylonian literary epistles but when this regularization actually took place is impossible to determine. In the earliest examples, the name of the person who sends the letter is fronted, as this is the new information that the recipient needs to hear first, but this requires an awkward relative construction with a deleted head (na.[b].e.a, "which PN says") and eventually the order is reversed, most likely for aesthetic reasons but also under the influence of the more familiar Akkadian epistles. Whatever the origins of the formula may have been, by Old Babylonian times the prospective form ù-na-a-dug_4 u.na.i.e.dug must have referred to the message of the letter and not to an oral greeting recited by the messenger, as is clear from the poetic letters of petition, which often have long bipartite introductions, the first headed by ù-na-a-dug_4 and the second by ù-na-dè-dah, "say furthermore."

The pragmatics as well as the interlingual relationship are similar to what one finds in the instruction sections of certain kinds of incantations in which Sumerian prospective forms are translated as imperatives in Akkadian.[29]

These structural differences notwithstanding, there is no indication in the collections or in the catalogs that letters and letters of petition were kept separate in the native tradition. Nevertheless, we are undoubtedly justified in following Hallo and considering the letter of petition as a specific category. The history of this form can be well traced and is instructive for the history of Sumerian literature: while it has its origins in the Ur III period, if not earlier, its floruit came in the middle of the Old Babylonian period, long after Sumerian ceased to be a spoken language. Indeed, one could argue that it is the only nonritual Sumerian genre that evolved and grew in Old Babylonian times.[30] Royal hymns and various prayers were still composed at this time, but most of the texts that were copied originated much earlier.

Royal letters of petition, unlike many other literary works, can be dated fairly precisely and thus, together with royal hymns, they are the perfect objects of study for literary historians. The earliest datable example of a letter of petition was written to king Šulgi of Ur, written by a military officer by the name of Abaindasa who had fallen upon hard times (AbŠ1 [4]). This short text, consisting of 27 lines in most redactions, shows all the characteristics of the form: the formulas are all there, and it

---

29. On the pragmatics of Sumerian epistolary practice, see also now Michalowski 2011.

30. On the literary revival under the Larsa kings, see the analysis in Brisch (2007), with special emphasis on the letter-prayers of the period.

is laden with metaphor and poetic parallelism. Indeed, the text is so filled with metaphorical imagery that it is impossible to ascertain what actually caused Abaindasa to fall out of favor with his liege. Fortunately, unlike any other text of this genre, this one has a larger epistolographic context, as there is an exchange of letters between the Grand Vizier Aradmu and King Šulgi concerning this matter to the king.[31]

The most recent known Sumerian archival letter (Sollberger 1966: 92) is dated to the time of Lipit-Eštar (1934–1924 B.C.) but literary letters in Sumerian mentioning Isin kings continued to be composed and used for school purposes. The *Sumerian Epistolary Miscellany* begins, after one transitional CKU letter, with pairs of letters between the kings Iddin-Dagan (1974–1954 B.C.) and Lipit-Eštar and their military officers (SEpM 2–5). The seventh king of the dynasty, Bur-Sin (1895–1874 B.C.), is listed as the recipient of a letter in the Uruk catalog (line 23′) but no manuscripts of this composition have been identified to date. A fragmentary ten-line letter to Enlilbani (1860–1837 B.C.) is known from a solitary manuscript from Nippur.[32] This ruler was well known to Old Babylonian schoolchildren, who had to study a very simple royal hymn to this king in the early days of their instruction (*Enlil-bani Hymn A*); later generations knew of him from an ominous anecdote recounted in the *Chronicle of Early Kings* (Grayson 1975: 155; Glassner 2004: 271). According to this story, he was a gardener who was installed as a substitute king by King Erra-imitti (1868–1861 B.C.), but when the rightful ruler died after drinking a "hot porridge," he remained on the throne as the new sovereign.[33] It is possible that there was also a letter to Sumu-la-el of Babylon (1880–1845 B.C.), a contemporary of Enlil-bani, according to the Berrien Springs literary catalog cited above, but no copies of the text have been recovered.[34]

The last Isin king who figures in the curriculum is Iter-piša (1833–1831 B.C.), whose four-year reign is otherwise only documented in the *Sumerian King List* and in a handful of documents, but no other literary texts in his name were preserved in the schools. A 24-line letter of petition to this king from a Nippur priest named Nabi-Enlil is documented in the pre- and post-WW II school exercises from Nippur, on a tablet from Ur, and from a tablet of unknown provenience.[35] The author identifies himself as a scribe as well as a nu-èš priest.[36] This is the only letter of petition addressed to an Isin king, and it is formally much closer to the one addressed by Abaindasa to Šulgi than to the elaborate, structurally more complex letters of petition of the Larsa dynasty. There are at least two other Sumerian literary letters written by individuals named Nabi-Enlil. One fragmentary missive is addressed to

31. Letters 5–9; see pp. 75–78 below.
32. Ni. 4326+9534; *ISET* 2 119, 9′–18′.
33. *pappasu emmetu.*
34. See p. 25 above.
35. 3 N-T 901, 48 (*SLFN* 23); 3 N-T 919, 455 (*SLFN* 23); 3 N-T 454 = UM 55-21-329; CBS 7857b; CBS 14041 + N 2740; *UET* 6/3 563 (*425); MS 2287, reconstructed by M. Civil.
36. Lines 7–8: ᶦna-bi-ᵈen-líl dub-sar nu-è[š . . .] lú šùd-dè lugal dumu nib[ruᵏⁱ . . .].

his "colleagues,"[37] but little can be made out of the contents at present. Still another letter of someone by that name deals with scribal education (ANL 9).

Ancient Greek, Arabic, Byzantine, Italian, Spanish Renaissance, as well as British and Continental eighteenth-century writings testify to the semiotic importance of letters in the rise of generic consciousness, in debates about the nature of fiction and in the development of one particular genre—the novel. Mesopotamian literature, focused on poetry more than on prose, never developed anything that we could label as a novel but the closest relative of such a form of storytelling were letter collections. Students in Old Babylonian schools studied these letters and often copied them in groups on large tablets or on successive smaller ones. Like most Sumerian literary exercises, the letters were no longer a part of the school curriculum after the middle of the second millennium, so as a genre they had no effect on later tradition. The internal history of the genre in the centuries before its abandonment cannot be recovered, for many of the reasons outlined earlier in this chapter, although one can see a definite elaboration of the letters of petition in the years between Šulgi of Ur (2093–2046 B.C.), when the first preserved letter of petition may have been composed, and the time of King Zimri-Lim of Mari (ca. 1770 B.C.), to whom the last known epistle of this type was addressed.[38] In other traditions, generic growth and innovation is often based on imitation and recovery of old examples, especially in weakly developed genres (see e.g., Javitch 1998), but with our current state of documentation, Sumerian literature in general defies such analysis. Letters are no exception. Nevertheless, certain characteristics of the genre, if we may now use the term with more confidence, are of interest for the general history of textuality and écriture, and one may conclude with two simple observations. The first is formal in nature: in many cultures, such as in the Arabic-language world, epistles played a crucial role in the development of prose (see, e.g., Latham 1983). Prose never attained any importance in Sumerian literature; indeed, the most substantial corpus of literary prose consists of the very letters under discussion here. Moreover, this form could not hold its own against the power of poetry and thus produced its own poetic form: the letter-prayer. The second observation is more substantive. C. Brant (2000: 377), writing about the European epistolary novel, noted that, "in the novel of letters, the author plays on the link between reality and fiction to sow seeds of doubt." There are reasons to believe that the Old Babylonian school masters used Sumerian letters—above all, the epistles of the house of Ur—in just such a fashion, as I have attempted to describe above. One may even go as far as to suggest that this questioning of received history, of royal power, of the role of writing, and of the scribal classes in the structure of the state was deeply embedded in these cuneiform exercises.

37. Ni. 4491 (*ISET* 2 121) gi₄-me-a-aš-ĝu₁₀-ne ù-[na-(a)-dug₄].
38. *Letter to Zimri-Lim*, edited in Charpin 1992; a copy was subsequently published in Guichard 1997, followed by a new translation by Durand (1997: 103–10).

Chapter 3

The Royal Letters in
Their Literary Setting

The letters of the kings of Ur are the topic of this book. Because we only know them from cuneiform tablets written during the eighteenth century B.C., approximately two-and-a-half centuries after the collapse of the Ur III state, they cannot be considered direct witnesses to the events they profess to relate. The texts that have survived are all exercises of young students, who studied these letters as they learned Sumerian in cities such as Nippur, Ur, Uruk, and elsewhere, long after the demise of the writers and recipients of these letters as well as of the language of their correspondence. The core of this work is the edition of these letters but, because of their double alterity and double reception, in Old Babylonian days as well as in our own time, they must be situated in both of their environments, as participants in the educational process and as purported historical documents from an earlier age. In order to effect this analysis, I offer here an overview of the material that will be discussed in the pages that follow.

The *Correspondence of the Kings of Ur* (CKU), as we know it today, consists of 24 Sumerian-language letters, reconstructed from 115 cuneiform tablets; most of these epistles have survived in multiple copies, but some are known from only a single source. Until now, this "corpus" has been known to modern scholars as "The Royal Correspondence of Ur," a title that was bestowed by W. W. Hallo in his pioneering work on literary letters (1968) and that served as the title of my doctoral dissertation, which included preliminary editions of most of these texts (Michalowski 1976). Decades have passed since that thesis was completed: the editions offered here have been constructed anew and the order of the items changed, raising the possibility of confusion, because some scholars have cited the letters according to the numbering used in my now-obsolete edition. The clearest way to avoid misunderstandings about these letters is to rename the corpus and to provide it with a new acronym—hence CKU. The old designation RCU will be reserved for reference to the 1976 dissertation.

A list of these letters follows, with an abbreviation that helps to identify the text, followed by the number assigned in Miguel Civil's catalog of Sumerian literary compositions and by the old RCU number.[1] A concordance between CKU and RCU is provided on p. 246 below.

The Correspondence of the Kings of Ur (CKU)

1. Aradmu to Šulgi 1 (ArŠ1; 3.1.1, A1; RCU 1)
1a. Aradmu to Šulgi 1a (ArŠ1a)
2. Šulgi to Aradmu 1 (ŠAr1; 3.1.2, A2; RCU2)
3. Aradmu to Šulgi 2 (ArŠ2; 3.1.3+3.1.11, A2a; RCU 3+4)
4. Abaindasa to Šulgi 1 (AbŠ1; 3.1.21, B1)
5. Šulgi to Aradmu 2 (ŠAr2; 3.1.61;+RCU 16)
6. Šulgi to Aradmu 3 (ŠAr3; 3.1.13.1; RCU 8)
7. Aradmu to Šulgi 3 (ArŠ3; 3.1.5; RCU 7)
8. Aradmu to Šulgi 4 (ArŠ4)
9. Aradmu to Šulgi 5 (ArŠ5; 3.1.6; RCU 6)
10. Aradmu to Šulgi 6 (ArŠ6; 3.1.4; RCU 5)
11. Urdun to Šulgi 1 (UrŠ1; 3.1.11.1; RCU 14)
12. Aradmu? to Šulgi? 7 (ArŠ7)
13. Puzur-Šulgi to Šulgi 1 (PuŠ1; 3.1.7; RCU 11)
14. Šulgi to Puzur-Šulgi 1 (ŠPu1; 3.1.8; RCU 9+10)
15. Šulgi to Išbi-Erra 1 (ŠIš1; 3.1.13.2; RCU 15)
16. Amar-Sin to Šulgi 1 (AmŠ1; 3.1.12; RCU 12)
17. Šulgi to Amar-Sin (ŠAm1; 3.1.13; RCU 13)
18. Šarrum-bani to Šu-Sin (ŠaŠu1; 3.1.15; RCU 17)
19. Šu-Sin to Šarrum-bani 1 (ŠuŠa1; 3.1.16; RCU 18)
20. Šu-Sin to Lu-Nanna and Šarrum-bani 1 (ŠuLuŠa1; 3.3.31)
21. Išbi-Erra to Ibbi-Sin 1 (IšIb1; 3.1.17; RCU 19)
22. Ibbi-Sin to Išbi-Erra 1 (IbIš1; 3.1.18; RCU 20)
23. Puzur-Numušda to Ibbi-Sin 1 (PuIb1; 3.1.19, A3; RCU 21)
24. Ibbi-Sin to Puzur-Numušda 1 (IbPu1; 3.1.20; RCU 22)

Origin and Date of the CKU Manuscripts

Origin

As noted above, the CKU is preserved on 115 clay tablets, all of them from the Old Babylonian period, with the exception of a Middle Babylonian manuscript from

---

1. The catalog remains unpublished, but some of the information has been used in the Oxford University online editions of Sumerian literary texts. That edition was for the most part done without collations and without utilization of unpublished materials and will therefore not be referenced here. Letters 1, 3, and 23 were once known as Collection A, hence the A numbers; see above, p. 22.

Susa. These tablets derive from Nippur, Ur, Isin, Kish, Susa, Sippar, and elsewhere. The exact breakdown is as follows:[2]

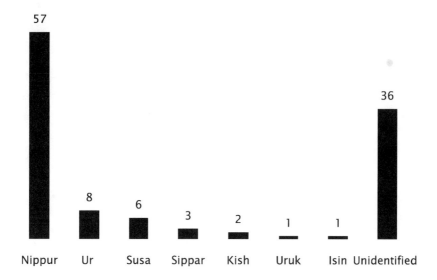

As is evident from the chart, the majority of the tablets—just over half—are from Nippur. The rest of the provenienced texts are available in much smaller numbers: eight texts from Ur, six from Susa, three from Sippar, and one each from Isin and Uruk. In terms of percentages, this may be represented as:

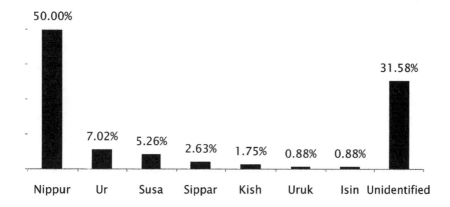

2. Well after the completion of this manuscript, I became aware of four unpublished tablets with CKU letters; they are not included here. Moreover, Niek Veldhuis identified a new duplicate to letter PuIb1 (23), which was posted on CDLI (P342755) when this book was already in press. It is included in the edition as source X4. It is not included in the counts in the charts on this page.

Few of the manuscripts were found in the course of controlled excavations, and even fewer have reliable, well-described information about the exact location and context of their discovery. A synopsis of what is currently known about the origin of these tablets follows.

Nippur

Ten of the tablets from the site are from the third post-World War II season of excavations at the site, and they are the only tablets that have well-established find spots (McCown and Haines 1967; Civil and Sjöberg 1979; Civil 1979a: 7–8).[3]

Excavation Number	Location	CKU Number/Source
3 N-T 8		4 (N1)
3 N-T 80		7 (N1), SEpM 2
3 N-T 306		21 (N1)
3 N-T 309		4 (N2)
3 N-T 311		1 (N1), 2 (N1), 23 (N1)
3 N-T 900,25	TA 205 level XI floor 1	1 (N2)
3 N-T 903,102	TA 205 level XI floor 2	2 (N3)
3 N-T 918,440 + 3 N-T 919,486	TA 191 level XI floor 1	1 (N3)
3 N-T 919,459	TA 191 level XI floor 1	23 (N1)
3 N-T 927,516	TA general area, sub X1	1 (N4)

With the exception of 3 N-T 80, all of these were discovered in House F, which was a private house used for scribal instruction in the first decade of the reign of Samsu-iluna of Babylon. The house provided archaeologists with almost 1,500 exercise tablets (Stone 1987: 56–59; Robson 2001).[4]

The other 47 Nippur CKU tablets derive from the excavations conducted by the University of Pennsylvania in the last four years of the nineteenth century. For all practical purposes, there is no reliable information on their original location. The literary tablets apparently were mostly found on "Tablet Hill," that is, in the same residential section in which the later trenches TA, TB, and TC were sunk. Although the early excavators at Nippur recovered tens of thousands of school texts, it is likely that most of them come from only a handful of private houses that were used for teaching, probably similar in style and layout to House F. Here is a description of the discovery of one such house, on Hill X, Site F (this has nothing to do with the post-WW II "House F"; Peters 1897, 2: 210–11):

---

3. On Nippur tablets, see also Wilcke 2000: 17–22.
4. 3 N-T 80 was found in the adjacent House I.

Here, in one room of a house of unbaked brick, about ten metres long by five metres broad, there had evidently been a depository of tablets; these had been placed around the walls of the room on wooden shelves, the ashes of which we found mixed with the tablets on the floor. We took out of this room thousands of tablets, and fragments of tablets, of unbaked clay. For four days eight gangs were taking out tablets from this room, as fast as they could work, and for four days the tablets were brought into camp by boxfuls, faster than we could handle them. These tablets were of later date than the ones found at E, as might be conjectured from the difference of level. Other rooms of this group contained tablets in fair numbers, but in no other had they been stored in the same way in which they had been stored in F. Close to F, to the northeastward, was a brick structure, on which tablets were found half-imbedded in bitumen. Between the two was a brick well, the bricks laid in bitumen. The débris in this well, like all the débris in that immediate neighborhood, was full of unbaked tablets, with occasional baked ones intermixed. We excavated the well to a depth of 14.5 metres, at which point, 4.5 metres below plain level, we struck water, finding for over thirteen metres, fragments of tablets, most of which were badly injured by water. Neither in this series of rooms, nor at E, did we find any pottery or household utensils.

This description, and similar descriptions embedded in the unpublished papers from the Pennsylvania expedition stored at the University Museum, provide ample proof that the majority of the Nippur literary texts were found in teaching establishments in the well-to-do parts of the city, in places similar to House F, as already noted above, as well as comparable locations at Sippar, Ur, and elsewhere. Note that the nineteenth-century excavators had undoubtedly discovered a house with a water basin used for recycling student exercise tablets of the kind found in other houses used for learning writing (Faivre 1995).

Ur

The eight CKU tablets from Ur were all discovered during Sir Leonard Woolley's 1922–1934 excavations at the site. Most of the Old Babylonian literary texts were found in three houses, No. 1 Broad St. and at 5 and 7 Quiet St.; they are currently housed in the British Museum and in the Iraq Museum. Some stray tablets of a similar type are registered as having come from elsewhere in the city or are without any find-spot information, but most of these were undoubtedly excavated at No. 1 Broad St. These houses, and the texts they contained, have been analyzed extensively by Charpin (1986: 419–86), Diakonoff (1990: 126–54), and, most recently, by Brusasco (1999–2000: 152–54, 159–61), Wilcke (2000: 11–13), Delnero (2006: 44–46), and Ludwig (2009: 4–8).

The following list provides the known findspots of the CKU tablets from Ur:[5]

---

5. I wish to thank Christopher Walker for his help in this matter; he provided the explanatory comments in the footnotes to this list.

Publication/Excavation Number		Location	CKU Number/Source
UET 6/2 173	(U. 7741)	No. 7 Quiet St.	4, Ur1
UET 6/2 174	(U. 16853)	No. 1 Broad St.	1, Ur1; 2, Ur1; 23, Ur1
UET 6/2 178	(U. 16857)	No. 1 Broad St.	4, Ur2
UET 6/2 179	(U. 16894B)	No. 1 Broad St.	4, Ur3
UET 6/2 181	(U. 17900V)	?[5]	2, Ur2
UET 6/2 183	(U. 16885)	No. 1 Broad St.	18, Ur1
UET 6/3 558		?	23, Ur2
UET 6/3 561		?	12, Ur1

Other literary letters known from Ur have similar contexts:

Publication/Excavation Number		Location	Letter
UET 6/2 175	(U. 16272)	?[6]	SEpM 16
UET 6/2 176	(U. 16894A)	No. 1 Broad St.	SEpM 16
UET 6/2 177	(U. 16849)	No. 1 Broad St.	SEpM 6
UET 6/2 180	(U. 16900G)	No. 1 Broad St.	SEpM 17
UET 6/2 182	(U. 7707)	? ("EM loose in soil")	*Letter to Utu*

As is evident from this list, the majority of the Ur tablets were found at No. 1 Broad St., a house that contained tablets brought together from a variety of places and which was probably destroyed around the tenth year of Samsu-iluna. Only one of the letter tablets—the epistolary collection *UET* 6/2 173—was found at No. 7 Quiet St., in a level that most likely dates from the time of the Rim-Sin rebellion. It is interesting that this compilation tablet is different in content from anything we know from Ur, or from elsewhere, for that matter.

Sippar

The three tablets excavated from this site are in the Sippar (Si) collection of the Istanbul Archaeological Museums and almost certainly derive from the excavations conducted in 1894 by Vincent Scheil (1902) at the site of Abu Habbah—that is, the site of the city that was called Sippar Yaḫrurum in Old Babylonian times.

---

6. According to C. Walker, "The only item in the dig register is a cylinder seal; therefore the entire tablet group U.17900 represents a duplicate numbering, therefore with no recorded provenance."

7. "The item recorded in the dig register is a mace-head of Shu-Sin; so the tablet has a wrong number and therefore no provenance."

Si. 420 (*USFS* 134)   = letter 3 (Si1)
Si. 524   = letter 23 (Si1)
Si. 557   = letter 24 (Si1)

Scheil found most of the Old Babylonian school-texts in one house (1902: 30–54; Lion and Robson 2005: 47–48). It is clear from Scheil's description that he discovered a teaching establishment similar to those excavated at Nippur and Tell ed-Der, and that many of the school exercises were found abandoned in an enclosure used to preserve wet clay and to recycle old tablets. Unfortunately, it is impossible to discern precisely which tablets were actually found in this house and which came from other work on the mound during the same excavations. All the finds were deposited in what is now the Istanbul Archeological Museum and cataloged with Si(ppar) numbers. There has been some suspicion that some of the tablets in the Si collection are actually Nippur pieces that were mixed in with them in the museum, but personal inspection of a number of the Si literary tablets in Istanbul convinces me that most of them are not from Nippur at all. My recollection is that the ones I saw were physically different from tablets uncovered in the southern city, and I am fairly confident that they were indeed found at Sippar. Thus, although some tablets from the Nippur excavations may have made their way into this collection, none of the three CKU tablets with Si numbers are from Nippur.

There are seven other tablets that may possibly have originated from Sippar; these are discussed in the section on provenienced sources below.

Kish

The two Kish sources derive from the 1912 excavations on the mound of Uhaimir and Inghara directed by Henri de Genouillac (1924 = *PRAK*).

AO 10630 (*PRAK* II C10)   = letter 24 (Ki1)
AO 10819 (*PRAK* I D60)   = letter 13 (Ki1)

The published reports of the excavations are less than informative, and almost nothing is known about the findspots of tablets, except that the Old Babylonian school texts were mainly found on the mound of Uhaimir. A number of tablets were published by de Genouillac (1924), arranged as series A through D, but these designations have nothing to do with their original locations. It is possible that the French excavators found some of the Old Babylonian school-texts in one large house, but it is impossible to confirm this conjecture (de Genouillac 1924: 23; Delnero 2006: 51–53; see now Ohgama and Robson 2010: 208).

Susa

The six Susa manuscripts come from two different contexts. Five are Old Babylonian practice texts on round tablets, and nothing is known about their findspots; the sixth is a Middle Babylonian two-column compilation tablet (see Susa below).

There is only one other CKU round tablet.[8] Only two other such "lentils" with lines from literary letters are currently known.[9] It therefore appears that in Mesopotamia proper letters were not used very early in the school curriculum.

MDP 18 51	= letter 4, Su1
MDP 27 87	= letter 2, Su1
MDP 27 88	= letter 2, Su1
MDP 27 207	= letter 4, Su2
MDP 27 212	= letter 23, Su1

The Old Babylonian Susa exercise tablets have unique characteristics and deserve a full treatment, but that lies beyond the scope of this study. Most of the round tablets are inscribed with elementary exercises such as lexical excerpts, divine and personal names, as well as proverbs, but also with lines from literary compositions such as *Message of Ludiĝira* (*MDP* 27 107) or *Gilgameš and Huwawa A* (*MDP* 18 49; *MDP* 27 93, 217). It seems that three of the most-commonly encountered core CKU letters were also used: ArŠ1 (2), AbŠ1 (3), and PuIb1 (23), but no other literary letters.[10]

On a Mesopotamian text of this type, one would expect the reverse to contain the student's version of what the teacher wrote on the obverse. At Susa, the reverse often contains an Akkadian translation, a syllabic transcription, or both, sometimes contained within a rectangular border that seems to imitate the shape of a portrait- or landscape-oriented imgida.

The date of the Old Babylonian school-texts from Susa is not precisely established; in the introduction to *MDP* 18, Scheil wrote that "ils s'étendent chronologiquement du temps d'Agade à celui du prince *Pala iššan*, c'est-à-dire assez avant dans la période correspondant à la première dynastie de Babylone" (Dossin 1927: i).

The other Susa tablet is the multicolumn text.[11] The format of this text is unusual: it is bilingual, in syllabic Sumerian and in Akkadian, and the two languages are not written in separate lines but run one into the other. The precise date of this tablet is difficult to establish. There are very few internal criteria to go by, because we do not have usable comparable material. It was found at Susa during the 1962–1963 campaign together with ten Akkadian-language omen texts in a pot in a cache that was hidden in a prepared pit in level AXII, locus 14, in the sector that the excavators named "Chantier A." There has been some controversy concerning the dating of the level and the ascription of the tablets to a particular stratigraphic context. The original editor of the literary texts, R. Labat (1974: 2), could only state that the tablets were undoubtedly later than the Old Babylonian period but had to be written prior to the time of the great Assyrian libraries. The proper placement of these finds had to be postponed until the archaeological sequences of the Ville Royale at

8. Si. 420 (Si1 of ArŠ2 [3]).

9. *BIN* 2 53 (SEpM 7) and CBS 4078 (Brisch 2007: 170, *Letter of Sin-iddinam to Utu*).

10. Unless *MDP* 27 104 contains a version of line 10 of *Letter of Gudea to His God* 10. The text reads: diĝir-ĝu₁₀ lú kur-zu nu-me-en / ba-ar-mi-en-tar-re.

11. Compilation tablet Sua; see pp. 56–56 below.

Susa were analyzed in full; this began with the publication of H. Gasche's (1973) exhaustive analysis of the pottery. In a review article of that book, E. Carter (1979: 121) presented her own scheme for the dating of levels in the Ville Royale and proposed that level AXII should be assigned to approximately 1400 B.C. Steve, Gasche, and de Mayer (1980) subsequently published a long rejoinder to Carter's review in which they provided more-precise information on the context of the literary texts from Chantier A. The matter is complicated by the fact that, although the tablets were found in level XII, they were in an intrusive feature and undoubtedly belonged to a later time, although one can only surmise as to the date and purpose of this pit (Steve, Gasche, and de Meyer 1980: 123, 125). On the basis of their reanalysis of the stratigraphy of Chantier A, the three scholars proposed that the pit had to have been dug from a later level and ascribed it to the period of abandonment of the area between levels XI and X–IX. Then R. D. Biggs and M. Stolper (1983) published an omen text from the Iranian site of Choga Pan West that shared many features with the unusual texts of the same type that were found in Susa together with the CKU tablet and presented persuasive arguments for dating all of them some time late in the fifteenth or early in the fourteenth century B.C.[12]

Whatever the exact date, it is clear that the tablet was written by someone who was using language and writing conventions that were different from those known to us from the OB Susa school-texts. While maintaining writings such as *šà* for the Akkadian pronoun *ša*, a convention that goes back at least as far back as the Ur III documents from that city, the CKU tablet does not seem to represent the type of Sumerian syllabic orthography that is characteristic of the older Sumerian school-texts from the city. Similar to other texts from the jar found at Susa, it represents a unique literary world whose contours are not well known, that was current in Iran in Middle Babylonian times and made its way to Mesopotamia as well (Rutz 2006: 64).

Uruk

Only one CKU tablet was found at Uruk, the compilation Uka containing ŠAr1 (1), SEpM 2, and possibly other SEpM items. The tablet was found together with 179 other OB tablets that were discarded in antiquity in a *Scherbenloch,* or sherd pit, located near the ceremonial complex in the center of the city (Cavigneaux 1996: 2–5). Although none of these literary tablets bears any date, the nonliterary tablets that were discarded together with them all date from Rim-Sin 31–42. The Uruk collection consists, for the most part, of standard school texts very similar in content to those found in Nippur. However, only four other literary letters were found in this group: SEpM, found on the compilation tablet, as well as two copies of SEpM 6 and a bilingual letter of petition to Nanna (Cavigneaux 1996: 59–61, nos. 113–15). This stands in contrast to the unique catalog of letter incipits from the sherd pit, which

---

12. See also Daneshmand 2004 for a similar omen tablet from Haft Tepe and Rutz 2006 for an astronomical omen in the same style from Nippur, copied from an original from Susa. See also Michalowski 2006f.

was discussed above (pp. 25–27). The catalog is broken and does not have the full listing of the royal letters, but what is preserved indicates that the Šu-Sin and Ibbi-Sin correspondence was known to someone in OB Uruk.

Isin

The one CKU source from Isin is a landscape-oriented practice tablet.[13] It was found in "Grabungsabschnitt NIIn, Bauteil 5: Raum 335N 35E 8: 332,15N.34,60E +7,24."[14] This tablet was found in the house at this locus; the house, as well as the street outside, contained numerous literary and administrative tablets, seemingly from the time of Samsu-iluna. It seems fairly certain that whatever else may have been going on in this building, instruction in cuneiform was part of the picture. For more detail and bibliography, see Wilcke 2000: 15–16 and Delnero 2006: 49–50.

Tutub

Two tablets in Berkeley are said to have come from Tutub (Khafadje), in the Diyala region (Foxvog 1976: 101). In reality, the provenience of these tablets is difficult to establish. Niek Veldhuis was kind enough to investigate the matter at the Phoebe A. Hearst Museum of Anthropology of the University of Califormia, Berkeley, on my behalf and informs me that many of the tablets that are reportedly from Khafadje were actually purchased by Henry F. Lutz in New York in May/June of 1930 from Alfred Kohlberg, while others were brought back by Lutz from Baghdad in 1929. Since controlled digging at the site began in 1930, these cannot come from the official excavations. It is therefore impossible to know if these two tablets actually came from Tutub or not.

Tablets of Unknown Origin

Little can be said about the 37 tablets of unknown provenience. The eight Yale Babylonian Collection tablets are said to have come from Larsa. Dyckhoff (1998; 1999: 108–13) has suggested that they are part of a large group of literary texts that come from a "library of the Enki temple in Larsa" that were subsequently scattered in a variety of European and American collections.[15] Until a full investigation of these tablets is undertaken, this remains an unsubstantiated hypothesis (Brisch 2007: 33–34). It is certainly possible that some of these tablets were found in an estate belonging to a family that was closely related to an Enki temple in Larsa, but this by no means suggests that they belonged to a temple library; more probably, this is another example of home-schooling by temple officials. Certainly, Enki/Ea is prominent in some of the Yale texts. There is an unpublished myth concerning this deity in the collection; three of the CKU letters were copied in Samsu-iluna year 1 by the stu-

---

13. IB 733 = IM 766444, ŠAm1 [17] Is1.

14. I am grateful to Claus Wilcke for this information.

15. Dyckhoff (1999: 110) suggests that the Yale tablets in the range from YBC 4000 through 10,000 came from this "library" in Larsa. All the texts used here fall between these two numbers.

dent Qišti-Ea, whose other exercises are also to be found among unpublished tablets at Yale, as noted below. It is perhaps relevant that, on the Yale tablet YBC 7149, the name of Lu-Nanna, governor of Zimudar, is written as Lu-Enki.[16]

One tablet in the Abbey of Montserrat in Catalonia is said to come from Babylon, but this ascription is shaky at best. Even less reliable is the annotation "said to be from Warka" that accompanies the publication of AN1930-581 (*OECT* 5 28 [p. 54]).[17]

Very little can be said about the majority of the unprovenienced sources of RCU that are scattered in museums and private collections. The first list contains tablets that are in the British Museum:

1. BM 54327 (82-5-22,479) + 82993 (83-1-21,156)
2. BM 54894 (82-5-22,1224)
3. BM 108869 = 1914-4-7, 35
4. BM 108870 = 1914-4-7, 36
5. BM 16897+22617 (92-7-9 13 + 94-1-15 419)

Texts 3 and 4 are from purchase, and nothing instructive can be said about them at present. The first two tablets are likely to be from Sippar, although it cannot be said which mound, Abu Habbah or Tell ed Der, is the probable source. The 82-5-22 collections also included tablets from a late archive from Babylon (van Driel 1989: 114–15), but there is no information on any possible Old Babylonian texts from that site in the mix.

Here one must refer to CBS 346 (*PBS* 10/4 8, ArŠ5 [9]), from the "Khabaza collection" of the University Museum in Philadelphia. The Sippar provenience of this tablet, while hardly certain, is most probable. The "Khabaza" tablets were purchased in London in 1888 and 1895 (Civil 1979b), and because most of the administrative texts in these lots are from Sippar, it is assumed that many of the literary texts from these acquisitions come from there as well. The CBS text is quite different in appearance, ductus, and format than the excavated tablets from Abu Habbah but is similar to some others in the Khabaza collection at the University Museum and to a few in the "Sippar Collections" of the British Museum. These texts are all bilingual, with the interlinear Akkadian lines written in smaller script; some passages are fully translated, while others are only partially glossed or omitted altogether in the Akkadian version. For examples of similar tablets, one might compare the three sources for the apocryphal *Lugalanemundu Inscription*,[18] all in Philadelphia, and *CT* 58 5 from the British Museum, but there are other texts of this type in both collections. The Khabaza collections in the University Museum of the University of Pennsylvania were acquired at about the same time as the Bu 82-5-12 group in the British

---

16. See the commentary to ŠaŠu1: 27 (18).

17. Inventory numbers in the Ashmolean Museum were formerly marked as Ashm.; this has been changed to AN.

18. On the sources, see Civil 1979b.

Museum and similarly seem to have been found at Abu Habbah or Tell ed Der (van Driel 1989: 112).

Finally, one should note that collective tablet Xa, which has all four letters of the Ibbi-Sin correspondence, may also have been written in Sippar. If one looks at the matrix of the letter PuIb1 (23), in lines 6–16 and 35–46 there is an overlap of text with source Si1, excavated in Sippar, and the number of unique variants shared between the two tablets strongly suggests that they belong to the same textual tradition.

Date

All the sources, as noted above, are Old Babylonian in date, with the exception of the Middle Babylonian Susa tablet (compilation tablet Su1), and possibly compilation tablet Xf (Ni. 3083 [*ISET* 2 115]). More precision is difficult to come by, since so few of the CKU tablets bear year-names. Fifteen of the manuscripts have colophons.[19] One has only "day 26" (F), and eight have only the month and day (A, B, C, D, G, J, M, N). Five tablets have the month and day, followed or preceded by the name of the scribe (A: Sin-išmeanni; B: Qišti-Ea; D: Ali-banišu; G: Zababa-[. . .]; J: Ibni-ilum).

Year-names are used to date five unprovenienced tablets, ranging from the 1st (1749 B.C.) to the 28th year of King Samsu-iluna of Babylon (1722 B.C.). Source X2 of letter 18 (ŠaSu1, col. C) was written on the third day of the eleventh month of Si1. Three other tablets, all written by one Qišti-Ea, were written that same year: manuscript X5 of letter 2 (viii.7) has no year-name but must belong to that year, as the same young man copied letter 13 (PuŠ1) on two consecutive tablets on the 20th and 25th days of month nine of Samsu-iluna's accession year (X4, X5). Three months later, he worked on YBC 4705, which contains the *Letter of Sin-iddinam to Nininsina* (Si1.xii.16; Brisch 2007: 76).

The last two dated tablets are compilation tablet Xa (col. O), a two-column tablet of unknown origin that contained the non-Nippur versions of the whole Ibbi-Sin correspondence, that is, letters 20–24, written by someone whose name ends in *-ia-a*, son of Kubulum, on Si27.v.17; and one by Šamaš-mušallim, written on Si28. ix.5 (ArŠ4 [8], X1, col. E).

The earliest-known manuscript of CKU may be a tablet from Uruk, since the sherd pit in which it was found contained tablets dated RS 31–42 (1822–1763 B.C.).[20] The tablets from No. 7 Quiet St. in Ur and House F in Nippur were written at some time before Si11 (1739 B.C.). The tablets from No. 1 Broad St. also date from

---

19. The colophons/subscripts are collected on pp. 247–248 below, listed by letters of the alphabet.

20. ArŠ1 source Uk1. Huber (2001: 205) claims that the earliest source of CKU goes back to the nineteenth year of Sumu-la-el of Babylon (1880–1845 B.C.). She notes that the Kish tablet *PRAK* II, D 60 (PuŠ1 [13], source Ki1) belongs to the archives of the Zababa temple restored in that year by the Babylonian king. But Zababa in the colophon is simply the beginning of the

before this year, but because they may have been brought there, from one or more other houses, their date is uncertain. The Nippur tablets, which make up the largest percentage of the sources, bear no dates, but archaeological information, although not unambiguous, suggests that many of them come from around Si10 (1740 B.C.) and at the latest from Si29 (1721 B.C.), or from the first two years of Iluma-ilu of the Sealand Dynasty (Civil 1979a: 8).[21]

The Royal Correspondence as School Literature

The literary letters, including those of CKU, are almost exclusively Old Babylonian school exercises written by young boys and perhaps occasionally by young girls in Sippar (Lion and Robson 2005, Lion 2009). The curricular approach to Sumerian literature has become fashionable of late, and the elements of this instruction have been recounted so many times that it makes little sense to go over it all in detail once again; therefore, I will only provide a brief description of the issues involved to provide the proper background for further analysis.

A few decades ago, a statement such as "all Sumerian literature was school literature" would have been greeted with some skepticism; but now, due to the exemplary detailed research of Hermann Vanstiphout (1978, 1979), Niek Veldhuis (1996, 1997), and Steve Tinney (1998, 1999), the core curriculum of the Old Babylonian schools in Nippur and places that used a similar syllabus is well known, at least as far the early phases of instruction are concerned.[22] As originally reconstructed by Veldhuis (1997: 63), "Phase 1" of instruction consisted of four graded sets of texts, beginning with sign- and personal-name lists, moving on to thematic lexical texts such as the tree- and wood-list, and then to more complex sign-lists such as *Proto-Ea*, *Proto-Diri*, and mathematical tables. Then students studied their first connected Sumerian sentences, as found in model contracts and proverb collections. Having mastered the elements of cuneiform writing, the young adepts were ushered into the world of Sumerian poetry. According to Tinney (1999: 162), the initial part of this phase involved learning a quartet of short hymns to kings and deities ("the tetrad"); this in turn was followed by "the Decad," a set of ten compositions of various kinds, hymns to the kings Šulgi and Lipit-Eštar, to the goddess Nungal, the temple of Ninhursanga at Keš, as well as myths (*Inana and Ebih*, *Enki's Journey to Nippur*), and a Gilgameš tale (*Gilgameš and Huwawa A*).[23] After this, the curriculum was filled

personal name of the student and has nothing to do with a temple, and thus this dating must be abandoned.

21. The commonly-held opinion that Nippur and other southern cities were completely abandoned toward the end of Samsu-iluna's reign may have to be revised in light of the new evidence marshaled by S. Dalley 2009: 7–8.

22. See also, among others, Robson 2001; Volk 1996, 2000; and Wilcke 2000. For a recent survey, with some new perspectives, see Delnero 2006: 27–147.

23. Full matrixes of all the Decad texts are now available in Delnero 2006: 1857–2473.

with other literary compositions, but it is unclear if there was any specific order that was generally followed or if teachers chose whatever they liked at this point. Thus, E. Robson (2001: 54) has identified a group of fourteen poems that seem to follow at some point after the Decad in House F at Nippur.

One of the primary criteria for assigning texts to specific phases of the curriculum is the physical character of the cuneiform tablets inscribed with school compositions. These were first defined by M. Civil (1979a: 5) in a study of lexical texts and refined by S. Tinney (1999: 160–61). They are:

Type I	Large tablets, cylinders or prisms
Type II	The obverse contains a two-column calligraphic exercise: the left side is written by the instructor, the right-hand side is the work of the student; the reverse contains a multicolumn excerpt from a longer list.
Type III	Small, one-column tablets that contain material extracted from a longer text.
Type IV	Small lentil-shaped tablets: these have one or more lines of text written by the teacher on one side and copied by the student on the other.

Tinney adjusted this typology, which was developed for lexical compositions, adding the following categories for school literary exercises:

Type S	One-column rectangular tablets containing between ten and forty or even more lines of text. At Nippur and Ur they are almost exclusively oriented in portrait fashion; at some other places, such as Isin and Uruk, landscape-oriented tablets of this type were also used. The Sumerian term for these is im-gíd-da. These correspond to Civil's Type III.
Type M	Larger tablets with two or more columns on each side.
Type P	Prisms that have from four to nine sides. Type M and P are subsumed by Civil's Type I.

Texts from the elementary phases of instruction, through the Tetrad, are usually found on tablets of the II and IV variety; beginning with the Decad, Types I and III predominate.

Eighty-four of the 114 Old Babylonian CKU tablets are one-column daily practice tablets (Type III). About a sixth sizable—19 tablets—are compilations that contain more than one letter; most of these have more than one column per side (these are usually referred to as Type M) but there are some that have only one column and, though they are technically Type S, in practice some of them are functionally more like Type M items, containing many more lines than the usual im-gíd-da. Three compilation tablets is a prism (P). Type IV round tablets ("lentils") are likewise rare;

the single example from Sippar and the five Susa items are the only indicators that excerpts from CKU were used somewhere at the earlier level of learning.

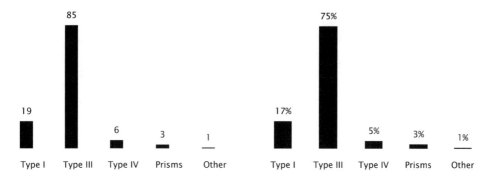

Statistically, the proportion of tablet-types is similar to the distribution established by Kleinerman (2009: 82; 2011: 81) for the SEpM and by Delnero (2006: 99–100) for the Decad:

	CKU	SEpM	Decad
Type I	17%	16.5%	24%
Type II	0%	0	less than 1%
Type III	75%	75.5%	72%
Type IV	5%	1.3%	less than 1%
P	3%	4%	4%

The Type III Practice Tablets

Because the majority of preserved CKU texts are preserved on single-column tablets, it is useful to take a brief look at the number of lines that these exercises contain. For obvious reasons, this analysis only takes into account exemplars from Nippur and Ur.

Type III CKU Tablets from Nippur		Type III CKU Tablets from Nippur	
ArŠ1 (1) 36 lines		ŠAr1 (2) 34 lines	
N2	20?–36	N2	1–34(?)
N3	1–20	N3	21–34
N4	1/20–36	N4	1–34
N5	1–13	N5	17–26
N6	20–36	N7	?
N8	1–?	N9	1–34
N10	1–20	N11	21–34

Type III CKU Tablets from Nippur	
ArŠ2 (3) 22+ lines	
N2	1–22
N3	1–?
N4	2′–20′
N6	1′–20′
N7	1′–20′(+)
AbŠ1 (4)[24]	
N1	
N2	
N3	
N4	
N7	
N8	
N9	
N10	
ArŠ3 (7) 15 lines	
N1	1–15
N3	1–15
N4	1–15
PuŠ1 (13) 34 lines	
N1	1–34
N4	1–34

Type III CKU Tablets from Nippur	
AmŠ1 (16) 12 lines	
N1	1–12
IšIb (21) 30 lines	
(short version)	
N1	1–14
N2	1–14
N3	1–30
PuIb1 (23) 51 lines	
N2	23–51
N3	23?–51
N4	1–51 (two column tablet)
N6	1–51
N7	?–51
N8	1–22
N9	1–23
IbPu1 (24) 36 lines	
N1	19–36[25]
N2	1–19
N3	1–36

Type III CKU Tablets from Ur	
ŠAr1 (33 lines)	
Ur2	1–33
AbŠ1	
Ur2	
Ur3	
ArŠ7 (20+ lines)	
Ur1	1–20+
ŠaŠu1 (18) 42 lines	
Ur1	1–23
PuIb1 (23)	
Ur2	1–36

24. All these tablets appear to contain complete versions of the composition, but because the number of lines differs in each case, it is difficult to gauge the exact count for each exemplar. The same holds true for the two Ur practice tablets. See the commentary to the edition.

25. N1 and N2 were written by the same scribe.

As a rule, the CKU daily exercises consist either of a complete letter or, in the case of longer epistles, only half the composition. Thus, each day a Nippur student learned anywhere from 14 to 36 lines of epistolary Sumerian. The much more limited Ur documentation suggests a similar practice in some school or schools in that city. This compares well with the figures established for the Decad, the ten elementary Sumerian literary compositions used at Nippur. According to Delnero (2006: 103–4), the average shortest number of lines on Type III exercises belonging to this group is 15, and the general average runs in the range between 28 and 37 lines. This type of evidence is not in itself conclusive, but it does suggest that at Nippur and Ur the CKU was studied at a relatively early level of instruction, in conjunction with, or perhaps even before or right after, the Decad.

If we look beyond Nippur, another indication for the way the CKU letters were used in school instruction comes from a set of tablets in the Yale Babylonian Collection that were written during the reign of Samsu-iluna by a student named Qišti-Ea. Wherever these texts may come from, the only other scribe by this name known to me is the "royal scribe" (dub-sar lugal) who inscribed a Louvre tablet containing the *Tale of the Three Ox Drivers from Adab*, dated to year 8 of Ammiṣaduqa—that is, 110 years later than the Qišti-Ea who wrote the Yale tablets—and thus he cannot be the same person.[26] The Yale tablets written by someone by this name are:

> YBC 4185: ŠAr1 (2): Si1.viii.7
> YBC 4654: PuŠ1 (13) Si1.ix.20
> YBC 4606: PuŠ1 (13) Si1.ix.25
> YBC 4705: *Letter of Sin-iddinam to Nininsina*: Si1.xii.16
> YBC 6713: *Two Scribes*, Si11.i.8
> YBC 7176: *Supervisor and Scribe*, Si11.iv.7[1]

If we assume that Qišti-Ea did not spend ten years in school, someone else by the same name must have written the last two. It took more than a month for Qišti-Ea to progress from CKU 1 to 13. Moreover, he waited four days before finishing the latter, because the two tablets from the ninth month contain two halves of the composition but are not dated on consecutive days. He then labored for another three months, perhaps working through a version of SEpM, before he tackled one of the Larsa letter-prayers (Brisch 2007: 34).

What of the tablets themselves and the manner in which they were used in the schools? Though the consensus is that Type III tablets represent daily exercises, there is no agreement on the function of the large Type I exemplars. Some years ago, Jerrold Cooper (1983: 46) famously observed that the larger tablets often do not have the best text and can contain more than the usual level of errors, but he did not offer any explanation as to why this might be the case. Nevertheless, his remarks remain important, as some modern redactors tend to give more credence to variants from

---

26. Cavigneaux (1987: 12) notes that, from the paleographic point of view, the tablet may have been copied in the Kassite period; see also Alster 1991–1993: 27.

the larger texts in their editions. Recently, Eleanor Robson (2001: 49), writing about mathematical exercises, stated:

> The short extracts on Type II/1 and Type III tablets were deployed in a student's first encounters with a composition, as he memorized it section by section. The longer passages on Types I, II/2, and P tablets, on the other hand, seem to be written in order to revise earlier work, consolidating individually memorized sections into lengthier segments.

Delnero (2006: 105–6) investigated the relationship between Type I and Type III tablets of the Decad and concluded that compositions were generally divided into four sections, each on a separate Type III tablet, to aid memorization, after which the student was required to write out the whole poem from memory. While working on a very different project that involves the reconstruction of the Old Babylonian "fore-runners" of the first two tablets of the canonical version of the lexical series HAR-ra = ḫubullu, I came to a similar conclusion that the best explanation for the longer tablets is that they are the ancient equivalents of exam texts. There are problems with this proposal, to be sure; for example, what are we to do with a composition such as *Nidaba Hymn C*, which is attested almost exclusively on Type I tablets? But as it stands, Delnero's proposition serves to explain the wide range of competence evidenced in these bigger formats, as well as the fact that on some such texts the level of accuracy deteriorates within the text, because some students did better than others. If one accepts this proposal as a working hypothesis, then the order and content of the compilation tablets provides some evidence for the reconstruction of the manner in which CKU letters were studied in Old Babylonian schools. I will investigate this matter below, but first I would like to end this section with comments about the nature of early school instruction.

It is now generally assumed that school children memorized texts from dictation and/or from model written exemplars and then wrote them down for teachers to check (Delnero 2006: 81). The problem is that none of the model tablets have survived, and therefore one suspects that most of the instruction was done by dictation. Nevertheless, certain features of school exercises, some of them present in CKU tablets, can only be explained by some form of recourse to a written original. There is a remarkable unity, for the most part, in the way that each text is divided into lines. The reasons for this may be purely syntactic, but the variations in the way lines are laid out are most often explained by the size of tablets or columns and not by scribal whim. One remarkable example of a feature that is best examined by redactional activity that leads to a common written manuscript, at least in the hands of some group of scribes or teachers, is an instance of crasis found in ŠAr1: 24 ([2]; see top of p. 53). Basic, commonly accepted rules of Sumerian morphology, as well as writing practices, require that the line be read as *lú igi-bar-ra-ka-ni lú li-bí-(ib)-diri, and indeed, this is what one finds in only two texts from different origins: N1, from House F in Nippur, and X2, from the Sippar Collection in the British Museum.[27] It

---

27. N1 is a compilation tablet (Na), and it does not often have the best text. It may even be that what to us is the correct writing here was actually a mistake or a hypercorrection as far as

lú igi-bar-ra-ka-ni lú-al-li-bí-ib-diri

N1	+	+	+	+	+	+	+	⸢	+	⸢	+		.
N2	o	.	+	+	+	.	.	+	+	+	⸢		.
N3	+	+	+	+	+	.	+	+	o	o	o		o
N5	.	.	o	o	o	o	o	o	o	o	o		o
N7	o	o	o	o	o	o	.	.	o	o	o		o
N8	o	o	o	o	o	o	+	+	+	⸢	.		+
N11	.	+	+	+	+	+	+	.	.	+	⸢		+
Ur2	o	o	o	o	o	+	+	ùlu	al-diri-ge				
X1	+	+	+	+	+	+	.	⸢a⸣	+	.	o		o
X2	+	+	+	+	+	+	+	⸢	+	+	in		+
X4	+	o	+	+	+a	+	+	⸢a⸣	.	.	⸢in⸣		o
X6	+	+	+	+	+	+	+	a	+	+	in		+

is impossible to know what N5 had at this point, but five Nippur duplicates have the crasis form lú-al-li-bí-(ib)-diri. It is always possible, of course, that all of these tablets came from the same house or from a group of related teaching establishments, but the fact that three of the four unprovenienced items (X1, X4, X6) have a different form of crasis (lú-a-li-bí-in/ib-diri) suggests that the eliding of lú with the verbal form in this line had at some point become a traditional part of the text, and it is hard to explain this without recourse to a written example for students to copy. After all, we know that schoolmasters sometimes sent texts to one another (Civil 1979a: 8), and this could be one form of dissemination of certain redactional features. This is not to say that all school texts were copied from actual physical examples, only to suggest that, although memorization from oral dictation may generally have been used at certain levels of instruction, at some point in their study students may have had recourse to sample tablets as well.

To get a better grasp on the curricular function of the CKU, it is useful to survey the distribution of the CKU letters on compilation tablets, their order as evidenced by catch-lines, as well as the geographical distribution of the sources.

Compilation Tablets

Here follows a brief description of all the compilation tablets, some of which actually belong to SEpM but begin or end with elements of CKU. The main reason for this listing is to help establish the order of the letters in the curriculum. Nineteen of these are Type M, three are prisms, one is an oval-shaped tablet with extracts from two letters, and two are of Type III (S) but contains two letters each.

the school tradition was concerned. This would work well with my hypothesis that many Type 1 tablets are examination pieces written from memory.

Nippur

A. Prisms (P)

Na CBS 7848+7856 (*SL* xxxviii). A fragment containing the first three sides of what was once a large prism that most probably contained all of SEpM (2–8 are preserved), beginning with ArŠ3 (7) = SEpM 1a.

Nb Ni. 9702 (*ISET* 2 122). Fragment of the bottom part of a prism; what remains of the first preserved side is blank, suggesting that it is the final side. Therefore, the other face must be the first side; it contains the last part of ŠAr3 (6) and the first three lines of ArŠ3 (7) = SEpM 1a.

Nc Ni. 9703 (*ISET* 2 120). This is a broken part of a prism that probably contained all of SEpM; the third preserved column, which was probably the last, has the end of a letter, followed by the only known manuscript of the beginning of ŠAr2 (5), but the face breaks off before the end and therefore there are no clues as to what followed. For a discussion of this prism, see Kleinerman (2011: 14).

B. Multiple Column Tablets (M)

Nd 3 N-T 311 (*SL* xxii–xxiii). This two-column tablet, from House F, was the basis for the reconstruction of the phantom Collection A. It contained ArŠ1 (1), ŠAr1 (2), and PuIb1 (23).

Ne CBS 7787 + N 1200 + N 1203 + N 1204 + N 1208 + N 1210-27a + N 1210-27b + N 1210-27d + N 1210-27e + N 1212 + N 1214 + N 1218 (+?) Ni. 4061 + Ni. 4188 (*ISET* 2 118). A two-column tablet that contained ArŠ2 (3), IbPu1 (23), and PuIb1 (24). The reconstruction of this tablet is almost, but not completely certain. It consists of two pieces, one in Philadelphia and one in Istanbul. The assumption that these two sections are probably part of the same tablet was crucial for the proper reconstruction of ArŠ3 (3). Soon after I made this discovery, Steve Tinney and then Jeremiah Peterson were able to join many small fragments to the larger CBS tablet in Philadelphia and kindly shared their discoveries with me. A hypothetical photographic join between the two sections is presented on the accompanying disc.

Nf Ni. 4149 (*ISET* 2 122). Two or more columns per side. In the original publication, the one inscribed side is marked "Obv.," but the order of the columns, which read from right to left, indicates that it is the reverse. However, the other side appears to be uninscribed, which is not what one expects of the obverse. The first preserved column has lines 1–9 of ArŠ1 (1); after the break, the text resumes in the next column with line 32 of the composition; from this one infers that the tablet had approximately 31 lines per column. The order of the surviving letters is ArŠ1 (1), followed by ŠAr1 (2).

Ng Ni. 4164 (*ISET* 2 117). This is a fragment of a multicolumn tablet with official letters and related texts. There are four compositions of this type in the preserved parts, including the otherwise unduplicated ŠuLuŠa1 (20), and the tablet undoubtedly contained more. The other three fragmentarily preserved letters on this tablet cannot be identified at the present time.

Nh Ni. 9706 (*ISET* 2 112). This is a sizable fragment of what was a very large tablet that had at least five columns on each side, as evidenced from the reverse. The remains of two columns on the obverse indicate that the tablet originally began with SEpM: the remnants of the text on col. i′ are impossible to identify but may be SEpM 8, and col ii′ has SEpM 9 (the *Tumal Inscription*). Only traces are preserved of the first column of the reverse, which must have contained SEpM letters. Column ii′ contains almost the entire last letter from that collection (SEpM 22: 2–12), followed by ArŠ1 (1). Judging by the reconstructed outline, it does not seem likely that any other CKU letters were included on this tablet. I therefore assume that the tablet contained the whole of SEpM, followed by ArŠ1 (1), ŠAr1 (2), ArŠ2 (3), and PuŠ1 (13).

Ni   Ni. 9854 (*ISET* 1 189). The remains of the obverse of a multicolumn tablet. One column has ŠA1 (1), and the next side has PuŠ1 (13). It is impossible to estimate if ArŠ1 (2) and perhaps another text was included between them.

Nj   UM 29-13-20 + UM 29-13-24 (both *SL* liii). Probably a three-column tablet that had SEpM 1–9, beginning with AbŠ1 (4) = SEpM 1.

Nk   UM 29-16-13 + N 3264 + N 3266 + N 3294 + N 3301 + N 3303 + N 3308 + N 3310 (all *SL* xxiv–xxv) + Ni. 9701 (*ISET* 2 114). Multicolumn tablet with the complete SEpM, beginning with AbŠ1 (4) = SEpM 1.

C. Single Column Tablet (S)

Nl   3 N-T 80 (A 30135, *SL* xxxi). One column tablet with ArŠ3 (7) = SEpM 1a, followed by SEpM 2. From house I.

Ur

A. Multiple Column Tablets (M)

Ura   U 7741 (*UET* 6/2 173). This two-column tablet from No. 7 Quiet St. had a medley of letters different from any other collection. The preserved section contains SEpM 19, an otherwise unattested *Inim-Enlila Letter*; AbŠ1 (4), SEpM 4, an otherwise unidentified letter; and SEpM 8.

Urb   U 16853 (*UET* 6/2 174) + *UET* 6/3 *537. A three- (or more) column tablet, this one from No. 1 Broad St, sandwiched the three most commonly attested CKU letters in between SEpM letters. The preserved order is (x), SEpM 7, ArŠ1 (1), ŠAr1 (2), PuIb1 (23), SEpM 17, and possibly more letters. Even if the tablet only had three columns per side, there is room for at least thirty lines before SEpM 7 in col i′.

B. Single Column Tablet (S)

Urc   *UET* 6/3 561 (*187). One-column tablet that contained ArŠ7 (12), preceded by another unidentified letter. See the commentary to letter 12.

Uruk

Uka   W 16743 gb (Cavigneaux, *Uruk* 143). This is a lower right-hand fragment of a tablet that contained parts of SEpM, followed by some parts of CKU. The original is in Baghdad and could not be inspected, and therefore it is difficult to determine the possible dimensions of the piece, but I suspect that it was a two-column tablet. From photographs, I was able to establish that the end of the last-preserved column on the obverse has traces of the first four lines of *Letter of Sin-tillati to Iddin-Dagan* (SEpM 2), and the final column has lines of ArŠ1: 25–28 (1), which continues on the first column of the reverse with lines 29–32, and then it breaks off. It is impossible to know what preceded SEpM 2 and how many more of the Isin letters were in the last column of the obverse. The remains of the top of the second column of the reverse are blank, and therefore the tablet ended with ArŠ1 (1) or perhaps with ŠAr1 (2).

Susa

Sua   Susa A XX/1 1962/3 (*MDAI* 57 1). This Middle Babylonian two-column tablet
contains ŠPu1 (14) and ŠIš1 (15). On the date, see pp. 42–43 above.

This tablet is unique: it is bilingual, with the Sumerian text running on into the
Akkadian, separated, when the language changes within a line, by an U sign, but
otherwise continuous, so that it does not respect lines as such, with words continuing from line to line. It also turns like the pages of a modern book rather than on
the bottom axis. There are examples of Old Babylonian tablets with lexical texts
that read in this manner, but I know of no standard literary exercises of this kind.
Indeed, the only other example of a literary tablet that turns in this manner is Xf
(see below).

Origin Unknown

A. Multiple Column Tablets (M)

Xa   A7475. This two-column tablet has all four letters of the Ibbi-Sin correspondence,
including the long versions: IšIb (21), IbIŠ1 (22), PuIb1 (23), and IbPu (24). There
is no information on its origins—only that it was purchased in Iraq by Henri Frankfort. The tablet is possibly from Sippar.

Xb   A w/n. This two-column tablet contains ArŠ1 (1), ŠAr1 (2), ArŠ2 (3), PuŠ1 (13),
ŠPuOBa1 (14a), and ŠPuOBb1 (14b).

Xc   BM 54327. This is a fragment of what must have been a two-column tablet, judging
by the curvature. When complete, it had ArŠ1 (1), ŠAr1 (2), a gap of around 70
lines, ŠuŠa1 (19), and PuIb1 (23). The scribe misjudged the size required and began
to run out of space in the last column, so that lines of PuIb1 (23) had to be skipped,
and eventually the composition remained uncompleted. The gap may have been
filled by either ArŠ2 (3) or PuŠ1 (13) and, most probably, by ŠaŠu1 (18).

Xd   BM 54894. This is a small left-hand fragment from the middle of what must have
been a rather large tablet that contained a version of SEpM, followed by CKU letters, similar to Nd. The obverse had a number of letters, of which only a few lines
(2–10) of SEpM 4 remain. The remains of the final column of the reverse have the
beginning of PuŠ1 (13); it is likely that this was the last CKU text on this tablet.

Xe   Crozer 206a. This is a two-column tablet that contained the first eight letters of
SEpM, beginning with AbŠ1 (4). Nothing is known about its origins, and its present location is likewise a mystery: the Crozier Seminary collection, last held by the
Rochester Theological Seminary in Rochester, NY, was sold at auction to anony-
mous purchasers.

Xf   Ni. 3083 (*ISET* 2 115). This tablet is housed in the Nippur collection in Istanbul,
but there are reasons to be cautious about its provenience. My doubts about the
origin of this tablet begin with paleography: the tablet simply does not look like an
Old Babylonian Nippur text; it may be either late OB or even MB in date. I am fully
aware of the subjective nature of such an assessment, but this is based on decades of
work with Nippur tablets in Philadelphia and Istanbul. Be that as it may, there are
more precise reasons for doubting the Nippur origin of this tablet.

There is another feature that sets this tablet apart from most OB, and certainly
from most Nippur school texts of this format, namely, that it turns like a modern

book: the columns on the reverse have to be read from left to right rather than from right to left. Thus the marking of obverse and reverse on the published copy has to be reversed. On this kind of tablet, see the comments on tablet Sua above.

Assuming that each column contained approximately 51 lines, Xf preserves the remains of five letters: PuŠ1 (13), ŠPu1 (14), AmŠ1 (16), ŠAm1 (17), ŠaŠu1 (18), and IšIb1 (21). Two of these—letters 17 and 18— are otherwise not attested at Nippur and one (AmŠ1) is documented by only one other Nippur duplicate.

Xg YBC 7149. This is a two-column tablet containing the Šu-Sin correspondence, ŠaŠu1 (18) and ŠuŠa1 (19).

B. Single Column Tablet (S)
Xh YBC 4596. This is a one-column tablet with ArŠ1 (1) and ŠAr1 (2).

C. Oval Exercise Tablet
Xi LB 2543 (*TLB* 3 172). This is an almost complete oval-shaped exercise tablet that has excerpts from AŠ1 (1) and ŠrA1 (2).

A survey of the documentation reveals that, from the curricular point of view, AbŠ1 (4) and ArŠ3 (7) belong to SEpM, although they are treated here as part of CKU on thematic grounds. Usually, Ur III royal letters were studied before SEpM, although there are at least two compilation tablets on which the order is reversed (Nf, Xd, possibly Xc). The Abaindasa letter of petition was edited by F. Ali (1964: 53–62) as the first item of his "Collection B"—that is, SEpM—and as a result it has been considered to be the "canonical" B1, with ArŠ3 (7) = SEpM1a as an alternative. But there is no reason to privilege one over the other, and the alteration between them seems quite free, in Nippur at least, since the latter is only documented in four tablets from that city. For example, one AbŠ1 source from House F has a catchline to SEpM2,[28] but in a house next door (I) someone copied ArŠ3 and SEpM on the same tablet.[29] If we tabulate the order of items on the compilation tablets, without including those that belong strictly to SEpM, adding the sequence in the *Uruk Letter Catalog* (ULC, lines 1–8; ( ) = restored), we obtain the results shown in the table on p. 58: This correlates well with the information derived from catchlines, which are only present on tablets from Nippur:

Letter	Sources	Letter	Sources
2→3	N3, N4, N11 [30]	7→SEpM2	N3, N4
3→13	N6	16→17	N1
→23	N4	23→24	N3
4→SEpM2	N2 [31]		

28. 3 N-T 309 = AbŠ1 (4), N2.

29. 3 N-T 80 = ArŠ3 (7), N1.

30. The catchlines are all lugal-ǧu$_{10}$-ra ù-na-a-dug$_4$, and while this could refer to some other Aradmu-Šulgi letter, it is most likely a reference to ArŠ2 (3).

31. The catchlines on letters 4 and 7 all read lugal-ǧá ù-na-dug$_4$; the use of ǧá for the pronoun is a way of indicating that this is SEpM 2 rather than one of the CKU letters.

	Nb	Nd	Ne	Nf	Nh	Ni	Urb	Xa	Xb	Xc	Xf	Xg	Xh	Xi	ULC
1		x		x	x	x	x		x	x			x	x	(x)
2		x		x	x (x)	x			x	x		x	x		(x)
3			x	x					x						(x)
6	x														
7	x														
13					x	x			x		x				
14a									x		x				
14b									x						
16											x				
17											x				
18										(x)	x	x			x
19										x		x			x
21								x			x				x
22								x							
23		x	x				x	x		x					x[32]
24			x					x							x

The order of items on the compilation tablets and the catchlines is our best source for the reconstruction of the native ordering of the CKU letters. There are some other lines of evidence that may offer supporting documentation. First, there is the evidence from House F, which had the following (Robson 2001: 58, revised):

Letter	Number of Sources
ŠAr1 (1)	4
ArŠ1 (2)	2
AbŠ1 (4)	2 (one has catchline to SEpM 2)
IŠIb1 (21)	1
PuIb1 (23)	2

This must be compared to the small collection of tablets found in House I (Robson 2001: 59), which had one tablet with ArŠ3 (7, followed by SEpM 2). This house had only a few literary tablets; aside from this tablet that had the first two items of SEpM, it had one with SEpM 9,[33] a tablet with one of the three surviving Nippur manuscripts of *Nidaba Hymn C*,[34] as well as one unidentified literary exercise.

32. See p. 429 below.
33. 3 N-T 109 (A 30146).
34. 3 N-T 213 (A 30179, *AOAT* 25 pl. XVI*).

		Nippur	Ur	Uruk[35]	Isin	Kish	Sippar	Susa	Unknown	Total
1	(ArŠ1)	10	1	1(x)					8	20
1a	(ArŠ2)								1	1
2	(ŠAr1)	11	2	(x)				2	6	21
3	(ArŠ2)	7					1		2	10
4	(AbŠ1)	10	3					2	3	18
5	(ŠAr2)	1								1
6	(ŠAr3)	1							1	2
7	(ArŠ3)	5								5
8	(ArŠ4)								1	1
9	(ArŠ5)								1	1
10	(ArŠ6)								1	1
11	(UrŠ)								1	1
12	(ArŠ7)		1							1
13	(PŠ1)	4				1			5	9
14	(ŠPu1OBa)								2	2
	(ŠPu1OBb)								2	2
	(ŠPu1MB)							1		1
15	(ŠIš)							1[36]		1
16	(AmŠ1)	2							1	3
17	(ŠAm1)				1				1	2
18	(ŠbŠ1)		1	x					3	4
19	(ŠŠb1)			x					2	2
20	(LuŠŠ1)	1		x?						1
21	(IšI1)	3							5	8
22	(IIŠ1)								2	2
23	(PI1)	9	2	x			1	1	5	17
24	(IP1)	4		x		1	1		2	8

Finally, there is the matter of the number of sources for each letter and their provenience, which are correlated in the table above. The existing data, which are hardly abundant, lead to the conclusion that the main body of Ur III letters that

35. Entries from *ULC* are entered as x.
36. Middle Babylonian.

schoolteachers drew upon in Nippur at the time of Samsu-iluna consisted of the Aradmu/Šulgi correspondence about the officer Apilaša (letters 1–3), one letter from general Puzur-Šulgi to Šulgi (13), as well as a missive from Puzur-Šulgi, the general of Kazallu to King Ibbi-Sin (23). Then, depending on criteria that are simply unknown to us, they chose either the petition letter of the captain Abaindasa to Šulgi (4) or a letter from Aradmu to the king about this officer and then moved on into the SEpM collection (7). Only two other letters have some presence at Nippur, augmenting this core batch of six or seven items: a letter from Išbi-Erra to Ibbi-Sin (21) and Letter 24, a reply from Ibbi-Sin to the general Puzur-Numušda (23). This expands the Nippur CKU core to eight or nine letters, but there are also single exemplars of four more (5, 6, 15, 20).

At the same time, compilation tablets demonstrate that at least two schoolteachers, one at Nippur and one elsewhere, utilized an even smaller set consisting only of the three Apilaša letters (1–3) and the Puzur-Šulgi missive (13) and that these were taught after SEpM (Nd, Xd). If one takes into account all of this information, it is apparent that the core of CKU in Nippur consists of letters 1, 2, 3, 13, 23, to which must be added the two alternating SEpM 1 letters, AbŠ1 (4) and ArŠ3 (5), and no 21. The Sippar Yaḫrurum (Abu Habbah) documentation points in a similar direction, since the only CKU tablets actually found in the OB "schoolhouse" in the city are part of letters 3, 23, and 24. The only Kish witness of CKU is also part of the core, namely, letter 13. Finally, at OB Susa, the existing evidence also represents the same small subgrouping (2, 4, 23).

The evidence appears as scattered, fragmentary, statistically unrepresentative, and heterogeneous, because the recovery situation at each of these cities is quite different; all of this only bolsters the hypothesis that there was a basic core set of fewer than ten CKU letters that were used in Old Babylonian schools in Nippur, Sippar, Kish, and Susa, and possibly elsewhere. The number of manuscripts from these sites supports this assumption; given the small percentages of the manuscripts from Sippar, Kish, and Susa in the overall number of CKU witnesses, the relatively uniform choice of core letters seems representative after all.

This north–south curricular harmony is disturbed by the evidence from Uruk, which provides only one actual CKU source, part of the ubiquitous letter ArŠ1 (1), but the catalog from the city includes the Šu-Sin correspondence, which is not part of the Nippur core. The main evidence for this reconstruction is found in the first preserved lines of the *Uruk Letter Catalog*, which was presented in full on pp. 25–27 above. The first legible lines have the two Šu-Sin letters (18 and 19), followed by IšIb1 (21), IbPu1 (24), PuIb1 (23), and then, after a letter prayer to Nanna that is only known from Uruk, by what is possibly AbŠ1 (4). It is impossible to know how the list began, but it probably had ŠAr1 (1) and ŠAr1 (2) and possibly ArŠ2 (3). One would like to know if PuŠ1 (13) was included or not, because it is quite possible that it was replaced by the Šu-Sin letters, as at Ur. [37]

---

37. Note, however, that compilation tablet Xf had both letter 13 and 18.

At Ur, the list is similar but not quite the same: ŠAr1 (1), ŠAr1 (2), 12, 18, 23, as well as AbŠ1 (4). The unduplicated no. 12 aside, Ur used the Nippur core (albeit thus far letter 13 does not show up there) but with the addition of the Šu-Sin correspondence (letter 18), as in Uruk. It may be only a matter of chance of discovery, but letter 13, the Puzur-Šulgi letter that describes the work on the fortifications at Bad-Igihursağa, is missing at both Ur and Uruk, and in its place teachers seem to have used the Šarrum-bani correspondence that concerns the construction of another line of forts, Muriq-Tidnim. This trio of epistles (18–20) will be discussed in detail in chap. 6.

Hypothetical CKU Core[38]							
N, Si, Ki	1	2	3	13	(21)	23	(24)	4/7
Ur	1	2		18 [19]	21			4
Uruk	1	[2	3]	18 19		23	24	4

Finally, a word must be said about the tablets of undetermined origin that constitute 32% of the total CKU documentation. As already noted, anecdotal information and guesswork aside, there are few clues to where they were discovered, and though some of them may come from major sites such as Larsa or Sippar, it is equally possible that some proportion of these tablets may have been found in peripheral sites and may have been written decades after the majority of the provenienced tablets.

The rest of the letters, outside of the core, are poorly attested and widely distributed, and this has important implications for the analysis of the Old Babylonian versions of Ur III royal correspondence. The quantity of extant sources tells a story. While 114 tablets may seem to be a large number, one has to keep in mind that this total covers 24 different, if related, compositions from various places of origin and that, core texts aside, most CKU letters are very poorly documented. In many ways, the general statistics presented above are in concert with the situation found in House F in Nippur. As observed by Robson (2001: 58), this locus produced only one or two manuscripts of letters and related texts, from CKU as well as from SEpM. The only exception to this is, as can be expected, ArŠ1 (1), which is represented by four exemplars. This contrasts markedly with the number of tablets from the so-called Decad and of some other examples of school literature found in the house, which are documented by up to thirty or more manuscripts, although there are also other hymns, "law codes," debates, etc., that are represented by single exemplars (Robson 2001: 53–56). Taking together all the evidence adduced above, it seems most probable that selections from the available corpora of CKU, SEpM, as well as sundry literary letters, not to mention ad hoc epistolary creations by teachers as well as by students, constituted a regular but relatively marginal part of the instructional

---

38. In this chart ( ) mark the "extended core" and [ ] denote reconstructed items.

materials utilized in Old Babylonian schools and that the choice of items very much depended on the preferences of individual instructors.

Beyond the Core

I have indentified the core of CKU on purely distributional grounds, without any consideration of the contents of the letters. Moving further, but taking into consideration only the general thematics of these items, it seems that Old Babylonian educators and their wards most often became familiar with the problems that the grand vizier Aradmu and his king Šulgi had with an officer by the name of Apilaša, with difficulties that the general Puzur-Šulgi encountered when he was repairing sections of large fortifications, and with elements in the early history of Išbi-Erra's usurpation of power at the time of King Ibbi-Sin, as related by Puzur-Numušda, governor of the city of Kazallu. In addition, they knew something about a lower-level Ur III officer, Abaindasa, who had been demoted and perhaps even imprisoned by Aradmu. Those who explored more of the Ur III royal correspondence learned about Išbi-Erra when he was still working for the state and studied Ibbi-Sin's answer to the governor of Kazallu. As already asserted, this appears to be the situation at Nippur, Ur, Sippar, and Susa, but it only pertains to 9 of the extant 24 CKU letters, and it still leaves us with 15 items of this correspondence that need to be accounted for.

Letters ŠAr2 (5), ŠAr3 (6), and ArŠ4 (8) belong to the Aradmu/Šulgi correspondence concerning Abaindasa. The first two may be variant recensions of one another, but because only the beginning section ŠAr2 (6) is preserved, this cannot be firmly established. Letters 5 and 6 are found in sequence on a Nippur prism (Nc), but this does not necessarily undermine the hypothesis that they are variants of one another, because there is another example of this kind of sequence in the case of ŠPu1 (14), which is found in two recensions on the same tablet.[39] The letter ŠAr2 (5) was also known outside of Nippur, as documented by a manuscript of unknown origin (X1), but ŠAr3 (6) is unduplicated at present.

Letters ArŠ1a (1a) and ArŠ6 (10) are represented by unique manuscripts and may all be one-off exercises, possibly by students rather than teachers. This is certainly the case with 1a, which is simply a muddled attempt at combining letters 1 and 2 to create a new letter. The only OB bilingual CKU letter, ArŠ5 (9), is duplicated by an unpublished text and therefore is no longer represented by a solitary manuscript. Item 15 of CKU (ŠIš1), purportedly written to Išbi-Erra by King Šulgi two decades after his death, known only from a bilingual MB manuscript from Susa, is a late concoction, perhaps written in late OB times or later.

Three letters may be secondary creations designed for curricular symmetry in order to provide epistolary pairs expanding the core: ŠPu1 (14) as an answer to PuŠ1 (13), IbŠ1 (22) as a reply to IšIb1 (21), and IbPu1 (24) in response to PuIb1 (23).

---

39. A w/n (compilation tablet Xb).

All of this accounts, more or less, for the curricular status of 17 of the 24 CKU letters. The situation is less clear when it comes to the two letters concerning a merchant by the name of Ur-dun (letters 11 and 12), and to an exchange of missives between Šulgi and his successor-to-be Amar-Sin (letters 16 and 17). The first two are, in all likelihood, one-off creations that utilized literary materials from various sources, including lexical texts and the SEpM, but the Amar-Sin correspondence, which has wider distribution but is still badly documented, is more difficult to evaluate. The fact that tablets with these letters were found at Nippur and Isin as well as on a tablet of unknown origin suggests that they had a more secure presence in school study than one might assume from the bad state of the preserved documentation.

In conclusion, the CKU, unlike SEpM, is not an established, mostly set group of texts utilized in a systematic manner in school instruction. Instead, it consists of a general, sometimes shifting core group of texts, with occasional additions, some of which are clearly ad hoc creations made by teachers or students, while others belong to a peripheral collection of materials that instructors could call upon to round out their teaching materials. The exact contours of this phenomenon are somewhat fuzzy due to the aleatoric manner in which the Old Babylonian literary sources have been recovered, but the general outline of the problem is clear: the CKU is not a native category but only a modern construct assembled for heuristic purposes, for ease of publication and citation. The CKU was not a fixed "corpus;" instead, it is better understood as an expandable set of epistles, purportedly between the kings of Ur and their subordinates, that were, by and large, studied together before, after, or alongside the SEpM and other literary letters.

Chapter 4

The Royal Letters in
Their Historical Setting 1

The Affairs of King Šulgi (Letters 1–12, 15–18)

Of the 24 CKU letters, 17 are written to and from Šulgi. These can be divided, on thematic grounds, into groups: the Apilaša affair (letters 1–3), the Abaindasa affair (4–8), miscellaneous Aradmu letters (9–10), the Ur-dun affair (11–12), the Puzur-Šulgi correspondence (13–14), the letter from Išbi-Erra to Šulgi (15), and the Amar-Sin correspondence (16–17). Here I survey these letters, with only a cursory discussion of items 13 and 14, because these will be analyzed in chap. 6, which deals with fortifications—that is, with the major topic of the Puzur-Šulgi/Šulgi epistles as well as of the correspondence of King Šu-Sin (letters 18–20).

The Apilaša Affair (Letters 1–3)

The most commonly attested epistolary exchange in Sumerian consists of three letters between the grand vizier Aradmu and King Šulgi concerning a military officer by the name of Apilaša (letters 1–3). Aradmu, the powerful grand vizier of the Ur III state, is the only correspondent who figures in more than two CKU letters; indeed, he is either the author or recipient of 10 or 11 of the 24 items in this set (1–10 and possibly 12), but only the Apilaša letters and missive 7 are part of the core group.

The lives of Aradmu and Apilaša are well documented, and nothing in the Ur III record contradicts the information contained in CKU. I begin the discussion of the first part of the literary royal correspondence with a brief look at the biographies of the main protagonists.

Aradmu

The information pertaining to this individual has been collected in other places and need not be reiterated here in full.[1] It is usually agreed that Aradmu is a form

1. Sollberger 1954–1956: 37; Goetze 1963: 9–12; Scharaschenidze 1976; Sallaberger 1999: 188–90; Dahl 2007: 22–24. Here I use the conventional traditional rendering, although some scholars prefer other forms such as urdu/ÌR-ĝu$_{10}$; on the reading of the name, see Appendix B.

of the name Arad-Nanna, well known as the highest military and political official of the Ur III state from some time late in Šulgi's reign into the reign of Ibbi-Sin. His primary title was sukkal-mah, "grand vizier," and under Amar-Sin he also took over direct rule of the Girsu province: at least from AS7 on he carries the title énsi Girsu, "governor of Girsu (province)."[2] From ŠS1 he was also designated as sukkal-mah énsi, "grand vizier and governor of Girsu (province)," but only in documents from Girsu (Sallaberger 1999: 192).[3] In the long inscription dedicated to Šu-Sin, he is described as sukkal-mah énsi lagaša[ki] (Frayne 1997: 324, lines 11–13). In CKU, as in most Ur III references to his name, he never carries any title.

There is some confusion concerning the early parts of Aradmu's career: it is generally assumed that he rose to the status of grand vizier with the accession of Amar-Sin (AS3, according to Huber 2001: 196 and Sallaberger 1999: 189), and this has been used as evidence of the fictitious nature of his correspondence with Šulgi (Huber 2001: 195–97). A reevaluation of the beginning of his long tenure at the side of the Ur III kings is therefore necessary here.

The office of the sukkal-mah appears to have its roots in Girsu, where it is first attested in documents from the Early Dynastic period in archival texts as well as in the *Reforms of Urukagina*, where it comes right after the ruler (énsi), but the title is also attested at Nippur and Uruk.[4] References to such an official continue throughout the Old Akkadian period in texts from Girsu and Adab.[5] The same tradition was maintained at Girsu when the city was once again independent, during the time that is usually referred to as the "Gutian period," when the so-called Second Dynasty of Lagaš ruled the city and its environs. We know that a certain Bazi was the sukkal-mah in the second year of the reign of Ur-Ningirsu I (*MVN* 7 512:6). An unnamed individual held this position in the twentieth year of Gudea (*MVN* 7 399:8), and the grand vizier of the last independent king of Girsu, Nammahani, was named Ur-aba (Edzard 1997: 202–3). If the tradition documented at the time of Urukagina is any measure, these officials were the "Grand Viziers" of the kings of the Lagaš polity. This hierarchical relationship was carried over when Lagaš was incorporated into Ur-Namma's state, but now the sukkal-mah answered to the king in Ur. In the immediate aftermath of the collapse of Ur, the title continues to be attested in Isin

---

2. First attested in the last month of AS7 (*PDT* 2 1161:2). The title sukkal-mah is the only one he uses in his seal dedicated to Šu-Sin (Frayne 1997: 347, line 6).

3. First documented in the basket tag *ITT* 2 810 (ŠS1.-.-), probably from the latter part of the year. Curiously, this combination of titles is attested only in "court protocols" (di til-la) or basket tags for collections of such documents, with one exception only (*TCTI* 620 t. iv 11–12).

4. See, for example, *VS* 14 159: ii 4; *VS* 14 171: vii 1; *VS* 14 173: ii 15; *VS* 14 179: vi 6; *DP* 132: iii 4; *TSA* 2 iv 9. For Urukagina, see Wilcke 2007: 32. Note also at Nippur *OSP* 1 137:1 and possibly *BibMes* 3 30: iii 2. See also the dedication of šu-na-mu-gi₄ [sukkal-m]ah-e for the life of Enšakušana of Uruk (Frayne 2008: 432; E1.14.17.3:2–3), and Lugalzagesi's title sukkal-mah den.zu (Frayne 2008: 435; E1.14.20.1:21–22).

5. See, for example, *ITT* 1 1282:6; Donbaz-Foster, *OPBF* 5 53:3; 128:14, *MCS* 9 276:6; Nippur: *OSP* 1 137; Adab: *OIP* 14 144: 5, 7 (= *PPAC* 1 A 795).

and Ešnunna, although little is known about the role of this official in post–Ur III times.[6] As is well known, in post–Ur III times the title sukkal-mah was borne by the rulers of Elam, in vague memory of their earlier overlords and of Aradmu's functions. In an inscription of Idaddu II, one of the last rulers of the "Šimaški Dynasty," it denoted the status of a secondary ruler of Elam, subject to the king (lugal) of Anšan, Šimaški, and Elam (Steinkeller 2007a: 222), and therefore was not that far removed from its Ur III meaning. Soon after, during the first half of the second millennium, the nomenclature used by the sovereigns of Elam changed, and sukkal-mah usually described the supreme ruler at Anšan, while his sons were addressed as sukkal when they administered the various parts of the state: Elam, Šimaški, and Susa. The understanding of these titles is somewhat complicated by the fact that at various times the former may have been used to designate both the concept of "supreme ruler" as well as that of "regent," according to Vallat (1994: 9).[7]

I should note that, in my estimation, the term "Gutian period" is a misnomer and should be avoided in discussions of early Mesopotamian history. It follows a tradition sanctioned by the Old Babylonian redaction of the *Sumerian King List*, a history-creating composition that illustrates an ideology that supports and justifies large, centralized statehood, as opposed to regional autonomy and city-states. The period between the collapse of the Akkad kingdom and the rise of the territorial Ur III state was a time when Sumer and Akkad were ruled in various ways from different cities. The area west and northwest of Nippur, around Kazallu and Marad, was occupied at least for some of this time by the forces of Puzur-Inšušinak from the Iranian highlands; in the south, Adab, Umma, and possibly a few other cities acknowledged some form of domination by Gutians from the eastern highlands, while others, such as Girsu, Uruk, and Ur, thrived independently. The native historiography, emblematically represented by the *Sumerian King List*, is very murky on the subject of this period, and every manuscript of the text that preserves this section has a different set of Gutian rulers, many of whom may be fictitious (Michalowski 1983b). The modern historian is by no means bound by such native views of history. Piotr Steinkeller (forthcoming) is preparing a more expansive criticism of received ideas about this period, and I am in agreement with most of his views on the matter.

I have raised this issue here to underscore the fact that, prior to the reign of Ur-Namma, Girsu stood at the head of a powerful independent polity, and nothing in our documentation sheds any light on the mechanisms—military, political, or economic—that the founder of the Ur III kingdom utilized to bring Lagaš into his territorial state. In the introduction to his so-called "Law Code," Ur-Namma claims

---

6. For Ešnunna see Whiting 1987: 83. In early Isin texts, the sukkal-mah functioned as maškim for transactions concerning diplomacy and war, just as Aradmu did in Drehem texts, such as, e.g. *BIN* 9 383, 388, *BIN* 10 149, *TLB* 5 8, etc.

7. The title may have had an afterlife farther north, in Georgia; according to Krebernik (2006: 91): "Falls das Wort im Onomastikon der georgischen Mythologie weiterlebt—Sukalmaḫi heißt dort der Vater des Helden Amirani—müßte es durch Elamische vermittelt worden sein."

to have done something to King Nammahani of Girsu, but the verbal root is difficult to read at this point and scholars have variously seen this as a violent overthrow ("he killed") or the instillation of a vassal/governor ("he elevated/installed," Civil in press). It is possible that one of the ways in which the king of Ur compelled Girsu to become a part of his kingdom was to appeal to the self-interest of the ruling elites in the city. The documentation for the early part of the Ur III period is scant indeed, but we know that the governor of Girsu, between the second and twelfth years of Ur-Namma's reign (at least) was named Ur-aba, and it is possible that this was the same person who had been the grand vizier under Nammahani.[8] This kind of continuity may indicate that other elite families were co-opted and acquired additional prestige and wealth under the new masters of the land. It may very well be that the "dynasty" of sukkal-mahs of Ur III times came from one of the most important lineages in Girsu and that the office of grand vizier was instituted by the government at Ur as part of that province's acquiescence to membership in the new state; this could also serve to explain why the title seems to have been kept in one family for much of the duration of the state founded by Ur-Namma.

The office of sukkal-mah is first attested, for Ur III times, in Š25 (*OBTR* 141:4; *TÉL* 250: r. i 5), but the name of the holder of the office is unknown. The first identifiable grand vizier of the state was Lani, who is known only from four impressions of a seal of one of his underlings, named Iddi-Erra. The earliest dates from Š29.12.- (*TCL* 2 5537) and the latest from Š32.12.- (*TCL* 2 5538; see also *Ontario* 1 166 [Š30.4.-] and *PDT* 1 374 [Š31.12.-]).[9] The latter does not mean very much, because the seal may have been in use for some time after Lani no longer held that position. The next grand vizier was Ur-Šulpae, son of Lani, who is known only from four references: *AnOr* 7 2 (Š36.9.-), from the impression of his seal on an undated bulla (*NFT*, 185), and on an envelope fragment (*NATN* 388), and in an unpublished document with a broken Šulgi year-name.[10] Therefore, unless someone else came in between, Ur-Šulpae's son Aradmu must have become sukkal-mah at some time after the last two months of Š36, not during the reign of Amar-Sin. Indeed, two texts provide direct evidence for his tenure in this high office under Šulgi.

First, he is indisputably already grand vizier in Š45, as documented in *BaM* 16 (1985) 217 no. 2, which contains the imprint of his seal, which reads:

^{d}šul-gi, nita kala-ga, lugal uri$_5$^{ki}-ma, lugal an ub-da limmu$_2$-ba, árad-[^{d}nanna], dumu ur-[^{d}šul]-pa-ʳèʾ, sukkal-[mah], árad-[zu]

O Šulgi, mighty male, king of Ur, king of the four corners (of the universe), Arad-Nanna, son of Ur-Šulpae, grand vizier, is your servant!

8. *RTC* 261, (UN2.-.-) to *RTC* 265: r. iʹ 8, iiiʹ 5 (UN12).

9. The reading of the second sign in the name, NI, is uncertain.

10. Newark Public Library 27:14 mentions dam ur-^{d}šul-pa-è sukkal-mah (courtesy of Marcel Sigrist).

Second, he continues in this role a year later, as evidenced by *TIM* 6 36:7, dated Š46.3.-, which must be read árad-^{d}nanna sukkal-⟨mah⟩ maškim.

Other information allows us to move this accession to high office back a few more years, to Š42 and perhaps even a year earlier. The basis for this is the career of a person named Ahuni, who is described as dumu sukkal-mah, "son of the grand vizier." If we assume that this refers to the current holder of that position—and all evidence suggests that there was only one such dignitary at any one time—then the dates of these documents tell a story, because he is attested in the following documents:

CT 10 44: 16	Š 42.-.-
MVN 13 641: 17	Š 47.5.-
NYPL 27: 4	AS 4.-.-
Nebraska 1: 26	AS 5.9.-

This line of reasoning is bolstered by the fact that, beginning with the last month of Š41 (*TCL* 2 5502+5503, Š41.12.-), Aradmu (as maškim) authorized Drehem disbursements connected with the royal family, their closest retainers, including the royal bodyguard, as well as foreign dignitaries and their entourages. There are at least 130 such texts from the remainder of Šulgi's reign; indeed, this would remain one of his official responsibilities for three decades—that is, for the rest of the duration of the Puzriš-Dagan depot.[11] Of course, Aradmu did not reside there; he also presided over the province of Girsu and at least one other administrative center, a place that was located not far from Nippur and housed the prisoners of war brought back from Šu-Sin's campaign against Simanum.[12] Officials acting under his authority ascribed documents and transactions to his name, but state officers of the highest ranks did not always have to be present for operations conducted under their authority.

In conclusion, it is fairly certain that Aradmu succeeded his father and grand-father as grand vizier at some point between the years Š36 and Š41 (he is undoubt-edly sukkal-mah by Š45) and retained that position throughout the rest of Šulgi's reign, those of his two successors, and into the first years of the last ruler of the dy-nasty, King Ibbi-Sin.[13] He is last attested in IS3 but may have held the position for up to a decade after that.[14] The next grand vizier is not documented until a decade later, when Ninlil-amagu was in this position (*UET* 3 45 seal, IS14.9.-). Eight years later, he had been replaced by Libur-Sin (*UET* 3 826 seal, IS22.6.-); we know next to nothing about either of these men and therefore cannot establish if either one of

11. He is last documented in this role in IS2.12.12 (*MVN* 8 207:7).

12. This archive is being prepared for publication by Benjamin Studevent-Hickman.

13. This sequence is apparently interrupted by the evidence provided by *MCS* 6 106 = *MVN* 37 (Š48.10.-), which carries a seal that read, according to the copy, ur-^{d}nin-mug, dub-sar, dumu lú-^{d}ba-ba$_6$, sukkal-^{r}mah^1. Collation, courtesy of Piotr Steinkeller, definitely excludes this reading of the final line.

14. He is last attested in two Girsu documents, both dated IS3.-.-: *TCTI* 1 897: r. v 15 and *Zinbun* 18 (1982) 96 1: r. ii' 6'.

them belonged to the same lineage as Aradmu, but by then the office would have had a different scope, because Girsu was no longer part of the kingdom. [15]

In light of these facts, one must also set aside the prosopographic arguments presented by Huber (2001: 196–97), who thought that Arad-Nanna/Aradmu was still a junior military officer in the last years of Šulgi. There are a number of other people named Aradmu and/or Arad-Nanna in documents from Šulgi's reign, but at present there is no reason to identify any of them with the person of the grand vizier. [16]

This was an extraordinary career; throughout the reigns of four kings, he was in charge of diplomacy, the military, and some of the border regions of the state during almost three decades of constantly shifting foreign alliances and continuous warfare. He was married to a princess of the house of Ur, and one of his daughters in turn married a prince of the realm. [17] His ceremonial, military, and diplomatic functions in the state are best observed in the Puzriš-Dagan texts, where he carries the responsibilities (maškim) for transactions involving the royal family, foreign dignitaries, and high members of the military. As already noted, in the latter part of Amar-Sin's reign, he was put in charge of the Girsu province, officially returning to the place that was most likely his ancestral home, thus obviating any tensions between his high rank and the role of the city governor. It may only be the lack of sources that leads us to this conclusion, but it does appear that his status increased as the years went on, and late in the reign of Šu-Sin, he took charge of the military administration over much of the eastern frontier, which he would have controlled from Girsu. The evidence for this comes from a dedicatory text inscribed on door sockets from a temple of Šu-Sin in Girsu (Frayne 1997: 323–24) that was built by Aradmu. In addition to his standard titles, the grand vizier is now also a temple administrator (saĝa) of the god Enki, as well as the general in charge of Ušar-Garšana, Bašime, Sabum and the territory of Gutium, Dimat-Enlila, Al-Šu-Sin, Urbilum, Hamazi, Karhar, Nihi, Šimaški, and Karda. [18] The multiple responsibilities parallel those given by Šu-Sin to his own uncle Babati, as we shall shortly see; the list of place-names suggests

15. Ninlil-amaĝu occurs once before, in IS2.3.- (*SET* 168: 5). There are no other references to Libur-Sin.

16. If we limit ourselves to Girsu, among these are Arad-Nanna; lú-kaš₄ (*ITT* 7690: 4, Š33.1.-); àga-ús (*ITT* 4 8089: 3, Š4.-.-); àga-ús lugal (*ITT* 4 7306: i 5, Š30.-.-); nar (*Princeton* 1 570: 1, Š35.1.-); and engar (*CT* 1 2 ii 12, Š37.-.-). There is one text that definitely refers to the person we are dealing with: *Nisaba* 7 3:10 (Š42.-.-, Girsu), kišib₃ igi-lam-lam dumu ur-ᵈšul-pa-è ki árad-mu-ta. It is clear that both Igilamlam and Aradmu were brothers, sons of Ur-Šulpae, the sukkal-mah.

17. His wife, nin-hé-du₇ appears as dam sukkal-mah in the undated Girsu tablet *ASJ* 9 (1987) 126 57: iii 13 (otherwise she is listed only as dam sukkal-mah, without a name). His daughter-in-law, géme-é-an-na, appears as é-gi₄-a árad-mu sukkal-mah (*OIP* 121 9:7; AS2.12.10); she was still alive, albeit ill, in AS6.4.5 ([géme]-ʳéʳ-an-na é-gi₄-a ʳaradʳ-muʳ u₄ʳ tu-ra ì-ʳme-aʳ, *MVN* 13 635:11). Both women are listed among princesses (dumu-munus lugal) in *CTMMA* 1 17: I 28 and ii 1 (AS6.7.-).

18. On all of these places, see Steinkeller 2010. For Bašime, 66 km north of Amarah, see now Hussein et al. 2010; on the location of Hamazi, see Appendix D below.

that this new status was connected to war with the lands of Zabšali that took place in Šu-Sin's sixth year and that it was bestowed upon Aradmu either during the preparations for, or in the immediate aftermath of this military effort. We should bear in mind, however, that many of these titles may have been more honorary than real, since the grand vizier already shouldered many responsibilities; indeed, a survey of administrative and legal texts in which his name appears makes it clear that he could not have been physically present at every transaction that he officially sanctioned. Therefore, there must have been officers to whom he delegated authority to act in his name, and we must assume that reference to his name is often institutional rather than personal.

Aradmu also carries the title énsi lagaša[ki] in his inscription, and this has created some confusion in the modern literature (see below). Thus, Dahl (2007: 24) cites this as evidence that the man "was able to add the governorship of Lagash to his impressive array of titles" and also states that this title was only used in his monumental inscription. This is only partly true: the title is also used in a dispute resolution from Girsu, which, unfortunately, has a broken date (*ITT* 2 1034 = *TCTI* 1 1034). The matter is more complex, however, and has to do with the terminology used to describe what was probably the largest province of the Ur III state (de Maaijer 1998).

In documents from Girsu and from other parts of the realm, the governors appointed to rule this area are always—other than the two instances cited above—designated as énsi ĝír-su[ki]. But on the seal inscriptions of local officials, the governor is always, without exception, referred to as énsi lagaša[ki], "governor of Lagaš (territory)." These governors, and following them the Grand Vizier as well, are using the traditional local terminology, which is explicitly explained by the goddess Nanše as she addresses King Gudea (Cyl. A6.15): ĝír-su[ki] é-saĝ ki lagaša[ki]-šè ĝìri-zu ki ì-bí-ús, "after you direct your feet to the city of Girsu, storehouse of Lagaš-land . . . ."

The significance of this is difficult to gauge; perhaps there is an element of oppositional fervor, which may also be seen, for example, in the use of a seal dedicated to the famous ruler Gudea during the time of Šu-Sin, but it is also possible that this is simply a local custom, with few ideological overtones.[19] Thus, Aradmu did not acquire a new title; in his own inscription and in one legal dispute he utilized the local terminology, while on documents from the governor's office his scribes continued to use the official title énsi ĝír-su[ki], just like his predecessors.

Apilaša[20]

Apilaša appears only in the Šulgi correspondence. In the letters, his only title is gal-zu unken-na, conventionally rendered here as "prefect," which is unattested

---

19. Aradzu seal of Ur-Šarura, *ITT* 2 4216 (ŠS6.11.0).

20. Kutscher 1968–69; Huber 2001: 202–5. On the name, see Hilgert 2002: 240. In Ur III documents, it is written a/á-pi/pi₅-la-ša; in CKU, it is consistently rendered a-pi-il-la-ša in Nippur sources and a-pi-la-ša in texts from other places.

in Ur III sources, and in CKU it is borne by only one other official, Šarrum-bani, the man sent by Šu-Sin to rebuild the Muriq-Tidnim fortifications.[21]

Apilaša's military career is documented in more than 60 documents from Drehem, Umma, Girsu, and Nippur, covering at least 22 years, from Š44 to ŠS9. By the time he first makes an appearance in the documentary record, he had obviously risen though the ranks to a top military position. In the 44th year of Šulgi, he delivers part of the booty from a highland place called Šuruthum (*MVN* 20 193: 5, Š44.4.-). In the following year, he is mentioned as one of the collectors of grain alongside generals such as Huba'a (*HLC* 52: r. 33, Š45.-.-, Girsu). This is also the case in many texts mentioning Apilaša from the time of Šulgi and Amar-Sin. He is first designated as šakkana, "general, commander," in the last year of Amar-Sin's reign (*TCTI* 2 3315:3, AS9.9.-), but by then he had already been appointed governor of a major city; it is probable that he held the rank much earlier.[22]

The references from the last years of Šulgi indicate that he belonged to the highest military echelons at the time; texts in which he is mentioned in the company of high military officials are marked by /m/.

45.-.-	*HLC* 52: 28 (Girsu)	m
46.1.24	*AfO* 24 pl. 15 S 213:3	m
4.5	*PDT* 1 168:17	m
5.13	*OIP* 115 203:17	m[23]
9.7	*PDT* 1 408:12	m
12.29	*PDT* 1 678:6	
47.12.8	*TRU* 109:9	
12.12	*OIP* 115 268:5	m

Sometime between the 15th and 30th day of the fourth month of AS7, Apilaša assumed the governorship of Kazallu, an important city in the frontier military zone in the area west and northwest of Nippur and south of Kish.[24] It is rare that we can pinpoint an official appointment with this degree of precision in this period, but in this case we have a document that records both the contributions of the previous governor, Šu-Mama, on the fifteenth day, and those of Apilaša, with his new title, on the last day of the month (*JCS* 14 [1960] no. 9).[25] This last text refers to him as governor, but his own seal inscription, impressed on the tablet, gives his title as "general of Kazallu." He continued to hold this post at least until ŠS3 (*JCS* 22 [1968/9]

21. On this title, see Appendix B.

22. He holds this title in three other Girsu texts, but two of them are undated: *RTC* 317: r. 38 (ŠS1.10.-); *DAS* 77:13; and *DAS* 329:4.

23. He delivers Šimaškian animals, undoubtedly from the booty garnered in the campaign against Simurum and Lullubum in the previous year.

24. On this zone ("mada"), see pp. 125–129 below.

25. Kazallu was governed first by Ititi (Š28.5- [*PDT* 1 516: 9]), then by Issariq (Š31.4.- [*YOS* 4 75: rev. 2']; Š33.3.- [*AnOr* 7 92:7–8]), then by Kallamu (Š43.2.- [*PDT*1 509:3]; Š46.8.- [*Nisaba* 8 App. 4+A: 4]), who was transferred to Ešnunna (Hallo 1953: 76), then by Šu-Mama from Š47.10.- (*TRU* 116: 4), until Apilaša took over.

63); a recently published tablet provides no title but places him in Kazallu in the first month of ŠS5, and we would assume that he was still in charge of the city.[26] He seems to have remained there for some time, but the lack of evidence makes it difficult to trace his residency in Kazallu, because no subsequent governor of Kazallu is attested in Ur III sources, if we exclude the CKU. Apilaša is last mentioned in the last years of Šu-Sin's reign, when he seems to have once again been involved in frontier matters.[27]

His tenure at Kazallu was interrupted once in AS8, and Apilaša must have been seconded to other duties, because just after his appointment a certain Ititi is mentioned as governor of Kazallu. How long this lasted is unknown, but less than two years later, in ŠS1, Apilaša was back at his post in charge of the city.[28]

The Aradmu–Šulgi letters concerning Apilaša provide unique perspectives on power relationships in an early Mesopotamian state. While most of the school literature presents King Šulgi as a superhuman figure of unlimited charismatic authority—political, intellectual, and martial—the CKU compositions offer a portrait of a realistic and canny ruler who is cognizant of the limits of his authority. In ArŠ1 (1), the grand vizier writes to his master, reporting that he has been sent on a royal mission to the eastern frontier to check on the situation in the territory controlled by the officer Apilaša, to assure the flow of taxes back to the homeland and to bring new instructions to the locals. There are three issues in the opening lines that require comment: the exact location of Apilaša's camp, the taxes imposed on the area, and his official title.

The general area that Aradmu has traveled to is referred to by the name Subir (ArŠ1: 3 [1]). The same term occurs twice more in CKU: in Aradmu's subsequent answer to Šulgi's reply and in the letter of Puzur-Numušda to Ibbi-Sin, where we encounter a certain Zinnum, who is a governor of/in Subir.[29] Much has been written about this geographical term, which changes reference over time and space; in third- and early-second-millennium sources, it refers to an area east of the Tigris in the mountains of Iran (Michalowski 1986, 1999a; Steinkeller 1998). In Old Babylonian literary texts, it is often coupled with Elam, and the division between seems to lie in the Diyala region (Michalowski 2008). The example of ArŠ2: 6 [3], where Simurum lies in the territory of Subir, is in harmony with this literary usage.[30] It is important

---

26. A Drehem tablet from a private collection mentions sheep given to Lamassatum, the bride/daughter-in-law (é-gi₄-a) of Apilaša, "when she went to Kazallu" (Hallo 2008: 114 lines 21–22).

27. *Trouvaille* 50:6 (ŠS9.-.-), where he is responsible for the undelivered dues from troops of Arman in the Diyala, and *ASJ* 16 107 7:8 (ŠS9.9.3). He is also responsible for deliveries of one ab-ba lú NE-da-DUN^{ki} in *BPOA* 7 2340:25–26, an undated Drehem account that probably comes from some time after ŠS6.

28. Ititi is listed in *PDT* 1 561:9 (AS8.5.-). Apilaša is mentioned next as governor of Kazallu in *SAT* 3 1219:3 (ŠS1.11.-).

29. ArŠ2: 6 (3) and PuIb1: 34 (23).

30. The text reads: zag si-mu-ur₄-ru-um ma-da su-bir₄^{ki}-šè.

to note, however, that the term Subir does not appear to have been included in the geographical language of the Ur III bureaucracy: there is not a single mention of the word in any text from the period.

The taxes that Aradmu is sent to regulate are designated as gun mada (ArŠ1: 4 [1]). In administrative texts from Ur III times, this is a technical term that designates a specific kind of obligation imposed on military outposts in frontier areas, as described in detail by Piotr Steinkeller (1987). However, as Pascal Attinger already observed (apud Huber 2001: 204 n. 153), the exact phrase gun mada never occurs in texts from the time of Šulgi; indeed, it only makes an appearance from the year ŠS3 on, although the actual tax is no different from what is earlier designated simply as gun. For some, this is proof of the spurious nature of this letter, but we must keep in mind that the difference between gun and gun mada only applies in the accounting terminology used at Drehem, and the change takes place at a time when various other reforms of the administration and technical language were introduced at this redistribution depot (Sallaberger 2003–4). There is no reason to associate the language of the letter so closely with the technical jargon of one administrative center, and therefore the meaning of these words in the letter may be more general— that is, it may refer to all forms of frontier taxation.[31]

Apilaša is referred to by the unusual title galzu unkena, which may signify that he was not a regular general of the region but a special emissary, involved with some unspecified task.[32] But the welcome accorded Aradmu was offensive to some degree, and, what is more, the insults were aimed not at him personally but at the king himself, since he was acting as a royal representative. When the grand vizier arrived at the gate of Apilaša's establishment, most probably an elaborate military camp, no one inquired, as etiquette required, about the king's well-being; those sitting did not rise in his presence and did not prostrate themselves before him. As argued in the commentary to ArŠ1: 10 (1), the expression of concern about the king's health was apparently a formalized greeting that was considered proper in such circumstances. Refusal to rise before a royal messenger was a serious offense in the ancient world, as is well illustrated in the much later myth of *Nergal and Ereškigal* (Foster 2005: 55) in which this is the main narrative trigger that opens up the entire drama. When a messenger arrives in the heavens from the queen of the Netherworld, all the gods and goddesses rise except one, and this creates a major diplomatic row between the two realms.

In the Aradmu letter, these offenses lead to further denunciations by the grand vizier. Not only is Apilaša acting in a high-handed fashion—in essence rejecting the ceremonial symbols of his subservient status—but he has also apparently usurped the very trappings of royal power and, by implication, is acting as if he were an independent ruler. He receives visitors on a dais—a symbolic object usually reserved for

---

31. It is this kind of general usage that most likely led to the inclusion of the expression in the lexical tradition. See gun ma-da = MIN (*bi-lat*) *ma-a-tu₄* (Hh II 371 [MSL 5 80]); also possibly in Nigga 469 (*MSL* 13 109).

32. See Appendix B.

deities and kings—in an elaborate enclosure made of carded animal skins and filled with treasure. To underscore Apilaša's alleged arrogant attitude, Aradmu calls his camp é-gal, the same word that is usually applied to the royal seat of power.[33] The vizier expresses his apprehension early on in his letter; but when Apilaša serves him a feast fit for a whole army and then has his bodyguards turn over the table before Aradmu can enjoy his meal, the situation becomes more than just tense. The vizier writes to the king that he is afraid that Apilaša's rebellious stance will end in real violence. Aradmu's rhetoric is carefully chosen and covers much ground, damning Apilaša in the eyes of the king.

Šulgi's reply comes as something of a surprise. Rather than support the most powerful member of his court and express indignation at the reported actions of his officer who was on assignment in the east, he turns the rhetorical game back against the grand vizier and defends Apilaša's actions. Briefly stated, the ruler of Ur expresses his own outrage at Aradmu's accusations; how could he have been so foolish to misunderstand the situation he had observed? Apilaša, stationed in a dangerous territory far from Ur, had no choice but to take matters into his own hands and to resort to ruthless methods; indeed, his actions were in fact the proper way of executing the king's own orders. Having cleverly chastised the grand vizier, he then turns around and asks both Aradmu and Apilaša to cease their feud and to arrive at a mutually satisfactory agreement. The discourse of the letter is designed to reveal both the wisdom of the king—who understands the limits of his power in frontier regions—as well as his clever manipulation of the people on whom he must rely as he rules his kingdom. The epistolary exchange continues, however, and in the only extant answer to a royal reply in the whole of CKU (ArŠ2 [3]), Aradmu takes cues from his master and utilizes his own rhetoric of subordination to diffuse the situation and to maintain his own high position. The letter is difficult to understand, but the general outlines of the grand vizier's discourse strategy are clear. He begins by reporting the general state of the entire Ur III state, which is, by implication, in magnificent shape due to his personal efforts. He then reports on brigands who have settled in the area outside the cities, where royal control is weak; but this passage is simply a defense of his own actions. He then turns to the main topic of his epistle, an explanation of his relationship with Apilaša, whom he has known from childhood. In this manner, he alludes to the intimate, close-knit nature of the elite groups that were close to the Crown and to his own status with them; Aradmu has nothing but praise for the wise king who recognized the other man's abilities and promoted him to his high rank. How could Aradmu ever be set against such a faithful servant of the Crown? The sycophantic language of the grand vizier reaffirms the hierarchical relationship between the king and his most powerful subordinate. He appeals to the patronage of the king, while at the same time implying a similar relationship between himself and Apilaša.[34]

---

33. See the commentary to ArŠ1: 9 (1).

34. I am using the term "patronage" in the limited sense that has been investigated by Raymond Westbrook (2005).

The opening lines of Aradmu's reply include an interesting geographical perspective on the borders of Šulgi's state (ArŠ2: 4–6 [3]):

> ⁴(The entire kingdom), from the sea of Dilmun land ⁵to the brackish waters at the foot of the Amorite Highlands ⁶to the borders of Simurum in the land of Subir.

Here the Persian Gulf is referred to as "the sea of Dilmun land" (a-ab-ba kur dil-mun^{ki}) but later in CKU, in a letter addressed to Ibbi-Sin at the very end of his reign, this body of water is designated as "the sea of Magan" (a-ab-ba má-gan-na^{ki}, PuIb1: 9 [23]). The former refers to the island of Falaika and its vicinity, while the latter is now thought to designate roughly the area of the United Arab Emirates/Northern Oman (Zarins 2008: 215). References to Magan, although hardly abundant, occur from Šulgi's time into the reign of Ibbi-Sin,[35] but the rare occurrences of Dilmun begin only with Amar-Sin's second year. Indeed, Dilmun is only mentioned three times in the Ur III record, in a cluster of texts concerning a group of "Amorite" maš-maš practitioners who arrived from there (AS2.6.3–4),[36] in a record of a boat loaded for a trip to Dilmun in IS1.6.14 (*UET* 3 1507), and in an enigmatic undated Girsu record that documents a group of royal bodyguards (àga-ús lugal), who had arrived from Dilmun but were ill (*RTC* 337).

To summarize: the three letters concerning the Apilaša affair provide a perspective on the image of Mesopotamian kings that is complementary to the overpowering poetic self-representation of the royal hymns and related literature. In the letters, King Šulgi is portrayed as a wise and judicious ruler who understands the limits of his own power and knows how to balance the various claims to authority among his subordinates, siding with a provincial governor against the grand vizier, but also controlling Aradmu without losing his loyalty.

The Abaindasa Affair (Letters 4–9)

The epistolary material concerning an officer by the name of Abaindasa is heterogeneous and badly documented. Five of the six letters belong to the Aradmu dossier and the sixth is a letter of petition from Abaindasa himself to Šulgi (AbŠ1 (4)= SEpM1). The latter is the only poetic letter of petition in the CKU, although some of the SEpM poetic epistles of this type were undoubtedly addressed to Ur III rulers or were later composed as such (Kleinerman 2011). Moreover, this composition, although preserved in 15 sources from Nippur, Ur, and Susa, as well as on three tablets of unknown origin, is extremely unstable, with a level of textual variation that is unmatched by any other CKU item. Indeed, in my experience, the textual variation in this text is unique in the standard OB literary corpus. Not only is the text open

---

35. The references to Magan are discussed in Englund 1990: 132–34 and now in Zarins 2008: 271.

36. mu amurrum maš-maš dilmun-ta e-ra-ne-šè: Owen, *Ebla 1975–1985* 287 A: 3 (AS2.6.-), *CST* 254: 2 (AS2.6.3), *TRU* 305:3 (AS2.6.4).

to manipulation by teachers and perhaps even students, but its place in the Nippur curriculum is also unfixed: on some tablets, it opened SEpM, while on others, it is replaced in this role by the prose letter ArŠ2 (7) = SEpM1a, which deals with Abaindasa but was sent from Aradmu to Šulgi.

Even though Abaindasa was the subject of more letters than anyone else in CKU, the whole affair is murky, and it is difficult to establish anything more than the broadest outline of the problems that beset him. Of the five prose letters (nos. 5–9), two are attested only at Nippur (ŠAr3 [6]; ArŠ3 [7]) but are documented only on a single prism that seems to have a unique, expanded version of SEpM. One is known only from a single manuscript from that city and from a somewhat different manuscript of unknown provenance (ŠAr2 [5]), another is documented by a unique tablet of unknown origins that is difficult to read in places (ArŠ4 [8]), and the final manuscript, possibly from Sippar, is definitely a spurious later scribal creation that only mentions Abaindasa in passing in broken context (ArŠ5 [9]). None of these compositions can be fully reconstructed at present.

One is tempted to create a single narrative from all of these letters, but the dossier is essentially a modern fiction, created from sources that were never read together in antiquity. From the Nippur perspective, the affair appears to have been documented primarily by the letter of petition of Abaindasa (AbŠ1 [4]) or by ArŠ3 [7], which alternated as the first item of the SEpM; that is, it is quite possible that students only knew one or the other, depending on the tradition that their teachers followed.

Abaindasa's letter of petition (AbŠ1 [4]), which is the most intelligible of the whole group, describes his lot in metaphorical terms and provides no information on the details of his experiences. All one gathers from the entire dossier is that he was an officer stationed in Zimudar and that he was dismissed from his position and imprisoned. The Zimudar reference (ArŠ3: 5 [6]) is somewhat suspect and may point to the Šu-Sin correspondence as the source of this contamination or perhaps as the inspiration for a complete fabrication. Aradmu investigated his case on behalf of the king, and it may be that Abaindasa was returned to his post. As matters now stand, the only full description of an episode in the ongoing Abaindasa drama is contained on a tablet of unknown provenance that is almost complete but extremely difficult to understand (ArŠ8 [8]).

Although partly impenetrable, this letter is critical for understanding the Abaindasa affair. It seems that Aradmu reports that the officer, cashiered from the ranks and thrown into prison, had been let free and reinstated as a result of royal intervention, perhaps due to the effectiveness of his letter of petition to Šulgi (AbŠ1 [4]). The second half of ArŠ4 (8) is extremely difficult to make out, but we may discern that Aradmu, unhappy with the king's ruling, is accusing Abaindasa of further mischief and insubordination. The "authenticity" of the missive is suspect, to be sure; furthermore, it may link the position of Abaindasa with the bad mada fortifications that are the likely subject of the Puzur-Šulgi correspondence, if the reconstruction and interpretation of a crucial line is correct (ArŠ4: 16 [8]):

[kí]ĝ lugal-ĝu₁₀ mu-un-šub bàd im-mi-in-dù

(Abaindasa) abandoned the task (assigned by) my king and applied himself to work on building the fortifications.

None of this makes very good sense, because we would think that the king would want Abaindasa to work on fortifications, but since the actual task (kíĝ) that is the subject of all of this correspondence is never specified, it may have concerned other matters altogether. Either the person who composed this had no idea about these affairs and knew them only from existing letters or the word bàd here does not allude to the bàd mada and this letter has nothing to do with the Puzur-Šulgi works.

This letter contains at least one line that is somewhat suspect (line 5):

ra-bi sí-ik-ka-tum ugula nu-banda₃ érin daĝal-˹la˺ lugal-ĝá˺-ke₄

The military rank *rabi sikkatum* is not attested in Ur III times.[37]

The impression one gets is that, at some points in the transmission of CKU, new letters concerning Abaindasa were added and some of the already existing letters were modified along the way, but which epistles or motifs may have originated in Ur III times and which ones were later elaborations is impossible to discern at present. It is also important to note that the name Abaindasa is unattested as such in any Ur III text; it is documented only once in the form a-ba-an-da-sá (*UDT* 58 r. iii 15, Š43.-.-, Girsu).[38] This form of the name is also known from Old Akkadian times (*MAD* 4 70:11, *ECTJ* 29: rev. iii 11). In the letters, his title is ugula éren zú-kešda (lugal), which is likewise unattested in Ur III.

Origins and transmission aside, the letters of the Abaindasa affair, much like the Apilaša correspondence, reaffirm the statecraft of King Šulgi, who knows when to defend junior officeholders against higher ranking officers and who is willing to overturn local verdicts. How this relates to actual Ur III practice is unknown, because we have no information on the role of the Crown—if indeed there was any—in controlling and affirming local decisions of this type, including judicial proceedings on the frontier, although we must assume that mechanisms for complaints by local officials existed. In light of the fact that at least some of the Old Babylonian students who were learning these texts were children of local officials and would eventually assume the roles of officials themselves, we can see the Ur III disputes between Aradmu and his master as distanced examples of relationships between the Crown and its officers. As W. F. Leemans (1968) noted some years ago, in Hammurabi's time, the king was personally invested in various provincial issues, arbitrating disputes on his own, but as N. Yoffee (1988: 104) has observed, "these decisions do not represent resolutions

---

37. See Pientka-Hinz 2006 and the commentary to the edition below.

38. This is an entry in a long list of workers, perhaps connected with àga-ús, assigned to various shrines in the temple complex of Nanše. This particular fellow is marked as deceased. See also *NATN* 955 I 17 a-ba-an-x-[x] (Nippur; the text is in Baghdad; collated on a cast in the University Museum, Philadelphia).

between disputants but were, rather, political acts of a king either supporting or occasionally restraining his own bureaucrats against complaints about their behavior." At some level, at least, the CKU exemplifies relationships of this kind but depoliticizes them to some degree by projecting them into the past.

Miscellaneous Aradmu-Šulgi Letters (Letters 9–10)

The correspondence between the grand vizier and his king also includes two solitary items that are without duplicates and without an answer; both are undoubtedly OB concoctions.

Letter 9 (ArŠ5) combines elements of the Puzur-Šulgi correspondence, namely, the construction of fortifications at Igihursaĝa, with the mention of Abaindasa. The text is bilingual, but the Akkadian version does not always match the original very precisely, and it appears that the scribe who wrote this version had a somewhat idiosyncratic knowledge of Sumerian compared with what we are accustomed to, at least from Nippur. It is also clear, however, that the author of this exercise, or perhaps of an earlier version, had other sources to draw on, even if some of it became garbled at some point in the making of the letter or in the process of transmission. The last preserved line of the obverse mentions the Ur III princess Kunši-matum, who was married off to the ruler of the highland principality of Simanum, only to be ousted, together with her husband, in some form of coup at the beginning of the reign of Šu-Sin (Michalowski 1975; Sallaberger 2007: 442). The king of Ur led a punitive expedition against Simanum and reinstated Kunši-matum on the throne of the allied state. The name seems to have survived in this letter but was misunderstood as an Akkadian intrusion and was therefore translated into Sumerian, creating additional confusion.

The last Aradmu missive of this "dossier" (ArŠ6 [10]) resembles the beginning of letter 3 in tone if not in wording, offering praise for the king and apparently moving on to report the grand vizier's achievements, but the fragmentary state of the only existing manuscript hinders any fuller analysis. The language of this section is more reminiscent of royal hymns than of the epistolary literature, very much suggesting a late date of composition. This supposition is further bolstered by the mention of the place names Gutium, Mari, and Rapiqum, because the first and last really have no place in a letter from Ur III times.[39]

The Ur-dun Affair (Letters 11–12)

The two letters concerning a merchant by the name of Ur-dun are known to us only in single manuscripts.[40] The first (UdŠ1 [11]), which was sent by this man to

39. Lines 5′–6′; see the commentary to the edition.
40. The reading of the second element of the name is uncertain; the reading Ur-dun is conventional (see the commentary to UrŠ1: 2 [11]).

a king, who must be Šulgi, is clearly a post–Ur III fabrication, written by someone who knew the Apilaša-affair letters as well as the Šu-Sin correspondence. Following the example of Aradmu, the merchant reminds the king that he had been sent on a royal mission, in this case to purchase juniper resin in the eastern mountains. But the high-handed Apilaša had sent for him and had his men confiscate Ur-dun's goods. In words that echo Aradmu's denunciations of the very same officer, the merchant describes how no one bothered to hear his complaint when he appeared at the prefect's palace. He then explains that Aradmu and Babati—the latter borrowed from Šu-Sin's letter to Šarrum-bani (ŠuŠa1: 35 [19])—were not available to help him, because they had gone on a mission from Zimudar to Simurum; notably, the only other letter in which these toponyms are both mentioned is the missive from Šarrum-bani to Šu-Sin (ŠaŠu1: 9, 14 [18]). The rest of the text is imperfectly preserved, but it appears that Ur-dun warns Šulgi that he fears the affair can only end in violence. As noted in the commentary to the edition of UrŠ1 (11), the borrowings from other letters as well as the questionable grammar of the letter strongly suggest that this is an Old Babylonian creation.

Letter 12 (ArŠ7) seems to have little in common with no. 11 except for the mention of the same merchant, Ur-dun. The solitary manuscript from Ur is incomplete, and we are missing the beginning and end of the letter. The contents indicate that the addressee must have been royalty, and therefore we suspect that once again Šulgi is involved. The identity of the writer remains unidentified for now, and it is only conjecture that Aradmu is involved. No juniper resin is mentioned; instead, it appears that precious stones of various kind are the subject of the narrative; perhaps the acquisition of precious materials from the highlands is the thematic link between the two letters. As noted in the commentary to the composition, it is filled with rare words and utilizes vocabulary taken from the lexical and school epistolary traditions, strongly suggesting that this composition, like the one that precedes it, is an Old Babylonian fabrication.

Hans Neumann (1992b, 2006) cautiously tried to connect this Ur-dun, known at the time only from UrdŠ1, with a merchant by that name who was active in Ur III times, although he was well aware of the problems involved. In view of the fabricated nature of these missives, I would argue that this fictitious character had nothing to do with his Ur III namesake; instead, he was lifted, for the purposes of fiction, from another Old Babylonian school text, one that was studied together with texts of an epistolary nature, namely, the *Announcement of a Lost Seal* that was part of the SEpM (text 14). This composition will be edited and commented upon by A. Kleinerman, so here I only offer a composite text and a translation of the main part of the text:

1. kišib$_3$ mu-sar-ra ur-dun dam-gàr-ra ú-gu ba-an-dé
2. inim pu-úh-ru-um-ma-ta
3. niğir-e sila-sila-e si gù ba-ni-in-ra
4. lú-na-me níğ-na-me ugu-na li-bí-in-tuku

An inscribed cylinder seal of the merchant Ur-dun has been lost. By order of the assembly, a herald (announced this by) blowing the horn throughout the streets. (From this day forward) he will not owe anyone any obligation.

Whatever the genealogy of letters 11 and 12 might have been, they are missing at Nippur and are clearly marginal within CKU.

The Puzur-Šulgi Correspondence (Letters 13–14)

In the CKU, Puzur-Šulgi is the general of a location named Bad-Igihursaĝa, a place-name that is unknown outside of the literary tradition. It is probably intended to be understood as the fortress that anchored the fortifications built by Šulgi that was celebrated in the names of his 37th and 38th regnal years; the historical circumstances of this entire construction are discussed in chap. 5.

The Letter from Išbi-Erra to Šulgi (Letter 15)

This fascinating epistle is obviously a late creation, attested only in a single bilingual Middle Babylonian version from Susa. What makes this text so interesting is that it was composed by someone who had imagination—possibly even a sense of humor—but also knowledge of the Sumerian literary and lexical tradition; moreover, this person knew well many of the other parts of the Ur III royal correspondence. There are absurdities, including the very synchronism between Šulgi and Išbi-Erra, as well as the amounts of silver and gold mentioned, which are excessive, to say the least. While technically not impossible, it is improbable that these two individuals, the second Ur III monarch and someone who came from Mari but is first attested a generation later, would have had any contact, epistolary or otherwise. Indeed, as we shall presently see, Išbi-Erra is mentioned only once in the extensive Ur III archival documentation, and by that time he was already the independent ruler of Isin.

The amount of gold that Babati is said to have received from the crown for Išbi-Erra—600 talents of silver and an equal amount of gold—is preposterous even by imperial Mesopotamian standards and in a sense anticipates the absurd amounts of treasure contained in a much later literary epistle, the first-millennium Akkadian-language *Letter of Gilgameš*.[41]

The derivative nature of this text is impossible to miss: the mention of the high commissioner Babati, with his title pisaĝ-dub-ba, is derived from the Šu-Sin correspondence, the subject of gold and silver for purchasing grain, as well as the very figure of Išbi-Erra was taken from the Ibbi-Sin letters, and a passage about the nature of punishments available to royal officers (lines 24–26) is lifted almost verbatim

41. This composition, thus far attested only in the late–seventh-century Assyrian literary collection at Sultantepe (ancient Huzirina), was first edited by Gurney 1957; see Foster 2005: 1017–19, with further literature.

from letter 2 (ŠAr1). Thus, although the linguistic features of both the Sumerian and Akkadian versions suggest a post-Old Babylonian date of composition, the intertextual gestures to much of CKU leads us to believe that perhaps this letter was already pieced together in Old Babylonian times, when all of the other epistles would have been available, and that the text we have shows marks of later redaction. Alternatively, we have to posit that the knowledge of some parts of CKU lasted longer than can presently be documented and that other Middle Babylonian manuscripts may ultimately surface. This is not completely unexpected, since we know that the second-millennium purge of the majority of Old Babylonian Sumerian-language literature was a complex affair that may have proceeded in stages, as can be observed from the material collected by N. Veldhuis (2000).

The late Old Babylonian/early Middle Babylonian literary tradition that was transmitted to the west, known from places such as Bogazköy, Ugarit, Amarna, and Emar, preserves very little memory of the Ur III kings, but this might have been different at Susa and elsewhere in the east. At present, however, we know little about the complex cuneiform traditions of second-millennium Iran, which appear, judging from the modest remains recovered to date, to have been quite different from what was preserved in the west.[42]

The Amar-Sin Correspondence (Letters 16–17)

The letters from Amar-Sin to Šulgi and the king's answer offer the biggest challenges to any editor of the CKU material. The state of preservation of the existing manuscripts, described in full in the commentaries to the editions, simply does not allow for reliable reconstructions. The fragmentary remains testify to the distribution of these letters in Nippur, Isin, and elsewhere, but the contents are difficult to evaluate. The subject seems to be much more prosaic than the usual CKU topics: it appears that Amar-Sin, who seems to have military responsibilities, is writing to the king about fields and irrigation work. If I understand the oblique reference to the area around Apiak correctly, the prince may have been stationed in the military zone discussed in the next chapter—perhaps even at the fortifications built by his father that are the main focus of the Puzur-Šulgi correspondence. Nothing can be said about the genealogy of either of these two letters; it may be that they are not derivative, because the main topic is not generic and is not borrowed from elsewhere, but at the same time it is possible that its atypical character may also indicate later composition.

42. On this Iranian tradition, see pp. 43, above.

Chapter 5

The Amorites in Ur III Times

The "Amorite question" has been one of the most debated and contested issues in the historiography of ancient Near Eastern studies for more than a century. It has occasioned such publications as *The Empire of the Amorites* (Clay 1919), with its pan-Amorite hypothesis, as well as its refutation by T. Bauer (1926, 1929), not to mention others such as *Who Were the Amorites* (Haldar 1971), or other more modern studies by D. O. Edzard (1957: 30–45), H. B. Huffmon (1965), G. Buccellati (1966), C. Wilcke (1969), and M. Streck (2000). The conversation changed radically as a result of the discovery, in the 1930s, of the archives in the palace of the kings of the city of Mari on the Euphrates River. French excavators discovered thousands of eighteenth-century-B.C. cuneiform tablets in the ruins of Tell Hariri (the modern name of the mound), written in the Babylonian language, containing hundreds of Amorite personal names, and many of these texts are available for study. The ongoing reexamination of these texts by Jean-Marie Durand, Dominique Charpin, and their collaborators has changed the way we view social, ethnic, and political relationships in northern Mesopotamia and Syria in the first centuries of the second millennium—so much so that they have insisted on renaming the Old Babylonian period (quite incorrectly, I think) the "Amorite Epoch" (e.g., Charpin and Ziegler 2003; Charpin 2004a, 2004b; Durand 2004). The dynastic lines in most of the principalities of the time may have had Amorite roots, but this is not necessarily an aspect that should be chosen to essentialize a historical moment. We really do not know how important this "ethnic" factor was in society and how deeply it was rooted in very different states and social groups. Although the documentation is extensive, our most abundant and informative source of information, the Mari archives, covers no more than 50 years, and the main body of the texts—primarily letters—spans no more than two decades or so (Charpin and Ziegler 2003: 1). As important as these texts are—and some have dedicated their entire lives to the study of the Mari materials—they provide us with a small and idiosyncratic entry into this ancient society; this is but a peephole, and our field of vision has definite boundaries.

The scribes of Mari wrote in Semitic Babylonian—more specifically, in one scribal dialect of Babylonian used in Ešnunna—but in all probability many of the inhabitants of Syria and northern Mesopotamia at this time spoke a variety of Amorite dialects. Amorite, although also a member of the Semitic branch of the Afro-Asiatic language family, was definitely distinct from Babylonian, and the two languages, related though they were, would not have been mutually understandable.[1] It is important to note that not a single sentence has been preserved in Amorite and that we know the language almost exclusively from personal names and loanwords. Amorites may be defined as Amorite speakers, but to us they are known only through their writings in Babylonian—that is, Akkadian.[2]

Defined in traditional Assyriological terms, the Amorite dialects were relatively new to Syria. In the Ebla archives of 700 or 800 years earlier, there is not a trace of the Amorite language, and the personal names of Syrians appear to have belonged to a different Semitic language group or, perhaps, even groups.[3] In the Sumerian records pertaining to Syria from around 2000 B.C., few if any people from the West have Amorite names, and in the small number of published Mari tablets that predate the period of the main archives, there is likewise no evidence for Amorite. Whatever social and historical forces underlie this situation, there can be little doubt that we are witness here to the replacement of one dialect continuum by another. These Amorite speakers lived not only in Syria; many of the urban centers of Babylonia were ruled by dynasts with Amorite names and lineages, and Amorite personal names are found in western Iran as well as in areas of the Persian Gulf. These peoples—and it is not at all clear who was new and who was old—utilized Mesopotamian cuneiform and the Babylonian language for communication, and only a limited repertoire of their own cultural traits can be detected behind the veneer of adopted written conventions. At the time of Yasmah-Addu, and even more so during the time when Zimri-Lim occupied the throne of Mari, central and eastern Syria was host to a number of Amorite ethnic groups, or tribes, that had come to live in both the cities and on the steppe. Some of their members lived in permanent residences in villages, towns, and cities, while others, designated in the local texts by the term *ḫanûm*/ha.na, were more mobile, moving along the pasture and water areas with their flocks (Gelb 1961: 37; Durand 1998: 417). The complex relationships between the settled people and their more mobile relatives are still being analyzed and debated.

The general portrait I have just sketched is one that describes matters on which there is much consensus. The picture becomes more difficult when we attempt to look more closely at the early history of these "Amorites" and try to ascertain the denotation of the term in the native sources.

---

1. This can be inferred from the words of Samsi-Addu, addressed to his son Yasmah-Addu at Mari: "You can't (even) speak Amorite with them!" (*a-mu-ur-re-e it-ti-šu-nu da-ba-ba-am ú-ul te-le-i*) referring to the local pastoral tribesmen (*ḫanûm*) [Ziegler and Charpin 2007: 61, lines 6″–7″]. Presumably, Yasmah-Addu spoke Akkadian. Amorite is also listed as a separate language that has to be translated in *Šulgi Hymn B* 213 and *Šulgi Hymn C* 119–124; see Rubio 2006: 167–70.

2. On the general background of these matters, see Heimpel 2003: 13–36 and Durand 2004.

3. The Ebla texts do, however, contain references to a MAR.TU[ki] as well as to daggers made in the "Amorite manner"; see Archi 1985. For possible local language variation in Syria as reflected in Ebla onomastics, see Bonechi 1991.

The high Old Babylonian period may be a time of "Amorite Dynasties," but, in Babylonia at least, youngsters studying the ancient Sumerian tongue were exposed to an ideology that was less than kind to outsiders, including "Amorites." In the older Sumerian texts, there are literary depictions of "the other" that are predictably less than flattering (Cooper 1983: 30–36). In this semantic universe, Sumer was the "homeland" (kalam) and others were depicted in terms of negations of what was perceived of as markers of civilization, much as outsiders were defined in the classical world. And so in Sumerian primary curriculum texts, such as *The Curse of Agade, Enki and the World Order*, or *Lugalbanda II*, these people are described as ignorant of agriculture and of the finer points of civilization, with neither permanent abode nor burial places, or as fools who live in the mountains (Cooper 1983: 31–33). It should be noted, however, that most of these negative depictions of Amorites are in fact Old Babylonian and shed little light on earlier ways of thinking about these matters. The only securely dated Ur III depiction of these people, which is found in a later copy of a royal inscription, is highly negative to be sure, but it is impossible to know how pervasive prejudices might have been at the time (Šu-Sin E3/2.1.4.1 v 24–29; Frayne 1997: 299):

> u₄-bi-ta MAR.TU lú ha-lam-ma[4]
> dím-ma ur-ra-gin₇
> ur-bar-ra-gin₇
> tùr x [x] x
> lú [še nu]-zu

> Then, the Amorites, who are evil, with minds like beasts, like wolves, who . . . sheep-stalls, who are ignorant of agriculture. . . .[5]

Any proper understanding of who was designated by the term MAR.TU in Ur III texts requires some discussion of how one understands the issues associated with ethnicity and tribalism in the context of early ancient Near Eastern history. Traditionally, the study of this history has focused on a succession of "peoples": Sumerians, Akkadians, Amorites, Kassites, Arameans, and many others. The identification of these groups comes from a mixture of ancient labels and linguistic classification, so that historically divergent peoples are directly associated with specific languages or dialect groupings. This approach made sense decades ago, but after a half-century of cross-cultural studies on ethnicity and social identity, it is truly wanting. Although Kamp and Yoffee (1980), Emberling (1997), and Emberling and Yoffee (1999) have attempted to steer the discussion of ethnic issues into a more theoretically and comparatively informed arena, their efforts have apparently had little effect on the way

---

4. This word seems to mean "evil (destroyers)"; see OB Lu A 36 = B 39 (*MSL* 12 158, 178 = *ša li-mu-ut-tim*); Limet compares the term "vandals." The same term is used to describe Šimaški and Elam (*Ur Lament* 244, *Eridu Lament* 4:10) and Gutium (*Lamentation over the Destruction of Sumer and Ur* 230).

5. The passage is broken, and what follows cannot be restored with confidence.

in which these matters have been considered, and this is evident when one surveys the subsequent literature that deals with the topic of the Amorites.

Most current discussion of the "Amorite problem" distorts the issue by creating a unitary semantic concept that combines notions of common origin, ethnic and linguistic identity, tribalism, and nomadism as a way of life. As I see it, this way of essentialist thinking about terms such as MAR.TU leads to convenient historical fictions. We take all of the references to the word from all periods and throw them all in the same basket, implying that they all denote the same loosely defined notion of an Amorite people. A handful of Early Dynastic references; two Old Akkadian military encounters at the Jebel Bishri in Syria; a few hundred Ur III designations of individuals as MAR.TU; not to mention the famous wall built to exclude them, are all seen through the lens of a much more abundant Old Babylonian document set, some of it from one or two generations of scribes from Mari in Syria. Seen in this manner, a master narrative emerges in which nomads or pastoralists move across Syria and Mesopotamia, from the desert to the sown; first raiding and harassing, then transgressing and finally dominating the urban areas of the Near East, from tent to city after city.

Underlying all of this is the assumption that the appearance of an Amorite language or dialect continuum in Syria and Mesopotamia, as documented in personal and tribal names, must be considered as evidence for intensive population spread—in other words, it is a symptom of an influx of new people from the west, sometimes imagined as great invasions. The ancient sources are silent about these issues, and therefore all historical and sociolinguistic reconstruction can only be based on theoretical principles and presuppositions. But comparative studies of language spread suggest that such phenomena are rarely the result of massive population shifts or replacement. Thus, for example, one influential archaeologist and linguist, Colin Renfrew (1992), has proposed that the spread of Indo-European must be explained as an example of an "elite-dominance" replacement process, whereby a small number of Indo-European speakers supplanted local elites, eventually leading to linguistic change. Johanna Nichols describes three known mechanisms of such change: language shift, demographic expansion, and migration:

> There are probably no pure cases: Language shift is normally in response to the presence of at least a few influential immigrants; demographic expansion involves some absorption of previous population rather than extermination; and migration leads to language shift (either to or from the immigrants' language). The terms *language shift*, *demographic expansion*, and *migration* refer to the predominant contributor with no claim that it is exclusive. Almost all literature on language spreads assumes, at least implicitly, either demographic expansion or migration as the basic mechanism, but in fact language shift is the most conservative assumption and should be the default assumption (1997: 372).

Nichols's "shift" is similar to, if less precise than, Renfrew's "elite-dominance" model. A recent study of genetic diversity in a linguistically complex area, the Caucasus, where many languages, some unrelated, are found in proximity to one another in a relatively small area, has demonstrated that linguistic diversity is not reflected in the distribution of genetic features (in this case, DNA), which led the researchers to Renfrew's model as the most probable explanation for language spread in the Caucasus (Nasidze and Stoneking 2001: 1205). More recent work on genetic analysis and language groupings has not solved the problem, and linguists such as Lyle Campbell (2006) have drawn attention to the errors that are often found in this type of analysis. Indeed, comparative work has revealed the complexities and many variables involved in large-scale language shift, with competing models in different disciplines favoring or avoiding the issue of broad population replacement as an explanation for such phenomena (e.g., Bellwood 2001).

These alternative models for the spread of language undermine the idea that the appearance of various languages or dialect groups in the Near East—such as, for example Sumerian, Akkadian, Hurrian, Amorite, Kassite, or Aramaic—can only be explained as a symptom of concentrated and substantial population movements and that the appearance of linguistically distinct personal and geographical names signals the arrival of new peoples moving in from the West or from the North. Some population movement certainly took place, but the relative numbers of peoples involved and the manner in which languages spread throughout the existing population are matters that need to be modeled and analyzed in each individual case; we cannot simply assume in each instance that waves of people overran large areas and brought new languages—and new cultures—with them.

In the case of Amorites, it is unlikely that the presence of speakers of this language continuum arrived in Mesopotamia in one fell swoop or that all aspects of Amorite self-definition can be ascribed to the same set of ideological constructs. We cannot dispute that evidence exists for native notions of Amorite identity in Old Babylonian times or at least for ideological constructs at state levels that utilize these ideas for social control, but it is important to analyze them in their historical context and to recognize the fluid nature of such ideas. This is not the place for a full analysis of these matters, and one example will have to suffice. I leave out the later genealogies found in the famous funeral ritual text from the time of Ammiṣaduqa, as well as the *Assyrian King List*, because they come from a different time and may appeal to ideas that stem from another era (Michalowski 1983b). An oft-cited example of the recognition of common ethnic identity comes from a letter of Anam, king of Uruk, written to the Babylonian ruler Sin-muballiṭ, in which Anam appeals for military assistance to his fellow monarch, reminding him that the two cities were "of one house" (*bītum ištēnma*; Falkenstein 1963: 58 iii 25). Many scholars, including Kamp and Yoffee (1980: 90) and A. Goddeeris (2002: 324), see this as evidence of a sense of common Amorite ethnic ties as members of the Amnanum tribe, but it is more likely that this refers, in a much more limited manner, to the dynastic marriage that had bound the two ruling families a generation earlier, when Šallurtum, the daughter of the Babylonian king Sumu-la-el—the founder of the dynasty—had married King Sin-kašid of Uruk (Röllig 1972–1975: 283). In other words, kinship alliance by marriage may be the issue here, rather than ethnicity, although quite obviously one does not exclude the other.

I have stressed the relatively recent arrival of the Amorite language on the canvas that we are scanning. There are also other developments that accompany these linguistic phenomena—tribalism and transhumance—but they also do not necessarily imply that a completely new population had moved into the area. There can be no doubt that, at the time of the Mari archives, native categorizations included notions of identity that were linked to Amorite tribal units and that these notions operated on local as well as state levels in Syria and to some degree in Babylonia as well (Michalowski 1983b). But tribal nomenclature was fluid, and there were a variety of forms in which rulers appealed to the population, pronouncing their legitimacy, claiming allegiance, and facing reminders of the tensions within their kingdoms. I suggest that the genealogies, far from being primordial, were recent in origin and may have been secondary at best. Taken further, we can see in these genealogies and tribal names invented realities that resulted from and reflected the complex relationships between city and countryside, settled and mobile, old and new. The shifting and peripatetic family relationships of the rulers of often-ephemeral polities, centered on old urban centers, required new legitimizing mechanisms, and the written evidence at our disposal was of negligible importance in the search for identity and power that must have been of paramount significance in those politically volatile ancient times. There can be no doubt that part of this reality was infused into a variety of identity labels and that there was a definite hierarchy of such terms in which the notion "Amorite" played a significant but variable role in various times and various places. What these roles may have been we are only beginning to understand.

This is, briefly stated, a summary of the Old Babylonian situation that often serves as a model for understanding earlier issues concerning Amorites. All current work on the Ur III Amorites is still based on the only substantial collection and analysis of this material in the standard work on the subject, Giorgio Buccellati's pioneering 1966 work, *The Amorites of the Ur III Period*. It was an excellent book for its time, but it was published almost 50 years ago; many texts have been published since then, and our historical and historiographic perspectives have changed in the intervening years. Lists of newly discovered Ur III Amorite names have been provided subsequently (Wilcke 1969; Edzard and Farber 1974; Owen 1981: 256–57), but a full reexamination of all the material is clearly overdue.

In modern works on the Amorites and Ur III times, there are six propositions that crop up over and over, perhaps best illustrated by three of the most recent publications on the matter—those by Michael Streck (2000), Brit Jahn (2007), and Walther Sallaberger (2007). These propositions are:

1. The Amorites Mesopotamian encountered in Ur III times were nomads.
2. Amorites came at Mesopotamia from the west.
3. Some Amorites underwent a process of sedentarization that can be traced in texts.

4. Amorites infiltrated the Ur III state in large numbers.
5. Hostile Amorites played a significant role in the collapse of the Ur III state.
6. Amorites took over power in Mesopotamian cities after the Ur III collapse.

Most authorities, particularly those cited above, would affirm these propositions as correct. Here I wish to demonstrate that not a single one of them can be substantiated on the basis of currently available information. Furthermore, I will argue strongly, on empirical as well as comparative and theoretical grounds, that these propositions are simply false. First, however, it is important to remember that there are essentially two kinds of Amorites in the Ur III archival records: (1) outsiders who are visiting, primarily for diplomatic reasons, and (2) those who live in Mesopotamia, either permanently or in passing. The few references in literary texts and inscriptions written during the period refer only to hostile Amorites on the eastern frontier. Most of the comments below concern those living within the borders of the Ur III state proper. Let us take up these issues one by one.

1. Were the Amorites Whom Mesopotamians Encountered in Ur III Times Nomads?

Although it is said that the Amorites were nomads, there is not a single piece of evidence from Ur III times to support this assertion. Once again, it is worth mentioning that the issue is undermined by a number of underlying problems. First and foremost, we have often essentialized the notion of "the Amorites," treating it as unitary by projecting historically determined information into the past. The matter is further complicated by confusion in Assyriological literature over if and how to distinguish the concepts of nomadism, pastoralism, transhumance, and tribalism.[6] Not all pastoralists are transhumant or fully nomadic, and while tribal organization is common among nomads and transhumant pastoralists, it is not a defining characteristic of either. Most important, there is good reason to question whether there ever were any nomads, in the classic sense, in the early history of the ancient Near East—although this depends on a subtle definitional matter. Anatoly Khazanov is quite adamant, stating that, "despite the opinion of certain scholars, there are no grounds for thinking that pastoralists of the third and even the second millennium B.C. were real nomads" (Khazanov 1984: 91). Though Brian Spooner (1986: 184), who has more research experience in Western Asia, has criticized this formulation, Khazanov's statement reflects the recognition that ethnographic information on nomadism in the area cannot be used uncritically to model historical situations prior to the domestication of the camel and the spread of Islam. Glenn Schwartz (1995: 240) likewise calls attention to the importance of the camel for the development of mobile forms of lifestyle.

---

6. See now the essays published in Szuchman 2009.

The development of pastoralism in the western Zagros region is important for our discussion, because this is one of the places where sheep and goats were originally domesticated. Kamyar Abdi (2003) has studied the archaeological evidence for this development with an eye on nuanced definitions of the terms. If Abdi is correct, by Uruk times, pastoral modes of life fully complemented agricultural forms of production in the western Zagros. Therefore, any hypothetical arrival of a nomadic Amorite population may have had an impact in cultural terms but would not have by any means introduced any new mode of life. It is more probable, if we are to formulate hypotheses, that the Amorite groupings documented in Ur III times in the Zagros constituted new sociopolitical units that resulted from a form of ethnogenesis in which new and old populations adjusted to one another. Among these groups, herding strategies were more determined by geography and climate than by ethnic tradition.

Because some Amorites at Mari in the time of Zimri-Lim seasonally moved their herds by no means implies that Amorites elsewhere, or in other times, lived in the same manner; but even if they did, this would not make them nomads in the modern sense of the term. Most recently, W. Sallaberger (2007: 448) has pointed to the fact that in Ur III times people who are designated as Amorites sometimes delivered fat-tailed sheep, and from this he concludes that they must have been nomads, because these animals, which have the ability to store extra energy in their tails, are particularly suited to a nomadic lifestyle. Breeds of such sheep, such as the Awassi, which are prevalent in the Middle East today, are well adapted to arid landscapes and are raised by nomadic and settled communities alike, but there is no good reason to correlate the raising of fat-tailed sheep with any particular lifestyle.[7] Moreover, as Steinkeller (1995: 51) has observed, fat-tailed sheep are commonly mentioned in the Drehem archives and therefore cannot be specifically identified with nomadic existence. As Sallaberger himself points out, the Amorites also brought other types of animals, including cows and oxen, creatures that are not well suited for nomads. The texts listed below that register booty from the Amurrum lands mention fat-tailed sheep, but other animals appear as well, predominantly equids. All of this evidence points to mixed husbandry, with various animals used for different purposes. And the sources themselves are completely silent about whether these groups were pastoralists or nomads. It is quite possible that some of them were nomadic, but more than this one cannot say; Norman Yoffee (2005: 146), in a discussion of people of the Amoritical persuasion, puts it succinctly: "being Amorite has little to do with any common subsistence pattern (pastoralists vs. agriculturalists), or a common residential pattern (nomads vs. city dwellers), or any common economic status." This becomes quite clear once the notion that the Mari situation is paradigmatic for the study of Amorite ethnicity in other times and other places is discarded. More recently, Diederik Meijer (in press) writes:

---

7. For example, in a survey of villages in the Bint Jbeil and Marjeyoun districts of South Lebanon, all of the sheep were of the Awassi fat-tailed breed (Rouda 1992: 115).

> The distinction made between Amorites and Akkadians in some ways is striking, but . . . no discrimination in the modern sense can be noted. Such often repeated notions that "they didn't bury their dead, they lived in tents, etc.," are obvious contradistinctions to the urban, settled way of life, undoubtedly used to bolster the cohesive spirit of the urban, settled population. . . , perhaps even to "indoctrinate" one's subjects against these unruly dangers from the steppe. But how closely correlated were these notions of "Amorite" and "unruly dangers from the steppe" really for the man in the street, at a time when the Amorites were accepted in the higher echelons of society?

The identification of the "Amorites" with nomadic lifestyle undoubtedly grows out of a conceptualization that creates radical distinctions between urban and rural, state and non-state, center and periphery, settled and mobile, and other binary oppositions, some of them actually rooted in ancient ideological formulations. But for some time now, it has been apparent that such categorizations impede rather than assist historical analysis. Indeed, some archeologists with very different points of view on many matters have been arguing that early cities in certain ecological zones were founded, in Syria at least, as centers for semipastoralists who occupied both urban and non-urban occupational niches. The best examples of research along these lines can be found in the work of Anne Porter (2002, 2004, 2007) and Bertile Lyonnet (1998, 2001, 2004, 2008); in addition, we must also mention studies by Giorgio Buccellati (1990, 2004, 2008), who suggests, following well-known theoretical postulates, that pastoralism in Syria was secondary to agriculture. All three scholars stress that there was a fluid back-and-forth movement between settled and mobile or semimobile ways of life. Here I must stress again that seasonal pastoralism should not be equated with fully mobile nomadism.

The comments just made concern the specific geographical and ecological realities of Syria, but the theoretical concerns about the misleading role of binary oppositions are important for understanding the very different situation found in Mesopotamia, particularly in its southern areas. Nonetheless, the notion that cities and settled countryside must be distinguished from the sometimes friendly, sometimes hostile nomads who are "outside" oversimplifies historical reality, even if it reflects categorizations occasionally encountered in the ancient literature, which sometimes presents stereotypes of barbarian outsiders (Cooper 1983: 30–33). Adams (1981: 136) notes that "the accounts of ancient scribes, officials, and literati do not supply us with entirely balanced and comprehensive testimony on matters from which their authors were socially remote and of which they were technically ignorant." Adams goes on to provide a powerful argument for the existence of large areas, within the borders of the Ur III state and not beyond, that were primarily but not exclusively dedicated to the raising of very large animal herds by pastoral semisedentary folk (1981: 149). In other words, the very large numbers of animals recorded in Ur III texts, and which were exploited for milk, wool, hides, and other products, came from within the alluvial plain. Although it is obvious from the Drehem records that the frontier regions to the east were also a source of animals of this kind, the state was not solely dependent on outlying regions for pasturing flocks, even if some flocks may have been moved seasonally into the flanks of the highlands. If Adams is correct, then we must discard the idea that all pastoralists were "outsiders"; some of them were an integral part of the "inside" economy.

It is true that the native Ur III and later literary stereotypes portray Amorites as people who raise animals and who are "ignorant of agriculture" (Cooper 1983: 32). In the *Curse of Agade* 45–46, which may be one of the earliest portrayals of the Amorites in this manner and which was composed in Ur III times or slightly earlier, they are described as breeders of both cattle and caprids:

MAR.TU kur-ra lú še nu-zu
gud du$_7$ máš du$_7$-da mu-un-na-da-an-ku$_4$-ku$_4$[8]

Highland Amorites, who are ignorant of agriculture,
Delivered to her (Inana) butting bulls and butting bucks.

Goats certainly are raised by mobile folk, but cattle typically are not. So while this depiction of Amorites characterizes them as people who raise animals but do not grow grain, it does not necessarily follow that in Ur III times they were imagined as nomads in the romantic mode that permeates some of our modern studies. Some may have moved from pasture to pasture in the highlands during the course of the year, but there is no evidence at present that the Amorites on the eastern borders of Babylonia lived some version of a fully nomadic lifestyle.[9]

Finally, I would like to question the explanatory value of the very problem: even if some Amorites in fact were nomads, how much would this really matter? The extensive research on this problem has only served to demonstrate that, as noted by Khazanov, it is very difficult to define nomadism, aside from the fact that nomads lack permanent dwellings. Brian Spooner (1971), already cited above, has insisted on an ecological focus in studies of nomadism, and his perspective is highly relevant for our work.[10] Once again, I stress that the historical situation revealed in the Mari letters is determined by unique ecological as well as political and ethnic circumstances and can by no means be considered as paradigmatic for the analysis of this problem in other times and places. Moreover, with all due respect to the brilliant work of our Paris colleagues, the Mari information is itself open to further analysis, braced by theoretical and comparative work. For example, it is unfortunate that the translation "Bedouin," first proposed by I. J. Gelb (1961: 37) for the native term, ḫanûm/ha.na, used for transhumant groups, has been widely adopted of late (Heimpel 2003: 34–36, with earlier literature). Of course, we understand that this translation is meant as a generalized analogy, but it is nevertheless unfortunate, because it brings to mind

---

8. The translation assumes that the prefix da is transitivizing here, in accordance with the theory espoused by Miguel Civil (2010: 528–29).

9. Deiderik Meijer (in press), writing about Bronze Age Syria, also focuses on pastoralism in contrast to nomadism—that is, herders of animals but not necessarily nomadic.

10. He is not alone; see, for example, more recently, Sørbø 2003.

many modern myths pertaining to a category of people whose identities have shifted in various ways throughout the centuries and whose culture has been associated, although not explicitly, with two elements that are obviously missing in the second millennium B.C., the camel and Islam (D. P. Cole 2003).

Comparative study has revealed the endless varieties of cultural, organizational, structural, and adaptive strategies developed by nomadic peoples all over the world and has provided ample evidence for a distinction between nomadism and pastoralism. According to Spooner (1971: 208):

> Nomadism is an extreme form of adaptation which generates extreme degrees of instability of minimal social groupings and requires a high degree of fluidity of social organization. There are, however, no forms of social organization or other cultural features which are found in all nomadic societies or found exclusively in them.

To press the point further, I refer to the work of Philip Carl Salzman, who summarized years of research in a comprehensive essay entitled "Pastoral Nomads: Some General Observations Based on Research in Iran" (Salzman 2002). He begins by asserting the distinction between "pastoralists," who raise livestock on natural pasture, and "nomads," who move from place to place. He begins with a summary that includes the following (2002: 245):

> [N]omadism is not tied to one economic system; some nomads have generalized consumption-oriented production, while others are specialized and market-oriented. Nor is nomadism limited to one type of land tenure; some nomads migrate within a territory that they control, while others have no political or legal claim over land that they use. . . . Pastoral nomads vary in political structure from state-controlled peasants, to centralized chiefdoms, to weak chiefdoms, to segmentary lineages.

He concludes (2002: 261):

> The peoples whom I have in this essay called "nomads" could equally—depending upon the particular case—be labeled "tribesmen" or "peasants," "Muslims" or "pagans," "Persian" or "Turkic" or "Baluch" or "Arab," "fierce warriors," or "pacific civilians." There are many aspects and dimensions to peoples' lives and to a people's culture. For us to select and emphasize one aspect as paramount would be a distortion of the always complex human reality. And such an essentialism and reductionism would be a distortion of nomadism, for to understand nomadism truly, we must grasp its dependence on human objectives and upon multiple social, cultural, and environmental circumstances and thus appreciate its variability, its malleability, and its impermanence.

I cite Salzman at length because his words force us to rethink what we mean by the term "nomad" in the context of early Mesopotamian history. As a result, we must also avoid using the word as if it were a unitary term that allowed us to associate various groups of people with one another over time and space just because they sometimes are denoted by the same descriptive terms in the native sources. One must therefore be careful not to automatically identify cultural and ethnic groups in different times and places simply because they are designated by the same label. Indeed, the explanatory value of terms such as "nomad" and "tribe" and the practice of associating cultural patterns such as a specific kinship system with mobile groups was questioned a quarter of a century ago by Rudi Lindner (1982) in an essay titled "What Was a Nomadic Tribe?" At this juncture, it is important to recall that Robert McC. Adams (1974) has warned us that the boundaries between people living in agricultural towns and villages and those who moved about on the outskirts of these towns, tending herds, was quite fluid in ancient Mesopotamia. There must have been considerable population flux between these modes of life due to the instability of farming conditions, and these modes of life must be seen as nodes on a continuum, rather than as contrasting means of subsistence. Furthermore, as Adams observes (1974: 2):

> The antipathy between the steppe and the sown is deeply rooted, of course, in West-ern religious and literary traditions, finding perhaps the most comprehensive expres-sion in Ibn Khaldun's statement that nomads are "the negation and antithesis of civilization." . . . That same attitude may be at least partially implicit in Sumerian myths and proverbs. . . . But these are the views of urban literati. . . . Hence norma-tive statements like these, important as they are for the continuities of Mesopota-mian literate civilization, must be treated with reserve as an expression of the forces and patterns of behavior actually prevailing in the countryside.

In light of this, we must be careful not to view nomads through romantic Western, or even later Middle Eastern lenses, but at the same time we also must remain skeptical about the perspectives of ancient Mesopotamian elites as well.

With regard to the subject at hand, the Ur III period, I repeat what I said above: there is no evidence that permits us to determine if the people on the frontiers of the kingdom who are described as MAR.TU were nomads, pastoralists, or both. Some may have been pastoralists who moved up and down between pastures during the year but lived part-time in durable homes; others may have been on the move, with-out permanent abodes; the evidence available at present is inconclusive on these points. But even if the MAR.TU raised livestock and moved from place to place, this would, in the end, tell us very little about them, because designating them vaguely— and anachronistically—as "nomads" would have little if any historical explanatory value.[11]

2. Did the Amorites Infiltrate Mesopotamia from the West?

Many authorities have assumed that, because there were peoples described as Amorites living in Syria, they must have made their way into Babylonia and Sumer down the Euphrates through the Jezira. Some published maps in, for example, the standard compilation on Ur III geographical names (Edzard and Farber 1974), show

11. Note, however, the nuanced approach to Mari-era nomadism in the remarkable study by J.-M. Durand (2004).

arrows implying this sort of movement. Wilcke (1969) had already questioned this conclusion, as had Lieberman (1968–1969), and in RCU, I argued that there was no historical basis for this movement. It is true that hostile as well as allied Amorites that had contact with the Ur III state were located in the mountain regions to the east of Mesopotamia, most probably in the valleys around the Jebel Hamrin, and this can be understood as supporting some, but by no means all, of the ideas of Bauer (1926, 1929). Some have accepted our conclusions but others have not, continuing to seek the Amorites in the west, unwilling to disassociate the specific historical situation from the general "western orientation" of MAR.TU/Amurru in other periods.

The eastern location of these Amorites can be discerned from an analysis of administrative documents from Drehem that mention kur MAR.TU, that is the "Amorite (high)lands;" many of these texts are concerned with war booty (nam-ra-ak), but it is also evident that there were also peaceful relationships with these areas. I will revisit this material below (p. 102),[12] but first we need to take a close look at the larger context of the military and diplomatic strategy of the Ur III state so that we do not see these texts, and the events that lie behind them, merely from a philological and literary perspective.

War and Foreign Relations during the First Half of the Ur III Period— An Overview

We know next to nothing about how Ur-Namma pieced together a new territorial state, bringing together a variety of polities that had been independent for approximately a century and driving out invaders from the highlands out of areas in the south such as Umma, as well as from the territory around Marad, Kazallu, Girkal, and Akšak. Foreigners aside, we simply do not know how much assent there was for his state building and which efforts required force. Suffice it to say that, at the end of his eighteen-year reign, the core of the Ur III state had apparently been established, but his ill-fated death on the field of battle undoubtedly threatened to undermine the very foundations of the nascent state. As I have argued elsewhere (Michalowski 2008), the battlefield death of a king was only possible as the result of the withdrawal of divine favor and thus constituted the worst possible negative omen: it signaled nothing less than divine abandonment. Ur-Namma's successor, Šulgi, worked hard to reestablish his authority by demonstrating his piety toward the divine world, and this is reflected in the year-names of the first half of his reign, which almost exclusively commemorate cultic activities, culminating in his divinization around year 21. It is telling that his 11th and 12th years were named in honor of "introducing" the city-gods into their towns, Der and Kazallu; the former is a transfer center that controlled the piedmont route into the highlands, and the latter is a major city in the northern defense territory, the mada.[13] It is likely that these two place-names defined the eastern and northern borders of the state at the time.

12. See also Steinkeller 2004; Sallaberger 2007.
13. On the mada as "frontier," see p. 132 below.

A diplomatic marriage with Mari under Ur-Namma had already created a personal bond with the state that controlled the Euphrates corridor to Syria (Civil 1962). In his seventeenth year, Šulgi arranged to have one of his daughters become queen of Marhaši, a powerful polity deep in Iran. But matters were not peaceful closer to home, and in year twenty he was forced to move against Der to secure a vital node on one of the most important roads into the highlands and even to the lowlands of Susa. This was the very same place that he had dealt with on a cultic level just a few years earlier.

A diplomatic marriage contracted with the highland polity of Anšan in year twenty-nine did not guarantee peace, however, because four years later the king of Ur had to wage a major war there, as commemorated in his thirty-fourth and thirty-fifth year-names. Now Šulgi and his advisers sought to pacify the areas on the eastern frontier, presumably to ward off raids against the homeland and to safeguard the routes through the eastern mountains that were critical for access to many of the luxury goods required for display and gift-giving to allies and clients but also for the export of cloth and grain.[14] The peace established by war and marriage with the powerful states in southwestern Iran—namely, Anšan and Marhaši—eventually calmed the far frontier, and the alliances appear to have remained intact until the last decades of the kingdom. Between these two polities and Ur lay the more troubling highland areas that were much less stable politically and militarily. Some of the people living there controlled the communication routes through the mountains: in the south, through Susiana; to the north, up the Diyala Valley and past the Jebel Hamrin; as well as even farther north, through the valleys around the Adheim and lower Zab rivers on the one hand and the passage known much later as Great Khorasan Road on the other. All of the areas were in the hands of smaller powers centered around cities or areas such as Kimaš, Hurti, Urbilum, Šuruthum, and, most important, an entity that is referred to in the texts as Šimaški.

The term Šimaški does not refer to a unitary state like the one centered in Ur but rather to a loose confederation of local people, towns, and cities whose scope and control ebbed and flowed but whose fate was undoubtedly influenced by the Mesopotamian state that they interacted with on both diplomatic and martial terms (Stolper 1982; Steinkeller 2007a; Potts 2008 [see chap. 6]). The term is used both in a geographical and in a political sense; politically, it encompassed many different subgroups, individual cities, and kin groups and had various rulers who were contemporaneous—though they may also have been organized in a hierarchical manner that makes it difficult to trace its development. In the end, however, pressured by Ur, the disparate elements that made up the areas of Šimaški finally consolidated into a powerful polity that also involved Anšan and eventually overran its western opponent, ending the already weakened state ruled by the House of Ur-Namma.

The ebb and flow of war in these areas can be mapped only partially, but even without a full picture, it is obvious that the endless, and ultimately futile, military

---

14. On Drehem as a redistribution center for elite gift giving, see Sallaberger 2003–4.

encounters in these regions must have put massive strain on the resources of the state, draining manpower, organizational capacity, and wealth. This is a long and complicated story, however, and here we are only interested in certain parts of the narrative, concentrating on the reign of King Šulgi and providing detail to the storyline sketched out above.

As already observed above, in the second half of Šulgi's reign, his administration, having consolidated the core of his kingdom, began a long process of pacification of areas directly to the east, northeast, and southeast. We can trace some of this activity in the year-names and in chance references in the administrative record, but this information is sometimes unreliable and more often incomplete. Moreover, Šulgi's claims of victory were often exaggerated to various degrees: for example, it took him nine such announcements before his armies supposedly subdued an entity called Simurum. We often tend to think of every victory that is celebrated by a year-name as a separate "campaign," but the record, as we will presently see, makes it more likely that these wars went on with very little respite for decades, even if the exact contours of the flow of this military activity cannot be established from the surviving documentation. Some of the year-names undoubtedly commemorated major battles or campaigns, but it is also more than likely that many of them were actually inspired by border skirmishes or low-level military encounters. The problem is that we rarely are in a position to distinguish between a major military undertaking, such as the one against Huhnuri during Amar-Sin's reign, or Šu-Sin's assault on Zabšali, and smaller, badly documented skirmishes.[15] Equally important, we should not underestimate the ideological nature of the year-name discourse, which undoubtedly often represented defeat or minor victories as major military successes. How we perceive this military history is very much a function of the year-names we read, and therefore we are often influenced, unintentionally, by ancient propaganda. But we should not always think of years as campaigns; the conduct of these wars was as much determined by physical and organizational factors as by the requirements of immediate politics or of broader strategy. Hot summers and cold winters, topography, access to food and water for people and for animals, as well as to supply lines, must all have played a significant role in the conduct of these wars.

The motivations for this sustained and complex military activity are nowhere to be found in the ancient literature, and we can only hypothesize regarding what factors drove Šulgi's regime to undertake these wars. All of them took place in the highlands, within the Zagros ranges. The best summary of the geography of these areas is still Louis Levine's (1973, 1974), whose personal knowledge of the topography was critical for his analysis of these mountain areas in Neo-Assyrian times.[16] Levine mapped out the various routes through the mountain valleys, and though we

15. The campaign against Huhnuri (AS YN7) is documented by an inscription found in Iran (Nasrabadi 2005); the war against Zabšali and surrounding regions (ŠS YN7) is documented in a variety of sources (Steinkeller 2007).

16. Subsequently, Timothy Potts (1994: 38–43) provided an excellent overview of the overland communication routes between Mesopotamia and the highlands.

cannot pinpoint the location of any of the places that fought against Ur, it is possible to approximate the general area that was the object of much of this military activity.

One such place is Assyrian Harhar, which Levine (1974: 117) suggested was located close to or directly bordering the Great Khorasan Road, in the central part of eastern Mahidasht. If this is indeed the Karhar of the Ur III texts—and this is by no means certain—then at least one of the polities that was the target of armies from Sumer has been located with some degree of probability. The defeat of Karhar is mentioned in four of Šulgi's year-names: YN24, 31, 33, and 45; interspaced with this are no less than eight claims of victory over Simurum, culminating, in YN45, with a version of the year-name that includes mention of a decisive rout of Urbilum and Lullubum, in tandem with Simurum and Karhar. These seemingly unending wars, stretching over more than two decades, known to us from self-serving claims of victory, suggest that Šulgi's armies were well matched by the forces of the highlanders. But the tenacious drive for victory over the highland polities requires some kind of explanation.

As observed above, the most obvious conclusion to be drawn is that Šulgi's administration had a strong interest in controlling the communication routes through the Zagros—those moving north toward what would later be Assyria, perhaps to Urmia and beyond, and those moving south along the Great Khorasan Road that ultimately led to the Hamadan plain and connected to further routes in various directions.[17] It seems that this was accomplished by the time of YN45; Karakar, if it was indeed where Levine places it, would have marked the southern, and Urbilum (Erbil) the northern, limits of this control, and the main goal of this policy would have been achieved, covering the main routes through the Zagros outlined in Levine's study. The next three years are named after victories over the lands of Kimaš and Harši. The locations of these polities are likewise a matter of speculation: many, following A. Goetze, have placed them in the vicinity of Kirkuk, but this is improbable, because two well-known passages in inscriptions of Gudea specify that Kimaš encompassed areas where copper was mined.[18] This, as Vallat (1993: 139–40) and Lafont (1996: 92) have argued, could refer to the documented copper sources of Kashan or Anarak, roughly in the area of the archaeological site of Tepe Sialk, which has revealed abundant evidence of copper smelting in antiquity, although there are other sources of copper in Iran.[19] Thus, it was only toward the end of Šulgi's reign that his kingdom achieved, for the time being at least, control of trade and of copper mining areas in the frontier, extending control, if only nominally in many places, beyond the Zagros.

17. One of the nodes in this communications nexus was Susa; the Ur III kings, according to Elisabeth Carter (1985: 46) "seemed to have viewed central Khuzistan and the Deh Luran regions as a kind of corridor through which valuable highland commodities could be channeled and transshipped to points northwest along the foothill road or eastward into the Zagros valleys."

18. See already Edzard and Röllig 1980. A discussion of these issues, with bibliographical information is provided in Lafont 2006.

19. Tomothy Potts (1994: 24) also summarizes succinctly the information on Kimaš and suggests that a location "near the mines of the Tiyari mountains north of Amadiyeh is possible."

Economic issues must also have been part of the equation, because the mountains and valleys of the Hamrin and Zagros could be exploited for natural resources,
labor forces, and pasture. But it would be a mistake to see such specific local benefits
as the only motivation for a costly and exhausting military policy, which must have
been organized and sustained with a broader set of concerns in mind. It is important
to recall here that, when Šulgi's father Ur-Namma was creating the Ur state, he had
to drive out highlanders who had occupied important parts of Babylonia—the Guti
in the south near Umma, Adab, and elsewhere, and Puzur-Inšušinak's forces that
were ensconced in the area of Marad and Kazallu west and northwest of Nippur.
Puzur-Inšušinak's polity may not have outlived its creator, but he had demonstrated
well that at any moment a variety of highland polities could coalesce into a powerful
enemy force that could overwhelm the lowlands. The armies of Ur had to make sure
that nothing like this would happen again in the frontier areas on Sumer's borders,
and such potential fears would have been well justified, because this is exactly what
happened a few decades later, when the various highland polities banded together
into a powerful coalition that eventually toppled the kingdom of Ur.

At the same time, Šulgi had to contend with powerful polities that lay beyond
the Zagros—for example, Marhaši and, most importantly, Anšan in Fars, ruled from
the city that is now Tal-e Malyan. Šulgi's diplomats arranged for an alliance through
dynastic marriage (YN30), but this did not prevent an eruption of hostilities, as is
documented by claims of victory over Anšan four years later (YN34), as already
mentioned above. In the following decades, before the collapse of Ur, the only documented contacts with Anšan appear to be peaceful, but it is impossible to trace the
shifting dynamics of this relationship and of the history of Anšan itself, which was
eventually merged with the polities of Šimaski (Steinkeller 2007a). But even with
these uncertainties, it is possible to imagine that some of the conflicts with areas that
lay between Anšan and Ur were in essence proxy wars that involved polities that
were in the buffer zone between the two larger states.

The end of the third millennium was a time of complex long-distance relationships between sophisticated cultures that stretched from the Mediterranean to Mar-
giana, Bactria, Baluchistan, Makran, and beyond. Lyonnet and Kohl (2008) have
provided a compact synthesis of the complex movements of people, ideas, representations, finished goods, and raw goods across these broad areas. Sumer was a major
player in this interconnected world, but it was hardly the dominant one. Elements of
spiritual and material culture were transmitted overland and by sea; some resources—
for example, lapis—had to come from one area only, while copper or workable stone
such as steatite could be obtained from multiple sources. We still cannot pinpoint
the origin of much of the tin used in Mesopotamia and Iran at this time, but it is
probable, as Lyonnet and Kohl (2008: 39) have suggested, that it came

> either from Afghanistan south of Herat. . . , or the tin-belt extending from the Kyzyl
> Kum to the Pamirs to the south of the Zeravashan Valley. It is probably not purely
> coincidental that the BMAC developed directly between these areas. We now know
> that some of those who were involved in tin mining, and probably in the prepara-

tion of metal ingots, belonged to Andronovo-related steppe groups who were installed in the Zeravashan Valley itself.[20]

The BMAC (Bactria-Margiana Archaeological Complex) refers to late third- and early second-millennium cultures reconstructed from archaeological sites in present-day northern Afghanistan and Turkmenistan. Daniel Potts (2008) has recently drawn the attention of Assyriologists to the BMAC in a remarkable study that sheds light on the exchange of luxury goods between that area, Elam, Anšan, and other parts of Western Asia, complementing the synthesis of Lyonnet and Kohl and providing concrete evidence for late third-millennium circulation of worked metal goods and shared artistic conventions over a large area of the ancient world.[21] The military activities of the Ur III state are but one element among competing strategies of participation in this complex communication network; indeed, while we by habit isolate martial acts for heuristic purposes, driven partly by the nature of the surviving data, it might be better to view them as but one node in a differentiated strategy directed at full participation in the broad interconnected world of the time, a strategy that involved devices that we would label with terms such as trade, gift exchange, kinship ties, vassalage, political and military control, or diplomacy.

It is impossible to determine, with the evidence at hand, how much of this was driven by detailed broader central strategic planning and how much was due to ad hoc decisions made either by the central government or by local commanders on the frontier or simply in reaction to immediate contingencies. Those of us who study early Mesopotamia have rarely asked such questions, but they have been broadly discussed by other historians of the ancient world, prodded, during the last century by Edward Luttwak's provocative, albeit highly flawed, monograph *The Grand Strategy of the Roman Empire* (1976). The book was not well received by historians of ancient Rome, but the ensuing debate brought new focus to the issues raised by the author, even if the criticisms of Classicists have not deterred specialists in other disciplines from taking it much too seriously.[22] Subsequent research on Roman frontiers and on the potential forms of military and diplomatic decision-making have shown just how difficult it is to analyze the contingencies of organization, information flow, communications, as well as the roles of central and peripheral officers in the defensive and offensive policies of the state, even though the available information on these matters is much richer than it is for the Ur III kingdom.[23] As summarized by Kagan (2006: 347):

20. Note also the recent suggestion that some of this tin may have originated in Gujarat/ Southern Rajasthan (Begemann and Schmitt-Strecker 2009).

21. I sidestep here his final conclusion that BMAC is to be identified as ancient Šimaški, a conclusion that I find highly unlikely. Note that Maurice Lambert (1974: 11–12), more than 30 years ago, had already drawn attention to the importance of Central Asian contacts, in reference to Old Akkadian times.

22. An early, devastating review was produced by Mann (1979). For a recent comprehensive review of the objections leveled against it, see Kagan 2006.

23. There are many works on this subject; my thinking on these matters has been particularly influenced by Fergus Millar (1982).

Because the Roman state did not apparently have a formal body that made imperial security decisions, and because records of such decision-making do not survive, it is very difficult to prove that the emperors or their advisors engaged in consistent or systematic planning. And the evidence from the narrative sources, combined with the archaeological record, suggests that ad hoc security arrangements far outnumber instances of systematic long-term planning, which occurred mainly (but not exclusively) at major turning points such as the reigns of Augustus (31 B.C.–A.D. 14) and Diocletian (A.D. 284–305).

In light of these analogies, I hesitate to ascribe to Šulgi, or to whatever group or groups in his state that might have been empowered to make strategic decisions, any well-planned long-term grand strategy beyond a general policy of securing defensible frontiers and control of communications routes that may have acquired a life of its own and led to many unpredictable consequences, with unexpected reactions.[24]

This is a complex set of issues that is worthy of a much fuller investigation; here I only touch on the major outlines of the story to provide some historical background for the main topic of this discussion. The chart on pp. 101–102 provides a compilation of all the existing documentation on Ur III wars based on the administrative texts. The narrative of Ur III warfare on the eastern, northeastern, and southeastern fronts, told through the medium of year-names, may appear to be triumphant, but when we look more closely, it is possible to dismantle the official story. The military conflicts in the highlands during the last 28 years of Šulgi until the sixth year of Amar-Sin, if not longer, may seem to be represented as a series of victories, but there are indications that there were defeats and setbacks as well as successes. A glance at the chart indicates that wars with Urbilum, Simurum, Šašrum, Šuruthum, Šimaški, Karhar, Harši, Hurti, and Kimaš, which all lay near one another up and down the Zagros, went on and on, and even though the year-names and the economic texts provide evidence of victories for the Ur III state, these successes seem to be short-lived and not to have resulted in stability on the eastern frontier. Victories over Karhar adorned the names of four regnal years, spanning more than two decades. Nine defeats of Simurum are mentioned, while Šašrum, supposedly crushed in Šulgi's fortieth year, remained a problem, together with its neighbor Šuruthum, until at least AS6, 14 years later. It took 22 years to subdue Harši. The case of Kimaš and Hurti, already referred to above, is illustrative of the difficulties faced by Ur: year 46 was named after a victory over these principalities. But administrative records show that hostilities continued; the records even mention celebrations of the capture of the king of Kimaš in the fifth month of Š46 and various announcements of subsequent victories, but it took another year before, once again, a year-name would proclaim military success (YN48). The peace thus established lasted for two decades; it is difficult to determine the exact status of Kimaš, be it vassal, ally, client state, or colony, but its relations with Ur remained strong at least until the very end of IS2, when the

---

24. A very different perspective on these issues will be presented by Piotr Steinkeller in a forthcoming essay.

Date[25]	Event	Source
Š20	Der defeated	YN 21
Š23	Karhar defeated	YN 24
Š24	Simurum defeated	YN 25
Š25	Simurum defeated	YN 26
Š26	Harši defeated	YN 27
Š29	diplomatic marriage w. Anšan	YN 30
Š30	Karhar defeated	YN 31
Š31	Simurum defeated	YN 32
Š32	Karhar defeated	YN 33
Š33	Anšan defeated	YN 34
Š33.11.-	n. Anšan	AOAT 240 80 6
Š36	Bad mada built	YN 37 & 38
Š40.5.-	n. kur Amurrum	*Ontario* 1 50
Š41	Šašrum defeated	YN 42
Š41.12.-	n. Simurum m. S	TCL 2 5502+5503
Š43	Simurum, Lullubum defeated	YN 44
Š44	Urbilum, Simurum, Lulubum, Karhar defeated	YN 45
Š44.3.-	n. kur Amurrum	*BIN* 3 321
Š44.4.-	n. Šuruthum	MVN 20 193
Š45	Kimaš and Harši defeated	YN 46
Š45.7.17	n. Urbilum	*Trouvaille* 86
Š45.11.15	n. Urbilum	MVN 13 423
Š45.12.2?	n. Urbilum	AUCT 2 326+336
Š46.4.27	Kimaš (destroyed)[26]	*TRU* 144
Š46.2.-	Kimaš (destroyed)[27]	YOS 4 74
Š46.5.3	celebration: king of Kimaš captured	OIP 115 428
Š46.5.-	n. Badadu Šimaški	*Princeton* 1 130
Š46.12.7	n. kur Amurrum	*SumRecDreh* 9
Š47	Harši, Kimaš, Hurti defeated	YN 48
Š47.2.0	n. Šimaški	JCS 31 175 H
Š47.2.-	n. Šimaški	ZVO 25 134 1
Š47.2.11	šà n.	*SmithCS* 38 7 (animals are Šimaški)
Š47.3.20	n. kur Amurrum	JCS 22 57
Š47.3.22	n. kur Amurrum	*Nisaba* 8 App. 3
Š47.3.22	n. kur Amurrum	BM 104355 (unpubl.)

25. In the chart, YN = year-name, n. = nam-ra-ak "booty," m. = military context. For comprehensiveness, the chart covers the entirety of the period, not only the reign of Šulgi.

26. Line 2: u_4 ki-maš^{ki}, "the day/when Kimaš (was defeated)."

27. Line 2: u_4 ki-maš^{ki}, "the day/when Kimaš (was defeated)."

Date[25]	Event	Source
Š47.5.-	n. kur Amurrum	*Amorites* 11 (pl. 4) = *OIP* 115 336
Š47.5.-	n. kur Amurrum & n. Šimaški	*PDT* 2 802
Š47.5.-	n. kur Amurrum	*OIP* 115 336
Š47.5.8	n. [ ]	*VN* 13 113
Š48.-.20	n. kur Amurrum, n. Urbilum	*Ontario* 1 53 (includes Badadu šimaški)
Š48.4.14	n. Hurti	*MVN* 15 201
Š48.6.16	n. Harši	www.smm.org SMM 12
Š48.7.-	n. Harši	*SAT* 2 611
Š48.7.-	n. Kimaš, Harši, [Hurti?]	*Princeton* 1 60
Š48.7.-	n. Harši	*TCL* 2 5485
Š48.7.-	n. kur Amurrum	*Amorites* 12 = *OIP* 115 287
Š48.10.-	n. Šimaški	*OIP* 115 355
AS1	Urbilum destroyed	YN 2
AS1.1.-	n. kur Amurrum	*RA* 62 8 11
AS2.1.-	news of Šašru defeat[28]	*AnOr* 1 83
AS3.2.-	ša n.	*AUCT* 2 284
AS3.7.28	ša n.	*AUCT* 1 028
AS.4.8.-	n. Šuruthum	*YOS* 4 67[29]
AS4.8.29	n. Šašrum Šuruthum	*TCL* 2 5545
AS4.8.30	saĝ n.	*TRU* 326
AS4.12.18	n. kur Amurrum	*SAT* 2 800
AS5	Šašrum, Šuruthum destroyed	YN 6
AS5.1.03	n. kur Amurrum	*PDT* 1 32
AS5.1.20	n. uru Nergal	*BIN* 3 532
AS5.1.20	n. uru Meslamtaea	*PDT* 1 120
AS6.1.-	news of Šašru defeat[30]	*UTI* 4 2315
AS6	Iabru, Huhnuri destroyed	YN 7
ŠS2	Simanum defeated	YN 3
ŠS3.-.-	news of Simanum defeat[31]	*MNV* 16 960
ŠS6	Zabšali defeated	YN 7
IS2	Simurum defeated	YN 3

28. Lines 3–4: á-áĝ-ĝá sig₅ ša-aš-šú-ru hul-a, "(on the occasion of) the good news of the defeat of Šašru."

29. An account of female prisoners of war with children, from Šuruthum (written ša-rí-it/ip-hu-um) destined to be ex-voto slaves for the temple of Šara, taken in charge by the governor of Umma. There are at least four other near duplicates of this text: *ASJ* 7 191, *Prima del'alfabeto* 33, *RA* 15 61, and *SAT* 2 1163.

30. Lines 3–4: á-áĝ-ĝá sig₅ ša-aš-šú-ru hul-a, "(on the occasion of) the good news of the defeat of Šašru."

31. Line 16: lugal-si-sá rá-gaba á-áĝ-ĝá sig₅ si-ma-núm^{ki} hul-a de₆-a, "for the messenger Lugal-sisa who brought the good news of the defeat of Simanum."

last known messenger returned from Kimaš through Garšana.[32] Two months earlier, representatives of Kimaš had sworn a loyalty oath in the Ninurta temple in Nippur (MVN 13 128: 16–18, IS2.10.25).

A glance at the chart presented above shows that by year 33 the Šulgi administration had ended openly hostile relationships with far-off Anšan, and from then on the wars took place in the Zagros and surrounding areas, some of them in what might be described as the buffer zone between the two states. The difficulties in locating ancient toponyms hinder any precise indentification of the locale of these wars, but it is safe to say that Urbilum undoubtedly marks the northern or northwestern limit and that the enemies of Ur controlled communications routes and access to resources. Most important, however, is the fact that wars with all of these places stretched up and down the Zagros and spanned three decades, all the way into the reign of Amar-Sin, targeting the same areas again and again, suggesting that the armies of Ur faced tenacious opposition. More ominously, their strategies were driven less by overall design other than the control of the marches than by the exigencies of events and by the intentions of their enemies.

Kur Amurrum

Having sketched in broad outline the eastern and northern military confrontations of the Ur III state, I now return to the issue of the location of the area that contemporary administrative texts label as kur Amurrum (MAR.TU), which may be rendered "Amorite mountain lands." A listing of Drehem texts that mention booty from the Amorite land provides some information but only makes sense when viewed within the context of the general martial situation outlined above:[33]

Date	Text	Delivering Officer	Animals
Š40.5.-	*Ontario* 1 50		kids
44.3.-	*BIN* 3 321	ĝìr Abuni	equids
46.12.7	*SumRecDreh.* 9	ĝìr Hun-Habur	FTS, goats
47.3.20	*JCS* 22 57	Lu-Nanna	equids
47.3.22	*Nisaba* 8 App. 3		equids
47.5.-	*OIP* 115 336		equids
47.5.-	*PDT* 2 802		goats, kids
48.-.20	*Ontario* 1 53	ĝìr Šu-ili nu-bànda	equids, FTS
48.7.19	*OIP* 115 287	ki Lu-Nanna šakkana	equids
AS1.1.-	*RA* 62 8 11		equids
4.12.18	*SAT* 2 800		FTS
5.1.3	*PDT* 1 32		FTS

32. Unpublished messenger text, courtesy of David Owen (IS2.xii-).

33. All these texts document animals from nam-ra-ak kur MAR.TU, "booty from Amorite mounain lands." It must be stressed that these accounts concern the fate of parts of the booty within the Drehem system, not the date of their seizure. See now also Sallaberger 2007: 407, with a very different analysis and conclusions. In this listing, FTS stands for "fat-tailed sheep" (gukkal).

A glance back at the listing of references to military operations on the chart above reveals that booty from Amurrum lands comes from the same time that wars were taking place against such places as Urbilum, Šimaški, Šaruthum, Kimaš, and Harši—that is, against locations to the east, northeast, and northwest, but not to the west of Sumer. The military officers who deliver this booty—often generals—are the same as those who are doing much of the fighting in the highlands: Abuni, Lu-Nanna, and Hun-Habur. The captain Šu-ili delivers goats and sheep in Š47.10.18, as do the generals Ṣilluš-Dagan and Šu-Enlil (*OIP* 115 262).

These people all took part in the expedition against Urbilum; in *Trouvaille* 86 (Š45.7.17) officers deliver metal objects from the plunder, and among them are Abu-ṭab, a subordinate of the general Abuni, acting on behalf of the prince Šu-Enlil, the leader of the expedition, as well as the general Hun-Habur. Five months later, Abuni was involved in another delivery from that booty (*AUCT* 2 326+336, Š45.12.2+). Note also that, in *Ontario* 1 53, the booty of Urbilum follows that of kur amurrum.

No year was named for any expedition against this Amorite land, suggesting that skirmishes with Amorites were not significant and took place on the way to the more important war areas. It is also possible that the hostile Amorites were not permanently associated with any specific geographical location and that the term "Amorite land" was a shifting component in Mesopotamian mental maps.

Not all relationships with the hostile Amorite lands were comprised of battle and strife. This was clearly a frontier region that could serve as a place of refuge, as is documented by a fragmentary Nippur text that records that a slave woman had escaped there for the third time, although the very fact that she had been apparently caught there implies that the Ur authorities had some way of retrieving runaways who fled to the area (*NATN* 354). Various people are documented as having traveled to and from there, including the chief Naplanum, who may have been the head of the Amorite royal bodyguards.[34]

The term kur MAR.TU is not, properly speaking, a specific location, which is why it never has a place-name classifier /ki/ but is a descriptive term that refers to the highlands in which certain Amorites were thought to live. As such, it has no borders and could possibly be used of more than one area.[35] It is important to observe that the use of kur in this term, traditionally rendered "highland," is probably better conceived simply as "hostile territory" or "borderland," since it is fairly obvious that this is not a single mountain. To be sure, in Ur III times, enemy lands were almost always located, by definition, in the highlands, but when Gudea informs us that he was in contact with highland Amorites, he specifically uses the term hur-saĝ "mountain (range)," not kur.[36]

---

34. See *MVN* 13 656; *MVN* 11 179; *Ebla 1875–1985* 286; *AUCT* 1 942; *AUCT* 1 133; *AUCT* 1 276; *OrSP* 47–49 38; *OIP* 121 543 (Naplanum).

35. Piotr Steinkeller (2004: 39 n. 68) suggests that the term was used of the entire piedmont region from the "middle course of the Tigris to the region of Susiana, within which the Amorite groups moved back and forth, pasturing their flocks."

36. On the meaning of hur-saĝ as "mountain range/chain," see Steinkeller 2007b.

In conclusion, all evidence leads us to think that, as far as the Ur III state was concerned, all hostile Amurrum resided in the borderlands flanking the Diyala Valley and perhaps in the Jebel Hamrin and in the valleys beyond, as well as further southeast along the Great Khorasan road, where they raised equids, sheep, goats, and cattle in areas that the Drehem administrators thought of as the Amurrum borderlands. This is not to say that peoples who were called Amurrum did not live elsewhere at the time, but only that those who were of enough concern to the Mesopotamian state to be mentioned in documents did so. There is also circumstantial evidence to suggest that some people designated as Amurrum were dwelling east of Mesopotamia already in late Sargonic times.[37]

3. Did Some Amorites Undergo a Process of Sedentarization That Can Be Traced in Texts?

More than forty years ago, G. Buccellati (1966: 355–60) devoted a chapter in his book on Ur III Amorites to the issue of the sedentarization of these "nomads" and their integration into Mesopotamian societies, and his conclusions have never been questioned. If Amorites were not nomads, then the issue of sedentarization is moot. But in order to disprove the notion completely, we need to take a closer look at the actual documentation concerning people who are labeled "nomads." This exercise is important because it sheds light on several issues at the same time. Before addressing the matter of "sedentarization" directly, it is important to analyze the word MAR.TU, because it has a direct bearing on the problem.

It is commonly accepted that the Akkadian word for "Amorite" is *Amurru(m)* and that the Sumerian is mar-tu or mar-dú. There is no evidence at present for any Amorite language equivalent of the term, if one actually existed; indeed, it is important to note that ethnic terms often are invented by outsiders and are not necessarily used by those to whom the label is applied.[38] The Akkadian word is rare before the Old Babylonian period; in early texts, MAR.TU functions both as a Sumerian word and as a logogram for Amurrum as a "people" and as the name of a deity (Kupper 1961; Klein 1997). The assumption that mar-tu/dú is the Sumerian word for this group is purely hypothetical and is not based on strong data. There is very little evidence for the reading of mar-tu/dú in Sumerian; indeed, the few existing "phonological" renditions of the word—Martu, Mardu, of even Ĝardu—have been deemed unhelpful for resolving the problem of the reading of this sign combination (Wilcke 1974–1977: 93; Marchesi 2006: 11).

The term MAR.TU is first attested in the third-millennium literary texts from Fara, Abu Salabikh, and Mari and is then more amply documented in the Ebla texts (Archi 1985), where it is clearly used as a logogram for an Eblaitic word that cannot

---

37. Note the mention of rá-gaba MAR.TU gu-ti-um in texts from this period (e.g., Lambert 1974: 2).

38. I sidestep the issue of the use of the term *amurrum*/MAR.TU in Old Babylonian times at Mari or in the edicts of the kings of Babylon.

be recovered at present.[39] The term is encountered more often in texts from the Old Akkadian period (A. Westenholz 1999: 97) but is most often found in Ur III documents (Buccellati 1966). I refer here only to the term MAR.TU and do not link these sporadic references with a historical narrative.

The thousands of Ur III occurrences are of no help in determining the reading of MAR.TU. There are, however, a small number of texts that may provide us with an important clue to the matter. The sign sequence a-mu-ru-um is known only from five Ur III documents, four of which are from Girsu and one from Nippur. The latter (*NATN* 909: 2) is fragmentary and should be left out of the discussion. The Girsu references are:

1. lú-ᵈnin-gír-su dumu a-mu-ru-um (*TUT* 160 r. viii: 22–23)
2. a-mu-ru-⸢um⸣ ì-dab₅ (*ITT* 4 7134:2)
3. má a-mu-ru-um (*ASJ* 2 30 86:1)
4. 10 a-mu-ru-um (*WMAH* 33 iii: 4)

There can be no doubt that nos. 1 and 2, and most probably 3, have to be construed as personal names. This is how Buccellati (1966: 133) interpreted nos. 1 and 4. The last example, however, requires closer examination. While it is always possible that it contains nothing more than a personal name, the immediate context suggests otherwise:

   iii 3. 4 gud TÚG.⸢KIN⸣
       4. 10 a-mu-ru-um
       5. [ugula] ⸢ur-ᵈig-alim⸣
       6. [x gud TÚG.KIN]
       7. [x] ⸢lú⸣-huğ-ğá
       8. [ugula ur]-⸢ᵈ⸣nanše
       9. [3ˀ gud] ⸢TÚG.KIN⸣
     10. [1 gud] ⸢ğiš⸣-ùr
     11. [ugula] ⸢lú⸣-diğir-ra
     12. [. . .] x x [. . .]
     13. 20 lú-huğ-ğá
     14. ašag₅ ur-ᵈ⸢en.zu⸣
     15. 3 gud TÚG.⸢KIN⸣
     16. 1 gud ğiš-ùr
   iv 1. [x] lú-[huğ-ğá]
       2. [ugula] ⸢lú-ᵈšul-gi⸣
          etc.

39. Literary text from Fara and Abu Salabikh: kur MAR.TU (*SF* 39 iv 15 and 17) = UD[= kur] MAR.TU (*IAS* 118 v 4) [mss. K. Zand]; Mari: sipa MAR.TU (Bonechi and Durand 1992: 153 iv′ 5′). Also in a Fara administrative document *WF* 78: ii 5. A type of dagger, ğír MAR.TU, which is often encountered in Ebla documents, is also attested in contemporary lexical texts from Southern Mesopotamia; see Civil 2008b: 88.

The pattern in this section of the text is clear: a number of oxen are followed by an entry with a designation of a group of people; here it is hired workers (lú-huǧ-ǧá), although earlier sections of the tablet do include personal names in this position. This strongly suggests that the spelling a-mu-ru-um is a syllabic writing for the normal designation MAR.TU; the entry in line iii 4 therefore has to be read as 10 Amurrum and rendered "10 Amorites." The occurrences of a-mu-ru-um in the other texts in this list (nos. 1–3) are undoubtedly personal names and have to be interpreted as full writings of the name MAR.TU that occurs in accounts from Girsu (see, e.g., *Rev. Sem.* 11 184: 3; *ITT* 4 7051: 4; *HSS* 4 2: ii 18; *CT* 1 2: 8, engar ["farmer"]; *ITT* 4 7955: 4, mušen-dù ["fowler"]; *ITT* 4 8106: 4, ugula ["foreman, captain"], etc.). This demonstrates that a-mu-ru-um is equivalent to MAR.TU, both as a personal name and as an ethnic or professional name. The conclusion is clear: there is no Sumerian word mar-tu/dú; in Sumerian, as in Akkadian, the word is Amurrum.

There is an important corollary to this analysis that brings us back to the main topic of this section. Buccellati (1966: 357), and others following him, assumed that the Girsu references cited above provided proof of the integration of Amorites into local society: since "Amorites" were farmers, fowlers, and the like, this was evidence for a process of sedentarization of nomads. If Amurrum is simply a personal name, then all instances of persons designated as MAR.TU holding these occupations disappear. A closer look at the evidence confirms this conclusion. In his section on "the Amorites as residents," Buccellati (1966: 340–42) summarizes the evidence for the occupations of people referred to as "Amorites." First, we must take out all references to individuals whose names are etymologically Amorite but who are not designated as MAR.TU. Second, we must eliminate functions, as opposed to occupations—that is, people who serve as "conveyors" (ǧìr) in specific contexts. Finally, we must dispose of all references to Amurrum who temporarily served as "musical organizers" (gala) at certain ceremonies, perhaps weddings (Michalowski 2006b). Once this is done, we are left with a much smaller collection of references and with a few exceptions that are entirely military. In texts from Umma and Girsu, we find documentation concerning a cohort of àga-ús amurrum, "Amorite bodyguards," who were stationed in the capital during the last two years of Šulgi's reign,[40] and in one Umma account, there is an ugula ǧeš-da amurrum, "captain of sixty Amorites."[41] A small group of undated accounts from Umma record beer rations for amurrum igi lugal-šè tuš-a, "Amorites stationed before the king"—that is, most probably, royal bodyguards.[42]

---

40. Girsu: *HLC* 1 311: 2, (Š46.11.-); *MVN* 12 112: 2 (Š46.11.-); *HLC* 1 305: 2 (Š46.12.-); Umma: *OrSP* 18 7 24: r. i 9 (Š47.2.-); *NYPL* 291: 2 (Š48.1.-); see also possibly *TSDU* 108: iii 22′ (n.d.).

41. *TSDU* 108: 15′ (n.d.), followed by rations for àga-ús.

42. *CHEU* 56: 5, *RA* 8 156: 5, *OrSP* 47/9 477: 5, *MVN* 13 726: 5, *SAT* 3 2083-6: 5.

The idea that some of these people may have been royal and elite bodyguards leads us to the best-known Amorite of Ur III times, namely, Naplanum. This man, who lived in Sumer for at least 19 years, from Š44 to ŠS6, is documented in more than 90 texts, sometimes with other members of his family.[43] Piotr Steinkeller (2004: 38) wrote that he was "one of the most important persons of his age" and located his Mesopotamian home in Kisig, close to Larsa, although I am not as certain that we can establish his base. The claim about Naplanum's importance is based partly on the sheer number of references to this individual and his family, as well as on the fact that he was undoubtedly the eponymous ancestor of the lineage that eventually took power in Larsa after the collapse of the Ur III state.[44] But what was Naplanum actually doing in Sumer? The fact that he appears so frequently in Drehem documents suggests that he was a foreign envoy or a visiting dignitary or even a ruler, member of the state elite, courtier, or member of the extensive house of Ur. If we set aside Drehem texts that record his receipt or delivery of animals apart from any context, he appears most often together with foreign rulers, with their ambassadors, or with members of the Ur III royal family. What sets him apart from anyone else in the Puzriš-Dagan archives is the large group of underlings who are part of his entourage, some of them definitely kin. He first appears in Š44 (MVN 13 704: Š44.3.21), but a year later he appears at the end—and therefore at the head—of a list of 21 Amurrum; all of them are receiving one sheep each from the booty of Urbilum (MVN 13 423, Š45.11.15). The information we have is insufficient for any secure conclusions, but in light of the facts we do have it is quite possible that Naplanum and his cohorts constituted the personal guard of the Ur III king and his entourage. In this case, they may have accompanied him on the campaign or been present for a victory celebration at home.

While we cannot prove this conclusion decisively at present, the concept of an elite foreign royal guard in Ur III times is hardly surprising and has many historical analogs. To cite one historian on the matter (Kiernan 1957: 68):

> Despots have often chosen to surround themselves with bodyguards of aliens: we see Byzantine emperors with their Varangians, French kings with their Scots and their Swiss Guards, Napoleon with his Poles, Franco with his Moors.

In the Middle East, examples include the early Janissaries or the Mamluks, but there are even more pertinent Mesopotamian examples of kings surrounding themselves with foreign elite legions. Julian Reade (1972: 106–7) observes that Sennacherib's bodyguard may have consisted of men from the Levant and that Elamites were part of a similar cohort around Assurbanipal. Most important, however, is Mario Liverani's (1995; 2001: 391) fascinating reexamination of the famous *Vassal Treaties of*

43. For references, see Fitzgerald 2002: 165–67 and Steinkeller 2004: 37–40.
44. Sallaberger (2007: 446) tries to link Naplanum with the Old Babylonian Yamutbal "tribe," because the latter were associated with Larsa, but this only holds for the lineage of Kudur-mabuk, not for the descendants of Naplanum.

Esarhaddon, discovered in the ruins of Nimrud; he views them not as vassal treaties but as loyalty oaths given by Medes who served as palace guards. I should also note that this view of the term Amurrum in Ur III and early Old Babylonian times is not new; others had made similar claims before, albeit mostly in passing. Among the scholars who claimed that in Babylonia the word Amurrum may, in certain circumstances, have denoted a profession rather than an ethnic description were F. Thureau-Dangin (1910: 18 n. 2) and I. M. Diakonoff (1939: 61).[45]

We have now narrowed down the context in which some of the people designated as Amurrum surface in the Ur III accounting record, with everything pointing in the direction of the military.[46] This parallels the Ur III-period use of the term elam, the other non-native bodyguard designation in texts from the period (Michalowski 2008b: 109). In this case as well, the same word is used in both Sumerian and Akkadian. The people named as elam apparently were guards in the employ of envoys from eastern, northeastern, and southeastern foreign lands, but Amurrum designated military personnel that for the most part protected the royal family and important individuals from abroad, as well as their representatives, although like all Ur III soldiers, they also performed many other duties as well. This is the professional role of most Amorites who actually lived in Sumer, and there is nothing in the currently known Ur III records that documents a process of "sedentarization" of a putatively nomadic people.

It is also true that the word Amurrum was utilized in Ur III times in a way that we might today describe as ethnic. The clearest case of this comes from documents from AS4 from an "industrial park" in Girsu that include rations for amurrum munus, "Amorite females," who were apparently prisoners of war (Heimpel 1998: 397–98). This is certainly the case in the full version of Šu-Sin's fourth- and fifth-year formulas that celebrate the construction of bàd amurrum *muriq-tidnim*, "the fortifications against the Amorites 'Muriq-Tidnim' (The One That Keeps the Tidnum at a Distance)," an event also commemorated in at least one royal inscription.[47] Slightly later, after the collapse of the Ur III state, this usage is encountered repeatedly in the early Old Babylonian letters from Tell Asmar (Whiting 1987) and in the early Isin literary letter to King Iddin-Dagan (SEpM 2).

I should be clear on this: I am only claiming a military role for some, not the majority, of people resident in Babylonia who are designated as Amurrum in Ur III

---

45. Thureau-Dangin presciently described the word for "Amorite" as a "gentilice employé comme nom de fonction; comparer p. ex. notre terme 'Suisse'." For a contrary view, see Buccellati 1966: 351.

46. This is not exactly new; Weeks (1985) and Whiting (1995) suggested, in different ways, that Amorites, being organized militarily, were in a position to take power in times of chaos. Charpin (2004a: 57 n. 134) criticized Weeks and rejected his ideas, claiming that they were based on out-of-date information. But although new information has improved our knowledge, there is much to be said for Weeks's main thesis, even if his analysis is not without problems.

47. For the year-name and inscription, see p. 124 below.

administrative records, but there are other occasions in other times when the term referred to an area, ethnic groups, as well as to a language, and while ultimately these meanings are all related, they are not the subject of the present investigation.

4. Did Amorites Infiltrate the Ur III State in Large Numbers?

In order to understand the function of these people in the state, it is important to examine the statistics. Buccellati (1966: 100) based his analysis on a corpus of 309 names of people who were designated as Amurrum.[48] By now, the number has almost doubled, but it is still a relatively insignificant number in the overall Ur III documentation available to us, which now numbers almost 75,000 published tablets (Molina 2008: 20). It is hard to believe that several hundred references constitutes evidence for a major infiltration of a new population into the land. Moreover, only 39.8% of these people have names that can be identified etymologically as Amorite. What does this say about attempts to recover ethnicity on the basis of personal names? The core problem is that naming and renaming patterns involve many variables, and it is impossible to reduce this to something that we label loosely as ethnicity. What is one to do with a family in which the father has a Hurrian name (Hašib-atal), his son an Akkadian name (Puzur-Šulgi), and whose bride or daughter-in-law (é-gi₄-a) bore a Sumerian name (Ereš-hedu; Limet 1972: 134)? The same holds true for the matter of native language as a marker of ethnic identity, now dramatically undermined by evidence that Yasmaḫ-Addu, who governed Mari on behalf of his father Šamši-Addu, usually considered to have been a classic "Amorite," could not speak Amorite and therefore could not communicate directly with the tribal units in his area of the kingdom (Charpin and Ziegler 2007). These cases force us as Assyriologists to question the traditional means by which we have assigned ethnic identity—that is, solely by means of language and onomastics—and, therefore, once again, we need to reexamine what we mean by the term "Amorite." Here, Buccellati's (1990, 2004, 2008) ideas about the urban/rural distinction are particularly pertinent.

As I have already attempted to demonstrate, in most cases, the term Amurrum is a professional designation in Ur III documents and should probably be translated as "elite Amorite guards" or the like, not as a general ethnic label. But even if one does not accept this conclusion, the ethnic identity of these persons is difficult to determine, even if one uses the evidence of personal names.

One-fifth of the individuals who were designated as Amurrum bear Sumerian names, leading some to suggest that this is evidence of acculturation. But the majority of these people are documented in Girsu texts, where 59 of the 89 Amurrum have Sumerian names (Buccellati 1966: 255). Consider these numbers:

---

48. Streck 2000: 34 has somewhat different numbers.

Total Amurrum	309
Amurrum at Girsu	89
Total Amurrum with Sumerian PNs	63
Amurrum with Sumerian PNs at Girsu	59

Note that of the 63 Ur III Amurrum who have Sumerian names, 59 are known only from Girsu documents. Are these statistics indicative of ethnicity, or do they simply provide evidence for naming patterns? It has been observed repeatedly that, during the Ur III period, personal names in the Girsu province are almost exclusively Sumerian. For example, Heimpel (1974–77: 173) calculates that they constitute 93.8% of all names. These calculations have been used by a number of scholars as proof of the persistence of Sumerian speakers in the south (Woods 2006: 94 with previous literature). I suggest that none of this data provides any information about ethnicity or spoken language but only about onomastic habits. It is even possible that people who carried Akkadian, Elamite, or Amorite names were registered in Girsu texts with ad hoc Sumerian names, but this may be difficult to prove.

Let us assume that there are at least 600 or 700 people designated as Amurrum in Ur III texts. Even if new definition of the word offered here is not accepted, given the wealth of epigraphic documentation for the period, this is a strikingly insignificant number, and this discovery supports the idea that there is no empirical evidence for a massive Amorite infiltration of Mesopotamia in Ur III times.

5. Did Hostile Amorites Play a Significant Role in the Collapse of the Ur III State?

This notion is derived almost exclusively from Old Babylonian literary sources, from the *Lamentation over the Destruction of Sumer and Ur*, as well as from the CKU. The Ur III and early Isin documentary record points to Šimaški as the main military foe that brought down the House of Ur-Namma. There were, however, hostile Amorite polities on the eastern borders of the state, but we have hardly any knowledge about them at the present time. The two political—perhaps ethnic—entities that fought Ur during the reign of Šu-Sin are Tidnum and Ia'madium.

Tidnum and Ia'madium

Much has been written about Tidnum, and recently Gianni Marchesi (2006: 7–19) has offered an exhaustive treatment of all references to this word in cuneiform sources, in previous scholarly literature on the subject, and of the root *DDN* in other ancient Near Eastern traditions. The classic philological method Marchesi uses has its value, but here I would like to take a somewhat different look at the matter. The word Tidnum, in various guises, is attested in Mesopotamia from at least as far back as the Akkad period into late Old Babylonian times and survives, in the lexical and literary tradition, into the first millennium. There can be little doubt that at root this is an Amorite subgroup name, but it does not follow that all occurrences of Tidnum (sometimes written as PIRIG̃.PIRIG̃) and its variants denote the same referent. The occurrences are so sporadic and isolated that any discussion of the issue at this time remains highly tentative. In light of the full documentation presented by Marchesi, only relevant references are repeated here.

1. Although the sign sequence PIRIG̃.PIRIG̃ is attested already in the archaic "Cities" lexical list, it is unlikely that this is already a reference to Tidnum.

2. The earliest attestation of the root is the place name da-da-nu[ki] in Syrian texts from Ebla.

3. The use of PIRIG̃.PIRIG̃ in connection with Eanatum of Lagash does not seem to have anything to do with the word under discussion, as Marchesi has shown quite clearly.

4. All extant references to Tidnum as a geographical/political entity are restricted to the Ur III period and to the time immediately preceding and succeeding it, as well as to literary texts that are dependent on Ur III traditions.

5. The first reference comes from *Gudea Statue B* (Edzard 1997: 34). This passage has been cited many times, but it nevertheless bears additional scrutiny. The king is rebuilding the Eninnu, the main temple of the state god Ningirsu, and he wishes to demonstrate that he can obtain precious items from the whole known universe. Therefore, in columns v and vi he describes in detail how he obtained wood and stone from a broad arc of source areas that begin close to the Mediterranean, then move eastward. First, he acquires "cedars" from the Amanus (v 28), then aromatic woods from Uršu, which he locates in the "Ebla ranges" (hur-sag̃ ib-la-ta, v 53–54), and then in vi 3–8 he brings down great blocks of stone from two highland areas that are described as:

> ù-ma-num
> hur-sag̃ me-nu-a-ta
> PÙ-sal-la
> hur-sag̃ amurrum-ta
> ^{na4}na gal
> im-ta-e$_{11}$

> (Gudea) brought down great (blocks of) stone from Umanum, in/of the mountain range(s) of Menua, and from PUsala in/of the mountain range(s) of Amurrum.

None of these places can be identified at present. The only toponym in this sequence that seems familiar is PÙ-sal-la, which has generally been read ba$_{11}$-sal-la and identified with Bašar, the ancient name of the mountain range known today as Jebel Bishri (Marchesi 2006: 12). Marchesi questions the reading ba$_{11}$ of PÙ and, consequently, of the identification of this toponym with the Syrian mountain range;[49] as a result, some doubt remains concerning its connection with Bašar. Finally, Gudea pre-

---

49. See also Sallaberger 2007. Heimpel (2009b: 27) is apparently unconvinced by Marchesi's doubts and promises a future discussion of this passage.

sumably goes farther east, describing how he brought "alabaster" from still another Amurrum highland area (vi 13–16):

ti-da-núm
hur-saĝ amurrum-ta
nu₁₁-gal lagab-bi-a
mi-ni-de₆

(Gudea) brought in blocks of alabaster from Tidnum, in/of the mountain range(s) of Amurrum.

Here Tidnum is a geographical name or an ethnicon that serves as a place-name. We cannot determine what is meant, except to suggest that it is a distinct place and farther east than Umanum and PUsala.[50]

6. The second occurrence, and the first alleged Ur III example, is found in a broken passage of a fragment of an Old Babylonian royal hymn in honor of the god Nergal, one that perhaps may be a copy of an Ur III poem of Šulgi (*Hymn U*), although it may very well be later in date. The pertinent lines read (*BL* 195: 23–26, van Dijk 1960: 13–15):[51]

ꞌkiꞌ dib-ba-zu érin ur-bi-šè hul m[i-ni-ib- . . .]
an-ša₄-anki ti-da-nu-um-m[a . . .]
ᵈnergal ki dib-ba-zu érin ur-bi-ꞌšèꞌ [hul mi-bi-ib- . . .]

Wherever you go, *evil falls* on all the troops,
Anšan, Tidnum . . .
O Nergal, wherever you go, [*evil falls*] on all the troops!

This broken passage is hardly revealing, although the association of Tidnum with the highland polity of Anšan once again suggests an eastern or northeastern location of these Amorites who were of concern to the Ur III kings.

7. The third reference is also embedded in Old Babylonian manuscripts of a poem that may have been composed in Ur III times, namely *Šulgi Hymn X* 116–117:

kur-ra é-bi-a igi mu-ni-bar-bar
tidnum-e u₆ du₁₀ ì-mi-dug₄

In the foreign land (the inhabitants) looked upon them (Šulgi's deeds) from their dwellings,
Tidnum admired (them) in joy.

---

50. For a different interpretation, see Marchesi 2006: 14. Keeping in mind the uncertainties about the identification of nu₁₁-gal, it is useful to point out that sources of alabaster are well documented in Iran; see Beale 1973: 136

51. The composition is known from a single manuscript of unknown origin. The ascription to Šulgi is based on van Dijk's reading of line 36 as ur-saĝ ꞌšul¹-giꞌ-ra z[i . . .], based on a collation from a photograph.

8. The set of references linked to the line of fortifications that are mentioned in Šu-Sin's fourth year-name: *Muriq-Tidnim*, "The One That Keeps the Tidnum (Amorites) at a Distance."

Just before these fortifications were built, the king's armies encountered enemies as they marched against the northern principality of Simanum, which had rebelled against Ur and deposed a ruling family that was tied to the house of Ur-Namma by means of a dynastic marriage (Michalowski 1975). An Old Babylonian copy of an inscription of Šu-Sin contains the lines (Šu-Sin E3/2.1.4.1 iii 38–44, Frayne 1997: 297):

amurrum l[ú kúr-r]a
ti-id-n[u-um]^{ki}
ìa-a-ma-d[ì-um]^{ki}
im-ma-da-[è-eš]
lugal-ˈbiˈ
mè šen-š[en-na gaba]
im-m[a-d]a-r[e]-eš

Hostile Amurrum came down against (him) from Tidnum and Ia'madium. Their chiefs confronted him in battle.

This passage, now fully restored by C. Wilcke (1990) and G. Marchesi (2006: 12), is particularly important. Tidnum is never mentioned in Ur III documents outside of the Šu-Sin year-name and the texts cited above, and this means that it had no diplomatic relations with the Sumerian state, or at least that none are known in the preserved record. The only Amorite subgroup name that is mentioned in these texts is in fact Ia'madium.[52] D. I. Owen (1993: 183–84) has collected all the references on the matter, which can be briefly summarized here.[53]

1. *Orient* 16 42 10: 3 (Š46.8.3) mu lú-kin-gi$_4$-a lú *ìa-ma!-dì-um*
2. Owen, *FS Hallo* 183: 11 (AS2.7.21) *du-ul-qá-núm* lú *ìa-a-ma-dì-um^{ki}*
3. *JCS* 7 (1953) 105: 8–9 (AS2.8.-) *dú-ul-qá-nu-um* amurrum *ìa-a-ma-dì*
4. *JCS* 7 (1953) 106: 14–15 (ŠS6ʔ.-.-) *i-pí-iq-re-e-ú* ˈamurrumˈ *ìa-a-ma-d[ì-um]*
5. *Amorites* 22: ii 31′ (ŠS 6.-.20) *i-pí-iq-re-e-ú* ˈamurrumˈ *ìa-a-ma-dì-[um]*
6. *Amorites* 21: 17 (ŠS 6.8.14) *i-pí-iq-re-e-ú* amurrum *ìa-a-ma-dì-um*

These texts inform us that ambassadors from Ia'madium were treated like those of other independent polities, including Syrian principalities such as Uršu, Ebla, and Mari, as well as Šimaški and other principalities in the Iranian highlands that were allied to the house of Ur. Contrary to Owen (1993: 181) and Sallaberger (2007: 450),

---

52. Note also the PN ìa-a-ma-tu, an Amurru who was part of Naplanum's cohort (*BibMes* 25 151 54:8, ŠS1.6.24)). There were, of course, other groups and chiefs at the time, but they rarely make an appearance in the archival record; see, for example na-ap-ˈtaˈ-núm lú kíĝ-gi$_4$-a na-ap-ra-núm, "Naptanum, envoy of Napranum," (*JCS* 57 [2005] 29 10: 17, n.d.).

53. See also Sallaberger 2007: 437–38.

I do not think that the order of entries in the Drehem accounts is in any way indica-tive of the geographical location of Ia'madium; some of these texts list it together with Syrian cities, but others include places in Iran. These texts provide fragmentary glimpses of three separate diplomatic events, one in Šulgi 46 (text 1), another in the second year of Amar-Sin (texts 2–3), and a third in Šu-Sin year 6 (texts 4–6). Each event is discreet; the Amar-Sin references document intense diplomatic activity at the beginning of the king's reign, and the Šu-Sin texts are probably evidence for complex international negotiations that accompanied the massive attack on Zabšali and neighboring lands in Iran that took place that year; this will be discussed further below. The fact that Ia'madium was vilified as an evil enemy only two years earlier is hardly surprising, similar to many other relationships between eastern principalities and Ur, swinging back and forth from military confrontation to alliance.

Therefore, in Ur III documents, Ia'madium was the only polity whose emissar-ies are qualified as Amurrum that had diplomatic relations with the Mesopotamian state, and, according to the Šu-Sin inscription, it must have been located close to another such unit, Tidnum, which remains undocumented in the archival texts. But geographical proximity and Amurrum identity aside (from the Mesopotamian point of view), the two shared one more important feature, in the Šu-Sin text at least: they were both governed by rulers whom the scribes of Ur designated as lugal. Of course, we have no way of knowing what the natives called their sovereigns, but the Sumerian designation is almost unique. In Ur III political language, there is only one lugal in the terrestrial realm, and that is the king of Ur. All other rulers are énsi at most, even the king of the powerful kingdom of Anšan, which dwarfed the Mesopotamian state.[54] One may be reading too much into this, but it is striking that the scribe who fashioned this inscription had such a high opinion of the rulers of Tidnum and Ia'madium that he described them as lugals. Perhaps Tidnum and Ia'madium were a well-organized force that constituted a true threat to the kingdom at this time, and this justified using this label for their leaders. But it is more likely that this is simply the way that scribes chose to render the idea of an ethnic chieftain in Sumerian, just as some time later Iaḫdun-Lim of Mari would use the word LUGAL to describe various sheiks in his well-known foundation deposit inscription (Frayne 1990: 606–7, lines 67–75, 96). References in some Mari letters to the Bene-iamina may reflect a similar scribal practice (Durand 2004: 158). Dominique Charpin (2007: 171) suggests that in passages like this the logogram LUGAL is used to express the term *sugāgum*, "tribal leader/king," an Amorite loanword into Mari Akkadian.

Tidnum, which proved to be such a bother that it was immortalized in the name of Šu-Sin's fortifications, seems to have escaped the grasp of Ur, leaving no trace in the Mesopotamian archival record, while Ia'madium, as noted above, did participate in a small number of diplomatic exchanges, three of which are known to us at pres-ent. As a military and political entity, the latter disappears from the historical record

---

54. The one exception was a ruler of Mari whose daughter married one of Ur-Namma's sons; see Civil 1962.

after Šu-Sin's sixth year, while the former leaves a few more traces. The poet who wrote the *Lamentation Over the Destruction of Sumer and Ur*, which describes the fall of the state built by Ur-Namma, counted Tidnum among the areas that contributed to the final fall of Ur, cursing them all in the final sections (lines 486–492):

u₄ ki-en-gi-ra ba-e-zal-la kur-ré hé-eb-zal
u₄ ma-da ba-e-zal-la kur-ré hé-eb-zal
kur ti-id-nu-um^{ki}-ma-ka hé-eb-zal kur-re hé-eb-zal
kur gu-ti-um^{ki}-ma-ka he₂-eb-zal kur-re hé-eb-zal
kur an-ša₄-an^{ki}-na-ka hé-eb-zal kur-re hé-eb-zal
an-ša₄-an^{ki}-e im-hul dal-la-gin₇ kuš₇ hé-ni-ib-su-su
šà-ğar lú níğ-hul hé-en-da-dab₅ ùğ hé-em-ši-gam-e

So that the storm that blew over Sumer will blow over the foreign counties,
That the storm that blew over the frontier will blow over the foreign countries,
Blow over Tidnum-land, blow over the foreign countries,
Blow over Gutium-land, blow over the foreign countries,
Blow over Anšan-land, blow over the foreign countries,
So that it will level Anšan like a blowing storm,
And seize it with a horrid famine,[55] its people be brought down low before it.

Here Tidnum is associated, as one would expect, with two general terms for large Iranian geographical areas, Anšan and Gutium, suggesting that the author thought of it as a major player in the geopolitical configuration of the time. Such glory was short-lived, however, because, save for two enigmatic references in somewhat later literary texts,[56] Tidnum as a political entity never appears again in the historical record.

The location of the people designated as Tidnum and Ia'madium is difficult to establish. The fact that they appear together as enemies of Ur who sided with Simanum suggests, but does not prove, that they are to be sought in proximity to one another, and the manner in which they appear in the Šu-Sin inscription cited above seems to indicate that the armies of the Ur III ruler encountered them as they made their way north to subdue the rebels of Simanum. Whatever one thinks of the real motivations behind the building of Muriq-Tidnim, the fact that the fortifications were supposedly directed against Tidnum indicates that at least a sizable portion of them had to be in its vicinity, and this means that they must be localized in the mountains that bordered the Diyala valley. Therefore, it is reasonable to assume that Tidnum as well as Ia'madium attacked the forces of Ur as they made their way toward Simanum, either from their encampments in the old strategic center around Apiak, Marad, Kazallu, and Urum, or from the newer military outposts in the Diya-

55. Note the transitivizing use of -da-.
56. *Nippur Lament* 231: ugu-bi-ta ti-id-nu-um/tidnum nu-ğar-ra íb-ta-(an)-zi-ge-eš-[àm], "They removed treacherous Tidnum from upon it (Umma)," *Letter of Lugal-nisağe* (SEpM 8: 4): ti-id-nu-um/tidnum^{ki}-e šu bí-in-ğar šibir-bi mu-un-dab₅-ba/ğar, "who subjugated Tidnum, seized its royal staff."

la.[57] The road that Šu-Sin's armies took on their way to Simanum is not described in the surviving narrative of the expedition. It is possible that they went up along the Tigris, but it is more likely that they moved up the Diyala, or started from the Diyala area, crossed the Hamrin range and then proceeded toward what would later be Assyria, in essence taking in reverse the roads that many years later Šamši-Adad V would traverse in his campaign against Babylonia (Levine 1973: 22). In this scenario, Šu-Sin's armies would have encountered hostile Amorites somewhere in the valleys surrounding the Jebel Hamrin.

In this context, it may be relevant to recall that there is an account from Ur, dated to IS4.8.-—less than a decade after the Simanum campaign—that mentions gifts (níĝ-šu-taka₄) for "Amorites of the bolt of the frontier (saĝ-kul ma-da)."[58] There are, quite obviously, different ways of interpreting this phrase; it may not be simply fortuitous that in much later Akkadian literary texts Ebih—that is, the Jebel Hamrin—is described as *sikkur mati*, "bolt of the land," most prominently in the "*lipšur* litanies" edited by Erica Reiner (1956: 134 line 37). The phrase occurs elsewhere in first-millennium texts,[59] but as Reiner (1956: 131) notes, there are indications that these litanies may have originated in Old Babylonian times.

The sparse and sometimes contradictory evidence on Tidnum that has survived is inconclusive and is open to a number of interpretations. It is important, however, to isolate the Ur III data that refer to a political entity from earlier, and especially from later, references that contain the same Semitic root but have no bearing on the historical issues that are under consideration here. By contextualizing the information in the political geography of the time, we can reach certain conclusions, always keeping in mind their highly speculative nature.

Just before the rise of the Ur III state, during the reign of Gudea, Tidnum was an Amorite subgroup name, one that was known to Mesopotamians, although the area in which they were encountered cannot be located at present. Some time during the Ur III period, at least two groups that had settled in the upper Diyala region and farther east in the valleys around the Jebel Hamrin and beyond came into contact with the Mesopotamian state—Ia'madium and Tidnum. The former was engaged in diplomatic relations with Ur, but the latter was not. Nevertheless, at least by the time of Šu-Sin they constituted a military threat; their geopolitical importance may have been amplified by their location, because they seem to have menaced the all-important trade and military routes that lead from the Diyala region into Iran. It is most probable that their own political emergence was also precipitated by their location, caught between the powerful highland polities of Anšan, Šimaški, and Zabšali and the Mesopotamian kingdom. It is highly unlikely that both Ia'madium and Tidnum were wiped off the map during their encounter with the forces of Šu-Sin; more

---

57. Sallaberger (2007: 449), implausibly to my mind, suggests, "the Yamadium were a main group of pastoralists of the Balikh and Khabur plains and/or around the Jebel Sinjar."

58. *UET* 3 1685: 4–5.

59. For other examples, see *CAD* S 258.

probably, they disintegrated in the aftermath of the fall of Ur, when the Diyala area became the seat of new political entities, some of them dominated by Amorite leaders, many of whom may at some time have been a part of these tribal confederations.

This is all that is known with any degree of precision about hostile Amurrum in Ur III times. The role of Amorites in the military events that led to the collapse of the state has been gleaned from the CKU, specifically, from the Šu-Sin, and most specifically, the Ibbi-Sin, correspondence (Wilcke 1969, 1970). As we will presently see, this evidence is tenuous at best and difficult to interpret, but everything points to the conclusion that these people had only a minor role to play in the disintegration of the Ur III kingdom.

6. Did Amorites Take Power in Mesopotamian Cities after the Ur III Collapse?

Historians of early Mesopotamia often claim that Amorite dynasties took power in the aftermath of the Ur III collapse. Most recently, D. Charpin (2003b: 43) wrote:

> Au moment où disparut le dernier roi d'Ur, des nomades amorrites, venues de Syrie, envahirent la Mésopotamie et fondèrent un certain nombre des dynasties, come à Isin ou à Larsa. . . .

My goal here is not to criticize one author but to exemplify a commonly held opinion, one that I in part shared until recently. Here I am proposing that a reexamination of the pertinent information does not fully support this conclusion. In light of the data collected earlier in this chapter, there is no evidence that the Amorites mentioned in Ur III texts were nomads, and those who posed a danger to Ur were located in the east or north, not the west. Moreover, the matter of the early histories and ethnic identity of the "dynasties" that were established in Isin and Larsa is likewise less than clear.

The main actor in the post–Ur III drama was Išbi-Erra, who had already taken over Isin and Nippur and possibly a number of other towns and cities before the fall of Ur; of him we will have more to say in chap. 7. A decade or so after this event, he was able to oust the Elamites from the old capital and add it to his new kingdom. The dynasty he founded at Isin lasted more than two centuries, but nothing about him or his successors can even remotely be linked to anything "Amorite," however one may interpret the term. Indeed, it appears that some of his descendants, most notably Iddin-Dagan, Išme-Dagan, and Lipit-Eštar, quite consciously appropriated many of the outer trappings of Ur III self-representation, thereby laying claim to continuity with the former regime in the land. And even though it is often asserted that Išbi-Erra was an Amorite officer in Ibbi-Sin's employ, there is not one piece of evidence to support the claim that he was either an officer or an Amorite. As already noted, the only indication that he ever served Ibbi-Sin comes from CKU, and even here his status and rank are unstated. Unless I am mistaken, the notion that he was a military officer goes back to T. Jacobsen (1957: 40 n. 45), but Jacobsen's comment was only an informed guess that was not directly supported by any contemporary evidence and only inferred from the CKU. Išbi-Erra is mentioned only once in the entire Ur III documentation, but this one citation refers to him as an independent ruler at Isin.[60] Literary references, including the CKU, link him with Mari, but again without any further information, and even if his original homeland was there, this does not in any way indicate that he was an Amorite of any kind (Michalowski 2005b).

I know of no evidence for Amorite presence in Mari during the Ur III period. The language of the written texts from the city and of many of the personal names that appear in them is a different Semitic language altogether. Finally, while it is often asserted that Išbi-Erra's name is linguistically Amorite, it is equally possible to analyze it as Akkadian: "Erra Has become Sated."[61]

In Ešnunna, a local dynasty freed itself from Ur III rule, and even if these kings did link themselves by means of dynastic marriages to Amorite chieftains in the area (Whiting 1987), they themselves were not of Amorite origin, as far as we can determine. Only in Larsa did an Amorite group take over, but they were uniquely positioned, because it is possible that they had made their home in nearby Kisig (Steinkeller 2004: 38–39) or elsewhere in the vicinity. If my speculations about Naplanum and his people are correct, this is hardly surprising. A well-organized elite military troop, bound by kinship ties, with intimate knowledge of the Ur III court, would have no trouble seizing power and holding a nearby city during a time of war and disorder. How they did this is a matter of pure speculation, because no contemporary sources illuminate the matter. Naplanum himself is last attested in ŠS6 (*PDT* 2 1172), and his son is mentioned in an unpublished Drehem text from IS2.9.20 (Buccellati 1966: 263), at a time when Larsa was still part of Ibbi-Sin's orbit (Fitzgerald 2002: 19). It seems likely that Naplanum, if he were still active or alive, would not have established any independent polity before IS3, which seems to be the watershed year for Ibbi-Sin's kingdom. In the Isin texts there is no mention of the great man, but there are two references to one e-mi/me-zum, otherwise unqualified, who may be the Jemṣium who is listed as the second ruler in the Larsa Dynastic List. As Fitzgerald (2002: 26–27) observes, he is listed together with Amorite chieftains, some of who are known from contemporary texts from Ešnunna, suggesting that Jemṣium was likewise a high-status individual. There is no way of establishing whether he was actually an independent ruler at Larsa or a vassal of Išbi-Erra. Royal inscriptions only begin with the fourth and fifth rulers of Larsa—Zabaya (1941–1933 B.C.) and Gungunum (1932–1906 B.C.)—and therefore we cannot determine the nature of kingship in the city before that time. It is not possible to establish the role or even the precise geographical location of this lineage before that time.

---

60. See p. 182 with n. 28.

61. Thus *CAD* Š/2 253 sub *šebû*. Others disagree; see, for a recent example, Selz 2005: 104 ("der Name ist amuritisch").

One must be careful not to conflate the political, demographic, and social land-scape of Old Babylonian times with events that took place generations earlier. A case in point concerns the alleged ascription of "Emutbalian" origins to Naplanum during the Ur III period. P. Steinkeller (2004: 40) cautiously has suggested that a connec-tion of this sort existed, based essentially on the fact that his entourage included a man by the name of Napšanum, who was a messenger of one ìa-a-mu-tum (*TCL* 2 5508: 12, Drehem, AS 4.1.6).[62] I find this unconvincing, but one must note that Steinkeller himself was aware of the very tenuous nature of this suggestion. Aside from the fact that connections with an envoy of a person named Iamutum does not make one a member of a putative Emutbal tribe, it is important to stress that the connections between Larsa and this corporate name are attested only for the last independent rulers of the city, Warad-Sin and Rim-Sin, as well as for their father Kudur-mabuk. But these persons constitute a completely new lineage on the throne of Larsa, and there are absolutely no grounds for projecting these genealogical claims back to earlier times, to the rulers who claimed descent from Naplanum. The fact that the first members of this lineage who ruled at Larsa used titles such as *rabiān amurrim* can be explained in a number of ways (Michalowski 1983b: 240–41; Seri 2005: 55–60), but it has nothing at all to do with Emutbal, as far as we know.

However, Steinkeller's cautious conjecture has fueled further speculation, lead-ing D. Charpin (2003a: 15) to suggest that already in Ur III times Naplanum and his group had migrated from the region south of the Jebel Sinjar in Syria and had brought with them new toponyms that they applied in Babylonia. I think that this is an anachronism, because it projects the claims of Kudur-Mabuk and his descendants several centuries into the past. More importantly, however, F. Joannès (1996: 353) had already argued that the issue at hand is not tribal affiliation but the naming of places and regions. Indeed, there is no evidence to support the notion that Emutbal was ever a tribal name to begin with—only a geographical designation, although Charpin (2003a: 17) remains unconvinced. More recently, W. Sallaberger (2007: 446) has taken this even further, reversing the direction of Charpin's toponymic renaming, stating that "the case of Yamut-balum may serve as a prime example of the extension of a Mardu tribal name from the South to Upper Mesopotamia." In other words, unless this is simply a redactional lapse, a hypothetical identification of Emutbalum in one Ur III text has now led to the historical scenario of an Amorite tribal movement from Babylonia to Syria.

---

62. The account lists animals given to various foreigners, beginning with Naplanum, his brother, his son, and his brother's wife, followed by Napšanum, and then two individuals, Šulgi-abi and Hun-Šulgi, and these are (all?) summarized as MAR.TU-me (line 16). Then follow the envoys of various eastern states, followed by members of the royal family. Hun-Šulgi, his subordi-nate Šulgi-abi, and in some texts also Šulgi-ili were important members of Naplanum's troop and were often present when foreign envoys and royal family members were present. It is unlikely, in my opinion, that the envoy Napšanum was part of Naplanum's organization; instead, the latter and his family and lieutenants were assisting and guarding Iamutum's ambassador, because this was part of their normal duties.

Instead, I suggest a somewhat different scenario for the developments that took place in the aftermath of the Ur III collapse, one that does not simply paint all the new polities as "Amorite" nor link them to an otherwise unattested large influx of new peoples in the preceding decades. In the Mesopotamian homeland, the main new political center was in Isin, which to some degree portrayed itself as the legitimate extension of the Ur III kingdom. From what little we know, it seems that the new kingdom had extensive relations with small polities in the Diyala and surrounding regions, many of which were now in the hands of Amorite chieftains, although some of the older urban centers, such as Ešnunna, were not. It is only somewhat later that Amorite leaders established themselves in Babylonian cities such as Larsa, Sippar, and Babylon. The approximate time of these events can be associated with the beginning of the reign of Sumu-la-el in Babylon, around 1880 B.C. by the Middle Chronology—that is, more than a century after the fall of Ur. Indeed, while one may ultimately see this as a long-term consequence of the Ur III collapse, the rise of "Amorite dynasties" for the most part takes place generations after the last king of Ur was carried off to Anšan.[63] The first Amorite royal family came to dominate Larsa some time around 1940 B.C., but these Amorites were not outsiders and certainly not nomads, because their ancestors had been living in Babylonia for generations.

With these general thoughts in mind, let us return to an earlier period and focus on "Amorite" matters that are highlighted in the CKU, especially the fortifications that were supposedly built against their dangerous intrusions. In light of the conclusions reached above, we must ask the question: if Amorites posed no significant threat to the Ur III kingdom, why would King Šu-Sin order the construction of massive fortifications that were ostensibly designed to keep them from infiltrating the Mesopotamian homeland?

---

63. Charpin (2004a: 80) and Charpin and Ziegler (2004: 29–30) already recognized that there might have been a "new wave" of Amorite infiltration into upper and lower Mesopotamia around 1900 B.C., the first taking place in Ur III times; they are proponents of Amorite invasions from the west, from Amurrum, which they situate in the mountainous region from east of Ugarit up to the Jebel Bišri.

Chapter 6

The Royal Letters in Their Historical Setting 2

Great Walls, Amorites, and Military History: The Puzur-Šulgi and Šarrum-bani Correspondence (Letters 13–14 and 19–20)

The Great Wall(s)

Ancient Mesopotamians are often accused of collapsing history by narrative concentration on emblematic personages and events. Modern historians, however, often share some of the same discursive strategies. One such characteristic moment that practically serves to define an era is the construction of a great wall that, according to many of our modern authorities, served to separate Sumer from hostile nomadic Amorite infiltrators in Ur III times. Indeed, no matter how sketchy the description of the period may be, one can be sure to find a mention of the wall that Šu-Sin claimed to have built, a wall he named Muriq-Tidnim[1]—"The One That Keeps the Tidnum (Amorites) at a Distance." The image of a massive wall separating Sumer from the barbarians certainly appeals to the imagination, but it may not accurately reflect historical reality. Lacking informative sources, some scholars have turned, by analogy, to the image of the Great Wall of China, which has become part of Western popular imagination going back at least into the sixteenth century and is reflected in art and literature as disparate as the works of Franz Kafka (1917) and Jorge Luis Borges (1964). R. D. Barnett (1963: 18), in his influential article on the "Median Wall" mentioned by Xenophon, already invoked the metaphorical connection:

> Nebuchadnezzar (604–561 B.C.) constructed a sort of Babylonian equivalent of the Great Wall of China; whereas that was intended to keep out the Mongols, this was intended to keep out the Medes, who were then threatening the Empire.

1. For the interpretation of the Akkadian participle as *mureʾʾiq*, see Marchesi 2006: 11–12 n. 33. Here, the conventional rendition of the name of the fortifications will be used.

He also made the most forceful connection between this notion and Šu-Sin's constructions based on a translation of the first eleven lines of ŠaŠu1 (18) that he had received from C. J. Gadd, who utilized the only source known at the time, a then-unpublished tablet in the British Museum found at Ur.[2] Barnett's (1963: 20) description, couched in language characteristic of his time, reads:

> Fifteen hundred years before Xenophon's time, the Sumerians found themselves faced with the problem of protecting their flourishing countryside and wealthy cities from the incursions of barbarian nomads from the north. The Third dynasty of Ur struggled to keep out the Amorite Bedouin or Martu as they were called, and Shu-Sin, King of Ur, dates the fourth year of his reign (2038–2030 B.C.) by the official description as that in which 'Shu-Sin constructed the wall called Muriq Tidnim—that which keeps out the barbarians'.

Most recently, another scholar (Marchesi 2006: 19) has reiterated the historical metaphor, asserting that:

> During the period of the Third Dynasty of Ur, a sort of Great Chinese Wall was built in order to keep them (=Tidnum) out of the territory of the Ur state."

One can easily see how the Chinese example influenced thinking about this construction, although much of what most of us think we know about the Chinese Great Wall is based on nationalism and myth (Waldron 1992). Ancient Near Eastern polities were certainly capable of building long defensive or offensive walls, as illustrated by Nebuchadnezzar's construction, or the Sasanian wall on the Gorgan Plain in northern Iran, 195 kilometers or more long, with a canal and 33 forts that reached from the Caspian Sea up to the highlands to the east, marking the northern border of the state; the latter is currently under study by Iranian and British archaeologists (Nokandeh et al. 2006; Rekavandi et al. 2007; 2008; Sauer et al. 2009). The excavators of this amazing construction claim, "if we exclude earthworks, the Gorgan Wall may be the longest wall anywhere in the ancient world" (Nokandeh et al. 2006: 121). There are traces, however, of an even longer ancient wall, more than 200 kilometers long, in Syria, that was probably built in the third millennium B.C.E. (Geyer et al. 2007: 278–79; Geyer 2009). The height of this wall is unknown, as is its purpose. As with so many similar constructions, it is impossible to know if the primary motivation for its construction was to keep people and/or animals in or out.

And yet if we are to believe the CKU, Muriq-Tidnim spanned a length of at least 269 kilometers and when finished may have covered another 100 kilometers or more; in other words, it may have been almost twice the size of either of these constructions. Of course, the analogy goes only so far. The Sasanian and Syrian walls were continuous stone-made constructions, but Šu-Sin's project was most probably a line of discontinuous fortifications.

---

2. Source Ur1 of the present edition.

What do we actually know about this phantom wall, or line of forts, from Ur III sources? The answer is: practically nothing, since our evidence consists of two year-names and half a sentence in a dedicatory inscription:

> Šulgi year-names 37 and 38: mu bàd ma-da ba-dù, "The year: the wall of the 'land' was built."
>
> Šu-Sin year-names 4 & 5: mu ^{d}šu-^{d}en.zu lugal uri$_5$^{ki}-ma-ke$_4$ bàd amurrum mu-rí-iq-ti-id-ni-im mu-dù, "The year: Šu-Sin, king of Ur, built the fortifications against the Amorites 'Muriq-Tidnim'(The One That Keeps the Tidnum [Amorites] at a Distance)."
>
> Šu-Sin inscription 17 (Frayne 1997: 328, E3/2.1.4.17: 20–26): u$_4$ bàd amurrum, mu-ri-iq,-ti-id-ni-im, mu-dù-a, ù g̃ìri amurrum, ma-da-né-e, bí-in-gi$_4$-a, "When he had built the fortifications against the Amorites 'Muriq-Tidnim' (The One That Keeps the Tidnum [Amorites] at a Distance) and turned back the incursions of the Amorites to their territories."

Perhaps because the evidence is so meager, it has fueled much speculation on the location and purpose of these fortifications. Indeed, it may be apt to cite the words of the great British historian R. G. Collingwood (1921: 37), written about a different but equally notorious military construction, words that could be appropriated to apply to the Ur III situation as well:

> The theories that have been advanced concerning the Roman Wall in England and its attendant works have been so many, so divergent, and at times so rapid in their succession as almost to justify the favourite taunt of irresponsible criticism, that their sequence is a matter of fashion or caprice rather than of rational development.

As far as I can determine, it is generally assumed that the Šulgi and Šu-Sin year-names, although 23 years apart, refer to the same project (e.g., Sallaberger 1999: 159, 2009: 37);[3] Muriq-Tidnim was an extension of the earlier bad mada, although nothing in the surviving Ur III documentation links these two ventures. The assumption is exclusively based on the information from CKU; indeed, the two projects have been lumped together under the common name "MAR.TU-Mauer" (Wilcke 1969: 1). Moreover, the Ur III references tell us nothing about the location of these constructions, their full length, or basic characteristics, and little, names aside, about their purpose. Although it is usually taken for granted that the "wall(s)" had to be continuous, it is more likely that one or both could have consisted of a line of fortifications or a combination of strongholds and walls. Most important, there is not a single direct reference to these massive building projects in the tens of thousands of known Ur III documents, and later texts, excluding CKU, are likewise silent on this matter. The only information on the location and possible length of the Šulgi construction is found in two CKU letters, 13 and 14 (PuŠ1, ŠPu1), written from the military officer in charge of the fortifications, or at least part of them, to the king. It

---

3. I have myself contributed to the confusion between the two by asserting, incorrectly, that Šu-Sin renamed Šulgi's wall Muriq-Tidnim (Michalowski 2005a: 200).

is only supposition, however, that these letters actually describe the bad mada. Because the authenticity of this epistolary information cannot easily be established, it is best to consider all other relevant data first and then compare the results with testimony from the Old Babylonian literary correspondence. Before proceeding, however, I would like to note that the lack of archival evidence should not be considered a good argument for dismissing all other forms of documentation on this subject; some have gone so far as to claim that Muriq-Tidnim might have been a small local construction.[4] It is true that the existing Ur III administrative documents record expenditures and other official acts connected with certain large building projects, such as the rebuilding of the Tumal during the time of Šulgi, or work on the Šara temple at Umma that is the subject of Šu-Sin's ninth year-name and is also documented in archival texts (Frayne 1997: 294).[5] But there are also many examples of large construction undertakings that have left no footprint in the recovered archives, even though they are known from royal building inscriptions and year-names. The fact that the construction of Muriq-Tidnim was heralded in two successive year-names testifies to the significance and the very scope of the undertaking.

The bad mada of Šulgi

The lack of Ur III archival information is not surprising in the case of the Šulgi constructions, since the work antedates the founding of Puzriš-Dagan, commemorated in the names of Šulgi's thirty-ninth, fortieth, and forty-first years, and therefore comes from a time when documentation is extremely sparse and is limited to the archives of Umma and Girsu, relatively far from the area of the fortifications. To get some insight into the purpose or nature of this construction, it might be best to start with its name, which, as already noted, is known to us only from the Šulgi year-names. The expression bad mada (bàd ma-da) is usually translated as "the wall of the land/des Landes/du pays," which is imprecise and seems to leave the impression that it was designed to protect the whole "country," that is, the state of Ur itself. But Sumerian ma-da—obviously a loan from Semitic (Jacobsen 1957: 40 n. 47)—does not mean "country" in this sense when it stands alone and does not qualify a geographical name (certainly not in Ur III times) but designates, more narrowly, the concept of "territory, countryside, march, frontier (area)," in the general as well as political sense, as distinct from the geographical term ki-en-gi, "Sumer," and ka-lam, "homeland."[6] When used in connection with a place-name, it has a somewhat

4. E.g., "The wall itself may have been built as a modest protecting wall against sheep and serving as a demarcation line" (Sallaberger 2007: 445). He has now changed his mind on the scope of these fortifications; see Sallaberger 2009.

5. On such projects, see now the forthcoming paper by Piotr Steinkeller, "Corvée Labor in Ur III Times."

6. It is only during the time of the Isin kings that, under Akkadian influence, ma-da comes to mean more and can be applied to the "homeland," as in Išbi-Erra's title lugal ma-da-na, "king of his own land." The semantics of all three terms require a full investigation, because their

different shade of meaning. For example, in Šu-Sin's description of the raid on Sima-num, the expression ma-da ma-da-bi describes the territories surrounding the city that were under its control (iv 29), and the same holds for Amar-Sin's claim earlier, in the formula for his seventh year, that he defeated Bitum-rabi²um, Iabru, as well as their surrounding territories.[7] Similarly, Ur III texts use mada GN to refer to the specific provinces of the state, such as Girsu, Umma, and so on. In administrative documents, mada often means "countryside," as in "the orchard of the estate of Amar-Šulgi, in the Isin countryside,"[8] or refers to small chapels in the Umma prov-ince.[9] As "frontier," mada is an areal concept and must be distinguished from zag, "frontier (line)."[10] I should add that these distinctions may not have been apparent to all teachers and students in Old Babylonian times and, therefore, some if not all of them may have interpreted the CKU usage of mada as the full semantic equivalent of Akkadian *mātum*.

The use of mada as "frontier" is documented in certain literary texts that go back to Ur III and somewhat later times; subsequently, semantic leveling with Ak-kadian *mātum* restricts the range of the term in Sumerian. The best example comes from the curse at the end of the *Lamentation over the Destruction of Sumer and Ur*, 486–87, where the storm is beseeched to return home:

u_4 ki-en-gi-ra ba-e-zal-la kur-re hé-eb-zal
u_4 ma-da ba-e-zal-la kur-re hé-eb-zal

So that the storm that blew over Sumer should blow over the foreign lands,
So that the storm that blew over the frontier should blow over the foreign lands!

This is followed by Tidnum, Gutium, and Anšan;[11] mada here is not a quasi-syn-onym of Sumer; instead, the progression is geographical, from Sumer to the frontier, then to the "Amorite" lands on the edge of the eastern frontier, and then on through to the large territory of Anšan in the southeast.

Similarly, in *Šulgi Hymn A* 45–47:

anzu[mušen] kur-bi-šè igi íl-la-gin$_7$ du$_{10}$-ĝu$_{10}$ hu-mu-sù-sù
uru ma-da ki ĝar-ĝar-ra-ĝu$_{10}$ ha-ma-su$_8$-su$_8$-ge-eš-àm
ùĝ saĝ-gi$_6$-ga u$_8$-gin$_7$ lu-a u$_6$ du$_{10}$-ga ha-ma-ab-dug$_4$

---

usage and meaning change over time; for example, as a logogram in Sargonic inscriptions, kalam corresponds to Akkadian *mātum*. Jacobsen (1953: 40 n. 47) argued that ma-da is to be under-stood as "level land that may be found at the edge of the desert." For a discussion of these terms, with somewhat different conclusions, see Limet 1978.

7. mu ᵈamar-ᵈen.zu lugal-e bí-tum-ra-bí-um[ki] ì-ab-ru[ki] ma-da ma-da-bi ù hu-úh-nu-ri[ki] mu-hul, "The year: King Amar-Sin destroyed Bitum-rabi²um, Iabru, their surrounding territories, as well as Huhnuri."

8. ᵍⁱˢkiri$_6$ é amar-ᵈšul-gi, ma-da isin$_2$[in.ki] (MVN 18 132:5–6; see also BCT 1 127 4:5).

9. éš-didli ma-da (*Nebraska* 37: r. iv12′; *Nik* 2:236 r ii 23; *AnOr* 1 88: r iii 5′, et passim); see Steinkeller 2007d: 193.

10. The latter is equivalent to Akkadian *pāṭu*, for which see Charpin 2004b: 53–55.

11. See p. 116 above.

Like Anzu, sighting his mountain (lair), I elongated my steps,
And so the (inhabitants of) the cities I had founded on the frontier stood up for me,
And the Black-Headed People, numerous as ewes, gazed at me with sweet
   admiration.

And in *Šulgi Hymn* C 87–88:

uru ma-da ki-bala gú-érim-ma mu-da-gub-na-$\tilde{g}u_{10}$-šè
mè-$\tilde{g}u_{10}$ a-ma-ru-kam ság nu-um-ši-íb-èn

When I stand up to the cites of the hostile rebel frontier,
My war (making) is as a flood wave that cannot be withstood!

The notion of the frontier is critical for our understanding of salient aspects of the
Mesopotamian geographical imagination. A frontier is not a line in the sand but
a liminal zone, an area of multifaceted interactions that can unite as much as it
separates, and is often the place where new cultural and political orders can establish themselves and grow, challenging established centers and resisting hegemony
(House 1980; Lightfoot and Martinez 1995). This fits in perfectly with certain aspects of the denotation of mada, as we shall presently see.

Seen in the light of what has been said above, bad mada must be rendered
as "wall/fortifications (guarding) The Territory/Frontier," but this then leads to the
question: what is the specific territory that required such protection?

As it happens, there is some neglected Ur III archival information that might
shed light on a province or area that was designated, in native terminology, as mada.
Two texts from Umma document the existence of an entire dossier of transactions
concerning the lú énsi ma-da-(ke_4-ne), "representatives of the governors of 'The
Territory/Frontier.'" The first, and the only dated text, mentions a reed basket with
accounts of these officials covering the years Š33–45,[12] and an undated tag from the
same city was used to label a basket with similar transactions.[13] Only one text of the
kind referred to in these tablets has been published to date, and it needs to be cited
in full (MVN 14 228, collations in MVN 16: 231–34):[14]

1. 348.0.0 še gur
2. mu i-sà-rí-ik-šè
3. kišib₃ hi-bí-DIĜIR
4. 2.2.3 dabin gur kišib₃ ᵈèr-ra-ul-lí
5. 120.0.0 še gur kišib₃ di-ni-lí
6. 572.0.4 še gur
7. kišib₃-bi 2-àm kišib₃ i-ṣur-DIĜIR
8. 51.0.3 1 sìla 12 gín še gur
9. kišib₃ ì-lí-be-lí

12. 1 ᵍⁱˢpisaĝ kišib₃/dub énsi ma-da (SANTAG 6 20:3).
13. pisaĝ-dub-ba, kišib₃/dub lú énsi ma-da-ke₄-ne, ì-ĝál (BRM 3 174:2).
14. I refrain from speculating on the specific nature of the transactions involved, but I doubt
that they have anything to do with the building of the Šulgi fortifications.

10. 55.2.5 5 sìla dabin gur
11. kišib₃-bi 2-àm
12. kišib₃ é-a-ma-lí-ik
13. lú énsi ka-zal-luᵏⁱ
14. 3.0.0 še gur kišib₃ puzur₄-ma-ma
15. 1055.0.0 še gur
16. kišib₃-bi 4-àm
17. kišib₃ é-a-ba-ni
18. 77.0.0 se gur
19. kišib-bi 2-àm
20. kišib₃ nu-úr-ᵈadad
    (line)
21. lú énsi már-ra-adᵏⁱ
22. 2.0.0 še gur kišib₃ puzur₄-sú
23. lú ur-ᵈEN.ZU énsi úrumᵏⁱ
    (line)
24. šu-nígin 2286.0.0 12 gín še zíz gur
25. kišib₃-bi 16-àm
26. kišib₃ dab₅-ba ki lú-giri₁₇-zal-taᵎ
27. ur-ᵈšára-ke₄ ba-an-dab₅ᵎ
28. kišib₃ lú énsi ma-da-ke₄-ne

The last line, "accounts of the representatives of the governors of 'The Territory/ Frontier,'" is the key to our understanding of one particular Ur III usage of the term mada. Although undated, the document can be assigned to the period covered by the reed container with similar accounts. Issariq, the person mentioned in line 2, must be the earliest known governor of Kazallu, first attested in the position in Š33.3.- (*YOS* 4 75:7). His successor, Kallamu, first appears in Š43.2.- (*PDT* 1 509:3), and so this transaction is probably earlier than that.[15] Issariq is followed by three persons; the first, Ḫib-ili, belongs with the governor; the second, Erra-ulli, is documented in another Umma tablet, where he is described as a man working for the governor of Kazallu;[16] and in line 13 Ea-malik is specifically described as the man of the governor of Kazallu. One may conclude that the whole section up to line 13 or 14 concerns Kazallu and that Din-ili (5), Iṣṣur-ili (7), and Ili-beli (9) are also associated with the administration of that city.[17] Thereupon follow representatives of the governor of

---

15. Ur-Su'ena, governor of Urum is first attested in Š42.7.15 (*Ontario* 1 12:2).

16. *BPOA* 6 1530: 3–4 (Š38.-.-) ᵈèr-ra-ul-lí, lú énsi ka-zal-luᵏⁱ. The tablet bears the seal of Erra-ulli and may be one of the sealed accounts summarized here. Note that the editors, Marcel Sigrist and Tohru Ozaki, recognized the association between the entries in the two texts, which concern the exact same transaction, providing a date for the *MVN* document.

17. There is a Dan-ili who appears in Umma texts, known from texts and his seal, as dub-sar. He is first attested in *SAT* 2 263 (Š33.7.-). This is undoubtedly not the same person as the representative of the governor of Adab in V. Scheil, *RA* 12 (1915) 164 r. ii 1 (AS4.-.-). In this

Marad: Ea-bani and Nur-Adad.[18] Ur-Sin is otherwise attested as governor of Urum
in Š42.7.15 (*Ontario* 1 12:2) sometime around AS7,[19] so this would be his earliest
appearance in the Ur III record. All the identifiable people fit into the time around
Š33 or slightly later, and judging by the Erra-ulli entry, it may be dated to Š38.

Seven of the eleven people mentioned here—excluding the officials in charge
of the transactions—are from Kazallu, Marad, and Urum. The rest remain unidentified at present, and until evidence is uncovered that proves otherwise, one may
assume, as a working hypothesis, that they also represented the governors of Kazallu
or Marad. Should new texts demonstrate otherwise—for example, if some of these
people were linked to Adab—the argument presented here would be invalidated. In
that case, one would have to render énsi ma-da-ke₄-ne as "governors of various
provinces;" but in fact one would expect something along the lines of énsi ma-da
ma-da-ke₄-ne for such a meaning.[20]

If my hypothesis is correct, these three records offer proof that there were numerous Umma accounts pertaining to the mada that have not been recovered to
date and that the *MVN* text is only one of many transactions from this period that
concerned these governors. To be sure, there are similar texts from Umma that list
"accounts" (kišib₃) of governors of cities and provinces of the Ur III state, including Adab, Marad, and Kazallu (*RA* 12 164, AS2.-.-, bricks), or Marad, Babylon,
Ešnunna, Nippur (*SNAT* 404, AS8.-.-, breads and flour), but such texts—and there
are others of this kind—never mention the "governors of the mada."

In light of these facts, tenuous though they may be, one can formulate two alternative hypotheses, both of which are difficult to substantiate: either the bad mada
was located somewhere in the Diyala or even beyond, in the areas where Šulgi was
engaged in almost constant warfare, or it was located closer home, in a different
mada region.

The Early Ur III Defense Zone

Although only these fragments of a larger dossier have survived, they do provide
clues that permit us to narrow down the meaning of a specific area that was designated as mada. It clearly denotes the area that included the cities of Kazallu, Marad,
and Urum, all of which lay just northwest of Sumer proper, west of Nippur, and just

text, Adab is followed by Marad and Kazallu, but this order is simply the bala order for AS 4, as
documented by the text published by W. W. Hallo in *JCS* 14 (1960) 113:21.

18. Ea-bani, who is not to be confused here with the governor of Ereš by the same name, is
the lú énsi már-da^ki in *BIN* 5 154:6–8 (Š36.-.-) and *Babyl.* 7 20 5:3–4 (Š36.8.-). It is impossible
to establish if Puzur-Mama ends the Kazallu section or begins the part concerning Marad.

19. YBC 130, with a broken date, summarized by A. Goetze (1963: 21), which is most probably from AS7.

20. For a different view of this matter, see now the forthcoming paper by Piotr Steinkeller,
"Corvée Labor in Ur III Times" [added in proofs].

south of Sippar. Kazallu and Marad were situated south of Kish, on the Abgal canal, northwest and west of Nippur, while Urum was north of the great city, between Kutha and Sippar, in the "district of Sin," according to the Ur-Namma "cadastre," as demonstrated by Steinkeller (1980: 24–27). After throwing off the yoke of Puzur-Inšušinak's polity, Ur-Namma proceeded to organize the area as he included it in his state. A record of this activity was probably inscribed on a public stele that has not survived, but the text that adorned it was copied in Old Babylonian times and is known from two tablets from Nippur known today as *The Cadastre Texts of Ur-Namma* (Kraus 1955; Frayne 1997: 50–56), and this is the composition that describes the area in question.[21]

To understand the military and ideological status of this region in Ur III times, one must go back even earlier, to the beginnings of the dynasty, as recounted by its founder, Ur-Namma, in the prologue to his "*Law Code:*"[22]

> u_4-ba akšak[ki] már-da[ki] ğír-kal[ki] ka-zal-lu[ki] ù maš-gán-bi ú-za-ru-um[ki] níğ an-ša$_4$-an[ki]-a nam-árad hé-éb-ak-e á [d]nanna lugal-ğá-ta ama-ar-gi$_4$-bi hu-mu-ğar

> At that time, by the power of my master Nanna, I liberated Akšak,[23] Marad, Girkal, Kazallu, their (surrounding) settlements and Uṣarum, which were all in servitude to Anšan.

This then, hypothetically to be sure, is the military area designated as mada, which included Kazallu, Marad, and probably Urum, along with other cities and towns. It is curious that Kish, which lay in the middle of this area, is not included in the list, but at some point it must have been integrated into the conceptual framework of this territory.[24] It is likely that some of the state army was positioned here and that the mada was conceived of as an in-depth defensive line against raids from the highlands, as a buffer that stood behind the first protective areas. In a sense, this is the frontier area of the state in the time of Ur-Namma but also throughout most of Šulgi's reign, as we shall presently see.

On the face of it, it seems unlikely that such an area would function as the frontier military staging area for the northwestern part of the Ur III state during the reign of Šulgi. The campaigns that originated there, targeting areas in the highlands, would have to be mounted through the Diyala Plain and the break in the Hamrin, which is essentially the route of the later Great Khorasan Road, while other armies would have marched from or through Susa. It would therefore appear to be more likely that the Diyala Plain would be more suited for this role and, indeed, there

---

21. There is a new piece of this composition that will be published by Piotr Steinkeller.

22. *Code of Ur-Namma* A iii 125–134, C i 1–10 (Roth 1995: 16, Wilcke 2002: 308), collated.

23. Frayne (1997: 48) and Sallaberger (1999: 134 n. 51) read Umma, rejecting the reading Akšak reported in Steinkeller 1991: 15 n. 1, which was based on my collation of the original tablet.

24. A Drehem account from Š43.5.- (*Princeton* 2 1 iv–r i 2′) includes a cluster of governors and officials from the same area (Girtab, Kutha, Kazallu, Kish, Marad) but without mention of mada. The only earlier Ur III reference to Kish is *CST* 45:5 (Š39.3.-).

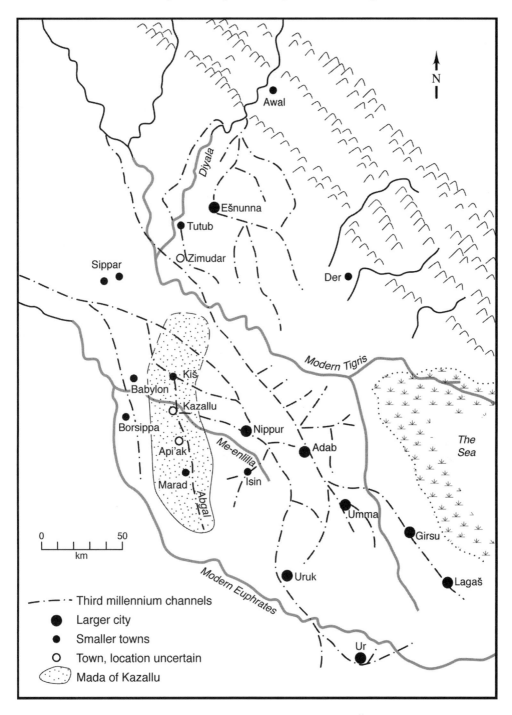

Fig. 2. The central part of the Ur III state: the hypothetical mada of Šulgi's time.

is evidence for precisely such a situation in the time beginning with the reign of Amar-Sin. But information on earlier Ur III presence and control east of the Tigris is neither abundant nor easy to interpret. A closer look at the geographical reality of early Ur III times helps to clarify the issue.

As already noted above, the mada must be associated with the areas described in the Ur-Namma cadastre text. The first section of this composition delimits precisely the borders of districts belonging to specific towns and their titular deities: Kiritab (Numušda), Apiak (Meslamtaea), possibly Urum (Sin), two or three others, and then Marad (Lugal-Marada), followed by a fragmentary section with other districts. The location of these towns has been the subject of much speculation in the past but can now be seen more precisely due to the work of Steven Cole, Hermann Gasche, and their collaborators, who have used a broad range of interdisciplinary tools to map out the complex and shifting runs of the river system of northern Babylonia in the late-third and early-second millennium (Cole and Gasche 1998; Gasche et al. 2002). According to their work, as well as that of their predecessors (Carroué 1991: 123–30; Frayne 1992: 48–51), the branch of the Euphrates (Buranun) that flowed through Kish split downstream of the city, with the Abgal flowing from the right, running through the territories of Kiritab, Apiak, and Marad; then, around Marad, the Me-Enlila watercourse branched off the right side of the Abgal, possibly running south to Nippur, Larsa, and beyond (Cole and Gasche 1998: 28–29).[25] If this is correct, then the first three districts of the *Cadastre* were located along the Abgal south of Kish. The same authors have also reinterpreted the location of the fourth district, centered on Urum, which they place farther north, just south of modern Baghdad, stretching from the Euphrates to the Tigris, bordering on the place at which the Diyala joins the Tigris.[26]

If we combine all of this information, it is highly probable that in the latter part of Šulgi's reign the whole area west of Nippur and up to the conjoining of the Tigris and the Diyala was designated as mada, "frontier territory." It is equally probable that this designation was abandoned when the frontier moved into the Diyala and into the highlands in the last years of Šulgi and in subsequent times. This would explain why the tax named gun, which was applied to the valleys and highlands outside of Babylonia, became gun mada during the reign of Šu-Sin, when the frontier had shifted.

Piotr Steinkeller (2010) has focused attention on a frontier district just north of the region that may have been the mada, south of Sippar on the Arahtum canal, that included such places as Dimat-Enlila, Ur-Zababa, Maškan-Amar-Sin, and Al-Šu-Sin. While Steinkeller suggests that the settling of this region was a state undertaking that may have begun already under Ur-Namma, it is possible that the

---

25. It must be noted that neither the Abgal nor the Me-Enlila is currently attested in Ur III administrative documents; both make an appearance, however, in the *Cadastre Texts of Ur-Namma* (Frayne 1997: 51, 53).

26. Steinkeller (1980) provides a full discussion of Urum but places the district of Sin closer to Sippar.

development of this agricultural and military area took place only after the construction of the bad mada and was actually a northern extension of the frontier that took place in subsequent years. Dimat-Enlila is mentioned for the first time in Šulgi's last year (*BE* 3/2 84, Š48.8.-), and the rest of them only appear in the record later, two of them founded, as their names indicate, under later kings. The region was already fully integrated into the Ur III administration by Amar-Sin's second year, when men from the area were included, together with workers from what had been the mada, in a large harvesting project that brought together men from different cities and their hinterlands, documented in a tablet that was analyzed many years ago by Albrecht Goetze (1963) in his classic study of the commanders of the Ur III state (*TCL* 5 6041, AS2.-.-).

Recall that the bad mada was the subject of two consecutive Šulgi year-names, years 37 and 38. This was followed by a two-year celebration of the building of Puzriš-Dagan. This suggests that the two events were linked and that these fortifications and the founding of an administrative center for the collection of provincial taxes were possibly but part of an elaborate restructuring of the territories and dues of the state. This supports my contention that these fortifications were meant to protect military staging areas and to provide a central mobilization point for offensive activity. Nevertheless, as I have repeatedly asked above, why would one create a military zone at some distance from the wars that were taking place in the highlands and from the vulnerable Diyala Plain?

One answer to such a question may lie in the concept of defense-in-depth. The term was first developed by Edward Luttwak (1976) in his much-criticized book on the grand strategy of the Roman Empire, already referenced in the last chapter. Although specialists on antiquity have rightly disproved most of his claims on the matter, the concept has been adopted in a variety of other contexts, from military and peace studies to chess and even computer safety.[27] Dankbaar (1984: 150) defines the issue in the following terms, within the context of modern warfare:

> [A]ttrition by firepower is achieved not so much by a formidable concentration of fire on one zone, but by confronting the attacker with a never-ending network of anti-tank groups, constantly engaging in small fights, using prepared positions, artificial barriers and natural obstacles, avoiding a big battle, but slowly absorbing the attacking force.

While one would not want to project these ideas literally into the past, it is possible to modify the notion somewhat and suggest that, in addition to serving as an inland mustering area, the mada was also conceived of as a secondary defensive area that was designed to repel any infiltrators or attackers who might have managed to skirt or penetrate any of the forward defenses on the outer frontier.

---

27. For example, C. J. Mann (1979: 180–81) dismantled Luttwak's claims on Roman defense-in-depth in an early review.

The Diyala Plain in the Time of Šulgi

References to the Diyala Plain and to the area immediately outside the Hamrin gates only begin to show up in the latter part of Šulgi's reign. The lower region of the valley in mentioned once in a fragmentary Old Babylonian copy of an Akkadian royal inscription, probably from Kutha (Frayne 1997: 14, lines 1'–5', collated):

⌈ù⌉ ⌈íd⌉-*da-ba-an,* ⌈iš⌉-*bi-ir-ma, ù in* ⟨*a*⟩-*pá-ri-im, kà-ma-ra-ma, iš-ku-un*

He then crossed the Ṭaban watercourse and built a rampart in the swamp. [28]

The beginning of the inscription is not preserved, but one must assume that it belongs to the reign of Šulgi. It is impossible, however, to relate this to any other information from the time, and therefore this piece of information is of little use to the historian in its present form. [29]

The main Diyala Plain city that was nearest to the core of the state, Ešnunna, is first documented in Š36 (MVN 21 8:2, Š36.5.-), and by Š45 had a governor whose name was Bamu. [30] Zimudar, even closer to the homeland, is first mentioned in Š46 (UCP 9-2-2 38:3, Š46.3.24), and its status is unclear. It pays taxes, but there is no governor there, nor, it seems, is it under the control of a general as it would be during the time of Šu-Sin. Most references from this time mention "men" (lú) of the city, and it seems to be a small transitional military post during this period. The town of Išim-Šulgi, apparently somewhere in the vicinity of Ešnunna, is mentioned only once during Šulgi's reign; the first of its many governors, Lugal-pa'e, is documented in Š48. [31] The same holds true for Garnene and Tablala, two outposts that were also close by. [32] Little is known of the area farther east; Maškan-šarrum and Kismar are documented together in Š45 and Š46 in a manner that is difficult to interpret:

(twelve animals) níg̃-gur₁₁ MAŠ.EN.KAK lugal^ki giš-mar^ki ù maš-kán-šar-ru-um^ki-ke₄-ne (*TRU* 144:11, Š45.4.27)

(twelve animals) níg̃-gur₁₁ MAŠ.EN.KAK ki-is-mar^ki, ù maš-kán-šar-ru-um ^ki-ke₄-ne (*MVN* 2 99:8–9, Š46.4.27)

---

28. I take the first verb as a faulty form of *ebērum*. Frayne (1997: 143) understood it differently and translated the passage "and the River Ṭaban he smashed and in a swamp he annihilated (the enemy)."

29. Unless, of course, one accepts the translation offered in the footnote above. Frayne (1997: 103) relates this passage to the conquest of Der in Šulgi's twentieth year and connects it with a passage in *Šulgi Hymn* C that is difficult to read and requires collation.

30. *PDT* 2 1246:3 (Š45.10.-); more than a year earlier he officiated (g̃ìr) over a delivery of equids from Ešnunna and may have already been governor there (*Princeton* 1 51:4, Š44.4.-). He also appears in the next year in *CST* 119:4 (Š46.7.-), but by Š48.10.- had been replaced by Kallamu (*OIP* 115 355:7), who was moved from Kazallu. Kallamu remained at his new post at least until AS7.7.26 (*NATN* 453:2). By ŠS2 Lugal-kuzu had been posted in Ešnunna (*Torino* 1 72:12, ŠS2.8.6).

31. *AUCT* 2 281 (Š48.8.-).

32. *SACT* 1 65:3, 6 (Š48.7.22).

The two transactions are dated one year apart to the day, but the almost identical list of animals makes one suspicious that the first tablet has a mistake and that the year should be Š46 rather than Š45. The term níĝ-gur$_{11}$ is generally assumed to mean "property," although it has been argued by K. Maekawa (1996) that in some cases it means, more precisely, "(confiscated) property." However, a survey of the Drehem references suggests that it must be some kind of a minor tax on military personnel from small outlying places. No one really knows what MAŠ.EN.KAK, later translated in Akkadian as *muškēnum*, really means in this era; perhaps these are low-status homesteaders in the area.[33] It is all the more interesting because it is one of only two other Ur III occurrences of such people in connection with a specific geographical name found in a very similar context from just two years later:[34]

(animals) udu ba-ug$_7$ šà níĝ-gur$_{11}$ MAŠ.EN.KAK me-dur-an^{ki} (MVN 15 195:20, Š 48.6.9)

The town of Meturan, known from Old Akkadian, Old Babylonian, and later sources, has been identified as Tell Haddad on the Diyala east of the Hamrin gates (Muhamed 1992), but it never appears, outside of this passage, in any other Ur III document. Kismar and Maškan-šarrum, however, became important military centers. Toward the end of Š46, Išar-ramaš, a man who ran affairs in the middle Diyala region for years, delivered animals from troops from nearby Abal[35] and then in Š47 from the "shepherds" (sipa) of Kismar.[36] Almost exactly a year later, the same man oversees deliveries from a group of shepherds who are listed by name but without any place-name, but who are clearly from the same area.[37] At least one of them, SI.A-a, rose to become a military officer (nu-banda$_3$) by AS5, as documented in a text that mentions Išar-ramaš again and the troops of Abal.[38]

Finally, the towns or hamlets of Puttulium and Sabum, which in all probability lay in the Diyala Plain, make their first appearance in Š48 (AUCT 1 743:2, 5, Š48.9.19).

The evidence is admittedly quite thin and its interpretation hampered by philological uncertainties, but it all points to a weak Ur III presence on the Diyala Plain

33. See OB Diri Nippur 7:29 (MSL 15 30); OB Diri Nippur 9:22 (MSL 15 32); OB Diri Oxford 498 (MSL 15 48); and Aa I/6 131 (MSL 14 228). This is not the place to discuss the reading and meanings of this difficult Sumerian word; the reading mášda is not used here, following the strictures of Civil 2008b: 88 n. 195.

34. Note a MAŠ.EN.KAK named Ĝišgaga who functions as ĝìr, delivering animals left over from an accounting of booty from Urbilum in Š48. He is described as MAŠ.EN.KAK lú ì-lí-am-ra^{ki}, an otherwise unattested place-name (*Ontario* 1 53:20, Š48.-.20)

35. JCS 52 7 6:2–3 (Š46.9.11).

36. MVN 13 868:14–15 (Š47.7.17). On Išar-ramaš, possibly the governor of Awal and Tašil, see Steinkeller 1981: 165.

37. OrSP 18 (1925) pl. 5 15 (Š48.6.26) mentions a number of shepherds under (ugula) Išar-ramaš. Among these are Ili-tappe, SI.A-a, and Puzur-Ebiḫ (puzur$_4$-a-bi-⟨iḫ⟩).

38. MVN 15 350 (AS5.9.24).

and in the valleys adjacent to the Hamrin to its north prior to the last years of Šulgi. The main administrative and military centers for the region still lay close to the homeland in places such as Ešnunna, Išim-Šulgi, and Zimudar. It seems likely that the stabilization of the Hamrin area and the lands beyond took place around Š47 and Š48. One must conclude that prior to this the staging areas for major military expeditions against Iran had been located within Babylonia itself, possibly in the district designated as mada. The armies from this area may have traversed the un-ruly Diyala Plain on their way to the highlands, or they may have skirted it by the piedmont route through Der. Henry Wright, who knows the area well, informs me:

> Armies going from Babylonia into the north-central Zagros valleys would have to proceed either northeast up the pass above Sar-i Pol-i Dokhtar, then southeast into the Islamabad area, or north up the Diyala and into the Sanandaj Area or southeast into the Mah-I Dasht and the Kermanshah Area. Once in either of these places, they would be in a series of large inter-connected north-central Zagros valleys. It is difficult, however, to go from these valleys southwestwards over the high and almost continuous mass of Kabir Kuh and get to the foothill region and Susiana. Alterna-tively, if they were going toward Susiana and the southern Zagros, they would have to go southeastwards to Der, and from there to Susiana and even beyond towards Anšan.[39] Once could, of course do a loop, moving directly via the plain of Ru-mishgan into the Saimarreh (upper Karkheh) or more circuitously via Nehavand and Khorramabad and into Susiana, returning to Mesopotamia via Der. There were routes marked by settlements in Uruk and Early Dynastic times, and groups of no-mads and traders with goods had been traveling them for centuries. However I do not know of an account of any army doing this before Hellenistic times.

I should also note that the general area that was considered to be mada at the time of Šulgi, which needs to be studied in full, was a trouble spot that created prob-lems for various rulers in third- and second-millennium Mesopotamia. When Rimuš ascended to the throne of Akkad, he had to put down a massive rebellion in Sumer. No sooner had he quelled this uprising, when "thereupon, on his return, Kazallu revolted. (Rimuš) vanquished it and slew 12,052 men inside Kazallu. He took 5,862 prisoners and captured Ašared, ruler of Kazallu, and tore down its (city) wall."[40] The area in question was also part of the "great revolt" against Naram-Sin, which included the cities of Kish, Kutha, Tiwe, Sippar, Kazallu, Kiritab, and Apiak, as well as Dilbat, Sippar, and Borsippa.[41] Centuries later, Hammurabi faced a conspiracy at Kazallu and its countryside, which at that time was named Mutiabal. After discover-ing that their elites were plotting with the ruler of Elam, he destroyed the city and deported its inhabitants to Babylon (Van De Mieroop 2005: 118–19). The punish-

---

39. On the importance of Der (Tell ʿAqar) and the roads that passed through it, see Postgate and Mattila 2004: 240 and now Frahm 2009: 51. Der figures prominently in the Ur III messenger texts from Urusaǧrig (personal communication, courtesy of David I. Owen).

40. Rimuš E2.1.2.4: 44–63 (Frayne 1993: 48).

41. Naram-Sin E2.1.4.6: i′ 14′–20′ (Frayne 1993: 104) and passim.

ment was apparently not severe enough, because Kazallu rebelled soon thereafter against his son Samsu-iluna. These are some of the more dramatic moments in the long history of Kazallu and its environs, but they are important because they signal the long-term strategic importance of a town that plays an important role in CKU.

The bad mada and Bad-igihursaĝa

If one accepts the information gathered above pertaining to an area designated as mada, then it is possible to go further and hypothesize that this provides some evidence on the location of the bad mada that is known from Ur III year-names. But once again, one must stress that this name never appears in the CKU. The only mention of any sizable fortifications in the Šulgi correspondence is found in letters PuŠ1 (13) and ŠPu1 (14), an exchange between the king and an officer by the name of Puzur-Šulgi or Puzur-Numušda. Is it possible that the subject of these letters is the bad mada commemorated in Šulgi's thirty-seventh year-name? Many seem to think that this is indeed the case (Wilcke 1969: 1; Sallaberger 2007: 445; 2009). If we assume that these letters do indeed refer to the bad mada, then, in light of the arguments laid out above, the Puzur-Šulgi works should be localized somewhere within or on the perimeter of the defensive zone of Urum, Marad, and Kazallu; but here we move from hypothesis to conjecture. None of these cities is mentioned in the correspondence, and the officer in charge is the commander of a place named bàd-(igi)-hur-saĝ-ĝá, which is unattested anywhere in the literary or documentary record outside of the CKU. As he addresses his master, he states (PuŠ1: 6–8 [13]): "My king, for the well-being of the army and his country has built the great fortifications of Igihursaĝa against the vile enemy for the sake of his people and his country."

There are two ways of understanding the toponym or descriptive phrase bàd igi hur-saĝ-ĝá: one can take it literally and translate it "fortification(s) facing the mountains" or "fortification(s) facing Hursaĝ."[42] Most scholars have preferred the first solution, but Douglas Frayne (1992: 19) has observed that the Ur-Namma cadastre text mentioned a place, or geographical feature, named an-za-gàr hur-saĝ-ĝá, "tower of the Hursaĝ," and linked it to the subject of the CKU letter; the use of hursaĝ fits well with Heimpel's definition cited in the last footnote. Frayne's felicitous discovery provides a reasonable, if not absolutely convincing, reason to place Bad-igihursaĝa within the defensive zone of the mada, although his conclusion has been contested (Huber 2001: 193). Therefore, in light of this, unless the CKU material concerning the issue is pure fabrication, one may think of Bad-igihursaĝa as a fort that anchored the "wall" of bad mada.

---

42. This is generally taken to refer to the mountains to the northeast of Sumer. On the interpretation of hursaĝ as "mountain range, hills," see now Steinkeller 2007b. Heimpel (2009b: 26 n. 3) has taken this interpretation further and states that it designated "anything that was not flat alluvium or a hill created by a ruined settlement." The references to the use of the phrase igi hur-saĝ-ĝá are collected in Appendix C below.

The Officials of the Puzur-Šulgi Correspondence

At this point, we must take a closer look at the people and places that are mentioned in CKU letter PuŠ1 (13) and attempt to harmonize this information with the archival record of Ur III times. From the prosopographic point of view, this epistle is the most troubling one in CKU. In contrast to most of the other items of the royal correspondence, none of the officials mentioned in the letter from Puzur-Šulgi to Šulgi, including the writer himself, can be identified in Ur III documents, and their respective areas of responsibility do not correspond to anything that we can find in the surviving texts of the time. To add to this, there was clearly a good degree of confusion in the transmission of the passage that corresponds to lines 15–22 of the reconstructed text: no two manuscripts contain the same line order, and there are significant variants in the names.

Puzur-Šulgi

The name of the writer is not without problems, as there is some textual confusion between the governor of Bad-Igihursağa (PuŠ1 [13], ŠPu1 [14]) and the governor of Kazallu who is one of Ibbi-Sin's correspondents (PuIb1 [23] and IbPu1 [24]). If we tabulate the different names of the two officers who exchanged letters with Šulgi and Ibbi-Sin, with reference to the sigla designating the various manuscripts of the composition, the problems of textual transmission become evident:[43]

	PuŠ1	ŠPu1	PuIb1	IbPu1
Puzur-Šulgi	N1, X1	X1, X3, X4	Ur1, Ur2, X1	X1
Puzur-Numušda	N4		N5, N8, N9	N2
Puzur-Marduk	Ki1			

The name Puzur-Numušda occurs only once attested in Ur III sources;[44] the variant Puzur-Marduk is clearly an editorial anachronism that requires no comment. However, the name Puzur-Šulgi is documented in tablets from Drehem, Girsu, Ur, and Nippur, ranging in date from Š41 to IS14. Two different persons are identified by professional designation: a lú ^gištukul (MVN 17 135:8, messenger text, no year-name) and a šár-ra-ab-du, son of Abija (MVN 8 207:rev. 4′ and seal, IS2.12.12).[45] Other messenger texts may contain references to the former, namely, RTC 388:3; MVN 5 250:24; DAS 144:3; and Nisaba 3 2 32:8. There was also another Puzur-Šulgi, active at least between AS8 and ŠS3, who was identified twice as the son of the general Hašib-atal, an officer who was stationed in Arrapha (JCS 31 166A:2; CT 32 36: ii

---

43. The letters and numbers refer to the individual manuscripts of the composition, defined in the edition below.

44. AUCT 1 294:3, a fragmentary document from Umma; date broken.

45. I cannot offer translations of these designations, although the former clearly has military connotations and the latter "may be involved with surveying and agricultural work" (CAD Š/II 67, sub šarrabtû).

8). Much lower on the social ladder was someone by that name whose seal, dedicated to a certain Ibani, is attested at Nippur in ŠS3, if the reading of the name is correct (*TMHnf* 1/2 76)

In addition, there are other attestations of one or more Puzur-Šulgi's in Drehem texts from the reign of Šulgi, beginning with year 41, but it is impossible to determine the exact title or function of any of them:

Nisaba 8 172:5	Š41.7.22
OIP 115 151:8	Š43.5.3
PDT 1 86:10	Š43.6.14
ŠA 39:1	Š43.9.00
Nik. 2 523:10	Š44.-.-

The contexts and dates strongly suggest that this is one and the same person and that he was part of the military establishment.

Whatever the origins of the letter, the passage that contains the names of officers in charge of segments of the fortification looks suspiciously as if it had been redacted with school mathematical exercises in mind. All of this is presented in detail in the edition of PuŠ1 (13), but the composite text for lines 15–21 is reprised here for ease of discussion:

15. nam ¹puzur₄-ᵈnu-muš-da énsi ul₄-lum-TUR.RAᵏⁱ
16. ninnu nindan uš sağ ba-ab-gíd murub₄-ba im-ma-an-ri
17. nam ¹lugal-me-lám šabra ⁽ᵈ⁾šeg₅-šeg₅
18. ía nindan uš-ni ha-ni-dar-dar
19. nam ¹ka-kù-ga-ni énsi ma-da murub₄ᵏⁱ
20. 35 nindan uš gaba dúr-bi ba-gul-gul
21. nam ¹ta-ki-il-ì-lí-šu kù-ğál ⁽ᵈ⁾ áb-gal ù ⁽ᵈ⁾me-ᵈen-líl-lá
22. nimin nindan uš-ni gúr ugu-bi-šè nu-ub-ğar

[15]In the sector under the responsibility of Puzur-Numušda, governor of Ullum-ṣeḥrum, [16]a 300 m. section *had sagged* and collapsed in the middle; [17]in the sector under the responsibility of Lugal-melam, the overseer of the Šeššektum canal,[18] 30 m. of his section can be breached; [19]in the sector under the responsibility of Kaku-gani, governor of the inland territory, [20]a 210 m. section, its face and based are damaged, [21](and) in the part under the responsibility of Takil-ilišu, canal inspector of the Abgal and Me-Enlila waterways, [22]240 m. of his section *does not have its perimeter laid out yet.*

Puzur-Numušda, Governor (énsi) of Ullum-ṣehrum (line 15)

This name, which only occurs in the solitary Nippur manuscript for this line (N1), is rare; indeed, it occurs only once in Ur III times, as already noted above. All the other sources have different names, which are also relatively rare, or even non-existent, in Ur III:

Šu-Marduk (Ki1) Unattested in Ur III; the name of Marduk is clearly an anachronism here. The same manuscript uses the name Puzur-Marduk for the sender of the letter.

Šu-Numušda (X2) Only two people are known by this name: one at Umma,[46] and a bodyguard (àga-ús) documented in a Drehem text.[47]

Šu-Nunu (X1) There are five examples of this name in Ur III, but none of them is even remotely related to the functionary in the letter.[48]

The place name Ullum-ṣeḫrum is attested in a variety of spellings from the Old Akkadian texts through Old Babylonian lexical lists; the first sign is variously written bil, bíl, bìl, and ul₄, and the last part is either TUR or TUR.RA. There was also a Billum (known already from Early Dynastic sources) and a Billum-rabium. The various spellings of this place-name are collected by Steinkeller (1986: 35). The reading ul₄ rather than ğír is based on the gloss ul in *MSL* 11 p. 16 (McEwan 1980: 159). Although it is impossible at present to identify the place-name, it was definitely located in northern Babylonia. If one assumes that Billum, Billum-ṣeḫrum, and Billum-rabium were located in proximity to one another, then the listing of bíl-lum in line 165 of the ED geographical list from Ebla and Abu Salabikh in the section dealing with northern Babylonia (Steinkeller 1986: 35; Frayne 1992: 19–20) provides evidence on the matter. Two Old Akkadian references to Billum-ṣeḫrum (*MAD* 5 69: ii 8′) and to Billum-rabium (*MAD* 5 101: ii′ 14) come from "Umm-el-Jīr," on which see Gelb's comments in *MAD* 5. Although the provenance of tablets that have been described as coming from this place is somewhat problematical, they are all from northern Babylonia, close to Kish. Frayne (1992: 19), moreover, points to the presence of an é-duru₅ i-bil-lum, "Hamlet of Ibillum," in the cadastre text, right after an-za-gàr hur-saĝ-ĝá, "The Tower of Hursaĝ," which supports the geography of the letter but suggests the reading Billum for the place-name.

Lugal-melam, Overseer (šabra) of the Šeššektum Canal

In contrast to the other personal names discussed here, there are almost 280 examples of this name in Ur III texts, although not one of them can be connected with the individual mentioned in the Puzur-Šulgi letter.

The waterway is not attested in a single Mesopotamian administrative text, and even the reading of the name is uncertain. Lexical texts provide information on a reading še/ig₅ for the sign URU×TU as well as ĜIŠGAL×TU (also EZEN×TU and KA×TU). Thus Proto-Ea 544 (*MSL* 14 53) has the readings ši-ig and si-ig, a tradition repeated in the later lexical texts; the Akkadian glosses indicate the meaning *šaqummatum*, "silence" (e.g., Aa VI/4 45–46 [*MSL* 14 442]; Reciprocal Ea Tablet A 191 [*MSL* 14 528]). All of this is somewhat confusing. The Standard Babylonian versions of HAR-ra XXII and Diri III provide the most direct evidence:

46. *BIN* 5 298:6 (AS7.8.3); *MVN* 14 573:8 (AS8.11.2); *MVN* 20 46:4; *MVN* 20 57:4, both with date broken.

47. *BOAM* 2 34 86:41 (ŠS2.7.29).

48. *CST* 263 r. iii 7 (AS6.2.-, Girsu); *Princeton* 1 7 (SS1.5.8, Drehem); *RA* 32 190:7 (ŠS9.-.-, prov. unkn.); *SAT* 3 1952:2 (IS2.2.-, Drehem); *YOS* 4 35 (IS2.12.-, prov. unkn.).

ᵈKA×TUˢᵉˢ⁻ˢᵉˢ-K[A×TU] = ŠU (Hh XXII 4 ii 20′ [*MSL* 11 25])

[. . .]-še²-eg² = ᵈĜIŠGAL×TU.ĜIŠGAL×TU (var ᵈĜIŠGAL×TU.TU)= [še]-eš-še-ek-tu (Diri III 198 [*MSL* 15 146])

The earlier documentation is somewhat more complicated. The entry does not seem to be attested in the preserved part of the "forerunners" to Hh XXII. There is an entry in the Ugarit version that may shed light on the Emar and Nippur redactions:

ᵈsig-sigᶻⁱ⁻ᶻⁱ⁻ⁱᵏ *zi-ni-ki* (Hh XX–XXII Ras Shamra. A iii rev. 15 [*MSL* 11 46]), which corresponds to:
ᵈSAL.SILA₄-sig *iš-me-e-tu₄* (Hh XX–XXII Emar [Arnaud, *Emar* VI.4 148]
ᵈSAL.SILA₄-sig (Hh XX–XXII Nippur F 333 [*MSL* 11 106])

If SAL.SILA₄-sig is another writing of the same watercourse name, then line 5 of the third kirugu of *Išbi-Erra Hymn B* is the only other Old Babylonian literary text in which it occurs (collated):

ᵈburanun-na ᵈidigna ᵈSAL.SILA₄-sig íd-kišᵏⁱ zag-bi im-mi-in-gu₇
He found nourishment on the banks of the Euphrates, Tigris, Sigsig², and Kish watercourses.

Jacobsen (1960: 478) identified íd-SAL.SILA₄-sig as the Sumerian writing of the Isinnitum canal, which branched off from the Euphrates north of Nippur, an interpretation that was followed by *CAD* I/J 197 and by Frayne (1992: 39). The lexical entry cited in *CAD*, which is one of the two data items that constitute the main basis for this identification, is now read as [íd-x.x] ki-en-gi /ʳki-uriʳ/ = *i-ši-ni-ʳtum*ʳ (Hh XXII 4 ii 16′ [*MSL* 11 25]). The other is a Sultantepe bilingual. This identification, which now has no solid basis, is also not supported by any archival evidence. The other is a bilingual hymn to Ninisina, *KAR* 6 15 and duplicates, recently reedited, with new copies and an Old Babylonian manuscript, by K. Wagensonner (2008: 281). In the Assur version, from the 10th or 11th century, íd ᵈSAL.SILA₄-sig-a is translated as *i-na i-si-ni-ti* (VAT 9304 [*KAR* 16]: 15). The earlier version does not preserve these signs. Could SAL.SILA₄ have been read as sigₓ/šegₓ in the literary mode? Whatever may have been the case, the identification of this Sumerian name with the Isinnitum is tentative at best and is not supported by any archival evidence.

The Isin canal is attested as i-si-nu in the ED LGN (Frayne 1992: 39) and in Ur III texts as íd-i-si-in⁽ᵏⁱ⁾-(na) (*RGTC* 2 270). It is therefore possible that these entries represent a separate manuscript tradition of the lexical text and that they stand for the ᵈšeg₅-šeg₅ᵏⁱ. This is far from certain, however, and the information on this watercourse name remains highly unclear; the fact that it is known primarily from the lexical tradition suggests that the CKU reference is spurious.

Finally, the use of the title šabra for the overseer of a waterway is also unknown in Ur III times, and in this letter it looks suspiciously like a back-translation from the title *šāpir nārim*, "governor of the river (system)," known primarily from Old Babylonian sources.

Kakugani, Governor of the "Inland" (murub₄) Territory

There are at least thirteen attestations of this personal name, from Š48 (*WMAH* 176: iii 4) to IS1 (*AnOr* 45 60: r. iv 14), mostly from Girsu but also once from Umma and once from Nippur. None of these references provides any information on the function of these individuals.

The geographical designation ma-da murub₄^{ki} is not attested in any text other than this one and ŠaŠu1:21 (letter 19). The only similar usage is found in a year-name of Sin-iddinam of Larsa: mu ia-ab-ra-at^{ki} uru murub₄ uru-didli ba-an-tuku/dab₅, "The year: Iabrat, (its) central city, and various surrounding settlements were taken" (Goetze 1950: 97–98). In the present letter, the term has to refer to an area within the military zone discussed above; in the Šarrum-bani missive, it has to refer to an area in the Diyala Plain or its surroundings. In all likelihood, this is to be interpreted as "central region," or simply "inland," and not as a specific toponym.

Takil-ilissu, the Canal Inspector (kù-ǧál) of the Abgal and Me-Enlila Waterways

There are only two attested occurrences of this personal name in Ur III documents: in a court protocol from Umma from the time of Amar-Sin (*SNAT* 373:19),[49] and in a seal inscription dedicated to Ibbi-Sin by the general Takil-ilissu, impressed on a tablet from Garšana (*CUSAS* 3 525, IS2.i.2). The interpretation of the name is uncertain, as discussed recently by Hilgert (2002: 485–86). Only three sources for PuŠ1 preserve the name in full: one uses the modernized Old Babylonian writing (Ki1), but X1 has *ta-ki-il-ì-lí-iš-su*, while X4 uses *ta-ki-il-ì-lí-sú*. There was clearly a tradition that preserved a garbled version of an earlier writing convention or attempted to archaize the name.

The waterways are not attested in Ur III administrative texts, although they are already known from Old Akkadian documents and from the *Cadastre Texts of Ur-Namma*. The combination of the two suggests that an area around Marad is the subject of this official.[50] Moreover, both canal names were familiar to persons living in Old Babylonian times.

The Fortifications of the Puzur-Šulgi Letter

Complex as this presentation of the facts has been, the analysis of geographic data from the PuŠ1 letter confirms only that the location of the Šulgi fortifications conforms reasonably well to information gleaned from other sources. Unfortunately, this only confirms that the author or successive redactors of the composition were aware of the lexical tradition and of the geographical reality of a specific part of Babylonia.

---

49. See Wilcke 1991.
50. On the location of these waterways, see p. **132** above.

Whatever its origins and redactional history, neither of which can be traced at the present time, the letter PuŠ1 (13) is part of the core of CKU. The reply from the king, ŠPu1 (14), however, is not, and is attested only in two different OB versions on tablets of unknown origin and in a bilingual Middle Babylonian tablet from Susa that has been further redacted. The letter begins with the king's highly rhetorical explanation of his reasons for building Bad-Igihursaĝa, and these are couched in language more familiar from hymns than from epistolary works. What follows seems to have been adapted from the Šu-Sin correspondence, including anachronistic references to Lu-Nanna, the governor of the province of Zimudar. There can be little doubt that letter 14 of CKU (ŠPu1) is a post–Ur III fabrication that was concocted, possibly in northern Babylonia, to create a symmetrical pair with PuŠ1 (13). By chance, it survived in the periphery long after the rest of the royal correspondence was deleted from the literary tradition.

This survey has marshaled quite a bit of factual information, but it fails to answer the main historical questions that come to mind, namely, does the narrative of letters PuŠ1 (13) and ŠPu1 (14) in any way deal with matters surrounding the construction or maintenance of the bad mada that we know from the Šulgi year-names? The general geographical context points in that direction, but that is all. I therefore provisionally connect Bad-Igihursaĝa with part of the bad mada, as earlier authors have already done, even if I remain agnostic about the historical veracity of parts of the Puzur-Šulgi letter. But even if the bad mada is the subject of these epistles, the affairs described in PuŠ1 (13) concern small local issues and not any large-scale defensive wall or line of forts. If these pieces are part of the bad mada, they are only small elements of a construction massive enough to warrant commemoration in two successive year-names. The letter, whatever its evidentiary status, implies that the "wall" is something that could be measured linearly, so it was not perceived as a line of forts but as an actual wall. One must keep in mind, however, that if we add up all the numbers in this letter, the deteriorating sections enumerated in PuŠ1 altogether amount to 130 nindan, approximately 780 meters, and therefore this is but one small part of a larger construction.

The Fortifications

There is not a shred of contemporary Ur III evidence concerning the purpose of Šulgi's fortifications. All the surviving information on military activities places warfare far from the homeland and not on its doorstep, but if I am right about the fact that the Diyala was not under full Ur III control until very late in Šulgi's reign, then the location of the staging area in the environs of Kazallu and east to the Tigris may be less surprising. Some historians have asserted that it was built against Amorite invaders, but this is merely a supposition that projects their interpretation of Šu-Sin's constructions into the time of Šulgi. The PuŠ1 (13) letter is no more informative, because it refers to enemies in a generic manner, without identifying the source of the danger that is apparently at the gates. The answer from Šulgi (ŠPu1, 14) does implicate the Amorites, but it is clearly spurious, as the reference to the Amorites is a paraphrase of a similar passage from the Šu-Sin correspondence; this passage will be cited below.

Recall that the bàd mada was the subject of two consecutive Šulgi year-names, years 37 and 38. This was followed by a two-year celebration of the building of Puzriš-Dagan. Earlier, I suggested that the two events were linked and that these fortifications and the founding of an administrative center for the collection of provincial taxes were possibly but part of an elaborate restructuring of the territories and dues of the state. This would support my contention that these fortifications were meant to protect military staging areas and to provide a central mobilization point for offensive activity.

Muriq-Tidnim

If the Ur III sources are silent on the reasons why the Šulgi fortifications were constructed, the purpose of the later Muriq-Tidnim is seemingly well documented. First and foremost, there is the very name itself, "The One That Keeps the Tidnum at a Distance," and second, there is the Šu-Sin inscription, cited on p. 124 above, commemorating the rebuilding of the temple of Šara in Umma "when he had built the wall against the Amorites Muriq-Tidnim and turned back the incursions of the Amorites to their territories." As far as the CKU is concerned, the letter from Šarrum-bani to the king sets out the motivations behind the work simply and directly (ŠaŠu1:1–7 [18]):

> [1] Speak to Šu-Sin, my king: [2] saying (the words of) the prefect Šarrum-bani, your servant:

> [3] You commissioned me to carry out construction on the great fortifications (bàd gal) of Muriq-Tidnim [4] and presented your views to me as follows: "The Amorites have repeatedly raided the frontier territory." [7] You commanded me [5] to rebuild the fortifications, to cut off their access, [6-7] and thus to prevent them from repeatedly overwhelming the fields through a breach (in the defenses) between the Tigris and Euphrates.

Šarrum-bani continues his narrative with the following information (ŠaŠu1:11–17 [18]):

> [11] When I had been working on the fortifications that then measured 26 dana (269 km.), [12] after having reached (the area) between the two mountain ranges, [13] the Amorite camped in the mountains turned his attention to my building activities. [14] (The leader of) Simurum came to his aid, and [15] he went out against me between the mountain ranges of Ebih to do battle. [16] And therefore I, even though I could not *spare* corvée workers (for fighting), [17] went out to confront him in battle.

In this manner, the literary correspondence unequivocally insists that the main purpose of the fortifications was to keep hostile Amorites away from the homeland of the Ur III kings. In this epistolary world the massive works were a patent failure, since a dozen or so years later a man by the name of Išbi-Erra was writing to Ibbi-Sin, Šu-Sin's successor on the throne (IŠIb1:7–12 [21]):

> [7] Word having reached me that hostile Amorites had entered your frontier territory, [8] I proceeded to deliver all the grain—72,000 kor—into (the city of) Isin. [9] But now all the Amorites have entered the homeland, [10] and have captured all the great store-houses, one by one. [11] Because of (these) Amorites I cannot hand over the grain for threshing; [12] they are too strong for me, and I am made to stay put.

The information cited here seems to leave no doubt: early in the time of Šu-Sin, the state faced a serious danger from a group, or groups, of Amorites identified as belonging to the Tidnum, an incipient state, ethnic group, or confederation. Moreover, the menace was so serious that it required an enormous expenditure of treasure and labor, including a line of fortifications at least 300 kilometers long, perhaps as long as 500 kilometers. Who, then, were these Amorites, and were they really so threatening that Šu-Sin's administration was forced to build what may have been, potentially, the longest military construction created in the ancient world? In the previous chapter, I argued that the Amorite problem on the eastern frontier was mostly limited to low-level hostilities and did not pose a serious threat to the Ur III state. Should we therefore take the name of the fortifications at face value, or is it possible that it was purposely misleading, and that they were constructed for offensive, rather than defensive purposes?

With little else to go on, we must turn to the evidence of the Šu-Sin correspondence and, as with the other CKU compositions, confront it with information contained in the available documentary record. Rather than criticize previous localizations and explanations of the construction, I will simply build my own argument, relying on my own interpretation of the sources.

According to ŠaŠu1 (18), the king has commissioned the author, named Šarrum-bani, to build Muriq-Tidnim and, at the time of his writing, the fortifications had reached the territory of Zimudar in the Diyala region, a place under the control of the governor Lu-Nanna. In his reply (ŠuŠa1 [19]), the king admonishes Šarrum-bani and relieves him of his duties, replacing him with his own uncle Babati. Felicitously, all three officials are well documented in Ur III texts in a manner that conforms to the image found in the royal correspondence.

Šarrum-bani

The name Šarrum-bani appears more than a hundred times in Ur III texts from Drehem, Girsu, Umma, and Nippur, and it can be demonstrated that a number of different individuals are involved, from a messenger (sukkal) to a kennel master (sipa ur-ra). As already observed by A. Goetze (1963: 16), one of these was a high-ranking military official who held the rank of šakkana, "general." He is designated by this title only twice in texts from AS7.1.20 (*Nisaba* 8 161:2) and in ŠS1.10.- (*TÉL* 61:9), but there can be little doubt that he held a high military rank much earlier, and his high status is reflected in the fact that he married a princess of the realm.[51] He first appears in Drehem tablets from the last six years of Šulgi's reign, and even though he is without overt title, the company he keeps in these accounts strongly suggests that he was already part of the highest ranks of the military, perhaps even already a general. His importance at this time is documented on a tablet that was made out when the king and queen, together with their closest entourage, dined at his estate.[52] He kept his military title when he also assumed the role of governor of Apiak in the northern defensive zone; he is attested in this position from AS5.3.- through AS8.1.29, but using other sources one can pin down his tenure more precisely. Although the city had a governor as early as Š31 (*OIP* 115 17: 8), only two names of such officials are known:

Šu-Tirum	SAT 2 785: 5	AS4.4.30
	OrSP 47/9 80: 10	AS4.9.-
Šarrum-bani	OIP 121 587: 8	AS5.3.-
	JCS 17 21	AS7?.-.-
	UDT 128: 5	AS8.1.29

This narrows the time of his appointment at Apiak to some moment between the ninth month of AS4 and the third month of the following year. How long he remained at the post after the eighth year of Amar-Sin is unknown; the only governor of the city known by name after this is none other than Babati, whose seal inscription, which will be discussed below, includes the title; it is first documented on ŠS3.10.-. In CKU, Šarrum-bani bears the title gal-zu unkena, "prefect."

Šarrum-bani continued his career throughout the reign of Šu-Sin. A possible reference to his estate and, therefore, presumably to his death or disfavor is documented in the very beginning of the first year of Ibbi-Sin's reign (*AUCT* 1 53:3, IS1.2.7).

According to the Šu-Sin correspondence, Šarrum-bani sought assistance from another officer, Lu-Nanna, who is described as the governor of the territory of Zimudar.[53]

Lu-Nanna

The name Lu-Nanna is common, and this complicates the study of the man's career; moreover, there may have been two or more generals by this name. Commanders named Lu-Nanna are attested in texts from Š46 through AS3; a Lu-Nanna is twice described as general of the town of Nagsu, which was located in the province of Umma (*TIM* 6 36:5 [Š 46.3.-] and *TCL* 2 5488:7 [Š46.4.-]).[54] A general Lu-Nanna

51. An unnamed wife (dam) of Šarrum-bani appears in a list of princesses (dumu-munus lugal) in *CTMMA* 1 17:44 (AS4.7.-); one assumes that this is the officer under discussion here.

52. This tablet, which was once in the USA and was published on the Internet, is now in the Gratianus Stiftung in Germany and will be published soon by Konrad Volk; see Volk 2004. The date formula is broken, but it is undoubtedly one of Šulgi's last years.

53. For previous discussions of this official, see Goetze 1963: 16–17, Lieberman 1968–69: 59–60, Owen 1973: 136, and Michalowski 1978a: 34–49.

54. The reading of the first sign, NAG, is uncertain in this name. For its location on the Iturungal canal, see Steinkeller 2001.

is mentioned in texts from Umma (*SAT* 2 601:5 [Š48.1.-]), Girsu (*HLC* 221:13, *DAS* 179:17, *TCTI* 1 1021+1022: v 28′, *RA* 19 40 18:10, *WMAH* 284: rev. iii′ 12′, all undated), and Ur (*UET* 3 1770:4′, date broken). Although no one can say for certain, it is likely that all of these references—the dated ones cover only six years—refer to the same individual.

After a hiatus of approximately six years, beginning with the first year of Šu-Sin, there is evidence for a Lu-Nanna serving as general of Zimudar, in the Diyala, where he remained for at least eight years. His tenure there continued into the early part of Ibbi-Sin's reign: in IS2, he is one of the officials in charge of delivering taxes from the Diyala region (*CT* 32 19 iii 1, 26, IS2.4.29).[55] In Ur III texts, he is always a commander (šakkana) of Zimudar, while in CKU letters he is a governor (énsi) of the province. The only imprint of his seal, preserved on a fragmentary envelope from Nippur published by David I. Owen, reads (*NATN* 776 [ŠS1.-.-]):

[d]ršu¹-den.zu
lugal kal-ga
lugal uri₅ki-ma
lugal an-ub-ʿdaʾ limmu₂-ba
lú-d[nanna]
ʿšakkanaʾ
zi-ʿmuʾ-[darki]
árad-[zu]

O Šu-Sin, mighty king, king of Ur, king of the four corners of the universe, Lu-Nanna, commander of Zimudar, is your servant.

In one receipt from Ur, his dues are delivered "in the town of Šulgi-Nanna, on the banks of the Diyala."[56] A document from Nippur demonstrates that his son was also involved with matters in the Diyala region (*NRVN* 1 176, IS2). The tablet is a simple loan of grain, to be repaid after the harvest, and the borrower, Ennam-Šulgi, is to pay back the loan in Ešnunna. From the seal impression on the tablet we learn that Ennam-Šulgi was the son of the general Lu-Nanna.

The third individual mentioned in the Šu-Sin correspondence is named Babati, and he is likewise well known from the Ur III record.

Babati

The Babati of the royal correspondence is the brother of Queen Abi-simti and uncle of King Šu-Sin; of this there can be no doubt. However, the Ur III archives document the activities of a number of people named Babati, and it is difficult to distinguish which person appears in each document. There were Babatis in Girsu and Umma, including an envoy (sukkal) and a bodyguard (àga-ús), but the queen's brother may also have been involved with certain matters in these provinces.

---

55. *UET* 3 75:2–3 (ŠS1.1.-); *ASJ* 4 140 2:2 (ŠS8.5.19); *PDT* 1 170:4 (d.b., ŠS); *UTI* 6 3800: ii 15′ (d.b, "treasury" text, ŠS or early IS).
56. šà dšul-gi-dnanna, gú íddur-ùl (*UET* 3 75:6–7, ŠS1.1.-).

The main sources of information on our man come from the Drehem archives, but even here it is difficult to unravel the documentation pertaining to this particular Babati as distinguished from the work of a bureaucrat (dub-sar) who is well attested throughout the reigns of Amar-Sin and Šu-Sin. The dignitary who holds our interest first appears in the third month of Amar-Sin's third year, described as "the Queen's brother" (šeš ereš, *BCT* 1 126: 4, AS3.3.3.19). His exact function at this time is difficult to ascertain, but he may have been serving in the military, possibly even with the rank of captain (nu-banda₃) or general (šakkana). One may draw this conclusion from a passage in a receipt dated AS5.1.23 (*JCS* 23 113 23:8–15) in which he is listed as delivering one lamb in the company of officers of the army, Nir-idagal, Išar-ramaš, Murhigaba, Ur-Eana, Huba'a, and Ur-mes, as well as the governor of Urusağrig. Just four months later, he appears, once again delivering a single lamb, together with two other captains (*PDT* 1 25:2 [AS5.5.19]). From a text dated five months later, one can conclude with little doubt that Babati had achieved the status of general, because he is listed in a long text that registers deliveries of one lamb each from most, if not all, of the generals of the state (*TCL* 2 5504: ii 18 [AS5.10.9]). When his nephew, Šu-Sin, officially took over the throne of Ur, Babati, as expected, continued his career among the elite and eventually rose in prominence, but first he had to officiate, together with his two sisters, Queen Abi-simti and Bizu'a, at the funerary rites of his brother Iddin-Dagan.[57]

By the end of Šu-Sin's second year, Babati had acquired a new role: he is now described as pisağ-dub-ba, "high commissioner," which was to be his main title for the remainder of his career (*Rochester* 217:5–6 [ŠS2.10.-]). Amazingly, this is his title in two spurious letters, UdŠ1 (11:12) and ŠIš1 (15:8); at some point, therefore, the author or redactor of this composition relied on material that went back to Ur III times. It was to be the first of many titles on his seal, discussed in full below, and when his son Girini-isa joined the bureaucracy, it was the word he used to describe his father's official role, as already noted by A. Goetze (1963: 23).[58]

As is often the case with terms for titles and professions, it is difficult to define the exact meaning of the word pisağ-dub-ba (Akk. šandabakkum). The word is commonly rendered "archivist," but as W. F. Leemans (1989: 231) observes, this does not properly describe the activities of persons who held the title; I follow Leemans in using the translation "commissioner."[59] Persons who bore it functioned in both royal and temple contexts. As used by Babati, the title is much more prestigious. There is an interesting later analogy to this: Anam, who was to rule Uruk following the

---

57. *TLB* 3 24 (ŠS1.12.-); for a full discussion, see Michalowski 2005a.

58. Seal on *AOS* 32 P4 = Frayne 1997: 357. The tablet is dated to the year ŠS9, with no month or day, but it must come from the very end of the year, because the seal inscription already extols Ibbi-Sin: ᵈi-bí-ᵈen.zu, lugal kala-ga, lugal uri₅ᵏⁱ-ma, lugal an ub-da limmu₂-ba, ğìri-ni-ì-sa₆, dub-sar, dumu ba-ba-ti, pisağ-dub-ba, [árad-zu], "O Ibbi-Sin, mighty king, king of the four corners of the universe, Girini-isa, "scribe," son of Babati, the high commissioner, [is your servant!]. The tablet belongs to the Guzana archive, discussed by Steinkeller 1982b: 640–42. For the Diyala area origin of this group of tablets, see p. 151 below.

59. On the function of this high official at Mari, see Maul 1997.

death of Sin-gamil, held this title before he assumed power, and his position was high enough that he left behind two monumental texts from the time when he was still a *šandabakkum* (Frayne 1990: 467–68). During the Kassite period, this title designated the governors of the city of Nippur (Sollberger 1968: 191–92).[60]

Sometime around the third year of Šu-Sin, the Ur III bureaucracy was transformed in a number of ways, and Babati, together with the grand vizier, Arad-Nanna, was granted many new powers; indeed, these two members of the extended royal family now seem to share military and diplomatic ranks second only to the king. After six or so years of glory, Babati disappears from the scene at about the same time as the rest of the family. The king and queen both die in the last months of ŠS9 and Babati is last attested in the previous year (*PDT* 1 483 [ŠS8.8.29]).[61]

This brief survey of the lives of the three protagonists of the Šu-Sin letters situates this epistolary exchange within the realia of Ur III times. This does not in any way prove that the letters are genuine copies of actual records, because even if they do go back in some form to the time of the Third Dynasty, they would have been heavily redacted and rewritten by one or more generations of scribes. It is also possible that they are later fabrications based on some documentary material that had survived the fall of Ur. Nevertheless, there is clearly some historical material in these compositions, even if it has been altered in a manner that is impossible to recover; indeed, no other texts of CKU, with the possible exception of PuIb1 (21), can be matched so closely with the archival record. At the same time, one must recall that the Šu-Sin correspondence is not part of the core of CKU and is unattested in Nippur, but it may have been part of such a collection at some earlier time. This is suggested by the *contaminatio* in PuŠ1 (13), where Lu-Nanna of Zimudar was inserted anachronistically, undoubtedly on the basis of ŠaŠu1 (19) or a similar letter, and also by the very existence of the *Lu-Nanna/Šarrum-bani Letter* (ŠuLuŠa1 [20]) at Nippur, which would otherwise seem completely out of context.

These text-historical and redactional problems must be kept in mind when using the evidence of the Šu-Sin letters for reconstructing events surrounding the building of Muriq-Tidnim. We must, no doubt, proceed with caution, but it would be folly to reject this material out of hand, given the close prosopographic fit between the letters and people who not only lived in the times described therein but also participated in some of the events that are narrated in the epistles.

---

60. See now *CAD* Š/1 373.

61. See Michalowski 2005b: 70. In this article, I state that "the position of pisag-dub-ba that had been his, was taken over by one Lugal-azida (*JCS* 19 28 3 seal, IS 1)." This argument may have to be set aside; first, Babati is never actually described as pisag-dub-ba lugal, but only as pisag-dub-ba; and second, it is possible that there was more than one pisag-dub-ba lugal in this period, as documented by the career of Nani, who worked at Girsu. He appears as pisag-dub-ba in sixteen texts, from AS7.8.11.- (*TCTI* 2 3764:2) to IS2.-.- (*TCTI* 2 3846:7), but in one of them, from ŠŠ4.-.- (*ZA* 53 [1959] 89 25:11) he may be pisag-dub-ba lugal, overlapping with both Babati and Lugal-azida. The final sign in the line is not well preserved and requires collation.

The Construction of the Fortifications

The major topic of this part of CKU is the building of Muriq-Tidnim, finished in the third year of Šu-Sin's reign. As described earlier in this chapter, the only contemporary information on this construction comes from a year-name and from an uninformative dedicatory inscription, and there is not a single direct reference to it in the archival material of the time. This does not mean, however, that such documentation cannot be used, if only obliquely, to assist us in an analysis of the complex events surrounding the construction of Muriq-Tidnim. The lack of concrete information has forced scholars to speculate and then to take speculation as fact. Some have taken it for granted that the Šu-Sin work was an extension of Šulgi's Bad Mada/Igihursaĝa (e.g., Wilcke 1969: 1; Gasche et al. 2002: 542; Sallaberger 2007: 445). Edzard (1957: 44), in his pioneering study of the Early Old Babylonian period, frankly admitted that we simply did not know its location. It was usually thought of as starting near Fallujah or Umm Raʾūs (Wilcke 1969: 9) or, simply, somewhat north of Baghdad (Whiting 1995: 1233); more recently Cole and Gasche (1998: 29) and Gasche et al. (2002: 542–43) have placed it farther south, running west of the Euphrates toward Zimudar, but there is no good reason to argue that either locale is correct. I will suggest that, if we take information relayed in the CKU and combine it with hitherto untapped data from Ur III sources, we will be able to reconstruct some of the geographical and ideological factors surrounding the matter of Muriq-Tidnim.

The epistolary exchange between Šarrum-bani and the king of Ur provides certain important concrete pieces of information: that the fortifications began at the Abgal watercourse; that they had reached the territory of Zimudar, spanning 26 dana, or approximately 269 kilometers; and that Šu-Sin replaced Šarrum-bani with his uncle Babati. While no Ur III document refers directly to any of these matters, there is one text that may provide indirect support for the presence of Šarrum-bani in the Diyala Plain in a military capacity at exactly the time specified by the Šu-Sin correspondence (MVN 3 257, ŠS3.4.-, collated):

1. 1(géš) 2(u) 7(aš) 3(barig) 2(bán) še gur
2. érin ugnim^{ki}-ma[62]
3. ì-íl-la-ne/dè
4. šu ba-ab-ti
5. šà kišib$_3$/dub šar-ru-um-ba-ni
6. lú-^{d}utu-ra ba-an-na-zi
7. kišib$_3$ šakkana^{na}-bi tùmu-da-bi
8. kišib$_3$ lú-diĝir-ra dumu
9. lú-^{d}utu-ka zi-re-dam
9–10. date
    seal:
    lú-diĝir-ra
    dub-[sar]
    dumu lú-^{d}utu

---

62. Written KI.SU.LU.KI.GAR-ma.

87.3.2 kor of barley were taken by the conscripted troops in the military encamp-
ment from the account of Šarrum-bani, consigned to Lu-Utu. When the sealed
receipt from the general is brought over, the document sealed by Lu-digira, son of
Lu-Utu will be destroyed. Date.
Seal inscription: Lu-digira, scribe, son of Lu-Utu.

This text is from the unprovenienced Guzana archive, reconstructed by Piotr Steinkeller (1982b: 641). There can be little doubt that this is the general Šarrum-bani
who had been working on Muriq-Tidnim; indeed, Steinkeller (1982b: 642) already
suggested that two texts in the archive that mention soldiers stationed "next to the
wall" (da bàd-da) might in fact refer to these fortifications, but he could not securely place its origin, because none of the geographical names mentioned in these
texts is known from any other Ur III document. There is one clue, however, that may
help us locate Guzana's depot somewhere in the lower Diyala region. A transaction
from this archive (*MVN* 3 278: 5, ŠS7) is said to have taken place in Dur-Šarrum
(bàd-*šar-ru-um*[ki]), which may be identified with the Middle Babylonian a.šà bàd.
lugal gú [id]ṭa-ba-an, "the field of the city of Dur-Šarri on the bank of the Ṭaban;"[63]
the Ṭaban watercourse was located in the Diyala Plain, and this makes a good case
for locating Guzana's establishment somewhere in the same vicinity.

Thus, we have been able to locate Šarrum-bani in the Diyala at the time specified
by CKU. As we have seen, this man's destiny was, in the epistolary literature at least,
linked to that of Babati. It may be pure chance, but there is one moment in Babati's
biography that may provide a direct point of contact with the royal correspondence;
indeed, it may be the only other such convergence between the Old Babylonian
literary letters and archival data from Ur III times. A document excavated in the
Diyala city of Ešnunna, dated ŠS3.10.- (Whiting 1976: 173–74) records an allotment
of flour to (king) Tiš-atal of Nineveh, on behalf of the governor of Ešnunna, but the
whole affair is certified by Babati, whose inscribed seal was rolled over the tablet.
Apparently, Tiš-atal was on his way to Sumer to swear allegiance to the king of Ur,[64]
but this does not concern us, for it is probably only tangentially associated with the
fortifications we are chasing. However, the very fact that Babati can be located in the
Diyala region exactly at the time that he is said to be there according to ŠaŠu1 (19)
can hardly be brushed off as coincidence. This is the earliest example of the use of
Babati's cylinder seal, which is now known from different sealings on tablets dated as
late as ŠS8.[65] The inscription is the longest of its kind from the period, and its size,
38 mm high and 28 mm in diameter, makes it "very possibly the largest seal known
from impressions of the Ur III period (when the average seal was little over 20 mm
in height)" (Mayr and Owen: 2004: 153)

Equally unique is an unprovenienced Old Babylonian version of a similar Ur
III text, published more than a quarter of a century ago by Christopher Walker
(1983) from the holdings of the British Museum. Unlike the seal inscription, which
was dedicated to Šu-Sin by Babati, the copy had been made from an item that was

63. *MDP* 2 87 33, see Nashef 1982a: 99. On the Ṭaban, see Nashef 1982b.
64. Zettler 2006, with clarifications by Steinkeller 2007c.
65. For references, see Mayr and Owen 2004: 153.

given by the king to his uncle, ending with the formula in-na-ba, "bestowed upon him." This formula has hitherto only been known from cylinder seal inscriptions, and therefore Walker understandably assumed that the text had been copied from a somewhat different seal of Babati that had survived to Old Babylonian times, but this now appears unlikely. A copper bowl from Tell Suleima, discussed below, provides proof that prestige objects other than seals with inscriptions utilizing the "in-na-ba" formula already existed in Ur III times, or at least in the reign of Šu-Sin, and it is likely that just such a royal gift had survived into later times.

The two inscriptions read as follows; the Ur III seal inscription is on the left, and the Old Babylonian copy of a dedication text is on the right.

1. ^{d}šu-^{d}en.zu	1. ^{d}šu-^{d}en.zu ki-áǧa ^{d}en-líl-le
2. nita kala-ga	2. lugal ^{d}en-líl-le
3. lugal uri$_{5}$^{ki}-ma	3. ki-áǧa šà-ga-ni ì-pàd
4. lugal an ub-da limmu$_{2}$-ba-ke$_{4}$	4. lugal uri$_{5}$^{ki}-ma
5. ba-ba-ti	5. lugal ki-en-gi ki-uri^{ke}
6. pisaǧ-dub-ba	6. lugal an ub-da limmu$_{2}$-ba-ke$_{4}$
7. šà-tam lugal	7. ⌜ba$_{4}$⌝-ba$_{4}$-ti dub-⌜sar⌝ šà-⌜tam⌝
8. šakkana	8. ⌜pisaǧ⌝-dub-ba ǧiškim z[i⌜]$^{[66]}$
9. maš-gán-šar-ru-um^{ki}-ma	9. ⌜énsi⌝ a-wa-⌜al⌝$^{[ki]}$
10. énsi	10. ù a-pí-ak⌜^{ki}⌝
11. a-wa-al^{ki}	11. kù-gál ma-da a du$_{10}$-ga
12. ù a-pí-ak^{ki}	12. šabra ereš min-a-bi
13. kù-gal	13. saǧa ^{d}be-la-NIR-ba-an
14. ma-da a du$_{10}$-ga	14. ù ^{d}be-la-at-šuk-nir
15. saǧa	15. šeš a-bí-si-im-ti
16. ^{d}be-la-at-šuh-nir	16. ereš$^{!}$(dam) ki-áǧ-ǧá-ni
17. ù ^{d}be-la-at-te-ra-ba-an	17. árad-zu
18. šeš a-bí-si-im-ti	
19. ama ki-áǧ-ǧá-na	
20. árad-da-ni-ir	
21. in-na-ba	

Šu-Sin, mighty man, king of Ur, king of the four corners of the universe, gave (this) to Babati, high commissioner, royal accountant, commander of Maškan-šarrum, governor of Abal and Apiak, canal inspector of the sweet water territory, temple administrator of Belat-suhnir and Belat-terraban,

Šu-Sin, mighty man, king of Ur, beloved by Enlil, king, beloved of Enlil who called him (to kingship already) in the womb, king of Ur, king of Sumer and Akkad, Babati, the scribe, accountant, trustworthy high commissioner, royal steward, governor of Abal and of Apiak, canal inspector of the

66. Walker (1983: 91) reads agrig l[ugal⌜], which is also possible.

brother of Abi-simti, his beloved mother, his servant.

sweet water territory, officer in waiting to both queens, temple administrator of Belat-suhnir and Belat-terraban, brother of Abi-simti, his beloved queen, is your servant.

The last part of the inscription refers to Babati's status within the House of Ur: he is the high priest of the goddesses Belat-šuhnir and Belat-terraban, divine patrons of the royal family (about whom there will be more to say in a moment), brother of the Dowager Queen, and—in the later copy only—officer-in-waiting to the "two queens," whom I take to be Abi-simti and Kubatum, that is, the Dowager Queen and the Royal Consort.[67] More perplexing are his new administrative and military duties that encompass three cities and their territories: Maškan-šarrum, Abal, and Apiak.

The Areas under the Control of Babati and the Run of Muriq-Tidnim

In order to unravel the symbolism of Babati's newly acquired domains, we must go back to the beginnings of the dynasty as documented in the claims preserved in the inscriptions of its founder Ur-Namma. The new king had to wrestle control of various strategic territories from Puzur/Kutik-Inšušinak, the king of the highland kingdom of Awan (André and Salvini 1989; Potts 2008). In a broken passage, he lists these lands in the following manner (Wilcke 1987: 109–11; Frayne 1997: 65 col. v'):

16'. a-wa-al^{ki}
17'. ki-is-ma-ar^{ki}
18'. maš-kán-LUGAL^{ki}
19'. [m]a-da éš-nun-na^{ki}
20'. [m]a-da tu-tu-úb^{ki}
21'. [ma-d]a zi-mu-dar^{ki}
22'. [ma-d]a a-ga-dè^{ki}

This inscription maps out the route of Puzur-Inšušinak's assault on Mesopotamia. The result of this invasion was described in the prologue to the *Code of Ur-Namma*, cited above on p. 130, wherein the new king of Ur stated that he had liberated "Akšak, Marad, Girkal, Kazallu, their (surrounding) settlements and Uṣarum, which had (all) been taken in servitude by Anšan."

It is clear that the highlanders had attacked Mesopotamia at some time after the dissolution of the Akkad state, coming through the break in the Jebel Hamrin and down the Diyala, and had established themselves in the area around Marad and Kazallu—that is, the later defensive zone described earlier in this chapter. Ešnunna

---

67. Others interpret this to refer to the two deities mentioned above, which I find difficult to believe (e.g., Frayne 1997: 341).

(Tell Asmar) and Tutub (Khafajah) are the only cities in this list that have been securely located, and then follow Zimudar and Agade, undoubtedly on the Tigris not far from Sippar (Wall-Romana 1990).

The location of Abal/Awal, which was governed by Babati and heads the Ur-Namma list, is of obvious importance for our investigations. The place is attested in a variety of sources, beginning with Old Akkadian texts from Susa, Gasur, and Tell Suleima (Edzard et al. 1977: 20–21; Rashid 1984).[68] A quarter of a century ago, F. Rasheed (1981: 55) proposed that it was Tell Suleimeh in the Hamrin Basin, but subsequently D. Frayne (1992: 67) and Y. Wu (1998a: 578; 1998b: 579) rejected this claim, suggesting instead that Tell Suleimah was the site of Batir. The main reason for this identification is the cult of a deity named Batiritum, who is documented in votive and seal inscriptions from the site, and two references to ba-ti-ir[ki]. Most of the information comes from Old Babylonian sources from the Hamrin basin. From Tell Suleimeh itself, we have a seal inscription of a guda priest of Batiritum, a tablet that mentions an oath by the weapons of the goddesses Šarratum and Batiritum, and a brick inscription of a petty ruler or sheik (*rabiān amurrim?*, Seri 2005: 58) of Batir who built or rebuilt a temple of Batiritum, all cited by Wu. Outside of Tell Suleima, there is an Old Babylonian extispicy report from the neighboring mound of Tell al-Seib (al-Rawi 1994: 38–40; Glassner 2005: 277–78) that reads, in part (lines 7–10):

> da-du-ša i-na ni-q[í ᵈb]a-ti-ri-t[im-ma?]
> ù né-pe-eš-tim ši-ru-u[m an?-nu?]-um? [. . .]
> iti da-du-ša a-na gu.za é [a-bi-šu i-ru-bu]
> ù ši-mu-ru-um ba-ti-[ir . . .]

> Daduša—in the sacrifice to Batiritum and in the oracular consultation, these were the signs. . . .Month when Daduša ascended the throne of his patrimonial house, and [. . . .] Simurum and/in Batir. . . .

There are Old Akkadian references to Batir in texts from Tell Suleimeh, but the geographical name is absent from Ur III administrative sources, which reveal only one mention of the goddess: a Drehem document records items that are the property of a certain Arzanu, the temple administrator of Batiritum, who came from Zimudar, and the transaction was officiated by a guard of the "man" of that city.[69] This may mean that the goddess was worshipped in Zimudar, but it is more likely that Arzanu only came through there on his way to Sumer. One other Ur III text from Tell Suleimeh still awaits full publication: a bronze bowl with a dedicatory inscription of Šu-Sin found in an elite grave rich in prestige items (Müller-Karpe 2002, 2003). The text

---

68. The toponym is written a-ba-al in Ur III sources, but a-wa-al in OAkk and OB texts; see Whiting 1976: 179–81 and Owen 1981: 247. The city of e-ba-al, which may have been in the same region, must be kept distinct from Abal for the time being.

69. *Ontario* 1 25:3–6 (Š47.7.13) níğ-gur₁₁ ar-za-nu sağa ᵈba-ti-ri-tum-ma, zi-mu--dar[ki]-ta, ğìr bí-la-bi àga-ús lú zi-mu-dar[ki]-ka, "(confiscated?) property of Arzanu, temple administrator of Batiritum, from Zimudar. Conveyor: Bilabi, bodyguard of the 'man' of Zimudar."

is incomplete, but it appears to document a gift (in-na-ba) from King Šu-Sin to a man whose name is broken off but who was a temple administrator (saĝa) of a deity whose name is likewise incomplete. It would hardly be surprising if it were none other than Batiritum. Of course, it is impossible to say if this was the grave of the temple officer or if someone else had been buried with an heirloom or booty, but it does provide some indication of Ur III presence in the area. Equally important, the inscription demonstrates that dedications with the in-na-ba formula, until now known only from cylinder seals, were used on other luxury objects as well in Ur III times; thus, the Old Babylonian copy of the Babati text need not have been taken from a seal but was more likely found on a larger votive object, as already observed above.

But the most important references to Batir are found in the rock inscriptions of Annubanini of Lullubi and Iddin-Sin of Simurum, both of which were carved *ina šadū'im batir*, that is "in the mountain(s) of Batir" (Al-Rawi 1994: 39). As J. de Morgan and V. Scheil (1893: 104) already observed more than a century ago, Batir is obviously first and foremost the name of a mountain and not of a city, and Batiritum, together with Šarratum, was probably worshiped in more than one place, but nothing would prevent her from being the patron deity of Abal. Both were probably local manifestations of Ištar. There may have been a village at the foot of the mountains that bore the same name, but it is unlikely that this would have been Tell Suleima. Therefore, echoing the same caution that Piotr Steinkeller (1981: 164) expressed some years ago, I would still insist that Awal/Abal was indeed the ancient name of this mound, and if not, it lay very close to it.

Both R. Whiting (1976) and P. Steinkeller (1981) have collected information on Hamrin and Diyala Plain place-names, but neither utilized the Ur-Namma listing. As P. Steinkeller observed, Abal is associated with Tašil, since the official Išar-ramaš seems to have been in charge of both cities. He is also associated with the town of Kismar (MVN 13, 868, Š.47.7.17), which was listed together with Awal in the Ur-Namma text and in an inscription of Ilušuma of Aššur. Tašil, in turn, is listed together with Maškan-šarrum, the other city governed by Babati, in an undated Drehem text (Owen 1997: 371). Maškan-šarrum has also been located in the same area, so it would appear that prior to the time when Babati took over these functions, the military rule of Abal, Tašil, and Kismar was in the hands of Išar-ramaš. A close look at his command reveals that he was in charge of this area from at least Š46 to AS5 or possibly even up to AS7.[70]

The copy of the Ur-Namma inscription provides the only solid information on the location of Zimudar. It is generally agreed that it was located in the Diyala region, but there has been little evidence for a more precise identification (Michalowski 1978a). In one Ur III text that mentions Lu-Nanna, who, as we have already

---

70. JCS 52 (2000) 52 7 6:1–3 (Abal, Š46.9.11) to MVN 15 350:4 (AS5.9.24). See already Goetze 1963: 18 (the text he publishes probably dates to AS7). Later occurrences of the same name may refer to someone else.

demonstrated, was the officer in charge of the city and region during the reign of Šu-Sin, the transaction takes place in Šulgi-Nanna, "on the bank of the Diyala."[71] A somewhat later document from Nippur records a loan of grain that was borrowed by Ennam-Šulgi, Lu-Nanna's son; he promises to return the capital in the city of Ešnunna after the harvest.[72] The logical geographical progression of the listing in the Ur-Namma inscription leads to the unavoidable conclusion that this city and its territory lay between Tutub, which is modern Khafajah, and the Tigris.

A number of other cities lay on this route from the Hamrin basin down the Diyala, including Maškan-abi. There were close administrative links between the various administrative centers along these lines, with Ešnunna most likely the dominant one, as far as Ur was concerned. The area also seems to have been religiously unified, because most of the major deities of the towns are connected with the underworld. Ešnunna had Tišpak, but it was also the place that housed a major temple of Belat-šuhnir and Belat-terraban, who often occur in religious ceremonies in Ur in tandem with Annunitum of Agade and with two underworld deities, Allatum, the goddess of Zimudar, as well as Meslamtaea, who was the patron deity of Kismar. In addition, Maškan-šarrum was sacred to Kaka, another minor netherworld god (Steinkeller 1982a). Over the years, many have tried to interpret the significance of the Ur III cult of Belat-šuhnir and Belat-terraban; most recently, Sallaberger (1993: 19) suggested that Šulgi's spouse, Šulgi-simti, who seems closely associated with the cult of these goddesses, might have come from Ešnunna.[73] It is clear that the joint cult of this pair in Ur together with deities from the whole Diyala region must have some important significance. Perhaps it is not Ešnunna that is key here, but Agade, and it is more likely that Šulgi-simti came from the old imperial city. But the fact that the kings of Agade are only rarely mentioned in Ur III texts suggests that if a line of the House of Ur actually derived from Old Akkadian elites, it was probably not from the main branch of the descendants of Sargon but from those who had come to power in the city when that dynasty collapsed. This explains the somewhat reticent cult of Sargon and Naram-Sin in Ur III times.[74] Nevertheless, Babati's title, which links him with the two goddesses, most probably signals his control over the city of Ešnunna.

Babati's governance of Abal and Maškan-šarrum would put him in charge of the areas immediately bordering on the Hamrin pass, perhaps on both sides of the opening. But Apiak is nowhere near that area; in fact, it lay on the Abgal watercourse, more than 200 kilometers from his other domains.

The Abgal, as we now know from the work of Gasche and Cole (1998: 27–29) and Gasche, Tanret, Cole, and Verhoeven (2002: 542) discussed above, was the branch of the Euphrates that split off at Kish, or just below it, and moved south

---

71. *UET* 3 75:6–7 (Š1.1.-): ša ᵈšul-gi-ᵈnannaᵏⁱ, gú ⁱᵈdur-ùl.

72. *NRVN* 1 176:6–8 (IS2.-.-): egir buru₁₄-šè, ⸢ša⸣ áš-nun-naᵏⁱ-ka, ág-e-dam, "to be measured out after the harvest in Ešnunna." The seal inscription explains that Ennam-Šulgi was the son of the general Lu-Nanna.

73. See the discussion in Sharlach 2002, with previous literature.

74. For all the Ur III references to the Sargonic kings, see now J. Westenholz 2008.

through Apiak to Marad and, presumably, further south. Among the towns associated with the defensive zone described above one stands out—often in tandem with Kazallu—namely the city of Apiak. As we have already established, the governor of that city prior to Babati was none other than Šarrum-bani, who, according to the CKU letters 18 and 19 was in charge of building Muriq-Tidnim until Šu-Sin replaced him with Babati. As already mentioned earlier, it may be pure coincidence, but the fact that the tablet that bears the earliest example of Babati's seal places him in the Diyala region in Šu-Sin's third regnal year, that is exactly at the time when the fortifications were being built, provides the one point of real contact, prosopography aside, between events that actually took place in Ur III times and those described in a CKU letter. The Šarrum-bani letter describes precisely the state of the work at the moment when he is writing, just before being relieved of his duties, and even if the precise interpretation of parts of this passage are open to discussion, the general tenor is clear (ŠaŠu1 [18] 8–13):

> [8] As I was leaving (for the assignment), [9] from the banks of the Abgal canal up to the territory of Zimudar, [10] I levied workers there.

> [11] When I had been working on the fortifications that then measured 26 dana (269 km.), [12] after having reached (the area) between the two mountain ranges, [13] the Amorite camped in the mountains turned his attention to my building activities.

Šarrum-bani had mustered workers from the banks of the Abgal, possibly from his own domains at Apiak, up to Zimudar, which clearly bordered Ešnunna. This does not specifically state that Muriq-Tidnim began at Apiak, but in light of the Babati seal inscriptions it appears more than probable. If we take the admittedly risky step of combining Ur III information with the testimony of the CKU, then it would follow that when Šarrum-bani was relieved of the task of overseeing the building of Muriq-Tidnim he also lost his job as governor of Apiak, and the man who replaced him took over both responsibilities. Seen in this light, the geographical scope of Babati's new position as defined in his inscriptions makes sense: the combined governorships of Apiak and Abal define the run of Muriq-Tidnim. It was apparently designed to stretch from the defensive region on the Abgal canal to the area between the Hamrin gates and beyond, although it is impossible to know if these ambitious plans were ever actually completed. In short, Babati's inscriptions from the time of Šu-Sin define his new responsibilities when he was appointed to finish Muriq-Tidnim and the areas that were put in his charge by the king define the planned end points of the fortifications.

The facts and analysis presented above, while obviously speculative, provide some evidence for the run of Muriq-Tidnim from Apiak into the Diyala region, perhaps as far as Awal, beyond the break in the Hamrin. Beginning at Apiak, these fortifications did not bifurcate the state into two; they only spanned part of the width of its territory. This differs with all existing reconstructions of its location. [75]

---

75. The one person who anticipated these conclusions, most presciently, was Michael Rowton (1982: 322).

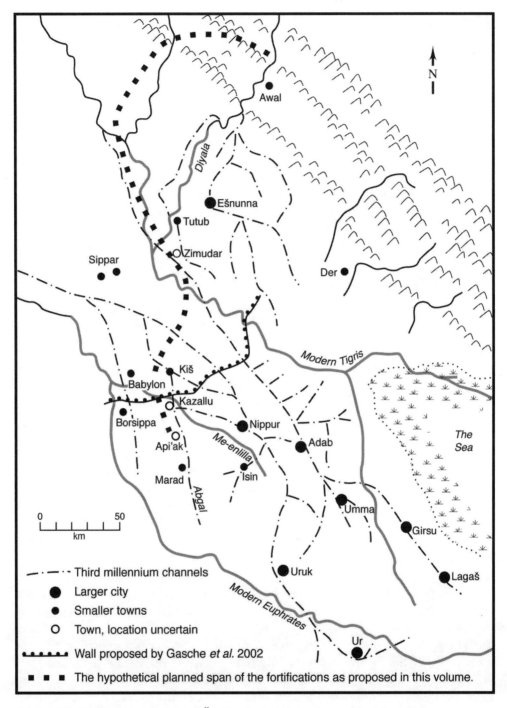

Fig. 3. The Ur III state in the time of Šu-Sin: the hypothetical run of the Muriq-Tidnim.

The Historical Setting of the Construction of Muriq Tidnim

Military Policies in the Time of Šu-Sin

We cannot view the construction of these fortifications, as announced in Šu-Sin's fourth date formula, in isolation from the major events of the surrounding years, because it is only part of a complex, shifting military policy that consumed much of the government's energies during his reign.

The reign of Šu-Sin marks a turning point in Ur III military strategy, and one must wonder what outside forces or transformations of political configurations outside of the realm brought about these changes. At the outset of his reign the new king was faced with a crisis in the far northeast and soon sent the forces of Ur north for the first time, attacking Simanum, Habura, Mardaman, and other areas on the Tigris north of the confluence with the Upper Zab (Sallaberger 2007: 442–44). This region had never been under direct Ur III control, but the state had influence there by means of allied, client, or even vassal states such as Assur and Simanum. In his inscriptions, Šu-Sin claims that he was forced to act when a local revolt ousted the ruling family of Simanum, which had been allied by marriage to the house of Ur when the princess Kunši-matum was betrothed to one of the sons of Pušam, ruler of the highland country (Michalowski 1975). Although the kings of Ur engaged in many such diplomatic marriage alliances, this is the only known instance when they intervened militarily to protect an allied ruling family, and one must suspect that there was more to this affair than just a palace coup. This was the only military campaign in the north; as far as we know, no Ur III army had ever moved into this region, and this clearly marks a new dynamic in state strategy. It is during this campaign that the Amorite polity of Tidnum is encountered—or at least mentioned in the surviving documentation—for the first time. The events of the second year were followed by the work on Muriq-Tidnim, which gave its name to two consecutive years, namely, years four and five.

The evidence is murky at best, but there are indications that there were many changes in strategy as well as organizational structure that took place in the second and third years of Šu-Sin's reign (Sallaberger 1999: 170). This was the time when Muriq-Tidnim was nearing completion, and it was a time when the official state calendar was reformed. As we have already observed, this is when Babati was given expansive new responsibilities, as recorded in his seal inscription. There is another interesting phenomenon that can be observed in this year that may be linked to the same cluster of events.

In his seminal work on the taxes contributed by military personnel from the border regions of the Ur III state, P. Steinkeller (1987) was able to describe in precise terms the obligations of various ranks of soldiers and officers that were due to the crown, and he described them all as gun mada (gun ma-da), "frontier taxes." The taxation does indeed seem uniform from Šulgi to the early years of Ibbi-Sin, but the actual term gun mada occurs only from the third year of Šu-Sin on; until then, the actual name of the tax is never specified. It is always possible that this term was used to label these taxes earlier; after all, the word appears in ŠAr1 (1), where it may be anachronistic, as already noted by P. Attinger (apud Huber 2001: 204 n. 153), but the fact remains that, in the Drehem administrative language, the term does not appear before ŠS3. Maeda (1992) saw in this a new form of taxation, but this is unlikely (Sallaberger 1999: 197). Earlier taxes—or perhaps, better, tribute—of this kind from the border and frontier lands encompassed a whole range of places, from occupied Susa and deeper into southwestern Iran, to allies or clients such as Nineveh and Simanum in the north, as well as various areas beyond the Hamrin. But the taxes from the time of Šu-Sin cover a much more limited territory; this may be a result of political and military problems that beset the Ur III kingdom at the time, as Steinkeller (1987) suggests, but it may also be a reflection of strategic readjustment and of concomitant administrative restructuring.

The list of places that supply gun mada is not easy to analyze, because many of them are unique or cannot be located at present.[76] The tablet that documents such taxes from the first two years of Ibbi-Sin's reign covers localities in the Diyala; with the exception of Zimudar and Išim-Šulgi, they are all relatively small army posts (CT 32 19). Notably, many of them seem to be located in the lower Diyala Plain, and places further north such as Maškan-šarrum, Kismar, or Abal are not included. Such taxes during the reign of Šu-Sin were sent from other places, including Azaman, Daltum, Išum, and Šu-Sin-idu, which are otherwise unknown, as well as Der, Urbilum, Šetirša, and possibly Simurum, which lie outside of the plain in the highlands. It is difficult to see any pattern here, but it may lead to the conclusion that while outlying posts were still holding on, settlements on both sides of the pass were no longer under the control of Ur and that processes that would lead to the loss of Ešnunna and other closer cities were already at work in the first two years of Ibbi-Sin's reign and perhaps even earlier.

To put this in a larger perspective, we must go back earlier and review some of the military events of previous years. The intensive, seemingly uninterrupted warfare of the last part of Šulgi's reign seems to have continued into the reign of his successor, Amar-Sin, when war with Urbilum resurfaced once again. After this, the new ruler appears to have concentrated his military activity in the nearby Lower Zab region, mounting campaigns against Šašrum and Šuruthum that are attested in documentation from his third and fifth year, and then against Huhnuri, far to the southeast of the area attacked by his previous expeditions (Nasrabadi 2005). This was hardly a time of peace, but it appears that many of the regions pacified or subjugated by his predecessor remained calm. This is also the time of a remarkable increase in diplomacy, as evidenced by the presence in Sumer of ambassadors and envoys from various principalities in Syria and Iran (Owen 1992; Sharlach 2005; Sallaberger 2007: 441). Many of them are undoubtedly independent of Ur, some bound by family ties to the successors of Ur-Namma, while others owed various levels of allegiance and

76. For a chart of the texts and list of places, see Maeda 1992: 163.

subservience. It is difficult to discern if all of these foreigners had traveled willingly, and it is possible that some of them were actually hostages who had been sent to Sumer to guarantee political and military arrangements. Some came from far-away Ebla, Uršu, and Tuttul in Syria, or from Mari on the Euphrates. Others had traveled from Simanum, Urbilum, Simurum, Harši, Šimaški, and Marhaši—that is, from various parts of northern Mesopotamian and Iran. A glance at the tables in Tonia Sharlach's study of Ur III diplomacy (2005) reveals the clustering of these embassies in the reign of Amar-Sin, although such relationships began much earlier, and would continue in some fashion after his death. A more thorough investigation of the full documentation raises more questions than answers, because the patterns that emerge are difficult to interpret, and some of the clusters of information as well as silences may be due to the chance nature of archival recovery and are therefore somewhat illusionary.

While the concentration of information on diplomatic relationships is certainly more abundant for the reign of Amar-Sin, it does carry over into the first years of the next king, Šu-Sin. Some of the foreigners remained while others were replaced at about the time the new king came to the throne, and it is impossible to determine if there is any correlation between these events. The distinct possibility that Šu-Sin was already running the state at some point before the death of his predecessor complicates matters further. The case of the envoys of Harši serves as a good example of the issues involved. In the period under discussion, a certain Marhuni first represented this polity; he first appears in AS1[77] and remained at his post until the sixth month of AS8.[78] Three months later, at most, he was replaced by prince Iša-wer, the son of Adda-gina, the ruler of the country, who may have only come for a short visit, as we can only document a three-day stay in Sumer.[79] Then, in ŠS1, a new envoy appears once, and after that we have no record of any such delegation from Harši. We are, as usual, at the mercy of the preserved fragmentary documentation and therefore cannot establish if the data reveal something about the flow of events or if all of this is but a reflex of partial archival recovery.

All of this diplomacy, if this is the correct term, appears to collapse in the sixth year of Šu-Sin, the year that the Ur III state mounted a massive attack against Zabšali and more than fifteen cities and territories that were part of the area of Šimaški (Steinkeller 2007a: 216–17). A unique pair of documents from the time of the Zabšali campaign records disbursement of flour and other commodities to various foreigners, including ambassadors and their assistants.[80] The main text (*Amorites* 22) is dated to day two of the sixth year of Šu-Sin, without mentioning the month, while the second

77. *HUCA* 29 (1958) 75 4:8–10 probably records his arrival at court: mu ma-ar-hu-ni, ù érin mu-da-a-re-e-ša-a-šè, lú ha-ar-ši[ki]-me, "on behalf of Marhuni and the troops that had travelled with him, people of Harši."

78. *BIN* 3 402:11 (AS8.6.10).

79. From AS8.9.13 (*OIP* 121 555:6) until AS8.9.16 (*BCT* 1 83:7–8).

80. I discuss here texts 4–6, which are listed above in the discussion on Ia'madium on p. 114.

text, (*JCS* 7 [1953] 106), which duplicates exactly the first two-thirds of the first one, is undated. The goods are destined for people from Šimaški and Hurti, as well as imprisoned messengers; from Banana of Marhaši and his translator, to Ari-buduk (of Šašrum), as well as to others, including Abu-ṭab of Mari, the Eblaites Izin-Dagan and Kurbilak, an Amurrum named Ipiq-reʾu from Iaʾmadium, as well as men of Aššur and Urbilum. The very same people from Mari, Ebla, and Iaʾmadium appear in the record only once again in a receipt dated two months later, to the eighth month of the very same year, which records the disbursement of provisions that were loaded on a boat when they returned to their homes (*Amorites* 21 [ŠS 6.8.14]). Only one other person from the longer list of foreigners is ever heard from again—namely, Ari-buduk of Šašrum, who seems to have returned a year later.[81] To put it more strongly, for reasons that are impossible to establish but which must have had something to do with the war that was being waged in the highlands, these envoys all appear in the record for the last time, and it may be that most of them, if not all, had left Sumer for good.

The Zabšali Campaign

The seventh regnal year of King Šu-Sin was named

(a) mu ^{d}šu-^{d}en.zu lugal uri$_5^{ki}$-ma-ke$_4$ ma-da za-ab-ša-li^{ki} mu-hul
The year: Šu-Sin, king of Ur, defeated the land of Zabšali.

But what exactly was Zabšali? The royal inscriptions that described these events read, in part:[82]

(b) u$_4$-ba, šimaški^{ki} ma-da ma-da za-ab-ša-li^{ki}, zag an-ša-an^{ki}-ta, a-ab-ba igi-nim-ma-šè, buru$_5$-gin$_7$ zi-ga-bi
At that time Šimaški (as well as) the lands of Zabšali, from the borders of Anšan to the Upper Sea, whose levy is like a flock of birds . . .

(c) u$_4$ ma-da za-^{r}ab^1-ša-li^{ki}, ù ma-^{r}da ma^1-da, šimaški^{ki}-ka, mu-hul-a
When he had defeated the land of Zabšali and all the lands of Šimaški . . .

The wording of (b) is somewhat ambiguous; Stolper (1982: 45), Frayne (1997: 303), Potts (1999: 135), Steinkeller (2007a: 217), and others took this to mean that Zabšali was part of Šimaški; indeed, they all accepted the translation of the opening words of the passage, either literally or by implication, as: "at that time Šimaški (which comprises) the lands of Zabšali. . . ." But it is seems more likely, on the combined evidence of the year-name, of the last-cited inscription (c), as well as on the basis of administrative texts that will be dealt with below, that in Ur III nomenclature Zabšali was perceived as a separate polity that was contiguous with the area generally

81. JCS 57 114 1:2–3 a-^{r}ri-du^1-bu-uk ^{r}lú ša^1-aš-ru^{ki}, dub-sag uru-a ku$_4$-ra-ni. He appears once again two years later, with the identical phrase (CST 455, ŠS9.12.14).
82. (b) Frayne 1997: 303 (E.3/2.1.4.3) lines ii 14–20, (c) Frayne 1997: 313 (E.3/2.1.4.6) lines 5′–8′.

designated as Šimaški by the scribes of Sumer. Indeed, throughout the descriptions of Šu-Sin's campaign, the territories of Šimaški and Zabšali appear as distinct geopolitical areas, not as synonyms.

The general location of the Zabšali lands, as perceived from Mesopotamia, is difficult to determine. Stolper (1982: 46), using the information embedded in *Išbi-Erra Hymn B*, concluded that it "locates one of the Šimaškian lands, Zabšali, immediately north of 'Elam'." I would read the passage in question as (*Išbi-Erra Hymn B*, Segment C: 4–5, collated):

> ba-ši-miki gaba a-ab-ʼbaʼ-[ta] zag za-ab-ša-[liki-šè]
> a-ra-waki sağ-kul elam[kima-ta] zag mar-ha-[šiki-šè]

> From Bašime, on the edge of the sea, to the borders of Zabšali,
> From Arawa, the lock-bolt of Elam, to the borders of Marhaši . . .

The interpretation of these lines as depicting, in rough terms, a south-to-north and a west-to-east axis is bolstered by recent archival and archaeological work. There is a good chance that Bašime/Pašime is to be located at or in the general area of Tell Abu Shija, 66 km north of Amarah in Iraq (Hussein et al. 2010). Marhaši most likely lay to the east around the Halil-rud alluvium (Steinkeller 2006), and if A-ra-wa, which is otherwise unattested, is the same place as Urua (URU×A), it may have to be located in the Deh Luran Plain, either at Tepe Musiyan (Carter and Stolper 1984: 212 n. 275) or more probably at Tepe Farukhabad (Wright and Neely 2009; Michalowski and Wright 2010).

Recalling that Šu-Sin's inscription describes his campaign as reaching the Upper Sea, it is reasonable to assume in conjunction with the evidence just cited above that the lands of Zabšali bordered on the "Upper Sea," which could be the Caspian Sea or Lake Urmia (T. Potts 1994: 33). No other new evidence on the matter has come to light in the intervening years, and such a hypothesis stands, to my mind, as the best we can do at present. The supposed northern location of Zabšali lands, and by implication of the parts of Šimaški attacked by the armies of Ur, has important implications for the analysis of the general flow of military and political events during the reign of Šu-Sin.

The possible breakup of long-nurtured diplomatic relationships, described earlier, in concert with the drain that the war put on troops and other state resources, may have had catastrophic long-term consequences for Ur, while Zabšali apparently recovered and would now play an important role in international events. The inscriptions trumpet the great extent of the enemy lands, "from the borders of Anšan to the Upper Sea," and the king claims victory over a coalition of more than 13 polities or cities (Steinkeller 2007a). After much maiming and slaughter, the king claims that he installed prisoners from Mardaman to work in the gold and silver mines in the highlands and brought the rulers of the conquered territories to Sumer. The mention of Mardaman prisoners is particularly suggestive, because they had to have been taken during the raid on Simanum, ostensibly conducted five years earlier.

Here, once again, Simanum and Zabšali are referred to together, as in the documents cited above, and it makes one wonder about the wars conducted against them, which we separate into two distinct events on the basis of year-names.

The grand hyperbole of Šu-Sin's inscriptions is impressive, but only four years after the great victories that they describe, Zabšalian ambassadors received rations in Umma on their way to or from Ur, and still another four years later, Ibbi-Sin gave a daughter in marriage to the ruler of Zabšali (IS YN 5).[83] Whatever punishment was meted out by Šu-Sin's armies was not fatal, and the land recovered and thrived, governed by a new leader loyal to Ur or by a local ruler who was strong enough to force his enemy into diplomatic alliance.

The Issue of Šimaški

The name of Šu-Sin's seventh year mentions only the defeat of Zabšali, but the associated royal inscriptions also describe various principalities, towns, or even villages as part of the lands of Šimaški, presumably its northern regions, as already noted above. The geopolitical concept of Šimaški denoted both a geographical area as well as a number of shifting polities, each led by individuals who were bound by kinship ties. Many have analyzed the history and location of Šimaški, but all modern work on the subject begins with Matthew Stolper's (1982) synthesis, supplemented by the discoveries and analysis of Timothy Potts (1994: 30–34), Daniel Potts (1999: 130–59, 2009), Katrien de Graef (2005: 113; 2006: 43–55; 2008), and Piotr Steinkeller (1988, 2007a). An Old Babylonian "king list" from Susa registers the names of twelve successive rulers of Šimaški, but as Stolper demonstrated, a number of these rulers can be identified in the Ur III and Early Isin administrative record. Steinkeller (2007a: 221) has recently collected all the information on this matter and concluded, "since Ebarat I (Yabrat), Kirname, and Tazitta (Taʾazite) are named concurrently in Ur III sources, the conclusion is unavoidable that they were contemporaries." Stolper (1982: 48) already noted that two other Šimaškian rulers from the list, Kindattu and Idaddu, are attested in a text from the time of Išbi-Erra (*BIN* 9 382). The details of all of this are of little consequence here, except to note, once again following Steinkeller, that these rulers and the polities under their control do not seem to have been targeted by Šu-Sin's armies, which fought only against some smaller Šimaškian polities that bordered on the lands of Zabšali.

The areas ruled by Ebarat and his kin survived this war without any apparent damage; indeed, as Steinkeller (2007a: 227) has argued, their lands did not take part in the war. We have no direct evidence for the immediate consequences of these events, but only six years later Ebarat's forces entered Susa and stayed there for at least two years, if not longer (De Graef 2005: 99). Two decades later, Šimaškian armies, apparently now led by Kindattu, would defeat Ur and occupy the city for a

---

83. *UTI* 5 3472:5–7 (IS1.12.-): lú-kíǧ-gi₄-a, an-ša-an^{ki}, ù za-ab-ša-ʾli^{ki}-[ke₄-ne].

decade. Stolper's compelling analysis of the political situation of the time deserves to be cited in full (1982: 51):

> The war was not an isolated foray, but an escalation; Ur had been campaigning on its eastern and northeastern marches almost incessantly since late in the reign of Šulgi. Conflict stiffened local opposition and created communities of interest among Ur's adversaries. Loose political affiliations perhaps antedated the campaign. Šu-Sin's war stimulated or accelerated political or military liaisons among the several regions.

In the end, Šimaški merged with Anšan, and their combined forces were able to challenge Ur (Steinkeller 2007a: 224). When this actually took place is impossible to discern at present. A Mesopotamian document from ŠS8 can be interpreted as treating Ebarat's part of Šimaški and Anšan as separate polities (*TÉL* 46, ŠS8.12.-). One text from Ur may refer to leather bags for the ruler of Anšan, perhaps meant to hold previous items to curry favor with the growing power in the southeast.[84]

The military and political actions of Šu-Sin's reign are usually analyzed as discrete unrelated events, but there may be profit in taking a different view, linking them together into the flow of history. The wars and diplomatic contacts documented in the fragmentary record do not represent by any means a full portrayal of what transpired during those years, and therefore any reconstruction of the times can only be hypothetical, at best. And yet the clues already described above, which connect the attack on Simanum, the construction of Muriq-Tidnim, and the assault on Zabšali, suggest that these campaigns were part of some larger scheme, that new forces were operating in the north and northeast that forced Šu-Sin's government to enact defensive measure of a completely novel kind.

At this juncture, it is important to draw attention to one striking fact: while Šimaškian lands had been mentioned time and again by the scribes of Ur, her latest enemy, Zabšali, is completely new in cuneiform sources. Like Tidnum, there is no mention of this polity before the time of Šu-Sin, when it first makes an appearance in inscriptions and in the name of his seventh year. In other words, there is not a single text documenting any contact— diplomatic, economic, or military—with either entity before hostilities began. The only possible exception to this is found in two laconic and undated ration texts that may come from Umma, but the provenience is uncertain: (a) *Santag* 6 382 (day 25) and (b) *MVN* 15 66[85] (day 30). Both are accounts of beer, and among the recipients are: $kaš_4$ za-ab-ša-li^{ki} (a: 4, b: 11) lú za-ab-ša-li^{ki} (a: 5, b: 13) and lú si-ma-núm^{ki} (a: 7).[86] The longer text (b) also mentions a "man" from Arrapha (6) and Sabum (ii 5). The peculiar spellings used in

---

84. Large number of animal skins to make $^{kuš}du_{10}$-gan for the lú an-ša-ʾan'[^{ki}-šè], *UET* 3 1290 (IS15.2.-).

85. Collated (UM 72-25-03).

86. There is also one a-[ba-ar]-du-uk (b: ii 1), who must be the sukkal of the same name who conveys (ĝìri) goods in connection with Kunši-matum, the princess married into the royal house of Simanum in ŠS1.3.9 (*MVN* 15 216:17), or even a-[ri]-du-uk, an envoy from Šašrum, who is known from tablets dated to the time of Šu-Sin (see the next paragraph).

these texts and the fact that none of the other individuals who appear in them can be identified suggest that they come from an otherwise unknown archive, although it is also possible that this tablet came from Umma but not from any of the major known archives from the city. The lack of a date formula makes it difficult to draw any firm historical conclusions from these documents, but the association of Simanum and Zabšali is perhaps more than pure coincidence.

Prior to the Simanum expedition, Ur III records concerning conflicts with Amorites mention only the nonspecific kur Amurrum, "Amorite highlands," discussed earlier, and the only "Amorite" polity that maintains diplomatic relations of some kind was Pamadium. The appearance on the scene of an additional Amorite polity, Tidnum, which joins the latter in attacks on Ur's armies marching toward Simanum may signal that the same processes that gave rise to the Zabšali confederation also had the effect of pressing disparate Amorite tribal or kinship groups into some larger political entity that, with greater numbers and unified tactical potential, created some level of danger for the progress of Mesopotamian forces along the Hamrin.

The novel appearance of both Tidnum and Zabšali in the Ur III record prompted strong actions on the part of the Mesopotamian kingdom. One can see in all of this the work of outside forces, as did, for example, Maurice Lambert (1979: 38), who blamed the crisis of these years on a massive Amorite invasion. Other interpretations come to mind, however. It is important to call attention to the fact that the years in which Šu-Sin occupied the throne are characterized by intensive contacts with the various leaders of Šimaški, in addition to the other events detailed above. One hypothesis that comes to mind is that the temporary weakening of Ur during the last few years of Amar-Sin's reign may have provided an opportunity for the revival and strengthening of certain Šimaškian polities to a degree that would have been too difficult to deal with. Even so, more open revolt against the Crown in the north and northeast, combined with the consolidations of the new powers invested in the Tidnum tribes or tribal confederation around the Hamrin and in the new polity of Zabšali could not be allowed to stand and were dealt with accordingly. Other forces, undetectable in the preserved record, may have been at play, of course, but it is useless to press the data and speculate further on these matters. It does seem likely, however, that the planning and construction of Muriq-Tidnim was not an isolated episode but was connected to events that spread out over the whole reign of Šu-Sin, although they were part of processes that began later and continued into the time of his successor.

It is perhaps instructive that the authors of the Šu-Sin inscriptions repeatedly described Šimaški, Tidnum, as well as Šimaski not as unified polities under the control of a single sovereign but as "lands" with many rulers. For example, in one passage, the prisoners of war are depicted as (Frayne 1997, E3/2.1.4.3 iii 22–29):

en-en bára-bára-bi šağa[a] mi-ni-in-dab$_5$-dab$_5$ énsi gal-gal ma-da ma-da za-ab-ša-li[ki] ù énsi-énsi uru[ki]-uru[ki] . . .

He took all their lords and leaders prisoner. And all the great rulers of all the lands
of Zabšali as well as all the rulers of all of (its) cities . . .

One should be wary of overinterpretation here, keeping in mind Robert Adams's
strictures concerning the degree of cultural knowledge of the authors of such texts,[87]
but on the rhetorical level, at least, it would seem that they wish to create a contrast
between the strictly hierarchical, centralized state of Ur, firmly ruled by a master of
the universe and the fragmented and inferior polities of the highlands. Is it possible
to speculate that this political language sheds light on some of the motivations that
lay behind the organization of the Zabšali invasion, which may have been designed
to interfere with and hinder processes of integration in the highlands, developments
that posed a serious potential threat to the lowland kingdom? If this was indeed the
case, the campaign, whatever its immediate effect may have been, was ultimately a
failure and may have even been counterproductive, hastening rather than impeding
the consolidation of highland polities.

The "Walls" Revisited

Let us now return to the subject of the fortifications built under Šulgi and Šu-
Sin. Although the surviving documentation impels us to think episodically, the
building of relatively important lines of fortifications cannot be reduced to two short
periods of building activity. Conceptually and organizationally, they were separate
undertakings, but from a broader point of view, one must see them as elements of
complex, long-term processes that began some time during the first half of Šulgi's
reign and continued, off and on, well into the time of Šu-Sin. The idea may go back
to the time of the founder of the dynasty, judging by the focus of the Ur-Namma cadastre text that charters the area protected by the Šulgi fortifications. The reason for
their construction and the consequences of the building activities are more difficult
to determine. On the preceding pages, I offered the hypothesis that the bad mada
of Šulgi's time was designed to protect military staging areas and provide a central
mobilization point as part of an in-depth strategy that supported the more forward
military defenses on the marches of the state.

The name of Šu-Sin's fortifications, one royal inscription, as well as the royal letters all point to a more specific central theme: defense against Amorite infiltration.
As noted at the outset of this chapter, the idea of such a defensive line has often
evoked comparisons with the Great Wall of China. The analogy turns out to be
apposite but not for the reasons that usually come to mind, and the historical analogies with border relations of early Far Eastern peoples can be instructive. The myths
about the Great Wall provide much inspiration to the imagination, but the fact is
that it is really a concatenation of various fortifications, not all of them continuous,

---

87. Adams 1981: 136; see p. 90 above.

built at different times for different purposes, and the wall did not, as is commonly thought, isolate China from its neighbors. Recall, also, that Lattimore (1940) argued many years ago that the wall actually served to consolidate hostile state formations in the borderlands, eventually leading to the downfall of the ruling dynasty of China.

The constant Ur III military activities in the highlands over the course of more than three decades may have led to similar results and only served to unite fragmented polities in the Zagros and different elements of the large polities or confederations of Anšan and Šimaški, and these, in turn, eventually toppled the Mesopotamian state. In the context of this broader historical picture, one may propose that the true purpose of Muriq-Tidnim was not so much the protection of the homeland from small Amorite raids but the securing of the agriculturally rich Diyala region and surrounding parts of the eastern frontier, strengthening defensive as well as offensive capacities against a broad range of highland principalities, and the preparation, provisioning, and establishing of the infrastructure supporting the attack on Zabšali and on certain elements of Šimaški, as part of a chain of events that began with the campaign against Simanum and perhaps even earlier but also as a result of the encounters with Tidnum during that expedition. The fact that the name of the fortifications is defensive can be viewed as an obvious tactical propaganda ploy; one never announces one's military intentions ahead of time, and military installations are often described as defensive no matter what their true purpose might be. Frontier constructions of this kind would have also served to discipline unruly local populations, to facilitate the exploitation of natural resources and labor sources of the area, in addition to priming the local economy, thus assuring a more stable platform for expansion into territories that lay beyond. However, it is a measure of our lack of concrete information on these matters that one could equally well suspect that the conflict with Zabšali grew out of a new and sudden danger that required swift action on the part of Ur.

The broad array of complex diplomatic activities described above precludes any overt aggressive military construction on the frontier, even if its purpose may have been quite evident. It is possible that the name was linked to the fact that the building operations, as well as the resulting military activity, were expected to be harassed by raiders from Tidnum, but nothing in the surviving documentation justifies a literal interpretation of the name of the defenses or of the justification for their construction that is found in the CKU. If my reconstruction is correct, the fortifications were much too long and the effort that went into them was much too extreme if their purpose was to ward off such a low-level threat. Therefore, one has to imagine Muriq-Tidnim not as a great wall but as a series of forts, army posts, and perhaps even short walls that served as bases for support of the royal army. It was not, by any means, conceptually an extension of the bad mada, although it might have begun in the area that the latter shielded; the purposes of the two construction projects were different, founded as they were in different times and in different political and military contexts.

According to older reconstructions, the Ur III fortifications not only divided the state from its enemies but also cut the core of the state into two parts, separating northern cities such as Sippar and Kish from the center (see, e.g., Gasche et al. 2002: 542–43). Although it has been claimed that these places were of secondary importance to the Ur III kings, there is little to support this conclusion, since we have limited information about contemporary life in these parts of Babylonia at the time. The reconstruction I have offered does not require such assumptions. According to my hypothesis, the starting point was at Apiak, which lay on the Abgal, which was not the western branch of the Euphrates system, so the fortifications did not reach the Arahtum canal to the west, and thus if this reconstruction is correct, would not have prevented access from Sumer to Dimat-Enlila, Kish, Sippar, Babylon, and surrounding areas that belonged to the northern part of the core of the Ur III state. Moreover, if Muriq-Tidnim were only a line of forts and not a continuous wall, then these cities would have still been easily accessible from the south. The analogy with the Great Wall, or rather with a certain mental model of the Wall, has made us think of Muriq-Tidnim as a barrier, but it was undoubtedly more than that.

According to the reconstruction offered here, Šu-Sin's fortifications were designed, if not actually fully built, all the way up the Diyala/Ṭaban plain past the Hamrin gates. This region was a true frontier zone, constituting one of the marches of the Ur III state. Shepherds, herdsmen, tribute bearers, messengers, ambassadors, traders, as well as native and foreign armies constantly traversed these areas. This is also where different ethnic groups and different languages intermingled, where cultural contact worked in all directions, and where settled and pastoralist dwellers of the mountains and valleys exchanged goods and ideas. The defenses in this region were built as much for moving armies as for stopping infiltrators. They may have had defensive purposes, but, more important, they constituted a link to these places, both as a staging route for the movement of troops but also as a two-way highway of ideas. At the same time, they were part of a self-defeating military strategy, for the military campaigns that began there only served to create opposition against Sumer in the highlands, an opposition that would eventually topple the Ur III state.

J. L. Borges (1964: 3), who understood such matters far better than we do, once wrote an essay on the Great Wall of China in which he observed that "burning books and building fortifications is a task common to princes." It would have pleased him to know just how well our knowledge of Šulgi's deeds, which probably included the discarding most of the Early Dynastic literary tradition in addition to the construction of a "great wall," confirms his prescient words.

Chapter 7

The Royal Letters in
Their Historical Setting 3

Ur, Isin, Kazallu, and the
Final Decades of the Ur III State
(Letters 21–24)

The Ur III Collapse

The fall of Ur is one of the dramatic moments of early Mesopotamian times, if modern historians are to be believed, but in many ways our received opinions about the episode are grounded in a vision of history and politics colored by the celebration of nations, ethnic unity, and centered in the glory of large and powerful states. We often depict the kingdoms of Akkad and Ur as classical moments of early Near Eastern history, when in fact they may be better viewed as aberrations in a historical flow dominated by localism and small political organizations. The picture of the last decades of Ur is muddled by lack of sufficient documentation; as a result, speculation and inference give license to the imagination, offering a broad field of play for the philologist and historian alike.

The classic description of the fall of Ur still belongs to Thorkild Jacobsen (1953), although he had already summarized his views a decade and a half earlier (Jacobsen 1941: 219–20):

> Events around the fall of the Third Dynasty of Ur are gradually becoming clearer. A rebellion in Babylonia around the tenth year of I(b)bi-Sin reduced that ruler to a mere petty king who may not have controlled much more than the territory around Ur itself. The rest of his empire broke up into similar small states; Nippur and northern Babylonia fell to Ishbi-Irra of Isin, henceforth I(b)bi-Sin's chief rival; the Diyala region had won independence under Ilushu-ilija, and so forth. Elam, another former vassal, took advantage of this breakdown in Babylonia. In the twenty-fifth and last year of I(b)bi-Sin, with its allies and neighbors the Sua people, it launched a dev-

astating attack against both Ur and Isin. While Isin lived to fight another day, Ur succumbed entirely. I(b)bi-Sin and most of his subjects were carried off captive to Elam, and Ur itself was looted and destroyed. In the ruins or at a nearby spot part of the invaders settled.

After more than 60 years, we can flesh out the narrative with new data and with minor revisions of the chronological framework, but the picture remains jumbled, fragmented, and there are large patches of empty canvas.[1] These blank spaces have been filled in with suppositions based on meager evidence and by much speculation, some of it based on preconceived notions rather than on facts. The standard presentation of the fall of Ur is that it was a catastrophe and invokes causes such as the influx of foreign ethnic elements such as the Amorites, environmental determinism in the form of climatic disasters and crop failures, or the rise of a bloated bureaucracy. One of the main sources of information for all this is the CKU, in the incomplete form that it has been previously available, as well as poetic texts such as the *Lamentation over the Destruction of Sumer and Ur*, *The Ur Lament*, later omens, and the fragmentary hymns of Išbi-Erra (van Dijk 1978; Sjöberg 1993; Vanstiphout 1989–90; Michalowski 2005b).

Catastrophic collapse may appeal to the imagination but has little historical or sociological justification (McAnany and Yoffee 2010: 5–6). The fall of the Ur III state apparatus was primarily a political and military affair, and the admittedly meager information currently available does not suggest that it led to a collapse of global civilization, which, as Marcella Frangipane (2009: 16) observes, is extremely rare. As she notes,

> Very often what is thought of as "collapse" was a merely a change, in other words a few elements—even important ones—were transformed within the overall system that fashioned a civilization, while other elements are simultaneously retained and adapted to the new conditions representing the continuation of what are often equally important aspects of traditional relations between the members of a given society.

Frangipane's apposite remarks, which echo may of the positions taken by contributors to Yoffee and Cowgill's collection of essays on the collapse of states and civilizations, serve as an introduction to a discussion of events from the fourth millennium B.C.E., but they serve equally well as a caution to the historian who looks at historical processes that took place early in the second millennium B.C.E.[2] The consequences of the fall of the House of Ur are difficult to gauge in any adequate manner because of a lack of textual information from the period covering the last decades of the kingdom and years subsequent to its fall. Ur was occupied by an eastern army, but in Nippur

---

1. New light on these events has been shed by Wilcke 1970; Gomi 1980, 1984; Lafont 1995; and Steinkeller 2008.

2. Yoffee and Cowgill 1988; most pertinent to our discussion are the contributions of Adams, Eisenstadt, and Yoffee. See also Sinopoli 1994: 169.

and Isin life continued without any evidence of disaster. At Ešnunna and Susa, new masters took over without any evident hiatus, but evidence is lacking from other places. The main damage, insofar as one can determine, took place early during the reign of Ibbi-Sin, but life in the south of the state, around the capital and in an area the size of which is impossible to gauge, continued with few ill effects for another two decades. From the long-term sociopolitical point of view, however, there is nothing tremendously cataclysmic about the fall of Ur, even if part of the native tradition, as preserved in texts such as the city laments, presents it in catastrophic terms. These poems identify state collapse with the ruin of civilization, but this is the point of view held by native proponents of centralized authority. It ignores, perhaps willfully, the opening up of new sets of community relationships that come about with the dissolution of rigid state apparatus and hierarchical social models that characterized the highly bureaucratized Ur III kingdom (Adams 2009). Moreover, as Yoffee (2005: 137) observes, the most frequent consequence of state collapse was the rise of new states that were often "consciously modeled on the state that had done the collapsing." In the case of the dissolution of Ur, it was Isin that performed this role, as Yoffee undoubtedly had in mind when he wrote those words.

Explanations of the Ur III Collapse

Proponents of the kind of historiography that finds causation in ethnic movements have ascribed much fault to the Amorites. As I have already described in chap. 5, administrative texts from the time document but a small number of Amorites within the country, most of them associated with the military, probably as elite bodyguards. The documents also refer to low-level conflicts resulting from a hostile Amorite presence on the frontier and beyond. The CKU letters refer to confrontations with Amorite tribes in the northeast, but the economic texts as well as the year-names make it clear that the Ur III government had bigger adversaries and more pressing military problems to deal with and that their main enemies were the larger polities in Iran that had little to do with Amorites. To be sure, hostile Amorites were counted among the enemies of Ur, as we have already seen, but there is absolutely no evidence outside of CKU that their presence in Babylonia was a significant factor in the processes that led to the disintegration of central power.

Within CKU, the information from the Ibbi-Sin correspondence implies that with the breakdown of Ur III control of the Diyala and the surrounding highlands, Amorite tribal groups were able to descend into the valley and mount raids into Mesopotamia proper. The situation described therein would have already resembled what can be observed soon after the Ur III collapse in Early Old Babylonian letters found at Ešnunna (Whiting 1987), but it is difficult to imagine that even if the CKU portrait is accurate, such low-level threats could have had any sizable influence on the process of the dissolution of the kingdom. To repeat the obvious once again, the primary reason for imagining a major Amorite threat is the name of the fortifications that were celebrated in Šu-Sin's fourth year-name, *Muriq-Tidnim*, "The One That

Keeps the Tidnum (Amorites) at a Distance." but too much weight has been given to this name, as I have argued above, and one cannot base an entire theory of collapse on a single name. Indeed, there is little to support "a model of intrusion, conquest, and assimilation of Amorite foreigners into Mesopotamian society" (Yoffee 2005: 146). It is therefore more than likely that we must adjust the commonly held opinion, summarized by the author of the most recent in-depth and most reliable history of Old Babylonian times (Charpin 2004a: 57):

> En ce qui concerne la fin du troisième millénaire, il est néanmoins certain que le movement de peuples désigné conventionnellemnt sous le terme d'«invasions amorrites» a joué une rôle essentiel.

Environmental determinists argue that declining crop yields precipitated the fall of Ur. In its milder form, this is seen as resulting from possible shifts in the course of the Tigris (Sallaberger 1999: 177), but others speak of crop failures and "the collapse of Ur III agriculture" due to climate change (Weiss 2000: 89).[3] The idea that agricultural failures may have been important in the disintegration of the Ur III state was first argued by T. Jacobsen (1953) and then further discussed by T. Gomi (1980, 1984). It is important to note that both Jacobsen and Gomi were very careful in their analysis, and that neither blamed lack of grain as the sole reason for the collapse of the state. The evidence they brought together is important, but it in no way supports the assertion of a collapse of agricultural production throughout northern and southern Babylonia.

It has also been argued that the Sargonic and Ur III states disintegrated as a result of an abrupt change in the climate of the region, which shifted to relatively arid conditions beginning around 4000 to 4200 years ago and continuing for a few centuries (Cullen et al. 2000; Weiss 2000). There can be no questioning the impressive marshalling of hard evidence for aridification and changes in the water-flow of the Euphrates around 2200 B.C. (Riehl, Bryson, and Pustovoytov 2008; Riehl 2008, 2009), but there are good reasons to be skeptical of the connections that have been made between these physical factors and collapse of both society and state. As interesting as these speculations may be, they tend to overlook a number of serious problems. First, our absolute chronology of Mesopotamia is not precise enough to allow correlation between scientific data on climate and specific historical events, and, furthermore, the dating of the supposed climate crises are also imprecise. Second, it is not clear how a lasting process of aridification can account both for the collapse of two state formations, Akkad and Ur, as well as for the rise of the second state on the ashes of the first. Moreover, as the argument goes, climate changes in

---

3. Older theories that ascribed the fall of Ur to agricultural failure caused by salinization of the soil were strongly criticized by Powell (1985), although a full study of the problem is still badly needed. Influential nonspecialists (e.g., Chew 2001: 37–38; Diamond 2005; Tainter 2006) have continued to repeat unsubstantiated claims for resource degradation, overconsumption, and overirrigation in ancient Mesopotamia, based on fanciful restating of older specialist literature but without empirical substance.

Syria drove Amorite tribes south, forcing them to encroach on land in Babylonia; as we have already seen, however, there is no evidence for such dramatic population movements at the time.[4]

One could argue that, in the wake of a serious agricultural crisis, Mesopotamians adapted their growing techniques to the new conditions and managed short-term successes, only to be defeated in the end by natural conditions. It may be reasonable to speculate about such processes, but little evidence from Mesopotamian sources has been marshaled to bolster these conjectures. Even if one were to accept the hypothesis that Ur III times were characterized by extreme weather conditions, there is no evidence that this had a significant impact on agricultural yield, because cultivators still managed to obtain an impressive 1:30 seed to yield ratio in the Lagash province, at least (Halstead 1990: 187), and the massive textual documentation from that area shows no evidence of any developing agricultural crisis. It has been argued that "reduced Euphrates stream flow probably explains unique linearization of Ur III irrigations canals (Adams 1981: 164) that attempted to counter stream channel meandering" (Weiss 2000: 89), but this is an overstatement of the evidence; such a layout of irrigation canals is linked to field shapes, and this type of field shape is not in any way characteristic of the period but of a geographical location—the Girsu province—and the data on Sargonic fields that is used in this comparison comes from farther north, from the area of Kish, a very different physical environment (Liverani 1997: 173).

Ration lists and other administrative texts from Ur indicate a shortage of grain in the capital starting at about the middle of Ibbi-Sin's sixth year and continuing at least into year nine (Gomi 1984). By this time, almost all the outlying regions of the state were no longer under central control, and it therefore comes as little surprise that the Crown had problems obtaining resources. As far as we know, this shortage was a three-year crisis in a single city, but it is more a symptom than a cause of a political predicament, and one cannot conclude from this that there was a prolonged multiyear crop failure in the whole of Sumer and Akkad. Unfortunately, we cannot trace the grain situation in the capital beyond this point, because the archive that provides this information stops in IS8, and for the following six years there are only 38 texts from Ur; when more abundant records resume, in the form of tablets from IS15–17, they come from a different archive that deals mainly with precious metals (Widdell 2003: 98–99) and therefore provide no documentation regarding the agricultural situation.

Ibbi-Sin's eighth regnal year is probably coterminous with the beginning of Išbi-Erra's independent rule at Isin and Nippur to the north, and nothing indicates that there were any agricultural problems in the area under the control of the new administration, but here once again we are hampered in our understanding by inadequate documentation. The central government managed to maintain control over Ur and its immediate environs for another 16 years. Up to this point I have avoided any ref-

---

4. A particularly fanciful and imaginative narrative of the fall of Ur, wrong in all details, based on these ideas, can be found in Fagan 2004: 6–7.

erence to the CKU, which in fact precipitated this entire line of inquiry, because it was a reading of the letter of Išbi-Erra to Ibbi-Sin (IšIb1 [21]) that prompted Jacobsen to produce his pioneering study. But this epistle has been somewhat misused, as we will presently see, and provides no evidence of any large-scale agricultural disaster.

The theoretical ramifications of the Ur III collapse are as murky as the relevant evidence. In a monograph that is perhaps the most detailed comparative analysis of the fall of complex societies, Joseph A. Tainter (1988) argues that their inevitable collapse cannot be ascribed exclusively to internal and external conflict, environmental factors, including catastrophes and resource depletion, but results from the pressures involved in maintaining complexity. Collapse tends to ensue when the investment of resources in such complexity maintenance becomes too costly, in terms of cost–benefit ratios, so that a state can no longer maintain proper organizational and other forces to resists stress surges. Although Tainter's comparative work is fascinating in many ways, it provides but another monocausal explanation of what are usually extremely complicated historical processes (Trigger 1989: 375) and limits "civilizational" collapse to political disintegration (Bowersock 1991: 120).

More recently, Yoffee (2005: 139) has returned to the subject and restated his position, taking a position that differs substantially from that of Tainter:

> Collapse, in general, tends to ensue when the center is no longer able to secure resources from the periphery, usually having lost the legitimacy through which it could disembed goods and services of traditional organized groups.

By shifting the trigger for collapse from economic cost ratios to ideology, Yoffee also moves the explanatory focus to different moments in the historical process: loss of legitimacy arises as a consequence of other social, economic, organizational, or military factors, but there are always other complex forces at play that lead to such dissolution of central authority.[5] In the case of the Ur collapse, we have very few facts to go on, so we cannot reliably discover and evaluate the various "stress surges" that led to the fatal loss of legitimacy by the central government.

None of the monocausal explanations of the end of the Ur III kingdom have proved convincing, and the reason for this may be that the affair was much more complex and aleatoric than one would like to believe. The sudden loss of both Susa and Ešnunna in IS3 suggests that the Crown did not have the military means to head off such disasters, perhaps because all of the wars in recent years had drained its martial resources. Unrelated to this may be the loss of the Umma and Girsu provinces, which happened a few years later. The evidence is tenuous, to say the least, but Maekawa (1989: 49) has shown that cereal production in parts of the Umma province fell somewhat in IS3, although there is no reason to believe that anything like this was happening in the Girsu province. Both areas were watered by canals that fed from the Tigris, and perhaps we are witnessing here the beginnings of a process that

---

5. Yoffee (2010) recently returned to these issues in a somewhat different manner, concentrating on the end of Assyrian state power.

came to a head three years later. Sallaberger (1999: 176–77), referring to work done by Heimpel (1990), already suggested that the change of the course of the Tigris may have been a factor in the fall of Ur, and Robert Adams, who drew my attention to the importance of this potential factor, notes that later Girsu information shows a diminished agricultural capacity, as documented by Richardson (2008). It is interesting to note that after Ur III times there is no evidence of any life in Girsu and Lagaš before the time of the Larsa rulers Nur-Adad and his successor Sin-iddinam, and then information resumes again in the time of Rim-Sin. All of this has been documented by Richardson and need not be repeated here. This correlates well with information gleaned from the year-names and inscriptions of these Larsa kings: both Sin-iddinam and Rim-Sin claim to have dredged the Tigris (Steinkeller 2001: 31–32). Could it be that, from the time of Ibbi-Sin until Nur-Adad or Sin-iddinam, the old channel of the Tigris that fed the alluvium and therefore led to Girsu was running in a different bed, or carried little water, and it was only in the time of these Larsa kings that it was restored to some approximation of its former location?

As Adams (2006: 39) himself has observed: "alluvial river systems are characteristically unstable, given to course changes through channel avulsion that would naturally disrupt established patterns of human use."[6] Alternatively, one may seek human agency in this matter, either as a result of cumulative action on waterworks or resulting from more deliberate interference; for example, a later Old Babylonian king, Abi-ešuh, claimed to have damned up the river.[7] Whatever the causes, if the "old Tigris" changed its course or carried lower water volume because of avulsions of tributaries farther upstream, then we could understand why all the provinces fed by its waters become silent. Many cities to the west and northwest of these areas, fed by the branches of the Euphrates, continued to exist, even though some of them no longer pledged their allegiance to Ur.

The end of the Drehem archives may perhaps be related to the loss of the frontier; Nippur and Isin were taken over by Išbi-Erra—a person who in a different time might have been called a warlord—who proclaimed independence, but seems not to have been actively seeking the immediate collapse of what was left of the Ur III state. If the CKU is to be believed, civic life continued in Kazallu, Girkal, Kish, and perhaps Borsippa. At the same time, the rulers of Anšan and Šimaški, in the mountains to the east, consolidated their political and military might and were eventually ready to overwhelm the armies of the Mesopotamian alluvium. It is impossible at

---

6. For an overview of the history of avulsions of the Tigris and Euphrates river systems, see Morozova 2005, with previous literature. "Avulsion is a process whereby a major river diverts from an existing channel to a lower elevation on the floodplain, initiating a new channel belt" (Morozova 2005: 407). Longer-term climatic factors may have also played a role in all of this, because there is evidence of long-term aridification around that time (Aqrawi 2001); nonetheless, it is difficult to correlate climate and geological time with somewhat uncertain absolute historical chronology, as already noted above.

7. YN O: mu a-bi-e-šu-uḫ lugal-e usu mah ᵈmarduk-ka-ta ⁱᵈidigna ĝiš bí-in-kéš-da, "The year King Abi-ešuh, by Marduk's supreme might, damned up the Tigris."

present to ascertain the connection between these various factors, and therefore our understanding of the last decades of the kingdom founded by Ur-Namma remains fragmentary and opaque. It may have been pure chance that all these different narratives converged at a time when the state was already weakened by military and organizational overreach; God may not play with dice, but History often does.

On the pages that follow, I will survey some of the patchy information from the last decades of the Ur III state. The focus will be primarily military and political, but this choice is dictated by the nature of the surviving sources and by the context of the present discussion, which is, after all, merely an extended commentary on the literary royal letters and not a full history of the times. Therefore, the spotlighting of these specific factors should in no way be taken to mean that they are the only components involved in the processes that led to the fall of Ur. I will then proceed with a discussion of the Ibbi-Sin letters in this historical context.

The Beginnings of Ibbi-Sin's Reign

Šu-Sin did not live to see the end of his ninth regnal year, and the new king, Ibbi-Sin, was immediately elevated to the throne, accompanied by ceremonies in important cult places (Sollberger 1953; Sigrist 1989; Sallaberger 1999: 172–73; Katz 2007: 174–82).[8] The succession seems to have taken place without any obvious strife; the new man on the throne of Ur was probably Šu-Sin's brother, another of Šulgi's sons.[9] The consequences of the change of occupant on the throne of Ur are difficult to gauge because it is impossible to discern the practical role of the monarch and how much agency can be ascribed to his person. Under the influence of native self-representational strategies, we tend to think of the history of these times as divided into reigns, but, truth be told, we simply do not know how power was distributed within the state, nor do we understand the patterns of decision-making among the elites. We are also in the dark about Ibbi-Sin's social and official position, prior experience, or community networks before he assumed the kingship of Ur.

Contemporary documents provide very little in the way of evidence of any changes in administration or of any looming problems. At first, economic activity seems to function as before, but taxes from the eastern periphery appear diminished

8. There is some question in the ancient sources as to whether Ibbi-Sin reigned 24 or 25 years. Here, a twenty-four-year reign is assumed, following the scheme presented by Sollberger (1980) and Frayne (1997: 361–66). This conforms to the number recorded in the two Ur III/Isin reign lists published by Sollberger (1954), now duplicated by still another list in Friberg 2007: 233. Manuscripts of the *Sumerian King List* contain different numbers: J: 24; P5: 25; Su1: 25; Su3+4: 25?; WB: 24; Leilan: 23? (information kindly provided by Gianni Marchesi, who is preparing a new edition of the composition; sigla follow Jacobsen 1939; Leilan = Vincente 1995. The numbers may change, because only the second source has been collated).

9. On the Ur III succession, see a forthcoming study by Jerrold Cooper and me; for the time being, the latest discussion of the issue is in Dahl 2007: 7–32.

in the first two years of the new monarch, [10] and then, suddenly, records simply stop in most places outside of Ur and the south so that, by his sixth year, Ibbi-Sin's administration controlled only Ur, Uruk, Adab, Nippur, and surrounding regions. [11] There are small signals that things had begun to go wrong earlier. At least three records from the last year of Šu-Sin's reign document that scheduled dues from the frontier had not been received. [12]

The archival situation is difficult to analyze because, outside of a few major cities, the documentation is relatively meager, but the consistency of the pattern tells a story. There are no dated Ur III tablets from Kisurra, Sippar, or Išan-Mizyad after IS2. The same holds true for the SI.A.A archive, which cannot be located at present. The related Turam-ili group ends with IS3, as do the texts from Ešnunna, Susa, Garšana, and Urusağrig. [13] Kish and Babylon are last mentioned in a Drehem text from IS2. [14]

The situation is more complex in other cities, as discussed most recently by Lafont (1995), with minor modifications by Sallaberger (1999: 175 n. 180). It appears that in Ibbi-Sin's second year the central government still held Ur, Girsu, and Umma, as well as Puzriš-Dagan, Nippur, and Isin—but not for long. Records from a town close to Nippur that housed prisoners of war from Šu-Sin's Simanum campaign end in IS4. [15] The tax collection offices at Puzriš-Dagan still functioned normally though IS2: although there seem to be eleven texts from IS3 and one from the following year (Lafont 1995: 7), for all practical purposes it had ceased to function after IS2. [16] At Umma, texts stop after year IS5 and at Girsu after year IS6. In none of these last-dated documents is there any clue to the end of the textual documentation, and so the historian can only speculate regarding events that might have had such distinctive consequences. The end of the tax collections from the frontier, documented by the disappearance of records at Drehem, indicates that something was going on in the eastern borderlands in IS3, months before the loss of both Susa and Ešnunna.

10. An account of such taxes (gun ma-da), covering year one and the beginning half of year two of Ibbi-Sin's reign, lists only places in the lower Diyala and close to the Tigris (Kakkulatum, Tutub, Zimudar, etc.) and none that can be securely located farther up the valley (CT 32 19, IS2.4.9).

11. The last mention of Uruk in an Ur III archival text is in *UET* 3 1133:6, which records that 13 slave girls were sent to that city in the sixth month of IS5. Adab is last mentioned, in broken context, in IS7.7.- (*UET* 3 1574).

12. *TAD* 66, *Trouvaille* 50, *Santag* 7 101 (nu-mu-de$_6$); all three dated ŠS9.-.-.

13. Information on Urusağrig courtesy of David Owen (personal communication).

14. Kish: *MVN* 10 144 r. iii:17 (IS2.9.3); Babylon: *MVN* 8:139: r. ii 8; and *BIN* 3 346 4, both dated IS2.6.14.

15. This archive is still unpublished; information courtesy of Benjamin Studevent-Hickman.

16. Lafont mentions 11 Drehem texts from IS3, without any detail. Most of the documents that have been ascribed to Drehem from this year are in fact from other places, such as Nippur or date to the time of Šulgi. Those that may come from Drehem are mainly from the leather archive (*SET* 290, month 4; *MVN* 13 594?, month seven; *ASJ* 4 [1982] 8, month broken; *SAT* 3 1998, month 12).

It may be coincidence, but the end of these archives correlates with an expedition against the northeastern state of Simurum; its defeat was heralded in the name of Ibbi-Sin's third year. Simurum had been a perennial problem for his predecessors: Šulgi campaigned endlessly against it, naming his forty-fourth year for the "ninth" defeat of the city. Drehem accounts from AS8 to ŠS2 document the presence of two "men" of Simurum, Kirib-ulme and Tappan-darah, followed by an énsi by the name of Silluš-Dagan, who is attested from Š42 through at least ŠS6 (Owen 2001b). Given the ambiguity of Ur III terminology, it is impossible to determine if he was an independent ruler or Šu-Sin's governor of the area, although at least in Šulgi's time he was definitely an appointee of the Crown. It is interesting to note, however, that he first appears just when, according to the Šarrum-bani letter, Simurum had joined the hostile Amorites against the state of Ur (ŠaŠu1: 14 [19]). Whatever the outcome of this event may have been, only four years after the last attestation of Silluš-Dagan, the king of Sumer once again went to war against Simurum and claimed victory, as related in the name of Ibbi-Sin's third year. But in the aftermath of this war, his empire began to collapse, and one cannot but wonder if the events are not linked: that this war in the northeast, coming only four years after a major war in the area focusing on Šimaški and Zabšali, overextended Ur's reach. More pertinently, it cannot be excluded that the year-name masks a military disaster. Soon after, the Ur III government negotiated a dynastic union with Zabšali in IS4, as documented by the year formula for the following year. Why would Ur conduct diplomacy with a remote highland polity, when most of the territories in between had dropped their allegiance to the house of Ur-Namma? And yet, even after the documentation from Umma, Girsu, and even Nippur had ceased, Ibbi-Sin's chancellery insisted on proclaiming victories over Huhnuri (IS9), as well as Susa and Adamdun (IS14), all in southwestern Iran.

Military and Political Events of Ibbi-Sin's First Years

The documentation preserved from the first two years of Ibbi-Sin's reign shows no evidence of any political, economic, or military problems, nor are there any signs of impending crisis. As described above, after assuming the throne, Ibbi-Sin's regime was probably forced into war in his second year and claimed victory. Some of the diplomatic relationships with lands to the east that appear to have been interrupted at the time of his predecessor's war against Zabšali were resumed, and taxes continued to come in from the core of the state as well as from limited areas of the frontier regions. To cite but some examples, vigorous diplomatic activity is suggested by the testimony of a yearly account from Girsu (*TEL* 46) that records provisions for highland guards and messengers from the Šimaškian ruler Ebarat, from Huhnuri, Anšan, from a place named Barbarahuba, and from Beli-ariq, the governor of Susa, disbursed in the establishment for messengers (é-kaš₄) in Guabba in the first month of ŠS8. In the first year of the new king of Ur, envoys from Anšan and Zabšali are attested in Umma documents.[17] Perhaps the best traces of diplomatic relationships at the beginning of Ibbi-Sin's reign are preserved in a Drehem account that makes mention of rulers of the far-off southeastern and northern principalities of Marhaši and Simanum, who seem to be present in person in Sumer, perhaps in order to affirm their alliances with the new king (*JCS* 10 15:15–20, IS1.3.25). As late as IS3, men from Mari are attested in Umma (*BPOA* 1 387:3–8, IS3.-.10).

The messenger texts from Girsu, Umma, and Urusaḡrig tell their own story. These documents record provisions and rations for envoys who traveled back and forth between Ur and the various polities and governors resident in Susiana and in the highlands, as well as to people moving around within the provinces and the center of the state.[18] The dated Girsu texts of this kind cease during Šu-Sin's last year, but because so many are undated, it is difficult to know what to make of this, and the document distribution may simply be due to circumstances of archival recovery.[19] In Umma, the messenger text archive ends almost precisely at the very end of IS2 (*Nisaba* 1 34, IS2.12.29).

The Urusaḡrig accounts record foodstuffs issued to envoys coming from and going to places such as Kimaš, Hurti, Šigriš, Šimaški, and Diniqtum, apparently through Der, which is the most commonly encountered toponym.[20] These contacts continue straight through the whole of IS2, although the records from that year have more references to Der than to the places that lay on the routes beyond. The one currently known messenger tablet from Urusaḡrig dated to IS3 mentions only Der. On the basis of these texts, it appears that diplomatic passage into the highlands was still unimpeded in IS2, although one is at a loss to explain why the messenger archives in Umma and Girsu end earlier. Documents from different archival sources in Umma and Girsu indicate that traffic with the highlands still occasionally went through the city in IS3, but for all practical purposes, all information on such matters ends at Umma in IS 2, as it does in Urusaḡrig.[21]

These signs of trouble dovetail with information from the redistribution center at Drehem; there are very few texts dated to IS3, and only one of them registers animals, the main commodity processed there.[22] Then, in the fourth year of the new king, the state suffers a sudden and debilitating defeat, losing control of the city of

17. Guards (elam) from Anšan (*MVN* 16 793:6 [IS1.7.-]), messengers (lú-kíḡ-gi₄-a) from Anšan, and Zabšali (*UTI* 5 3472:5–7 [IS1.12.-]).

18. A succinct analysis of the Girsu and Umma messenger texts, with previous literature, can be found in Sallaberger 1999: 295–315.

19. The last known Girsu messenger text is *TCTI* 2 4708, dated ŠS9.10.-.

20. Once again, I am indebted to David I. Owen for information on Urusaḡrig.

21. Elam guards came from Adamdun to Umma in IS3.1.- (*Nik.* 2 340:5), and similar personnel came from Susa to Girsu in IS3.7.- (*BPOA* 1 126:2); see also *SNAT* 200:1–3, where the same people receive dates a month earlier (IS3.6.-). People from Mari received rations over a ten-day period during an unspecified month of IS3 (*BPOA* 1 387, IS3.-.-)

22. *AOS* 32 WO1 (IS3.9.11).

Susa to the Šimaškian king Ebarat. The final known dated Ur III text from the site comes from IS3 (*MDP* 18 79) and from this time on, for two or three years at least, tablets carry Ebarat's year-names (De Graef 2005: 99, 2008).[23] The conquest seems to have been rapid and unanticipated, because all indications are that relations with Susa and beyond were normal right up to the moment of the takeover. The city still delivered taxes to Ur in Ibbi-Sin's second year,[24] highland guards from Adamdun (beyond Susa) received rations at Umma at the beginning of his third year,[25] and they received dates at Girsu in months six and seven.[26] In the sixth month, a boat-load of grain was prepared for shipment to Adamdun.[27] One assumes that such a transport would have been unloaded in Susa or in its vicinity for overland transport. If Susa was besieged or had already fallen, the route to Adamdun would certainly have been blocked, and no one would have risked sending a boat laden with grain to the area. The violent end of the Ur III garrison in Susa may perhaps be traced in the archaeological record; De Graef (2005: 107–8) suggests that the destruction evidenced at the end of Ville Royale B level VII may be attributable to the Šimaškian takeover of the city.

But the fall of Susa was not the only calamity experienced by the Ur III state toward the end of IS3. Approximately at the same time, the other entry into Iran, through the Diyala Valley, was lost as well. The city of Ešnunna, which controlled access from Babylonia to this vital military frontier area, declared independence, and the local governor Ituria or his son Šu-iliya became independent rulers (Reichel 2001a: 56–57). The local elites, taking advantage of political and military conditions that we cannot discern, threw off decades of control from Ur and resumed their independent political existence. The last known Ur III text from Ešnunna is dated to the ninth month of IS3 (Whiting 1987: 33 n. 3). At some time after this, the city was no longer a part of Ibbi-Sin's realm. This is usually viewed as just one more symptom of the breakdown of central control, resulting in various cities splitting off from the government at Ur. But the case of Ešnunna is by far more complicated and significantly more important for understanding the process of breakdown of the state.

Let us recall that Ešnunna was the most important military and administrative center in the lower Diyala. In essence, it controlled access to this frontier zone all the way into the Hamrin Basin, which was the nerve center for one part of the Ur III military corps and also the key to martial, diplomatic, and commercial access to Iran. It is highly improbable that the elites of the city could have declared independence if the military establishments up the Diyala, including the Muriq-Tidnim forts, were

23. The order of the month-names used at Susa cannot be reconstructed at present, and therefore one cannot be more precise.

24. *BCT* 1 117:5 (IS2.4.7) lists sheep šà gun šušin[ki]; strictly speaking, the taxes could have been delivered at some time earlier.

25. *Nik.* 2 340:5 (IS3.1.-).

26. *SNAT* 200 (IS3.6.-) and *BPOA* 1 126:2 (IS3.7.-).

27. *UET* 3 1057. This shipment of grain was from Sumer and Babylonia to Susa and Adamdun; for other examples, see Steinkeller 1987: 33 n. 68.

still in the hands of the central government, but the sources are silent on these matters. There is not much to go on, and it may just be pure chance, but recall that the provincial taxes from the first two years of Ibbi-Sin's reign do not mention any cities beyond the lower Diyala plain. Perhaps Awal, Maškan-šarrum, and the other military posts north of Ešnunna had already passed into the hands of the Šimaškian Ebarat, keeping in mind that this would be only a few years after Šu-Sin's claims of great victories over parts of Šimaški. One can also imagine that Ebarat or his allies had launched a double-pronged attack and had taken these areas as they prepared to move on Susa; but other scenarios are equally possible. Whatever happened in the Hamrin and the Diyala late in IS3 or early in the next year, the frontier was now independent of Ur, and Ešnunna likewise declared its independence from the realm.

From the strategic point of view, Ešnunna was the equivalent of Susa: both controlled the main routes from Mesopotamian into Iran, and now both were no longer part of the Ur kingdom. The military and political policy that went back to the time of Šulgi, anchored in almost endless war and complex diplomatic activity, was erased and extinguished within the span of a few months. Seen in this perspective, it is reasonable to assert that the collapse of the frontier and of access to the east dealt a debilitating blow to the integrity of the Ur III state, one that triggered a variety of consequences that lead to its ultimate political collapse. There must have been critical parallel military and organizational developments that weakened the state from within, because all available evidence suggests that Ibbi-Sin's armies could do nothing to stop any of this or to take back the areas that had seceded from the realm. But in light of current knowledge, it is reasonable to assume that most of the symptoms of organizational and structural disintegration that are observable after IS3 came about in direct consequence of the resurgence of Šimaški and of the dissolution of the military defenses in Susiana and the Diyala. Amorites, the weather, hypothetical developments in Syria—none of these had anything to do with this phase of the Ur III collapse.

The Usurpation of Power by Išbi-Erra

To complicate matters further, a man by the name of Išbi-Erra declared himself the independent ruler of the city of Isin and nearby Nippur. But although he figures here and there in Mesopotamian historiography, his identity and the chronology of his usurpation are not easily explained. He is mentioned only once in the entire Ur III archival documentation, and then only after his assumption of the throne of Isin (*UET* 3 1421:5, IS14.6.16).[28] We know of him from texts dated to his own reign, from later copies of a small number of royal hymns, from CKU, from the *Sumerian*

---

28. The document records rations for ⸢puzur₄⸣-ᵈšul-gi and puzur₄-lu-lu, the latter described as lú-⸢kíǧ⸣-gi₄-[a] iš-bi-èr-ra, and they are both lú ì-si-inᵏⁱ-me-éš (lines 3–5). The tablet is in Baghdad and cannot be collated.

King List, and from the anecdotal *Tumal Inscription*.[29] According to the letter of Ibbi-Sin to Puzur-Numušda (PuIb1, 23), he seems to have come from Mari. A fragment of a later copy of an Išbi-Erra hymn likewise proclaims his Mari origins (Michalowski 2005b). The rulers of this Syrian city had been closely allied with the house of Ur, and there is circumstantial evidence suggesting that the troubles affecting both dynasties may have been related, but this is admittedly highly speculative (Michalowski 2004). Whatever his origin, Išbi-Erra was successful in his bid for independent power, but the exact date and the circumstances surrounding this event are difficult to establish from information outside of the CKU.

Old Babylonian school texts aside, the reign of Išbi-Erra is documented primarily by a substantial group of illegally excavated accounts from a craft archive that is presumed to come from the city of Isin, a handful of tablets from Nippur, and a year-name list of unknown provenance, all of which have been analyzed by Van De Mieroop (1987). The chronology of Išbi-Erra's reign has to be reconstructed on the basis of the date-list, broken on the top and bottom, that preserves 23 consecutive year-names, to which must be added 12 additional year-formulas known from economic texts (Baqir 1948). The problem is how to fit the additional year-names at the beginning and end of the date-list; various schemes have been proposed and are summarized by Van De Mieroop (1987: 120–28), who offers a new reconstruction, which seems to be the best that we can hope for, given the current state of the documentation. According to him, the first-known year-name of the new king was actually his fourth, and therefore we are still missing years one through three. Moreover, he argues for a synchronism between IS8 and IE4—the last Ibbi-Sin year documented from Nippur and the first year of the Isin craft archive, a position that appears to have been generally accepted.[30]

It is difficult to establish the exact moment when Išbi-Erra became independent from Ur. In symbolic terms, independence would have been proclaimed by the instigation of a dating system recognizing the reign of the new king, but it is more than likely that for all practical purposes Išbi-Erra could have been acting independently for some time before this happened. As already noted, the Isin documents begin in what most scholars believe to be his fourth year, but there is no guarantee that we have the whole archive, and this is surely a chance find from one of many in the capital city. The slightly earlier tablets from Nippur are more informative. They come in two distinct groups: tablets dug up at the end of the 19th century from private houses (PH) and the archives of the Inana temple (IT) excavated after WW II.[31] Tablets with Ibbi-Sin dates extend to year seven, with a spike in year six and a decline in year seven. The last such document from this area comes from IS7.5.7-12 (6 NT 378),

---

29. These have been discussed recently by Frayne 1982, Vanstiphout 1989–90, and Michalowski 2005a.

30. See, for example, Lafont 1995: 9 and Charpin 2004a: 60.

31. Zettler 1992; Lafont 1995: 8–11. I have benefited from discussing these matters with Richard Zettler.

and then there are two texts dated IE4 and 6, respectively, that also belong to the same archive.[32] The situation is somewhat different in the private houses, where the documentation appears to extend into IS8, spiking in years two and three (Lafont 1995: 9). The evidence for IS8 at Nippur is not very solid, however. Only two texts from PH are dated to this year, *NRVN* 118 (month 2) and *NATN* 533 (month 3).[33] Both records are dated to early months of IS8, and one could assume either that Išbi-Erra imposed his dating scheme in the middle of the year or that in a few private archives the change of power was not yet acknowledged, by omission or by design. Moreover, if Išbi-Erra's control over Nippur was originally sanctioned by the Crown, as is reported in CKU but cannot be otherwise confirmed, then it is possible that Ibbi-Sin dates could have continued to be in use for a time, even though the city was effectively under new rule.

Finally, one must say a word about the Ur III administrative tablets found at Ur, which can be seen in a new light as a result of work done by Magnus Widell (2003). It is now clear that all of them were found in secondary contexts and therefore came from incomplete, disturbed archives. Nevertheless, some patterns can be discerned. Widell (2003: 98) was able to demonstrate that the largest numbers of Ibbi-Sin texts, found in the third season of excavations at Ur, derive from two distinct archives, one containing tablets from IS1–8 (peaking between IS5 and 8) and another containing mostly materials from IS14, with some from IS15 and IS16. The clustering demonstrates the limitations of our knowledge about the last decades of the Ur III kingdom.

Is there anything to be learned from this accumulation of information, all of it imperfect and from a limited range of heterogeneous sources? As described above, the Nippur evidence, while not abundant, does not undermine the hypothesis that Išbi-Erra began his own dating system in the city in the year corresponding to IS8, but concrete evidence is sparse, and there may have been an overlap in dating by both kings. But even if we assume that this synchronism holds, it still does not solve all of our problems. The Ur III Nippur IT archives cease in IS7, but they also contain two Išbi-Erra tablets, one dated IE4 and another dated IE6.[34] The former has the very same year-formula that marks the earliest-known tablet from the Isin craft texts. One wonders if this is simply coincidence or if this is really the first real year of Išbi-Erra's reign and his first three years are essentially a fiction, used locally somewhere before he actually obtained control of Nippur and Isin. Almost everywhere one looks, there is some disruption of archival activity around the end of IS2 or IS3 and again around years IS7 and IS8. This supports the idea that there was some political or military

---

32. 5 N-T 77 and 5 N-T 656, see Zettler 1992: 42–43 n. 33. As Zettler informs me (personal communication), all but fifty or so of the IT tablets come from a secondary context, from the fill of the platform built as a foundation for the Parthian temple (SB Level II).

33. Not all texts that supposedly come from Nippur were actually written or even found there. Nevertheless, *NRVN* 118 is from the city, because it is sealed by a scribe in service to the governor of Nippur and Ur-Ninurta, son of Munimah, who sealed *NATN* 533, is known from other Nippur texts, as is his father.

34. 5 N-T 77 and 5 N-T 656, respectively; see n. 23 above (p. 181).

set of events around the end of IS2 and then again approximately three or four years later when year-names of Išbi-Erra—beginning with his year four—appear at Nippur and Isin. These two tablets, which mention the same people who were in charge of the Inana temple in the time of Ibbi-Sin, bear witness to the administrative continuity that reached into the reign of Išbi-Erra, unaffected by the change of sovereign authority in the city (van Driel 1995: 396).

This first-attested year-name of Išbi-Erra—the one that is currently designated IE4—commemorated a victory over Kiritab, a city in the marshy defense zone of Akkad located not far from Marad and Kazallu, in the area that may have designated the mada in Šulgi's time, at least. This event, which would have happened just before the new king established himself in Nippur and Isin according to our scenario, suggests that he had both an army and a nearby base of operations before moving militarily on that city or that he already held Nippur before his own year-names began and already was operating from there. After his eighth year, Ibbi-Sin was boxed in around Ur, with even Girsu and Umma having left the fold, and it is unclear just how far up the Euphrates his control reached. The only military victories he could claim in his year-names were over enemies in the east, Huhnuri (YN9), Susa and Adamdun (YN14), and the "Amorites" (YN17), but the logistics of these victories are difficult to discern, and it is possible that some of these battles may have been fought in the alluvium, not in the highlands, and some may have been less successful than the Crown would want us to believe.[35] After 24 years on the throne, he lost his kingdom to armies from these very regions, and the house of Ur-Namma was no more; 9 years later, Išbi-Erra drove out the last Elamite garrison from Ur.

The Ibbi-Sin Correspondence (Letters 21–24)

The last four letters of the CKU purport to come from the time of the last king of Ur and consist of single epistolary exchanges between Ibbi-Sin and Išbi-Erra and between the monarch and Puzur-Numušda, his governor of Kazallu. How does this correspondence fit into the skeletal reconstruction of the political history of the times presented above?

The fragmentary and confusing documentation for the last decades of the Ur III state has tempted historians to reach for the RCU to illuminate the shadows, but even if one takes into account the general transmission and redactional problems of these literary letters already discussed earlier, the Ibbi-Sin epistolary quartet is unique, and their value as historical sources is difficult to evaluate. The distribution of the sources of the letters is uneven: two of the four letters have long and short versions, and at least one scribe compiled them into a connected narrative that is different from other epistolary collective tablets (A 7475, compilation tablet Xa).

---

35. Note the skepticism of Sallaberger (1999: 174) concerning the rhetoric of some of Ibbi-Sin's year-names. See also p. 191 below.

Let us take these issues one at a time, starting with the matter of source distribution, tabulated in the following chart:

IšIb1(21)	IbIš1 (22)	PuIb1 (23)	IbPu1 (24)[36]
3 Nippur	2 unknown	9 Nippur	4 Nippur
5 unknown		2 Ur	1 Kish
		1 Sippar	1 Sippar
		1 Susa	2 unknown
		5 unknown	

Only the two letters addressed to Ibbi-Sin are attested in House F in Nippur,[37] and the overall number of sources for each is quite different, 8 for IšIb1 and 18 for PuIb1—the latter the biggest number of manuscripts of any CKU item—but the distribution of these sources is very different. In general, it seems that the Puzur-Numušda letters are more broadly attested in the best-known scribal centers, and Išbi-Erra epistles are better documented outside of them, written on tablets of unknown origin. Moreover, the unprovenienced manuscripts of the first and final epistles in this quartet belong to longer redactions that differ substantially from the Nippur, Kish, and Sippar versions. All of these issues make it difficult to reconstruct an ideal Old Babylonian reception context, because it is impossible to know if anyone outside of the circle of the teacher and student involved in the writing of the collective tablet Xa that contains all of these letters was ever exposed to the full range of the epistolary history.

The Išbi-Erra–Ibbi-Sin Correspondence (Letters 21–22)

According to IšIb1 (21), Išbi-Erra had been dispatched to Kazallu to purchase grain for the capital. This fits in well with possible shortage of grain in the city in IS6–8, if we are to follow the evidence marshaled by Gomi (1984). By this time, dated tablets from Umma and Lagaš had ceased, and one must assume that Ur would have been unable to obtain food supplies from these provinces and therefore needed deliveries from farther north. The letter also mentions Amorite incursions into the area south of Kazallu and refers to a war with Elam. As A. Falkenstein (1950), C. Wilcke (1970), and others have long observed, the Išbi-Erra correspondence must date just before IS8 or early in that year, when Nippur passed into the hands of the future king of Isin. This also explains why the year after the empire essentially collapsed would be named after a victory over Huhnuri, "the bolt to the land of Anšan," and why Išbi-Erra had to defeat Kiritab in his third year (IE4), which would have

36. Strictly speaking, there are four tablets with this letter from Nippur, but N2 and N1 were written in sequence by the same student and therefore should be counted as one manuscript for our purposes.

37. Sources N1 of IšIb1[21] and PuIb1 [24].

been equivalent to IS7. Granted, it is difficult to know what was meant by the term "Elam" (elam^{ki}) in Ur III usage, but there is evidence that it designated the highland regions to the east and did not include Susiana (Michalowski 2008b). By this time, Susa was in the hands of Ebarat or Kindattu, but they would probably have been referred to as rulers of Šimaški.

Any discussion of the historical inferences of CKU must disregard the answer from Ibbi-Sin (IbIš1 [22]), which is undoubtedly an Old Babylonian fabrication stitched together from elements of other letters. Moreover, there are only two extant manuscripts, both unprovenienced, and both utilize very poor Sumerian that makes little sense in places. The composition and transmission of this letter is curious, to say the least, because the two versions differ substantially and yet share the same overall disregard for many rules of Old Babylonian Sumerian grammar. The source of much of the missive is not the epistle that it answers but the Puzur-Numušda correspondence (PuIb1 [23] and PuIb1 [24]), which is refashioned, without much historical sense, to fit the purpose. But although this letter seems to have been marginal in antiquity, today it is one of the most cited or paraphrased items of the CKU. Many historians have interpreted the letter as a blackmail message wherein Išbi-Erra, having been sent on a mission to purchase grain, wants to sell it back to the king for twice the price. The only source available until now, *OECT* 5 27, was published in 1976, but a somewhat imperfect hand-copy made many years earlier by Petrus van der Meer had been in circulation for some time among Sumerologists. Samuel Noah Kramer (1976: 9) realized well that the narrative deals with accusations of cheating, not blackmail, but this seems to have escaped the notice of many. The spurious nature of this text requires us to withhold all reference to it in the historical reconstruction of Ibbi-Sin's reign, even if it sheds interesting light on what some Old Babylonians thought about such matters.

What is puzzling in the whole affair is the focus on Kazallu. One would not normally expect this region to be a source of large amounts of grain and, therefore, if the CKU were in any way to be believed, it seems likely that the harvest actually took place farther upstream, perhaps in the Sippar region, and that Kazallu was only a relay point at which the sale took place.

E. Robson (2002: 351) and, following her, W. W Hallo (2006: 98), have claimed that IšIb1 (21) is likewise a school concoction, created in part to illustrate mathematical exercises. She writes:

> The letter reads suspiciously like an OB school mathematics problem: the first paragraph gives the silver-grain exchange rate and the total amount of silver available (72,000 shekels); in the second the silver has been correctly converted into grain. Next that huge capacity measure is divided equally among large. . . . As is typical for school mathematical problems, the numbers are conspicuously round and easy to calculate with. The numbers in the final, damaged part . . . are reminiscent of the final multiplicands of a standard multiplication table or the sexagesimal fractions $\frac{1}{3}$, $\frac{1}{2}$, [$\frac{2}{3}$], $\frac{5}{6}$. The letter, at one level, is no more than a pretext to show simple mathematics and metrology at work in a quasi-realistic context.

This is an attractive proposal, but it does not stand up to scrutiny; it is based on incorrect older readings of the numbers. Moreover, elements such as figures were undoubtedly redacted over time and would not, in themselves, discredit the whole composition, even if some changes may have been motivated by instructional goals. All the literary letters, including the Isin dynasty literary epistles (SEpM 2–5), use simple, round numbers, primarily multiples of 600. In the case of this letter, the fractions in the damaged passage are not in the composition as it is currently reconstructed. Robson utilized the Oxford on-line edition of the text and read lines 13–16:

> Let my lord repair 600 barges of 120 gur draught each; 72 solid boats, 20. . . , 30 bows, [40] rudders (?), 50 . . . and 60 (?) boat doors on the boats (?), may he also . . . all the boats.

This passage is admittedly difficult; my reconstruction of the text is different, and although it is hardly secure, the fractions are not present.

The figures in the text have attracted attention because they may reflect school mathematics more than practical and historical concerns. But there are other issues at stake as well, ones that might reveal the motives or thoughts attributable to the correspondents, or at least of one of them. Išbi-Erra reports that he has acquired 72,000 kor of grain; this, like 7,200, is a standard "very large number" in CKU, and even if it did at one point represent a historical reality, it has been adjusted for didactic purposes. Later in the letter, he declares (IšIb1: 28 [21]): "There is (enough) grain in my city to provision your palace and all of its residents for fifteen years." Note the use of the noun šà-gal, "provisions, food, fodder"; in Ur III times, this term is "used for barley rations for animals but also for captives and for the érin class of workers/soldiers" (Gelb 1965: 232). Taking the standard Ur III ration of 60 liters per month for a grown man, this would be enough to feed 2,000 workers for 15 years, but if we take into account that the total figure refers to grain before it has been threshed, the number of workers supported would be much smaller. However, this does not take into account the unspoken assumption that the elites of the capital, and especially of the palace, would require much better alimentary treatment. Presumably, Išbi-Erra is claiming that he has even more grain on hand in Isin and is ready to save his king from any shortages in the capital, but it is also possible that the numbers are meant to be ironic or even threatening.

There are other problems with the text, however. Ever since Thorkild Jacobsen (1953) edited the first 13 lines of IšIb1 (21), historians have used this letter and its answer as evidence of nefarious blackmail that led to the loss of Isin and Nippur and, eventually, to the downfall of the Ur III state: Išbi-Erra takes advantage of a grain crisis in Ur to force Ibbi-Sin to pay him double for provisions that he was sent to purchase with funds provided by the crown. A closer investigation of the narrative and of the figures involved complicates matters and raises other questions. I should note that this discussion is only concerned with the "short version" of IšIb1 (21), because it is clear that the non-Nippurean additions of the "long versions" are without any doubt Old Babylonian in date and have no historical relevance whatsoever.

Išbi-Erra, whose role in the Ur III kingdom is never defined, writes to his king, reminding him that his brief was to travel to Kazallu, in the old Šulgi defense zone, to purchase grain, and he did so at the price of one kor (ca. 300 liters) per shekel of silver. The line reads (IšIb1: 5):

šakanka 1 gur-ta-àm še sá-di/sá ba-an-dug₄
As the market price of grain was equivalent to one (shekel) per kor . . ."

Jacobsen (1953: 41) complicated matters in his commentary to the text, stating:

> Assuming that . . . Ishbī-Erra's grain-buying expedition, which bought at the exceedingly favorable rate of two *gur* to a shekel, could only have taken place at harvest time, we may with a fair degree of probability assume that he wrote early in Ibbī-Suen's sixth year.

But this is not what the text says. One can only surmise that Jacobsen confused the letter from Išbi-Erra with Ibbi-Sin's reply in IbIš1 (22). The king's response, which is reported in the spurious epistle, will be left out of the historical discussion, because it only illuminates the manner in which some non-Nippurean school circles viewed the affair, as noted above.

With Jacobsen's commentary set aside, the central issue is that the numbers presented here do not testify, at first glance, to any grain shortage in the Kazallu region, because Išbi-Erra reports that the price of grain there is one kor per one shekel of silver, and this is the standard average rate encountered in most Ur III documents (Gomi 1984: 231). A closer reading of what follows reveals that this is the price of unthreshed grain—on the stalk—while the normal rate is always calculated in relationship to the grains of barley. The king claims that Išbi-Erra purchased the grain at half the going rate, but delivered, or offered to deliver it, at the normal price of one shekel per kor, as if it had already been threshed.

Išbi-Erra then informs the king that he wanted to transport his acquisitions to a safe threshingfloor for processing but that hostile Amorites had entered the mada, and therefore he has taken all of the grain into the city of Isin for protection. He goes on to state that the Amorites have now entered the mada and have taken over all of its fortresses. Previous translations have rendered mada by the neutral term "country," but in light of the discussion presented in chap. 4, I will assume here that mada is a technical term referring to the defensive frontier territory, although it also possible that the meaning here is closer to "countryside."[38] If, for the sake of the argument, we situate this letter in the historical reality of Ibbi-Sin's early years, we must assume that the Diyala Valley region has already been lost, and the military would have retreated back to the old Šulgi defense zone around Apiak, Marad, and Kazallu, and that this is the area once again designated as mada. The exact date may

---

38. For example, Jacobsen 1953: 47: "Reports that hostile Martus had entered the plains having been received (lit., 'heard') 144,000 *gur* grain (representing) the grain in its entirety was brought into Isin."

be unclear, but the time of year is obvious: it must be during or right after the harvest, because there is not even time to thresh the grain. The urgency of the matter explains the price, which is normal for the period, but only for threshed barley and not for grain on the stalk. Up to this point, the author's explanations make sense, but then he provides further clarification of his situation: because of security issues, he is stuck in Isin with the unthreshed barley; if only the king would provide him with a flotilla of armed barges, he could send it all to a safe place for drying and processing. Apparently there is no space in Isin to do this, which may seem to be a disingenuous claim, but we lack any further clarification of the matter.

More disconcerting is the claim that the armed fleet is necessary because of hostile Amorites. This implies that the enemy is actually threatening the areas between Isin and Ur, and there is no way, at present, of establishing the veracity of this assertion, since the historical record of the time is limited to year-names and a handful of administrative documents. Moreover, Išbi-Erra proposes bypassing the hostiles by means of two watercourses, the Idkura and the Palištum, but neither of these is attested from any Ur III document. If Idkura is indeed located in the vicinity of Isin, this may provide some indication of the geographical horizon that lies behind the text, but the details escape us for the moment.[39] Finally, one might very well inquire why he cannot deliver the barley in its unthreshed form to Ur and have it threshed in the city. This may all very well be Old Babylonian fantasy, but the rhetoric reveals a form of blackmail, albeit of a kind that is different from what has been assumed by most historians: both correspondents know that none of this is true. The issue is not really grain but royal sanction for Išbi-Erra's control of Isin, which is already in his hands, because that is presumably where his letter originates.

At this point, it is necessary to refer, if ever so briefly, to the spurious letter that contains Išbi-Erra's answer to the king of Ur. As already noted, for almost half a century, this epistle has been cited as evidence that the usurper blackmailed Ibbi-Sin by demanding to be paid a double price for the grain that he had obtained in Kazallu. The history of various interpretations has been well summarized by Kutscher (1982: 585–86) and will not be repeated here. The veracity of IbIš1 (22) aside, the figures in this text are not intended as a request for double payment but reflect school traditions of the kind addressed by Robson and cited above in connection with IšIb1 (21). Because the amounts of grain reported by Išbi-Erra are weighed in an unthreshed state, the person or persons who invented the response concocted an answer that recognized the fact and addressed the issue in numerical terms.

In the final section of his letter, Išbi-Erra urges the king not to be discouraged by the progress of a war with Elam. As already noted, the only conflict with "Elam" that this could possibly refer to is the series of events that was commemorated in the name of Ibbi-Sin's ninth year, describing his defeat of Huhnuri on the borders of

---

39. See the commentary to IšIb1 (21).

Anšan; this was already observed by Wilcke (1970: 54).[40] If the letter were in harmony with actual historical events, it would mean that the war with Huhnuri was not going very well. The name of Ibbi-Sin's ninth year is incomplete; at present one can read it as (Steinkeller 2007a: 223 n. 31):

mu ^{d}i-bí-^{d}en.zu, lugal uri$_5$^{ki}-ma-ke$_4$ hu-úh-nu-ri^{ki} sag-kul ma-da an-ša-an^{ki}-šè (var.: elam^{ki}) á dugud-(bi) ba-ši-in-DU [x] SUM? sa bí-in-ğar
Year: Ibbi-Sin, king of Ur, brought massive (military) force to Huhnuri, the lock of the land of Anšan/Elam (and) . . .

This formula marks the first of many hyperbolic year-names of Ibbi-Sin that have no parallel anywhere, certainly not in Ur III times. These year-names make one wonder if the grandiose claims are intended to mask minor accomplishments or even failures. The road to Huhnuri was last traversed by Ur III armies in the time of Amar-Sin, 20 years earlier (AS YN 7), as far as we know, but with Susa lost after IS3, the way could not have been easy this time.[41] Either Ibbi-Sin's troops had to make their way around the city and surrounding garrisons, or they had to retake it, and no evidence for such an effort is presently known. It is therefore equally likely that the war against the "Elamites" actually took place closer to home, not in Susiana and beyond. While it is possible that the event that is described as a defeat of Huhnuri in the name of Ibbi-Sin's ninth year may have actually been an attempt to reconquer Susa, there is no evidence that the Mesopotamians ever succeeded in doing so.[42]

The letter of Išbi-Erra certainly makes it clear that Ur was in need of grain and that it had to be procured from the northern part of the alluvial plain. It claims that Amorites were raiding the area around Kazallu and had even descended into the homeland, presumably into some of the areas that lay between Isin and Ur, and explains how Išbi-Erra obtained control of Isin and Nippur by sanction of the Crown. As bad as the situation may have been, it was not fatal; if indeed these events took place around IS8, then the kingdom still had a decade and half left before its final demise.

40. Jacobsen 1953: 40 suggested that the letter reflects events referred to in the year formula IS6.

41. The location of Huhnuri remains uncertain. Since the publication of an inscription of Amar-Sin found at Bormi that may be from this city, it has often been assumed that Huhnuri was somewhere in this vicinity (Nasrabadi 2005). As Henry Wright informs me: "It is unlikely that this text attributed to Bormi is in its original place. The site was been surveyed three times in the 1960s and 70s by myself, Eliabeth Carter, John Hansman, and Pierre de Miroschedji. It produced many ceramics, some inscribed bricks, and even an unbaked tablet fragment, but nothing earlier than Middle Elamite, when it was quite an important town. I suppose it was dragged from its original site, perhaps nearby in the unsurveyed eastern portion of the Ram Hormuz plain or perhaps as far away as Izeh or Behebahan, by a Middle Elamite literati. François Vallat, however, tells me that we do not have an eyewitness account of the recovery of the text, and it is possible it was not actually found at Bormi itself."

42. Sallaberger 1999: 173–74. For a different interpretation, see, e.g., Steinkeller 2007a: 223, who assumes that Ibbi-Sin's armies may have been able to retake Susa.

Even if we discount Ibbi-Sin's answer, there is nothing in the Išbi-Erra letter that contradicts anything we know from the historical record, even if this does not in any way guarantee its veracity. The situation is equally complex in the case of the Puzur-Numušda correspondence, albeit for very different reasons.

The Puzur-Numušda–Ibbi-Sin Correspondence (Letters 23–24)

It is a challenge to attempt to fit the bits of factual information contained in the Ibbi-Sin–Puzur-Numušda epistolary exchange into any historical context. The governor of Kazallu writes to the king, reporting a message he had received from Išbi-Erra, who demanded that he abandon Ibbi-Sin and switch sides (PuIb1 [23]). In the letter contained within the letter, the Isin king describes various events of his reign, and it is clear that these events took place over a number of years. Following Wilcke (1970: 57), many have dated this part of CKU to Ibbi-Sin's nineteenth year, but if my interpretation is correct, this correspondence—if it is not complete fiction—must be placed a few years later, during the very last part of his reign, as was already suggested by Jacobsen (1953: 44), possibly as late as the last year or two.[43]

And yet, all of this strains credulity: how can one imagine that, late in the reign of Ibbi-Sin, a dozen years after Išbi-Erra conquered nearby Kiritab, the king of Ur still controlled Kazallu and Girkal? Granted, we know absolutely nothing about Kazallu after the last known Ur III reference in ŠS 9.ix.18 (SAT 3 1892:8), and Girkal is unattested in this period. Nevertheless, is it difficult to imagine a pocket of governors loyal to Ur in this area late in Ibbi-Sin's reign. The Isin texts are of little help here, although texts dated to the reign of Išbi-Erra include sporadic references to Apiak, Marad, Mur, and Kiritab, located in the same general area, as well as to Borsippa and Kish farther upstream (Van De Mieroop 1987: 110), which suggests that Isin had unimpeded contact with the region.

Puzur-Numušda to Ibbi-Sin (PuIb1, Letter 23)

This complex Puzur-Numušda letter is unique in the Sumerian literary epistolary tradition. On the structural level, it is the only one that contains one letter within another. Moreover, the text that follows is divided into two sections, so that after the embedded letter the narrator twice asserts, "it was just as he had predicted (that is, 'said')," and in each case this is followed by an explanation of how Išbi-Erra's predictions came to pass.[44] I will return to these compositional devices, but first one must discuss the historical context of the epistle.

In PuIb1 (23), the prediction phrase provides a way of asserting that Išbi-Erra had fulfilled his boastful predictions while also commenting and expanding on his

---

43. For a somewhat different opinion, see Whiting 1987: 25 ("at the latest during Išbi-Erra 11").

44. bí-in-du$_{11}$-ga-gin$_7$-nam (PuŠ1: 23, 42).

achievements, grouping them in two sections, because the events that are narrated took place over a period of time. Išbi-Erra asserts that he has divine sanction to take over Sumer and offers a litany of possible future actions, including the ominous pledge to take over Kazallu, the very city of Puzur-Numušda, ending his own letter with the boast to rebuild the outer wall of the city of Isin and to rename it in his own fashion, establishing a tradition that would be followed by his successors on the throne of Isin. Puzur-Numušda then reports to Ibbi-Sin his belief that these predictions had come true (line 29), beginning his comments with the last promise, the rebuilding of the walls of Isin, an event that is also known from Išbi-Erra's twelfth year-name, equivalent, according to the dating scheme adopted here, to Ibbi-Sin's eighteenth year.

Immediately after confirming the fulfillment of this particular promise, Puzur-Numušda relates a series of political and military events (lines 43–46), including the capture of Nippur, which took place at least 11 years earlier, and it is impossible to ascertain if there is any chronological order or logic in this passage. After this section, the narrator once again uses the phrase in question, this time relating back to the first of Išbi-Erra's predictions (lines 7–13), to take over the banks of the Abgal and Me-Enlila branches of the Euphrates that lay south of Kish, and then once again moves on to add new information about the enemy's military progress. It is possible that the conquest of Kiritab in year three (YN 4) was part of this strategy. The structure of Puzur-Numušda's comments refer, in reverse order, to Išbi-Erra's initial and final predictions, thus using a complex trope to assert the veracity of everything else that the man of Isin had predicted, adding even more detail to underscore the seriousness of the dire situation that he now finds himself in. At the same time, he lays the ground for the admission that he will not be able to resist Išbi-Erra's coming onslaught on Kazallu and will be forced by superior odds to abandon his post.

The complex rhetoric of the letter creates a multilayered discourse that is open to many different interpretations, creating a "reality effect," if one is permitted to invoke Roland Barthes' (1968) much overused concept, by reciting specific names and places that require comment, replicating historical narrative to imitate and establish textual realism and to create a tension between implied reality and fiction. In lines 32–39 these are:

1. Niĝdugani of Nippur

Puzur-Numušda reports that Išbi-Erra took control of Nippur and stationed his own guard over the city and that he captured Niĝdugani, temple administrator (saĝa) of Nippur (lines 32–33). Although this is listed after the building of the wall of Isin, in historical terms it had to have taken place a few years earlier. No such person has been identified to date in the Ur III administrative record, although the name appears occasionally in accounts from Drehem, Umma, Girsu, and, most interestingly, Nippur. There were at last three individuals by that name in the city: a "scribe," son of Lu-duga (*NRVN* 1 212:4 and seal, n.d.[restored]), a captain (nu-banda₃ *NATN* 468:9, ŠS6.7.13), and a high official who served both as "cupbearer," and "gardener of the god Enlil," known only from the seal inscription of his son Ur-Meme, who inherited his father's position in Enlil's gardens (*NRVN* 1 36, ŠS9.8.-).

During this period, the title saǧa designated the highest administrator of temples or temple estates, and the association with a city seems to be out of place. Nippur was administered by a governor (énsi), and this is what one would expect in the context. There are, however, three examples of a saǧa of Nippur or of its god Enlil. The first is an Old Akkadian seal, known from multiple impressions, of one lugal-níǧ-zu énsi of Nippur and saǧa of the god Enlil (*RIME* 2 E2.6.2.1). The second, likewise Old Akkadian, is mentioned in an orchard sale document: *JCS* 35 151 no. 6:5; ur-ǧidri saǧa nibru^ki. The third dates from the time of Šulgi—it bears no year-name— and was published in *RA* 74 47 116:11 (the governor of the city is mentioned two lines earlier).

The last Ur III references to a saǧa of Enlil and a governor of Nippur come from IS2 and IS3, respectively. The first is in the form of a seal inscription of a servant of lugal-á-zi-da saǧa ^den-líl-lá (*NATN* 858, IS 2.3.8; the same man was pisaǧ-dub-ba lugal saǧa ^den-líl-lá on his own seal, *JCS* 19 28:3, IS1), and the second is a tablet with a seal inscription of a servant of the governor Dada (*MVN* 3 116, IS3.-.-). The office of the governor of Nippur was held, for most of the duration of the Ur III period, by the descendants of Ur-Meme, which had connections with the Inana temple (Hallo 1972; Zettler 1984; Hattori 2006), and the last of this line was Dada, who is attested until IS8; a dedicatory seal of one of his scribes was used on the penultimate Ur III tablet from the city, dated IS8.2.-.[45] This suggests that, even if Dada was not physically present in Nippur at the time of Išbi-Erra's takeover, he was Ibbi-Sin's last serving governor there. Given the paucity of information, it is not impossible to imagine that, by the time Nippur changed hands, the governor had fled and the city administration was in the hands of a saǧa, but at present this can only remain speculation.

2. Zin(n)um and the Land of Subir (line 34)

Previous translations of PuIb1: 34 (23) identify Zinnum as the "governor of Subir,"[46] but, for reasons that are explained in the philological commentary to the line, I prefer to render it as "(His ally), the ruler/governor Zinnum, took prisoners in Subir." Certainly the notion of an énsi of Subir is difficult to accept, because "Subir" serves as a general areal designation in early Mesopotamian usage and is never used to refer to a political entity. The documentary evidence gives us no clues as to the areas that might have been imagined as Subir in Ur III times; although the geographical term occurs in CKU, it is not used even once in the surviving Ur III documentation. Its appearance in some letters of CKU may be anachronistic; one

45. *NRVN* 118; see Zettler 1984: 5.
46. E.g.,Whiting 1987: 23; Wu 1994: 9. The normalization and linguistic identity of the name are uncertain.

assumes that the general orientation is in the Trans-Tigris area, north, northeast, and northwest of the Diyala, but this is all that one can say.[47]

As first noted by Whiting (1987: 26 n. 77), a person named Zinnum (*zi-nu-um*) is the recipient of a diplomatic gift in an early Isin dynasty tablet, but even though the fact that he receives such a bequest suggests that he is an important foreigner, nothing more is known about him.[48] More important has been the claim, made by J. J. van Dijk (1978: 199), that the Zinnum of PuIb1 (23) is also documented in the final lines of the third kirugu of *Išbi-Erra Hymn B*. Here are the first preserved lines on the first column of the reverse of CBS 14051. My readings and interpretations differ somewhat from van Dijk's original edition and from the on-line ECTSL version, but most of this is irrelevant for the purposes of our discussion:

1'. [. . .] ⌜im?-ma?-an?⌝- [. . .]
2'. [x x x x] x x x x-šub-dè ur₅ mi-ni-in-⌜dug₄?⌝
3'. [x x (x)]x ⌜níĝ⌝-gur₈ gil-sa-a-bi barag-šè mu-un-dù
4'. [ti?-id?]-⌜nu⌝-um[49] lú šu-ta šub-ba-bi ᵈen?-ki? maškim-bi-im
5'. ᶦᵈburanun-na ᶦᵈidigna ᶦᵈkir₁₁-sig íd-kiš^ki zag-bi im-mi-in-gu₇
6'. eden bar-rim₄ líl bu-bu-da enmen-e mi-ni-in-ug₇
7'. ki-in-da-tu lú elam^ki-ma-ra inim-bi ba-an-na-de₆
8'. an-ša-an^ki-e šimaški šeg₁₁ ba-ab-gi₄ kur im-ma-an-te
9'. ⌜ugnim⌝-ma-ni pu-úh-ru-um-bi inim mu-na-ni-ib-bé
10'. ki-ru-gú eš₅-kam-ma

. . .
. . . . thus he spoke?(:)
. . . he placed (all) its goods and treasures into sacks,
And as for the scattered forces of *Tidnum, Enki was their protector*;
(Some) he fed at the banks of the Tigris, Euphrates, Kirsig,[50] and Kish watercourses,
(But) killed (others) by thirst in the phantom-filled desert.
Word of this was brought to the highlander Kindattu;
Anšan and Šimaški screamed out (in horror); he approached the highland
And addressed his assembled armies.
The third kirugu.

I have collated the tablet a number of times. It is written in a very small hand and is admittedly not easy to read. As much as I respect the knowledge and effort that it

---

47. ArŠ1: 3 (1) and ArŠ2: 6 (3, in association with Simurum). On the concept of Subir, see Michalowski 1986, 1999a, 2008, as well as Steinkeller 1998. See now also Arkhipov 2002: 93–94.

48. *BIN* 9 332:18, dated IE9. The same name appears also in the undated tablet *BIN* 10 188:7.

49. This is, admittedly, a tenuous restoration, and there may not be enough space to justify it. Note that ⌜ti-id⌝-nu-um⌜ki⌝ is mentioned in *Išbi-Erra Hymn Hymn A*, in a very fragmentary context (A iii 5).

50. On this watercourse, see above, p. 141.

took to offer the first edition of this difficult and fragmentary composition, try as I might, I cannot see the traces of the first sign in the beginning word in line 4′ that van Dijk read as [z]i-nu-um.[51] The second sign of his reading is not as clear as his copy suggests, and while my own suggestion may not be much better, Zinnum's name is simply not present.

3. Hamazi (line 35)

The city or territory of Hamazi is first attested in a famous third-millennium diplomatic letter from the Syrian city of Ebla (Neumann 2006: 2–3). Ur III documents from the reign of Amar-Sin record the names of two persons who were designated as énsi, Lu-Nanna and Ur-Iškur, but then in the latter part of Šu-Sin's reign Hamazi was part of the extensive border territories that were controlled, perhaps only nominally, by the grand vizier Arad-Nanna (Owen 1988: 116 n. 10). Ur-Iškur appears as late as ŠS7.11.29 (*PDT* 1 475), when his bride, or daughter-in-law, Tabur-ḫattum, traveled to Hamazi from Sumer. The Sumerian names of the two men may suggest that they were governors appointed by the Crown, as do certain texts that suggest that Hamazi contributed frontier taxes to the Ur III state.[52] There can be little doubt, however, that Tabur-ḫattum was a royal daughter and, therefore, her marriage to the ruling house of Hamazi suggests that it was a client state—though its status must have fluctuated from independence to official incorporation into the kingdom of Ur.[53] It is difficult to pinpoint where Hamazi lay, but the location could not have been very far from Mesopotamia; all evidence points to the east, to the immediate border region (Steinkeller 2010: 373 n. 19; see Appendix D).

4. Nur-aḫum (Nur-Ea), Ruler of Ešnunna (Line 36)

Ešnunna became independent of Ur at the time of Šu-iliya or perhaps even under his predecessor Ituria, who was originally the appointed governor of the city (Wu 1994: 2–11; Reichel 2001: 17). In true historical terms, Nur-aḫum was an independent ruler whose scribes used the Sumerian term énsi as a logogram for Akkadian *iššiakum*, "king," although his predecessor Šu-iliya carried the Babylonian title *šarrum*. At Ešnunna, the name is always written *nu-úr-a-ḫu-um*; curiously, in CKU it is rendered as *nu-úr-a-ḫi*, just as in the only Ur III attestation of the name (*TCCBI* 2 35: 8, ŠS5.-.-, Nippur).

---

51. Van Dijk read the line as [z]i-nu-um lú-šu-ta-šub-ba-bi edin-bar-rim$_4$(maškim?)-bi-im, and translated, "Quant à Zinnum, celui qui s'était échappé, c'était dans la terre brûlée de la steppe." The ECTSL rendition is: "As for Zinnum, who escaped from them, Enki is their *maškim*." Vanstiphout (1989–90: 55) also accepted the reading of Zinnum'a name in the line.

52. E.g., *JCS* 31 166 A (AS8.5.8), or *PDT* 2 959 or *MVN* 15 179, neither of which can be precisely dated but must come from late in the reign of Šu-Sin or early in the time of Ibbi-Sin.

53. Tabur-ḫattum, who is not always mentioned by name, is attested for almost a decade, beginning with a cluster of texts from three successive days (17–19) in the eleventh month of AS9, when Šu-Sin was already on the throne (*BIN* 3 382: 5; *Ontario* 1 160:2; *Torino* 1 261:2) until ŠS7.11.29 (*PDT* 1 454: 3).

There is no better example of the difficulties of utilizing the CKU letters as historical sources than the matter of the first years of independence of Ešnunna in the waning years of the Ur III dynasty. Excavations at Tell Asmar, the modern name of the city mound, have provided material and inscriptional data that provide some information on these matters. In the first major publication of this material, Thorkild Jacobsen (1940) provided a tentative reconstruction of the transition from Ur III to independent rule in Ešnunna without mentioning the CKU, which was then hardly known to the scholarly world. Subsequently, Falkenstein (1950) and Jacobsen (1953) himself revealed the complex textual tradition of the Ibbi-Sin correspondence, and since that time, all others who have studied the matter have used this additional data in their analysis, adding them to the information gleaned from the Asmar excavations.

Briefly stated, the currently accepted historical scenario can be summarized as follows: In the latter half of Ibbi-Sin's third year, Ešnunna's governor Ituria, or possibly his son, Šu-ilija, turned his back on the king of Ur and declared autonomy. Shortly thereafter, however, an invasion by "Subarians/Subartu" ended this experiment in independence, but the situation was saved: Nur-aḫum, the "legitimate" ruler of Ešnunna, was reinstated with the help of Išbi-Erra of Isin (Whiting 1987: 26; Wu 1994: 6; Reichel 2001a: 18; 2001b: 103; Saporetti 2002: 52). The supporting evidence for this historical reconstruction consists of a year-name recovered from two tablets from Ešnunna and of a passage from the Puzur-Numušda letter (PuIb1 [23]), as interpreted originally by Jacobsen and accepted by all subsequent followers. The pertinent lines of the epistle are:

34. ᶦzi-in-nu-um énsi su-bir$_4$ᵏⁱ-a šaḡaᵃ i-ni-in-dab$_5$
35. ha-ma-ziᵏⁱ nam-ra-aš im-mi-in-ak
36. ᶦnu-úr-a-hi énsi èš-nun-naᵏⁱ
37. ᶦšu-ᵈen-líl énsi kišiᵏⁱ-a
38. ù ᶦpuzur$_4$-ᵈtu-tu énsi bàd-zi-ab-baᵏⁱ
39. ki-ni-šè ba-an-gur-ru-uš

There are grammatical difficulties and ambiguities here that can result in different translations; here is what I have settled on, justified in the commentary to the edition:

[34](His ally), the ruler/governor Zinnum, took prisoners in Subir [35] (and) plundered Hamazi. [36] Nur-aḫum, ruler of Ešnunna, [37] Šu-Enlil, ruler of Kish, [38] and Puzur-Tutu, ruler of Borsippa [39] *came over to his side.*

Whiting (1987: 23), following Jacobsen, rendered it as follows:

He (Išbi-Erra) took captive Zinnum, ensi of Su-bir$_4$ᵏⁱ, plundered Hamazi, (and) returned Nur-aḫum, ensi of Eshnunna, Šu-Enlil, ensi of Kish, and Puzur-Tutu, ensi of Bad-Ziabba, (each) to his place.

These events were then linked to the enigmatic year-name:

mu ᵈtišpak lugal-e sağduₓ(SAG×DU) su-bir₄-a-ke₄ tibir₂-ra bí-in-ra-a
The year that (the god) King Tišpak smashed the head of Subir.

Jacobsen (1940: 171) argued that this was the name of Nur-aḫum's first year, and it was the basis for the following observation by Whiting (1987: 24):

> Since the Kazallu letter and the Eshnunna year date seem to agree on the fact that Nur-aḫum came to the throne in the wake of a defeat of Subartu, it seems likely that the two sources refer to the same event and that Nur-aḫum was placed on the throne by Išbi-Erra. A corollary to this conclusion is that the reign of Nur-aḫum's predecessor, Šuilija, was brought to an end by a defeat at the hands of Subartu and that the city of Eshnunna was in imminent danger of falling into its hands when Išbi-Erra intervened.

More recently, Reichel (2001a: 18) claimed that:

> Ešnunna's powerful position seems to have ended around 2010 B.C. with an invasion of Subartu, an event known from a letter written by Puzur-Numušda of Kazallu to king Ibbi-Sin of Ur.

If my interpretation of the pertinent passage in PuIb1 (23) is correct, there is no evidence for any "Subarian" intervention in the dynastic succession at Ešnunna, even if a year-name from the city testifies to a military confrontation with some forces from a region described as Subartu; all of these speculations on the history of Ešnunna should be laid aside.

5. Šu-Enlil of Kish (Line 37)

Although a number of individuals having the name Šu-Enlil are known from Ur III times, not one of them is a governor and none are connected in any way with the city of Kish. The Babylonian city is first attested on Š43, but its governor is not mentioned by name (*Princeton* 2 1 r. 5 i 2′). The city was still in the orbit of the Ur kingdom in IS2.9.3 (MVN 10 144 r. iii 17) but disappears from the Ur III records thereafter. An important individual named Šu-Enlil, unfortunately without any title, appears in two texts from Ešnunna in texts that date from the time of Nur-aḫum, and R. Whiting (1987: 23) suggests that he is "presumably the ensi of Kish mentioned in the letter." As with all other individuals mentioned in PuIb1 (23), with the possible exception of Girbubu, I have translated énsi as "ruler" rather than "governor," on the assumption that, by the time this letter was purportedly written, cities so far north of Ur could not have been under the direct control of Ur, with the possible exception of a small enclave around Girkal and Kazallu.

6. Puzur-Tutu of Badziaba (Line 38)

A governor of Babylon named ⌜puzur₄-tu⌝-tu is mentioned in MVN 8 139 rev. ii 8 (IS 2.6.-). Frayne (1997: 379) identified this man with Puzur-Tutu of Badziaba of the letter, noting that Borsippa is located only 18 kilometers from Babylon.[54] Other than this, the name occurs only once in a text from AS7 (*Ontario* 1 70:6).

The place-name written as bàd-zi-ab-ba^{ki} is unattested before the Old Babylonian period, and the identification of Badziaba with Borsippa is uncertain. In later times, it is well attested as a logographic writing for the name of the city, but it is only a surmise that it was used for Borsippa in OB times or earlier. The writing bàd-zi-ab-ba^{ki} occurs only twice outside of CKU in OB: in a Nippur "forerunner" to Hh XX–XXII (line 32, *MSL* 11 105), and in a school text dubbed *The Slave and the Scoundrel* by its editor, Martha Roth (1983: 276 line 34). In documents and letters of the OB period, the standard writing is bar-zi-pa, which is already attested in texts from Isin from the time of Išbi-Erra (*BIN* 9 415 [IE25.3.16]; *BIN* 9 479 [IE25.7.-]; *Rochester* 243:24 [IE28.2.7]; *BIN* 9 391 [IE28.3.24]) and Šu-ilišu (*BIN* 9 452 [ŠI1.10.11?]). It is also mentioned in year-names of early kings of Babylon: Sumu-la-el YN28 and Apil-Sin YN1c.

Following the repetition of the sentence "it was just as he had predicted" (line 42), Puzur-Numušda mentions two more proper names (lines 44–45).

7. Iddi of Malgium (Line 44)

The philological difficulties of line 44 are discussed in the commentary to the text. Malgium, which lay somewhere on the Tigris close to the Diyala Valley (Kutscher and Wilcke 1978: 101 n. 28), is not otherwise attested, to my knowledge, before the time of Gungunum of Larsa (YN 19).

8. Girbubu of Girkal (45)

Until very recently, neither the personal name nor the city had been attested in Ur III archival texts, but the general location of the latter could be deduced from the introduction to the *Code of Ur-Namma*, where it is listed in tandem with Akšak, Marad, and Kazallu.[55] According to Frayne (1992: 23), Girkal lay in the old Šulgi defense zone, immediately adjacent to Apiak. In March, 2011, when this book was already in page proofs, Piotr Steinkeller kindly informed me that the name occurs in an Ur III tablet from the Schøyen Collection, MS 2643, which will be fully published by Jacob Dahl; the photograph had been posted on the CDLI web site with the number P251672. A person by the name of gir-bu-bu, who serves as ugula in connection with workers from Adab, is listed on the last line of what seems to be the reverse. The tablet is unprovenianced and undated, but it includes two individuals with names that incorporate Šu-Sin's name, and therefore it must have been composed either in that ruler's time or early in the reign of Ibbi-Sin. The document may come from Umma, but because it mentions a number of otherwise unknown people

---

54. Modern Birs Nimrud, "located 17 km southwest of Babylon as the flow flies," according to Zadok (2006: 389).

55. See p. 130 above.

and waterways (in addition to the Tigris and íd-lugal), it is possible that it comes from some other locality in the province, perhaps from the same place as the tablet published by Michalowski and Daneshmand (2005).

As I understand Puzur-Numušda's rhetoric, he is trying to convince the king of Ur that his own situation is hopeless and that he must abandon Kazallu to Išbi-Erra. All the major cities in the northern part of the kingdom have already allied themselves with the Isin monarch, as has Ešnunna on the other side of the Tigris. Only neighboring Girkal tried to oppose Išbi-Erra's man in Malgium, but its army was defeated and its leader taken prisoner.

Ibbi-Sin to Puzur-Numušda (IbPu1, Letter 24)

The king's answer to Puzur-Numušda pushes the limits of epistolary history-making. The king chastises Puzur-Numušda for not confronting Išbi-Erra in tandem with Girbubu, the governor of neighboring Girkal. Because he had just learned that Girbubu had been captured by the Isin king, one must assume that this is a rhetorical gesture, because the governor of Kazallu is now left without any allies in the region.

Among the issues raised is a war with Elam, which may refer to the final struggle with eastern powers that led to the fall of Ur and to the subsequent battles that Išbi-Erra fought with those very same forces—battles that appear to have been described in poetic form in his *Hymn B* (van Dijk 1978) and can also be traced, albeit imprecisely, in administrative records from Isin (Steinkeller 2008). According to this letter, however, the easterners as well as the man of Isin are both portrayed as enemies of Ur.

A long passage in the letter has a bearing on historical events and on the dating of the missive itself. The crucial lines read as follows (IbPu1 [24]: 18–26, short version A):

> [18] Enlil had earlier already come to hate Sumer, [19] appointing a monkey descending from its mountain (home) to the stewardship of the homeland. [20-21] But now Enlil has handed kingship to a *(mere) peddler of exotic spices*, one who chases the wind, to Išbi-Erra, who is not even of Sumerian descent. [22] Moreover, once the assembly of the gods (decided) to scatter the (inhabitants of the) Sumer, [23] Father Enlil, having conveyed his commands, proceeded to overthrow the homeland. [24] "As long as Ur *is imbued with evildoers,* [25] Išbi-Erra, the man of Mari, will tear out its foundations, [26] and Sumer will be measured out," thus he spoke!

In lines 14–17, there is a contrast, as well as a disjunction, between two persons—one unnamed but characterized in simian terms and the other, likewise represented as foreign, who is specifically identified as Išbi-Erra. This is an important distinction; there can be no doubt that in the semantic universe of this letter, the word "monkey" does not refer to Išbi-Erra, as has often been thought, but must be a characterization of someone else, undoubtedly "Elamites."[56] Is it difficult to avoid the conclusion that

---

56. So, for example, Sjöberg 1993; Wilcke (1968: 60 n. 20) already suggested that this refers to Elamites.

this refers to events that provided the enigmatic name of Ibbi-Sin's twenty-third, and penultimate, year: mu ᵈi-bí.en.zu lugal uri₅ᵏⁱ-ma-ra ᵘᵍᵘugu₄-bi dugud kur-bi mu-na-e-ra, "The year: The *formidable/dumb* monkeys *struck out* from its mountain against Ibbi-Sin, king of Ur" (Sjöberg 1993: 211: n. 2). Note that the Gutians are described as having the form of monkeys (ulutin ugu₄-bi) in the *Curse of Agade* 156, and the same expression is used to portray Amorites in the *Marriage of Amurrum* (line 127). Here it also characterizes highlanders, perhaps the Amorites, according to IbIš1A 14' (22), but the untrustworthy nature of the latter text makes it highly unlikely. Therefore, one must conclude that the Ibbi-Sin letter, as well as the year-name, refers to Kindattu and his cohorts, or to another Šimaškian leader. Most important, if this holds true, it sets the Puzur-Numušda correspondence at the very end of Ibbi-Sin's reign; it also suggests that, in this epistolary universe at least, the last king of Ur was at odds with both Išbi-Erra and with his enemies from the east.

The lines that follow further support the late setting of these letters. Lines 20–22 relate an oracle from the god Enlil, and the only way to make any sense of his words is to assume that Ibbi-Sin was no longer in the capital, forced to withdraw to the countryside, where he was still waging war against the enemy. If this were indeed the case, it explains why there are no documents from Ur from the king's last year. On the other hand, such a historical reconstruction contradicts the poetic portrait of Ibbi-Sin's last days in Ur from the *Lamentation over the Destruction of Sumer and Ur* (lines 105–106):

> Ibbi-Sin sat in anguish in his palace, all alone,
> In the Enamtila, the palace of his delight, bitterly he cried.

More specifically, an earlier passage in the poem describes the fate of the last king of Ur, as decreed by the great divinities of Sumer (lines 34–37):

> That its shepherd be captured all alone in his palace by the enemy,
> That Ibbi-Sin be taken to the land of Elam in fetters,
> That from the sand dunes of Sabum, on the edge of the sea, to the borders of Anšan
> Like a bird that has flown his nest, never to return to his city . . ."

The historical record leaves us with little information that could inform a choice between the two literary depictions of the last days of the last king of Ur. The fragmentary *Išbi-Erra Hymn B*, in its opening section, apparently described some of these events, but only traces of the narrative remain:

> He went south in splendor . . .
> Like snake spitting venom he approached with evil intent,
> [His army] wiped out the . . . of Sumer,
> . . . in the desert of Ur
> He killed many people.[57]

---

57. Col. ii 3–7 (van Dijk 1978: 192; Vanstiphout 1989–90: 54). This composition is badly preserved, and too many lines were restored by its first editor. I have collated the original tablets

The apologetic and self-legitimating nature of Išbi-Erra's "historical" hymns caution against taking them at face value. There is, however, some evidence that Išbi-Erra's armies fought with Elamites in the south at a time that must be correlated with the very last year, or possibly the last two years, of Ibbi-Sin, as Piotr Steinkeller (2008) has discovered. Three accounts from Isin, dated IE15 = IS24, refer to battles with Elamites, and one of them relates that the army was at one point in Uruk during these campaigns.[58] These events were used to name Išbi-Erra's sixteenth year:

> mu ᵈiš-bi-èr-ra lugal-e ugnim šimaški ù elam-(e) bí-(in)-ra
> The year King Išbi-Erra defeated the armies of Šimaški and Elam.

If the chronology is correct, this suggests that at the last moment Išbi-Erra moved south to save Ibbi-Sin or to protect his own kingdom from the enemy armies that had attacked from the east.[59] In the epistolary universe of CKU, however, the rulers of Ur and Isin were at odds to the very end, or very near it.

Whatever his motivations, Išbi-Erra only succeeded in saving himself; the Ur kingdom fell to the armies from the east, and it would be almost a decade before the forces of Isin would be able to drive the Elamite garrison out of the old capital. All indications are, as much as one can be certain in light of such slight evidence, that Išbi-Erra and Ibbi-Sin were forced to fight off elements of the same invasion from the east, but while the former managed to come out on top, the latter was unable to resist, was defeated, and, if later traditions are to be believed, was led off to Anšan weeping, never to return.[60]

Structural and Literary Aspects of the Puzur-Numušda Correspondence

The epistolary exchange between the governor of Kazallu and the soon-to-be-toppled last king of Ur is unique in the literary letter corpus—indeed, in all of Su-

---

more than once and find many of the restorations difficult to accept. Until new duplicates surface, very little can be said about this poem, but my personal impression is that it mainly deals with the aftermath of the fall of Ur and describes Išbi-Erra's victories over the forces that were responsible for the defeat of Ur.

58. *BIN* 9 152, 338; *BIN* 10 124 (the latter mentions Uruk).

59. Steinkeller reconstructs the events differently, preferring to see two separate encounters between the armies of Isin and those of Kindattu. I see no reason not to assume that the texts of IE15 and the name of YN16 refer to the same events. I am also assuming that Ibbi-Sin was on the throne for 24 years; Steinkeller is more cautious and does not commit himself to a 24 or 25-year reign.

60. According to a first-millennium astronomical omen, "if the Yoke Star in its appearance faces towards the west, you watch the whole sky, and if no wind stirs, there will be famine, a disastrous sign. (It is an omen) of Ibbi-Sin, who went to Anšan in captivity, weeping" (Koch-Westenholz 1995: 35 n. 1). One text provides an alternative "stumbling (on the way)" for "weeping" (Reiner 1974: 261). For similar portents, see Glassner 1997: 110. See p. 213 below.

merian literature—for its structural and intertextual complexity. All of the RCU was read with a considerable dose of hindsight in Old Babylonian times, driven, if nothing else, by the very fact of its attribution to long-dead correspondents. The drama of the last days of Ur, however, known to latter-day readers from a variety of other poetic and mantic sources, provided a canvas for reflection and commentary on historical and epistolary veracity, the reliability of messages from the divine world, and finally, at the risk of considerable anachronism on my part, on the very nature of fiction and discourse.

The letter to the king (PuIb1 [23]) begins—uniquely in all of Sumerian literary epistolography—with an embedded first-person message from Išbi-Erra (lines 6–28). This message, moreover, begins with a third-person summary of an oracle that the ruler of Isin had received from the god Enlil (lines 6–13). All of this is presented as the words of Išbi-Erra, as relayed by an envoy, but there can be little doubt that this is intended to represent a prototypical scene of a sender's messenger reading aloud a letter at its destination. In this manner, a message is embedded in a letter that, in turn, is dropped verbatim into yet another epistle.

These concentric referential circles reach a full climax in the king's reply, in which he references the full text of the previous letter, complete with all of its embedded messages. This *inclusio* is accomplished in an unusual manner, by citing the first and last lines of PuIb1 [23] (IbPu1: 6–8 [24]):

> ⁶How could you send someone to me (with a letter beginning) thus: ⁷"Išbi-Erra has presented his matter before me," ⁸(and ending with) "and as far as I am concerned, when he finally strikes, I will have to flee!"

But the succession of messages does not end at this high point; the text of IbPu1 turns back and becomes a narrative mirror image of the text that it quotes, as it proceeds to narrate a rival communication from the god Enlil (IbPu1: 20–22 [23]), but unlike the one described by Išbi-Erra, this message is reported as direct speech, perhaps intended to justify the fact that it must supersede the previous one in this multilayered narrative exchange.

The only other letters that refer directly to some previous correspondence are the first two epistles of CKU, and by paraphrasing rather than directly quoting, they offer two different perspectives on the instructions that motivated the preserved exchange but are not attested directly in any letter. In the first letter of CKU, the grand vizier Aradmu reports to King Šulgi (ArŠ1: 2–8 [1]):

> ⁸You commanded me, ³while I was on an expedition to Subir, ⁴to firmly secure the taxes on the frontier territory, ⁵to thoroughly investigate the state of (this) frontier, ⁶⁻⁷to confer (with the elites of Subir) about the prefect Apilaša and have them come to agreement, ⁸*so that he could bring to them* (i.e., the Subir elites) *up-to-date instructions.*

In his reply, the monarch summarizes his interpretation of his own instructions thus (ŠAr1: 6–16 [2]):

[6] As far as I am concerned, you were to make the frontier territory secure as my representative, [7] to organize the people and keep them obedient, [8] and once you reached the cities of the frontier, to discern their attitudes [9] and to learn what their dignitaries are saying, [10] so that my battle cry would fill the mountains, [11] my mighty battle weapons fall upon the foreign lands, [12] and my "storm" cover over the homeland! [13] *"Drop (chasing) winds in the wilderness and robbers in the fields!* [14] Until you have reached my prefect Apilaša, [15] *ignore all of this so that you can . . . your face before him (without delay)*!" [16] Thus did I command you!

This disagreement about interpretation, at the very outset of the school study of CKU, sets the stage for an underlying questioning of textual authority that will be taken up, more radically, at the very end, in the final section of the Ur III royal correspondence, in the Ibbi-Sin/Puzur-Numušda letters.

The succession of letters within letters in the last items of CKU anticipates, millennia earlier, the device known to literary and film critics as *mise en abyme*, a term originally adapted to literary analysis by André Gide in 1893 that was resurrected and elaborated in various ways in the second half of the twentieth century. While there are many works on the subject, including a well-known full-length work by Lucien Dällenbach (1977) and an important essay by the same author, opinions differ as to the narrative significance of this rhetorical device.[61] As Ron (1987: 434) summarizes the latter, "*mise en abyme* always ironically subverts the representational intent of the narrative text, disrupting where the text aspires to integration, integrating where the text is deliberately fragmentary." This is an issue that requires a much broader discussion, and I will return to it in a different context, but for the present purpose it will suffice to argue that the use of these mirroring devices in the two Sumerian letters serves to undermine the illusion of closure imposed by the literary form and at the same time underscore their artfulness. To take this even further, they subvert any notions of historical veracity and point the reader steadfastly in the direction of fiction. At the same time, this kind of structural mirroring and embedding brings attention to what Patricia Rosenmeyer (2001: 172) has designated as the kinetic function of letters in narrative, "actively causing and reacting to events."

The artifice of the Puzur-Numušda letter (PuIb1 [23]) is further accentuated by the exegesis of the embedded Išbi-Erra missive that is offered by the author. This is done in two parts, both introduced by the formula "it was just as he had predicted," in lines 29 and 42.[62] The only other Sumerian literary composition that has such a structural element is *Gilgameš and Aga* (line 93), although the sentence also occurs in one nonstandard manuscript of *Gilgameš, Enkidu, and the Netherworld* from Ur.[63] The first passage in question reads, in translation (*Gilgameš and Aga* lines 69–81; 89–99):

61. For a slightly revised vision of his ideas, see Dällenbach 1980. An important and succinct critique of various approaches to the problem is presented by Ron (1987).

62. bí-in-du$_{11}$-ga-gin$_7$-nam, literally, "it was just as he had said."

63. *UET* 6/1 60: r. 14′; see Cavigneaux and Al-Rawi 2000a: 8; Gadotti 2005: 302. The context is difficult, and both offer very different interpretations.

"Slave—that man, is he your king?"
No, that man is not my king!
If that man were my king,
If that was his furious brow,
If those were his bison eyes,
If that was his lapis beard,
If those were his beneficent fingers (pointing blessings),[64]
Would not millions fall, would not millions rise,
Would not millions . . . in the dust,
Would not all the lands submit,
Would not the entrance to the frontier be filled with dust,
Would not the prows of barges be cut off?
Would not Aga, king of Kish, be taken prisoner in the midst of his own army?
. . .
Then Gilgameš peered over the city wall:
Upon seeing him, Aga fixed his eyes (on Enkidu, and said):
"Slave—that man, is he your king?"
"Yes, that man is my king!"
It was just as he had predicted:
Millions fell, millions rose,
Millions . . . in the dust,
All the lands submitted,
The entrance to the frontier was filled with dust,
Prows of barges were cut off,
And Aga, king of Kish, was taken prisoner in the midst of his own army.

There are good reasons to believe that *Gilgameš and Aga* is an Old Babylonian creation, quite possibly composed as a parody lampooning the whole Ur III divine-kingship tradition, and therefore one must wonder if there is any intertextual connection between the Puzur-Numušda epistle and this particular Gilgameš story.[65] But while the Gilgameš passage provides a simple contrast between rhetorical question and answer, between hypothetical negative and assertion, using precisely the same topics with different grammar, the letter uses the phrase "it was just as he had predicted" in a more complex and subtle manner. The *Gilgameš and Aga* passage rips into the heart of the image of charismatic divine kingship; the very appearance of the ancient hero, emanating godly aura, his fingers on the parapet and only his head showing, is enough to make the world tremble and the enemy king to surrender with his army. The ironic mode is signaled here, as in the Ibbi-Sin letters, by the mirroring *mise en abyme* of the passage.

In his letter, Puzur-Numušda echoes the very words of Išbi-Erra but then proceeds to explain the man's actions further in his own words. The use of the same phrase here is not identical, but it serves similar narrative reception purposes.

----

64. I owe this interpretation of šu-si sa₆ to Jerrold Cooper.
65. Wilcke (1998) already argued for an OB date of this composition, but he based his proposal on grammatical criteria that I do not find convincing; see p. 216 below and Rubio, in press.

A very different set of references to the historical/literary tradition is embedded in the long version of the letter of Išbi-Erra to Ibbi-Sin. In a section that comprises words of supposed encouragement by the once and future usurper to the king whose place he will soon take, we find the following words (IšIb1 [21]: 35–55):

> [35]Ur, city of wisdom, linking the upper and lower regions; [36]having been built by Great Prince (Enki), the exorcist, (it is a city) whose façade is precious (to the people), [37]one endowed with cosmic rites, whose foundations and ground plans are secure (among all the) lands, south to north,[38] *it will surely be spared and its (favorable divine) decision announced!*
>
> [39](Temple) Ekišnuĝal, shrine that envelops the upper and lower regions, without rival—[40]the Elamite, an evil vicious dog, [41]will not defile it, nor render asunder its guardian deities! [42]*My king, all the loudest noisemakers have run away.*
>
> [43]Ibbi-Sin, beloved by the gods as he came out of the womb—[44]An, Enlil, and Enki, looked so favorably upon him! [45]Established . . . so that its front be secure. [46]As long as the gates of Ur stay open, [47]. . . will be saying, "Who is really king?" [48]But it is you who are the king to whom Enlil gave no rival! [49]So do not. . . , so be of good spirits! [50]*(He/they) has/have taken revenge*, and secured its foundations for you. [51]Not being . . . may your spirit be happy! [52]As long as my king is alive, he will exercise kingship over Ur, [53]and (I will do) for him whatever my king might command me to do! [54]Please, I will not neglect (your orders)! [55]By Utu, I will not change my allegiance!

There are no direct quotations, but the poetic language used by Išbi-Erra may be imagined to invoke, albeit in reverse, the diction of the two compositions that had a strong presence in the school curriculum, *The Lamentation over the Destruction of Ur* and *The Lamentation over the Destruction of Sumer and Ur*. Moreover, the expression "Who is really king?" is taken verbatim from *The Sumerian King List*, making a direct allusion to the last days of the Akkad dynasty.[66]

The appeal to literature itself situates these two letters, and by implication the whole range of school epistles, in the realm of fiction, as I have already suggested. At the very least, it questions their value as historical witnesses, creating a semiotic web of indeterminacy and undermining the illusion of narrative closure as implied by the "reality effect." If so, this may be still another marker, in native Mesopotamian terms, of the fictionality of the Puzur-Numušda correspondence, although readers would react to this differently, depending on their attitude toward the verisimilitude of these literary compositions. That is not to say that the letter "is not true," in pragmatic positivistic terms—only that some Old Babylonian readers would have reasons to read the text on a variety of levels if they caught the internal signals by which the two letters undermined their own narrative authority.

The author, or authors, of the tradition represented by the longer versions of IšIb1 (21) and IbPu1 (24) exploited these complex textual strategies further. The most important surviving witness to this dynamic process of reinterpretation is the

---

66. See the commentary to the letter.

collective tablet of unknown provenience that contains all four items of the Ibbi-Sin correspondence, including the long version of the first and fourth letter and one of only two surviving manuscripts of the second letter (IbIš1 [22]). This tablet, which is dated to the twenty-seventh year of Samsu-iluna, represents a tradition that developed outside of Nippur, Ur, and the other cities that used similar instructional materials and was written just as Nippur was being abandoned by many of the elite.[67] All the other tablets with longer versions of this correspondence are likewise unprovenienced; it is possible that two of them are from Larsa, but the reasons for thinking so are not very convincing and there is a remote possibility that the tablet with the full collection was written in Sippar, although this does not necessarily mean that its conceptual innovations originated there (Michalowski 2006a: 254–55).

It is impossible to know, given gaps in our present knowledge, if this particular collective tablet is but one token of a broader textual tradition, the solitary work of one student, or a one-of-a-kind exercise created ad hoc by an inspired teacher. Whatever its origins, the end result is an exceptional narrative: the concatenation of four letters created a connected story about certain aspects of the final moments of the last king of Ur, constituting what can be justifiably called the first epistolary novel. The plot centers on the contentious relationships between the king and two individuals: the man who would succeed him as the next ruler of Sumer and the last of his loyal provincial governors. But this version of the story takes the contradictions concerning textual authority and shifts them to a slightly different area, amplifying certain aspects to focus on divine sanction that is invoked by the protagonists.

The long version of IbPu1 (24) contains a novel section that is absent in the short version from Nippur and elsewhere. In these new lines, Ibbi-Sin describes in detail a divine message he had received in the form of a liver omen (IbPu1: 33–45 [24]):

> [33]Father Enlil, by means of his angry commands, has overthrown the homeland. [34]Come now, he has returned to my side! [35]*My complaints were submitted by humble prayer*, [36]and Great Lord Enlil heard me out; [37]he cast his favorable glance upon me, [38]set his holy heart on mercy, [39]and established for me my favorable omen. [40]And after I had the follow-up reading made concerning his *pars familiaris* and my *pars hostilis*, [41]the weapon-mark on my right side, its trunk is straight, and that (good news) gave me joy; [42]on the weapon-mark on his (i.e., Išbi-Erra's) left side a filament is suspended, it is placed (against) the other side. [43](The message was:) "My enemy shall fall into my hands, he shall be killed, [44]the people will come out of darkness into the light, and lie in peaceful habitations." [45]Utu, lord who makes the decisions of the heavens and the earth, has provided (this) omen.

This remarkable passage contains the only Old Babylonian liver omen in the Sumerian language, and it clearly represents a clever attempt to create a whole new vocabulary, since all of the technical extispicy terms were Akkadian. Moreover, the form of the omen, with a protasis and apodosis, mirrors the learned omen compendia,

---

67. A 7475; described above on p. 56 as compilation tablet Xa.

not the practical concerns of the omen reports of the time, and thus all of this points to the world of learned speculation and scholarship rather than to Sumerian school literature or to everyday mantic practice.[68] Indeed, there are good reasons to believe that extispicy became a dominant form of divination only during the Old Babylonian period and that prior to that time the main form of predicting the future from animals was from their behavior, not from their organs. Most important, extispicy is completely absent from the intellectual horizon of Sumerian poetics, and therefore the insertion of an imaginary Sumerian omen, complete with invented Sumerian technical terminology, marks the oppositional and polemic nature of this textual insertion.[69]

There are many fascinating aspects of this passage, but in this context one stands out above all others: the reader, armed with historical knowledge and the resulting hindsight, knows that the omen, as reprised and interpreted by Ibbi-Sin, was false, because the Old Babylonian readers were well aware, as are we, that it never came true and that the last descendant of Ur-Namma was led into captivity, his kingdom in ruins. This is also true of the Nippur versions, but in them the matter is only noted in passing without the explicit amplification of the issue. The invocation of extispicy is important here, because it serves to displace the blame for the fall of Ur and Sumer to foreign forces from the mundane world of both Ibbi-Sin and Išbi-Erra and to situate it in the transcendent sphere, as I shall argue below; but for now, I would like to stay with the matter of the omen.

Does this text undermine faith in divine messages and in their interpreters or does it question royal veracity? Does it subvert belief in epistolary narrative or just play games with different versions of history? One can only speculate on the answers to these questions, but there can be little doubt that the author or authors of the long version were very much concerned with the power of textual authority—both with tablets inscribed by humans and with exta inscribed by gods—in a new intellectual universe that was concerned with the process of interpretation and the very meaning of signs. In the self-congratulatory literature from the court of Išbi-Erra, Enlil is frequently invoked as the patron of the new master of Sumer, most ominously in *Hymn B*, where a broken passage at the beginning seems to imply that the end of Ur was decreed by the high god:[70]

---

68. I discussed this passage in Michalowski 2006a and do not repeat most of that analysis here. The transliteration and translation offered here, based on new collations, differ in small details. Other than this literary fabrication, the earliest known Sumerian omen comes from Kassite Nippur (Veldhuis 2000: 74).

69. I discussed this in a paper entitled "Observations on Divination and *Extispicy* in Early Mesopotamia" at the Rencontre Assyriologique Internationale in Paris, July 2009; it will be published in the near future.

70. *Išbi-Erra Hymn B* col. i 4′–7′ (van Dijk 1978: 191; Vanstiphout 1989–90: 54). The Sumerian (collated) reads: $^{4′}$[. . .]-ib-dug$_4$ $^{5′}$[. . .] uru^{ki} du$_6$-du$_6$-da šed-e-dè $^{6′}$[. . .]-dè nam im-ma-ni-in-tar $^{7′}$[. . .]-bal ^{d}en-líl á-dah-bi-im.

... was decreed, by the command of Enlil
... to count the city as ruins,
... to ..., he decreed it fate,
... was overturned, and Enlil assisted in these (events).

Perhaps this text was too obscure to matter, but to any reader, this passage could not but invoke a very different literary composition that was better known in antiquity, a poem that describes the death and journey to the Netherworld of the founder of the Third Dynasty of Ur (*Ur-Namma Hymn A* 8–9):

The god An altered his sacred established words, ...
The god Enlil deceitfully changed established destiny.[71]

This literary association, which could have been triggered by both the short and long redactions of IbPu1 [24], creates a form of semantic closure that dialectically pushes against the open semantic indeterminacy pursued by other narrative strategies in the Ibbi-Sin correspondence. In this literary universe, the parallelism between the destinies of the first and last kings of Ur, both deceived by their divine master Enlil, mirror the historical focal points of the dynasty, bookended by highland invasion and occupation.

These thoughts bring me back to some of what I wrote in the introductory chapter on Sumerian letters, where I invoked the subversive—and I would also say kinetic—image of letters in texts such as *Enmerkar and the Lord of Aratta* and in the Sumerian tale about Sargon and Ur-Zababa. In both poems, letters function as strong movers of plot, and in both they subvert the existing order of things. The Sargon story, in which a letter, unknown to its carrier, contains an order for his very own execution, is particularly significant, because it focuses attention on the deadly implications of epistolography.[72] The composition is known from only two manuscripts, one of which was found in House F in Nippur, which also contained exemplars of the CKU.[73]

The fictional and world-creating semantic and structural aspects of the Puzur-Numušda correspondence fit in well with views about epistolary exchanges that surface in these stories. Indeed, if I may be permitted to cite Claudio Guillén (1986: 78) once again:

In the history of our civilization letters have signified a crucial passage between orality to writing itself—or a practical interaction between the two. As écriture, it begins to involve the writer in a silent, creative process if self-distancing and self-modeling, leading perhaps, as in autobiography, to fresh knowledge or even to fiction.

71. The lines are difficult; for the Sumerian, and for a slightly different translation, see Flückiger-Hawker 1999: 102.
72. See pp. 20–21 above.
73. Both are edited in Cooper and Heimpel 1983, but it is not at all certain that both tablets belong to the same composition (see now also Attinger 2010: 1 n. 2).

Mesopotamian Perceptions of the Fall of Ur

I began this chapter with the statement that the fall of Ur was one of the dramatic moments of Mesopotamian history. For us moderns, this is certainly the case, if for no other reason than it provides a rhetorically apposite ending for chapters in history books. As an example of prevailing opinion, I cite the combined opinion of two major scholars, A. K. Grayson and W. G. Lambert (1964: 9), even if it was written almost half a century ago:

> Although Ur was captured by an enemy many times throughout its long history, the occasion which impressed the Babylonians most was its fall under Ibbi-Sin at the beginning of the second millennium.

But was this event truly important in antiquity? Were there significant memorial traditions concerning Ibbi-Sin and the collapse of his kingdom in Mesopotamian writings? In answering such questions, one must be careful not to select data from various texts from different times, taking them out of context and assembling them into a seemingly coherent narrative. A brief survey of the pertinent information, starting with the surviving Old Babylonian materials, sheds important light on the matter.

As already described above, the Ur III collapse is the subject of four distinct textual traditions: the CKU, the city laments, hymns of Išbi-Erra, and divination compendia. As we have seen earlier in this chapter, the different elements of the Ibbi-Sin correspondence are unevenly distributed and do not coalesce into a coherent consistent narrative. The city laments are a poetic genre that differs radically from the prose of the literary letters, although their secondary context, as school literature, places them alongside the CKU. What sets them apart from the letters, however, is their central standing in the curriculum, as measured by the comparatively large numbers of duplicates of both poems, which contrasts with the relatively marginal educational use of the letters, which are known in a much smaller number of copies. Moreover, they differ in their origin. Many years ago, Thorkild Jacobsen, writing about the *Lamentation over the Destruction of Ur*, suggested that laments were related to other cultic texts such as balaĝs and therefore were recited at ceremonies associated with the reconstruction of temples.[74] Such a hypothesis places their commemorative poetics within the context of the immediate present, where the past is only a matter invoked to provide a legitimating background for the glory of the monarch whose patronage allows the rebuilding to move forward. Since poems of this genre focus on the destruction of temples and on the interruption of cultic activities, their metaphorical language, geared toward collapse and renewal, is by definition catastrophic. But even if the laments can be analyzed together from a generic point

---

74. "When we consider that the balaĝ formed part of the service at the rebuilding of temples, that the present composition aims directly at the rebuilding of Ur and its holy places, and that the date of its composition can be narrowed down to the time before that rebuilding began, there seems little reason to doubt that we are here reading the very balaĝ written for and used at the restoration of Ur by the Isin kings" (Jacobsen 1941: 223).

of view, only one of them—*The Lamentation over the Destruction of Sumer and Ur*—actually mentions Ibbi-Sin by name and refers directly to the various enemies who were thought to have taken part in the final assault on his kingdom. I shall return to the *Lamentation* below, but first it is necessary to take a brief look at the other Old Babylonian texts that focused on the events surrounding the fall of Ur.

Two poems, *Išbi-Erra Hymn A* and *Išbi-Erra Hymn B*, describe events linked to the fall of Ur from the perspective of the administration of the ruler who contributed to its collapse but who represented himself as the avenger and heir to the throne of Sumer and Akkad. Unlike other compositions of this type, they uniquely describe historical events with some specificity, even if their fragmentary state of preservation hides much of the detail. But not only are these poems different from other royal hymns, they are also known from only one manuscript each, both from Nippur, and are undoubtedly marginal in the Old Babylonian school curriculum. This is hardly surprising, because the same holds true for all of the hymns of both Ibbi-Sin and his rival, Išbi-Erra.

Unlike his father Šulgi, whose self-praise was drummed into the memories of aspiring scribes with unrelenting lines of poetry, the last king of Ur was hardly known to the schoolboys of Nippur. Of the five existing hymns in the name of Ibbi-Sin, only one is attested in more than one exemplar.

Išbi-Erra, even if he was the founder of the Isin dynasty whose kings commissioned many hymns that were subsequently incorporated into the curriculum, was also but a shadowy figure in Old Babylonian schools, rarely encountered by students outside of their work on portions of CKU. Of his five hymns, only two are documented by more than one source—*Hymn C* and *Nidaba Hymn C*, which mentions his name but is usually not classified as one of his hymns. The former, a short tigi in honor of the goddess Nanaja, is preserved on one Nippur tablet and two of unknown origin. The latter is the only relatively widely distributed hymn that mentions Išbi-Erra's name, if only in passing.[75]

One cannot avoid the conclusion that literary texts concerning Išbi-Erra were very rarely utilized in Old Babylonian schooling and that this contrasts markedly with the strong presence of his latter-day successors Iddin-Dagan, Lipit-Eštar, and especially Išme-Dagan, who is represented by no less than 21 royal hymns (Ludwig 1990; Tinney 1995). The poetry of these Isin rulers looks back for its inspiration to the works written in the name of Šulgi, not to the short-lived literary innovations of Išbi-Erra.

The *Lamentation over the Destruction of Sumer and Ur* allocates no culpability for the collapse of the state to any Mesopotamian mortal, unhesitatingly assigning all responsibility to the transcendent sphere. Ibbi-Sin, Išbi-Erra—who is never mentioned in the poem—and even the highland forces that carry out the destruction are

---

75. The hymns of Ibbi-Sin have been edited by Sjöberg (1972); for the Išbi-Erra hymns, see Michalowski 2005a. *Nidaba Hymn C* had broad distribution but few manuscripts, attested in single exemplars from Uruk, Kish, Isin, and three from Nippur (see my forthcoming edition).

only actors in a drama orchestrated by higher powers: the gods and goddesses, fate, and history.

How different this all is from the *Lamentation*'s generic prior text, the *Curse of Agade*. In the latter, the collapse of the state is the direct result of the hubris and impetuous impiety of the king of the land, Naram-Sin, but behind all of this one can detect the manipulative hand of the god Enlil, whose provocative silence pushes Naram-Sin into action. The poem begins with a description of the heights achieved by the Agade regime and of the riches that fill the temples of its gods. But all of this apparently did not please the god Enlil, and the "words from the Ekur (temple) were as silence."[76] The gods and goddesses withdraw their protection of the city, and then the king has a dream forecasting its fall. After seven years, he apparently decides to rebuild Enlil's temple in order to obtain favor but cannot obtain favorable omens to undertake the task. Finally, aggravated by divine silence, he destroys the sacred shrine of Sumer, thus assuring divine retribution and the end of his kingdom. By contrast, Ibbi-Sin is never accused of any misdeeds and is merely an actor in a drama directed from on high, deprived of any meaningful agency. This is understandable because the Sumerian language texts in which he appears belonged to the school curriculum that had Ur III roots but was reconfigured during a time Išbi-Erra's successors on the throne of Isin ruled Nippur. These kings claimed to be the rightful successors of Ur, and their legitimating strategies would not have been well served by dwelling on the collapse of Ibbi-Sin's kingdom.

Finally, there is the matter of the so-called "historical omens." I shall disregard the issue of their historical veracity, which is irrelevant to the present discussion (Reiner 1974; Cooper 1980). Omen apodoses mentioning Ibbi-Sin and Išbi-Erra are known from Old Babylonian omen compendia, and the former is already mentioned in the earliest surviving extispicy texts, the Early Old Babylonian liver omens from Mari (Rutten 1938). Although Reiner (1974: 261) has rightly described these types of apodoses as "historiettes" rather than "history," the narrow focus of the omens that recall the last days of Ur undoubtedly reflect the limited memories of these events that resonated through time. The Ibbi-Sin apodoses most often refer simply to disaster, those of Išbi-Erra to his routing of the Elamites who had occupied Ur. The Old Babylonian omen apodoses concerning these rulers are:

Ibbi-Sin[77]

Early Old Babylonian Liver Models from Mari

> a. *a-mu-ut, ṣú-ḫa-ra-im, si i-bi-*ᵈen.zu, *ba-táq, ma-ti-šu i-ba-al-ki-ti-šu*, "omen of the *diminishing (of the land)* pertaining to Ibbi-Sin, *the end of the country*, they? will rebel against him" (Rutten 1938 no. 6)

76. *Curse of Agade* 57: inim é-kur-ra me-gin₇ ba-an-ğar.
77. See already Jacobsen 1953: 38–39 n. 18. Omens concerning Ibbi-Sin have been collected by Weidner 1929: 236–37; Nougayrol 1945; Goetze 1947: 261–62; Glassner 1997: 109–10.

b. *i-nu-mi, i-bí-*ᵈen.zu, *ma-su, i-ba-al-ki-tù-šu, a-ni-u-um, ki-am i-sá-kin*, "when the land revolted against Ibbi-Sin, this is how (the liver) was constituted" (Rutten 1938 no. 7)

c. *a-mu-ut, i-bí-*ᵈen.zu, *sá u-ra-am*, elamᵏⁱ *a-na ti-li, ú kàr-me₅ iš-ku-un*, "omen of Ibbi-Sin, under whom Elam turned Ur into ruins" (Rutten 1938 no. 8)

Old Babylonian Omen Compilations

d. *a-mu-ut, i-bi-*ᵈen.zu *ša ma-tum ip-ḫu-ru-nim*, "omen of Ibbi-Sin, against whom the land gathered (in revolt)" (*YOS* 10 36 i: 1314)

e–g. *a-mu-ut i-bi-*ᵈen.zu *ša ša-aḫ-lu-uq-tim*, "omen of Ibbi-Sin—of disaster," (*YOS* 10 13: 1; 14: 10–11; 22: 12)

h. *a-mu-ut i-bi-*ᵈen.zu, *ša-aḫ-lu-uq-tum*. "omen of Ibbi-Sin—disaster," (*YOS* 10 56: i 40-41)

i. *te-er-tum ši-i, ša ša-aḫ,-ma-as-ti, i-bi-*ᵈen.zu, "this is an omen of the turmoil (during the time of) Ibbi-Sin," (*YOS* 10 31 xiii: 2–5)

Išbi-Erra

Early Old Babylonian Liver Model from Mari

j. *a-mu-ut, iš-bi-èr-ra, sá* elamᵏⁱ, *da-giʲ-íl-šu, ú* elamᵏⁱ *íl-ga-a*, "omen of Išbi-Erra, who (first) put his trust in Elam, and then captured Elam," (Rutten 1938 no. 9)

Old Babylonian Omen Compilation

k. giš.tukul ˡ*iš-bi-èr-ra, ša e-la-am-tam is-ki-pu*, "weapon-mark of Išbi-Erra, who drove out Elam," (*YOS* 10 46 v 5-6)

The sample is admittedly quite small, but within it one can observe that the Mari livers and the later Babylonian omens share general perspectives on the two rulers but differ in detail. Omens (a) and (d), as well as (j) and (k) express similar viewpoints, but the wording is significantly dissimilar. Ibbi-Sin, in the Old Babylonian tradition, seems associated quite simply with "disaster," and these apodeses (e–i), find strong echoes in canonical omen compendia, as in the following two examples:

šaḫluqtu (níǧ.ha.lam.ma) *amūt* (bà-*ut*) *i-bí-*ᵈ30 *šar uri* (ˡlugal uri₅ᵏⁱ), "disaster; omen of Ibbi-Sin, king of Ur " (*CT* 20 13 r. 12)

amūt (bà-*ut*) ˡ*i-bí-*ᵈ30 *šá šaḫluqti* (níǧ.ha.lam.ma), "omen of Ibbi-Sin, of disaster" (*TCL* 6 1: 35)

The celestial omen series *Enūma Anu Enlil* included four omens concerning Ibbi-Sin, three of them relating how he was led in tears—or stumbling—into captivity to Anšan (Glassner 1997: 110–11; see also n. 60 above, p. 202).[78]

---

78. The literary tradition expands this motif in the cultic sphere. According to the Emesal Damu lament eden-na ù-saǧ-ǧá Ibbi-Sin was buried in Anšan; see Jacobsen 1997: 78. The lament must go back to the Ur III period, if not earlier (Cooper 2006: 42), but was revised in Old

Although the figure of the last king of the House of Ur-Namma is present throughout the history of the Babylonian omen tradition, the same cannot be said of his rival, Išbi-Erra. There are only two Old Babylonian omens concerning the king of Isin, as transliterated above, and, as far as I can discern, there are only two more in the later tradition, only one of which is complete:[79]

> *amūt* (bà-ut) *iš-bi-*ᵈ*èr-ra šá maḫira* (gaba.ri) *la* (nu) *irši* (tuk-ʿšiʾ), "omen of Išbi-Erra who had no opponent" (Leichty 1970: 83 l. 105)

The cultural significance of these omens is difficult to evaluate, however, because of uncertainties concerning the textual context of Old Babylonian compendia. Almost all of them are unprovenienced, and while it has been speculated that some may have originated in Sippar or Larsa (Glassner 2009), the evidence is circumstantial at best. The fact that the only well-provenienced compendia appear to come from contexts distinct from that of standard Sumerian school tablets is indicative of the difficulties we have in understanding the place of these compositions in Old Babylonian written culture.[80] Glassner (2009) argues that they are instructional materials, but even if he is correct, they must have come from environments that were very different from the Sumerian-language-based teaching establishments known from eighteenth century Nippur, Ur, and even Sippar, in which Akkadian-language extispicy was not only absent but rarely, if ever, even mentioned. This other context—which must remain hypothetical for the time being—must have also been the place where the long version of IbPu1 (24), with its extensive Sumerian "omen" in lines 33–45, was elaborated, expanded, and adapted for a worldview informed by the new semiotic system of divination from the organs of sacrificial animals.

Whatever the case may have been, these omen texts come from very different cultural environments than the laments, the CKU, or the royal hymns of Ibbi-Sin and Išbi-Erra that were marginal even within the Nippur curriculum. It is important to keep in mind, moreover, that the very notion of "historical omens" is a modern idea that may not have been recognized in Old Babylonian times, because these omens are scattered among the various compendia and are never brought together in antiquity. If, rather than viewing them as a group, we contextualize them in their proper settings among the thousands and thousands of omens that have survived

---

Babylonian and later times, when the resting places of Ibbi-Sin, Išbi-Erra, and his followers on the throne of Isin as well as the rulers of the first Babylonian dynasty were added.

79. The second is *CT* 30 10: rev. 4, which preserves little apart from the name (Weidner 1929: 238).

80. This is difficult to establish, because exemplars that are supposed to be from Larsa and Sippar have no specific provenience. But even if some of the British Museum exemplars are from "Sippar," it is clear that there were many different physical environments there that yielded non-archival tablets and that omens did not necessarily come from the same places as Sumerian school texts. Those from Tutub, Nerebtum, and Tell Yelkhi are not associated with other school texts (for bibliographical details see Jeyes 1989: 7–8). Koch-Westenholz (2000: 21 n. 48) says that the Susa tablet *MDP* 57 no. 4 is Old Babylonian, but it is definitely Middle Babylonian in date.

from ancient Mesopotamia, their cultural and literary impact is considerably reduced. The four celestial omens concerning Ibbi-Sin are embedded in the series *Enūma Anu Enlil*, which consisted of no less than seventy tablets, not to mention excerpts and commentaries (Reiner 1995: 12). Viewed in their proper environments, they melt into the mass of other omens and disappear from our view.

It is only in the latter part of the second millennium, or perhaps even later, that historical omens become important enough to be utilized in different literary contexts, most notoriously in the *Chronicle of Early Kings*, which appears to have been created out of such apodoses (Grayson 1966; 1975: 45). But such intertextual relationships take place in a very different literary context in which omens, rituals, and liturgical texts, all of which are almost completely absent from the Nippur and related school curricula, assume an essential and perhaps even a central place in the Babylonian literary tradition. As Maria deJong Ellis (1989: 162) wrote:

> In terms of literary interrelationships, clear connections exist between oracles, historical omens, prophecies, royal autobiographies and "pseudo-autobiographies," and the other classes of literary-historical texts. In content, many oracles show the terminology of the omen apodosis, which should not be surprising since on a practical level omens are at the very least to be connected with the manipulation of the divinatory mechanisms. On the most basic level of literary analysis, if a text is incomplete, it is often difficult to tell the difference between a "prophecy" or a "chronicle" and a compilation of omen apodoses. . . .

Although other literary-historical figures known from the omen compendia turn up in the *Chronicle of Early Kings*, neither Ibbi-Sin nor Išbi-Erra make an appearance in this composition. The last king of Ur does turn up in another late composition that has links with the omen tradition, the so-called *Weidner Chronicle*, which is actually an artfully constructed fictitious royal letter, ascribed anachronistically to Old Babylonian times, but the text is not well preserved at this juncture, and it is impossible to know what Išbi-Erra stands accused of here.[81]

When one steps back and looks over all of this material, it becomes evident that I have put together a heterogeneous assembly of data from various times and places that creates an illusion of a uniform tradition. But once one takes this all apart and then recontextualizes the scattered and badly documented material back within the flow of Mesopotamian writings, one sees that the subject of the fall of Ur is more conspicuous by its absence than by its presence; the issue that comes to the fore is the suppression of the broader aspects of its memory, rather than the collection of diverse philological references.

81. Rev. 33 (al-Rawi 1990: 13) *ḫi-pí* ᵈšul-gi *i-pu-šú a-ra-an-šú im-bi*-ᵈ30 dumu-ʳšúʾ *i*-⟨ ⟩. The source used by the Sippar scribe who left us the only text that preserves this line was already damaged when it was copied, as indicated by *ḫi-pí*.

Chapter 8

Afterword

The preceding chapters of this book offered surveys of the Sumerian literary letter tradition and the manuscripts and school settings of the CKU and attempted to relate the information contained in the royal correspondence to historical information gleaned from Ur III documentary sources. The main point that I have tried to stress throughout this book is the tenuous nature of CKU as a "corpus," so that even in Old Babylonian times we have to assume that only a small core of these letters constituted a regular part of schooling in Nippur and in places that used a similar set of teaching tools around the time of Samsu-iluna. Others were either composed ad hoc by schoolmasters or teachers or were part of traditions that were preserved outside of the central educational syllabus. Even in Nippur, however, the CKU letters were not used as often as were the other core literary texts of the loosely defined curriculum. And although there are indications that, when the royal letters were taught, they were often used in groupings and not individually, it is clear that the very notion of The Royal Correspondence of Ur/Correspondence of the Kings of Ur as a corpus is modern and cannot be projected into ancient times.

The consequences of such an approach are somewhat messy, but philologists—or at least some of them—prefer clearly defined groups and principles, recoiling from fuzzy sets and open definitions. At this juncture, all the uncertainties of the literary letter collections resurface and cloud our interpretive perspectives. How did the texts that we have come into being? Were some or all actually created under the Ur III kings or were they all composed later, and if so, when? The provenienced copies at our disposal were written during a narrow time-frame between reigns of Rim-Sin (1822–1763 B.C.) and Samsu-iluna (1749–1712 B.C.), but we have no way of knowing when, hypothetically, some letters might have been taken out of archives and incorporated into the literary tradition or when the imitations were composed. The very historicity of these texts has been a matter of some concern because they have been used by modern historians as primary sources for the reconstruction of events of the Ur III and early Isin periods (e.g., Jacobsen 1953; Rowton 1969; Wilcke 1969, 1970).

Over the last decade, two authors have made very different statements about the "authenticity" of the Ur III royal correspondence (Huber 2001; Hallo 2006). I should say at the outset that I am troubled by both of their positions, on methodological

216

grounds, because I cannot accept the very notion of authenticity as an ontological and heuristic concept; but this is not what I want to focus on in these pages. In defense of both authors, I note that they were working with inferior versions of the texts and with an undifferentiated notion of the CKU as a "corpus."

Fabienne Huber (2001) provocatively asserted that the royal correspondence was apocryphal, that it was all composed in the Old Babylonian period and should therefore be banished from all discussions of Ur III political history. She was apparently following the direction established by her teacher, Pascal Attinger, during a seminar at the University of Geneva in 1995 (Huber 2001: 170). I am sympathetic to her point of view, which has injected a salutary element of skepticism into the discussion, but I cannot accept the main lines of argument presented in her study, even if certain individual points are well taken. Huber uses three arguments to establish the late origins of the letters. Her first point is "philological"—that is, she identifies certain Sumerian morphological and syntactic features that she claims are Old Babylonian in origin and therefore point to a late creation of the letters. I find this unconvincing on a number of levels. We must take into account the fact that the literary letters as a whole comprise the only extensive set of Sumerian-language prose writing outside of the highly stylized and syntactically limited genre of royal inscriptions. As such, the comparison with royal hymns and other poetic texts or inscriptions, for that matter, cannot reveal very much about the issue at hand. Moreover, this kind of "dating by grammar" largely ignores the fact that all Sumerian-language texts were redacted and reformulated on the graphemic, phonemic, morphological, and even the semantic levels, most probably again and again, to conform to an artificial Standard Old Babylonian Sumerian that was used in the teaching establishments of the eighteenth- and seventeenth-century Mesopotamia and even beyond its borders. Some of the features she discusses are found primarily in texts that are clearly markers of late composition. But the use of enclitic *-ma*, the incorrect agreement-makers in verbal forms, and other elements are easily explained as elements introduced in the redactional process; other features, including certain "Akkadisms," could equally well have been already present in hypothetical Ur III versions.[1]

Huber's second line of reasoning against the authenticity of the correspondence rests on the recognition of "plagiats" between individual compositions. Some of these are clear indications of late composition, as is her first example, a comparison between ArŠ1 (1) and UrŠ1 (11); the latter is undeniably post-Ur III in date. Some of her other examples, however, are less convincing, as when she points to the repetition of elements that may be constitutive of epistolary style and to redactional contamination from one letter to another to make her case.

The third argument is based on prosopography/toponymy and is, to my mind, equally unconvincing, because the data that she uses entirely comprises names of persons and places found in various Old Babylonian manuscripts, including imaginative variants that clearly should not be considered in this kind of analysis. Moreover,

---

1. The "dating by grammar" issue has been addressed by Hallo 2006 and by Rubio, in press.

we differ in our assessment of the careers of some of the officials, including those of Aradmu and Apilaša, as documented in Ur III texts and described in the preceding chapters of this work, and, once again, in the value of textual contamination, as is the case with the anachronistic insertion of the name of Lu-Nanna, governor of Zimudar under Šu-Sin, in letters purporting to be from the time of Šulgi. Details are found in the appropriate places in earlier chapters; here I would like to summarize my own views on the matter.

First, I would exclude from the debate all obvious variants that are conditioned by later forces, as for example, Lu-Enki for Lu-Nanna, or Šu-Marduk for Puzur-Numušda. Once this is done, the situation becomes rather clear: of the twenty-nine persons mentioned in CKU, only eight cannot be identified with actual people who lived in Ur III times. To recapitulate, these people are:

1. Aba-indasa. The author of AbŠ1 (4), and a protagonist in four other letters (5–9), of which at least one ArŠ5 (9) is undeniably post-Ur III.
2. Ur-dun. The author of UdŠ1 (11), and mentioned in ArŠ7 (12), both of which are undoubtedly apocryphal.
3. The four officials mentioned in PuŠ1 (13), Puzur-Numušda, Lugal-melam, Ka-kugani, and Takil-ilissu, who are discussed in detail earlier. It is interesting that not one of the members of this cluster can be identified at present, but if the letter concerns repairs of the fortifications that are named bad mada, the letter could have been composed sometime around the year Š37 and therefore may have been earlier than the foundation of Puzriš-Dagan, which was commemorated in Šulgi's thirty-ninth year-name, that is, from a time in which such officials would not appear in the preserved documentation.
4. Niğdugani, saĝa of Enlil, and Iddi of Malgium. Of the 7 persons mentioned in the letter from Puzur-Numušda to Ibbi-Sin (PuIb1 [23]), only these two officials cannot be identified in the Ur III and early Isin documentary record.[2] In light of the relative paucity of sources from the reign of Ibbi-Sin, this is hardly an argument for late invention.

In summary—and I must stress that this is only an overview of Huber's main points— it is impossible to prove that all the surviving letters of the CKU were complete fictions fabricated in Old Babylonian times. Unfortunately, I find myself equally at odds with W. W. Hallo's (2006) strong defense of their authenticity, even if he is willing to admit that a few of the CKU compositions are definitely not Ur III.

So where do I stand on this issue? In purely practical terms I argue that, at a certain point in the development of the Nippur Old Babylonian teaching materials, some elements of authentic Ur III letters were incorporated into the curriculum, but that it is impossible to discern the various levels of redaction that transformed them into the school texts we are familiar with. Teachers were at liberty to concoct new letters on the patterns of existing letters or to ask their students to do so, but only in a few cases can we unequivocally recognize the new creations. This process is more evident outside of the areas that used the Nippur teaching corpus, since we see much less reliance on fixed texts in peripheral copies. I should also add that the hypotheti-

---

2. For a possible occurrence of Girbubu, see p. 199 above.

cal originals might not have all been purely archival letters; it is equally possible that some of them were elaborate epistles created as reports for semipublic consumption at court. We may never be able to reconstruct the history of this correspondence, but until we recover the royal archives of the kings of Ur, which may still lie in one of the palaces outside of the capital city, any further speculation on the subject is futile, as are most speculations about moments of pure origin in culture.

In my estimation—and this is admittedly a subjective personal impression—it is easier to say which letters are clearly Old Babylonian than to identify those that have a good chance of being derived from Ur III originals. Of the 25 items edited here, 7 are definitely late: ArŠ1a (1a), ArŠ5 (9), ArŠ6 (10), UrŠ (11), ArŠ7 (2), ŠIš1 (15), and IbIš1 (22), as are the long versions of IbIš1 (21) and IbPu1 (24). I am agnostic about 4 of the 5 letters that make up what I have called the Aba-indasa affair (letters 4–9; 9 is definitely late), and the same holds true about the Amar-Sin correspondence (letters 16–17). It seems fairly certain that many of the fabricated letters were answers to existing letters, because some teachers or scribes, most of them outside of Nippur, strove for symmetry on the pattern of the first three items of the "core" and on the Isin correspondence embedded in SEpM (items 2–5), where a letter to a king is followed by a royal response. Once one has set all these epistles aside, one is left with CKU letters 1, 2, 3, 13, 21, and 23—that is, essentially, the Nippur core with the addition of the Šu-Sin letters (18–19). I do not state categorically that all of these letters ultimately derive from authentic documents—only that there is a good probability that some of them might be descended, although filtered in a variety of ways, from Ur III documents of some kind. The fact that this judgment happens to correspond to the core use of these same texts in some Old Babylonian schools may or may not be coincidence, but more than this one cannot say.

The discussion about the authenticity of literary letters, perceived as a form of historical verisimilitude, is rooted in certain traditional philological notions of textuality, history, genre, and truth, but one could argue that epistolarity points us beyond such presuppositions. Letters, real or imaginary, have a unique semiotic status, with potentially endless chains of readings and misprision. In evaluating such texts, one has to take into account the primary act of the composition and its eventual decoding at its ultimate destination. But one must also presume that such texts may have new lives beyond the primary communicative act; some letters may be written with further readers in mind, as was the case with many Classical authors, or a letter may be lost or intentionally derailed, leading to other acts of reading. At each point, the text acquires new contextual meaning, leading to further communicative acts, some of which may not be epistolary at all. Let us assume, for the sake of argument, that some of the CKU letters may have actually been taken out of some royal archive and eventually reedited for instructional purposes. Does such a scenario result in texts that we might consider to be genuine historical sources and guarantee any degree of authenticity? As I see it the answer must be negative, as much as one would like to plead otherwise, because in being ripped from their archives, rewritten to conform to later standards, and recontextualized with new literary neighbors, the letters were semantically deformed and the stories they tell are Old Babylonian to a large degree. Even if we were to brush aside such considerations, we must still take into account the potential emotive and factual distortions embedded in them by their authors or by their scribes, distortions that are difficult if not impossible to identify in single or coupled letters that are only a small part of a larger conversation that is forever lost to us.

The effort to achieve historical certainty must also take into consideration that letters seen as literature confront the very nature of fiction, mimicking their own practical standing in the world, straddling the divide between private and public discourse, between writing and orality, and between the imagined and the real. It is no wonder that, in many different literary and cultural traditions, letters are thought to be crucial in the development of genres such as the novel. Some of us want the royal literary letters to be literally "true," because without them the stories we tell about Ur III and Isin times would be less interesting. But the fact is that even if one accepts a certain notion of historical proof, for reasons already mentioned above, we can never unravel the strands of choice, abandonment, revision, perdition, and invention that produced the textual corpus at our disposal. These issues are not unique to our area of study. Already half a decade ago, the Finnish scholar Heikki Koskenniemi (1956: 50), in the introduction to his survey of Greek letter-writing, rejected much received wisdom, observing that for all practical purposes one cannot make a distinction between real and fictitious Greek letters.

The CKU can be read in the context of school instruction, as discussed in chap. 3, or as literary artifact, as, for example, in the preceding chapter, where I briefly discussed the development of poetic prose in the direction of more complex united storylines. But the move toward something that we could call narrative fiction was a dead end, and the story of the combined four letters of the Ibbi-Sin correspondence is unique in Sumerian literary history. The importance of poetic literary letters, as well as the concomitant move toward epistolary prose narrative peaks in Old Babylonian times, but seems to lose its momentum, and drops out in later periods. The Old Babylonian period is also when Akkadian-language letters become ubiquitous in both royal and private communication; this is also when Akkadian begins to rise in status as a literary language. It is ironic, and perhaps not coincidental, that once epistolary communication becomes commonplace, the literary equivalents begin their eclipse, although recent publications provide evidence that literary letters made a comeback of sorts in much later times.

During the Old Babylonian period, Akkadian-language letter-writing was taught to some students as part of schooling, perhaps in places where writing instruction was focused on pragmatic issues and not on the old classics.[3] In Sumerian, letters of

3. See Michalowski 1983a: 222–27, with earlier literature. The whole issue needs to be studied anew in light of the recent publication, in photograph only, of 22 new Old Babylonian Akkadian-language school letter-exercises, some of them duplicates, most of which seem to come from the same archive (Wilson 2008: nos. 5–7, 10–12, 35, 45, 71–73, 161–66, and 168–72).

petition to deities and kings are couched in elaborate poetry, but the Old Babylonian "letters to gods" are written in simple prose and are inscribed in the documentary, not in the literary, hand. Six texts of this kind are known at present from Babylonia, as well as two royal letters to gods from Mari (van der Toorn 1996: 131). Occasionally, the divine world reached for the letter as a means of communication. A rare example of such an instance is found among tablets from the archive of the administrator of the Ištar Kitittum temple in Ishchiali (ancient Neribtum or Kiti), which include two epistles from the goddess to her king, Ibal-piel II of Ešnunna, composed in a complex, difficult language and filled with rare words and expressions (Ellis 1987, 1989: 138–40). The verbal complexity of these letters contrasts markedly with the prosaic nature of the contemporary Akkadian letters to gods, so that it is unlikely that the two text types are in any way pragmatically related.

There are at present only four elaborate Old Babylonian epistles that can be classified as "literary letters."[4] The first is an unusual literary letter addressed from Sin-muballiṭ, brother of King Rim-Sin of Larsa, who was apparently in charge of Maškan-šapir. Andrew George (2009: 117) in his edition noted: "the composition makes much use of balanced structures typical of Babylonian poetry and can be categorized as a highly elevated prose." The second is a bilingual letter of petition addressed to the Mari king, Zimri-Lim, found in the palace of the Syrian city and is therefore probably a genuine appeal to the ruler rather than a teaching tool; but it demonstrates a full command of Sumerian as well as Akkadian literary conventions and is the work of a scribe who was familiar with the southern tradition of literary letters of petition.[5] The third is an Akkadian letter of petition that seems to have been deliberately patterned on the matrix of the Sumerian letter-prayer (Kraus 1983: 207; van der Toorn 1996: 134); it even uses the Akkadian equivalents of the Sumerian opening formula, addressing the recipient three times with terms derived from the lexical tradition.[6] The phraseology is so close to what one finds in Sumerian that it is not out of the question that this poem may have been originally composed in Sumerian and translated into Akkadian. The fourth is a missive, found in at least four duplicates, from king Samsu-iluna to various high officials in the subdivisions of the city of Sippar (Janssen 1991); unless the letter was originally sent in multiple copies, this epistle may have entered the scribal curriculum at the time. To these must be added the two much simpler, genre-bending letters of Sargon of Agade that are combined with lists of professional names (J. G. Westenholz 1997: 141–69). The Nippur and Ur exemplars may be variants of the same composition.

The scribes of the latter part of the second millennium and first-millennium Assyria and Babylonia copied older royal letters and even composed new fictions in this form, including a satirical missive from Gilgameš (Gurney 1957; Kraus 1980)

4. Add to this, perhaps, the unaddressed Akkadian letter published by George (2009: 114–15).
5. *Letter to Zimri-Lim.*
6. See above, p. 30.

and an elaborate historiographic text that was known, for many years, as the *Wei-dner Chronicle*. It now turns out that this was a letter, purportedly written by an Old Babylonian king of Babylon to a king of Isin (al-Rawi 1990). The letter circulated in Akkadian, but at least one manuscript was written as a Sumerian and Akkadian bilingual (Finkel 1980: 72–74). Another late creation purporting to be addressed by Samsu-iluna to one Enlil-nadim-šumi is known from three duplicates, two of which were discovered in Assurbanipal's libraries (al-Rawi and George 1994: 135–39). These belong to a substantial list of literary letters of Babylonian and Assyrian kings that are now known from copies that range from approximately the eighth to the second centuries B.C. that have been brought together and studied in a preliminary manner by Eckhart Frahm (2005).[7] In addition to the missives ascribed to Samsu-iluna, there are items that claim to have an origin in Kassite, Neo-Assyrian, and Neo-Babylonian times. As Frahm observes, some of them are clearly spurious, while others may be copies, or adaptations, of real letters, and many of them are character-ized by high literary diction. Since the author has announced his intent to provide a more detailed study of these compositions, I shall say no more about them, except to observe that they are much more heterogeneous than the CKU, in origin, style, and time of copy. They also surface in a very distinctive literary world, in which re-dactional activity, royal, temple, and private tablet collections, as well as educational processes all combined to provide a very different semantic and pragmatic context for the royal literary letters.[8]

The literary letter of petition was not dead, however. Sometime during the last decades of the Assyrian Empire, a scribe by the name of Urad-Gula composed a long, immensely elaborate example of such a composition to his king, most likely Assur-banipal, full of allusions and quotations from literary texts (Parpola 1987). Although later schoolboy copies of royal correspondence are known, this text is perhaps the last grand example of innovation in the Mesopotamian literary letter tradition.[9]

From all of this, one may conclude that, while the concept of letters as literature seems to crop up at various times, after the Old Babylonian period, it is never as-sociated with the kings of Ur, although we must keep in mind the still unparalleled bilingual Middle Babylonian CKU tablet from Susa, which may be a solitary witness to a tradition that remains hidden to us for now.

The picture that emerges from all of this conforms, if only in general contours, with what we observe in the later Mesopotamian literary tradition: outside of the omens (Cooper 1980), the Ur III dynasty has been narrowed down to one king only,

---

7. See also Llop and George 2003: 9–11.

8. Ronnie Goldstein (2010) has now proposed a novel interpretation of the Seleucid con-text of the pseudo-epigraphic letters of Assurbanipal that concern the collecting of tablets for his libraries. She observes (2010: 207): "Wishing to recall their own cultural heritage, and threatened by the strong Hellenistic culture in Seleucid times, these scribes evoked the days of Ashurbani-pal's great library, stressing the important place of Babylonia in it, so claiming their important place in the history of knowledge."

9. For more details on literary letters, see Hallo 1981.

namely, Šulgi.[10] The whole dynasty is mentioned in the so-called *Weidner Chronicle*, but otherwise only Šulgi's name lives on in the great libraries of the first millennium, most notably in the text Assyriologists have labeled the *Šulgi Prophecy* (Grayson and Lambert 1964; Borger 1971). The date of composition of this fascinating text is not easy to determine (Ellis 1989: 148 n. 104), and some have suggested that it goes back to the end of the second millennium (Borger 1971: 23). Although its generic identity is a problematical issue, there seem to be observable connections between this composition, as well as similar ones, and the astronomical omen tradition (Biggs 1985). The name of Šulgi has cropped up in fragments from the Neo-Assyrian Nabu temple in Nimrud (Wiseman and Black 1996: nos. 65, 65, 69); the three pieces may be part of the same tablet, but this has not been confirmed. Robert Biggs (1997: 174), who first analyzed these pieces, cautiously suggests that they may belong to the *Šulgi Prophecy*. More recently, a fragment of a related Neo-Babylonian pseudoepigraphical Šulgi "inscription" from Ur has come to light (*UET* 6/3 919; Frahm 2006). Finally, there is also a unique late first-millennium copy of a letter addressed to the second Ur III king, excavated at Babylon, written in an imitation of Ur III script (Neumann 1992a; Michalowski 1993: 117–18; Neumann 2006: 19–20). According to its colophon, it was copied from a tablet found in the temple of the moon-god Sin in Ur, but the veracity of this statement is difficult to evaluate. These late traditions concerning the second king of the Ur III dynasty have their own dynamic and are unrelated in any way to the earlier Sumerian language literature about this monarch.

Of the more than 70 literary letters that have survived from Old Babylonian teaching rooms and courtyards, only 3 or 4 survived into later times. CKU items 14 and 15 are preserved in the fourteenth-century bilingual Susa tablet; the first, from Šulgi to Puzur-Šulgi, is probably apocryphal but is attested in Old Babylonian versions, while the latter, a ridiculous, possibly comical missive from Išbi-Erra to Šulgi, is as yet unduplicated and had all the marks of post-Old Babylonian composition. The final item of SEpM, which deals with scribal matters, crops up in bilingual Middle Babylonian form in Boghazköy and Ugarit and in later garb in Assur and Neo-Babylonian Babylon (Civil 2000: 109–16). The only early royal epistle that appears to survive into the first millennium is the letter-prayer of the Old Babylonian Larsa king Sin-iddinam, addressed to the sun-god Utu, known at present from early unilingual manuscripts from Nippur, Sippar, and elsewhere, as well as in a bilingual version from Emar and Kuyunjik.[11] Of the CKU there is not a trace after the fifteenth-century tablet from Susa.

The CKU, in its various incarnations, was a constituent of Old Babylonian education in Nippur, Ur, Uruk, Isin, Kish, Sippar, Susa, and elsewhere. During the Kassite period these texts became obsolete, as did much of the literature that was created

---

10. An early first-millennium astronomical compendium even refers to the whole dynasty as the *palû* ("reign, dynasty, time in office") of Šulgi: MUL.APIN II ii 18 (Hunger and Pingree 1989: 96; see already Finkelstein 1966: 104 and, most recently, Heimpel 2003: 14 n. 32).

11. *Letter of Sin-iddinam to Utu.*

in Ur III and early Old Babylonian times, and with minor exceptions, was lost for millennia, only to be recovered by modern archaeologists and looters. The present edition, imperfect as it may be, is dedicated to bringing this Sumerian royal epistolary prose literature back to a new life.

Appendixes

Appendix A:
The Reading of the Name of the Grand Vizier

The name of the great official of the Ur III state is conventionally rendered "Arad-Nanna" or "Aradmu"; the latter is written with the signs ÁRAD (ARAD×KUR) and MUHALDIM, and is conventionally read as árad-mu or, in more modern fashion, as urdu-ĝu₁₀. The Sumerian "pronunciation" of the first sign, which stands for "slave, servant," has been rendered variously as /arad/, /urdu/, or /urda/. There are two reasons for this discrepancy: the data from lexical texts as well as the evidence from etymology. All of the pertinent information has been gathered together by I. J. Gelb (1982) and J. Krecher (1987), who reached very different conclusions, and it will not be repeated here. I only note that I would not take seriously the writing ur-du-um-gu in *MDAI* 57 1, since the mid-second-millennium Susa scribe of this tablet was hardly an authority on Sumerian pronunciation and was more concerned with playing syllabic games than with linguistic authenticity.[1] Gelb viewed the word as a loan from Akkadian, but Krecher provided a tortuous Sumerian etymology that I find unacceptable.[2]

A perusal of the information from the lexical texts suggests that, in the first millennium lexical tradition, primarily in the syllabaries, the received interpretation of árad was both /urdu/ and /arad/. The Old Babylonian documentation is clearer on the topic: ProtoEa offers the reading /arad/.

ur-du : ⌜ARAD×KUR⌝ (Proto-Ea 790 [*MSL* 14 61])
ur-du : ⌜ARAD×KUR⌝ = [*wa-ar-du-um*] (Proto-Aa 790:1 [*MSL* 14 102])
ur-du : ARAD = *wa-ar-du-um* (Secondary Proto-Ea/Aa no. 1.3 iii 16
    [*MSL* 14 134])

---

1. This is the Susa source for ŠPu1 (letter 14) and ŠIs1 (letter 15); the specific writing of the name is in lines 21 and 37 of the former (ŠPu1MB). On the peculiarities and date of this tablet, see p. 56.

2. See Steinkeller 1993: 121 n. 38, who also rejects this argument. Others have accepted this analysis; see, for example, Wilcke 2007: 53.

First-millennium syllabaries offer the readings /urda/ (/arda/) and /arad/ :

ur-da : ARAD×KUR = MIN(*ar-du*)	(Aa VIII/2 218 [*MSL* 14 502])
ur-da : ARAD×KUR = MIN(*ar-du*)	(Ea VIII 145 [*MSL* 14 481])
[á]r-da : ARAD = *ar-du*	(Aa VIII/2 213 [*MSL* 14 502])
[á]r-da : ARAD = *ar-du*	(Ea VIII 140 [*MSL* 14 481])
arad = á[r-da]	(Lu fragment; *MSL* 12 142])
a-rad : ARAD = MIN(*ar-du*)	(Aa VIII/2 216 [*MSL* 14 502])
MIN(a-rad) : ARAD×KUR = MIN(*ar-du*)	(Aa VIII/2 217 [*MSL* 14 502])
a-rad : ARAD = MIN(*ar-du*)	(Ea VIII 143 [*MSL* 14 481])
a-rad : ARAD×KUR = MIN(*ar-du*)	(Ea VIII 144 [*MSL* 14 481])
[a-rad] : arad = [*ar*]-*du*	(Sb Voc. II 345 [*MSL* 3 150])

This suggests that the pre-Sargonic version of the word, written HAR.TU, should be read ur_5-tu or àr-tu, but forms that are followed by a sign beginning with the consonant /d/ point to u/arad when the form contains a bound morpheme.[3] It is possible that the discrepancy in readings is due to the two different Akkadian forms of the word for "slave, servant," Babylonian (*w*)*ardu*(*m*) and Assyrian *urdu*(*m*). It may be that the loan in Sumerian originally came from a Semitic dialect in which the lexeme was similar to the later Assyrian rather than the Babylonian form, but in later times the word was either loaned again or simply adjusted to correspond to the contemporary Babylonian (w)*ardu*(*m*).

The second sign in the name, MUHALDIM, has the syllabic readings mu as well as $\tilde{g}u_{10}$. The latter is used almost exclusively for the non-oblique form of the first-person singular bound possessive pronoun. I suggest that, lacking any direct evidence for Ur-III-period pronunciation, one chooses -mu because the name does not mean "My Slave," but is instead a hypocoristic form of Arad-Nanna. It seems improbable that people would refer to the person who was second in status only to the king in such a manner. It is therefore most likely that in Ur III times, at least, the name was read as something like "A/Urdumu," but one cannot be certain of how Old Babylonian students and teachers interpreted the name, which was no longer used in the culture, and it is possible that some of them would have playfully rendered it as Uradğu or Aradğu, as did the scribe of the Susa tablet hundreds of years later. Therefore, to steer clear of confusion and to avoid disharmony with the received folk tradition of Assyriological literature, I consistently refer to the grand vizier as Aradmu. This is a conventional modern rendition, similar to Tiglath-pilesar or Assurbanipal, even if he was somewhat lower in rank.

3. For examples, see Krecher 1987, although he reaches different conclusions and creates an unlikely form urdud. For other discussions of HAR.TU, with earlier literature, see Steinkeller 1989: 130 n. 389 and Steible 1993: 209–11.

Appendix B:
The Title galzu unkena

Although the title is unattested in any document prior to the Old Babylonian period, two officers are designated as gal-zu unken-na in CKU: Apilaša and Šarrumbani. In one lexical text, it is translated as *rab puḫruli*, "chief of the assembly," and it is usually listed after the zabar-dab₅ and the gal unken-na, Akkadian *mu'irrum*.[4] To my knowledge, its only literary attestation is in a hymn to Ningišzida, known from a solitary manuscript, which reads (*Ningišzida Hymn A: 27*):

palil gal-zu unken-na ǧárza-e hé-du₇
"Member of the vanguard/foremost, g., fit for high office/to be a high officer."

It is possible that this line refers to the martial qualities of Ningišzida, but the nouns are ambiguous.

It is obvious that the title has nothing to do with the "assembly," although perhaps the original etymology might have been somehow connected with unken.[5] The same holds true for the title gal unken-na = *mu'irrum*, a designation for an agricultural official or more generally a "commander director."[6] In fact, these two titles seem to have nothing in common except for the similarity in the way they were written, and therefore they were listed next to one another in the lexical texts.[7]

There are three occurrences of gal.zu unken.na as a logogram in Old Babylonian archival sources: (a) *YBT* 5 163, (b) *UET* 5 247 and (c) *AbB* 13 119:10. Of these, (a) is the most informative; in this Rim-Sin period document, rations are provided for people who may or may not be part of the personnel of the Ekišnugal temple in Ur.[8] The first four are: the g., the zabar.dab₅, the pisaǧ.dub.ba, and only

4. Proto-Lu 15 (*MSL* 12 33) and Lu I 17 (*MSL* 12 96, bilingual).

5. The role of "assemblies" in ancient Mesopotamia continues to be a contested issue; see for the present Seri 2006: 159–80.

6. Thus *CAD* M/2 178. See Yoffee 1977: 83 and Seri 2006: 171–74. Charpin (2007: 180) summarizes his own earlier statements on the issue, taking a different approach, linking the title to the "assembly."

7. See *CAD* M/2 180. The Sumerian reading of gal unken.na is problematical; see Sjöberg 1969: 96–97.

8. For this text, see Charpin 1986: 234–35.

then the saĝa—that is, the chief administrator of the temple complex. During this period, the functions of those who held the second and third of these titles is not always clear, but in many contexts they appear as high military officials. As Charpin (1986: 236) noted, the title under discussion here is also found in (b), from the time when Rim-Sin occupied Ur, in which a g. together with several judges renders a legal decision. The letter (c) is less informative, because the immediate context is broken, but the general topic concerns a "tax field" (a.šà gú.un), and it is possible that we are dealing with military colonists. All of this suggests that in Old Babylonian times the g. was a rather high-ranking military officer, in the south at least, but the scarcity of references makes it unlikely that this was a commonly encountered position and therefore perhaps the title was only given to officers assigned for special tasks.

None of these references, however, are of help in establishing the meaning of the title during the Ur III period; indeed, it is possible that it was not even used at that time. Although the evidence is insufficient at this time to provide a definitive explanation of the title, it appears that in CKU it designated a special envoy appointed by the king for the performance of specific tasks. Both Apilaša and Šarrum-bani held the title šakkana, "general/military governor," prior to their appointment as gal-zu unken-na.[9] This, in connection with the nature of their missions, suggests that the title was one that remained within the sphere of the military establishment of the Ur III state. On the surface, the situation seems very much like what we encounter during Old Babylonian times, but all of the evidence is indecisive and more than this one cannot say. In the translations, I have rendered the title in English as "prefect," but this is only a conventional approximation of its true meaning.

9. It is only conjecture that Apilaša was a general before his appointment as gal-zu un-ken-na. Šarrum-bani served as a general after he was governor of Apiak and prior to his tenure as gal-zu unken-na. See pp. 70–72 above.

Appendix C:
"Facing (the) Hursag̃"

The designation igi hur-sag̃-g̃á may be interpreted as "facing the Hursag̃" or as "facing the mountain ranges." In actual documents, the designation appears only in two contexts outside of CKU. The first occurrence is in a year-name of Sumu-la-el:[10]

> mu ég igi-hur-sag̃-g̃á mu-un-si-ig
> The year: Sumu-la-el piled up the irrigation embankment facing Hursag̃.

And, the second is in the name of the nineteenth year of Hammurabi:

> mu bàd mah igi-hur-sag̃-g̃á^{ki}
> mu bàd mah igi-hur-sag̃-g̃á^{ki}
> The year: (Hammurabi built) the great fortification(s) facing Hursag̃.

In neither case could this designation refer to the Hamrin or any of the major Zagros mountain ranges. While it is difficult to establish the precise parameters of Sumu-la-el's kingdom during the course of his reign (Goddeeris 2002: 347–49), it seems unlikely that he would be digging anything in the mountains, but he did control Kazallu and Marad and could have done work in this region. As far as Hammurabi is concerned, his kingdom could not even come close to the Hamrin, because the powerful state of Ešnunna would have stood in his way at the time of his eighteenth and nineteenth regal years. Therefore, wherever his "great fortifications" may have been, they were not literally facing the mountains. But his year-name has additional significance for this edition: there is always the possibility that there never was an Ur III Bad-Igihursag̃a and that Old Babylonian scholars inscribed the name of Hammurabi's constructions into the CKU.

The designation "facing the mountains" is known from the lexical tradition, more precisely from the composition HAR-ra = ḫubullu.

(a) tir-ga igi hur-sag̃-g̃á^{ki} (Hh XX-XXIV OB Forerunner 1 vi 41 [*MSL* 11 133])

(b) te-ir-ga igi hur-sag̃-g̃á (Hh XX-XXIV OB Forerunner 9 rev. i 6 [*MSL* 11 144])

(c) tir-qa-an igi hur-sag̃^{ki} = *pa-ni ša-di* (Hh XX-XXII Ras Shamra Rec. A ii 44′ [*MSL* 11 45])

---

10. Sumu-la-el 32/33. The name also crops up in the Emar "forerunner" to Hh XXVII as ég u₄-ki igi hur-sag̃-g̃á; see Civil 1994: 114.

(d) [tir-ga-(an) igi hur-sağ^{ki}] = ⸢šá pa-an KUR-*i*⸣ (Hh XXI Section 10
     1 [MSL 11 18])

(e) tir-qa-an igi hur-sağ^{ki} = *tir-qa-an šá-di-i* = šá ^dbu-la-[la] (Hg E to Hh
     XX-XXIV rev.ᴵ 15 [MSL 11 35])

(f) [t]ir-ga-an igi hur-sağ^{ki} = ŠU MIN šá IGI KUR-*i* = *ár-man*; PA-*din*
     (Hg B V to Hh XX-XXIV iii 6 [MSL 11 36])

In the two late HAR-gud commentaries (e) and (f), the entries are accompanied by
additional listings:

(g) tir-qa-an igi gu-ti-um^{ki} = *tir-qa-*⸢*an*⸣ *šá pa-an gu-ti-i* = URU LU-*ti*
     (Hg E to Hh XX-XXIV rev.! 14 [MSL 11 35], before e)

(h) [ti]r-ga-an igi gu-ti^{ki} = ŠU MIN šá IGI *gu-ti-i* = *ḫar-ḫar* (Hg B V to
     Hh XX-XXIV iii 7 [MSL 11 36], after f)

Goetze (1964: 118), who commented on these passages, provided an explanation of
(f): "The gloss Arman Hattin would locate it in the vicinity of Arman/Halba and
the Hattin(a) of the Assyrians." Whiting (1976: 181 n. 21), citing Goetze, identified the Terqan facing Gutium with the Ti-ir-qa of Early Old Babylonian texts,
which he located east of the Tigris. It must be kept in mind that the HAR-gud
explanations are quite late and may reflect geographical speculations that are of
little relevance to earlier usage, but the association of the Tirqa facing Gutium with
har-har in (h) seems to agree with an Old Babylonian letter that mentions the city
together the Karkar (Whiting 1976: 181 n. 21). D. Charpin (2003a: 29 with n. 144)
has drawn attention to this passage and also provides additional information on the
eastern Tirqa, which he places in the vicinity of Simurum.

There is one possible Ur III occurrence of the eastern Tirqa in a fragmentary
account from Drehem that lists taxes from a number of places east of the Tigris
(*Trouvaille* 54). Line 3 of the first preserved column of this text reads, according to
the copy, érin ti-ni-qa^{ki}, but Gelb (1938: 83) proposed to read the second sign as
ir, and this has apparently been accepted by other scholars—for example, by Whiting (1976: 180–81, with earlier literature), Owen (1997: 389), Luciani (1999: 3), as
well as in Steinkeller's (1987: 28 n. 56) list of cities that paid provincial taxes, which
includes Tirqa. However, collation of the tablet, which is in Istanbul, apparently
shows that neither de Genouillac's drawing nor Gelb's emendation are correct: the
line now reads [érin ti]-sa^ĭ-ga^{ki} (Yıldız and Gomi 1988: 20).

All of this demonstrates that the phrase igi hursağa was used in Old Babylonian
times twice in a manner that may have to be translated as "facing Hursağ," but, if
truth be told, this is simply a supposition based on circumstantial evidence. The in-
tuitively more proper notion "facing the mountains" is only known as a descriptive
phrase in lexical texts and pertains to only a single toponym. If one were to make
a connection between Bad-Igihursağa and the Tirqa that faced the mountains, one
would probably have to locate the fortifications in the vicinity of Dašil and Awal, in
the Hamrin plain. In this case, one would have to assume that the CKU letter PuŠ1
(13) is mostly if not completely spurious.

Appendix D:
The Location of Hamazi

The governor Puzur-Numušda, in his letter to King Ibbi-Sin, recounts that Išbi-Erra, having taken over Nippur and Isin, had, among his other achievements, plundered the land of Hamazi (PuIb1: 35 [23]). He also describes Išbi-Erra's claims that the god Enlil had promised him dominion over the homeland (kalam) and that it would stretch (line 5),

ma-da ha-ma-zi^{ki}-ta en-na a-ab-ba má-gan-na^{ki}-šè
from the land of Hamazi (down) to the Sea of Magan (i.e., the Persian Gulf)

The location of this land or city, which Piotr Steinkeller (1998: 79) justly describes as "rather mysterious," has been much debated over the years, but without new information the matter will undoubtedly remain unresolved for some time to come. The geographical name occurs in Early Dynastic dedicatory inscriptions, in a letter from Ebla, in the *Sumerian King List*, in lexical texts, and in two literary "epics" about Enmerkar of Uruk, but none of these references are of any use in precisely localizing the place, althought they all point to the east.[11] Jacobsen (1939: 98 n. 166) was certain that it should lie "in the mountainous regions of Kirkuk, near modern Sulaimaniyyah." Part of his reasoning was based on references in the Old Akkadian texts from Gasur (Nuzi). Someone named Šu-Eštar of Hamazi is mentioned twice (HSS 10 143 rev. 7', 153 rev. ii 7–8), and one Ititi from there occurs in still another document (HSS 10 155: 24–25), but the latter text also includes someone from Assur, which demonstrates that place-names in these texts are not necessarily very close by.

Steinkeller (1998: 85), in his thorough review of references to Hamazi, speculates that it might have been the older name of Ekallatum, which he locates north of Assur or Qabara, on the Lower Zab. Unfortunately, he provides no more solid evidence for this than his predecessors have, and these suggestions, while tantalizing, are still hypothetical. But if we are to take seriously the claim that Hamazi was ravaged by Išbi-Erra early in his reign and that it constituted the northern limit of his kingdom, a location north of Assur, while not impossible, seems somewhat improbable.

---

11. For references, see Edzard 1972, Astour 1987: 8, and Steinkeller 1998: 84–85.

After the three Gasur references, the only occurrences of Hamazi in documents come from Ur III times. Most of them are of not geographically helpful but five texts point to a trans-Tigridian location. All of them record taxes or dues from frontier regions: in *PDT* 1 171, Hamazi is followed by Der; in *MVN* 15 179 (n.d.), Hamazi is followed by Maškan-Dudu and Ešnunna; in *JCS* 31 166 A (AS8.5.8), it is in the company of hamlets that may lie in the Diyala and beyond, including Arrapha and Lullubum, and the same holds true for *PDT* 2 959 (n.d.). In *AUCT* 1 93:22 (AS5.4.10), deliveries from the city are precede by those of Ṣilluš-Dagan and Hašib-atal, who must be the commanders or even rulers of Simurrum and Arrapha, respectively.[12] All of this suggests but does not prove that Hamazi lay in the vicinity of Arrapha and Gasur, south of the Lower Zab, much in concert with the ideas of Jacobsen (1959), Edzard (1972), as well as Edzard and Farber (1974: 73).[13]

12. On the former, see Owen 2001b; on the latter, see Goetze 1963: 5.
13. "Grose Lokalisierung im Osttigrisland zw. Oberem Zab und Diyala."

Part 2

The Correspondence of
the Kings of Ur:
Text Editions

Introduction to the Text Editions

This section contains editions of all 24 letters of the CKU. The presentation for the most part follows, with minor deviations, the matrix system first used by Jerrold Cooper in his edition of the *Curse of Agade* (Cooper 1983: 72) and further developed by Miguel Civil in his publication of *The Farmer's Instructions* (Civil 1994: 207).[1] A reconstructed ideal text is followed by matrixes that provide maximum clarity in the representation of the individual witnesses and allow for the immediate perception of similarity and difference. It must be stressed that the reconstructed text is a redactional fiction created for analytical, citation, and translation purposes that does not correspond to any actual version of the composition that existed in antiquity. The issue of how to edit cuneiform texts has never been seriously debated, and it is a matter that is far too complex to be dealt with here in a satisfactory manner; only a few observations pertinent to the present edition will be noted.

The theory of textual editing has made much progress in recent decades, and the traditional methods of reconstruction, which attempt to strip away levels of textual changes in order to arrive at a pristine hypothetical original that would fully represent the author's intent, has largely been abandoned in many disciplines. The classic presentation of newer thinking about the materiality of textual traditions is that of Jerome McGann, whose 1983 monograph, *A Critique of Modern Textual Criticism*, has influenced a whole generation of scholars. Susan Cherniack offered a succinct summary of the theory followed here in the introduction to a study of Chinese textual transmission (Cherniack 1994: 8):

> [T]he goal of the critical edition, contemporary textual theorists argue, is undermined by the scholarly apparatus attached to the edition's reading text. The use of the apparatus changes the reading experience. As we move between one version of the work and another, the shape of the text shifts. What we encounter is not the work as the author wrote it but what Jerome J. McGann calls a "shape-shifting" entity—an ever changing work of composite authorship, which reveals itself as an ongoing social project, with contributions from sundry readers, editors, collators, printers, and booksellers. From this perspective, the variations among the versions may be seen to mark events in the life of the work, like rings on a tree. . . . Whether or not the critical text succeeds in fulfilling the author's intentions (and this is usually unverifiable), we can say with McGann that it is certainly "not a text which ever existed before." It is *not* the author's text reconstituted somehow. Like all previous

1. See also Michalowski 1989: 21–27.

versions, it is a new text, which emerges in a particular historical context but carries with it the entire history of its evolution.

Various ways of dealing with texts have been proposed, some of them attuned toward postmodernist visions of editing that would erase any intentionality on the part of the editor, but as Small (1999: 56) observes, this kind of activity "is inescapably value-laden, simply because editing deals not with text but with relevant or identified text, that is, with works and versions." Even hypertext and other technological solutions cannot overcome this problem, and "different editorial and critical orientations would generate different narratives from which to hang the facts of the textual situation" (P. Cohen 1996: 736). It is therefore possible to make a very different edition of the CKU that might reveal new insights, but at a certain moment one has to choose one's methods and proceed accordingly.

These theoretical observations pertain to certain types of manuscript cultures, but their general tenor applies to the Mesopotamian situation as well, as long as one takes into consideration pertinent culture-specific ramifications. In the case of Old Babylonian literature, the historical depth is difficult to gauge, and the tree-ring metaphor invoked by Cherniack only takes one so far. My main reason for invoking these postulates is to make certain that there are no misunderstandings about the critical texts presented here. The issue of variation, however, is another matter altogether.

Letters turned into literature constitute a perfect example of what Roland Barthes (1968) famously called the "reality effect," if I may be permitted to invoke this expression once again. In everyday practice, letters are one-of-a-kind elements in a communicative chain; hence, they are by definition unique. Multiple copies of epistles mark them as members of a different code and, as a result, their semiotic status is altered as they are removed from their own web of meaning and are entered into a different intertextual universe. But real or not, because an epistle reproduces, imitates, or riffs on a specific communicative act, one expects the text to be fixed and unalterable, ever the more so when royal authority is involved. To be sure, when letters are used in cuneiform schooling, one expects a certain level of textual deviation that is similar to what one finds in other pedagogic material—that is, variation that can be ascribed to the way in which texts were dictated, written from memory, and copied from instructors examples. The results of such processes, using the so-called decad, have now been exhaustively studied by Paul Delnero (2006), following upon the more limited investigations of Gene Gragg (1972) and Pascal Attinger (1993: 95–139). Even if we still do not fully understand the many sources of textual variation, we now do have a fairly good picture of the kinds of ways in which manuscripts of the same Old Babylonian literary composition may differ one from another. I have not provided a full listing of all such variants in CKU because it would be pointless; these texts should be considered with all other prose letters for any meaningful analysis of these kinds of phenomena in Sumerian literary prose.

But even without an exhaustive tabulation, it is clear from the textual matrixes that there is an unusually high level of variation in some parts of the CKU, so much so that one has to inquire as to why epistolary literature would exhibit such levels of difference, contrary to all generic expectations. Some texts from the CKU "core"—for example, the first three letters, ArŠ1 (1), ŠAr1 (2), and ArŠ2 (3)—look no different than the texts of the Decad, as far as textual variation is concerned, with the usual array of grammatical and orthographic disparity. But once we progress to the fourth letter, AbŠ1 (4), the disparity between witnesses is striking; indeed, I know of no other Sumerian literary composition that is characterized by such a large degree of textual dissimilarity. Each and every manuscript has a different set of lines, so that the composite text as reconstructed here is an utter fiction. Some of them are so short as to even omit the name of the sender of the letter of petition altogether. One could argue that this letter is composed in poetry, not prose, and that this may at least partially account for the lack of textual stability. But the next letter in the "core," PuŠ1 (13), also exhibits a textual fluidity that is unexpected in an epistle: in a passage describing parts of fortifications that are need of repair, each manuscript has a different line order, and the names of officials in charge of each segment are often different from one exemplar to another. When one looks outside the "core" and beyond Nippur and the places that used a similar curricular set, the textual tradition becomes even more unstable. This is particularly true for the royal responses to letters from officials—that is, for the letters whose historicity is most suspect, such as ŠPu1 (14) and IbIš1 (22), for which each preserved manuscript has to be considered a different recension. Perhaps the most acute example of such a cavalier attitude toward textual stability are the "non-Nippurean" long editions of two of the letters of the Ibbi-Sin correspondence, which add extensive poetic passages that are not found in provenienced manuscripts.

How are we to explain this state of affairs? In view of the fact that the distribution of tablets with CKU does not differ substantially from that of other school compositions, there is little likelihood that this can be attributed to chance. It is also unlikely that the large degree of variation can be attributed to place in the curriculum. There may be unrecoverable generic forces at play that affect literary epistles precisely because they imitate real ones, but there is little one can say about such matters without more insight into native genre theory. Perhaps this is a function of the fact that the CKU may have been added to the curriculum relatively late: as already discussed above, it is impossible to trace the existence of these letters before the time of Rim-Sin, but this is also the case with a large portion of Old Babylonian Sumerian literary texts. It is interesting—and this has also been discussed earlier—that although the SEpM is documented at Mari there is apparently no trace of CKU among the recently discovered Old Babylonian school texts from the Syrian city, but the date of these tablets is not clear at the present time. If the CKU had not been part of the curriculum in earlier Old Babylonian times, then perhaps the textual instability reflects the fact that the textual tradition was not considered truly fixed, especially outside of the Nippur-centric scribal areas. While this is certainly possible, I find it highly unlikely.

Because these are students' exercises, the level of variation reflects a wide range of professorial preference as well as varying degrees of individual student competence.

Ideally, each manuscript of each letter should be transliterated and translated separately, but such a treatment of 115 different tablets would be impractical and self-defeating. In a few cases, when the nature of the texts required it, I have edited texts in different manners for practical purposes, and if this alarms seekers of perfect consistency, so be it. The symbols in the matrixes, for the most part taken from Civil (1994: 207), are as follows:

+   sign is fully present
o   sign is not present due to damage to the tablet
.   sign is broken but recognizable
-    sign is omitted
x   sign is unidentifiable
*   line is omitted
:   line continues

The sigla of individual manuscripts are coded by provenance: I = Isin, Ki = Kish, N = Nippur, Ur = Ur, Uk = Uruk, Si = Sippar, Su = Susa, X = unknown.

For convenience, the letters are numbered sequentially for internal purposes of this volume and are also identified by a name and abbreviation that includes a separate, open-ended numbering scheme that allows for future additions. This is followed by other names or numbers that have been applied to the letter in the past, as well as by the unique number assigned in Miguel Civil's unpublished catalog of Old Babylonian literary texts, which is also used by *The Electronic Text Corpus of Sumerian Literature* (ETCSL; online: http://etcsl.orinst.ox.ac.uk/). Because there are differences between the new edition and my out-of-date RCU, a concordance of the two is provided below (see p. 246). Following the list of sources, previous editions and selected translations are mentioned. Fuller bibliographical information is provided by ETCSL and is not repeated here. I have not made use of the ETCSL composite editions, which do not provide a full list of variants, were made with few collations, and without access to most of the unpublished sources. I say this not to criticize this resource, which has its uses, but only to signal the fact that the new editions were made on the basis of the direct examination of the majority of the manuscripts, concentrating on the original materials rather than on previous work on the subject. I personally collated almost all of the 115 manuscripts of CKU on the originals; in the editions this is the unmarked category. With very few exceptions, all other tablets were either checked against photographs or were collated by colleagues, as noted under the list of sources for each letter. Only five items could not be accessed in any manner.

    The accompanying disc contains digital photographs or scans of all the tablets utilized in the reconstruction of the CKU, with the exception of the nine mentioned below under no. 1. Most were taken by the author. I am indebted to the kindness of colleagues who graciously provided me with digital pictures; other acknowledgments are found in the preface to this book.

    1. Not included on the disc are the following nine tablets: IM 13347 (*TIM* 9 38), IM 13712

(*TIM* 9 39), IM 44134 (*TIM* 9 40), *MDP* 27 87, 88, 207, 212, Ni. 4586, and NYPCL 334.

2. I have not been able to obtain photographs or collations of five tablets: Relph 16, IM 13712 (*TIM* 9 39), as well as *MDP* 27 87, 88 and 212.

3. Photographs of thirteen texts were taken by others: Aw/n and A 7457 (courtesy of the Oriental Institute), AN1922-163 (*OECT* 5 26, E. Robson; the tablet is too fragile for photography), Cotsen 40832 (Wilson, *Education* 159 [p. 251]), Cotsen 52157 (Wilson, *Education* 158 [p. 250]),[2] HS 1438, HS 1456 (*TMH NF* 4 42–43, J. Cooper), HS 2394 (M. Krebernik, K. V. Zand), MM 1039 (M. Molina), *MDAI* 57 1 (M. Ghelichkhani), *MDP* 18 51 (P. Damarshand), Ni. 9866 (*ISET* 1 133 [191]), Si 420 (Scheil, *USFS* 134, both G. Beckman) and Cornell 63 (L. Kinney-Bajwa). My own photographs of the three Schøyen Collection tablets are supplemented by official photographs from the Collection provided by Andrew George.

4. Ten texts were collated on photographs, and I did not have the opportunity to work directly with the originals: HS 1438, HS 1456 (*TMH NF* 4 42–43), LB 2543 (*TLB* 3 172), IM 78644 (IB 733), MM 1039 (*AuOr* 15 36), W 16743 gb (Cavigneaux, *Uruk* 143), Cornell 63, Cotsen 40832 (Wilson, *Education* 159 [p. 251]), Cotsen 52157 (Wilson, *Education* 158 [p. 250]), as well as NYPCL 334.[3]

5. Three published were texts collated by others: *MDP* 27 207 (M. Malyeri), IM 13347 (*TIM* 9 38, P. Steinkeller) and IM 44134 (*TIM* 9 40, J. Black).

6. I could not obtain digital images of three tablets; two of these are presented here as digital scans of paper photographic prints: IM 78644 (IB 733) and W 16743 gb (Cavigneaux, *Uruk* 43). The third, Relph 16, was scanned from a hand copy by T. G. Pinches, discovered by Irving Finkel, but the current location of the tablet is unknown.

No hand-copies are appended to this edition. Some years ago, I began to copy the unpublished sources of CKU, but the purchase of my first digital camera allowed me to set these rather imperfect drawings aside and use the new technology to its full advantage. By then I had already come to accept the fact that, unlike some of my more talented colleagues, I am not a very good copyist. Inaccurate hand-copies may satisfy formal requirements, but they are of little practical use; unless they are very precise, they can be misleading as far as paleography is concerned, as are, to my mind, all "regularized" drawings of tablets that do not preserve the exact shape of signs as well as other features such as lining and "ten marks." Such drawings are, in essence, nothing more than subjective transliterations expressed by other means and are of little assistance when readings are in doubt. In such moments, only precise, expertly drawn representations are of any use. Most Assyriologists can easily identify the copy hand of the great scholars of the past just by looking at a page, and this testifies to the personal nature of this work. But even the best copies are ultimately two-dimensional representations of three-dimensional reality and are never truly precise. For more than a century, they have been a necessary part of our endeavors, since traditional photography was expensive to reproduce and there were no other practical alternatives. I share the opinion of those who argue that the advent of affordable

---

2. Photographs kindly supplied by Ivy Trent.

3. Photograph: http://cdli.ucla.edu/cdlisearch/search/index.php?SearchMode=Text&txtID_Txt=P342755.

digital photography allows for a much better presentation of most cuneiform texts than does the traditional hand-copy, one that also offers a better chance to make many more texts available in a less time-consuming and more affordable manner. Moreover, photography, while never perfect, allows for better study of cuneiform paleography, a highly neglected area of Sumerology. Having said this, I should nevertheless acknowledge the wonderful paleographical handbook of Old Babylonian Sumerian produced by Catherine Mittermayer (2006), which has quickly become indispensable.

The transliteration system followed here is a fairly traditional one that is meant to represent the manner in which the texts were written and not approximate an idealized phonological transcription—hence the use of standard sign values, although I have bowed to current conventions and have indicated the "nasal g" by means of ĝ. The cuneiform writing system used conventional rules to represent the Sumerian, rules that do not attempt to provide a precise phonological and morphological representation of the language. Therefore, a transliteration is not a transcription and is meant to provide the modern reader with a transparent way of perceiving which signs are used in the text and how the editor understood them. Recently, attempts have been made to introduce new "readings" of signs in a more-or-less systematic manner (P. Attinger apud Mittermayer 2006; Attinger 2007: 36–37). Attinger is undoubtedly correct that our transliteration system is unsystematic and inconsistent; I sympathize with some of these views, but I cannot accept this new way of representing Sumerian texts for a number of reasons, and I think it unnecessary at this time. His proposals amount to a revision of a large percentage of the commonly accepted readings but is presented, for the most part, without full evidence or any analysis of the documentation, and some of them are based on questionable assumptions about historical phonology and about the way in which lexical texts encode Sumerian. I have no doubt that many of his renditions are more correct, on some level, than the ones we currently use, but this is not the way to implement changes in the way a field works. There are many different problems in the decipherment of the phonological shapes of Sumerian words. To provide but one example: if, as M. Civil (2007: 13) observes, the graphic syllabification may not match the phonological shape of words in cuneiform writing: "thus ŋi-ir 'foot' alternating with ŋi-ri may in principle represent /ŋir/, /ŋri/, or /ŋiri/; ka-la-ak 'strong' can be /kalk/, /klak/, or /kalak/, and so on."

There are many other similar problems with the understanding of the manner in which a logo-syllabic writing system was used to represent the long-dead Sumerian language, and therefore we cannot expect to create a transliteration system that will accurately represent the phonological shape of utterances. In a sense, such projects are ultimately futile and misguided because they create the illusion that the cuneiform system used to write Standard Old Babylonian Sumerian accurately represented the language as it was read aloud, but this misses the conventional nature of cuneiform writing, which was constantly changing as it was applied to languages other than Sumerian, even occasioning feedback into the way it was used to represent the source language (Cooper 1999). There is no assurance that the kind of uniformity sought by scholars existed in the teaching establishments of Mesopotamia. To be sure, there were elementary "pronunciation" guides, such as the Proto-Ea syllabary, but this composition was only used in Nippur (Michalowski 1983c: 151), and one must assume that there existed in antiquity a broad range of variation in the perception of Sumerian, subject to local and individual teacher/student idiosyncrasies and received traditions. Any attempt at revising our current, admittedly inconsistent and inadequate system of transliterating Sumerian texts must result from a detailed, linguistically informed graphemic investigation. In the end, I am of the opinion that the role of the editor is to represent texts the way they were written rather than to make assumptions on how they were read. Transliteration is a convention, and any new set of such conventions that is unsupported by such analysis will only serve to defamiliarize the texts and make it more difficult for others to read, without adding any new information.

Finally, I would like to comment on the translations of the letters. Epistolary texts are by their very nature highly idiomatic (Charpin 2008). Moreover, they compress complex information into a limited textual space and are often sketchy and elliptical, assuming knowledge of prior letters in the communicative chain, as well as oral commentary from the persons delivering the tablet. Our inadequate understanding of complex prose syntax of the language further hampers the understanding of Sumerian letters. After all, letters comprise the only large corpus of Sumerian prose, but our understanding of the grammar of Standard Old Babylonian Sumerian—highly contested as it continues to be—is based to a large extent on poetry. In addition, there is a detectable high percentage of interference from Akkadian in these texts, which is most apparent in the large number of idiomatic calques. Indeed, it often seems that at some level of deeper structure, the underlying abstract constitution of the letters is indeed Akkadian. This tells us nothing about the period in which they were composed, because interference of this kind could have already taken place in Ur III times. Even those who believe that Sumerian was the main spoken vernacular in the south in that period—and I do not share this view at all—will admit that some forms of Akkadian were widely spoken as well, at least in some parts of the areas controlled by the kings of Ur.

Some readers may be struck by the fact that I have avoided any discussion of the linguistic aspects of the CKU. I have purposely avoided providing any "grammar" of these letters for a number of reasons. The heterogeneous nature of the whole "corpus" and of the manuscripts of each individual composition makes it impossible, to my mind, to provide a consistent grammatical description. Each and every variant is dependent on too many different individual student and teacher decisions for any statistically-valid morphological study. It is obvious that many of the grammatical forms, particularly observable in the verbal morphology, are "incorrect" if viewed from our reconstructions of Standard Old Babylonian Sumerian. It would be equally fallacious to correct such forms or, in many cases, to translate them literally according to our idealized reconstructions of the language. Perhaps when all the other prose letters are properly edited, someone may be tempted to offer a syntactic analysis of Old Babylonian literary Sumerian prose, as distinct from the more circumscribed and stylized language of poetry.

Because translation is not a value-free act and is dependent on so many factors, including one's own opinions about the Sumerian lexicon and grammar, on knowledge of cultural practices, on intuition, and on a feel for the target languages, there will always be unlimited alternative renditions of any ancient text. In the case of the letters, the situation is complicated by a number of factors that have been discussed on these pages, among them the problem of a multileveled alterity, as well as redactional and editorial problems. Moreover, the translator is constantly vexed by concerns over semantics and reference in relationship to different periods of Mesopotamian history. Should one understand words and concepts in a manner that is in harmony with Ur III usage, or should one strive to recover meanings that would resonate better in Old Babylonian times?

One short example will serve to illustrate the many challenges that open up endless possibilities of rendering these compositions in a modern language. In the first letter of CKU, the grand vizier Aradmu reports that a high officer by the name of Apilaša, stationed on the far frontier, had usurped many symbolic and practical trappings of royalty and had insulted the king in the person of the high official who is writing the letter we are reading. To illustrate Apilaša's threatening stance, Aradmu informs the king that "he had stationed no less than five thousand of his *choice* guards to his right and left" (ArŠ1: 21 [1]). The word that I have translated as "guard," is àga-ús. There is some debate as to the meaning of this term: Lafont (2009: 9–11) has recently proposed that it refers to the soldiers of the "standing army," much as the corresponding Akkadian term *redûm* does in Old Babylonian texts—that is, at the very time when the versions we are reading were being used in schooling. I remain unconvinced, based partly on the conviction that military organization differed over time and hold to the older notion that such people were special elite guards, distinct from ordinary soldiers/workers of the Ur III state (de Maaijer and Jagersma 2003/4; Allred 2006: 57–61; Michalowski 2008: 111). But in Old Babylonian times readers may have interpreted the word in precisely this manner. To them it implied that Apilaša is being accused of standing at the head of his own private army, an army that answers only to him and not to the Crown, ready to menace the grand vizier. The horror!

Of course, my interpretation of the word àga-ús could be wrong, but that is not really the issue here. What matters is that we have absolutely no way of knowing whether some or all of the teachers and students who were involved in the production of the surviving manuscripts of this letter understood it in contemporary terms, as referring to conscripted soldiers, or if they comprehended the historical shift in meaning. If they did not, shall we translate it they way we imagine some of them might have understood it or stick with reconstructed Ur III meanings? The letters, even though they are often arranged in pairs—a letter to a king and an answer—are only small parts of conversations. Mired in the multifaceted alterity of purported time of origin, progressive redaction, and reception, leading into the eighteenth century b.c.e., and then into the twenty-first century c.e., their meaning is not fixed in the clay but becomes a constantly shifting ground for analytical reading. Therefore, I have tried to render these texts in contemporary English, avoiding the literal renderings of compound verbs and of idiomatic expressions that often crop up in modern presentations of Sumerian texts. Others will offer different translations, not only because of disagreements over readings of signs, lexicography, and grammar but also because of differences in the conceptualization of ancient history, literature, and epistolography. I was guided here by the words of the poet Jerome Rothenberg (1981 [1969]: 91), a proponent of "total translation:"

> Translation is carry-over. It is a means of delivery & of bringing to life. It begins with a forced change of language, but a change too that opens up the possibility of greater understanding.

More than two decades later, Rothenberg (1992: 65) observed that translation is not

> a reproduction of, or stand-in, for, some fixed original, but that it functions as a commentary on the other and itself and on the differences between them.

The Correspondence of the Kings of Ur: List of Letters

1. Aradmu to Šulgi 1 (ArŠ1, 3.1.1, A1, RCU 1)
1a. Aradmu to Šulgi 1a (ArŠ1a)
2. Šulgi to Aradmu 1 (ŠAr1, 3.1.2, A2, RCU2)
3. Aradmu to Šulgi 2 (ArŠ2, 3.1.3+3.1.11, A2a, RCU 3+4)
4. Abaindasa to Šulgi 1 (AbŠ1, 3.1.21, B1)
5. Šulgi to Aradmu 2 (ŠAr2, 3.1.13.1, RCU 8)
6. Šulgi to Aradmu 3 (ŠAr3, 3.1.61, RCU 16)
7. Aradmu to Šulgi 3 (ArŠ3, 3.1.5, RCU 7)
8. Aradmu to Šulgi 4 (ArŠ4)
9. Aradmu to Šulgi 5 (ArŠ5, 3.1.6, RCU 6)
10. Aradmu to Šulgi 6 (ArŠ6, 3.1.4, RCU 5)
11. Urdun to Šulgi 1 (UrŠ1, 3.1.11.1, RCU 14)
12. Aradmu? to Šulgi? 7 (ArŠ7)
13. Puzur-Šulgi to Šulgi 1 (PuŠ1, 3.1.7, RCU 11)
14. Šulgi to Puzur-Šulgi 1 (ŠPu1, 3.1.8, RCU 9+10)
15. Šulgi to Išbi-Erra 1 (ŠIš1, 3.1.13.2, RCU 15)
16. Amar-Sin to Šulgi 1 (AmŠ1, 3.1.12, RCU 12)
17. Šulgi to Amar-Sin (ŠAm1, 3.1.13, RCU 13)
18. Šarrum-bani to Šu-Sin (ŠaŠu1, 3.1.15, RCU 17)
19. Šu-Sin to Šarrum-bani 1 (ŠuŠa1, 3.1.16, RCU 18)

20. Šu-Sin to Lu-Nanna and Šarrum-bani 1 (ŠuLuŠa1, 3.3.31)
21. Išbi-Erra to Ibbi-Sin 1 (IšIb1, 3.1.17, RCU 19)
22. Ibbi-Sin to Išbi-Erra 1 (IbIš1, 3.1.18, RCU 20)
23. Puzur-Numušda to Ibbi-Sin 1 (PuIb1, 3.1.19, RCU 21)
24. Ibbi-Sin to Puzur-Numušda 1 (IbPu1, 3.1.20, RCU 22)

Concordance between RCU and CKU

RCU	CKU		CKU	RCU
1	1		1	1
	1a		1a	
2	2		2	2
3	3		3	3+4
4	3		4	
5	16		5	16
6	9		6	8
7	7		7	7
8	6		8	
9	14		9	6
10	14		10	5
11	13		11	14
12	16		12	
13	17		13	11
14	11		14	9+10
15	15		15	15
16	5		16	12
17	18		17	13
18	19		18	17
19	21		19	18
20	22		20	
21	23		21	19
22	24		22	20
			23	21
			24	22

Colophons

Fifteen of the 115 CKU tablets have colophons, and five of these have year-names: Samsu-iluna 1 (H, I, L), 27 (O), and 28 (E). All are Old Babylonian, with the exception of K, which is Middle Babylonian from Susa. Colophon G is from Kish; all the other Old Babylonian CKU tablets with colophons are unprovenienced, although N may be from Sippar. Because there is up-to-date study of such subscripts it is impossible to make any reliable statements on the matter, but my impression is that this is a relatively high number due, one would assume, to the large percentage of unprovenienced CKU sources, since colophons are never used in Old Babylonian school texts from Nippur and are rare at Ur.

Colophon A
    ArŠ1 (1) X8
    [im-gíd-d]a' ^{d}sin(30)-*iš-me-a-ni*
    [iti . . .]x u$_4$ 3-kam (month x, day 3)

Colophon B
    ŠAr1 (2) X5
    im-ᶜgíd-daᶜ *qi-iš-ti-é-a*
    iti ᶜapinᶜ-[du₈]-ᶜaᶜ u$_4$ 7-kam (month 8, day 7)

Colophon C
    ArŠ2 (3) X2
    ᶜiti zízᶜ-a u$_4$ ᶜ25-kamᶜ (month 11, day 25)

Colophon D
    ŠAr3 (6) X1
    [i]ti *še-kin-kuru*$_5$ u$_4$ 19-kam (month 12, day 19)
    [i]m-gíd-da ᶜ*a*ᶜ-*lí-ba-ni-šu*

Colophon E
    ArŠ4 (8) X1
    im-gíd-da ᶜ^{d}UTU?ᶜ-*mu-ša-lim*
    iti gán-gán-ᶜèᶜ ᶜudᶜ 5-kam
    mu *sa-am-su-*ᶜ*i-lu-na*ᶜ lugal-e
    á-áĝ-ĝá ᶜ^{d}enᶜ-líl-lá-t[a . . .] (month 9, day 5, Si 28)

Colophon F
    UdŠ1 (11) X1
    u$_4$ 26-kam (day 26)

Colophon G
    PuŠ1 (13) Ki1
    iti ᶜzíz-a u$_4$ᶜ [x ka]m
    im-gíd-ᶜdaᶜ ^{ld}za-ba$_4$-ᶜba$_4$ᶜ-[...] (month 11, day x)

Colophon H

PuŠ1 (13) X5

i[m-gíd-da *q*]*í-iš-ti-é-a*

iti g[án-gán]-⟨è u$_4$⟩ ⌈20⌉-kam

⌈mu⌉ [*sa*]-⌈*am-su*⌉-*i-lu-na* lugal-⌈e⌉⌉ (month 9, day 20, Si1)

Colophon I

PuŠ1 (13) X4

im-gíd-da *qí-iš-ti-é-a*

iti gán-gán-è ⟨u$_4$⟩ 25-kam

mu *sa-am-su-i-lu-na* lugal-e (month 9, day 25, Si1)

Colophon J

ŠPu1 (14) X2

iti ⌈ne-ne-ğar u$_4$⌉ [x]-kam

im-gíd-da *i*[*b*]-*ni*-DIĞIR (month 5, day x)

Colophon K

Šiš1 (15) Su1

ŠU ^{d}KUR.GAL-*ta-a-a-ar* DUB.SAR TUR (hand of Enlil-tajjar, junior scribe)

Colophon L

ŠaŠu1(18) X2

20 mu-bi-im

iti u$_4$-zíz u$_4$ 3-kam

mu *sa-am-su-i-lu-na* lugal (month 11, day 3, Si 1)

Colophon M

IšIb1 (21) X2

šu⌉ *i-lí-re*-[*me*]-⌈*ni*⌉ (hand of Ili-remeni)

iti zíz⌉-a [u$_4$ x-kam] (month 11, day x)

Colophon N

IšIb1 (21) X4

šu-nígin 32 mu-bi-im

⌈iti zíz⌉-a u$_4$ 15-kam (month 11, day 15)

Colophon O

compilation tablet Xa (X1)

⌈4⌉ lugal-ğu$_{10}$-ra

[mu]-bi 182-àm

[šu x]x-*ia-a* dumu *ku-bu-lum*

[iti ne-ne]-ğar u$_4$ 17-⌈kam⌉

[mu *sa-am-su*]-⌈*i-lu*⌉-*na* lugal-e

[níğ babbar-ra] ⌈sízkur a-ki-tum⌉

[ul šár-r]a-k[am] (month 5. day 17, Si 27)

1. Aradmu to Šulgi 1

(ArŠ1, 3.1.1, A1, RCU 1)

Composite Text

1. lugal-ǧu$_{10}$-ra ù-na-a-dug$_4$
2. ^{l}árad-mu árad-zu na-ab-bé-a
3. kur su-bir$_4$^{ki}-šè har-ra-an kaskal si sá-sá-e-ra
4. gun ma-da-zu ge-en-ge-né-dè
5. a-rá ma-da zu-zu-dè
6. ugu a-pi-il-la-ša gal-zu unken-na-ka
7. ad gi$_4$-gi$_4$-da gù-téš-a si-ke-dè
8. inim u$_4$-da ka-ne-ne-a hé-en-tùm á-šè mu-e-da-a-a-áǧ
9. ká é-gal-la-šè gub-a-ǧu$_{10}$-ne
10. silim-ma lugal-ǧá-ke$_4$ èn li-bí-in-tar
11. dúr na-ma-ta-an-zi ki-a nu-ub-za
12. ba-an-da-mud-en
13. te-ǧá-e-da-ǧu$_{10}$-ne
14. é kaskal-la kuš ga-ríǧ-ak šukur kù-sig$_{17}$ kù-babbar
15. ^{na_4}gug ^{na_4}za-gìn ǧar-ra-ta
16. a-ab-dù-dù-a ùšu sar-àm i-íb-tuš
17. kù-sig$_{17}$ ^{na_4}za-gìn-na mí zi-dè-eš im-me
18. ^{ǧiš}gu-za barag ^{túg}šutur-e ri-a i-íb-tuš
19. ^{ǧiš}ǧìri-gub kù-sig$_{17}$-ka ǧìri-ni i-íb-ǧar
20. ǧìri-ni na-ma-ta-an-kúr
21. àga-ús saǧ-ǧá-na iá li-mu-um-ta-àm zi-da gùb-bu-na íb-ta-an-gub-bu-uš
22. àš gud niga ǧéš udu niga níg-zú-gub-šè in-gar
23. šu-luh lugal-ǧá-ke$_4$ sá bí-in-dug$_4$
24. ká-na èn nu-tar-ra-bi lú na-ma-ši-in-ku$_4$-re-en
25. ku$_4$-ku$_4$-da-ǧu$_{10}$-ne
26. ^{ǧiš}gu-za gàr-ba kù-sig$_{17}$ huš-a ǧar-ra lú ma-an-de$_6$ tuš-a ma-an-dug$_4$
27. á-áǧ-ǧá lugal-ǧá-ke$_4$ ì-gub-bé-en nu-tuš-ù-dè-en bí-dug$_4$
28. min gud niga niš udu niga ^{ǧiš}banšur-ǧu$_{10}$ lú ma-an-gar
29. nu-kár-kár-dè àga-ús lugal-ǧá-ke$_4$ ^{ǧiš}banšur-ǧu$_{10}$ íb-bal-a-aš

30. ní ba-da-te su ba-da-zi
31. iti ezen-^{d}nin-a-zu u$_4$ iá-àm zal-la-àm
32. lugal-ğu$_{10}$ á-še mu-e-da-a-a-áğ
33. iti u$_5$-bí^{mušen}-gu$_7$ u$_4$ diš-àm zal-la-àm
34. lú-kaš$_4$-e mu-e-ši-gi$_4$
35. u$_4$ sa$_9$-àm šen-e ba-te
36. lugal-ğu$_{10}$ hé-en-zu

[1] Speak to my king, [2] saying (the words) of Aradmu, your servant:

[8] You commanded me, [3] while I was on an expedition to Subir, [4] to firmly secure the taxes on the frontier territory, [5] to thoroughly investigate the state of (this) frontier, [6-7] to confer (with the elites of Subir) about the prefect Apilaša and have them come to agreement, [8] *so that he could bring to them (i.e., the Subir elites) up-to-date instructions.*[1]

[9] When I stood at the gate of the (local) palace, [10] no one inquired about my king's well-being, [11] no one rose from (his) seat for me, nor did anyone prostrate himself (before me); [12] this (all) made me very worried.

[13] But when I drew nearer, [14-16] (I discovered that Apilaša) was dwelling in a *portable structure* constructed by means of finely combed fleece (panels stretched between) staked poles inlaid with gold, silver, carnelian, and lapis-lazuli covering an area of thirty sar (ca. 1080 sq. m.). [17] He was all decked out in precious stones and metals. [18] He sat on a throne on a dais placed over a fine carpet,[2] [19] and had set his feet on a golden footstool. [20] He would not remove his feet in my presence! [21] He had stationed no less than five thousand of his *choice* guards to his right and left. [22] (He ordered) six grass-fed oxen and sixty fattened sheep placed (on tables) for a meal; [23] and he took over the performance of my king's cleansing rites. [24] No one bothered to bring me in through the very gate at which no-one had inquired about your (well-being).

[25] As I entered (anyway), [26] someone brought me a chair with red gold encrusted knobs and told me: "Sit!" [27] I answered him: "When I am on my king's orders I stand—I do not sit!" [28] Someone placed[3] two grass-fed oxen and twenty grass-fed sheep onto my table, [29] but even though I had given no offense, my king's (own) guardsmen overturned my table. [30] I was so frightened that my skin crawled!

[31-32] My king, you gave me orders the evening of the fifth day of the Ninazu Festival Month;

[33-34] I am sending you a courier the evening of the first day of the Swan-Eating Month. [35] It is midday, and war is brewing! [36] Now my king is informed (about all of this)!

1. Alt. transl.: so that as part of the daily instructions he could bring them (the people of Subir) good news.
2. Alt. transl.: under an awning.
3. Var.: heaped up.

Commentary

Although this was the most commonly studied letter in the OB schools, it is full of lexical and syntactic difficulties. For this reason, but also because this translation differs from all previous ones, including a number of my own, a detailed commentary is required.

1. A constant problem that has come up in working with the CKU has been the rendition of lugal.ĝu (lugal-ĝu$_{10}$), literally, "my lord" or "my king." This occurs most frequently in the address phrase of letters addressed to kings: lugal-ĝu$_{10}$-ra ù-na-(a)-dug$_4$. For Akkadian-speaking scribes, this corresponded, almost morpheme for morpheme, to the opening letter formula *ana bēlija qibīma*, as discussed above. It is quite possible that the Sumerian phrase is actually a calque from Akkadian; nevertheless, lugal.ĝu means more than "my king" in Ur III Sumerian. In administrative texts from Drehem, the name of the living king is almost never invoked, except to refer to statues. Instead, the term that is used is lugal.ĝu, even in third-person reference; correspondingly, one often finds ereš.ĝa (ereš-ĝá), literally, "my queen/mistress," when the queen is mentioned (P. Michalowski, *Syro-Mesopotamian Studies* 2/3 [1978] 88–89). It is important to remember that, in the political language of the Ur III state, with a few exceptions that need not concern us here, there was only one real lugal in the mundane world, namely, the sovereign of Ur; all other rulers were described as énsi, as were the provincial and city-governors of the state itself. At the same time, the word lugal can be used, more simply, to mean "master," much like Akkadian *bēlu*, for the master of a slave, for example. From this, one may infer that the phrase is an important formal manner of address, and I have struggled with the translations, going back and forth between "my liege," "his majesty," "Milord," and simply "my king." For subjective aesthetic reasons, I have settled on the latter, although stylistically, and even perhaps ideologically, this is perhaps not the best solution.

3. The use of the verb si . . . sá, "to make straight," with kaskal, "road, expedition," corresponds here to the Akkadian idiomatic use of *šutēšuru* in the meaning, "to proceed, march on." The rare ending -ra/e found on nominalized verbal forms has been discussed by J. Krecher (ZA 57 [1965] 27) and a host of others, most recently by Christopher Woods.[4] Both suggest that it serves to topicalize or stress the end of subordinate clauses and also has a secondary temporal or spatial meaning, hence the translation "while I was. . . ." Woods argues that this is still another function of the demonstrative -re.

On the synonymic word pair kaskal har-ra-an-na and on the poetic structure of the opening lines, see above pp. 28–29.

---

4. Christopher Woods, "The Element -re and the Organization of Erim-ḫuš," paper read at the 213th annual meeting of the American Oriental Society, April 4th, 2003.

5. The expression a-rá zu requires comment. In Sumerian, the noun a-rá means "times (mathematical)" as well as "customary way, manner of behavior." Its Akkadian equivalent, *alaktu*, has a broader meaning, semantically parallel to English "way," because already in Old Assyrian and Old Babylonian it can also refer to "road, way, passage, etc." Students would have known the expression a-rá zu from the early level "tetrad" excercise *Lipit-Eštar Hymn A* 39: dub-sar a-rá zu ᵈnidaba-ka-me-en, "I am a scribe who knows the ways of Nidaba." Closer to the general semantic context of the letter is the use found in the *Ur-Namma Hymn A*, B 10–11:

> ᵍᶦˢtir ha-šu-úr ⌈ba-da⌉-an-sìg a-rá ⌈kalam-ma⌉ ba-e-sùh
> ᵍᶦˢeren kalam-ma-⌈ke₄⌉ ba-da-bal a-⌈rá kalam⌉-ma ba-e-kúr

> (Ur-Namma,) the stand of cypress trees was struck down; the mood of the homeland was confused,
> The juniper tree of the homeland was overturned; the mood of the homeland was altered.

Here, as in our passage, the expression appears to be a synonym of dím-ma ma-da = *ṭēm mātim*, on which see p. 401 below.

There is only one other example of the Sumerian expression with duplication of the verbal root: Waradsin 29 59 [E4.2.13.21] a-rá nam-lugal-la-ğá ùğ-ğá zu-zu-dè, "to inform my⁈ people of the conditions of my kingship." This usage is what one would expect—zu "to know, learn" and zu-zu "to teach"—but this can hardly apply here, and therefore it is most probable that the duplication is intensive: "to thoroughly investigate." However, in view of the high level of underlying Akkadian syntax and semantics in some of the CKU letters, it is also highly probable that the present line was also understood, by some at least, as "to investigate the roads through the frontier;" in fact, a double meaning may very well be intentional. Indeed, it is possible that a-rá zu may be a calque from Akkadian *alaktam lamādum*, which has been thoroughly analyzed by T. Abusch, *HTR* 80 (1987) 15–42.

Text X1 has additional material that may perhaps be restored as: [suhuš ma-d]a gi-ne-dè, "to secure the foundations of the land."

8. This line is unique; it has caused problems for all who have worked on this text and remains open to different interpretations. The verb is probably ka . . . de₆, "to bring news," discussed by M. Civil, *AOAT* 25 92. Since this is a calque of *pû*+suffix+*abālum*, the syntax of the phrase has to be understood as Akkadian. The noun is qualified by u₄-da. One could understand this in an adverbial manner, as in á u₄-da, "daily expenses/wages/work," for which see R. de Maaijer and B. Jagersma, *AfO* 44/5 (1997–98) 286, or as "today, present" as in munus u₄-da-e-ne in Ukg 6 iii 20′ and 23′, for which see D. O. Edzard, *Sumerian Grammar*, 19, who notes that this is an adjectival compound. The plural form here is what drives the translation of lines 6–7; the force of ugu in line 6 is difficult to gauge and, were it not for this plural form, one would consider the rendition "to council (with) Apilaša and come to mutual agreement."

The final verb is á . . . áǧ, "to send news, command, instruct." In CKU it is almost always construed with /-še/ on the first element. This idiosyncratic usage is rarely attested; for the most part OB Sumerian utilizes pronouns rather than -še$_{1/3}$ (Karahashi, *Sumerian Compund Verbs* 72-74). This element must be the deictic particle /-še/, and the use of it here probably reflects confusion with á-še = *anumma*, "now, here." Students in OB schools would have been familiar with the rhetorical use of the verb governing purpose clauses from the early level exercise *Iddin-Dagan Hymn B* (part of the "tetrad").

9. Note the intentionally ambiguous use of the term é-gal to designate Apilaša's residence. On one level, Aradmu is implying the usurpation of royal power, anticipating the lines that follow; rhetorically, the line really means "when I had arrived at his residence that was a veritable royal palace." On a more prosaic level, the word é-gal can be used to designate roadside establishments as well as royal palaces; apprentice scribes would know this from their study of the ubiquitous hymn *Šulgi A*, in which the king boasts that he built roadside establishments, or caravanserai (é-gal), for travelers along the roads of Sumer (line 29). Similar ambiguous rhetoric is probably found in the final part of *Inana and Šukaletuda*; the goddess predicts that after his death Šukaletuda will be remembered in songs performed in royal palaces (line 298: é-gal lugal) but that he will dwell in the caravanserai of the wilderness (line 301: é-⌈gal⌉ eden-na é-zu hé-a). Note that there were at least seven places designated as é-gal in the Umma province alone in Ur III times (P. Steinkeller, *FS Adams* 193). There is one Ur III document from Nippur that mentions an é-gal énsi-ka located in nearby Tumal (*TMH NF* 1–2 174:7–8). Since Tumal did not have its own governor, this must refer to the temporary residence of the man who ran Nippur; see also, possibly the Girsu document *TÉL* 271:4 (é-gal énsi ba-an-ku$_4$).

10. This expression has a very specific technical meaning in this context. The term silim-ma is not "hail" or "bon santé" but a very specific obligation to inquire about the king's well-being and safety. It seems to allude to a blessing that was used in the time of Šulgi that might be idiomatically rendered as "Long Live the King." The wording of this blessing is explicitly provided in ArŠ4: 6–7 (letter 8): silim-ma lugal-ǧá-ke$_4$ èn mu-tar-re-eš lugal-me u$_4$ da-rí-šè hé-ti gù bí-in-⌈dé⌉-eš, "they inquired about my king's well-being and shouted out 'Long Live the King!'" Almost the same wording is found in a subscript written at the end of the Ur III version of the *Sumerian King List* (which ends with the reign of Ur-Namma): ⌈d⌉šul-gi lugal-ǧu$_{10}$ u$_4$ sud-šè ⌈ha⌉-ti-il, "May Šulgi, my king, live a life of long days!" (P. Steinkeller, *Fs. Wilcke* 274). This official blessing is also encoded in OB personal names such as Hamatil, Ušareš-hetil (Mari and Ešnunna), and Til-ani-hesud (Akk. Balassu-lirik; see, most recently, D. Charpin, *OBO* 160/4 262, idem, *Hammurapi* 142–43). In Ur III, we commonly find RN/lugal/nin/PN-ha-ma-ti and, once, ᵈŠu-ᵈSin-hé-ti (*CUAS* 88:3). This was obviously a common element of royal protocol, as evidenced by a passage in a letter from Jamīum to Zimri-Lim in Mari: "the entire army cried out 'Long Live Our King' (*bur bêlī*)!" (*ARM* 26/2 327 2′–3′); the same cry was addressed to Hammurabi, according to *ARM* 26/2 363 5–10; see also J. M. Durand, *LAPO* 17 9d.

This use of the term is also attested in an Ur III document from the Drehem "treasury"; in *JCS* 10 (1956) 30 10, a messenger receives silver rings (lines 3–4): mu silim-ma a-bí-sí-im-ti, ⌜unug⌝^{ki}-ta mu-de$_6$-a-šè, "because he brought the salutations of (Queen) Abi-simti from Uruk."

11. To my knowledge, the idiom, or compound verb, dúr(. . .)zi is otherwise unattested. Compare the commonly attested dúr . . . ğar, "to sit, dwell."

12. The reading of this line is not clear, and it appears that it already offered problems to the ancients: some Nippur students solved the problem by omitting it altogether. Every text has a different version of this line. With reservations, I base my interpretation on mud = *galātu*, "to be or become restless or nervous," or *parādu*, "to be scared, terrified," assuming that túm in N9 and X3 reflect aural misinterpretations. The use of mud as *qulu*, "silence, torpor," for which see now M. Jaques, *Le vocabulaire des sentiments* 217, is clearly related. One assumes a rhetorical progress; here, Aradmu is very worried, but after the rest of the story, he is absolutely terrified (line 30).

14. It is difficult to ascertain the exact meaning of the rare é kaskal-(la). The word is documented as é kaskal in two Sargonic period texts (*OIP* 14 43:1, *Nik.* 2 53:5 [ereš é kaskal-šè gin-né]), and only twice in Ur III. The first is an incomplete Umma text (*CUAS* 93:2); the second is an account from Urusagrig that includes provisions for a royal messenger, u$_4$ é kaskal lugal sa gi$_4$-gi$_4$-dè im-gin-na-a, "when he traveled to prepare the royal *travel tent*" (LH 5458 8–9, courtesy D. I. Owen). Note that the scribe of N1 was thinking of the more common é dána, rather than é kaskal-la but thought better of it and complemented the term with -la.

IGI.KAK with the reading šukur = *šukurru* stands for a lance or spear for war and hunting but can also have other uses, more specifically as a pole or stake to create fencing—in our case, to hold the fleece panels. This is clearly the case in *the Lamentation over the Destruction of Sumer and Ur* 45: sipa-dè ^{giš}šukur-ra amaš kù-ga šu nu-nigin-dè, "that the shepherd(s) not enclose the sacred sheepfold with a fence." The image of a fence made up of fleece panels held up by metal poles is what lies behind the otherwise impenetrable passage in *Šulgi Hymn B* 339–41:

> piriğ igi ^{urudu}šukur-ra ga-raš^{sar}-gin$_7$ šab-šab-e
> nemur(PIRIĞ.TUR) šu zi-ga igi ^{giš}ga-ríğ-ak gi-gin$_7$ ša$_5$-ša$_5$-dam
> zi-bi ur-gir$_{17}$-gin$_7$ ^{urudu}dur$_{10}$ UŠ.NE.NE-ga

> Lions (trapped) by copper stakes are cut off like leeks,
> Furious *leopards* (trapped) by fleece panels are broken like reeds,
> Their life is . . . like dogs by an axe.

This is the meaning also implied by Diri Nippur 145 (*MSL* 15 18), which provides the equivalence with ḫa-al-wu/mu-ú-um. This must be the same word as ḫalwu, "border wall," listed in *CAD* H 57 as a Hurrian loan with distribution limited to Nuzi.

17. The compound verb mí . . . dug$_4$ has many nuances; see P. Attinger, *Eléments* 603–19. On p. 612, he reads the line as [na$_4$ (?)] ⌜za$^?$⌝-gin$_3$⌜ ku$_3$-sig$_{17}$ ku$_3$-babbar ⌜^{na_4}gug⌝ mi$_2$ zi-de-eš$_3$ im-me, and proposes a translation: "Il (Apillaša) ne (prend soin comme il se droit =) s'intéresse vraiment qu'au lapis, à l'or, à l'argent et à la cornaline." We differ in the reading of the line, but I would not completely rule out his interpretation. The verb is mí zi-dè-eš . . . dug$_4$ and corresponds to Akk. *kīniš kunnu*, "to honor." The translation of the syntactic connections in lines 16–19 reflects the use of the non-perfect (17) followed by perfect (18 and 19).

18. The complex TÚG.MAH can be read ^{túg}šutur or túg-mah, all with the meaning "finest quality cloth/garment"; see M. Green, *JCS* 30 (1978) 150. The reading šutur is adopted here in view of the complement -ré in U1. This does not mean that all the other students who studied this text understood it in the same manner. It is also possible that some scribes understood this to be a royal robe, as in *Winter and Summer* 230: ^{d}i-bí-^{d}en.zu ^{túg}šutur ^{túg}hur-saĝ ù-mu-ni-in-mu$_4$, "after (King) Ibbi-Sin had donned the special robe, the 'mountain range' robe. . . ." Thus, the line would mean, "sat himself on a throne, dressed in a special (royal) robe." There is another meaning of the word, however, which is probably more pertinent to the present passage. As W. Heimpel, *N.A.B.U.* 1994 72, has argued, in certain contexts TÚG.MAH designates a tent or perhaps an awning. The understanding of barag follows the traditional interpretation, strengthened by Heimpel's definition TÚG. MAH. However, M. Civil, "The Unveiling of the *parakku*" (unpublished communication read July 21, 2005, at the RAI in Chicago) has argued that this was really a large ceremonial tent; in this case, one would have to translate "he sat inside a (ceremonial) tent under an awning."

For barag and ^{túg}šutur together in an economic document, see *Tutub* 46 iii 3–4 (Sargonic).

19. The noun ^{giš}ĝìri-gub is used to designate an object that is set under foot; in connection with thrones, it designates a footstool. D. Soubeyran, *ARM* 23 333, draws attention to the representation of such footstools on cylinder seals, where they belong to deities and kings. This illustrates well the symbolic implications of Apilaša's actions.

21. The high number of guards is undoubtedly hyperbolic and should not be taken literally, although there are examples of very large number of àga-ús in Ur III texts (Lafont, *CDLJ* 2009/5). The use of the Semitic loan for "one thousand" has thus far only been attested in literary royal correspondence (ArŠ7: 8 [7], Ni. 4164 [*ISET* 12 117] "rev." i: 2 [see p. 330], SEpM 8–10). There is an Ur III text from Nippur that mentions 6 *li-mi* 2 *me-at* bricks (*NRVN* 1 318: 1) but it is probable that this was actually written in Akkadian. The earliest examples of both large numerals in a possibly Sumerian context is the ED document IAS 519 (Biggs and Postgate, *Iraq* 40 [1978] 107).

The term àga-ús saĝ-ĝá is rare and difficult to define properly. The earliest attestation known to me is in the seal inscription of one *e-em-ši-um*, ugula àga-ús

sağ-gá, árad su-mu-èl (D. Frayne, RIME 4, E4.3.7.2004). The translation is based
on the lexical equation érin sağ-gá = KI.MIN (=ÉRIN) be-e-ru, i.e., bēru (Lu II iii
I' 7' [MSL 12 119; see CAD B 21, "elite troops").

The translation "no less than" seeks to render the force of the copula; I have
assumed that the verbal form is transitive, but it is possible, in view of the reinter-
pretations of the use of Sumerian shifters that are characteristic of many forms in the
literary letters, that it is intransitive and means simply "stood (pl.)."

23. It is difficult to understand the use of sá . . . dug$_4$ in this context. In view of the
change of tone in the following line, it is possible that Apilaša performs the ritual on
behalf of the welfare of the king. More probable is that, in this series of implied usur-
pations of royal power, Apilaša is accused of performing rituals that properly belong
to the king, as in Šulgi Hymn C (Seg A) 28: sağ mu-tag šu-luh nam-lugal-lá-ka
šu gal mu-ni-du$_7$, "I touched (the Etemenniguru) and magnificently perfected it
with royal š. purification rites," and many similar passages where these purification
rites are the prerogative of deities and kings. P. Attinger, Eléments 96, is clearly thinking in this direction when he renders this line as: "il (Apillaša) s'est arrogé les rites
de purification de mon roi."

The nature of šu-luh purification needs a fuller study. These are clearly major
rites and seem to be linked to dining. This is well illustrated by the passage in Gudea
Cyl. A x: 7–14, in which Ningirsu proclaims:

> ^{ğiš}banšur mu-íl
> šu-luh si bí-sá
> šu si-sá-a-ğu$_{10}$ an kù-ge ù-a ba-zi-ge
> níg šu-ğá du$_{10}$-ga-àm
> a ugu$_4$·ğu$_{10}$
> du$_{10}$-ga-bi mu-gu$_7$
> an lugal diğir-re-ne-ke$_4$
> $^{d\ulcorner}$nin-ğír-su$^\urcorner$ lugal išib an-na
> mu-šè mu-sa$_4$
>
> I lifted the tray,
> And performed the ritual hand washing;
> Then my properly prepared hands woke holy An;
> The sweet morsels from my hands
> My progenitor
> Eats with pleasure.
> An, king of the gods,
> Then named me
> "King Ninğirsu, An's purification priest."

The association between išib an-na and royalty is attested for Lipit-Eštar Hymn A:
23 and, more to the point here, for Rim-Sin Hymn E: 1–2: [. . .] x x [. . .] šu-luh
kù-ga túm-ma [^{d}ri-im]-^{d}sin išib an-na sízkur sikil-la túm-ma, "fit for (performing) the holy š. rites, Rim-Sin, purification priest of An, fit for (performing) the
pure š. rites."

24. The word for "gate" ends in /-n/; I understand the opening phrase as a complex anticipatory genitive, (a)kan.a(k) en nu.tar.bi. On the Sumerian word for gate, probably /(a)kan/, and its reduplicated equivalent /kankan/ (found in some sources of Proto-Ea 238 [*MSL* 14 41] and here in X8), see M. Civil, *FS Biggs* 19.

Note the use of lú here; the term does not refer to a high officer who asks him to enter but a mere nobody.

28. The reading and meaning of the verb is uncertain. The choice of ğar is based on N2 and Ur1; but other sources have sá/di but the final sign is broken in a number of manuscripts. X7 seems to have s[á], possibly even t[ùm], but the remains are ambiguous. The meaning "heap up" for sá is based on the usage found in *Enki and Ninhursaĝa* 49 c–e (*UET* 6/1 1 ii 3–5): kur me-luh-ha^{ki} ^{na_4}gug níg al di kal-la ^{ğiš}mes šà-gan ğiš ab-ba sig$_5$-g[a] má gal-gal hu-mu-ra-ab-s[á], "May the foreign land of Meluhha load precious desirable cornelian, perfect mes wood and beautiful aba wood into large ships for you," and futher down in *Enki and Ninhursaĝa* line 49o (restored).

29. The first verb in this line has troubled previous editors. The interpretation offered here is based on kár = *ṭapālu*, "to slander, insult." Note the variant nu-kár-ak-dè in N6, which seems to be in harmony with lexical entries such as lú-kár-ak = *ṭa-ap-lum* (OB Lu D 240 [*MSL* 12 208]). One could also take into consideration a reading gur(u)$_6$ = *našû*, and translate the line: "Before I could rise and depart, my king's (own) guardsmen overturned my table." A remote possibility is that kár should be taken as Akkadian *napāḫu*, in the meaning "to be bloated, full" ("although I was not yet satiated. . . .").

The final verbal form is problematical. The only complete form is in-bal-a-šè in N1, not the most reliable source. This suggests a causative construction. The admittedly unsatisfactory composite version follows Ur1 and X1.

30. Students could not have ignored the instructive parallel with *Šulgi Hymn A* 70: lugal-me-en ní ba-ra-ba-da-te su ba-ra-ba-da-zi, "but because I am King, I have absolutely no fear!" Aradmu is clearly indicating his subordinate rank. The two almost synonymous verbs ní . . . te and su . . . zi are used in a traditional hendiadys as a rhetorical figure, hence the translation.

31–36. The final lines of the text are different in two manuscripts, N1 and Ur1, which are included in the matrix but also transliterated separately. It is obvious that the Old Babylonian scribes had difficulties with Ur III menology and were not sure of the writing nor of the order of the month names; the Ur student seems to have had the most difficulties. Within the official state calendar, the Swan-Eating Month (iti u$_5$-bí^{mušen}-gu$_7$) was month three (four after ŠS 3 and at Ur), and the Ninazu Festival Month (iti ezen-^{d}nin-a-zu) was month five (six after ŠS 3 and at Ur) but both names were out of use by the OB period. Note that all preserved Nippur sources omit the bird determinative and at least one (N1) writes gu$_7$ as KA.[5]

5. For the probable identification of the bird as a swan, see P. Steinkeller *apud* N. Velduis, *Religion, Literature*, 296.

For a similar formulation in an OB letter from Mari, see ARM 26 151: 24–27 iti *ki-is-ki-is-sí-im*, u₄ 14-kam ba.zal-*ma*, *tup-pa-am an-né-em a-na se-er be-lí-ia, ú-ša-bi-la-am*, "at the end of the fourteenth day of the month Kiskissum I am sending this tablet to my king."

34. This is the only occurrence of a lú-kaš₄ in CKU; they were simple couriers who carried messages, as distinguished from the lú-kíg̃-gi₄-a, who are also brought oral instructions and possibly read the letters aloud to the recipient. This corresponds to the Old Babylonian distinction between *lāsimum* and *mār šiprim*, as described by D. Charpin, *Lire et écrire* 176. Note that in Ur III archival texts the former do not occur as frequently as the latter.

The verbal form must be understood as the Sumerian equivalent of the "epistolary perfect;" it refers to the performative nature of the action. For the concept, as applied to other ancient Near Eastern languages, see D. Pardee and R. M. Whiting, *BSOAS* 50 (1987) 1–31.

35. This line is crucial for the understanding of the final passage. There are one or two signs missing in nearly all manuscripts. The key word is šen, which is only complete in found in N6 and X8. The signs šen and alal have been discussed by P. Steinkeller, *OA* 20 (1981) 243–49, but the meaning here is elusive. Lexical texts provide the Akkadian equivalent *qablum*, "battle, quarrel, strife," but in literary and historical texts this is usually rendered by the reduplicated form šen-šen, often in hendiadys with mè; see, for a rare unreduplicated example, *UET* 6/2 350: 4 mè šen im-ma-te.

The Ur1 text has a unique variant for the beginning of the line, ⸢u₄⸣ nu-mu-⸢un-da⸣-sa₉-a; it is possible that this is related to the likewise unique, if difficult, Ur ending of *Gilgameš, Enkidu, and the Netherworld* in *UET* 6/1 60 rev. 10′ u₄ nu-mu-un-da-sá-a àm-da-diri àga-bi in-ši-tag-ne.

Sources

N1 = 3 N-T 311 (IM 58418) i (*SL* xxii; *Sumer* 26 171)   = 1–36
N2 = 3 N-T 900,25 (*SLF* 21)   = 23–27; 32–35
N3 = 3 N-T 918,440 (*SLF* 22) + 3 N-T 919,486 (*SL* 41; *Sumer* 26 174)   = 1–20
N4 = 3 N-T 927,516 (*SL* xvi; *SLF* 21; *Sumer* 26 174)   = 18–26
N5 = CBS 7096   = 8–19
N6 = CBS 8875 (*SL* xxvi; *Sumer* 26 175) + N 6672   = 20–36
N7 = Ni. 4149 (*ISET* 2 122) rev. i′ 1–9; ii′ 1–5   = 1–9; 32–36
N8 = Ni. 4490 (*ISET* 2 122) =   1–3x
N9 = Ni. 9706 (*ISET* 2 112) rev. ii′ 12′–30′   = 1–21
N10 = UM 29-15-555 (*SL* xxxvii; *Sumer* 26 177)   = 1–6; 16–20
Ur1 = U. 16853 (*UET* 6/2 174) + *UET* 6/3 557 (*532) ii′ 1′–13′   = 20–36
Uk1 = W 16743 gb (Cavigneaux, *Uruk* 143) ii′ 1′–4′; iii′ 1–4   = 25–32
X1 = A w/n i   = 1–30

X2 = BM 54327 i 1'–8'		= 5–12
X3 = BM 16897+22617[6]		= 1–21; 24–36
X4 = LB 2543 (*TLB* 3 172) 6–8		= 18–21
X5 = MS 3275		= 1–25; 33–36
X6 = HMA 9–1815 (*JCS* 28 [1976] 102[7])		= 16–29
X7 = YBC 4596 obv.		= 1–36
X8 = Cotsen 52157 (Wilson, *Education* 158 [p. 250])		= 4–36
Z[8] = MS 2199/1 1–9, 16–18		= 1–9; 14–15?; 21

X2 possibly from Sippar, X3 and X7 possibly from Larsa. The Tutub provenience of X6 is doubtful (see p. 44 above).

Uk1, N1, and X4 collated on photographs (collations of X4 also by H. Waetzoldt, *OA* 15 [1976] 332).

Tablet typology: compilation tablets: N1, N3, Ur1, Ur2, X1, X2. The rest are all Type III, except X7 (one column with two letters) and X4 (oval exercise tablets with excerpts of letters 1 and 2).

Bibliography: Editions: F. Ali, *SL* 27–33; F. Ali, *Sumer* 26 (1970) 146–51. Translation and transliteration: P. Michalowski, *LEM* 63–64. Translations: S. N. Kramer, *The Sumerians*, 331–32, P. Michalowski, *Royal Letters*, 77.

Concordance of sigla used here (*CKU*) and by F. Ali in *SL* and in *Sumer* 26 with additions in *RCU*:

N1	A		A	N1
N3	F + 3 N-T 918,440		B	N7
N4	H		C	N10
N6	G		D	N8
N7	B		E	N9
N8	D		F	N3
N9	E		G	N6
N10	C		H	N4
Ur1	I		I	Ur1
X1	L		J	X7
X2	M		K	X4
X4	K		L	X1
X7	J		M	X2

6. 92-7-9-13 + 94-1-15-419.

7. Formerly UCLM 9-1815. Photo on line at CDLI (http://cdli.ucla.edu/dl/photo/P247912. jpg). The tablet has deteriorated somewhat since it was copied by D. Foxvog and since I first collated it. Recollated in February, 2011.

8. This is not, properly speaking, a source of the letter. These are lines that were used to create a new one together with elements of the answer, and it is edited here as ŠAr1a. The appropriate lines are incorporated into the matrix for comparative purposes.

Textual Matrix

1. lugal-ğu$_{10}$-ra ù-na-a-dug$_4$

```
N1   .    .    .    + .  o .
N3   o    o    o o  .    . .
N7   +    +    +    + .  o o
N8   .    +    +    + +  - +
N9   o    .    .    + +  - +
N10  +    +    +    o o  o o
X1   o    o    o .  + +  .
X3   .    .    o    o o  o o
X5   +    +    + .  o    o o
X7   +    +    +    + +  + .
Z    o    .    .    . .  - +
```

2. ¹árad-mu árad-zu na-ab-bé-a

```
N1   .  .  .  .  .    +  + o  .
N3   o o  o  o  .  +  .  + +
N7   + + +  +  +  +  .  o  o
N8   + . +  +  +  +  +  + +
N9   + o o  o  o  .  +  + +
N10  + . +  +  +  o  o  o o
X1   o o o  o  o  .  +  + .
X3   -. .  .  .  .  . o  o
X5   + . +  +  +  .  o  o o
X7   - + +  +  +  +  -  + +
Z    o o o  .  o  .  . + +
```

3. kur su-bir$_4$^{ki}-šè har-ra-an kaskal-la si sá-sá-e-ra

```
N1   .  .  .  . .  .  . .  .   +  .  . o o .
N3   o o o o o o o  . .   +  o o o . +
N7   + + + + + + + + +    +  + + . o o
N8   . o o . + + + + +    ra o o . . . .
N9   . o o o o o o o o    o  o . + + .
N10  + + . . + + . o o    o  + . + . o
X1   o o o o o o o o o    .  . + + + +
X3   .  .  .  . .  .  . . o   o o o o o o
X5   + . + + + + + + +    -  . + + . o
X7   + + + + + + + + +    -  + + + + dè
Z    .  o .  . .  .  . . +   -  + + + - dè
```

4.   gun   ma-da-zu   ge-en-ge-né-dè

	gun		ma-da-zu			ge-en-ge	-né-dè	
N1	.	.	.	+	+	+	+en+	.
N3	o	o	o	o	o	.	+ +	+
N7	+	+	+	.	+	+	+ o	o
N9	+	o	o	o	o	o	o o	.
N10	+	.	+	+	+	.	o o	o
X1	.	.	.	.	.	+	. +	+
X3	+	+	+	⌜za⌝	.	o	o o	o
X5	gú-un	+	+	⸗	+	+	. o	o
X7	gú-un	+	+	⸗	+	+	+ +	+
X8	o	o	o	o	.	.	. ?	.
Z	⌜gú⌝-un	⌜kalam–ma⌝	.	+	+	ne	⸗	

5.   a-rá ma-da zu-zu-dè

	a-rá		ma-da		zu-zu	-dè	
N1	+ +	.	+	+	+[9]	.	
N3	o o	o	o	o	.	+	
N7	+ +	+	+	+	.⌜ù⌝o		
N9	+ +	.	o	o	o o		
N10	. +	+	+	+	+ o		
X1	o .	.	+	+	.⌜ù⌝.		
X2	o o	o	o	o	o .		
X3	+ +	+	+	.	o⌜ù⌝.		
X5	+ +	+	+	+	+⌜ù⌝o		
X7	+ +	+	+	+	+ +		
X8	o o	o	o	.	. +		
Z	á-⌜áǧ-ǧá⌝		zu⌝-zu-dè				

5a. X1 [x x]x x ge-⌜ne-dè⌝[10]

6.   ugu a-pi-il-la-ša gal-zu unken-na-ka

	ugu	a-pi-il-la	-ša		gal-zu		unken-na	-ka
N1	+	+ + .	. +	+	+ +		+	+
N3	o	o o o o	o .	+	+		+	+
N7	.	+ + + +	+ +	+	.		o	o
N9	+	+ + .?	o o	o	o o		o	o
N10	.	. . . .	. o	o	o		o	o
X1	o	o o o o	. +	.	.		+	šè
X2	o	o o o o o	. .	.			+	šè
X3	.	+ + ⸗ .	. .	.	.			⌜šè⌝
X5	+	+ + ⸗ +	+ +	+	+		+	o
X7	+	+ + ⸗ +	+ +	+	+		+	šè
X8	o	o o . +	+ +	+	+		+	šè
Z	+	+ + ⸗ +	+ .	.	+		+	šè

9. Preceded by an erased zu.

10. Probably to be read [suhuš] ⌜ma-da⌝ ge-⌜ne-dè⌝, borrowed from ŠAr1 7 and 33 (letter 3).

7.   ad-gi₄-gi₄-da gù-téš-a sì-ke-dè

	ad	gi₄	gi₄	da	gù	téš	a	sì	ke	dè
N1	.	+	+	+	+	+	+	+	+	+
N3	o	o	o	o	.	o	o	o	.	+
N7	+	+	+	+	.	.	.	o	o	o
N9	.	+	+	.	o	o	o	o	o	o
X1	o	o	o	⌜dè⌝	+	.	+	.	+	+
X2	o	o	o	o	.	.	.	+	.	+
X3	.	.	+	⌜dè⌝	+	+	+	.	.	.
X5	+	+	+	dè	+	+	+	+	⌜ge⌝	.
X7	+	+	+	dè	+	+	+	.	ge	+
X8	o	.	+	dè	+bi	+	+	+	⌜ge⌝	.
Z	.	+	+	dè	+	+	-	+.?		+

8.   inim u₄-da ka-ne-ne-a hé-en-tùm   á-še mu-e-da-a-a-áĝ

	inim	u₄	da	ka	ne	ne	a	hé	en	tùm		á	še	mu	e	da	a	a	áĝ
N1	+	+	+	+	+	+	+	+	em	+		+	+	+	+	+	+	+	+
N3	o	o	.	+	+	.	.	.	.	.		o	+	+	+	-	+	+	+
N5	o	o	o	.	.	.	o	o	o	.		.	⌜še⌝	+	.	o	o	o	o
N7	+	+	.	.	.	.	o	o	o	o		o	o	o	o	o	o	o	o
N9	+	+	+	+	+	.	.	o	o	/		+	+	+	+	+	+	+	.
X1	o	o	o	o	.	+	-	+	+	+		.	+	+	+	+	-	+	+
X2	o	o	o	o	o	o	o	o⌜ébʔ⌝	.			.	ša	+	+	+	-	-	+
X3	.	o	.	.	+	+	+	+	.	/		o	o	o	.	.	-	.	.
X5	+	+	+	+	.	+	-	+⌜em⌝	.⌜muʔ⌝	/		+	še	+	.	+	-	+	.
X7	+	+	+	+	+	+	+	em	+			+	še	+	+	+	-	-	+
X8	+	+	+	+	+	+	+	+	+	+		+	+	⌜me⌝-da-an-ak					
Z	+	+	-	+	+	+	-	+	eb	+	/	+	še	me-da-ak					

9.   ká é-gal-la-še gub-a-ĝu₁₀-ne

	ká	é	gal	la	še	gub	a	ĝu₁₀	ne
N1	+	+	+	+	+	+	+	+	+
N3	o	o	.	-	+	+	+	.	.
N5	o	.	+	+	+	.	o	o	o
N7	.	.	.	o	o	o	o	o	o
N9	+	+	+	+	+	+	+	+	.
X1	o	o	o	o	.	.	.	+	+
X2	o	o	o	o	o	.	.	.	+
X3	o	o	.	.	⌜ta⌝	.	o	.	.
X5	+	+	+	+	.	+	+	+	.
X7	+	+	+	+	+	+	+	+	+
X8	+	+	+	+	+	.	-	+	+

10. silim-ma lugal-ǧá-ke₄ èn li-bí-in-tar

N1	.	.	+	+	+	+	+	+	+ +
N3	o	o	.	+	+	.	+	+	+ o
N5	o	.	+	+	.	o	o	o	o o
N9	+	+	+	+	+	.	+	.	o o
X1	o	o	o	o	o	.	.	-	⌈ib⌉ +
X2	o	o	o	o	o	.	.	.	+ +
X3	o	o	.	.	.	.	o	.	. .
X5	+	+	+	+	.	+	+	+	. +
X7	+	+	+	+	+	+	+	+	+ +
X8	.	.	.	ǧu₁₀-	+	.	bi	en	+

11. dúr na-ma-ta-an-zi   ki-a nu-ub-za

N1	+	.	+	+	+	+	+	+	+	.
N3	o	o	o	.	+	.	.	+	+	+ +
N5	o	.	+	.	+	.	o	o	o	o o
N9	+	nam	+	+	+	+	+	+	.	o o
X1	o	o	o	.	.	.	.	+	+	+ .
X2	o	o	o	o	o	o	.	.	.	+ +
X3	o	.	.	+	.	.	o	.	.	. +
X5	+	+	+	.	+	.	+	+	+	+ .
X7	+	+	+	+	+	+	+	+	+	+ + :
X8	.	x	nu-⌈na?⌉-ma-da-zu	.	+	.	-	zu		

12. ba-an-da-mud-en

N1	#
N3	#
N5	#
N9	ba-⌈an⌉-túm-mu-dè :
X1	[. . .]x-⌈mud⌉-dè-en
X2	[. . .]-⌈da?⌉-mud?-dè-en⌉
X3	⌈ba-an-túm⌉-mu-dè :
X5	ba-an-da-⌈mud-en⌉
X7	ba-an-da-mud-da
X8	⌈ba-an-da⌉-mu-dè

13.   te-ĝá-e-da-ĝu$_{10}$-ne

```
N1   + + +.  +   .
N3   o o .   +   .   .
N5   .  + - +    .   o¹¹
N9   + + - .    o   o
X1   o o o o   .   +
X3   .  o o o  o   .
X5   + + - + +    +
X7   + + ++ +    +
X8   + ge - .   .   .
```

14.   é kaskal-la kuš ga-ríĝ-ak   šukur kù-sig$_{17}$ kù-babbar

```
N1   + + gíd +  .   .  + +   ᵘʳᵘᵈᵃ+   + +   + +
N3   o o     .  +   .  . .   / .       + .   + +
N5   o o     .  +   +  . o   .         . .   . + :
N9   + +     +  +   +  + .   / ⌈kak⌉   + +   + + :
X1   o o     o  .   +  + +   .          + +   + +
X3   o o     o  o   +  . .   o         o o   o . :
X5   + +     +  +   +  + +   / +        + +   . + :
X7   + +     a  +   +raš+ +  +          + +   + + :
X8   + .     e  o   .  . .   šu-gur .   .     + + :
Z    - -        - - -  - -   .          + +   - - :
```

15. ^{na_4}gug ^{na_4}za-gìn ĝar-ra-ta

```
N1   . +   + + +   + + :
N3   . +   + .  .  + +
N5   o o   o o o  o o o
N9   - .   o o o  o o o
X1   o .   + + +  + . :
X3   o .   o o o  o + .
X5   . .   . + +  . o o
X7   . +   + + +  + + -
X8   . .   - - -  . . - :
Z    - +   - + +  + + + íb-ta-⌈gi₄⌉-gi₄
```

11. Possibly read ⌈te-e⌉ at the beginning of the line. There does not seem to be enough room for line 12.

16.   a-ab-dù-dù-a ušù sar-àm i-íb-tuš

```
N1    + +  +  +  + +   .   +   ⸢ +  .
N3    o +  +  +  + /o   .   .   o o o
N5    o +  +  +  + .    .   o   o o o
N9    + +  +  +  + +     .   o   o o o
N10   .  .  .  .  . o   o  o   o o o
X1    ⸢ .  +  +  + /o   o  +   + + +
X3    o o  o  o  . o    o  o    .  .  .
X5    .  +  +  .  .  .   .  .   + +  .
X6    o o  o  o  o /o   o  o    o x x :
X7    + +  +  +  + +     +   a   + + +
X8    ⸢ +  +  +  . +    +  ⸢   ⸢ +  .
```

17.   kù-sig$_{17}$ ^{na_4}za-gìn-na mí zi-dè-eš im-me

```
N1    .  .        +  +  +   +  +   + + +  + +
N3    o  .        .  o  o   o  o   .  o o o  o
N5    .  +        ⸢  +  +   ⸢  +   .  o o o  o
N9    +  +        ⸢  +  +   ⸢  .   .  o o o  o
N10   .  .        ⸢  +  +   .  .   o o o o  o
X1    o  .        +  +  +   +  +   .  .  + +  +
X3    o  o        o  o  o   o  o   .  +  + +  +
X5    .  +        .  .  .   ⸢  +   .  +  + +  o
X6    .  ⸢kù-babbar⸣ .  .  .  .   .   + + + +  +[12]
X7    +  +        +  +  +   +  +   + + + +  +
X8    +  +        .  .  +   .  ní  .  .  + +  +
```

18. ^{giš}gu-za barag ^{túg}šutur-e ri-a i-íb-tuš

```
N1    + +  +  +     + +   ⸢   + + + +  +
N3    o o  o  .     + .    o  o o  .  + o
N4    traces
N5    + +  +  +     + .    ⸢   .  .  o o o
N9    + +  +  +     + o    o  o o  o o o
N10   + .  o  .      .  .   o  o o  o o o
X1    o  .  .  .    + + ré + +  .  ⸢ + +
X3    o o  o  .     + .    o  o o  .  + +
X4    + +  +  +     + +   ⸢   + + + +  .
X5    .  +  +  +     + .   .  + +  .  .  .
X6    .  +  +  +     + +   +  + + ⸢ + +
X7    + +  +  +     + +   +  + + ⸢ + +
X8    + +  +  .      + .   o⸢rí⸣ + ⸢ + +
```

12. There are remnants of two signs and space for two more at the beginning of this line; probably had end of 16.

19. ᵍⁱˢĝiri-gub kù-sig$_{17}$-ka ĝiri-ni i-íb-ĝar

```
N1    . .   +   +   .   +   +   +   + + .
N3    o o   .   +   .   o   .   +   + . o
N4    + +   +   +   .   o   o   o   o o o
N5    . .   .   o   o   o   o   o   o o o
N9    + +   +   .   .   o   o   o   o o o
N10   + +   +   .   o   o   .   .   o o o
X1    o .   +   +   +   +   +   -   + +
X3    o o   o   .  .⌜ga⌝.  o   .   ⌜ì⌝ . +
X4    + +   +   +   +   -   +   +   i-ni-gub:
X5    . +   +   +   +   +   .   +   . . ⌜gub⌝
X6    . +   +   +   +   +   +   +   - + + :
X7    + +   +   +   + ga +   +   +   + + + :
X8    + .   .   .   .   -   .   +   - - . :
```

20. ĝiri-ni na-ma-ta-an-kúr

```
N1    .   +   +   +   +   +   +
N3    o   .   +   +   .   o   o
N4    +   +   +   .   o   o   o
N6    .   +   .   o   o   o   o
N9    .   .   .   .   o   o   o
N10   +   +   +   .   o   o   o
Ur1   o   o   o   .   .   o   o
X1    .   .   +   +   da  +   +
X3    o   o   .   .   +   +   +
X4    .   o   o   o   o   o   o
X5    +   +   +   +   +   +   .
X6    +   +   nu-mu-un-da-an-kúr
X7    +   +   +   +   +   + zé-er
X8    +   .   .   o   o   o   o
```

21. àga-ús saĝ-ĝá-na iá li-mu-um-ta-àm zi-da gùb-bu-na íb-ta-an-gub-bu-uš

```
N1    + +  + +  +  +  + +  + +  .  + +  +  + + + +  + +
N4    + +  + .  .  o  o o  o o  .  + .  o  o o o o  o o
N6    o .  + .  o  o  . +  + .  o  . +  .  + + + o  o o
N9    . .  . o  o  o  o o  o o  o  o o  o  o o o o  o o
Ur1   o o  o .  .  .  . .  o o  o /o .  .  + ⌜ba⌝+ + .  . o o
X1    o .  + +  +  +  + +  + +  /o o .  .  + + + +  + +
X3    o o  . .  +  +  + -  + +  . /o o  o  o o o o  o o
X4    + +  + +  -  +  ME.LI        +  . .  o o o o  o o
X5    + +  + +  +  o  . +  + .  +  + +  + ba .  . o  o o
X6    + +  + +a ni +  + im - + +  + + á.  -  . . .  . - . . .
X7    + +  + an +  +  + +  + +  +  + +  + ba + + +  + +
X8    . .  . .  +  .  - - x[13] + +  .  o .  .  . x o o  o o
Z     o .  + +  -  +  + .  . x  x x .  + á+ + x o o o  o o o
```

13. ⌜me⌝?

22. àš gud niga ĝéš udu niga níĝ-zú-gub-šè in-ĝar

Ms.	àš	gud	niga	ĝéš	udu	niga	níĝ	zú	gub	šè	in	ĝar
N1	o	o	o	x	.	.	.	+	+	+	+	.
N4	+	.	+	+	o	o /	+	+	+	+	o	o
N6	.	+	+	niš	+	+	+	.	o	.	+	+
Ur1	.	+	.	+	+	+	àm -	+	.	.	.	o
X1	o	o	o	.	.	+	-	+	+	+	+	.
X5	+	+	+	+	.	o	o	.	+	.	o	o
X6	+	+	-	+	+níta	+	-	+	+	+	.	.
X7	+	+	+	+	+	+	-	+	+	+	+	+
X8	o	o	o	o	o	o	o	o	x	+	o	o

23. šu-luh   lugal-ĝá-ke_4 sá bí-in-dug_4

Ms.	šu	luh	lugal	ĝá	ke_4	sá	bí	in	dug_4
N1	o	o	o	o	.	.	.	.	.
N2	.	o	o	o	o	o	o	o	o
N4	+	+	+	.	o	o	o	o	o
N6	+	+	+	+	.	o	o	.	+
Ur1	.	+	+	+	+	šu[14]+	+		⌜du⌝
X1	o	.	.	+	+	.	.	.	.
X3	o	o	o	o	o	o	o	o	x
X5	+	+x	.	o	o	o	o	o	o
X6	+	+	.	+	+	+	.	.	.
X7	+	+	+	+	+	+	íb	-	+
X8	.	+ ha' ke_4	+	+	+	+	.'	o	o

23a Ur1 [k]á é-⌜gal-la⌝-ta ⌜ì⌝-gub-bu-n[e] (see line 9)

24. ká-na èn nu-tar-ra-bi lú na-ma-ši-in-ku_4-re-en

Ms.	ká	na	èn	nu	tar	ra	bi	lú	na	ma	ši	in	ku_4	re	en
N1	.	o	o	o	o	.	+	+	+	+	+	+	+	+	+
N2	+	.	o	o	o	o	o	o	o	o	o	o	o	o	o
N4	+	+	+	+	o	o	o	o	o	o	o	o	o	o	o
N6	+	.	+	.	+	.	.	o	⌜na-ma-da-ku_4-re⌝						
Ur1	[ká]	⌜en nu-mu-un-tar-ra-ba[15]⌝						[lú]	⌜nu-mu-un-ši-in-ku_4-ku_4⌝						
X1	o	.	+	+	.	.	+	.	.	.	-	.	.	.	.
X3	o	o	o	o	o	o	o	o	⌜nu⌝-mu-ši-ku_4-re						
X5	+	+	.	+	.	o	o	o	o	o	o	o	o	o	o
X6	.	o	o	.	.	.	a ba	.	o	o	o	o	.	.	o
X7	+	+	+	+	+	+	+	+	+	+	+	+	+	+	-
X8	+	ká	en	+	+	+	+	nu	mu	-	.	o	o	o	

14. It is unclear if this is a true phonetic variant or a graphic error for sá. This student had an idiosyncratic hand and also sometimes used this shape for šè.

15. There is a small vertical line in the middle of the sign that almost makes it look like zu but collation suggests that it is not a real wedge. There does not seem to be room at the beginning of the line for more than one sign.

25. ku₄-ku₄-da-g̃u₁₀-ne

```
N1   o  o  .  +  +
N2   .  o  o  o  o
N4   +  +  +  .  o
N6   +  +  +  .  .
Uk1  x  o  o  o  o
Ur1  .  .  .  +  .
X1   .  +  +  +  +
X3   o  o  o  o  .
X5   .  .  o  o  o
X7   +  +  +  .  +
X8   +  +  +  +  o
```

26. ᵍⁱˢgu-za gàr-ba kù-sig₁₇ huš-a g̃ar-ra lú ma-an-de₆ tuš-a ma-an-dug₄

```
N1   o o .  .  .  + +   +  -  +   + +   + +   + +   + +   + +
N2   +. o  o  o  o o   o  o o o   o .   o o   o o   o o   o o
N4   .  .  .  .  .  o   o  o o o   o o   o o   o o   o o   o o
N6   +. +  +  +  +  .   +  + + +   + +   + +   + +   + +   + +
Uk1  . o o  o  o  o o   o  o o o/  . o   o o   o o   o o   o o
Ur1  . +  .  +  +  + +¹⁶  -  - +  ./  .  .  o   .  + +   bí i[n] o
X1   o. +  +  +  +  .   .  +. ./  o .   +   .  .  + +   .
X3   o o o  o  o  o o   .  .  + +  šutur-e ri-a   + +   + +   +
X6   o o o  o  o  o o   o  o o o   o o   .  +   o o   o o   o o
X7   ++ +  +  +  +  + +   +  + +   .  .  .  .  +   + +   + +   +
X8   ++ .  +  +  +  +   +  .  .  .  +. .  o   o o  ·o o  o o
```

27. á-ág̃-g̃á lugal-g̃á-ke₄ ì-gub-bé-en nu-tuš-ù-dè-en bí-dug₄

```
N1   o .  ,  .  + +   + +   + +   + +   + + +   +   +
N2   .  .  o  o   o o   o o   o o   o ʊ   o o o   o   o
N6   .  + +  +   + +   +. .   +   + +   + + +   +   +
Uk1  . o o  o   o o   o o   o o   o o   o o o   o   o
Ur1  .  .  o  o   .  .   . .   .  o   .  .  ꜥaꜣ - -  +i[n]o
X1   o o o  o   o .   + +   +. ./  o o   o o .   +   .
X3   o o o  o   o .   . .   + +   o o   o + +   +   +
X6   o o o  o   o o   o o   o o   o o   o o o   o   .
X7   ++ .  .   .  +   + +   +. .   .  o .   +   +
X8   ++ +  +   + +   . .   - -   .  .   - - -   .ꜥinꜣꜣo
```

16. Written zi.

28. min gud niga niš udu niga ^{giš}banšur-ĝu$_{10}$ lú ma-an-ĝar

```
N1   ⌜diš⌝ +  .  .  +  +  + +   +   +  +  +  sá
N6   +   +  +  +  +  .  . +   +   .  +  +  .
Uk1  diš .  o  o  o  o  + .   o   o  o  o  o
Ur1  diš +  +  àš +  +  + .   o   o  o  o  .
X1   o   o  o  o  o  o  o .   .   .  +  .  x x
X3   o   o  o  o  o  o  o .   +   .  .  +  sá
X6   o   o  o  o  o  o  o o   o   o  o  o  x
X7   +   +  +  +  +  +  + +   ĝá  .  o  ⌜un sá?⌝
X8   +   +  +  +  .  +  + +   +   +  +  .  .
```

29. nu-kár-kár-dè àga-ús lugal-gá-ke$_4$ ^{giš}banšur-ĝu$_{10}$ íb-bal-a-aš

```
N1   .  .  .  da +  +  + + +   + +  +  in +  +  +
N6   +  +  ak +  .  .  . . .   + .  .  o  o  o  o
Uk1  +  +  +  x  o  o  o o o   + .  o  o  o  o  o
Ur1  +  +  +  +  +  +  . o .   + +  +  +  .  o  ⌜eš⌝
X1   o  o  o  o  o  o  o . o   o o  o  o  .  ⌜e⌝o
X3   o  o  o  o  o  .  + + +   + .  +  -  +  o  o
X6   o  o  o  o  o  o  o o o   o o  o  o  o  x
X7   +  ĝá .  +  +  +  + + .   . +  -  ⌜in⌝o o  o
X8   +  .  + x+ +  +  + + -   + +  .  x  o  o  o
```

30. ní ba-da-te su ba-da-zi

```
N1   .  o  +  +  +  +  +  +
N6   +  +  .  o  o  o  o  o
Uk1  .  .  o  o  o  o  o  o
Ur1  #
X1   o  o  o  o  o  o  .  .
X3   o  o  o  .  .  +  .  +
X7   .  .  +  +  .  .  +  .
X8   .  .an+ +  +  +  +  +
```

31. iti ezen-^{d}nin-a-zu u$_4$ iá-àm zal-la-àm

```
N1   +  .  .  .  + +  + +  + +  +
N6   .  o  o o  o o  o o  o o  o
Ur1  +  +  + +  + +  + udilia-kam ba-[ab?]-⌜te⌝
Uk1  +  .  o o  o o  o o  o o  o
X3   o  o  o .  + +  + +  + +  a
X7   o  o  .  + + +  . o  o o  o
X8   .  .  ni-na + + + kam+ -  .
```

32. lugal-ĝu$_{10}$ á-še mu-e-da-a-a-áĝ

```
N1    .   +   .   +   +   + +   + + +
N2    .   o       o o   o   o o   o o o
N6    +   +   +   .   o   o o   o o o
N7    o   o       o o   .   + +   + + +
Uk1   .?  o       o o   o   o o   o o o
Ur1   +   +   +   še  +[17]  -   +   o o o
X3    .   o   .   še  +   + +   + - +
X7    o   o   +   o   o   o o   o o o
X8    +   .       +   +   me-da-an-ʾáĝʾ
```

33. iti u$_5$-bí^{mušen}-gu$_7$ u$_4$ diš-àm zal-la-àm

```
N1    .   +   +-  KA  +   +   +   +   +   +
N2    +   .   oo  o       o   o   o   o   o o
N6    +   ʾu$_4$-bí-KA$^{mušen}$ʾ   o   o   o       o   o   o
N7    o   o   oo  o       o   o   .   +   + +
Ur1   +   u$_5$-gu$_7$$^{mušen}$        u$_4$  diš-kam  ba-[(da)-zal/te]
X3    .   .   o o   .       +   +   +   +   + +
X5    .   o   o o   o       o   o   o   o   o o
X7    o   o   . .   .       .   +   k[am].   .   .
X8    +   u$_4$ . .   -       .   .   kam  +   - +
```

34. lú-kaš$_4$-e mu-e-ši-gi$_4$

```
N1    .   .   .   +   -   + + in
N2    +   .   o   o   o o o
N6    +   +   še  +   .   o o
N7    o   o   o   o   o .in+
Ur1   ʾlugal-ĝu$_{10}$ʾ lú ʾkaš$_4$ʾ-[e]/ ʾlú hu?ʾ-mu-unʾ-ši-ʾin-gi$_4$-gi$_4$ʾ
X3    +   +   o   .   + + .
X5    +   +   .   o   o o o
X7    o   o   o   .   - + o
X8    +   +   +   me-ši-in-ʾgi$_4$ʾ
```

35. u$_4$ sa$_9$-àm šen-e ba-te

```
N1    .   +   .   .   + + +[18]
N2    +   +   .   o   o o o
N6    +   +   +   +   . o o
N7    o   o   o   o   o o +
Ur1   ʾu$_4$ʾ nu-mu-ʾun-daʾ-sa$_9$-a ʾšen-eʾ ba-te
X3    .   +   +   .   . + +
X5    +   +   a   .   o o o
X7    o   o   o   o   o . +:
X8    +   +   -   +   + + +:
```

17. The scribe wrote a sign, possibly ha, erased it, and then wrote an incomplete mu.
18. Preceded by an erased te.

36. lugal-ǧu$_{10}$ hé-en-zu

N1	.	o	.	.	.
N6	.	+	+	.	.
N7	o	o	o	.	+
Ur1	.	+	+	+	+
X3	.	.	.	.	+
X5	+	+	o	o	.?
X7	+	.	o	o	o
X8	+	+	+	+	+

In N1, N7, N9, U1, Uk1, and X7 followed by ArŠ1(2).

Three manuscripts have different line orders:

N1:

> iti ⌜ezen-^{d}nin⌝-a-zu u$_4$ iá-àm zal-la-àm
> ⌜lú-kaš$_4$-e⌝ mu-ši-gi$_4$-in
> ⌜iti⌝ u$_5$-bí-gu$_7$(KA)u$_4$ diš-àm zal-la-àm
> ⌜lugal⌝-ǧu$_{10}$ ⌜á⌝-še mu-e-da-a-a-áǧ
> ⌜u$_4$⌝ sa$_9$-⌜àm⌝ ⌜šen⌝-e ba-te
> ⌜lugal⌝-[ǧu$_{10}$] ⌜hé-en-zu⌝

"I am sending you this messenger the evening of the fifth day of the Ninazu Festival. [32]My king, you gave me orders the evening of the first day of the Swan-Eating Month. Now it is midday, and war is brewing. Now my king is informed (about all of this)!"

Ur1:

> iti ezen-^{d}nin-a-zu u$_4$ udilia-kam ba-[ab⌝]-⌜te⌝
> lugal-ǧu$_{10}$ á-šè!^{19} mu-da-[a-(a)-áǧ]
> iti u$_5$-gu$_7$^{mušen} u$_4$ diš-kam ba-[(da)-zal/te]
> ⌜lugal-ǧu$_{10}$⌝ lú-⌜kaš$_4$⌝-[e]
> ⌜lú hu$^?$-mu-un⌝-ši-⌜in-gi$_4$-gi$_4$⌝
> ⌜u$_4$⌝ nu-mu-⌜un-da⌝-sa$_9$-a ⌜šen-e⌝ ba-te
> ⌜lugal⌝-ǧu$_{10}$ hé-en-zu

"My king gave me orders when the fifteenth day of the Ninazu Festival Month approached. On the first day of the Swan-Eating Month my king sent *him* [*(these) messengers*]. *It is not yet the middle of the day* and war is brewing. Now my king is informed (about all of this)!"

19. The scribe had some problems at this point. The sign is really šu, followed by an erasure; the following mu is also badly written.

X7:

[iti u₅]-˹bí^mušen˺-gu₇ u₄˺ diš-˹kam zal-la-àm˺
[lugal-ğu₁₀] á-[še mu-e-da-a-(a)-áğ]
[iti ezen]-˹d˺nin-a-zu ˹u₄˺ [x-kam-ma-àm]
[lú-kaš₄-e] ˹mu˺-ši-[in˺-gi₄-in]
[u₄ sa₉-àm šen-e] ˹ba˺-te lugal-˹ğu₁₀˺ hé-en-zu]

"My king, you gave me orders the evening of the first day of the Swan-Eating Month. I am sending you this messenger the evening of the x-th day of the Ninazu Festival. Now it is midday, and war is brewing. Now my king is informed (about all of this)!"

Colophon A (X8)

1a. Aradmu to Šulgi 1a

(ArŠ1a)

X1 = MS 2199/1

Tablet: Type III.

1. [lugal]-ʳğu₁₀-ra ù-naʳ-dug₄	ArŠ1:1
2. [⁽¹⁾árad-mu] ʳáradʳ-[zu] ʳna-abʳ-bé-a	ArŠ1:2
3. ʳkurʳ [su]-ʳbir₄ᵏⁱ-šè har-ra-anʳ kaskal si sá-sá-dè	ArŠ1:3
4. ʳgúʳ-un ʳkalam-ma geʳ-en-ge-ne	ArŠ1:4
5. á-ʳáğ-ğá zuʳ¹-zu-dè	ArŠ1:5
6. ugu a-pi-la-ša ʳgal-zuʳ unken-na-šè	ArŠ1:6
7. ad gi-gi-dè gù-téš sì-ʳkeʳʳ-dè	ArŠ1:7
8. inim u₄ ka-ne-ne hé-eb-tùm	ArŠ1:8
9. á-šè me-da-akʳ	ArŠ1:8
10. sìg-sìg eden-na lib₄-lib₄ a-šà-ga ú-gu dé-e-ne	ŠAr1:13
11. en-na a-pi-la-ša sa e-ne	ŠAr1:14
12. igi-zu hé-dib igi-zu ib-ši-UD	ŠAr1:15
13. lú ʳgalʳ-gal-bi inim-bi hé-zu	ŠAr1:9
14. za-ʳpa²-áğ²ʳ-zu kur-kur-ra hé-eb-ul	ŠAr1:10
15. x x ta hur-sağ-ğá x x x ba-ra²-ğá-ğá	?
16. ʳšukurʳ kù-sig₁₇ gug za-gìn ğar-ra-ta íb-ta-ʳgi₄ʳ-gi₄	ArŠ1:14–15?
17. ⁿᵃ⁴nir₇ kù-ʳsig₁₇ʳ gug za-ʳgìnʳ x x [. . .] x	?
18. [àga]-ʳúsʳ sağ-ğá iá li-ʳmu-umʳ x x x [z]i–da á-gùbʳ-ʳbuʳ x[. . .]	ArŠ1:21

Reverse

One illegible line.

¹Speak to my king, ²saying (the words of) Aradmu, your servant:

⁹You commanded me ³to undertake an expedition to Subir, ⁴to secure the taxes on the frontier territory, ⁵to inform (them) about (your) orders, ⁶⁻⁷to confer (with the elites of Subir) about the prefect Apilaša and have them come to agreement, ⁸*so that he could bring to them* (i.e., *the Subir elites*) *up-to-date instructions.*²

1. Followed by an erased zu.
2. Alternative translation: so that as part of the daily instructions he could bring them (the people of Subir) good news.

[10] *Drop (chasing) winds in the wilderness and robbers in the fields!*[3] [11] Until you have reached my prefect Apilaša, [12] *ignore all of this so that you can . . . your face before him (without delay),*" [13] so that their (local) dignitaries learn their orders, [14] so that your battle cries should cover the land(s). [15] . . . [16] staked poles/lances inlaid with silver, carnelian, and lapis . . . [17] nir-stone, gold, carnelian, lapis, . . . [18] Choice guards, five thousand strong, (stood to) his right and left . . .

Commentary

This is an one-off attempt at creating a new letter from Aradmu to Šulgi by pasting together pieces of the first two letters of CKU, that is, ArŠ1 (1) and its response, ŠAr1 (2). This student exercise ends inconclusively: it is clear that the whole thing makes little sense. The text shares some unique variants with source X8 of ArŠ1 (1), and both may come from the same place (e.g., the verbal form in line 9).

4–5. The source text (ArŠ1: 4–5 [1]) has gun ma-da-zu ge-en-ge-né-dè, a-rá ma-da zu-zu-dè. The substitution of kalam-ma for ma-da-zu is simply wrong, resulting from lexical identification of both kalam and ma-da with Akkadian *mātum*. The use of á-áğ-ğá for a-rá ma-da may have been triggered by problems with understanding the use of the reduplicated predicate (see the commentary to ArŠ1: 5 above). The infelicitous alterations may have been motivated by a desire to create a completely new text based on the two source letters.

17. This line, while it plays off the previous one, does not derive from any known letter. The only passage known to me that has the sequence kù-sig$_{17}$ gug za-gìn is from *Enlil-bani Hymn A* 107, part of the "tetrad" used in early stages of education, but the latter is without the precious nir$_7$ (*ḫulalum*) stone that opens the list here.

3. Alternative translation: make winds and robbers disappear from the wilderness!

2. Šulgi to Aradmu 1
(ŠAr1, 3.1.2, RCU 2)

Composite Text

1. ᴵárad-mu-ra ù-na-a-dug₄
2. ᵈšul-gi lugal-zu na-ab-bé-a
3. lú in-ši-gi₄-in-na-zu lú-dun-a-zu in-nu-ù
4. šu-zu-ta-àm á-áǧ-ǧá šu la-ba-ra-ab-te-ǧá-e
5. a-na-aš-àm níǧ-a-na an-ga-àm bí-in-ak-a-ni ur₅ ì-me-a nu-e-zu
6. ǧá-e níǧ ǧá-e-gin₇-nam ma-da ge-né-dè
7. uǧ si sá-sá-e-dè gù-téš-a sì-ke-dè¹
8. uru ma-da ba-te-ǧá-dè-na-zu umuš-bi zu-zu-àm
9. lú gal-gal-bé-ne inim-bi zu-àm
10. za-pa-áǧ-ǧu₁₀ kur-kur hé-eb-si
11. á kala-ga á nam-ur-saǧ-ǧá-ǧu₁₀ kur-re hé-en-šub-šub
12. u₁₈-lu-ǧu₁₀ kalam-ma hé-eb-dul
13. sìg-sìg eden-na lib₄-lib₄ a-šà-ga ú-gu dé-ni-ib
14. en-na a-pi-il-la-ša gal-zu-unken-na-ǧu₁₀ sá an-né-en
15. igi-zu è-ta-ab igi-zu hé-en-ši-UD
16 . á-šè mu-e-da-a-áǧ
16a. a-na-aš-àm ǧá-a-gin₇-nam nu-un-ak
17. tukum-bi gal-zu-unken-na-ǧu₁₀ ǧá-a-gin₇-nam nu-ub-gur₄
18. ᵍⁱˢgu-za barag ᵗᵘᵍšutur-e ri-a nu-ub-tuš
19. ᵍⁱˢǧìri-gub kù-sig₁₇-ka ǧìri-ni nu-ub-ǧar
20. énsi nam-énsi-ta
21. lú ǧárza ǧárza-ta
22. ní-te-ní-te-a li-bí-ib-ǧar ù nu-ub-ta-gub-bu
23. lú nu-un-gaz igi nu-un-hul
24. lú igi-bar-ra-ka-ni lú-a li-bí-in-diri
25. a-na-gin₇-nam ma-da íb-gi-ne
26. tukum-bi ki um-mu-e-a-áǧ

    1. Var.: suhuš ma-da ge-en-ge-né-dè.

275

27. šà-zu šà zú-kešda ba-ra-na-ĝá-ĝá
28. ì-gur₄-re-en àga-ús-zu nu-e-zu
29. nam lú-u₁₈-lu-bi ù nam-ur-saĝ-ĝá-ka-ni igi-zu bí-in-zu
30. tukum-bi émedu-ĝu₁₀ me-en-zé-en
31. igi min-na-zu-ne-ne-a im-sar-e gù hé-em-ta-dé-dé-ne
32. gù-téš-a sì-ke-dè-en-zé-en
33. suhuš ma-da ge-né-dè-en-zé-en
34. a-ma-ru-kam

¹ Speak to Aradmu, ² saying (the words) of Šulgi, your king:

³ (Apilaša), the one I sent you to—is he not your own trusted subordinate? ⁴ Did he not receive (his) orders from your very own hands? ⁵ What is more, how could you so misunderstand the true meaning of all that he has been doing?

⁶ As far as I am concerned, you were to make the frontier territory secure as my representative, ⁷ to organize the people and keep them obedient, ⁸ and once you reached the cities of the frontier, to discern their attitudes ⁹ and to learn what their dignitaries are saying, ¹⁰ so that my battle cry would fill the mountains, ¹¹ my mighty battle weapons fall upon the foreign lands, ¹² and my "storm" cover over the homeland! ¹³ *"Drop (chasing) winds in the wilderness and robbers in the fields!*² ¹⁴ Until you have reached my prefect Apilaša, ¹⁵ *ignore all of this so that you can . . . your face before him (without delay)!"* ¹⁶ Thus did I command you!³

¹⁷ If my prefect had not expanded (his powers), just as I would have,⁴ ¹⁸ if he had not sat on a throne on a dais placed over a fine carpet,⁵ ¹⁹ had not set his feet on a golden footstool, ²² had not by his very own authority appointed and removed ²⁰ governors from the office of governor, ²¹ office holders from official positions, ²³ had not (punished anyone) by death or blinding, ²⁴ (and) had not promoted those of his own choosing over others—²⁵ how else could he have secured the frontier? ²⁶ If you (truly) love me ²⁷ then you will not be so set against him!

²⁸ It is you who have expanded your powers so that you no longer understand your (own) guardsmen! ²⁹ He has made you learn (the hard way) the responsibilities of those people, as well as the responsibilities of his own warriors!

³⁰ If you are indeed both my most faithful retainers,⁶ ³¹ (you will listen together while) they read out this tablet before the two of you.⁷ ³² Both of you must come to an agreement ³³ and secure the foundations of the frontier territory! ³⁴ It is urgent!

2. Alt. transl.: make winds and robbers disappear from the wilderness!
3. Two texts have an additional line 16a; see commentary.
4. Var.: If you had not expanded my prefect's powers as my representative.
5. Alt. transl.: under an awning.
6. Var.: If you (sing.) are indeed my faithful retainer. . . .
7. Viz.: have them read out aloud my inscribed tablet before your (pl.) very own eyes.

Commentary

3. The term lú-dun-a clearly denotes a relationship of subordination between two people, but more precise legal and social ramifications of the word are difficult to define (the reading of the second sign is uncertain). Lexical equivalencies from Lu are *a-RA qa-a-te* (*MSL* 12 142:18′), *a-wi-il qá-ta-tim* (*MSL* 12 166:280), *ḫa-[i-ṭu]* (*MSL* 12 202:4); but the word is not the same as Akkadian *qātātu*, "guarantor," as that is Sumerian šu-du$_8$-a. *CAD* Q 171, under *amil qātāti*, translates it as "ward, (bonded) dependent." In administrative texts, the context is always PN$_1$ lú-dun-a PN$_2$. The term is already attested, albeit not very frequently, in pre-Sargonic texts (e.g., *SR* 94:3; *CT* 50: 28: iv 1; vii 3′, *CT* 50 26 v 3 [ugula 1.] *VS* 25 10:3, *VS* 25 55: iv 3) as well as in Sargonic (*TMH NF* 5 12:3, 6, *BIN* 8 153:3, *OSP* 1 50:2; see F. Thureau-Dangin, *ITT* 1 27 n. 3 for other examples) and Ur III sources.

Unlike the earlier examples, almost all the Ur III occurrences are found in connection with the šakkana, that is, with the highest military rank, and most of them are àga-ús, "(body)guards." These generals are Abuni (*TrDr* 83:13; *AUCT* 1 276: 14–15; *TIM* 6 34:7–8), Ea-ili (*MVN* 11 186:13, 15; *TCL* 2 5488:4–5), Šeškala (*UTI* 6 3800:11), and possibly Lugalkuzu (*TIM* 6 34:11–12). Other occurrences are connected with a certain Puzur-ili, who may have headed a leather workshop (*SCT* 38 14:7; *MVN* 3 354:12). A "captain" (nu-bánda) who was a lú-dun-a of one šeš-sag, serves as witness in a text from Ur (*UET* 3: 43) and six individuals receiving silver rings are described as gàr-tum lú-dun-a lú maš-kán-šar-[ru-um^{ki}] (*PPAC* 4: 7). Different from all the above is the example from an Ur III cylinder seal inscription, *SAT* 3 2199: ^{d}èr-ra-qú-ra-ad, zadim ^{d}nin-líl-lá, lú-dun ^{d}en-líl-lá, "Erraqurad, lapidary of Ninlil, 'subordinate' of Enlil." The cumulative evidence suggests that they are stand-ins; they are intimate subordinates, perhaps "adjutants" of very important military officers, but this specific meaning may be limited to Ur III times.

The word is rare in literary texts: *Schooldays* 88: u$_4$-me-da-aš lú-dun-a-zu sa$_6$-ge hu-mu-ra-ğá-ğá-ne/hu-mu-ra-i-ni-in-ku$_4$-re[8]: *Tree and Reed* 243: lugal-ğu$_{10}$ ğiš lú-dun-a-ğu$_{10}$; *SP Coll.* 13 39 […] x húb-bi-gin$_7$ igi lú-dun-a-za-ka ⌜ti⌝ (nu)-mu-ni-íb-bal-e-en, "do (not) duck sideways before your own faithful retainer like an . . . acrobat."

3–5. The rhetorical import of these lines is open to a number of interpretations. Previous translations have taken for granted that these words refer to the messenger who brought the previous letter. Thus, P. Michalowski, *LEM* 65, rendered the passage in the following manner: "That man whom you have sent to me, he cannot (really) be your trusted subordinate! Surely he does not take his orders from your hand! How is it that you are unaware of what he is doing?" Upon further reflection, one may suggest that, in view of what follows, it might be better to assume that the lú-dun-a of line 3 is anticipatory and that it refers to Apilaša.

8. S. N. Kramer, *JAOS* 69 (1949) 204, restored from Ni. 9751 rev. 10 and Ni. 4567 rev. 18 (both *ISET* 2 82).

5. This line seems to have created problems for the ancients, and the manuscript tradition is confused. The somewhat redundant fully reconstructed line reflects the Nippur tradition. Both texts from Ur differ from one another; Ur1 has a unique set of variants, while Ur2 resembles the two sources of unknown origin, which probably came from the same place (X5, X6). The term a-na-aš-àm corresponds to Akkadian *ana mīnim, ammīnim*, "why" (with negative verb); níg-a-na is used here in the same sense as *mimma ša*, "whatever, (about) everything"; and an-ga-àm (only in Nippur manuscripts) corresponds to *appūna*, "moreover, furthermore, indeed." More difficult is ur₅ì-me-a, which is, otherwise, only attested in a reconstructed lexical passage [ur₅] ⸢ì⸣-me-a = *ki-ma ki-a-am* (OBGT I 879 [MSL 4 60]).

6. I take níg ǧá-e-gin₇-nam to be a calque from Akkadian *ša kīma jāti*, "my representative." Elsewhere in CKU, as in lines 16a and 17 below, ǧá-e-gin₇-nam, without níg, means, "as I instructed."

9. The grammatical form, and hence the meaning of the final verb, differs in many of the manuscripts. The only Nippur witness to the line has zu-àm; X4, X5, and X6 have zu-a, which can be imperative or an abbreviation of zu-àm. The text from Ur has hé-en-zu. Thus, all the texts that are not from Nippur may be interpreted as "so that their (local) dignitaries know their orders."

13. The readings and meanings of PA.PA and IGI.IGI are uncertain, even though the obvious parallelism suggests similar or antithetical meanings. I understand this, as well as the following two lines, as an admonition from the king to Aradmu forbidding him to be distracted by anything until he reaches Apilaša. I also assume that the description of the activities of lawless people in the plain in ArŠ2: B1′–7′ (3) is related to this line and contains Aradmu's defense against this accusation, and this has influenced my understanding of the present line. The interpretation offered here is provisional at best and is based on PA.PA as sisig or sìg-sìg = *meḫûm*, "storm," *šārum*, "wind" (also *zaqīqum*, "fantom," *šaqummatum, šaḫurratum*, "stillness, silence") and IGI.IGI as lilib or lib₄-lib₄ = *šarrāqum*, "thief" (on the latter, see also A. Cavigneaux and F. al-Rawi, *Gilgameš et la mort* 38). The choice of these particular readings is based on ArŠ2: B2′ (letter 3) lú-la-ga lú-sa-gaz-e eden si-si-ig-ga-bi níg-gul-bi bí-ak, " Even rustlers and robbers break up the earth (for cultivation) in the (wind)-swept wilderness."[9] I assume that the "rustler" and the "wind-swept wilderness" are oblique references to Šulgi's rhetorical exhortation.

In Ur III and earlier documents, the verb ú-gu . . . dé usually means "to run away" when used of persons and animals and "to be lost" when used of objects.[10] In Old Babylonian literary texts, it can also mean "to vanish, disappear," but there is no other example of the verb in the imperative or of any parallel passage. So is the

---

9. Alt. transl.: I have made rustlers and robbers break up the earth (for cultivation) in the wind-swept wilderness.

10. For a discussion of certain aspects of this verb, including its treatment in the lexical tradition, see P. Steinkeller, *Sale Documents* 69–70.

king telling his grand vizier to deal with matters by making the "disappear," or is he exhorting to "forget" such issues and move on to Apilaša without distraction?

15. As presently preserved, this line is filled with difficulties. There are only two Nippur sources: the inferior N1 and the badly preserved N10. N1 is in Baghdad and can only be collated from the field photo; the first verbal form is è-x-ta-ab; x appears to be a badly written ta that may have been erased. Only the bottom parts of signs are preserved in N10, but collation confirms the probability of reading ⌜è-ta-ab⌝. Ur2 is also broken, but and the first preserved sign in the line appears to be [a]b. The two unprovenienced Yale tablets X5 and X6, which are undoubtedly from the same place although probably from different hands, both have è-ni-ib. It is possible that the verb è should be understood as *ḫâṭum*, "to watch over, explore": "explore the area ahead of you, *so that he can appear before you (without delay),*" or perhaps "*so that he can clear (the way) for you.*" I do not understand the final verb, which is hé-en-ši-UD in three sources; only the Ur2 text, which is not the best, provides TU as the root. Is this a syllabic variant (kud for húd), or is it semantic (kud = *erēbum*)? Note the clustering of the variants in all three unprovenienced texts.

16. All non-Nippur manuscripts add an additional line here (16a): a-na-aš-àm ĝá-(a)-gin₇-nam nu-un-ak. It is not clear if these texts connected this line with line 16 or with what follows. It is possible that the source of the interpolation—if that is indeed the case—is ŠuSa1: 23–24 (letter 19), where the two are clearly related and mean "Thus I did command you! Why did you not act in accordance with my instructions?" although in the Šu-Sin letter the final verb is second person (nu-ak) rather than third. Even if this was the source, it appears that the new line has been reinterpreted (nu-un-ak) and was designed to introduce what follows.[11] I would therefore consider it analytically part of the next paragraph: "¹⁶ᵃ (As to your accusations), why should he not act according to my instructions?"

21. The only occurrence of lú-ĝárza outside of CKU is in OB Lu C5 4 (*MSL* 12 195) and OB Lu A 374 (*MSL* 12 169); in both cases, it is rendered as *be-el pa-ar-ṣí*, "office holder, intimate participant." Note the identical formulation in an Old Babylonian Akkadian language omen: *šar-rum be-el pa-ar-ṣi-im i-na-as-sà-aḫ-ma be-el pa-ar-ṣi-im i-ša-ak-ka-an*, "the king will remove an office-holder and install (another) office-holder" (*YOS* 10 46 ii 16–17, cited *CAD* P 202). This confirms that Apilaša is in part usurping royal prerogatives and that the monarch accepts this fact, as do the lines that follow, all of which have Akkadian analogies. Note the sequence of a perfect verbal form followed by a non-perfect one to indicate the sequence of action.

22. The fully reduplicated form of the reflexive pronoun ní-te is unique. Note the idiomatic use of the verbs ĝar and gub together to denote the appointment and firing of officials; this probably reflects Akkadian usage, as documented, for example, in

---

11. The distribution of the interpolation is of interest since it is not found in the two Nippur manuscripts. Note that at present the Šu-Sin/Šarrum-bani correspondence is not attested from that city.

the OB letter *AbB* 14 218:8–11 *a-na na-sa-ḫi-im ú ša-ka-nim qá-at-ka i-te-li na-sa-ḫu ù ša-ka-nu ša qá-ti ša qá-ti-x*, "Have you really *obtained the authority* to remove and install people? Removing and installing people is, in fact, only *my* responsibility."

23. igi . . . hul is rendered by *lapātu* or *abātu ša inī* in late lexical texts (SIG$_7$. ALAN G1 ii 6″ [*MSL* 16 283], Antagal VIII 125 [*MSL* 17 174], Antagal G 56 [*MSL* 17 222], Antagal G 168 [*MSL* 17 225]). The use of this in CKU, as well as in other contexts, implies that such actions can be done only upon orders of the king. Another example of blinding as a royal prerogative is found in an Old Babylonian omen (*i-n[i-in* LÚ]-ʿ*im*ʾ*-ma* LUGAL *i-na-sà-aḫ*, "the king shall tear out the eyes of the *awīlum*," *YOS* 10 17:61); in Akkadian, *nasāḫum* is used alongside *napālum* and *ḫuppudum* (only in CH) for the act of blinding. There is one definite reference to the Ur III practice of blinding prisoners of war in an OB copy of a Šu-Sin inscription; see R. Kutscher, *Brockman* I 96 (the verb is igi . . . du$_8$).[12] The Akkadian lexical equivalents are somewhat problematical. The Akkadian verb *abātum* "to destroy" is clearly secondary, derived from its normal Sumerian correspondent gul. The other verb, *lapātum*, literally, "to touch," is more difficult to define in such contexts. The literal translation, "to touch," does not help us. The expression *i-ni-šu-nu li-il-pu-t[u]-ma* is documented in a Mari letter (*ARM* 14 78 = *LAPO* 18 929, 1 10′); K. van der Toorn translates this as "let them gouge out their eyes" (*RA* 79 [1985] 190). The same verb is attested with the tongue as an object in a few OB contracts; see M. deJong Ellis, *JCS* 27 (1975) 147–48.

24. Note the extraordinary transmission of the crasis form (lú-al-li-bí-ib-diri for lú-a li-bí-ib-diri) in all manuscripts from Nippur with the exception of N1, which was found in House F (lú li-bí-ib-diri; see also pp. 52–53 above). Could these five tablets have come from the same house? The N1 text is not always the best, however. The "correct" form is found in three texts of unknown provenience (X2, X4, X6: lú-a li-bí-in-diri, with no final -a in X2). The scribe of Ur 2 may have been working from a tradition that also had a crasis form but one that was reinterpreted with lú-ùlu as an imitation of Ur III lú-ù, and a verb with the prefix al-. For another example of crasis in this text, see sá (an)-né-en in the Nippur manuscripts of line 14. See also p. 53 above.

29. There is broad confusion concerning the first bound pronoun in this line, ranging from third-person singular and plural to second-person singular. Two texts omit it altogether. This confusion concerns both the referent of the pronoun and the understanding of nam(-) in this line. All previous modern renditions have taken this to be the abstract derivational morpheme but the use of the genitive nam ur-sag-gá-ka-ni/ĝu$_{10}$/Ø suggests that it is the homophonous and etymologically related noun nam that is used here in the meaning "province, responsibility," corresponding to Akk. *pīḫātum* (Hh I 126 [*MSL* 5 17]), and that the tone is clearly sarcastic; see

---

12. On blind workers in Ur III times see now Wolfgang Heimpel, *KASKAL* 6 (2009) 43–48.

also PuŠ1: 15ff. (letter 13). Our own confusion about this may mirror ancient differences about the interpretation of this line, since nam-lú-ùlu and nam-ur-saĝ are commonly encountered in the school texts. Note, however that nam-lú-ùlu can be used to refer to troops, as in *Letter of Lipit-Eštar to Nanna-kiaĝa* (SEpM 5) 15–16 uru-bi šu-zu-ta la-ba-ra-è, nam-lú-ùlu-zu ĝar-bí-ib, "Do not let those cities out of your grasp, station your forces (there)!" Note also *Letter of Iddin-Dagan to Sin-tillati* (SEpM 3) 7–8 me-lam-ĝu₁₀ kalam-ma ba-e-dul, ù za-e nam-ur-saĝ nam-kala-ga-zu kur-bi-šè ba-e-te, "My glory spread over the homeland but you brought your martial glory and power to that foreign land."

30. The predicate pronoun is second-person plural in N1, N8, and X4 (me-en-zé-en). The writers of N11 and Ur2 understood this as za-e me-en, that is, first-person singular, addressed only to Aradmu. This is not consistently carried out in the lines that follow, although the Ur2 scribe continued the singular forms in lines 32 and 33. The excerpt exercise adds the unrelated phrase tukum-bi lugal-ĝá an-na-kam, "if my king is agreeable," taken from PuŠ: 16 (letter 13) or from some other letter.

The same scribe provides a syllabic rendering of émedu (AMA.A.TU), "houseborn slave:" a-tu-mu. The word is already attested in ED texts; for references and earlier literature see J. Krecher, *WO* 18 (1987) 9–12. Krecher uses this in support of an assumed word *eme, "woman," which I do not believe exists. As I see it, émedu is originally derived from *ama-a tuda, "born in the woman's quarters (of the household)."

31. Note the use of im-sar-ra, "inscribed tablet;" except for ArŠ5: 12, where it is rendered in Akkadian as *ṭuppum*, elsewhere in the *CKU* letters and written instructions are referred to as á-áĝ-ĝá or as ù-na-a-dug₄. The precise meaning of this word eludes us at present; in later lexical texts, it is the equivalent of *ṭuppu(m)* (see the dictionaries), but in Ur III times it was certainly not simply a synonym of dub, "tablet," as evidenced by the basket tag *AUCT* 2 92, which lists 160 dub, followed by 4 im-sar-ra.

The verb gù ... dé, "to call, name," is used with the technical meaning of "to recite, read aloud," with ablative dimensional prefix in OB school texts (F. Karahashi, *Sumerian Compound Verbs* 109). This is already attested in *Gudea Cyl. A* v 21–vi 2, albeit without the ablative; the king sees the goddess Nidaba in a dream, who is holding in her lap, and consulting, a lapis lazuli tablet on her lap, covered with "stars," that is, cuneiform signs. The last lines of the passage reads (v 25–vi 2):

nin₉-ĝu₁₀ ᵈnidaba ga-nam-me-àm
é-a dù-ba mul kù-ba
gù ma-ra-a-dé

That was, beyond any doubt, my sister Nidaba,
The (instructions) for that temples construction, from those sacred 'stars'
She read out to you.

Sources

N1 = 3 N-T 311 (IM 58418) ii (*SL* xxii–xxiii, *Sumer* 26 171)[13]   = 2–34
N2 = 3 N-T 903,102 (*SL* xxxiv, *Sumer* 26 176)   = 23–30
N3 = CBS 6513 + N 3096 (*SL* xxxiii, *Sumer* 26 177)   = 21–34
N4 = Ni. 2317 (*SLTNi* 126)   = 3–8; 30–34
N5 = Ni 2723 (*SLTNi* 136)   = 17–22; 24–26
N6 = Ni. 4149 (*ISET* 2 122) rev. ii′ 6–8   = 1–4
N7 = Ni. 4389 (*ISET* 1 144 [86])   = 23–30
N8 = Ni. 9706 (*ISET* 2 112) rev. iii′ 1′–14′   = 21–34
N9 = Ni. 9709 (*ISET* 1 180 [122])[14]   = 1–5; 31–34
N10= Ni. 9854 (*ISET* 1 189 [131]) obv. i′ 1′–9′   = 15–21
N11= UM 29–13–330 (*SL* xxxiv, *Sumer* 26 176)   = 21–34
Ur1 = U. 16853 (*UET* 6/2 174) + *UET* 6/3 557 (*532) obv. ii′ 14′–19′;
  iii′ 1′   = 1–5, 33
Ur2 = U. 17900v (*UET* 6/2 181)   = 1–16a; 20–33
Su1 = *MDP* 27 87   = 1–2
Su2 = *MDP* 27 88   = 1–2
X1 = A w/n ii 1′–21′   = 15–35
X2 = BM 54327 ii 1′–12′   = 16a–28
X3 = LB 2543 (*TLB* 3 172) 1–4   = 25–26, 28–30
X4 = HMA 9–1820 (*JCS* 28 [1976] 103)[15]   = 6–11; 20–33
X5 = YBC 4185   = 1–17
X6 = YBC 4596 rev.   = 1–34
Z[16] = MS 2199/1 10–15   = 13–15, 9–10, 27

X2 possibly from Sippar, X5 and X6 possibly from Larsa. The Tutub provenience of X4 is doubtful (see p. 44 above). The clustering of variants suggests that the Yale tablets X5 and X6 must have come from the same place.

N1 and X3 collated on photographs (collations of the latter in H. Waetzoldt, *OA* 15 [1976] 332). Su1 and Su1 assigned here provisionally; they could be the open-

---

13. The tablet was collated on a cast held by the University Museum and on a field photograph that is reproduced on the accompanying compact disk. The right edge is not shown on either, and therefore one must rely on F. Ali's hand-copy, which was apparently made from the original tablet in Baghdad, for signs that are not visible on the photograph and cast.

14. Listed as Ni 9707 in *SL* 34. The reverse, which is not included in the published handcopy, is heavily destroyed, but some signs of the last four lines can be read, ending in a double line.

15. Formerly UCLM 9–1820. The tablet has deteriorated since it was copied and then collated by D. Foxvog and me. Recollated in February, 2011.

16. This is not, properly speaking, a source of the letter. These are lines that were used to create a new line together with elements of the previous letter, and it is edited here as ArŠ1a (letter 1a). The appropriate lines are incorporated into the matrix for comparative purposes.

ing lines of any of the letters from Šulgi to Aradmu. Neither could be located at the present time.

Tablet typology: compilation tablets: N1, N8, N10(?), Ur1, X1, X2, X6. The rest are all Type III, except X5 (one column with two letters), Su1, Su2, which are Type IV lentils, and X3 (oval exercise tablets with excerpts of letters 1 and 2).

Bibliography: Editions: F. Ali, *SL*, 34–41, F. Ali, *Sumer* 26 (1970) 152–59. Transliteration and translation: P. Michalowski, *LEM* 64–66. Translation: S. N. Kramer, *The Sumerians*, 332–33. C. Wilcke 1970 62–64 (lines 14–35), C. Wilcke 1993 65–66: translation, commentary (lines 6–26), P. Michalowski, Royal Letters, 77–78.

Concordance of sigla used here (*CKU*) and by F. Ali in *SL* and in *Sumer* 26, with additions in *RCU*:

N1	A		A	N1
N2	I		B	Ur2
N3	H		C	N9
N4	E		D (+)	Ur1
N5	F		E	N4
N6	T		F	N5
N7	Q		H	N3
N8	J		G	N11
N9	C		I	N2
N10	P		J	N8
N11	G		K	Su1
Ur1	D (+)		L	Su2
Ur2	B		M	X6
Su1	K		N	X5
Su2	L		O	X3
X1	R		P	N10
X2	S		Q	N7
X3	O		R	X1
X5	N		S	X2
X6	T		T	N6

Textual Matrixes

1.   ¹árad-mu-ra ù-na-a-dug₄^17

```
N6   oo   o   o o  .  -  +
N9   o.   +   + +  +  -  +
Ur1  oo   o   .  + + +  .^18
Ur2  o+   +   + + + + +
Su1  -+   +   + /+ ne - +
Su2  -+   +   + /+ ne - +
X5   .o   .   + + .  + +
X6   oo   o   o o o . o
```

2.   ᵈšul-gi lugal-zu na-ab-bé-a

```
N1   o.   .  +    + +  .  .  .
N6   oo o o    o o . + +
N9   ++ + +    + . + + o
Ur1  oo o.     .  .  . o .
Ur2  o. + +    + + + + +
Su1  ++ + +    + /+ + + +
Su2  +. o o    o /+ o o o
X5   ..  .  .    + . + + +
X6   .o o o    . . + . .
```

3.   lú in-ši-gi₄-in-na-zu lú-dun-a-zu in-nu-ù

```
N1   + + + +  + + +  + .  + +  + + o
N4   . o o o  o o o  o o  o o  o o o
N6   o o o o  o o o  o .  + +  o . +
N9   . + + +  - + +  /+ da  - +  + + +
Ur1  o o o o  .  .  .  . x  o o  x x x
Ur2  o . + +  - + +  + +  + +  + + -
X5   + . + +  . + +  + +  + +  + + .
X6   + . o o  o . +  .  .  . .  + + .
```

4.   šu-zu-ta-àm á-áǧ-ǧá   šu la-ba-ra-ab-te-ǧá-e

```
N1   . + + +  + + +    + + +  + + + + .
N4   + . . o  o o o    + . o  o o o o o
N6   o o o o  o o o    o o o  o o . . o
N9   + + + +  + + +    /. . +  + + + + .
Ur1  o . .x .  x x ⸢ak⸣   . . +  . + [ti] ti
Ur2  o . + –  + + +    + + +  + – + + +
X5   + + + +  . + +    + + +  – + + + +
X6   + . . .  . + +    . . +  + + + + .
```

17. N9 and Ur2 must have had the first sign.

18. The spacing of the break at the beginning of the line indicates that Ur1 had the personal name marker.

5.　　a-na-aš-àm níĝ-a-na an-ga-àm bí-in-ak-a-ni ur₅ ì-me-a　　nu-e-zu

N1	+ + + +	+	+ + + + +	+ + +	- + +	+a + +aš +	- +
N4	+ + + .	o	o o o o o	o o o o	o o .	o o o	o o
N9	o o o .	+	+ + + .	o	/o o o	. + +	+ . o	o o o o
Ur1	⌜a⌝-na-aš-⌜àm⌝	níĝ-⌜nam⌝-gin₇	⌜hé-en⌝-⌜ak⌝-a⌝	ur₅	i-me	nu-um-[zu?]
Ur2	o . + +	+	- - - -	+ + + + +	. +	+ +	+ - +
X5	+ - + +	+	+ + - -	- + + +	+ - +	+ + +	+ + +
X6	+ + + +	+	+ + - -	- + + +	+ - +	+ + +	. . .

6.　　ĝá-e níĝ ĝá-e-gin₇-nam ma-da ge-né-dè

N1	+ ++	+	+ +	+	+	+	+	+
N4	+ +.	o o o	o	o	o	o	o
Ur2	o o o	.	- +	+	+	+	+	+
X4	o o o	o o o	o	o	o	o	.
X5	+ ++	+	- +	+	.	+	+	+
X6	+ ++	+	- +	-	+	+	.	+ +

7.　　un si sá-sá-e-dè gù-téš-a sì-ke-dè

N1	+	+ + + + +	+	.	+ +	.	.
N4	+	+ + .	o o o o	o o o o o
Ur2	o	o o .	- +	suhuš ma-da	ge-en-ge-né-dè
X4	o	o o o o o o	o o o o	.
X5	+	+ + + + +	⌜suhuš ma⌝-da	ge-en-ge-né-dè-en
X6	+	+ + + + +	suhuš ma-da	⌜ge-en⌝-ge-né-dè

8.　　uru ma-da ba-te-ĝá-dè-na-zu umuš-bi zu-zu-àm

N1	+ᵏⁱ	+	+ + + +e +	+ +	+	+ + + +
Ur2	o	o o .	e+.	+ + +	+	+ + + +
X4	o	o .	o o o o	o o	o	o . za +
X5	+	+ + + + .	+en+ +	+	+ + + a
X6	+	+ + + + +	+en+ .	+	+ + + a

9.　　lú gal-gal-bé-ne inim-bi zu-àm

N1	+ +	+ + + +	+ + +
Ur2	o o o o	.	+	+ hé-en-zu
X4	o o o o o o	o o ⌜a⌝
X5	+ + + + +	.	. + a
X6	+ + + + +	.	+ + a
Z	+ .	+ + -	+	+ hé-zu

10.　　za-pa-áĝ-ĝu₁₀ kur-kur　　hé-eb-si

N1	+ + + +	+	+	+	+ +
Ur2	o o o o	+	+	ra	⌜hé⌝-en-dul
X4	o o o o	o	o	o o x¹⁹
X5	+ + + +	+	+	⌜ra⌝ o - dal
X6	+ + + +	+	+	⌜re⌝ + - dal
Z	+ .? .? zu	+	+	ra	+	+ ul

19. The sign is either si or dul, not dal (now all gone).

11.   á kala-ga á nam-ur-sağ-ğá-ğu$_{10}$ kur-re hé-en-šub-šub

N1	+ +	+	+ +	+ +	+ +	+	+ +	+ +	.					
Ur2	o o	o	o +	+ +	+ -	o	. +	+ +	+ bu					
X4	o o	o	o o	o o	o o	o	o o	o .	.					
X5	+ +	.	+ +	+ o	. +	+	ra .	o .	.					
X6	+ +	+	+ .	. +	+ -	+	ra +	- +	+					

12.   u$_{18}$-lu-ğu$_{10}$ kalam-ma hé-eb-dul

N1	+	+ +	+		+	+ +	+	
Ur2	o	o o	o		.	hé-en-dal		
X5	.	+ +	+		.	.	⌜en⌝ .?	
X6	+	+ +	+		+	+ en	+	

13.   sìg-sìg eden-na lib$_4$-lib$_4$ a-šà-ga ú-gu dé-ni-ib

N1	+	+ +	+ +	+	+ + +	+ +	.	+ +				
Ur2	o	o o	o o	.	+ + +	+ +	+	+ +				
X5	+	+ +	. +	.	o . .	o o	di	+ .				
X6	+	. .	+ +	+	+ + +	+ +	+	+ +				
Z	+	+ +	+ +	+	+ + +	+ +	+	e ne				

14.   en-na a-pi-il-la-ša gal-zu-unken-na-ğu$_{10}$ sá an-né-en

N1	+	+	+ +	+ +	-	+	+ +		+	+	+ +	+	.		
Ur2	o	o	o o	o o	o	o	o o		o	o	+ -	+	+		
X5	+	+	+ +	- +	+	-	- -		-	-	. -	⌜e⌝	né		
X6	+	+	+ +	- +	.	-	- -		-	-	+ -	e	né		
Z	+	+	+ +	- +	+	-	- -		-	-	+ -	e	ne		

15.   igi-zu è- ta-ab igi-zu hé-en-ši-UD

N1	.	.	. ⌜éb⌝	+	+ +	.	+ + +	+ (x=⌜éb?⌝)			
N10	.	.	. .	.	. .	o	o o				
Ur2	o	o	o o	.	+ +	+	in +	TU			
X1	+	.	o x	o	o o	o	o o	o			
X5	+	za	è-né-eb	+	+ .	+	+ +				
X6	+	za	è-né-eb	+	+ +	+	+ +				
Z	+	+	hé-dib	+	+ -	ib	+ +				

16.   á-šè mu-e-da-a-áğ

N1	#						
N10	o	+	ì	- +	+ .		
Ur2	o	o o	.	+ o	.		
X1	.	o o	o o	o o			
X5	+ +	+	+ .	+ +			
X6	+ +	+	+ +	+ +			

16a. a-na-aš-àm ğá-a-gin₇-nam nu-un-ak

N1	#										
N10	#										
Ur2	o	o	o	o	o	o	o	o	o	o	.
X1	x	o	o	o	o	o	o	o	o	o	o
X2	o	o	o	o	o	o	o	o	.	o	o
X5	+	+	+	+	+	+	.	+	+	+	+
X6	+	+	+	+	+	‑	+	+	+	+	+

17. tukum-bi gal-zu-unken-na-ğu₁₀   ğá-a-gin₇-nam nu-ub-gur₄

N1	.		.	.	+	+		.	.		+	+	.	+	+	+	+
N5	.		+	+	+	+		+	.		+	+	+	+	+	+	+
N10	.		+	+	+	+		+	+	⌜níğ⌝	.	+	+	+	+	‑	+ re-en
X1	x		o	o	o	o		o	o		o	o	o	o	o	o	o
X2	o		o	o	o	o		o	o		o	.	+	.	o	o	. re
X5	+		+	+	+	.		.	.²⁰		+	‑	+	.	+	+	+ re
X6	+		+	+	‑	+		+	+		+	+	+	+	+	+	+ re

18. ᵍᶦˢgu-za barag ᵗᵘᵍšutur-e ri-a nu-ub-tuš

N1	.	.	+	+		+	+		‑	+	‑	+	.	.	
N5	+	+	+	+		+	+		+	+	+	.	+	+	
N10	.	+	+	+		+	+		+	+	+	+	.	+	
X1	.	.	.	.		+	.		‑	.	.	o	o	o	
X2	o	o	o	o		o	o		o	o	o	o	.	+	
X6	+	+	+	+		+	+		+	+	+	+	+	+	

19. ᵍᶦˢğiri-gub kù-sig₁₇-ka ğiri-ni nu-ub-ğar

N1	.	.	‑		.	.		.	.	‑	+	+	.	
N5	+	.	+		+	+		+	+	+	+	+	.	
N10	o	.	+		+	+		+	.	+	+	um	+	
X1	+	+	+		+	+		.	+	+	+	.	o	
X2	o	o	o		o	o		o	.	+	+	+	+	
X6	+	+	+		+	+ga	+	+	+	+	+	+ ğar		

20. énsi nam-énsi-ta

N1	+	.	+	+
N5	.	+	.	o
N10	.	.	.	.
Ur2	o	o	.	o :
X1	+	+	.	.
X2	+	.	.	. :
X4	o	o	.	o :
X6	+	+	+	+ :

20. The scribe wrote ğu₁₀ right after na, realized that it had to be spaced at the end of the line, erased it, and then wrote it in its proper place.

21. lú ğárza   ğárza-ta

```
N1    + +          + .
N3    + +          . o
N5    . +          . o
N8    traces
N10   o .            . o
N11   . +          + .
Ur2   o .    nam + o
X1    + .          + +
X2    + +    lú   + . :
X4    . +    ⌜nam⌝ o o :
X6    + + nam lú   +¹²¹ ⸗
```

22. ní-te-ní-te-a   li-bí-ib-ğar ù nu-ub-ta-gub-bu

```
N1    + + + + +  + + + +   + +    . . .    .
N3    + . . + +  . o o o   + .    + ⸗ +    + ⌜uš⌝
N5    o o . .  o  o o o o   o o   o o o    o
N8    o o o o o  o o o o    o .   + + .    ⸗
N11   + + + + +  + + + +    + o   . ⸗ +    +
Ur2   o o o o[à]m + + .   o   o o o   . +    +
X1    + + + + +  . + íb . / + +   +⌜àm⌝- +
X2    + + + + +  + + in +   + +   íb + +    .
X4    . . . ta .  o o o o   + .   . ⸗ .    .
X6    + + ni ta +  + in + +   + +  +an +    ⸗
```

23. lú nu-un-gaz igi nu-un-hul

```
N1    . . . +   + + + +
N2    o o . .   . . ⸗ .
N3    + + + .   . . . .
N7    o o o o   . . o o
N8    o o o .   + + ⸗ .
N11   + + + .   + + + +
Ur2   o o o o   o + + +
X1    + + + +   . . + +
X2    + + ub +   + + ub +
X4    . o o +   . o o o
X6    + + + +   + + + +
```

21. Written ğarza (PA.AN¹).

24. lú igi-bar-ra-ka-ni lú-al-li-bí-ib-diri

N1	+	+	+	+	+	+	+	-		+	-	+	.
N2	o	.	+	+	+	.	.	+		+	+	-	.
N3	+	+	+	+	+	.	+	+		o	o	o	o
N5	.	.	o	o	o	o	o	o		o	o	o	o
N7	o	o	o	o	o	o	.	.		o	o	o	o
N8	o	o	o	o	o	o	+	+		+	-	.	+
N11	.	+	+	+	+	+	+	.		.	+	-	+
Ur2	o	o	o	o	o	+	+	ùlu al-diri-ge
X1	+	+	+	+	+	+	.	˹a˺		+	.	o	o
X2	+	+	+	+	+	+	+	-		+	+	in	+
X4	+	.	+	+	+a	+	+	˹a˺		.	˹in˺	o
X6	+	+	+	+	+	+	+	a		+	+	in	+

25. a-na-gin₇-nam ma-da íb-gi-ne

N1	+	+	+	+		+	+	+	.	.
N2	o	.	.	+		+	+	+	+	x
N3	.	.	+	.		.	+	+	+	.
N5	.	.	+	.		o	o	o	o	o
N7	o	o	o	.		.	+	.	o	o
N8	o	o	o	o		.	+	+	+	né
N11	.	.	+	.		.	.	.	.	.
Ur2	o	o	o	o		o	.	+	+	+
X1	.	.	.	+		+	+	.	.	o
X2	+	+	+	+		+	.	gi-né-dè
X3	+	+	+	+		+	+	+	.	na
X4	+	+	.	+		+	+	+	.	+
X6	+	+	+	+		+	+	+	+	né

26. tukum-bi ki um-mu-e-a-áǧ

N1	+		+	+	-	+	.	o	o
N2	.		+	+	+	+	.	+˹a˺o
N3	.		+	+	+	+	+	+	.
N5	+		+	+	.	o	o	o	o
N7	.		+	+	im-me-a-˹a?˺-[...]
N8	.		.	o	.	+	+	+	.
N9	.		o	o	-	+	+	+a+
N11	.		.	.	.	-	+	+	.
Ur2	o		o	o	o	+	-	-	+
X1	.		+	+	.	.	+	+	.
X2	.		+	+	˹a mu˺x	o	o	o
X3	+		+	+	-	-	-	-	+
X4	.		+	+	im-mi-áǧ :
X6	+		+	+	-	+	+	-	+[22]

22. Written KA.

27. šà-zu šà zú-kešda ba-ra-na-ğá-ğá

```
N1    + + + +   +    .  o o o o
N2    . .  + +²³ +    + + .  o o
N3    o o . + +    + + . .  +
N7    o o . + +    + + . o o
N8    + . . . .      . . + + +
N11   + + + +  +    + + + .
Ur2   o o o .  +    + + + + +
X1    . . + . .    + . + + .
X2    + . . . o    o o o o o
X3    #
X4    + . . . .    + + .an+ +
X6    + + + +  +    + +an+ + +
Z     ? ? ? +   + ni + + - + +
```

28. ì-gur$_4$-re-en àga-ús-zu   nu-e-zu

```
N1    ++  -  + + . o    o o o
N2    . .  -  + + + -    + + o
N3    o.  + + . . o    o o .
N7    . .  + + + + -    + . o
N8    +.  . . o o .     . . +
N11   ++  + . + . -     . + .
Ur2   o o  o . + + +     + - +
X1    ++  + . . + +     + -?.
X2    . o  o o o o o    o o o
X3    ++  + + + + +     - + .
X4    o o  o . +   + sağ-ğá-ni ì-ʼzuʼ-x?
X6    ++  + + + + +     + + +
```

29. nam lú-u$_{18}$-lu-bi ù nam ur-sağ-ğá-ka-ni igi-zu bí-in-zu

```
N1    +   + + - ni + .    o o . . + + + . .
N2    .   + + + + . .    . o  o o o + . o o o
N3    o   o . + . . o    o o  o o o o o o o o
N7    .   . + - ba + +    + . o + + + + . o o
N8    .   + . - + + .    . . o o o + . . . .
N11   +   . . + + . .    . + + - ğu₁₀ + + . +
Ur2   o   o o . ni + +    + + - + + o . ù-bí-du₈
X1    .   + + - - + +    . . . + + + . o o o
X3    +   + + - - - + +    + + + + - . . x o x
X4    o   . . ʼa niʼ. .    . . ʼaʼ- . + + + + .
X6    +   + + - zu + +    + + . . . o o o o o
```

23. The student began to write kešda but thought better and wrote zú over it.

30.   tukum-bi   émedu-ǧu$_{10}$ me-en-zé-en

N1	+	+	.	+	+	.	+	.
N2	.	o	o	o	o	o	o	o
N3	traces, possibly end of 29							
N4	.	o	o	o	o	o	o	o
N7	.	.	.	o	o	o	o	o
N8	+	+	.	.	+	+	.	.
N11	.	+	.	+	za-e-me-⌈en⌉			
Ur2	.	+	+	+	za-e-me-en			
X1	+	+	.	.	.	o	o	o
X3	(space)a-tu-mu mi-zé / tukum-bi lugal-ǧá an-na-kam							
X4	.	+	+	+	+	+	+	.
X6	+	+	+	+ e[n]	o	o	o	o

31.   igi min-na-zu-ne-ne-a   im-sar-e   gù hé-em-ta-dé-dé-ne

N1	+	mìn	+	+	.	-	ta	+	+	+	+	+	⌈íb⌉	+	+	+	.
N3	o	o	o	.	+	.	o	o	o	o	.	-	.	+	+	.	o
N4	+	+	àm	+	.	o	o	o	o	o	o	o	o	o	o	o	o
N8	+	+	⌈a⌉¹	+	+	+	-	+	+	.	+	+	+	+	.	o	o
N9	+	mìn	.	.	o	o	o	o	o	o	o	o	o	o	o	.	
N11	+	+	⌈àm⌉	.	.	o	o	.re-en	+	.	+	.	+	+	e	
Ur2	o	o	o	o	+	+	-	+	+	ra	.	+	+	+	+	e
X1	+	mìn	+	+	+	.	šè	+	+	r[e]/	+	.	íb	.	+	+e	.
X4	o	.ni	+	+	-	-	+	+	re	+	+	+	+	+	+	
X6	+	mìn	+	-	+	+	+	+	ra	+	.	o	o	o	o	o

32.   gù-téš-a sì-ke-dè-en-zé-en

N1	+	+	+	+	.	+	+	+	+
N3	o	o	+	+	+	+	+	+	.
N4	+	+	+	.	o	o	o	o	o
N8	+	+	+	+	+	+	.	o	o
N9	o	.	.	.	x	x	-?	.	.
N11	.	+	.	.	+	.	.	o	+
Ur2	o	o	o	+	+	+	-	-	-:
X1	+	+	.	.	+	+	eb	+	+
X4	.	+	+	hé-eb-sì	:				
X6	+	+	+	+	ge	+	.	o	o

33.   suhuš ma-da ge-né-dè-en-zé-en

N1	+	+	+	+	+	eb	-	+	. :
N3	o	o	+	+	+	+	+	+	+
N4	+	+	.	o	o	o	o	o	o
N8	+	+	.	.	.	⌜éb⌝o	o	o	o
N9	o	.	.	+	+	.?	.? .?	.	
N11	+	+	+	.⌜en⌝	.	.	+	+	
Ur1	o	o	o	/⌜ge-en-ge⌝-ne					
Ur2	+	+	+	ge-en-ge-ne					
X1	+	.	.	.	né-eb	-	+	+ :	
X4	+	+	+	+	né-dè	-	-	-	
X6	+	+	+	+	né-éb	-	.	o	

34.   a-ma-ru-kam

N1	+ +	+	.	
N3	. .	+	.	
N4	+ .	o	o	
N8	. .	.	o	
N9	o .	.	.	
N11	+ +	+	+	
Ur1	#			
Ur2	#			
X1	+ +	+	.	
X4	#			
X6	o .	+	o	

X4 after a double line; lines 32/33 repeated at least five times

Catchlines (all refer to ArŠ2 [3]):
N3 lugal-ğu₁₀-⌜ra⌝ ù-n[a-dug₄]
N4 lugal-ğ[u₁₀-ra ù-na-(a)-dug₄]
N11 lugal-⌜ğu₁₀⌝-ra ⌜ù-na⌝-dug₄

In X1 followed by ArŠ2 (3), in N8, N18, X2 by PuŠ1 (13), and in N1 and Ur by PuIb1 (23).

Colophon B (X5)

3. Aradmu to Šulgi 2

(ArŠ 2, 3.1.3 + 3.1.11. A2a, RCU 3+4)

Composite Text

Part A

1. lugal-ĝu$_{10}$-ra ù-na-dug$_4$
2. ^{l}árad-mu árad-zu na-ab-bé-a
3. lugal-ĝu$_{10}$ níĝ-na-me-šè á-še mu-e-da-a-a-áĝ
4. a-ab-ba kur dilmun^{ki}-na-ta
5. a mun$_4$ gaba kur amurrum^{ki}-šè
6. zag si-mu-ur$_4$-ru-um ma-da su-bir$_4$^{ki}-šè
7. uru^{ki}-didli ma-da-ma-da-bi^1
8. a-šà a-gàr-bi ù ég pa$_5$-bi
9. igi bí-in-kár è-dè en-nu-ùĝ bí-dab$_5$
10. uru^{ki}-uru^{ki} ĝiš-tuku lugal-ĝu$_{10}$
11. ki x x a-bi ì-KU šu-úr im šu bí$^?$-dab$_5$
12. bàd-bi en-nu-ùĝ kala-ga bí-gub
13. ugnim-bi gú-ĝiš bí-ĝar-ĝar
14. x du$_{10}$ ús x du-ús bí-dúr-ra
15. a-gàr a ĝar-ra-bi a-ta im-ta-è
16. kankal zal-la-bi sahar bí-ak
17. x x a-šà-ga ĝiš-gi ambar-ra
18. a bal saĝ-ĝá saĝ-sìg-ge x-bi
19. x x x x-ma ^{ĝiš}buniĝ-ta im-ta-ak
20. [. . .]x a la-ba$^?$-an$^?$-dé$^?$-ke›-eš [. . .] ⌜kal$^?$-ga$^?$ bí$^?$⌝-x
21. [. . .]x a-šà-ga kíĝ x x
22. [. . .]x-ge(-)en-na-bi [. . . n]e-ne bí-in-zu

Part B

1′. eden a du$_{11}$-ga íd-da mi-ni-ĝar-ĝar íd-da mi-ni-luh-luh
2′. lú-la-ga lú-sa-gaz-e eden si-si-ig-ga-bi níĝ-gul-bi bí-ak

---

1. Var.: iri^{ki}-didli-bi ⌜ugnim-bi⌝-ne.

3'. nita-bi-e-ne munus-bi-e-ne nita-bi ki šà-ga-na-šè ì-du-ne

4'. munus-bi ^{ĝiš}bala ^{ĝiš}kirid-da šu ba-e-si-ig har-ra-an šà-ga-na du-ù-ne

5'. eden níĝ-daĝal-la ĝá-rig$_7$ mu-ni-ib-ĝar

6'. za-lam-ĝar maš-gána-bi ki um-mi-ĝar-ĝar^2

7'. lú-kíĝ-ak-bi lú-gud-apin-lá a-šà-ga u$_4$ mu-un-di-ni-ib-zal-e

8'. á-áĝ-ĝá šul-gi lugal-ĝá-ke$_4$ gú-ĝu$_{10}$ nu-mu-da-šub

9'. gú bí-dù ĝi$_6$ an-bar$_7$-ba á-bi-šè ì-du-dè-en

10'. ^Iá-pi-il-la-ša u$_4$ tur-ra-ni-ta šu-ĝá mu-un-dim$_4$-e

11'. lú al-me-a-gin$_7$ šà-ĝu$_{10}$ ì-zu igi-zu um-mi-zu

12'. lugal-ĝu$_{10}$ igi-bar-ra diĝir-ra lú-ù-bi i-ni-in-zu

13'. lú ĝárza gal kur-kur-ra-ke$_4$ ugu-bi im-mi-diri

14'. lugal-ĝu$_{10}$ níĝ gal-gal ba-e-diri gaba-ri-ĝu$_{10}$ šu i-ni-i[n-gi$_4$?]

15'. du$_{11}$-ga-ab gi$_4$-bi^3 inim-zu inim dugud-da níĝ-zu níĝ gal-la-àm

16'. inim sa$_6$-ga-ni šà-za ì-ĝál u$_4$-šú-uš ì-ĝál-e

17'. lú-u$_8$-lu-àm igi-zu an-sa$_6$

18'. šà-ĝu$_{10}$ šà zú-kešda a-gin$_7$ hé-en-ta-ĝá-ĝá

19'. ma-da suhuš bí-ge-en gù-téš-a bí-sì-ke

20'. lugal-ĝu$_{10}$ lugal nu-mu-e-da-sá šà-zu hé-éb-du$_{10}$-ge

Part A

^{1} Speak to my king, ^{2} saying (the words) of Aradmu, your servant:

^{3} (Concerning) everything that my king commanded me (to do): ^{4} (The entire kingdom), from the sea of Dilmun land ^{5} to the brackish waters at the foot of the Amorite Highlands, ^{6} to the borders of Simurum in the land of Subir—$^{7-9}$ I have inspected the various cities, their (surrounding) territories, their fields and agricultural tracts, and their levees and irrigation ditches; I have imprisoned (all) fugitives.[4] ^{10} All the cities obedient to my king ^{11} . . . ^{12} I strengthened the garrisons on their walls; ^{13} I made their troops submit (to you). ^{14} . . . ^{15} I have drained flooded tracts ^{16} and had earth work done on *dissipated* plots that had been abandoned. ^{17} . . . in the fields, and canebrakes in the marshes . . . $^{18-19}$ Wherever the drawing of water was not sufficient (to irrigate gardens), I had . . . pour water by means of buckets. $^{20-22}$ (too fragmentary for translation).

Part B

$^{1'}$ Having brought water to the wilderness, they *establish* watercourses, they wash in the watercourses.

$^{2'}$ Even rustlers and robbers break up the earth (for cultivation) in the (wind)-swept wilderness.[5] $^{3'}$ As for their men and women, their men go wherever they wish,

2. Var.: ⌜za⌝-lam-ĝar maš-gána-⌜bi⌝-ta ú-sal mu-un-nú-nú.

3. Var.: du$_{11}$-ga-du$_{11}$-ga-ab.

4. Alt. transl.: *I have established a lookout for any leaks.*

5. Alt. transl.: *I have made rustlers and robbers break up the earth (for cultivation) on the wind-swept steppe.*

⁴′ and their women hold spindles and needles, wandering on whatever roads they wish. ⁵′ They set up animal pens in the far-flung wilderness, ⁶′ and after pitching their tents and encampments,⁶ ⁷′ their laborers and tenant farmers then spend their days (working) in the fields.

⁸′ I have not neglected the orders of Šulgi, my king! ⁹′ I resisted, but now I attend to those orders (without sleep) at night or during the midday siesta!

¹⁰′ Apilaša, from childhood, has been loyal to me. ¹¹′ *And when he became a (grown) man,* I recognized him in my heart, and once it was clear to you, ¹²′ my king, with divine insight, you recognized that person, ¹³′ and promoted him above all the (other) high officials in the foreign territories. ¹⁴′ My king, you surpass all great deeds, you [take revenge] on my opponents. ¹⁵′ Give a command; change it! ⁷Your orders are imperative orders; your deeds are great deeds! ¹⁶′ (Apilaša's) supplications are in your heart, daily they are. ¹⁷′ He is the mortal who has found favor in your eyes, ¹⁸′ so how could I ever be set against him?

¹⁹′ I have secured the foundations of the frontier and made obedient (all of its inhabitants). ²⁰′ No king can rival my king! ²¹′ May your heart be glad!

Commentary

In view of my reconstruction of CBS 7787+ (source N1 of this composition), it appears that what has been thought of as two separate letters (ETCL 3.1.3 + 3.1.11) are actually one and constitute a reply to ŠAr1. There is no overlap between the two preserved sections, but there seem to be between two and five lines missing.

Although the composition is relatively well attested and was clearly part of the regular set of CKU letters at Nippur, the reconstruction of the text is still uncertain and must be considered preliminary until better-preserved sources are recovered. Many difficulties remain. Note also that this is the only CKU text excerpted for early scribal training on a round practice tablet outside of Susa (source Si1).

8 and 15. For a discussion of a-gàr = *ugāru*, see M. Stol, *FS Kraus*, 351–58, and, more recently, G. Marchesi, *OrNS* 70 (2001) 313–17, who opts for a rendition "(communally held) meadow." It is clear from numerous references in administrative and literary texts alike that the a-gàr was cultivated and cannot be a meadow. Therefore I am inclined to follow Stol ("irrigated fields").

The translation follows the meaning of a ğar established by M. Civil, *Farmer's Instructions* 68–69 ("to irrigate, to be submerged"), so that the literal meaning would be, "have caused the submerged fields to come out." Just recently, W. Heimpel, *Workers and Construction Work in Garšana* 277–79, claims that it means "to set/prepare for watering." While I find much of his argument convincing, it does not fit the present context very well. Translate perhaps: "the fields that are ready for (proper)

6. Var.: They rest safely in their tents and encampments.
7. Var.: Give commands!

irrigation have emerged from (the spring) inundation." Interesting in this context
is a set of six almost-identical often-cited short documents from Girsu in which the
high adminstrator (saĝa) of various temples swear that they will not irrigate/prepare
for irrigation fields without the permission of the grand vizier—that is, of Aradmu
(sukkal-mah-da nu-me-a, a ba-ra-ĝá-ĝá); see M. Civil, *Farmer's Instructions*,
68–69, B. Lafont, *RA* 88 (1994) 97–106, idem, *Eau, pouvoir et société*, p. 17; idem,
Sur quelques dossiers, pp. 167–68 (adding the sixth text); Heimpel, *Workers and
Construction Work in Garšana*, 277–78.

9 and 12. In line 12, the word en-nu-ùĝ is used in the sense of Akkadian *maṣṣartum*,
"guard, watch." The combination with kala-ga occurs otherwise only once, in a
Rim-Sin royal inscription (RS I 8:43 [E4.2.14.20], in conjunction with a wall); it
seems to be a calque from the Akkadian use of *maṣṣartum* qualified by *dannum*; see
CAD M/1 335. Line 9 is more difficult. First, the verb igi . . kár, "to inspect, investigate," is followed by what seems to be UD.DU-dè in N1 and X1; the -dè is not
there in N6, and the whole complex is missing in N2. Here en-nu-ùĝ is governed by
the verb dab₅. To my knowledge, the only other example of this combination is in an
Ur III letter-order from Girsu, *ITT* 3 6511 (=*TCS* 1 54, *LEM* 127) 6: e-ne-àm inim
en-nu-ĝá-[ta?] ma-an-dab₅, "it was (PN) who detained him for me by command
of the prison (warden) on my behalf" (translation uncertain). With reservations, I
have assumed that the verb /ed/ refers to escaped soldiers and workers who have all
been caught and detained.

16. The term zal-la-bi is difficult. The approximate translation is based on ég zal-
la = *pa-áš-ru* (Hh 22 Section 9: 6′ [MSL 11 29]), discussed briefly by M. Civil,
Farmer's Instructions 115 ("not in use," but note Civil's comments on the philological
difficulties of this section of Hh).

18–19. The translation of these lines is provisional at best. As W. Heimpel, *Workers and Construction Work in Garšana*, 241–42, has recently shown, a bal refers to
pouring water, not to drawing it. The rendering of saĝ-sìg as "deficit," or the like,
follows K. R. Veenhof, *Mélanges Birot*, 296.

1′. This line would only make sense if we knew what preceded it; the direct objects
must have been in the lines above.

2′–7′. The lack of preceding context hinders the interpretation of these lines as
well. Presumably, the description of lawless men and women settling down, building
encampments, and raising crops on the eden ("desert, wilderness;" often rendered
as "plain")—that is, outside of the normal agricultural areas—must be related to
Šulgi's admonitions in ŠAr1: 13–16 (3). Presumably, Aradmu is explaining why he
had taken time on his journey to Apilaša to inspect the eden. Thus, the passage
concludes with the words (lines 8′–9′): "I have not neglected the orders of Šulgi, my
king! I resisted but now I attend to these orders night and day!"

2′. lú-la-ga is rendered in lexical texts by ḫa-ba-tum (OB Lu A 282 [*MSL* 12 166]) and sà-ru-um (OB Lu A 283 [*MSL* 12 166]). The Sumerian is more specific, however; W. Heimpel (*BSA* 8 [1995] 106–7) has suggested that it is the word for "cattle rustler."

Note also the literary trope of danger from brigands/rustlers in the wilderness: *Sheep and Grain* 128–29: muš-ĝìr lú-la-ga níĝ-eden-na-ke₄ zi-zu an-eden-na ku-kur ba-ni-ib-bé, "Scorpions and rustlers, creatures of the wilderness, threaten your life in the high wilderness," with variant lú-lul-la-ke₄ for lú-la-ga.

Although the immediate context is missing, it seems that the lines that follow pertain to these unruly people. Therefore, Aradmu seems to be reassuring the king that all is so well that even rustlers and brigands have settled down—or have been settled by him—and are involved with taming the land and agriculture.

The meaning of the line is complicated by si-si(g), which I take to be an abbreviation or corruption of the rare im si-si(g). It occurs in the *Flood Story* 201: im hul-hul im si-si-ig dù-a-bi ur-bi ì-su₈-ge-eš, "all the sweeping gales were gathered together." More important is the parallel line in *Išme-Dagan Hymn* A + V Segment A 219: lú-sa-gaz-e eden im si-si-ga níĝ-gul-bi hu-mu-ak, "I have made bandits break up the earth (for cultivation) in the wind-swept wilderness" (in broken context; others have interpreted this passage differently).

3′–7′. These lines are repeated in letter ŠPu1 MB1 9–14 (letter 14). For lines 5′–6′, see the commentary to that letter below.

5′. The pairing of bala and kirid seems to be a traditional metaphor for aspects of femininity (see, for example, *Enki and the World Order* 434 ᵍⁱˢbala ᵍⁱˢkirid šu-šè hé-em-mi-šúm). Though the translation "spindle" for bala seems well established, the meaning of kirid (Akk. *kirissu*) is problematic; it is usually rendered as "hair clasp," but W. Farber, *FS Reiner* 98, argues for "needle." Both are traditional accoutrements symbolizing femininity in Mesopotamian literary texts; for wider ancient Near Eastern use of the spindle trope, see H. A. Hoffner, *JBL* 85 (1966) 326–34.

7′. The exact definition of lú-kíĝ-ak and lú-gud-apin-lá is somewhat hazy. The former occurs only once outside of CKU, in a Sin-iddinam inscription [no. 6, E.: 33], and the latter is quite rare. The rendering of lú-gud-apin-lá as "tenant farmer, cultivator," follows P. Steinkeller, *JESHO* 24 (1981) 114 n. 5.

9′. The interpretation of this line is hindered by the state of preservation of the witnesses. Only one Nippur manuscript fully preserves the beginning of the line (N4); X2 is problematic and seems to bear the traces of textual corruption and reinterpretation. Note, in that source, the use of á-ĝi₆-ba, which is otherwise unattested in OB literary texts, although it is known from administrative documents.

The first verb is gú . . . dù, which is often translated "to neglect, despise," (F. Karahashi, *Sumerian Compound Verbs* 95) but which carries a more nuanced meaning "to be remiss, to turn against, resist," may be a better rendering. Note that it is used of rebellious kings in the inscriptions of Samsu-iluna.

The rare idiom á-bi-šè gin, "to apply oneself to a task," is also encountered with somewhat similar usage in *Supervisor and Scribe* 18: u_4 na-ab-zal-e gi_6 na-ab-še$_{17}$-e-en á-bi-šè gin-na, "Don't (idly) pass the day, do not (even) relax at night—apply yourself to that task!"

10′. This is the only example known to date of a finite form of the rare verb šu . . . dim$_4$. It is otherwise only attested in the expression agrig šu-dim$_4$-ma, "loyal steward" (Anam 4 6 [E4.4.6.2], *SP* 3 60+Bilingual Proverbs [= *abarakku sanqu*; B. Alster, *Proverbs* I 91], ^{d}gu-la agrig šu-dim$_4$${}^{di-im}$-ma-ke$_4$ [VS 17 33:25]) and úku šu-dim$_4$-ma-(àm), "the poor are loyal" (SP 9 Sec. A 2, B. Alster, *Proverbs* I 177). B. Alster, *Proverbs* II 419 and *CUSAS* 2 104 also argues for the meaning "to become rich, to prosper" for the verb, but this does not seem to fit the context here. Note M. Civil's rendering, *JNES* 23 (1964) 7, of šu-dim$_4$-ma as "one who keeps tight control, energetic," commenting on Message of Ludiĝira 18: šu-dim$_4$-ma-(àm) níĝ-gur$_{11}$ mu-un-šár-šár, "She applies herself energetically (to running the household), she enriches (its) assets."

11′. al-me-a is rare. The assumption here is that the verbal form is derived from the copula "to be" and is the same as al-me-a in early incantations (da)-ĝu$_{10}$ ^{d}nanše al-me-a, "since Nanše is at my side," *MDP* 14 91: 23–24, W. W. Hallo, *OrNS* 54 [1985] = N. Veldhuis, *CDLB* 2003: 6 line 18, and unpublished examples). The temporal use of -gin$_7$ has been discussed by M. Civil, *Farmer's Instructions* 92.

13′. ugu-bi diri is a calque from Akkadian *watārum eliana*; see J. Krecher, *UF* 1 (1969) 150 and F. Huber, *ZA* 91 (2001) 179.

14′. The restoration of the verb as šu . . . gi$_4$, "to take revenge," follows a suggestion by Steve Tinney.

18′. This line links the text with ŠAr1: 27 (letter 2) and suggests that it is an answer to that letter.

20′. Note the final eršahuĝa-like passage, which is more reminiscent of letter-prayers than of prose literary letters.

Sources

N1 = CBS 7787 + N1200 + N1203 + N1204 + N1208 + N1210-27a +
    N1210-27b + N1210-27d + N1210-27e + N1212 + N1214 +
    N1218 (+?) Ni. 4061 + Ni. 4188 (*ISET* 2 118) i–ii   = 1–19; 1′–20′
N2 = CBS 8385 + N 3290   = 1–22
N3 = N 2884   = 1–5
N4 = Ni. 2191 (*ISET* 1 64[122] = *BE* 31 54)   =2′–20′
N5 = Ni. 9706 rev. ii 13′–34′ (*ISET* 2 112)[8]   = 1–21
N6 = Ni. 9711 (*ISET* 1 63 [121])   =1′–20′

8. The surface of this tablet is much worn. Unless there are parts of a sign clearly missing, recognizable signs are marked by +.

N7 = Ni. 9866 (*ISET* 1 133[191])   =6′–10′
Si1 = Si. 420 (V. Scheil, *USFS* 134)   =10′
X1 = A w/n ii 22–33   = 1–12
X2 = BM 108869   =1′–20′

Tablet typology: compilation tablets: N1, X1. The rest are all Type III, except Si, which is a type IV round practice tablet.

Photograph of Si1 by Gary Beckman.

Textual Matrixes

Part A

1.   lugal-ğu$_{10}$-ra   ù-na-dug$_4$

N1	.	.	+	.	o	+
N2	o	o	+	+	+	+
N3	.	.	o	o	o	o
N5	+	+	+	+	+	+
X1	.	+	+	+	+ a	+

2.   ⸢árad-mu   árad-zu   na-ab-bé-a

N1	o.	.	.		.	.	.	+	+
N2	oo	o	.		+	+	+	+	+
N3	⸗+	+	o		o	o	o	o	o
N5	++	+	+		+	+	+	+	+
X1	..	+	+		.	+	+	+	+

3.   lugal-ğu$_{10}$ níğ-na-me-šè   á-še   mu-e-da-a-a-áğ

N1	o	+	.	+	+	.	.	.	+	.	+	+⸗	+
N2	o	.	+	+	+	+	o o	o		.	+	+++	
N3	+	⸗	+	+	.	o	o o	o		o o	o o o		
N5	+	+	+	+	+	+	+ +	+	⸗ .	⸗ ⸗ +			
X1	.	+	+	+	+	.	+ +	+	. .	+⸗ .			

4.   a-ab-ba   kur   dilmun^{ki}-na-ta

N1	. .	o o	.		+ .	.
N2	o o o	o	+		+ +	+
N3	+ . .	o	o		o o	o
N5	+ + .	+	+		+ +	.
X1	+ + +	+	.		⸗ +	+

5.   a   šeš   gaba   kur   amurrum^{ki}-šè

N1	+ +	.	.	.		. +
N2	o o	o	.	+		+ +
N3	o .	o	o	o		o o
N5	+ .	.	+	.		⸗ +
X1	+ +	+	+	.		⸗ ta

6. zag si-mu-ur₄-ru-um ma-da su-bir₄ᵏⁱ-šè

N1 +   +   .   .   +   ⸢   +   +   +   +   .   +
N2 o   o o o   .   +   +   +   .   .   ⸢a⸣.⸢
N5 +   + +   + ...⸣ .   + +
X1 +   + +   +   + +   .   +   +   +   + ta

7. uruᵏⁱ-didli ma-da-ma-da-bi

N1 .   ⸢.   .   +   +   +   +ʳᵏⁱ⸣.
N2 o   o o   .   +   .   .   .
N5 +   + +   +   +   +   + +
X1 +   + +   bi ⸢ugnim-bi⸣-ne

8. a-šàa-gàr-bi ù ég pa₅-bi

N1 o   . ++   +   +   +   +   .   .
N2 o   o o.   +   +   +   +   .
N5 +   + ++   .   .   +   +   +
X1 ⸢íd⸣+   + ++   +   .   .   .   +

9. igi bí-in-kár è-dè en-nu-ùŋ   bí-dab₅

N1 o   o   .   +   + +   .   ⸢   .   +   +
N2 o   o o   .   ⸢   ⸢   +   +   +zu   .   x
N5 +   + + +   .   ⸢   +   ⸢   +   +   +
X1 .   .   ⸢   .   +.   .   .   .   +

10. uruᵏⁱ uruᵏⁱ ŋiš-tuku lugal-ŋu₁₀

N1 o   o .   + +   .   .   +
N2 o   o o o .   +   +   +
N5 +   + + + +   +   +   +
X1 .   . ȯ o .   .   . |

11. ki x x   a-bi ì-KU šu-úr im šu bí⸣-dab₅

N1 [   ]-⸢a⸣-bi ì-kùš ⸢   im šu⸣ bí-x
N2 [x   x-b]i ì-KU šú-úr   šu bí-íb-ŠU
N5 ki x x   a-bi ì-KU šu-úr im šu bí⸣-dab₅
X1 [ ] x x   [   ] im šu bí-x

12. bàd-bi en-nu-ùŋ kala-ga bí-gub

N1 o   o o o   + +   + .   o
N2 o   o o   + + +   + +   +
N5 +   + + +   . .   + +   +
X1 o   o o o   + o   o o   .

13. ugnim-bi gú-ŋiš bí-ŋar-ŋar

N1 o   o .   +   + o o
N2 .   ⸢   + +   + + +
N5 .   +   + +   + + +

14.   x du$_{10}$ ús x du-ús bí-dúr-ra

N1   [x x x] x-bi [. . .]x
N2   [. . .]x du-ús bí-dab$_5$-bé
N5   x du$_{10}$ ús x du-ús bí-dúr-ra

15.   a-gàr a ğar-ra-bi a-ta im-ta-è

N1   o .   + +   + + . o . . .
N2   o o   o o   . + + + + x
N5   + +   + +   . + + + + +

16.   kankal zal-la-bi sahar bí-ak

N1   .   + + . x   . .
N2   o   o + + +   . .
N5   .   + + .   + +

17.   x KU a-šà-ga ğiš-gi ambar-ra

N1   x +   + . . + + .   o
N2   o o   o o . + . .   +
N5   x x   + + + + + +   +

18.   a bal sağ-ğá sağ-sìg-ge x-bi

N1   + +   + +   . + . o o
N2   o o   o .   + + . x +
N5   o o   x +   + + + x +

19.   x x x x-ma ^{ğiš}buniğ-ta im-ta-ak

N1   x x x x + - .   . o o o
N2   [   ] . +   + + + +
N5   [. . .] x x -   buniğ$_x$^{9}- .? .? .

20.   [. . .]x a   la-ba?-an?-dé?-ke$_4$-eš [. . .] ⌜kal?-ga?⌝ bí?⌐-x

N2   [. . .]x + +   . . .   + + [. . .].   . . x
N5   [. . .]o o . + . . .   + [. . .]   .   . . x

21.   [. . .]x a-šà-ga kíğ x x

N2   [. . .]x + + +   +   x x
N5   [. . .]o o o o   x   x x

22. [. . .]x-ge(-)en-na-bi [. . .n]e-ne bí-in-zu
N2 [. . .]x-+   + + + [. . .]. + + + +

Part B

1'.   eden a du$_{11}$-ga íd-da mi-ni-ğar-ğar íd-da mi-ni-luh-luh

N1   +   o . . o o o o o o o o o o o
N6   .   + . + + + + + + + o o o o o
X2   o   o . + + + i + - + ì-dun ì - + .

    9. A.LAGAB×A.

2′.   lú-la-ga   lú-sa-gaz-e   eden   si-si-ig-ga-bi   níĝ-gul-bi   bí-ak

N1	+ + +	o o o	o o	o o o o o	o o o	+ +
N4	+ + +	+ + +	. +	+ + + + +	+ + .	o o
N6	+ + +	+ + +	‿ +	+ + + ‿ .	+ + +	+ +
X2	o . +	+ + +	‿ .	. + + ‿ ‿ĝiš	+ + +	+ +

3′.   nita-bi-e-ne   munus-bi-e-ne   nita-bi   ki   šà-ga-na-šè   ì-du-ne?

N1	+	+ ‿ + +	. o o o	o	o o o o o	x o o
N4	+	+ + + +	+ + . +	+	+ + + +	++ .
N6	‿	‿ ‿ ‿ ‿	‿ ‿ -lú+	‿	+ . .	⌜ni⌝-ta⌝an-na-da-x-du-ù
X2	#

4′.   munus-bi   ĝišbala   ĝiškirid-da   šu   ba-e-si-ig   har-ra-an   šà-ga-na   du-ù-ne

N1	+	+ + +	+.	o o o o o o	+ + +	+ + o	o o o
N4	.	. + +	+ +	+ + + +. .	o . +	+ . +	+ + +
N6	.	‿ + +	+.	o o o . sì ga	. . .	. + +	ì-⌜du⌝-⌜ne?⌝
X2	.	⌜e⌝ + +	+.	‿ + + + + +	+ + +	+ + +	ì-DU

5′.   eden   níĝ-daĝal-la   ĝá-rig₇   mu-ni-ib-ĝar

N1	+	+ + +	o o	o o o o
N4	.	. .	+ ba¹⁰ + +	+ + + +
N6	.	o o	. . .	+ . ⌜in⌝.
X2	.	+ +	‿ é-ŠU.ŠÚ.DIB	mu-ni-si-ig (after 6′)

6′.   za-lam-ĝar   maš-gána-bi   ki   um-mi-ĝar-ĝar

N1	. + +	+ .	o o o	o o o
N4	+ + +	+ +	+ + +	+ + +
N6	. . .	. .	+ta . .	. ⌜in-ĝá-ĝá⌝
N7	o o o	o .	+ +.	o o o
X2	. + +	+ +	. ta ú-sal	mu-un-nú-nú

7′.   lú-kíĝ-ak-bi   lú-gud-apin-lá   a-šà-ga   u₄   mu-un-di-ni-ib-zal-e

N1	+ + +.	o o o	o o o o	o o	o o o o o o
N4	+ + + +	+ + +	a+! . + +	+	mu-un-di-ni-ib-zal-e
N6	. . . +	+ + +	+	.	mi-ni-ib-⌜zal-zal⌝-e
N7	o o . +	+ + +	+ . . o o	⌜mu⌝-un-⌜di⌝-ni-ib-zal-⌜e⌝
X2	+ + + a.	+ + +	+ + + +	+	mu-ni-íb-zal-e

8′.   á-áĝ-ĝá   šul-gi   lugal-ĝá-ke₄   gú-ĝu₁₀   nu-mu-da-šub

N1	+ + + .	o o	o o	o o	o o o o
N4	+ + + +	+ +	+ +	+ +	+ + + +
N6	o o o o	+ .	. .	o .	x x . +
N7	o . + +	+.	. o	o .	+ + + o
X2	+ + + ⌜d⌝	++ +	+ +	+ +	+ + + +

10. Preceeded by an erased ba.

9'. gú bí-dù ği₆   an-bar₇-ba   á-bi-šè ì-du-dè-en

N1	+	+	x	o		o	o	o	o o	o o	o o	o	o	
N4	+	+	+	+		+	+	+	.	+	+ + +	+	.	
N6	o	o	o	o		o	o	⌜bi⌝	+ +	.	. +	.	.	
N7	o	o	o	.		+	+	⌜a⌝	o o	.	+ +	o	o	
X2	+	+	-	á-ği₆-ba	+	+	+		+ +	+	+ +	-	+	

10'. ¹á-pi-il-la-ša u₄ tur-ra-ni-ta šu-ğá mu-un-dim₄-e

N1	+	+ + +	+	.	o	o	o	o o	o	o o	o	o	o	o		o
N4	..	+ + +	+	+	+	.	o	o	+	+	+	+	+	.?		
N6	oo o	o o o	+	+	+	.	+	.	-	+	ni	.		o		
N7	oo o	o o	.	.	.	o	o	o	o	o	o	o	o	o		
Si1	+a +	- + +	/ +	+	+	+ +	/ +	+	+	+	.		-?¹¹			
X2	..	. - +	.	+	+	+	+	+	+	+	ba-dim₄-e					

11'. lú al-me-a-gin₇ šà-ğu₁₀ ì-zu igi-zu um-mi-zu

N1	+	+	+	+ +		o	o	o o	o	o	o	o o		
N4	+	+	+	+ +		+	+	+.	+	+	+	+	.	
N6	o	.	.	. .		. .		+ +	.	+!¹²	-		bí	+
	o	.	+	+ +		+ +		+ +	+	+	im	+	du₈	
X2	+	+	+	+.		+	+	+ +	+	+	+	+ +		

11a'.N6 [lú] ⌜al⌝-me-a-gin₇ šà-ğu₁₀ ì-zu igi-zu im-mi-zu

12'. lugal-ğu₁₀ igi-bar-ra diğir-ra lú-ù-bi i-ni-in-zu

N1	.		+	+ +	.	o		o	o o o	o o	o o		
N4	+		+	+ +	+ +		+	+ +.	o o	o o			
N6	o	.		+ +	a	+	-	+	. x	+ +	. .		
X2	+		+	+ +	-	+		. .	.	⌜NE⌝ + +	+ +		

13'. lú ğárza gal kur-kur-ra-ke₄ ugu-bi im-mi-diri

N1	o o		o	.	.	. +	.	.	o o o		
N4	+ +		+	+	+	+ +	+	+	um +	+	
N6	.	.	+	+	+	+ +	⌜úgu⌝	.	. . .		
X2	.	+	+	+	+	+ +	.	⌜ba⌝	. . .		

14'. lugal-ğu₁₀ níğ gal-gal ba-e-diri gaba-ri-ğu₁₀ šu? i-ni-in-[gi₄?]

N1	.	.	.	.	+	.	o.	.	.	. .	o	o o	o o	
N4	#													
N6	.	+	+	+	+	+	-.	+	. .	.	. x	o o		
X2	.	+	+	+	+	+	+ +	+	+ +	.	. +	.	o	

11. The same text inscribed on obverse and reverse by the teacher and by the student. The line is entered as a composite of both sides. It is difficult to ascertain if the root of the verb is the final sign or if there was something after that.

12. The scribe was running out of space in the last line of the obverse and wrote what looks like igi-bar for igi-zu, probably also thinking of ù, resulting in some confusion. He then wrote the line again on the reverse of the tablet, attempting to correct himself but changing the predicate. Were two different versions available to him?

15'. du_{11}-ga-ab gi_4-bi   inim-zu   inim   dugud-da   níĝ-zu   níĝ   gal-la-àm

```
N1  .  +  .   . .        .   .   .       o   .   .   +  .  .
N4  +  + +   + +       +  +  +      +    +  .  +  +   + + +
N6  +  .  ⌜du₁₁⌝-ga-ab-⌜bé⌝ .   .   .       o       o  +  +  +   .  .  .
X2  .  .  du₁₁-ga-ab       +   .   .       .   .   .   .  .  .
```

16'.   inim sa_6-ga-ni   šà-za   ì-ĝál u_4-šú-uš   ì-ĝál-e

```
N1  +   +   +  na + +      + +   .  .   +  x +   +
N4  +   +   + -   + +      + +   + +  +   + ku₄ʔ
N6  .   .   +  +   .  ⌜zu-kaʔ⌝ +. +   .   .   .  . -
X2  .   .   +  .   .  o         o o   o o  o x.ʔ .ʔ
```

17'.   lú-u_8-lu-àm igi-zu   an-sa_6

```
N1  +  .  +  +  +   +  .  +
N4  +  +  +  +  +   +  +  +
N6  +  .  .  .  .   .  .
X2  .  .  .  .  .   .  ì-in .
```

18'.   šà-$ĝu_{10}$ šà zú-kešda   a-gin_7 hé-en-na-ĝá-ĝá

```
N1  + +   .  + +      + .    .  -  + + +
N4  + +   + + +      + +    +  + .  + .
N6  + +   + .  .      + .    .  .  .  + .
X2  + +   + .  .      + +    + ni -  + +
```

19'.   ma-da suhuš   bí-ge-en   gù-téš-a   bí-sì-ke

```
N1  +  + +    -  + ⌜né⌝ .   +  -  + + ⌜gaʔ⌝
N4  +  + +    +  + +      +  +  + + + +
N6  +  + .    .  . +      +  .  .  - + .
X2  +  + .    ⌜bí-in-gc⌝ gù-⌜téš⌝a bí-⌜in-sì⌝
```

20'.   lugal-$ĝu_{10}$ lugal   nu-mu-e-da-sá   šà-zu   hé-éb-du_{10}-ge

```
N1  +  .   .     .  . + + .e + +   .  + + +
N4  +  +   +     + + + + + + +   + + +
N6  +  +   +     + + . . . + +   .  x + .
X2  .  .   .     .  .  .  .  + +   em + +
```

Catchlines:
N4 ⌜ᵈ⌝i-bí-ᵈen.zu lugal-$ĝu_{10}$-[ra ù-na-(a)-dug_4] (PuIb1 [23]).
N6 ⌜lugal⌝-$ĝu_{10}$-ra ù-na-⌜a-dug›⌝ (PuŠ1 [13], less probably AbŠ1 [4]).
In N5, X1 followed by PuŠ1 (13), in N1 by PuIb1 (23).
In N5 followed by PuŠ1 (13)
In X1 followed by PuŠ1 (13)
Colophon C (X2)

4. Abaindasa to Šulgi 1

(AbŠ1, B1, SEpM1, 3.1.21)

Fully Reconstructed Ideal Text

1. lugal-ĝu$_{10}$-ra ù-na-a-dug$_4$
2. máš hur-saĝ-ĝá á sa$_6$-sa$_6$-ĝá
3. anše kur hur-saĝ-ĝá umbin hu-rí-in^{mušen}-na
4. ^{ĝiš}nimbar ki sikil-e mú-a zú-lum ^{na_4}za-gìn lá-mu-úr
5. ù-na-dè-dah
6. ^{1}a-ba-in-da-sá ugula érin^1 zú-kešda
7. saĝ-ki zalag lugal-la-na-šè šà lugal-a-ni-ir du$_{10}$-du$_{10}$-ge-ra
8. árad-zu na-ab-bé-a
9. ì-kala-ga lugal-ĝu$_{10}$ ga-ab-ús^2
10. igi-tuku igi-zu-šè ga-gin
11. inim-ma-zu ra-gaba-zu hé-me-en
12. a gub-ba-àm a mu-da-ak-e
13. tumu gub-ba-àm še mu-un-da-lá-a
14. ^{ĝiš}má gub-ba-àm ^{ĝiš}ĝisal mu-un-sì-ge
15. dub-sar-me-en na-rú-a ab-sar-e
16. inim ugnim-ma mu-da-[. . .]
17. inim pu-úh-ru-um-ma šub-ba e$_{11}$-dè-bi mu-un-da-sì-ge
18. ĝiš-gin$_7$ tir-ĝá mu-un-dù-ù-nam mu-sír-re im-gam-me-en
19. ^{ĝiš}gu-za-ĝá lú mu-un-da-lá-a šu-mu éše im-ma-lá
20. uru-ĝá túg dàn-na mi-ni-mu$_4$-ra túg mu-sír-ra ba-mu$_4$
21. lag-e a mi-ni-íb-tu$_5$-tu$_5$-a sahar igi-ĝá ba-e-gub
22. ur-e ad$_6$ íb-gu$_7$ gaba-bi íb-zi-zi-i
23. ušumgal-e saĝ ĝiš um-mi-íb-ra-ra ka-ta-tak$_4$ íb-tuku
24. ĝiš-gi izi ub-gu$_7$ niĝin$_5$ ì-tuk-tuku
25. ^{d}utu ìa un-gu$_7$ ga-ára un-gu$_7$ ^{ĝiš}banšur úku-ra-šè šu-ni íb-ši-in-tùm
26. zi-ĝu$_{10}$ ba-e-i šu-ĝu$_{10}$ ha-za-ab

---

1. Var.: àga-ús.
2. Vars.: kala-ga-me-en lugal-ĝu$_{10}$ ga-ab-ús; kala-ga-me-en àga-ús-zu hé-me-en.

27. dumu nu-mu-un-kuš-me-en lú èn-tar-re la-ba-an-tuku
28. ğá-àm me-na-àm³ šà ᵈšul-gi lugal-ğá ki-bi ha-ma-gi₄-gi₄
29. lugal-ğu₁₀ èn-ğu₁₀ hé-tar-re ki dağal-ğu₁₀-šè hé-em-mi-ib-gi₄-gi₄

1. Speak to my king:
2. To my mountain goat, fair of limb,
3. Eagle-clawed highland horse,
4. To my date palm growing in a sacred place, laden with glistening dates,
5. Say moreover:
6/8. Saying (the words of) Abaindasa, officer of the armed forces,
7. Who, (to obtain) his master's favor, is a constant delight to his master's heart:
9. Being strong, I want to follow my king,⁴
10. Having vision, I want to go in your vanguard,
11. At your command please let me be your messenger!
12. Even when water is still, I can make water flow;
13. Even when the wind is still, I can winnow grain;
14. Even when the boat is still, I can row!
15. I am a (trained) scribe—I can inscribe a stele!
16. I can . . . the orders of the army.
17. The orders of the assembly . . .
18. As if I were planting a tree in my own woodlot, I kneel in the dirt;
19. As if someone had managed to tie me to my own chair, my hands are tied with rope;
20. In my own city, where I used to dress in fine clothing, I am forced to wear dirty rags;
21. Forced to wash in clods of dirt, there is dirt on my face.
22. A beast devours cadavers but then retreats,
23. Even after the king of beasts makes a kill, he slackens his jaw;⁵
24. Even after the canebrake is consumed by fire, the pond remains (intact),⁶
25. And even Utu, after consuming (offerings of) ghee and cheese, still reaches out to (accept offerings from) a pauper's table;
26. (But now) my life hangs by a thread; please take my hand!
27. I am a widow's son; I have no one to show concern for me.
28. Ah but me—when will Šulgi, my king, restore me to my position?
29. May my king show his concern for me and restore me to my prosperous position!

3. No two manuscripts agree on the first two words of the line.
4. Vars.: I am strong, I want to follow my king; I am strong, so let me be your soldier.
5. Var: it spares some remains.
6. Var.: it spares some ponds.

Commentary

2–4. The metaphors of the opening lines are not directly paralleled in any other composition, but the general tenor is consistent with the kind of imagery that is found in Šulgi hyms, especially in the opening lines of *Šulgi Hymn D*. Note also *Šulgi Hymn A* 48: máš hur-saǧ-ǧá ki ùr-bi-šè húb sar-sar-re-gin₇, "As a mountain goat running to its lair (I entered the Ekishnugal)."

6. The use of zú-kešda in the sense of "troops" in Sumerian was established by C. Wilcke, *Das Lugalbandaepos* 195. According to M. Stol, *OBO* 160/4 777, the term érin zú.kešda (lugal) appears as a logogram in Old Babylonian texts, standing for *kiṣir šarrim*, who are the "Truppen der Armee des Königs." To my knowledge, it is not attested earlier, and therefore its usage in the correspondence concerning Abaindasa may very well be anachronistic.

7. F. Ali, *SL* 53, read the first three signs as KA-šu-U₄, but collations do not support this reading. This line, which is absent from all Nippur manuscripts, as well as one from Ur, contains a number of grammatical problems. No two sources have the same exact text:

```
Ur1    saǧ.ki zalag lugal.ani.ak.še šag lugal.ani.ra dug.dug.e.ra
Ur3    saǧ.ki zalag lugal.ani.ak.ta šag lugal.ani.a dug.dug.e.ra
X1     saǧ.ki zalag lugal.ani.ak.e šag lugal.ani dug.dug.e.ra
X2     saǧ.ki zalag lugal.ani.ak.še šag lugal.ani dug.dug.e.ra
```

The most problematical element is the final /-ra/; most likely this is a misplaced dative, which does not belong here, because this line pertains to the sender of the message, Abaindasa, and not to the recipient. It is also possible that it is the rare /-ra/ ending encountered in ArŠ1: 3 (letter 1); see the commentary to that line.

9. This line has many variants that do not show any obvious clustering. The main text follows N2; N8 is broken but may have been similar. All other sources have a different first part of the line. The three Ur texts differ: Ur1 is similar to N1 but Ur2 omits the line and Ur3, in concert with X1, has kala-ga-me-en àga-ús-zu hé-me-en, "Because I am strong, let me be your bodyguard."

12–14. These lines are difficult because they are without good parallels and are rife with variants. On the one hand, one is tempted to understand the repeated gub as "to be appointed to work/a position" and translate:

> He who assigned to water duty must know how to do water work,
> *He who is assigned to the barley sheaves* must know how to winnow,
> He who assigned to boat duty must know how to *man* the oars.

A somewhat different approach was taken recently by P. Attinger, *ZA* 95 (2005) 256, who renders gub-ba by "est à disposition." I would not rule out either interpretation. The translation offered here—not without misgivings—is influenced, in connection with line 14, by the parallel metaphor in W. L. Lambert, *JNES* 33 (1974) 290: 21: a gub-ba! ᵍⁱˢgi[sal-mu hé-m]e-en = *ina me ni-ḫu-ti lu-u gi-šal-li at-ta*, "in still waters be my oar." Further support comes from the Susa round practice tablet Su2, which may have an Akkadian translation on the reverse. The last two lines seem to read (the text requires detailed personal inspection): *i-na šaʾ-ri-im ne-ḫi-im a-ri-a-am šu-li-i*.

13. The line is highly problematical. Ur1 has še . . . lá, which is OB Sumerian for "to winnow." As M. Civil, *Farmer's Instructions* 96 has shown, the Ur III term for this activity is še . . . dé; in manuscripts Ur3 and Su1 the verb is sì (sig₁₀), which is most probably to be interpreted as *šapākum*, "heap up." The echoed im and ak in N2 are clearly erroneous and are influenced by the previous line and the beginning of this one. The confusion may be due to the lexical difference between Ur III and OB usage. Moreover, it is difficult to explain IM at the beginning of the line. The obvious interpretation is im/tumu, "wind," as that would explain the interpretation offered by the scribe of Ur3, who wanted to see winnowing here. This does not explain the use of the verb sì (sig₁₀) here; it may very well be that that at some point IM was incorrectly interpreted as *sarrum*, "stack (of sheaves of barley)," actually a loan from Sumerian zar, or even as *zārûm*, "winnower;" the basis would have been lexical: lú-IM = *sà-(ar)-rum* (OB Lu A 33 [MSL 12 158; OB Lu B i 36 [MSL 12 178]); (OB Lu D 151 [MSL 12 207]), which normally means "liar, criminal." Note the Akkadian translation of line in Su2: *i-na ša-ri-im ne-ḫi-im, za-ri-a-am šu-li-i*.

15–17. It is possible that a faint echo of these lines is found in the somewhat garbled passage in *Letter to Zimri-Lim* 16′–17′:

> [dumu é-dub-ba-a-me-en] ᵣsagᵣ lugal-ĝá-šè ᵣgubᵣ-bu-dè im-mi-ús
> dumu é ṭup-pí a-na-ku a-na ᵣreᵣ-[eš be-lí-ia] a-na ú-zu-ᵣuzᵣ-zi-im [ ]
> [á-áĝ-ĝá lugal-ĝá zú]-ᵣkéšᵣ-e u₁₈-lu lugal-ĝá ᵣĝeštuᵣ KA RI KAK
> *wu-ur-ti be-ᵣlí-iaᵣ ka-ṣa-ra-am ma-ši-it ᵣbeᵣ-[lí-ia] ᵣḫu-usᵣ-sú-sà-am e-le-i*

> I am a scribal graduate, I am . . . to serve my king,
> I am able to draw up in good form my king's commands, and to remind my king of what he has forgotten.[7]

20. The adjective /dana/ = *zakûm*, "clean," can be written with four different but visually often indistinguishable signs: most often it is dan₆ (UŠ×TAG₄) or dàn (ĜÁ×TAG₄), but sometimes it can be written dán (ĜÁ×ME.EN) or dan₄ (ĜÁ× GÁNA-*tenû*); see *ePSD* and C. Mittermayer, *aBZL* s.v. In OB school texts, the difference between the first two is often difficult to discern; when the end part of a sign is not well preserved, one cannot establish which one was actually used. This is the case in N1, N2, and N9.

22. gaba . . . zi has been translated "to depart, retreat" (F. Karahashi, *Sumerian Compound Verbs* 83, with previous literature). The verb has a more nuanced mean-

---

7. See B. Foster, *Before the Muses*, 223.

ing, "to retreat, withdraw, turn tail," and is used almost exclusively of animals or inanimate subjects. Contrast the marked rare example of an animate subject in the hymn *Šulgi Hymn B* 66 (concerning lions): za-pa-áǧ-bi-šè gaba-ǧu$_{10}$ ba-ra-ba-ta-zi, "but I did not retreat from (the sound) of their roar!"

23. The word ušumgal is presumed to be a mythological beast, often translated "dragon." In poetry, this word occurs in contexts in which this meaning makes little sense, but translators still insist on it. In magical texts and poetry, a distinction is made between ušum and ušum-gal, which refer to a snake-like beast, and ušumgal, which is a metaphor for "lion," perhaps idiomatically equivalent to English "King of Beasts." It is used separately or paired with piriǧ, another name for "lion," and with ur-mah in hendiadys constructions. See, for example, *Šulgi Hymn A* 3: piriǧ igi huš ušumgal-e tu-da-me-en, "I am a fierce-eyed lion, born of the 'King of Beasts'." Instructive is the passage in *Gudea Cyl. B* iv 20–21:

> ur-mah piriǧ ušumgal eden-na-ke$_4$[8]
> ù du$_{10}$ ǧar-ra-àm

> Even the lion, the p., 'King of Beasts' of the wilderness,
> Was lying down in sweet sleep.

The matter of the words for "lion," or "lioness," in ancient Near Eastern languages, particularly in Sumerian and Akkadian, is quite complex; I deal with this in a forthcoming article.

The compound verb saǧ ǧiš...ra is usually used with a human (or divine) agent and clearly means "to kill, to beat to death;" see the examples in F. Karahashi, *Sumerian Compound Verbs*, 138–39. The only other reference in which the action is performed by a lion suggests that it refers to the attack of the animal: *Gilgameš, Enkidu, and the Netherworld,* 23–26:

> lugal-ra a ^{ǧiš}má saǧ-ǧá-ke$_4$
> ur-bar-ra-gin$_7$ téš mu-na-gu$_7$-e
> ^{d}en-ki-ra a ^{ǧiš}má eǧir-ra-ke$_4$
> ur-mah-gin$_7$ saǧ ǧiš im-ra-ra

> The waters attack the King at the prow of the boat
> Like a wolf pack,
> The waters strike at Enki at the stern of the boat
> Like lion(s).

I know of only one other occurrence of ka-ta tak$_4$ in the lexical entry Sag A iii 36 [MSL SS 1 22]), where the Akkadian is the equally obscure ú-zu-ba-at pi-i. According to *AHw* 3 1448b, uzubbatu, "Verschonung," is otherwise only attested in first-millennium personal names. The meaning seems to be "dropping from the mouth," idiomatic for "to spare." The broader metaphorical frame of reference links this to a

---

8. For this line, see also *Šulgi Hymn B* 59 and possibly *Šulgi Hymn C* B1.

passage in a Sin-iddinam inscription (Frayne 1990: E4.2.9.1: 79–83), an eden-na, pirig̃ šu ba-an-zi-ga, g̃ìri-gin-na ba-an-gub, íb-tag$_4$ ⌜hé-em-ma-an⌝-gaz, "In the high wilderness, the lion, having risen, stood on the pathway so as to be able to kill stragglers/deserters."

The distribution of tak$_4$/tuku in both lines is due to the quasi-homonymic nature of the verbs but also reflects the aesthetic that dictates the repetition of the same word in two consecutive lines. The fairly consistent difference between Nippur and elsewhere is not significant, because most texts from Nippur are badly preserved at this point.

27–29. The verb èn...tar is used here in the sense of Akkadian *warkatam parāsum*, "to take care, be concerned with (a person, situation)," (*CAD* P 166 173) rather than in the more commonly attested meaning, "to ask, inquire," (Akkadian *šālum*). This is made explicit in *Letter-Prayer to Zimri-Lim 22′*: [lugal-g̃u$_{10}$] èn-g̃u$_{10}$ hé-tar-re ki-bi-šè-⌜g̃u$_{10}$⌝ hu-mu-un-g[i$_4$-gi$_4$] = *be-lí wa-ar-ka-ti* ⌜li⌝-ip-[ru-us-ma] *a-na aš-ri-[ia li-ti-ra-an-ni*], "May my king show his concern for me and restore me to my position."

Line 27, which is only present in two sources, Ur1 and X2, must be compared with *Letter-Prayer of Ininka to Nintinuga* (SEpM 19) 16: lú èn-tar-re la-ba-(an)-tuku, "I have no one to show concern for me." Note that Ur1 is inscribed on a collective tablet that also included SEpM 19 (col. i 1′–4′).

The idiom šà ki-bi gi$_4$ often occurs in the final lines of other literary texts, most notably in eršahug̃as; see already M. Civil, *Fs Oppenheim*, 89. It is often translated literally but means "to be favorably disposed to once again." In epistolary literature, see *Letter of Gudea to His God* 10: dig̃ir-g̃u$_{10}$ lú kúr-ra-zu nu-me-en šà-zu ki-bi ha-ma-ab-gi$_4$-gi$_4$, "O my god, I am not your enemy, so please be well disposed to me once again!"

Sources

N1 = 3 N-T 8 = IM 58335 (*SL* xxxvii)
N2 = 3 N-T 309 = A 30231 (*SL* liii)[9]
N3 = CBS 8007 (*STVC* 110) + Ni. 4592 (*ISET* 2 21)
N4 = HS 1456 (*TMH NF* 4 43, collations C. Wilcke, *Kollationen* 73)
N5 = UM 29-13-20 + UM 29-13-24 (both *SL* liii) i 1–6
N6 = UM 29-16-139 + N 3264 + N 3266 + N 3294 + N 3301 + N 3303 + N 3308
    + N 3310 (all *SL* xxiv-xxv) + Ni. 9701 (*ISET* 2 114) i 1′–7′
N7 = UM 29-15-535
N8 = N 1555
N9 = N 3461
N10 = CBS 10069

---

9. The surface of the tablet is worn and made difficult to read by a cover of shellac for preservation.

Ur1 = U. 7741 (*UET* 6/2 173, No. 7 Quiet St.) ii 2′–iii 7
Ur2 = U. 16857 (*UET* 6/2 178, No. 1 Broad St.)
Ur3 = U. 16894B (*UET* 6/2 179, No. 1 Broad St.)
Su1 = *MDP* 18 51
Su2 = *MDP* 27 207
X1 = Crozer 206a i
X2 = YBC 6458
X3 = Cotsen 40832 (Wilson, *Education* 159 [p. 251])

N1 collated on cast; N4, collated by S. Tinney and on print photographs provided by Manfred Krebernik and on digital photographs provided by Jerrold Cooper. Su2 collated by Mrs. Mernoush Malyeri.

Tablet typology: compilation tablets (Type I): N5, N6, Ur1, X1, the rest are all Type III, except Su1, Su2, which are Type IV round practice tablets.

Concordance to F. Ali, *SL* 53:

A	Ur1		N1	I
B	N2		N2	B
C	Ur2		N3	F+G
D	Ur3		N4	H
E	N5		N5	E
H	N4		N8	J
F	N3		Ur1	A
G	N3		Ur2	C
I	N1		Ur3	D
J	N8			

No other text in CKU is subject to the degree of textual manipulation that was allowed for Abaindasa's letter of petition. Leaving aside the Susa sources, the letter is preserved on four compilation tablets: two from Nippur (N4, N6), one from Ur (Ur1), and one of unknown origin (X1). There are twelve Type III manuscripts—that is, one-day imgida exercises—and although some are in fragmentary state, it seems that they contained some version of the complete composition. Unlike any other letter, AbŠ1 seems completely fluid; students/teachers appear to choose at will which lines they will use and which they will omit. Not all the pieces are completely preserved but within what we have, only three tablets contain exactly the same lines—N5, N7, and N10—but since all three are incomplete, one cannot be certain that they were identical in content. This textual flexibility is not limited to Nippur. The three tablets from Ur are subject to the same lack of uniformity. Significantly, the three sources from that city were found in different houses: Ur1 at No. 7 Quiet St. and the other two at No. 1 Broad St., and yet the variations do not cluster according to place of origin.

Source Distribution[10]

	N1	N2	N3	N4	N5	N6	N7	N8	N9	N10	Ur1	Ur2	Ur3	X1	X2	X3	Su1	Su2
1	-	+	+	-	+	-	-	-	-	-	+	+	+	+	+	+	+	
2	-	+	+	-	+	-	-	-	-	-	+	+	+	+	+	+	+	
3	-	+	+	-	+	-	+	-	-	-	+	+	+	+	+	+	+	
4	-	+	+	-	+	-	+	-	-	-	+	+	+	+	+	+	+	
5	-	+	+	-	+	-	+	-	-	-	+	+	+	+	+	+	+	
6	-	+	+	-	#	-	#	-	+	#	+	#	+	+	+	#		
7	-	#	#	-	#	-	#	-	#	#	+	#	+	+	+	#		
8	-	+	+	-	#	-	#	+	+	#	+	#	+	+	+	#		
9	-	+	#	-	#	-	#	+	#	#	+	#	+	+	-	#		
10	-	+	#	-	#	-	#	+	#	#	#	#	#	+	-	#		
11	-	#	#	-	#	-	#	+	#	#	+	#	#	+	-	#		
12	-	+	#	+	#	-	#	+	#	#	+	#	+	+	-	#		+
13	-	+	#	+	#	-	#	+	#	#	+	#	++	+	-	#		+
14	-	#	#	+	#	-	#	+	#	#	+	#	+	+	-	#		
15	-	+	#	+	#	-	#	+	#	#	+	#	#	+	-	#		
16	-	+	#	+	#	-	#	+	#	#	#	#	#	#	-	#		
17	-	+	#	++	#	-	#	#	#	#	+	#	#	+	-	#		
18	-	+	+	+	+	-	+	+	+	+	+	+	+	+	-	+		
19	+	+	+	+	-	-	+	+	+	+	+	+	+	+	-	+		
20	+	+	-	+	-	-	+	+	+	+	#	+	+	+	-	+		
21	+	+	-	+	-	+	+	+	-	+	+	+	+	+	-	+		
22	+	+	-	+	-	+	+	+	-	-	+	+	+	+	-	+		
23	+	+	-	+	-	+	+	+	-	-	+	+	+	+	+	+		
24	-	+	-	+	-	+	+	+	-	-	+	+	+	+	+	+		
25	-	+	-	+	-	+	++	+	-	-	+	+	+	+	+	+		
26	-	#	-	-	-	#	-	#	-	-	+	#	#	-	+	#		
27	-	#	-	-	-	#	-	#	-	-	+	#	#	-	+	#		
28	-	+	-	-	-	+	-	+	-	-	+	+	+	-	+	+		
29	-	#	-	-	-	#	-	-	-	-	+	#	#	-	+	#		

To provide a flavor of the difference between the preserved manuscripts, I offer a translation of an idealized shorter version (the line numbers are those of the full edition):

    1. Speak to my king:
    2. To my mountain goat, fair of limb,
    3. Eagle-clawed highland horse,
    4. To my date palm growing in a sacred place, laden with glistening dates,
    5. Say moreover:
  6/8. Saying (the words of) Abaindasa, officer of the armed forces,

---

10. In the table - = line broken, + = line present, ++ = line present and followed by one or more additional lines, # = line omitted.

18. As if I were planting a tree in my own woodlot, I kneel in the dirt;
19. As if someone had managed to tie me to my own chair, my hands are tied with rope;
20. In my own city, where I used to dress in fine clothing, I am forced to wear dirty rags;
21. Forced to wash in clods of dirt, there is dirt on my face.
22. A beast devours cadavers but then retreats,
23. Even after the king of beasts makes a kill, he slackens his jaw;
24. Even after the canebrake is consumed by fire, the pond remains;
25. And even Utu, after consuming (offerings of) ghee and cheese, still reaches out to (accept offerings from) a pauper's table;
28. Ah but me—when will Šulgi, my king, restore me to my position?

Textual Matrix

1. lugal-ǧu$_{10}$-ra   ù-na-a-dug$_4$

N2	.	.	.	+	.	⁓	.
N3	.	.	+	.	+	⁓	.
N5	.	+	+	+	+	+	+
Ur1	o	o	.	.	.	o	o
Ur2	.	.	.	+	+	⁓	+
Ur3	o	.	+	+	+	.	o
Su1	+	+	+	+	ne	⁓	+
X1	.	+	+	.	.	⁓	.
X2	+	+	+	.	.	⁓	.
X3	+	+	.	o	o	o	o

2. máš hur-saǧ-ǧá á sa$_6$-sa$_6$-ǧá

	máš	hur-saǧ-ǧá		á		sa$_6$-sa$_6$-ǧá	
N2	+	+	+	+	+	+	+	.
N3	.	+	+	+	+	+	+	.
N5	.	+	+	+	+	+	+	ǧu$_{10}$
Ur1	.	.	+	+	+	+	.	o
Ur2	.	.	+	+	+	+	+	ǧu$_{10}$
Ur3	.	+	+	+	+	+	.	o
Su1	.	.	.	.	.	.	.	⌜ǧu$_{10}$⌝
X1	+	+	+	+	+	+	.	⌜ǧu$_{10}$⌝
X2	+	+	+	+	.	o	o	o
X3	+	+	+	o	o	o	o	o

3.   anše kur hur-saĝ-ĝá   umbin hu-rí-in^{mušen}-na

	anše	kur	hur	saĝ	ĝá	umbin	hu	rí	in	mušen	na
N2	+	+	.	+	+	+	.	.	+	+	+
N3	+	+	+	+	+	+	+	+	.	o	o
N5	+	+	+	+	+	+	+	+	+	+	+
N7	o	o	o	o	o	.	+	.	.	o	o
Ur1	.	+ra	+	+	+	+	.	.	o	o	o
Ur2	+	+	+	+	+	.	+	+	+	-	+
Ur3	.	+	+	+	+	+	+	+	+	-	.
Su1	.	x	.	.	.	/ traces[11]					
X1	+	+	+	+	+	+	+	+	+	-	+
X2	+	+ra	+	.	.	o	.	.	o	(-)	o
X3	+	+	+	+	. ⸢ke$_4$⸣[12]	+	.	+	+	+	+

4. ^{ĝiš}nimbar ki sikil-e mú-a zú-lum ^{na_4}za-gìn lá-ĝu$_{10}$-úr

	ĝiš	nimbar	ki	sikil	e	mú	a	zú	lum	na$_4$	za	gìn	lá	ĝu$_{10}$	úr
N2	+	+	+	+	+	+	+	.	+	+	+	+	+	.	.
N3	.	+	+	.	.	.	.	+	+	-	+	+	.	o	o
N5	+	+	+	-	+	+	+	+	+	+	+	+	+	+	ĝá[13]
N7	o	.	+	+	o	o	o	.	+	+	.	o	o	o	o
Ur1	+	+	+	+	+	+	+	+	+	+	+	.	o	o	o
Ur2	+	+	+	+	+	+	+/	+	+	+	+	+	+	-	+
Ur3	+	+	+	+	+	+	+	+	+	-	+	+	.	.	.
Su1	traces						/	+	+	+	+	+	-	+	-
X1	+	+	+	+	+	+	+/	+	+	+	+	+	+	+	+ :
X2	+	.	+	.	o	+	o/	+	+	.	o	o	o	.	.
X3	+	+	+	+	.	+	+[14]/	+	+	+	+	-	+	+	+

5.   ù-na-dè-dah

	ù	na	dè	dah
N2	+	+	+	.
N3	.	+[15]	.	.
N5	.	+e	+	+
N7	.	+	+	.
Ur1	+	ne	+	.
Ur2	+	ne	+	+
Ur3	+	ne	+	.
Su1	+	ne	á	+ dah
X1	+	+e	+[?]	+
X2	.	.	o	o
X3	+	ne	+	+
X4	+	+	+	+

11. See p. 323 below.
12. A modern piece of clay with etched in wedges has been inserted here.
13. Probably trunacted úr.
14. Preceded by an erased a.
15. Erasures before and after na.

6. ᴵa-ba-in-da-sá   ugula   érin   zú-kešda

N2	++ +	+	+	+	+		+		+	+
N3	.+ +	+	.	o	+		+		+	+ lu[gal]
N5	#									
N7	#									
N9	oo .	.	.	.	.		.		.	o
N10	oo .	.	o	o / o			.		.	.
Ur1	++ +	an	+	+	+		àga-ús		+	+
Ur2	#									
Ur3	++ +	⌜nam⌝++		+			àga-ús		+	+
X1	++ +	an	+	+	+		àga-ús		+	+
X2	-..	⌜an⌝	.	./	.		⌜àga-ús⌝.		.	.
X3	#									
X4	oo o o	.	+	+			+		+	+:

7. saĝ-ki zalag lugal-la-na-šè šà lugal-a-ni-ir du₁₀-du₁₀-ge-ra

N2	#														
N3	#														
N5	#														
N7	#														
N9	#														
N10	#														
Ur1	+	+	+		+		+ +	+	+	+		+ + +	+		+ +
Ur2	#														
Ur3	+	.	+		+		+ +	ta / +	+	⌜la⌝ na	-	+	+		+ +
X1	+	+	+		+		+ +	ke₄/ +	+	la ni	-	+	+		+ +
X2	.	.	.		.			a ni .	/.	. o	.	-	.		. .
X3	#														

8. árad-zu na-ab-bé-a

N2	+	+	+	+	+	+
N3	+	+	+	.	+	.
N5	#					
N7	#					
N8	o	o	o	.	o	o
N9	.	+	+	o	o	o
N10	#					
Ur1	+	+	+	+	+	+
Ur2	#					
Ur3	+	+	+	+	+	+
X1	+	+	+	+	+	+
X2	.	o	o	o	o	o[16]
X3	#					

16. Followed by traces of two lines.

9.   ì-kala-ga   lugal-ĝu$_{10}$ ga-ab-ús
N2   + +   +   +   +   + + +
N3   #
N5   #
N7   #
N8   o o   o   .   +   o o o
N9   #
N10 #
Ur1 kala-ga-me-en +   +   +   + + +
Ur2 #
Ur3 kala-ga-me-en àga-ús-zu   hé-me-en
X1   kala-ga-me-en àga-ús-zu   hé-me-en
X3   #

Ë10. igi-tuku igi-zu-šè ga-gin
N2   +   + + ni +   + +
N3   #
N5   #
N7   #
N8   o   . + + +   o o
N9   #
N10   #
Ur1   #
Ur2   #
Ur3   #
X1   + tuk + + + +   + + (after 11)
X3   #

X1 has an additional line: Λ DIŠ Ú-àm ^{giš}banšur mu-da-ak-e

11.   inim-ma-zu ra-gaba-zu hé-me-en
N2   #
N3   #
N5   #
N7   #
N8   .   . . + +   + .   o o
N9   #
N10   #
Ur1   +   + + + +   + + + +
Ur2   #
Ur3   #
X1   +   +[17] + + +   + + + +[18]
X3   #

17. Followed by erased NI.
18. The line ends with four squeezed signs that I cannot read; it seems to be a verb begin-ning with ga-.

12.   a   gub-ba-àm a   mu-da-ak-e
N2   +   +   . ⸢a⸣ +   +   + + +
N3   #
N4   .   .   . .   o   o   o o o
N5   #
N7   #
N8   +   +   + +   +   +   + . o
N9   #
N10   #
Ur1   +   +   + -   +   +un+ + + (after 14)
Ur2   #
Ur3   o   o   o x   x   im-ma-ak-en (after 13)
Su2   +a+   + -   .   +   + - -¹⁹
X1   .   +   + -   +   +   + x x
X3   #

13.   tumu gub-ba-àm še mu-un-da-lá-a
N2   +   +   + a   IM mu-da-ak-e
N3   #
N4   +   +   + +   še x [ ]
N5   #
N7   #
N8   +   .   + -   še mu-da-⸢ak⸣-[. . .]
N9   #
N10   #
Ur1   +   +   + -   še mu-un-da-lá-a
Ur2   #
Ur3   o   o   o o   še mu-un-sì-ge
Su2   i   .   + -   še mu-sì
X1   .   +   + -   +   mu-⸢da⸣-x-⸢e⸣
X3   #

Ur3 has additional line: [. . .] ⸢bar?⸣-ĝá mu-un-dadag-ge

19. See full transliteration below. The final sign seems to be da but could be a combination of da and ak.

14.   ^{ĝiš}má gub-ba-àm ^{ĝiš}ĝisal mu-un-sì-ge

N2   #
N3   #
N4   + +   +   + +   + +   o   o   o o
N5   #
N7   #
N8   + .   .   + +   +.   o   o   o o
N9   #
N10 #
Ur1 + +   +   + -   + +   +   +   + + (before 12)
Ur2 #
Ur3 - .   .   . o   + +   +   +   + + (before 13)
X1   + +   +   + -   + +   +   -   + . (before 12)
X3   #

15.   dub-sar   me-en   na-rú-a   ab-sar-e

N2   +   +   + +   + +   .   .   .   +
N3   #
N4   +   +   + +   + + o   o   o   o
N5   #
N7   #
N8   .   +   .   .⌜dub⌝ .   + +   .   o   o (after 16)
N9   #
N10 #
Ur1 +   +   + +   + + +   +   +[20]re ⌜en⌝
Ur2 #
Ur3 #
X1   ⊦   ⊦   + +   + + +   mu + ⌜re⌝
X3   #

16.   inim   ugnim-ma   mu-da-[. . .]

N2   .   +   o   .   .   [. . .]
N3   #
N4   +   +   +   .   o
N5   #
N7   #
N8   + KI.AD.ĜAR+   +   .   [. . .]
N9   #
N10 #
Ur1 #
Ur2 #
Ur3 #
X1   #
X3   #

20. Preceded by an erased sign.

```
17.  inim  pu-úh-ru-um-ma  šub-ba  e₁₁-dè-bi  mu-un-da-sì-ge
N2   o      .  + + x   o   o   o   o   o   o   o   o   o   o o
N3   #
N4   +      +  x+²¹ ++   .    o   o   o   o   o   o   o   o o o
N5   #
N7   #
N8   #
N9   #
N10  #
Ur1  +      +  +  +  +   +    +   +   +   +   +   +   +   + + +
Ur2  #
Ur3  #
X1   +      +  +  +  -   +    +   +   +   +   +   mu-dab₅?
X3   #
```

N4 has another line after 17: inim sa₆-ge gaba-ri x[. . .]

```
18.  ğiš-gin₇  tir-ğá  mu-un-dù-ù-nam  mu-sír-re  im-gam-me-en
N2   o  o      .  .    .    .   .  o  o      o   o  o  o  o    o  o
N3   +  +      +  .    .    +   +  +  .      +   +  .  .  +  m[a]  o
N4   +  +      +  +    +    -   +  .  o      o   o  o  o  o    o  o
N5   .  .      .  +    +    +   +  -  +      .   .  ⌜e⌝.  +    +  +
N7   o  .      +  +    .    .   o  o  o      o   .  ⌜e⌝+  +  ⌜e⌝  o
N8   +  o      o  o    o    o   o  o  o      o   o  o  o  o    o  o
N9   .  +      +  +    +    -   +  un o      o   o  o  o  o    o  o
N10  o  o      o  o    o    o   o  o  o      o   o  .  +  +    -  +
Ur1  +  + ğiš  +  +    +    -   +  -  na     +   +  +  +  +    e  -
Ur2  +  +      +  +    +    + tùm - -        +   +  e  +  +    e  -
Ur3  o  o      o  .    .    .   +  +  +      o   .  .  .  +    e  -
X1   +  +      +  +    .    -   +  -  +      +   +  +  +  +    +  +
X3   +  + ğiš  +  +    +    +   +  -  +!     .   +  .  ì  +    e  -
```

21. The scribe has trouble with úh and began to write something else, erased it, and then wrote the right sign. He then repeated the line, once again with a problematical úh, partially erasing the offending sign: inim pu-x-úh-ru-um-m[a].

19.   ᵍⁱˢgu-za-ǧá lú mu-un-da-lá-a   šu-ǧu₁₀ éše im-ma-lá

N1	. .	. .	. .	.	.	. o	o o	+ .		.	.	.	o
N2	o o	o +	+ +	+	dam.	o	o o	o	o	o	o	
N3	+ +	. .	. .	.	. .	. o	o o	o	o	o	o	
N4	. .	+ +	+ +	+ +	. o	o o	o	o	o	o		
N7	o o	. +	+ +	.	o	o o	o	.	⌜uš⌝	+	.	+
N8	+ +	⸗ ⸗	. .	.	o o	. .	. o	o	o	o	o	
N9	o .	+	ǧu₁₀	+	.⌜da-an⌝	o o	o o	o	o	o	o	
N10	o o	o +	+ +	+ .	o o/	o o	.	+	+	+		
Ur1	+ .	+ +	+ +	+ +	+ +	+ +	.	+	+an+			
Ur2	+ .	+ ⸗	+ +	+ ⸗	+ +	+ +	.	.	+ +			
Ur3	o o	o .	. .	. +	+ +	+ +	+	+	+an+			
X1	o o	o .	+ +	+ +	+ +	. .	.	.	. .			
X3	+ .	+ +	+ +	+ +	+ +	. .	+	+	+ +			

Followed by another line in X1.

20.   uru-ǧá túg dàn-na mi-ni-mu₄-ra   túg mu-sír-ra ba-an-mu₄

N1	.	+	.	.	+	+	+	o o	o	.	+ +	+	x	o
N2	o	.	+	+	+a+	+	+ +	+	+	+ o	o o	o		
N4	o	.	.	dan₆	+a +	+i[n]o	o	o	o	.	+	+	+	o
N7	o	o	o	⌜dan₆ a na⌝	.	.	o	o	o	o o	o o	o²²		
N8	+	+	+	+	.⌜a⌝.	.	o o	o	o	o o	o o	o		
N9	o	o	.	.	o o	o o	o	o	o	o o	o o	o		
N10	o	o	.	+	+ +	+	. ./	o	o o	.	. ⸗	+		
Ur1	# (see next line)													
Ur2	+	+	+	+	+ +	+	+ +	+	+	+ +	+ +	+		
Ur3	o	o	.	dan₄	+ .	+	+ +	o	.	+ +	+ +	+		
X1	ʊ	.	.	.	+ +	+	. o	o	ϙ ο	.	. .	.		
X3	+	.	+	dan₄	+ +	+in⸗	.	+	+ +	+	+ ⸗	+		

21.   lag-e a mi-ni-íb-tu₅-tu₅-a sahar igi-ǧá ba-e-gub

N1	o	.	+	+	+ ⸗	+	. o	.	+	+	+	. +		
N2	.	+	+	+	+	⌜ib⌝.	+ +	+	+	+	+	. .		
N4	o	o o	.	+	+	+	. o	o	.	+	+	+ +		
N6	o	o .	+	+ .	. o	o	.	+	+	o	o o			
N7	o	o o	o	o o	.	+ o	o	.	.	+	+ +			
N8	.	. .	+	. o	.	. o	o	o	o	o	o o			
N10	o	o o	+	+	⌜ib⌝.	o o	/o	o	.	. . o				
Ur1	+	.	+	níǧ-dan₆-dan₆-a	+	+	+	+	+ + bu					
Ur2	+	+ +	+	+ ⸗	+	. + +	+	+	+ +					
Ur3	+	+ +	+	+ in	+	. .	+	+	+	+	+ +			
X1	o	o o	+	+ ⸗	+	+ +	.	o	o	o o.				
X3	.	. +	+	+ in	+	+ +	.	+	+	+	+ +			

22. Traces of an indented line, possibly ⌜mu-sír-ra⌝.

22. ur-e ad₆ íb-gu₇ gaba-bi íb-zi-zi-i

	ur	e	ad₆	íb	gu₇	gaba	bi	íb	zi	zi	i
N1	.	+	+	ub	+	+	+	+	+	.	+
N2	+	+	+	+	+	+	+	.	+	+	-
N4	o	o	.	+	+	+	.	o	o	o	o
N6	.	.	.	i+	+	.	o	o	o	o	o
N7	o	o	.	.	+	+	+	.	.	+	.
N8	.	o	.	.	.	.	.	o	o	o	o
Ur1	+	.	+	+	+	+	+	+	+	+	-
Ur2	.	+	.	.	+	+	+	+	+	+	+
Ur3	+	re	+	+	.	.	+	+	du₈	du₈	
X1	o	o	o	.	+	+	+	+	.	.	-
X3	o	o	.	+	+	o	.	+	+	+	.

23. ušumgal-e sağ ğiš um-mi-íb-ra-ra ka-ta-tak₄ íb-tuku

	ušumgal	e	sağ	ğiš	um	mi	íb	ra	ra	ka	ta	tak₄	íb	tuku
N1	.	.	+	+	+	.	.	o	o	o	o	o	o	o
N2	+	+	+	+	+	+	-	+	+	+	+	+	+	+
N4	o	.	ğiš	sağ	-	+	.	o	o	o	o	o	o	o
N6	.	+	+	+	+	+	ib	+	.	o	o	o	o	o
N7	.	+	+	+	⌜im-mi⌝		o	o	o	+	+	+	.	o
N8	o	.	+	+	.	+	.	.	-	+	.	o	o	o
Ur1	.	+	+	+	-	-	+	+	.	+ab.	ì+	tak₄		
Ur2	+	+	+	+	-	-	+	+	+	.⌜tak₄⌝.	+	+		
Ur3	+	+	+	+	-	-	+	+	+	+	tak	+	+	tak₄
X1	o	o	.	+	+	+	+	.	.	o	o	.	.⌜tuk⌝.	
X2	o	o	o	o	o	o	o	o	o	/o	o	.	.	tak₄
X3	.	.	.	-	-	-	+	+	+	+	+	+	+	tak₄⌜?⌝

24. ğiš-gi izi ub-gu₇ niğin₅ ì-tuk-tuku

	ğiš	gi	izi	ub	gu₇	niğin₅	ì	tuk	tuku
N2	+	+	+	+	.	.	⌜mi⌝	ni	+
N4	o	o	.	-	.	o	o	o	
N6	+	.	+⌜i	íb⌝	+	.	o	o	o
N7	+	+	+	ub	+	o	o	o	o
N8	o	.	+	íb	+	+	.	.	.
Ur1	.	.	+	íb	+e	+	e + ⌜tak₄⌝		tak₄
Ur2	+	+	+	íb	+	+	+	+	+
Ur3	+	+	+	+	.	+	+	⌜tak₄	tak₄⌝
X1	o	o	o	o	o	o	o	.	+
X2	.	.	+	íb	+[23]	e/	+	tak₄	tak₄
X3	.	+	.	+	+	+	+	.	+

23. Written as ka.

25. ᵈutu ìa un-gu$_7$ ga-ára un-gu$_7$ ᵍⁱˢbanšur úku-ra-šè šu-ni íb-ši-in-tùm

```
N2   .+  .  + +  + ra  + +  + +    +   + +  + + + + - +
N4   oo  o  . .  o o    o o  o o    o   o o  o o o o o o
N6   +.  +  . .  . x    o o  o o    o   o o  + + . o o o
N7   ..  +  + .  o o    o o  . +    +   o o/ o . . o o o
N8   oo  .  + +  + x²⁴  + +  + .    .   . +  + . o o o o²⁵
Ur1  ..  +  - +  + +mu-un +  . +    +   + +  + + im + + +
Ur2  ++  +  + +  + +    + +  + +!   .   + +/ + + + + + +
Ur3  ++  +  . +  + . -  + +  + +    +   + +  + + + + + +
X1   oo  o  o o  o o    o o  o o    o   o o  o o o o . ˹túm˺₉
X2   ++  +  - +  + +  - +²⁶/ - +    +   + +/ + + + + - túm
X3   .+  +  . .  + ra  ? ?/  + .    +   + +  + + + + + +
```

26. zi-ğu$_{10}$ ba-e-i šu-ğu$_{10}$ ha-za-ab

```
N2   #
N6   #
N8   #
Ur1  . .  + ++ + +    + +a+
Ur2  #
Ur3  #
X2   + +  + - + +    + + +
X3   #
```

27. dumu nu-mu-un-kuš-me-en lú èn-tar-re la-ba-an-tuku

```
N2   #
N6   #
N8   #
Ur1  +   + + + + +  + +  + + + + . + +
Ur2  #
Ur3  #
X2   +   + + - + +  + +  + + - + + - +
X3   #
```

28. ğá-àm me-na-àm šà ᵈšul-gi lugal-ğá ki-bi ha-ma-gi$_4$-gi$_4$

```
N2   ˹ğá-àm˺ me-na-˹àm˺  . .+  + .   . . + + . . . .
N6   ğá-a    me-na-àm    + -.  . o   o + + + . . o
N8   o o     o o .       + -.  o o   o o o . o o o
Ur1  ğá-e    me-e-a-na-àm + ++ + +  ğu₁₀ + + + + + +
Ur2  ğá-a    me-na-àm    / ++++ + +  + /+ + - + + +
Ur3  ğá-e    me-en-na-a  + ++ + +  ğu₁₀ + + + + + +
X2   ğá      me-en-a     + - + + +  ğu₁₀ /. + + + + +
X3   ğa      me-˹en˺-na-àm + ++ + +  ğu₁₀ /. + ˹ha˺ an + +
```

24. Erasure, or broken ára.
25. Followed by three additional lines; see p. 324 below.
26. Written as ka.

29. lugal-ğu$_{10}$ èn-ğu$_{10}$ hé-tar-re   ki dağal-ğu$_{10}$-šè hé-em-mi-ib-gi$_4$-gi$_4$

N2	#																	
N6	#																	
Ur1	.	+	+	+	+	+	+	+	+	+	+	+	+	+	+	+	+
Ur2	#																	
Ur3	#																	
X2	+	+	+	- hu-mu-un-tar-re	/+	+		bi	+	+	+	+	íb	+	.		
X3	#																	

Catchline N2: lugal-ğá ù-na-⌈dug$_4$⌉ (SEpM2).
In N6, Ur1, X1, and probably in N5 followed by SEpM2.

Su1 is a round tablet from Susa with an elementary exercise based on this letter:

Obverse:
⌈zú-lum⌉ ^{na4}za-gìn-⌈mu⌉
⌈ù⌉-ne-á-dah-dah
⌈zú⌉-lum ^{na4}za-gìn-mu
ù-ne-á-dah-dah

Reverse:
In a rectangle:
1. lugal-ğu$_{10}$-ra
2. ù-ne-dug$_4$
3. ù-ne-á-dah-dah
4. ⌈máš hur-sağ-ğá⌉
5. ⌈á sa$_6$-sa$_6$-mu⌉
6. ⌈anše⌉ x hur⌉-sağ-ğá⌉⌉
7. traces (seems to end in ⌈mu⌉)
8. traces
9. traces
10. zú-⌈lum ^{na4}za-gìn-mu⌉
11. ù-ne-á-dah-dah
12. ^{d}nidaba

On the right of the rectangle, written horizontally:
   zú-lum ^{na4}za-gìn-mu
   ù-ne-á-dah-dah

The central part of the reverse is very worn, and only traces of signs remain. Lines 7–9 should correspond to the second part of line 3 and the first part of line 4.

Su2 is a round practice tablet with lines 13 and 12 a repeated set of lines on the obverse and at least six lines on the reverse. A fragment on the left edge is now missing; this transliteration is based both on the copy in *MDP* 27 207 and the collation of the tablet in its present state by Mrs. Mernoush Malyeri. In the matrix, the text is entered only once.

1. a-a gub-ba ⌜a⌝ mu-da/ak⌝
2. i ⌜gub⌝-ba še mu-sì
3. a-a gub-ba a mu-x[. . .]
4. i ⌜gub⌝-ba še m[u- . . .]

The reverse is difficult to read. The first four preserved lines are illegible to me and would require detailed study of the original tablet, which is unavailable to me at present. Many of the Susa practice tablets of this type have on the reverse a syllabic version of the Sumerian lines from the obverse, followed by an Akkadian translation, and it may be that this lentil was of that kind. The first lines of the obverse were therefore probably syllabic; then came the translations of the two lines. I can only read the final preserved lines:

i-na ša-ri-im ne-ḫi-im
za-ri-a-am šu-li-i

N8 has three unique lines between 25 and 28:

[. . .]x a gal-gal-la dù-a igi-ni im-m[a- . . .]
[. . . l]ugal-ĝu₁₀ ĝéštu-ĝu₁₀-⌜še⌝ [. . .]
[. . .]x zi mu la⌝-x-x-[. . .]

5. Šulgi to Aradmu 2

(ŠAr2, 3.1.13.1, RCU 8)

Sources

N1 = Ni. 9703 (*ISET* 2 120) iii 2′–9′   =1–8
Tablet: prism.

1. ⌈árad-m[u-ra ù-(na)-a-dug₄]
2. ⌈ᵈšul⌉-[gi lugal-zu na-ab-bé-a]
3. ⌈ᵣa⌉-[ba-in-da-sá-a ugula érin zú-kešda (lugal)]
4. ⌈lú⌉ [. . .]
5. ⌈inim-zu-šè⌉ [. . .] h[é- . . .]
6. érin-bi-šè x [. . .] nu-x[. . .]
7. ba-ni-ib-zà[h?1 . . .] i-[. . .]
8. érin-b[i . . .] x [. . .]
   rest of text broken

¹ [Speak to] Aradm[u], ² [saying (the words) of Š[ulgi, your king]:

³ A[baindasa, captain of the royal army,] ⁴ a man . . . ⁵ According to your message . . . ⁶ To those troops . . . not . . . ⁷ He escaped⁷ . . . ⁸ Those troops . . .

1. Only HA (of HA.A = zàh) is preserved. The only other possible restoration would be ha-[lam. . .].

6. Šulgi to Aradmu 3

(ŠAr3, 3.1.61, RCU 16)

Composite Text

1. ᴵárad-mu-ra ù-na-a-dug₄
2. ᴵᵈšul-gi lugal-zu na-ab-bé-a
3. u₄⁽ᴵ⁾a-ba-an-da-sá ugula érin zú-kešda
4. [x] ù-na-a-dug₄-bi šu-ni mu-un-tak₄-a
5. [x x]-šè⁽ᵎ⁾ dugud(-)RI-dè NIR-da íl-la-zu hu-mu-un-ši-in-gi
6. a-na-aš-àm érin-bi-ta mu-un-zi-zi
7. en-nu-ùĝ-ĝá mu-ni-in-ku₄
8. [saĝ⁽ᵎ⁾ ba]-e-tùm-tùm-ma NIR-da šà-zu-a ba-e-ši-íl-la
9. [lú]-kúr-ra ba-ra-è-a érin-bi-ta gi₄-gi₄-mu-un-na-ab
10. [x (x) ur]-ᵈnamma a-a ugu-ĝu₁₀-ta
11. [x x]x-ra ha-ra-an-kalag šu⁽ᵎ⁾ x-nam
12. [x x]-bi ba-ab-ĝar-re-en-a
13. x x-bi/ga-šè ha-ra-an-kalag x-nam ha-ba-zu-zu
14. u₄ ù-na-a-dug₄-mu šu-ni šu tag₄
15. érin-bi-šè gi₄-gi₄-mu-un-na-ab
16. [. . .]-bi sa₆-ga-zu pàd-dè
17. uru⁽ᵎᵏⁱ⁾-bi nam-ba-an-pe-el-le-en
18. nam-gur₄-bi érin-bi-šè níĝ mu-ra-ab-dug₄
19. ki-saĝ-ĝál-la igi-zu-šè ᵍⁱˢgu-za-àm ha-ra-ab-dúr-dè-en
20. a-ma-ru-kam

¹ Speak to Aradmu, ² saying (the words) of Šulgi, your king:
³ When Abaindasa, captain of the armed forces, ⁴ sent that letter (to me/you)
⁵ . . . important . . . so that he *could confirm* the punishment that you imposed on him.
⁶ Why did you remove him from that regiment ⁷ and throw him in prison? ⁸ Having reduced the punishment that you had imposed by your own volition, ⁹ now that the enemy is coming against you, reinstate him into that regiment!
¹⁰ [*By the order of*] Ur-Namma, the father who begot me, ¹¹ . . . fortress . . . ¹² . . . I/you establish/appoint . . . ¹³ . . . fortress . . . ¹⁴ As soon as my letter concerning him has

326

been sent, [15] reinstate him into that regiment! [16] . . . [17] You must not diminish (the importance) of that city: [18] its importance to that regiment is something that has (already) has been explained to you, [19] so you should install him in a stronghold before you as if on a throne! [20] It is urgent!

Sources

N1 = Ni. 9702 (*ISET* 2 122) i 1′–10′   9–20
X1 = AN1922-163[1] (*OECT* 5 26)   1–20

X1 has deteriorated since it was copied and since I first collated it in 1985.[2]

Tablet typology: Prism: N1, Type III: X1.

Bibliography: Edition: S. N. Kramer, *OECT* 5 13–14.

Textual Matrix

1.   X1 ^{T}árad-mu-ra ù-na-a-dug$_4$

2.   X1 ^{Td}šul-gi lugal-zu na-ab-bé-a

3.   X1   ⌜u$_4$⌝ ¹a-ba-an-⌜da⌝-sá ugula érin zú-kešda

4.   X1   [x] ⌜ù⌝-na-a-dug$_4$-bi šu-ni mu-un-tak$_4$-a

5.   X1   [x x]-šè⌐ dugud(-)RI-⌜dè⌝ NIR-⌜da⌝ íl-la-zu hu-mu-un-ši-in-gi

6.   X1   [a-n]a-⌜aš⌝-àm érin-bi-ta mu-un-zi-zi

7.   X1   [e]n-⌜nu⌝-ùĝ-ĝá mu-ni-in-ku$_4$

8.   X1   [saĝ⌐ ba]-e-tùm-tùm-ma NIR-da šà-zu-a ba-e-ši-íl-la

9.   [lú]   kúr-ra   ba-ra-è-a   érin-bi-ta   gi$_4$-gi$_4$-mu-un-na-ab
N1   o   o   o   o   o   o o   o   o   o   o   .   .   o   o   o
X1   o   .   +   .   .   . +   +   +   .   .   o   .   +   +

10. [x   (x)   ur]-^{d}namma   a-a   ugu-ĝu$_{10}$-ta
N1   o   o   o   .   +   + +   +   .   o
X1   o   o   o   . .   o o   +   +   +

11. [x   x]x-ra   ha-ra-an-kalag   šu⌐ x-nam
N1   [   ]x +   +   +   ⸗   .   .   x   o
X1   o   oooo   .   +   +   o   o   .[3]

---

1. Formerly Ashm. 1922-163.

2. Much of the decay has affected the upper part of the reverse. The current state of the tablet can be seen on the digital photographs included here; a scan of an older museum photograph is included for comparison. The transliteration is based on the earlier state.

3. Followed by the traces of a line on lower edge.

12. [x x]-bi   ba-ab-ğar-re-en-a
N1   [   ] + + + +   . .   o
X1   o oo   o o .   + + +

13. x x-bi/ga-še ha-ra-an-kalag x-nam   ha-ba-zu-zu
N1   o x +   + + + - .   o o   + + o o
X1   o o o   . . . . o   x .   . + + .

14. u₄ ù-na-a-dug₄-ğu₁₀ šu-ni   šu tag₄
N1   + + + - +   +   ab o   o o
X1   o . + + +   +   + +   + +⁴

15. érin-bi-še   gi₄-gi₄-mu-un-na-ab
N1   +   + + + . o o o o
X1   .   . . + + + + + +⁵

16. [...]-bi sa₆-ga-zu pàd-dè
N1   Omits or on previous line.
X1   [...] . .   . . . +

17. uru$^{?ki}$-bi nam-ba-an-pe-el-le-en
N1   .$^?$ + + +   + + + + . o
X1   o o oo o   o o o . . +

18. nam-gur₄-bi érin-bi-še níğ mu-ra-ab-dug₄
N1   + + + +   + + x o o oo o
X1   o   o o o   . . + . . + +

19. ki-sağ-ğál-la igi-zu-še ^{giš}gu-za-àm ha-ra-ab-dúr-dè-en
N1   + + ki + + + . o + + +   h[é]o o o o o
X1   o . . o . . + + . . -   . .   + + + +

20. [a]-ma-ru-kam
N1   omits or on previous line.
X1   o . + +

In N1 followed by ArŠ3 (7).

Colophon D (X1)

4. There must have been half a line of text before this in X1.
5. As in the line above, in X1, this version had words at the beginning of this line that are not present in N1.

Commentary

The reconstruction of this letter is highly tentative, and there may be less harmony between the two sources than meets the eye. X1 has more of the text than N1 but is an inferior manuscript, with many errors. The difficulties are compounded by the current state of preservation of the former. The translation offered here is highly provisional, and everything is subject to revision. The pronominal elements in verbal forms are difficult, and third person may be used when first person is intended; therefore érin-bi may have to be rendered "his regiment," rather than "that regiment." It is possible that this and ŠAr2 (letter 5) are variant recensions of the same letter.

4/14. šu . . . tak₄, "to dispatch," discussed by M. Civil, *AuOr* 8 (1990) 109–11, is used regularly in administrative letters but not in literary ones. The only other occurrence is in letter SEpM 4:4, together with ù-na-dug₄. The unreliable source X1 has the form šu-ni šu-tak₄ in line 14, but this is hardly correct; N1 clearly had something else but only the sign ab- is preserved.

5/8. NIR-da, read either nir-da or šer₇-da, has been vigorously discussed, most recently by M. Civil, *FS Hallo* 75–78, who argues for the meaning "capital offense." The use of this noun with the verb íl is otherwise unattested in Sumerian, but it may be a calque of Akkadian *šērta našû*, "to bear punishment," or even of *šērta emēdu*, "to impose punishment." Compare perhaps *Šulgi Hymn B* 229: NIR-da saĝ ì-túm-túm-ĝá ma-da gal-gal-ĝá suhuš ma-ab-ge-en-ge-en, "*As I reduce punishments/offences*, I solidify the foundations of my great far-flung lands."

5. The sign before dugud appears to be -šè, but this is hardly certain. The interpretation of dugud(-)RI-dè is problematical, because there is no other evidence for /dʳ/ as the final consonant of the root.

18. The níĝ before the finite verb form, preserved only in X1, makes little sense, as one would expect the verb to be subordinated. One cannot be certain, but the poor remains of the equivalent sign in N1 resemble mu more than níĝ.

19. The interpretation of this line, as well as the preceding ones, is highly conjectural and admittedly makes little sense. The two sources are not in perfect harmony. For ki-saĝ-ĝál, possibly "secure place, stronghold," see S. Tinney, *Nippur Lament* 165. N1 has ki-saĝ-ki(-)ĝál, and therefore perhaps we should think of Izi C iii 12–13 [MSL 13 177]): ki-saĝ-ki = (a-šar) [. . .], ki-saĝ-ki = MIN *sak-ki-e*, "place of *s.*-rites:"

7. Aradmu to Šulgi 3

(ArŠ3, 3.1.5, SEpM1a, RCU 7)

Composite Text

1. lugal-ǧu₁₀-ra ù-na-dug₄
2. árad-mu árad-zu na-ab-bé-a
3. ¹a-ba-in-da-sá ugula érin zú-kešda lugal níǧ lugal-ǧu₁₀ ma-an-gi₄
4. lugal-ǧu₁₀ bar inim-ma ha-ba-zu-zu
5. u₄ zi-mu-dar^ki-ra-šè igi-ǧu₁₀ bí-in-ǧar-ra
6. kaskal lugal-ǧu₁₀ érin zi-ga-ǧu₁₀
7. ¹a-ba-in-da-sá érin-bi igi ù-bí-in-kár
8. min li-mu-um érin-bi nu-ǧál
9. x x-ne nu-un-DU nu-un-gi₄
10. ha-ra-kalag lugal-ǧu₁₀ mu-un-tag₄ mu-un-dab₅
11. NIR-da-bi NIR-da lugal-ǧu₁₀ [ba-e]-dugud
12. [. . .]-ma lugal²[. . .] x
13. [. . .]x ni x[. . .]-ǧar
14. níǧ lugal-ǧu₁₀ ab-bé-na-ǧu₁₀
15. lugal-ǧu₁₀ hé-en-zu

¹Speak to my king, ²saying (the words) of Aradmu, your servant:

³(Concerning the matter of) Abaindasa, captain of the royal armed forces, that my king sent me (a message) about; ⁴my king must be informed about the matter.

⁵When I focused my attention on Zimudar, ⁶I was in the process of mustering troops for my king's military service,¹ ⁷but when Abaindasa inspected those troops, ⁸2,000 of those men were missing. ⁹He had not gone to . . ., nor had he returned. ¹⁰He had abandoned the fortress, *o my king, and then (re)captured (it)!* ¹¹That crime was a very serious crime against my king! ¹²⁻¹³ . . .

¹⁴Whatever you, my king order me to do, (I will do)! ¹⁵Now my king is informed (about all of this)!

---

1. Alt. transl.: my king's expedition.

Commentary

In some redactions of SEpM, this composition takes the place of SEpM1. In all four extant manuscripts, it is followed by SEpM2 or by its catch line (see p. 323 above).

4. I know of no other example of bar inim-ma; the translation is conjectural, based on bar . . . ak, "because of."

5. I know of no other example of kaskal lugal in Sumerian. On the face of it, it should mean "royal expedition," but even if it meant that earlier, in OB times it was probably understood as a qalque from Akkadian *ḫarrān šarrim*, which, according to M. Stol, *FS Houwink ten Cate* 300–303 and idem, *OBO* 160/4 748, meant "royal military service." See also J. G and A. Westenholz, *CM* 33 88, citing this line.

11. The reading of the verb is conjectural; most probably this line is echoed—or echoes—ArŠ4 (8): 23.

Sources

N1 = 3 N-T 80 (A 30135, *SL* xxxi) obv. 1–15   =1–15
N2 = CBS 7848²+7856 (*SL* xxxviii) i 1′–10′   =5–15
N3 = Ni. 2786 (*ISET* 2 120)   =3–12; 14–15
N4 = Ni. 4586 (transliteration S. N. Kramer)[3]   =1–11; 15
N5 = Ni. 9702 (*ISET* 2 122) i 11′–13′   =1–3

Tablet typology: Prism: N2, N5, Type III: N1, N3, N4.

Textual Matrix

1. lugal-ğu$_{10}$-ra   ù-na-dug$_4$

N1	o	o	o	.	+	+	
N4	o	o	.	.	+	.	
N5	+	+	+	.	o	o	

2. árad-mu   árad-zu   na-ab-bé-a

N1	o	o	o	o	.	+	+	.
N4	o	.	.	.	.	.	.	.
N5	+	+	+	+	.	o	o	o

---

2. First published as *PBS* 13 46.
3. No photograph is included here; the tablet will be published by Asuman Dönmez.

3. ¹a-ba-in-da-sá ugula érin zú-kešda lugal níǧ lugal-ǧu₁₀ ma-an-gi₄

N1	ooo o o	. a	+	+	+ +	+	+	.	+	.	. +
N3	.. . . . .	o ⌜àga⌝-ús⌝	o o	o	+	+	+	+	o o
N4	ooo . . .	. àga-ús	+	.	+	o	o	.	+	. +
N5	.. + + +	. o	o	o o	o	o	o	o	o o o

4. lugal-ǧu₁₀ bar inim-ma ha-ba-zu-zu

N1	o	o	o	+	+	+ + +	dè
N3	.	+	+	+	+	+ . o o
N4	o	o	o	.	.	. + + .

5. u₄ zi-mu-dar-raᵏⁱ-šè igi-ǧu₁₀ bí-in-ǧar-ra

N1	. .	+ +	+ - +	+	+	+ ib + +
N2	o o o o	o o o o	. . . . .
N3	+ + +	+	+! . .	o o o o o o
N4	o o o o	. . . . . . + + .

6. kaskal lugal-ǧu₁₀ érin zi-ga-ǧu₁₀

N1	o	o	.	+	+ + +
N2	o	o	o	o	. + +
N3	+	+	+	+	. o o
N4	o	o	o	o	. + +

7. ¹a-ba-in-da-sá érin-bi igi ù-bí-in-kár

N1	oo o o + + a +	+	+	+ + + +
N2	oo o o o o o	o	+	+ + - .
N3	+++ + . . .	o	o	o o o o
N4	oo o o o . .	⌜ba⌝	.	. . + +

8. min li-mu-um érin-bi nu-ǧál

N1	o	o . +	+	+ + .
N2	o	o o o	.	+ + +
N3	+	+ + +	.	+ o o
N4	o	o o o	o	. . +

9. x x-ne nu-un-DU nu-un-gi₄

N1	o o .	+ + +	+ o .
N2	o o o o	. .	+ + +
N3	x x .	. . .	. o
N4	o o o	o o o	o . +

10. ha-ra-kalag lugal-ǧu₁₀ mu-un-tag₄ mu-un-dab₅

N1	o o o	.	+	+ + o	+	+ +
N2	o o o	o	o o . + o	. +
N3	+ . +	.	. + o o	o o o
N4	o o o	o	o o x x	. . +

11. NIR-da-bi NIR-da lugal-ğu$_{10}$ [ba-e]-dugud[24]

N1	o	o	.	+	.	o	o	o	x	.
N2	o	o o o		o	o	o		o o	.
N3	.	. .	o		o o		.	o o o
N4	traces

12. [. . .]-ma lugal$^?$[. . .]x

N1	[. . .]+ . [. . .]
N2	[ ]x
N3	[. . .]x . . [. . .]

13. [. . .]x ni x[. . .]-ğar

N1	o	x	+	x	o	.
N2	o	o	o o	o	+	
N3	traces

14. níğ lugal-ğu$_{10}$ ab-bé-na-ğu$_{10}$

N1	o	o	.	+	o	o	o[5]
N2	o	o	o	o o	.	+	
N3	.	.	.	. .	.	o	
N4	traces

15. lugal-ğu$_{10}$ hé-en-zu

N1	o	o	+	o	o
N2	o	o	o	.	+
N3	+	+	+	+	o
N4	o	o	.	.	.

In N1 and N2 followed by SEpM2.

Catchline N3: lugal-ğá ù-na-[dug$_4$] followed by upside down lugal-ğá ù-na-dug$_4$
Catchline N4: [. . . -ra ù-n]a-du[g$_4$]

Both catch lines reference SEpM2.

---

4. Only the very end of the final sign is preserved in both N1 and N2.
5. Possibly room for [ga-ab-ak].

8. Aradmu to Šulgi 4

(ArŠ4)

Source

X1 = MS 2199/2
collated by Konrad Volk.
Tablet: Type III.

Text Transliteration

1. ⌈lugal-ĝu₁₀-ra⌉ ù-na-a-⌈dug₄⌉
2. ⌈árad⌉-mu árad-zu ⌈na-ab⌉-bé-⌈a⌉
3. u₄ lugal-ĝu₁₀ kíĝ ⌈lugal?⌉ è-[dè] mu-e-ši-in-⌈gi₄?⌉
4. u₄ érin-bi-šè bí-in-⌈te⌉-a-ĝu₁₀
5. ra-hi sí-ik-ka-tum ugula nu-bànda érin daĝal-⌈la lugal-ĝá⌉-ke₄
6. silim-ma lugal-ĝá-ke₄ èn mu-un-⌈tar-re⌉-eš
7. lugal-me u₄-da-rí-šè hé-ti gù in-na-⌈dé?⌉-eš
8. kíĝ-bi-šè te-ĝá-da-mu-ne
9. kíĝ lugal-ĝu₁₀ mu-un-gi₄ igi ù-bí-kár
10. lú NIR-da NIR-da ⌈šu?⌉ bí-in-šúm
11. lú nam-tag nam-tag bí-íb-íl-e
12. lú kíĝ-bi tab-ba-a-ni mah-bi al-lá-e
13. ⌈á⌉-ni ud-bi-e kù al-lá-e
14. ⌊a-⌈ba-an⌉-da-sá ugula ⌈érin⌉ ⌈zú⌉-kešda ⌈lugal⌉-ĝá-ke₄
15. lú érin-a gi₄-gi₄ lugal-ĝu₁₀
16. [kí]ĝ lugal-ĝu₁₀ mu-un-šub bàd im-mi-in-dù
17. [lug]al-ĝu₁₀ ⌈inim⌉-ma ⌈nu-húl?⌉-le-dè
18. ᵈšul-gi-x-x-x lú-kaš₄-e im-⌈mi⌉-in-⌈gin?⌉-na?
19. gú mu-un-dù-a-ak-ke₄-⌈eš⌉ lú-kíĝ-gi₄-⌈a-ĝu₁₀⌉ nu-x-x
20. x x lugal x di-ne ĝá-e ù-x-du-x
21. x x-bi mu-un-gul NIR-⌈da⌉ bí-íb-⌈íl-e⌉
22. ⌈ù⌉ érin-bi-šè íb-⌈zi⌉-zi

334

23. NIR-da-bi NIR-da lugal-⌜g̃u₁₀⌝ ba-e-⌜dugud⌝
24. lú mìn-kam-ma šu-ni-ta ha-ba-ab-lá-e
25. ⌜NIR⌝-da ⌜šu⌝-ni-ta ⌜bí-íb⌝-g̃ar
26. [níg̃?] ⌜lugal-mu⌝ ab-bé ga-mu-na-ab-⌜dù?⌝
27. [luga]l-g̃u₁₀ hé-en-zu
28. [u₄?]-⌜bi-ta⌝ lugal-⌜g̃u₁₀?⌝ inim-ma nam-⌜ba⌝-ab-šub-bé-en
29. [in]im ⌜lugal⌝-g̃u₁₀ ba-ra-ab-⌜bal⌝-e
Colophon D

[1] Speak to my king, [2] saying (the words) of Aradmu, your servant:
[3] When my king dispatched me to . . . the task, [4] once I approached those troops, [5] the generals, lieutenants, and captains of my king's far-flung troops [6] inquired about the health of my king; [7] and shouted out 'Long Live the King!'" [8] When I was close to the work(-site), [9] after I inspected the work that my king had sent me to, [10] the one guilty of a capital offence was handed over for execution, [11] the sentenced had to bear their punishment. [12] The one who doubled his work-(load) was very well paid, [13] his wages were paid out in silver for each day.

[14] Abaindasa, the captain of the royal armed forces, [15] who had been returned to the ranks by my king, [16] abandoned the task (assigned by) my king and applied himself to work on building the fortifications. [17] My king, because the orders were not being . . . [18] Šulgi-x dispatched? a messenger, . . .[19] but because he rebelled . . . but could not send my messenger. [20] . . . [21] He destroyed/broke . . . and had to bear punishment [22] and was ousted from that troop. [23] That crime was a very serious crime against my king! [24] After he was entrusted to a second man [25] (that man) carried out the punishment.

[26] Whatever my king orders me, I will do. [27] My king should know (about all this). [28] From this very [day] on, I will never neglect my king's orders! [29] My kings [orders?] must never be transgressed!

Commentary

The transliteration was made from photographs in November of 2005. I was able to make collations, but due to the imperfect state of preservation of the tablet, a proper edition will require more time with the original. Subsequently, the tablet was baked and cleaned, and I was fortunate enough to obtain new photographs courtesy of Andrew George. Later, in June 2009, Konrad Volk kindly collated my edition against the original.

The writing on this tablet continues uninterrupted from the obverse to the reverse, covering the lower edge. Two of the three lines on that edge (20–21) are difficult to read; additional conservation may make it all easier to decipher. The Sumerian of this letter leaves much to be desired, even more so than some of the other CKU items.

5. The title ra-bi sí-ik-ka-tum is a loan from *rabi sikkati/um*, a high military rank in early OB but unattested in Ur III. It may designate the approximate equivalent to "general," that is Ur III šakkana and later OB *šāpir Amurrî* (ugula mar.tu, Babylon, Hammurabi and later) or *rabi Amurrî* (gal mar.tu, Mari and Ešnunna).[1] The earliest attestations are found in the literary correspondence of the Isin kings Iddin-Dagan and Lipit-Eštar (letters SEpM2–5). The sequence of military ranks does not correspond to anything we know from any specific period and probably represents an 18th-century garbling of early OB titles.

6–7. On this salutation, see the commentary to ArŠ1: 10 (1).

18. The reading of the beginning of the line is highly uncertain but it undoubtedly contains a personal name that begins with Šulgi.

22. The verb zi, when used of workers/troops, means "to muster," but here it is used with the allative case, which is unusual. The broken context does not help matters, but it is possible that this has to be connected with ŠAr3: 6–7 (6) a-na-aš-àm érin-bi-ta mu-un-zi-zi, en-nu-ùĝ-ĝá mu-ni-in-ku$_4$, "Why did you remove him from that regiment and throw him into prison?" Otherwise, one would have to ignore the case ending and render the line as "he mustered all of these workers/troops."

23. This line apparently also occurs in ArŠ3: 11 (6).

28–29. The restorations in these lines are conjectural; one would expect a genitive construction with lugal-ĝu$_{10}$ in both lines. Either this is simply a bad rendition from the Akkadian (which underlies much of this text, as it does with other letters) or it is a parenthetical interjection, literally, "From this very [day] on, I will never neglect orders, O my king! [(Your) orders?], O my king, must never be transgressed!"

---

1. See R. Pientka-Hinz, *FS Haase* 53–70. On military ranks in OB times, see, most recently, D. Charpin, *OBO* 160/4 282 and M. Stol, *OBO* 160/4 801–13. For a somethat different Old Assyrian usage of the title, see, most recently, C. Brinker, *AoF* 37 (2010) 49–62.

9. Aradmu to Šulgi 5

(ArŠ5, 3.1.6, RCU 6)

Source

Si1 = CBS 346 (*PBS* 10/4 8)   1–14
Tablet: Type III.
Bibliography: Editions: C. Wilcke, *WO* 5 (1969–70) 2–3, B. Sullivan, *Sumerian and Akkadian Sentence Structure*, 153–55.

Text Transliteration

Obverse

1. [lugal-ğu$_{10}$-ra] ù-ne-[dug$_4$]
2. ⌜l⌝árad-mu árad-zu na-ab-bé⌝-[a]
3. lugal-ğu$_{10}$ inim-zu inim an-na níğ nu-kúr-[ru-dam]
   ⟨ ⟩ *a-wa-at-ka a-wa-at a-nim ša* ⌜*la*⌝ [*ut-ta-ka-ru*]
4. nam-tar-ra-zu diğir-gin$_7$ šu-zu ğar-⌜ra⌝-[(àm)]
   ⌜*ši*⌝-*ma-tu-ka ki-ma* DIĜIR *šu-ut-lu-ma-*[*ni-kum*]
5. bàd lugal-ğu$_{10}$ šu mu-un-gi$_4$ kíğ-bi ⌜ki⌝-b[i-šè im-ma]-ğar
   ⟨ ⟩ ⌜*ša*⌝ *be-lí ú-ša-lim-x ši-pí-ir-šu* ⌜*a*⌝-[*na aš-ri-šu aš*]-*ku-un*
6. ğiri lú kúr-e ^{ka}kalam-šè ba-⌜bad⌝-[(re$_6$)]
   še-ep na-ak-ri a-⌜*na*⌝ *ma-tim pa-ar-*⌜*sa-at*⌝
7. ⌜mu⌝ mah lugal-ğu$_{10}$ ⌜sig⌝ igi-⌜nim⌝-ma
   šu-ma-am ṣi-rum ša be-lí-ia ⌜*iš-tu*⌝ *ma-tim e-li-*⌜*tim*⌝ *a-na* ⟨ ⟩
8. ^{d}utu-è-ta u$_4$-šú-uš zag-šè kalam til-la-a mi-ni-in-túm-⌜túm⌝-mu
   ⌜*iš*⌝-*tu* ⟨ ⟩ *a-na* ⟨ ⟩ *a-na pa-ṭe$_4$* ⌜*gi*⌝-*mi-ir-ti ma-tim i-tam-mi-*⌜*ra*⌝
9. amurrum gú-érim bí-in-ğar ní-bi ⌜im-ma⌝-x-x [. . .]
   ki-ša-tum šu? ú-x-al na-ak?-[*ri* . . .]
10. ^{l}kur-gam-ma-bi ⌜^{d}šul⌝-gi-ra túm-⌜mu?⌝ x [. . .] x(eras.) har-ra-an-kalag igi
    hur-⌜sağ⌝-[ğá-ka . . .]
    ku-un-ši-ma-tum a-⌜*na*⌝ ⟨ ⟩ [. . .] *a-na ḫal-ṣí ša pa-*⌜*ni*⌝ [*ša-di-i* . . .]

337

11. ⌈ù⌉ a-ba-àm-da-⌈sá⌉ [. . .]
    〈   〉
12. ⌈im-sar-re lugal-ğu₁₀⌉ [. . .]
    ⌈ṭup⌉-pí x(eras.) be-lí-⌈ia⌉ [. . .]
13. níğ lugal-ğu₁₀ ab-[bé-na-(ğu₁₀ ga-ab-ak)]
    ⌈ša⌉ be-lí [i-qa-bu-ú (lu-pu-uš)]
14. [lugal]-⌈ğu₁₀⌉ [hé-en-zu]

¹ Speak to my king, ² saying (the words) of Aradmu, your servant:
³ My king, your pronouncements are as the pronouncements of An that cannot (ever) be changed. ⁴ Your destiny has been bestowed to you as to a god! ⁵ And as for the fortifications that my king commissioned me to finish, I have restored the work to its previous condition. ⁶ (As a result) the enemy's access to the frontier territory has been blocked. ⁷⁻⁸ My king's name supreme illuminates (everything) from North to South, from East to West, to the borders of the entire homeland. ⁹ The enemy Amorites. . . . ¹⁰ Kurgamabi (Akk.: Kunši-matum) to Šulgi . . . the fortress Igihursağa . . . ¹¹ And Abaindasa . . .

¹′ The tablet(s)/written (instructions) that my king . . . ²′ Whatever you, my king or[der me to do, (I will do)].

³′ Now my king [is informed] (about all of this)!

Commentary

The tablet that preserves this letter is most probably from Sippar (Abu Habba; part of the so-called Khabaza Collection at the University Museum, Philadelphia). From our vantage point, it is difficult to know if it is the work of a clever, innovative student or of an incompetent one (an unpublished duplicate shows quite a bit of variation). The pastiche combines standard hymnic language, as in lines 3, 4, and 7, with ideas taken from other CKU letters. The tablet is fragile, overbaked, and has deteriorated somewhat over the years; the transliteration reflects the state of affairs before conservation.

1. The writing ù-ne-dug₄ (for ù-na-a-dug₄) is found primarily in northern and peripheral texts but also at Ur. As is the case with all known bilingual letters, except for the *Letter to Zimri-Lim* and one glossed manuscript of SEpM6 (Uk1), the Akkadian version does not include the opening formula.

3. Compare *Letter of Ursaga to a King* (SEpM 6) 7: inim-zu inim diğir-ra-gin₇ hur nu-gi₄-gi₄-dam, "your command is like that of a god, it cannot be revoked."

4. šu-zu. . .gar is an unorthodox writing for šu-zi. . .ğar, as the Akkadian translation indicates. It cannot be ruled out that the writer had in mind šu-zu-šè ğar, because the Sumerian verbs are semantically almost equivalent, but the parallel with *Lugale* I 25 supports the Akkadian translation (OB: ᵈnin-urta du₁₁-ga-zu nu-kúr-ru nam-tar-ra-zu šu-zi-dè-eš ǧ[a]r, Late: ^{d}nin-urta du$_{11}$-ga-zu nu-kúr-ra nam-tar-ra-zu šu-šè bí-[. . .] = ^{d}MIN *qí-bit-ka ul ut-tak-kar ši-ma-tu-ka šu-ut-lu-[ma]*). The equivalence šu-zi. . .ǧar = *šu-ut-lu-mu-u[m]* is also documented in Nigga B 132 (*MSL* 13 118). šu-zi. . .ǧar is a poetic equivalent of šúm, just as the Akkadian *šutlumum* is a poetic equivalent of *nadānum* (see W. P. Römer, *HSAO* 1 196; T. J. H. Krispijn, *FS Veenhof*, 253–54).

5. The first verb is apparently šu. . .gi$_4$ = *šullumum*, "to guard, to finish (a task)." This equivalence is also attested lexically (šu-gi$_4$ = *šu-ul-lu-mu-um*, Nigga Bil. B 139 [*MSL* 13 118]) but the usage is otherwise unknown in Sumerian, to my knowledge. Once again, the author was thinking in Akkadian, although the Sumerian is syntactically somewhat deficient. This makes little sense here; Sullivan, *Sumerian and Akkadian Sentence Structure*, 153 proposed reading "kin!" rather than šu, and the Akkadian equivalent as *ú-ša-⟨aš⟩-p[i?-ru-n]i*, but collation does not support either reading.

The end of the line is now broken, but the tablet at one time had -ǧar. The restoration of both versions is tentative and is based on the assumption that the penultimate visible sign in the Sumerian is ki rather than di. The verb ki-bi-šè. . .ǧar means both "to firm up, consolidate," as well as "restore" (Å. Sjöberg, *ZA* 63 [1973] 15–16).

6. It is difficult to gauge if the Sumerian or the Akkadian are primary here. M. Civil quoted this line in *MSL SS* 1 90, noting the equivalence between Akkadian *šēpa parāsu* and the Sumerian ǧìri bad. In the MB exercise cited there on p. 89, the Sumerian is somewhat different: ǧìri si-il-la-ab = *še-pa-am pu-ru-us*. The usage here is most likely a back-translation from the Akkadian *šēpam parāsum*, "to block access." See, perhaps, also *Šulgi Hymn B* 70: gù šubtum-ma ki ǧìri ku$_5$-da-ba eden-ba hu-mu-un-si-si-ig, "I silence the clamor (of battle) in ambush at the place where the road is blocked off, in the wilderness" (translation uncertain).

7. Note the writing *ṣi-rum* for *ṣi-ram*.

8. The translation of the verb is based on the Akkadian (*namārum*). I do not understand the relationship between this and the Sumerian equivalent túm-túm.

9. The scribe clearly had problems with Sumerian; he took apart gú-érim, "vile/enemy," and glossed the first element as *kiššatum*, "totality," on the basis of gú = *kišādum*, "neck," thinking of gú = *napḫārum*.

10. I discussed this line in *JAOS* 95 (1975) 717. *Kunši-mātum*, literally "Submit, O Land," was the name of the Ur princess who was married into the house of the north Mesopotamian principality of Simanum. Eventually, this led to the intervention by Šu-Sin's forces, when the royal family of Simanum was ousted from power. The historical issues are debated in the *JAOS* article; here the concern must be philological. Kunši-matum is well attested in Ur III sources (see above, p. 159), and it is unlikely that a Sumerian equivalent to the name kur-gam-ma-bi would have been used in a contemporary letter. In order to explain this peculiar situation, two possibilities might be entertained here. One envisages an OB scribe providing a learned translation of the Akkadian name back into Sumerian. It is likewise possible that the error was more complex. The original had kur gam-ma-bi, "the land that had submitted," and when that was mistranslated as *kunšī mātum*, "bow down, O land," it reminded someone of the Akkadian name Kunši-matum (attested as an elite priestess name in OB Mari [J. M. Durand, *LAPO* 18 386–87]), and the Sumerian was then reinterpreted as a personal name. It is quite possible, in this scenario, that the OB scribes had no idea that there actually was an Ur III princess by that name.

Note that the scribe modified the name of the Bad-Igihursaĝa fortifications into Harankalag-Igihursaĝa and then translated this literally into Akkadian.

11. Note that there is no personal name classifier in this line; the passage is broken and therefore it is impossible to ascertain if the scribe was once again confused or if he intended to refer to the man who is the subject of so many other Šulgi letters.

10. Aradmu to Šulgi 6
(ArŠ6, 3.1.4, RCU 5)

Source

X1 = IM 13712 (*Sumer* 15 [1959] pl. 6; *TIM* 9 39)
Tablet: Type III.
Not collated. P. Steinkeller and J. Black both tried to check the original but the
tablet could not be located in Baghdad.
Bibliography: Edition: J. J. van Dijk, *Sumer* 15 (1959) 10–12.

Text Transliteration

Obverse

1. ⌜lugal⌝-ĝu$_{10}$-ra ù-na-a-dug$_4$
2. [$^{(1)}$árad-m]u árad-zu ⌜na⌝-ab-bé-a
3. [lugal]-⌜ĝu$_{10}$⌝ ma-da daĝal-la ⌜nam-en-na⌝-aš mu-ra-an-šúm-ma-a
4. [g]ù-téš-a sì-ke ⌜dím-ma⌝-bi aša-⌜àm⌝
5. [u]n ú-gin$_7$ lu-lu ^{d}šul-gi-ra sipa ⌜níĝ$^?$-gi⌝-na-bi
6. [na]m-lú-ùlu sig ⌜igi-nim-ma⌝ diĝir-bi za-e-⌜me-en⌝
7. ⌜igi$^?$⌝-bi ⌜ma-ra-ši-ĝál⌝
8. [u]n daĝal-la ú-gin$_7$ lu-lu ⌜a⌝ mah ^{id}idigna ^{id}buranun-na-ta
9. [. . .]x ^{id}idigna-⌜šè⌝ ⌜lugal⌝-ĝu$_{10}$ sá ma-ab-du$_{11}$-ga
10. [. . .]x ⌜íb⌝-zi-zi
11. [...b]a$^?$-⌜da⌝-an-ĝar
12. [. . .]x-ak-en
13. [. . .]-⌜kal-la⌝-bi
14. [. . .]x x bí-si
Rest of obverse broken

Reverse

1′ [. . .]x
2′ [. . .]-⌜an-tuk⌝-a

3′ [. . .]x-me-en
4′ [. . . .]x x x
5′ [. . .] ⸢dumu?⸣ ma-da⸢¹⸣ gu-⸢tu-ú?⸣-um^ki
6′ [. . .]x ⸢ma/má?⸣-rí^ki ù ra-pí-qum^ki
7′ [x?] x tuk-tuku-ne igi-ǧá ì-ǧál
8′ níǧ lugal-ǧu₁₀ ab-bé-na ga-ab-ak

¹ Speak to my king, ² saying (the words) of Aradmu, your servant:
³ Your Majesty, the far-flung territories that have been given to you to rule—⁴ they are obedient, and of one mind. ⁵⁻⁶ You are the rightful shepherd of Šulgi's people, numerous as blades of grass, ⁶the god of mortals/the population, of the lower and the upper (lands), ⁷ *they look to you (with reverence)*! ⁸ The teeming peoples, numerous as blades of grass, from the mighty waters of the Tigris and Euphrates,⁹ . . . of the Tigris, that my lord has *entrusted to me*, . . .

⁵′ . . . citizens? of the land of Gutium, ⁶′ . . . Mari? and Rapiqum, ⁷′ who have . . . are before me. ⁸′ Whatever you, my king, order me to do, I will do.

Commentary

3. The line is damaged; without the opportunity for collation, one can only speculate on the proper reading. J. J. van Dijk, *Sumer* 15 (1959) 10, transliterated it as: [lugal]-mu ma-da-dagal-la nì na[m-r]a-aš mu-ra-an-sì-ma-a but this seems improbable. One could also restoration the broken section as kadra or níǧ-ba. In defense of my reading, see *Letter to Zimrilim* 14: kur-kur daǧa[l nam-en-na-aš mu-na-an]-šúm-uš = *ma-ta-ti [r]a-ap-ša-ti a-na be-li-im id-di-nu-šu*, "(and) have given the far-flung lands to him to rule," and ŠPul: 4–5 (14): kur-kur ùǧ daǧal-la an-né ᵈen-líl-le, nam-en-na-bi ma-an-šúm-mu-uš = *mātāti niši rapāšti Anu u Enlil, ana bēli iddinūni* (reconstructed).

5. Compare *Letter of Sin-idinnam to Utu* 25: érin-a-ni ú-gin₇ lu-lu-(a)/àm nu-mun-a-ni daǧal-la, "their troops are as numerous as blades of grass, their offspring far-flung." The sign before gi-na may have been erased. The most probable reading would be inim, but the remains are too short for this sign. Note that sipa níǧ-gi-na (if correctly read) is an epithet of Nur-Adad and Sin-iddinam.

The syntax of the line is problematical: I take it to be a complex anticipatory genitive: uǧ u.gin lu.lu šulgir.ak sipa niǧ.gin.a.bi.

7. The interpretation of the verbal form igi-bi ma-ra-ši-ǧál is conjectural. Another possibility is to view this as a variant of igi . . . ǧar, "to present the matter," commonly found in Ur III protocols of legal proceedings and in the Ibbi-Sin correspondence. See p. 400 below.

9. The final verb is not clear. One could read silim-ma ab-du₁₁-ga, "after having hailed . . ."

5′–6′. Two of these three place and "ethnic" names, Mari and Gutium, are known from Ur III texts; the first requires no comment:

a. Gutium. This geographical/ethnic name is almost always written gu-ti-um$^{(ki)}$ from Sargonic through Old Babylonian times. In the time frame of interest to us, it is known from the *Utuhegal Inscription*, the *Curse of Agade* (155), as well as from various royal hymns of Ur III kings (*Ur-Namma Hymn C*: 90, *Šulgi Hymn B*: 267, *Šulgi Hymn D*: 230, 346), from the *Lamentation over the Destruction of Sumer and Ur*, and from the *Sumerian King List*, always written gu-ti-um$^{(ki)}$ (the Ur III version of the *King List* has um-ma-núm^{ki} [P. Steinkeller, *FS Wilcke* 280]). All of these are, of course, known only from Old Babylonian versions and may not reflect Ur III writing conventions. It is not attested in any Ur III document but occurs in Arad-Nanna's dedication to Šu-Sin, where it is written ma-da gu-te-bu-um^{ki} (D. Frayne, *RIME* 3/2 324: 18) and gu-du-ma-ka in an unpublished Ur III clay cylinder with a copy of the *Laws of Ur-Namma* (courtesy of M. Civil). An Ur III? tablet copy of a monumental inscription of Ur-Namma preserves dumu gu-tim-um-ma and ma-da gu-tim-um^{ki} (D. Frayne, *RIME* 3/2: 67: iii′ 4′ and iv′ 4′).

b. Rapiqum, whose precise location has not been determined, is not attested before Old Babylonian times. It is generally agreed that it was situated on the Euphrates, either close to Ramadi or to Fallugah (Charpin 1999: 95). Rapiqum was strategically important in OB times, but there is not a single reference to a place by that name in Ur III or earlier documents; this suggests that we are dealing here with an anachronism.

Edzard and Farber, *RGTC* 3: 157, followed by D. Charpin, *FS Renger* 102 n. 27, proposed that the Ur III place name ra-NE^{ki} is to be read ra-bí/pi$_5$-qí. This is highly improbable for philological as well as geographical reasons. I know of no other Ur III example in which final /ki/ could be read in such a fashion in a place name, and the few occurrences of ra-NE^{ki} do not favor a Euphratean setting but instead point to a trans-Tigridian location. The GN occurs only three times, and in two of the three it is associated with other localities that lay beyond the Tigris. Thus, in *BIN* 3 139:3 (AS 7.8.13) and in *PDT* 2 959 the érin ra-NE^{ki} are listed together with those from places such as Išum, Arman, Tiran, Hamazi, and Karhar, all of which lay in the east. The third occurrence of this toponym, *OIP* 122 72, only tells us that there was a man by the name of za-an-nu-um who was a lú ra-NE^{ki}.

11. Ur-dun to Šulgi 1

(UdŠ1, 3.1.11.1, 14)

Source(s)

X1 = YBC 5011   = 1–20
Tablet: Type III.
Bibliography: Translation: H. Neumann, *TUAT* nf 3 (2006) 17–19.

Text Transliteration

1. lugal-ĝu$_{10}$-ra ù-na-a-ʿdug$_4$ʾ
2. ur-dun dam-gàr árad-zu na-ab-bé-a
3. kù lugal-ĝu$_{10}$ mu-e-ne-šúm-ma
4. kur sù-rá-šè šim ^{ĝiš}eren-na
5. sa$_{10}$-sa$_{10}$-dè mu-e-ši-gi-na
6. u$_4$ kur-šè ⟨BI⟩ ku$_4$-re-na-ĝu$_{10}$
7. šim ^{ĝiš}eren-na bí-sa$_{10}$-sa$_{10}$-ĝu$_{10}$
8. ᴵa-pi-la-ša gal-zu-unken-na ma-an-gi-ma
9. šám-ĝu$_{10}$ mu-da-an-kar-re-eš
10. ká é-gal-la-ni ù-um-gub
11. lú na-me ka-ĝu$_{10}$ èn nu-bi-tar
12. ᴵarad-mu arad-zu ù ba$_4$-ba$_4$-ti pisaĝ-dub-ʿbaʾ
13. zi-mu-dar^{ki}-ra-ta si-mu-ur$_4$-ʿruʾ-um^{ki}-šè
14. ì¹-re-eš-ma
15. [(x) i]n-ne-zu-ʿmaʾ
16. [lú-kí]ĝ-gi$_4$-a-ne-ne in-ʿšiʾʾ-g[i$_{(4)}$ʾ. . .]
17. [(x)]x lugal-ĝá ba-e-ni-x[. . .]
18. ʿusu$_9$ʾ nu-tuku á-dar-re-bi nu-mu-ʿda-ĝarʾʾ
19. du$_{11}$-ga lugal mu-ra-an-šúm
20. níĝ lugal-ĝu$_{10}$ ab-bé-na-ĝu$_{10}$

Colophon F

    1. Followed by an erasure.

[1] Speak to my king, [2] saying (the words) of Ur-dun, commercial agent, your servant:

[3] My king gave me capital [4-5] and dispatched me to a distant highlands to purchase juniper resin. [6] But once I had entered the highlands [7] and purchased the resin, [8] the prefect Apilaša dispatched (his people) to me, and [9] they appropriated my purchases. [10] When I stood at the gate of his (local) palace, [11] no one wanted to investigate my complaint.

[12] And as for Aradmu, your servant, and Babati, the high commissioner, [14] they had gone [13] from Zimudar to Simurum, [15] *and to inform them.* . . , [16] [they have sent] their messengers. [17] My king. . . . [18] This confiscation cannot be undone without using force. [19] O king, (my messenger) has given you my accounting (of the matter). [20] Whatever you, my king, order me to do, (I will do).

Commentary

This text contains syllabic writings: gi for gi_4 (5, 8), bi for bí (11), ba_4 (PISAG̃) for ba (12) and was clearly written or even composed by someone whose grasp of Sumerian grammar and writing was idiosyncratic, to say the least. The addressee is not mentioned by name, but one can safely assume that it was construed as a Šulgi letter. Only letters from his reign mention Aradmu and Apilaša. Indeed, as cleverly explained by F. Huber (*ZA* 91 [2001]: 181), the writer of this text used ŠAr1 (1) as a model for the beginning of this letter. The addition of Babati and of the city of Simurum, both taken from the Šu-Sin correspondence, is but one more indication of the spurious nature of this letter.

2. The conventional reading of the name of the sender is uncertain. J. Bauer, *BiOr* 50 170 and *JAOS* 115 (1995) 295 prefers Ur-šul and suggests that this is an abbreviation for a theophoric name such as ur-^{d}šul-pa-è or ur-^{d}šul-šà-ga-na but without any justification. The name is well attested in Pre-Sargonic Girsu (there is even a dam-gàr, *BIN* 8 175: 2–3) and in Ur III. Two Drehem texts provide the explicit writing ur-dun-na (*Trouvaille* 24: 7, *RA* 9 [1912] 55 SA 224); an Umma tablet has ur-^{d}dun (*YOS* 4 237: iv 96). The abbreviation appears unlikely, because both Ur-dun and Ur-Šulpae are common Ur III names and I know of no instance where both mark the same individual (the name Ur-Šulšagana does not occur during this period).

3. I have understood the final -ma in this line as the Akkadian conjunction, as is the case in line 8 below. The verb has a third-person plural dative prefix; this can only be analyzed as an anticipation of the names of Aradmu and Babati in line 12 but is probably simply wrong, as is the verbal form in line 5. The author had problems with Sumerian prefixes and confused first and second singular as well as third-person plural forms.

4. The traditional translation "cedar" for eren is imprecise. It is clear that ancient plant names did not correspond precisely to modern ones from a taxonomic point of view. This label was used in Sumerian for a range of conifers, aromatic woods that produced sap, perhaps including "cedar," which the Mesopotamians obtained from the west, as well as pine and, more precisely, juniper. There is no pollen evidence that cedars ever grew in western Iran. Juniper (*Juniperus excelsa*), however, covered much of the Zargos in early times.[2] There is evidence, both literary and archival, that in the third and second millennia, parts of the eastern mountain areas were thought of as kur ᵍⁱˢeren-na (P. Michalowski, *JCS* 30 [1978]: 118), a term that is referenced obliquely here but is present in another OB literary letter: *Letter of Iddatum to Sumu-tara* 3–4: lú-kíǧ-gi₄-a kur ᵍⁱˢeren-na zag x[. . .], igi-ǧu₁₀-šè gú mu-un-ǧar-re-eš-ma, "envoy(s) from the Juniper Mountains . . . have gathered before me." For a discussion of the various problems involved, see J. Klein and K. Abraham, 44th *RAI*: 65–66; the Semitic etymology of eren and the translation "juniper" will be discussed in detail by Leonid Kogan in a forthcoming study.

5. The writing gi must stand for gi₄, "to send, dispatch," with the prefix -ši-. The final vowel a must stand for the copula -àm, hence mu.e.ši.gi.en.am, literally "I sent to you;" hardly a correct form given the context.

6. In view of the grammatical knowledge and writing habits of this scribe, it is difficult to second-guess his or her intentions. It seems that after kur-šè the scribe began to write ŠIM, in dittography from the line above and/or in anticipation of the following line, thought better of it, and just moved on.

8. The translation is based on the assumption that the verb gi is a syllabic writing of gi₄, as in line 5. One would, however, expect the prefix -ši-.

9. This is a crucial line in the text, because it spells out the actual wrong committed by Apilaša. The verb is kar (with -da-), in the meaning of *ekēmu*, "to take away (by force)," in the third-person plural. The object is šám-mu, which requires explication. At first glance, one is tempted to understand this as níǧ-šám, "price" (P. Steinkeller, *Sale Documents* 161). This makes little sense; it may be preferable to view this as a form of níǧ-šám-ma, "purchases" (note níǧ-šám-ma, SEpM 15: 14 but here meaning "price"); see now C. Wilcke, *Early Ancient Near Eastern Law*, 78.

10–11. This is clearly derived from ArŠ1: 9–10 (1) ká é-gal-la-šè gub-a-gu₁₀-ne silim-ma lugal-ǧá-ke₄ èn li-bí-in-tar. The verbal form nu-bi-tar is incorrect. The reading ka is based on the assumption that the predicate is a calque from Akkadian *pû*+PRO *ša'alu*; see the examples in CAD Š/1 277.

12. Note the almost automatic arad-zu after Aradmu's name; note also arad, as opposed to árad in line 2. The scribe mindlessly inserted this from his studies of letters from the prime minister to the king. Note the writing ba₄-ba₄-ti for ba-ba-ti; the value ba₄ of PISAǦ is usually used only in the writing of the name of the Kish deity

---

2. This is a complex issue that requires a longer study; see, conveniently, Naomi F. Miller, *Journal of Ethnobiology* 5 (1985): 1–19.

dza-ba₄-ba₄; the only other example of such a writing in this personal name comes from the OB copy of his seal inscription published by C. Walker, *JCS* 35 (1983) 91:7. The figure of Babati, with his title, is taken from ŠuŠa1: 35 (letter 19).

15. H. Neumann, *TUAT* n.f. 3, 19 n. 91 writes: "Die Zeichenspuren am Anfang der Zeile (kollationiert) legen einen Kohortativ nahe: [g]i₄-in-ne-zu-m[a]." I do not see the remains of gi₄ at the beginning of the line. I also doubt that the OB scribe who concocted this letter would have known about the Ur III usage of gi₄- to express the cohortative mode.

18. The restorations in this line are uncertain. The translation is based on á . . . dar, "to cheat, confiscate," for which see A. Falkenstein, *NSGU* II 110, R. de Maaijer and B. Jagersma, *AfO* 44/5 (1997–98) 285 and F. Karahashi, *Sumerian Compund Verbs*, 75; *PSD* A/II 50 renders the line "not having . . . their illegal seizure (confiscation) (of the purchased cedar resin) cannot be. . . ."

19. I take the third-person singular agent of the verb to be the messenger who is carrying the tablet ("epistolary perfect").

12. Aradmu? to Šulgi? 7

(ArŠ7)

Source

Ur1 = *UET* 6/3 561 (*187) obv.; rev. 1'–19'   =1–20
Tablet: Type III.

Text Transliteration

1. [lugal-ĝu₁₀-ra ù-na-(a)-dug₄]
2. [⁽¹⁾árad-mu árad-zu na-ab-bé-a]
3. [. . .]
4. [. . .]
5. [x] (blank space) è-[x] x x
6. [x x x] x gi gíd? u₄-da-gin₇ ur₅? an gal-ta ⌜an⌝-pa-šè e₁₁-[(x)]
7. [x x] árad é lugal-ĝu₁₀ ba-UD-da x-lu
8. [mu ur-d]un dam-gàr-ra-ke₄-eš ⌜níĝ lugal⌝-⌜ĝu₁₀⌝ ma-an-gi₄
9. [ur-d]un árad-zu-gin₇ á-áĝ-ĝá ⌜ì⌝-áĝ⌝-ĝá lugal-ĝu₁₀ ì-zu
10. [x x]x ur-dun nu-du₁₀-ga-ni-ta mu¹-ta-ni-tehi
11. [x] x-ĝá-ni lul sì-sì-ke bí-⌜in⌝-šúm
12. [lugal-ĝ]u₁₀ bar-ĝá èn hé-⌜bí⌝-in-tar níĝ-šà-⌜ga⌝-na ha-ma-an-ak?
13. [(x) x]x-ĝu₁₀ a-gin₇ me-er-⌜ga⌝ gi₄-bi nu-⌜du₁₀-ga-bi?⌝ mu-ra-an-dug₄ lugal-ĝu₁₀
    ì-⌜zu⌝
14. [x x z]i-ta ur-dun dam-gàr-ra ⌜ur₅⌝-gin₇ ka bal-bal-e
15. [x x]x⌜ki?⌝-šè zag-bi-ta na₄-⌜nir₇-babbar₂⌝-dili na₄-duh-ši-a ⌜na₄⌝-za-gìn-na na₄-
    ⌜gug⌝ bar-bi sá-a
16. [x x]x na₄-nir₇⌜(⟨ZA⟩MIR) x ⌜na₄-gug/nir₇?⌝(-)zú-lum dili GAM.GAM NUN.
    KÁR kù-zu x x-bi-a DUB.DUB-me-eš
17. [x x]x ĝál-ta ⌜na₄⌝ [x] ⌜na₄⌝ eme₅ gal kár-kár ĜIŠ? dili-àm x du₁₀-du₁₀-⌜ge
    šu?⌝-x-àm

1. There are additional wedges after mu; either the scribe had problems with the sign or
tried to write du₁₀.

18. [x x]x-la-g̃u₁₀ ⸢kíg̃⸣-bi in-ne-lá
19. [x x]x-àm ⸢ur⸣-dun ⸢šu in-ne-zi-zi-dè⸣ [. . .]
20. traces

Rest of tablet broken

[¹Speak to my king: ²saying (the words of) Aradmu, your servant:]
 [³⁻⁴. . . ⁵. . .] ⁶. . . like the day/sun, coming out from the great above to the zenith, ⁷. . . servant who . . . my master's estate, . . .
 ⁸Concerning the matter of the merchant Ur-dun, that my master dispatched me about, ⁹Ur-dun, as your servant, *was given* instructions; but you, my master, know (this). ¹⁰But Ur-dun approached . . . in deceit. ¹¹(and) his . . . were full of lies. ¹²May my master inquire about my wellbeing, . . . ¹³Why did my . . . speak deceitfully to you not once but twice? But you, my master know (this). ¹⁴By means of. . . , addressing the merchant Ur-dun in the following terms: ¹⁵"To the city [of x], from its border . . . *pappardillu*, chlorite, lapis, carnelian . . ." ¹⁶⁻²⁰ (untranslatable)

Commentary

This letter is preserved only on a broken tablet from Ur. The obverse is almost completely destroyed, and only a few fragmentary signs on the right edge have survived. There are traces of a double line three or four lines up from the bottom of the obverse; this suggests that the letter begins at this point. The traces of the solitary sign visible at the end of that line may be interpreted as ⸢zu⸣, and it is possible that this is the remnant of the closing formula lugal-g̃u₁₀ hé-en-zu.

When two letters are paired on a tablet, one expects a letter to and from the same individual, usually a king. The sender of the second letter cannot be Ur-dun, because he is mentioned in the third person, and so the author is most probably Aradmu and the recipient must be Šulgi. The clues are too sparse to establish if the top of the obverse contained a similarly unique letter or, less probably, the missive from Ur-dun to Šulgi (UdŠ1, 11). The only readable signs on the obverse of this tablet are in 3′, which ends with [. . . -n]a⸣-g̃u₁₀. This could be associated with UrŠ1 6 (11): u₄ kur-šè ⟨BI⟩ ku₄-re-na-g̃u₁₀. This, however, would require 14 more lines of text, and the Ur tablet only had 6 or 7 before the double line. If it indeed contained UrŠ1, then the lines were longer; many of then containing the equivalent of two lines of the one surviving Yale source for that composition, and some lines may have been omitted.

The lack of duplicates and, above all, the use of rare words suggests that this is an Old Babylonian scribal concoction, most probably composed in Ur. The text is extremely difficult, but in view of the contents of the first three preserved lines, it was possibly a poetic letter of petition rather than a prose literary letter, and therefore the beginning may have to be restored appropriately. Note the use of vocabulary derived from the lexical and school epistolary traditions. Needless to say, the translation is a mere approximation. The tablet was studied in person and on photographs but I also benefitted from collations kindly done by Steve Tinney.

10. The restoration of the beginning of the line is most uncertain but much depends on this, because it is not clear from the text, as it presently stands, if Ur-dun is the villain or the victim.

The adjective nu-du₁₀-ga is most likely a calque from Akkadian *la ṭābum*, "wicked, deceitful," that is normally used of words or utterances; see *CAD* Ṭ 26–27.

11. The rare lul . . . sì means "to deceive;" see M. Civil, *FS Lambert*, 109. It is attested in lexical texts and in two Gilgamesh passages (*Gilgamesh and Huwawa A* 152B and *UET* 6 58: 20 [*Gilgameš, Enkidu, and the Netherworld*, Ur Version]). Note, moreover, *Letter of Inim-Inina to Lugal-ibila* (SEpM 22) 7–11: na-an-ga-ma lú na-me lul i-ri-ib-sì-ke, ugu ad-da-na-šè ga-àm-gin a-ra-ab-bé, en-na ĝiškim ĝá-e ù za-e inim ì-bal-en-da-na, lú-(ù) mu-e-ši-in-gi₄-gi₄-(a), lú-tur šu nam-bí-bar-re-en, "From now on (be on guard) for anyone for would try to deceive you and say "I have to go (home)" on the authority of his father! Until you and I have exchanged passwords and I have sent you (my) representative, you must not let the youngster out!"

12. For the first half of the line in letters, see *Letter of Ursaga to a King* (SEpM 6) 10 lugal-ĝu₁₀ bar-ĝá èn (li)-bí-in-tar dumu uriᵏⁱ-ma-me-en and also *MDP* 27 104: 1–2 diĝir-ĝu₁₀ lú kúr-zu nu-me-en ba-ar mi-en-tar-re.

The only other occurrence of níĝ-šà-ga+PRO . . . ak is in *Išme-Dagan Hymn A+V* 97 á-tuku níĝ-šà-ga-na nu-ak lú lú-šè nu-DI, "so that strong men not do simply as they please, that one man does not . . . another man."

13. The word me-er-ga, "one," is otherwise quite rare and occurs only in texts that lie outside the Nippurean Old Babylonian school tradition—the three OB references are from Ur—with one exception in lexical compositions. The only poetic usage known to me is *Rim-Sin Hymn B* 35 (to Haya): nam-ereš diĝir-re-e-ne-ke₄ me-er-ga-bi al-ak-e diĝir sag-du nu-tuku, "(Nidaba) uniquely performs the duties as queen of the gods, and has no divine rival." Like the present letter, this hymn is only attested at Ur (it may actually be in honor of Rim-Sin II); see the sequence mi-ir-ga = *iš-te-en*, [g]i₄-bi = ⌈ša⌉-*nu-ú-um* in the OB lexical text/commentary from Ur, *UET* 7 93:3–4, discussed by Å. Sjöberg, ZA 86 (1996) 220–37 and the Late Babylonian grammatical text *CTMMA* 2 246: 33, me-er-ga = *iš-te-en* (= NBGT IV 33 [*MSL* 4 164]). See now T. Balke, JCS 62 (2010) 46–7.

14. In UdŠ1 (letter 11), Ur-dun writes about his purchase of juniper resin, but the only commodities in this letter are precious stones. In the *Letter of Šamaš-ṭab to Ilak-ni'id* (SEpM 17): 15 the writer asks the recipient to keep in mind his desire for na₄-duh-ši-a, na₄-igi, and na₄-nír-gig/na₄-nír-muš-ĝír/na₄-nír-muš-sù-ud. The na₄-nír-babbar₍₂₎-dili stone is otherwise attested in lexical texts (see *PSD* B 31 and *CAD* P 107 sub *pappardilû*) and is occasionally listed in archival documents (*UET* 34

548 2, 3, 10; *UET* 3 1498 ii 25; *HUCA* 34 (1963) 14 138 [OB]). The identification of na$_4$-duh-ši-a as "chlorite" has been proposed by P. Steinkeller, *JMS* 1 (2006) 2–7.

16. See, perhaps, *AAICAB* 1/1 Ashm. 1911-240 obv. ii 4:2 na$_4$-nir$_7$-zú-lum ka-ba kù-sig$_{17}$ gar, or nir$_7$ zú-lum, and gug zú-lum in *YOS* 4 267: ii 23, 26 (Ur III). In the lexical texts, there is only na$_4$-zú-lum = *aban suluppi*, Hh XXIV 255 (*MSL* 11 85), Nabnitu XXI 166 (*MSL* 16 1961), NB Stone List ii 8 (*MSL* 10 65).

17. The rare eme$_5$(SAL.HÚB)-gal must be a kind of stone or a qualifier; see 4 gug zú-lum eme$_5$-gal (*YOS* 4 267: ii 26–27) and 17 še kù-babbar dalla eme$_5$-gal-šè (*SANTAG* 6 336: 3), both Ur III. Perhaps this is an abbreviated writing of algames (UD.SAL.HÚB), sometimes translated as "steatite". It is impossible to ascertain if there was an UD sign before SAL in this line.

18–19. Note the change to third-person-plural dative in the verbs. In line 19, the verb is uncertain but it is šu . . . zi, "to be angry, cheat, plunder" (F. Karahashi, *Sumerian Compound Verbs*, 173).

13. Puzur-Šulgi to Šulgi 1
(PuŠ1, 3.1.7, RCU 11)

Composite Text

1. lugal-ĝu$_{10}$-ra ù-na-a-dug$_4$
2. ^{I}puzur$_4$-^{d}šul-gi šakkana bàd-igi-hur-saĝ-ĝá
3. árad-zu na-ab-bé-a
4. lugal-ĝu$_{10}$ kù-sig$_{17}$ ^{na_4}za-gìn diĝir-re-e-ne-ka in-ne-en-dím-dím-ma
5. zi-ni-šè-àm in-nu-ù
6. lugal-ĝu$_{10}$ zi ugnim ù kalam-ma-ni-šè
7. bàd gal igi-hur-saĝ-ĝá mu lú kúr hul-ĝál-šè
8. ùĝ kalam-ma-ni-šè mu-un-dù
9. ugnim lú-kúr-ra im-ma-zi
10. diš-àm lú igi-ĝá záh-bi i-im-túm-ma
11. dib-dib-bé inim ma-an-dug$_4$-ma igi-šè ba-gin
12. ĝiškim lú kúr-ra ĝá-e ì-zu
13. lú kúr im-ma-til usu-ĝu$_{10}$ ì-tur
14. bàd nu-mu-un-da-kal-la-ge en-nu-ùĝ nu-mu-da-ak-e
15. nam ^{I}puzur$_4$-^{d}nu-muš-da énsi ul$_4$-lum-TUR.RA^{ki}
16. ninnu nindan uš saĝ ba-ab-gíd murub$_4$-ba im-ma-an-ri
17. nam ^{I}lugal-me-lám šabra ^{íd}šeg$_5$-šeg$_5$
18. iá nindan uš-ni ha-ni-dar-dar
19. nam ^{I}ka-kù-ga-ni énsi ma-da murub$_4$^{ki}
20. 35 nindan uš gaba dúr-bi ba-gul-gul
21 nam ^{I}ta-ki-il-ì-lí-šu kù-ĝál ^{íd}áb-gal ù ^{íd}me-^{d}en-líl-lá
22. nimin nindan uš-ni gúr ugu-bi-šè nu-ub-ĝar
23. u$_4$ lú kúr im-ku-nu-a ugu-bi-šè ù-nu-ub-zu
24. lú kúr mè-šè usu-ni im-til
25. ugnim-bi šà hur-saĝ-ĝá-ka íb-tuš
26. tukum-bi lugal-ĝá an-na-kam
27. 7200 érin lú-kíĝ-ak-ne ha-ma-ab-íl-e ul$_4$-la-bi hu-mu-ši-gi$_4$-gi$_4$
28. 70 àga-ús lú su-da-lu-nu-tum^{ki}-a
29. ugu-ĝu$_{10}$-šè hé-em-su$_8$-bé-eš

30. dím-ma-ğu$_{10}$ hé-dab$_5$ ki-tuš-bi ga-ba-da-an-kúr
31. hé-zu ği$_6$-ta u$_4$ ul-lí-a-šè nam-tag-ni dugud
32. árad ^{d}šul-gi lugal gi-na-me-en[1]
33. nam-mu-da-til-en
34. lugal-ğu$_{10}$ hé-en-zu[2]

[1] Speak to my king, [2] saying (the words) of Puzur-Šulgi,[3] general of Bad-Igihursağa, your servant:

[4-5] Is it not for the sake of his own well-being that my king fashions (objects) of silver and gold for the gods? [6] My king, for the well-being of the army and of his homeland, [7-8] has built the great fortifications of Igihursağa for the sake of the vile enemy and of the people of his homeland.

[9] But now the enemy army has mustered (for battle). [10] A certain individual who was brought before me as a deserter [11] gave me some information as he was passing (through) and then went back out (again). [12] Now I really know the enemy's passwords!

[13] The enemy has concentrated (all his forces) for battle but my forces are insufficient (to keep them off). [14] It is impossible to strengthen the fortifications against him, nor (properly) guard it. [15] In the sector under the responsibility of Puzur-Numušda,[4] governor of Ullum-ṣeḫrum, [16] a 300 m. section *had sagged* and collapsed in the middle; [17] in the sector under the responsibility of Lugal-melam, the overseer of the Šeššektum canal, [18] 30 m. of his section can be breached; [19] in the sector under the responsibility of Kakugani,[5] governor of the inland territory, [20] a 210 m. section, its face and base are badly damaged, [21] (and) in the part under the responsibility of Takil-ilišu, canal inspector of the Abgal and Me-Enlila waterways, [22] 240 m. of his section *does not have its perimeter laid out yet.* [23] Although I cannot know ahead of time when the enemy will advance against (the fortifications), [24] (it is evident) that the enemy has concentrated (all) his forces for battle, [25] and his troops are encamped in the mountain valleys.

[26] If my king is agreeable, [27] he will raise for me a very large contingent (viz., 7200) of workers and send them here immediately. [28-29] Seventy *Sudalunutum* troopers should also come here to me. [30] I am resolved, and so I shall dislodge them (i.e., the enemy), [31] so let this be known, for his (the enemy's) sins have been grievous from (primeval) night to the end of days! [32] (Be assured), I am the true servant of my lord Šulgi,[6] [33] and I will definitely finish (this work)! [34] Now my king is informed (about all of this)![7]

1. 32a (N4 only): [ù-na]-a-dug$_4$-ğu$_{10}$ ⌜níğ-gú-šub⌝-bu-bi in-nu-ù.
2. 34a (N4 only): ⌜a⌝-ma-ru-k[am].
3. Var.: Puzur-Numušda, Puzur-Marduk.
4. Var.: Šu-Marduk, Šu-Nunu, Šu-Numušda.
5. Var.: Šu-Numušda.
6. One text adds: [32a] My letter, it will not be neglected, will it?
7. One text adds: [34a] It is urgent!

Commentary

The redactional difficulties of this composition provide a particularly stark example of the difficulties of creating a "composite text" of a composition that has a very fluid textual tradition in witnesses found in different places. Textual variants cluster in a manner that reveals consistent differences between the Nippur sources and those from elsewhere, and the solitary Kish witness sometimes goes its own way. The reconstruction is hampered by the fragmentary state of the Nippur tablets, which provide good evidence for the beginning and end but do not document well the middle part of the letter.

Of the four Nippur manuscripts, all of which come from the 19th-century excavations of the site and have no precise provenience, two are one-column tablets (N1 and N4) and two are on collective ones (N2 and N3). Because of the fragmentary state of these sources, it is impossible to establish if they all had a similar "redaction" or if the differences from the other manuscripts are limited to one or two of these tablets. I should stress that one should not think of this as a generic Nippur version, because it may simply represent the idiosyncrasies of one or two teachers or their students. It is unlikely, however, that more-complete sources from the city will surface in the foreseeable future.

The variants in the opening section are such that rather than indicate differences in every line, I offer a separate Nippur composite text of the passage:

1. lugal-ğu$_{10}$-ra ù-na-a-dug$_4$ N1, N4
2. ^{1}puzur$_4$-^{d}nu-muš-da šakkana bàd-igi-hur-saĝ-ĝá   N1, N4
3. árad-zu na-ab-bé-a   N1, N4
4. lugal-ğu$_{10}$ kù-sig$_{17}$ ^{na4}za-gìn diĝir-re-e-ne-ka in-ne-en-dím-dím-ma   N1, N4
5. zi-ni-šè-àm in-nu-ù   N1
6. lugal-ğu$_{10}$ silim-ma ugnim ù kalam-ma-na-šè   N1
7. bàd gal igi-hur-saĝ-ĝá mu lú hul-ĝál-šè   N1
8. mu-un-dù   N1
9. ugnim lú kúr-ra im-ma-an-zi   N1

^{1}Speak to my king: $^{2-3}$saying (the words) of Puzur-Šulgi, general of Bad-Igihursaĝa, your servant:

$^{4-5}$Is it not for the sake of his own well-being that my king fashions (objects) of precious metals and jewels for the gods? ^{6}My king, for the safety of the troops and his homeland $^{7-8}$has built the great fortifications of Igihursaĝa against the vile (enemy).

^{9}But now the enemy troops have mustered (for battle).

4. This line is different in all manuscripts.

10–11. The difficulties in these lines were apparently already felt in antiquity, as shown by the ambiguities inherent in the line division. N1 had both of them on one line, but N2 apparently divided it in the manner adopted here; this was also the interpretation of the scribes who wrote X2 and X4. The student from Kish (Ki1) had dab₅-dab₅-bé as part of line 10.

12. giškim is used here as a technical term referring to secret signals or passwords; on such nuances of the word, see M. Civil, *FS Lambert* 109.

13. One would expect that usu til would mean that the enemy forces have been weakened, but as in *Nippur Lament* 226, the context requires a different interpretation. Here, as elsewhere in this letter, idiomatic usage reflects Akkadian usage, in this case, *emūqam gamārum*, "to concentrate military forces"; see S. Tinney, *Nippur Lament*, 170. There is some textual confusion with line 24; the reconstruction of the latter remains problematical.

15. On the noun nam, see commentary to ŠAr1: 29 (2).

15–22. There is a good deal of variation in the order of these lines and in the personal names of the officials that are mentioned (on the names and the variants in lines 15 and 19, see pp. 138–142 above). In view of this, the somewhat arbitrary order accepted here reflects source X4/5, the only one that preserves the whole sequence. X2 begins without an official, at line 18. The distribution and order in each manuscript can be reconstructed as follows:

N2	N3	Ki1	X1	X2	X4/5
*	o	15	19	18	15
16	o	18	16	19	16
15	o	17	17	20	17
18	o	22	18	o	18
17	o	19	21	o	19
22	o	20	22	o	20
19	o	21	15	o	21
20	21	16	20	o	22

16. The compound verb or, perhaps better, idiom saĝ(. . .)gíd, is otherwise attested, to my knowledge, only in the *Uruk Lament* 1a 3: [. . .]-ni saĝ a-na-aš ba-ab-ᵣgídᴵ [uĝ saĝ ĝi₆-ga] a-ba-a in-lu-lu-un, which M. Green (*JAOS* 104 [1984: 266) read gíd as su₁₃ and translated the line "Why was . . . expanded? Who was it who made [the black-headed people] become so numerous (anyway)?" with reference to the outline in her commentary (p. 278), rendering it as: "he expanded (the wall) 50 ĜAR.UŠ but let it collapse in the middle." It is doubtful if this verb has anything to do with saĝ . . . gíd = *nekelmûm*, "to be angry," for which see F. Karahashi, *Sumerian Compound Verbs*, 137.

21–. After line 21, the two Nippur tablets have a line order that is different from all the other texts from Kish and elsewhere and possibly even from N1. They both seem to repeat line 14; note that X1 omits lines 24–25. Ideally, the Nippur order should have been used for the reconstruction of the composite texts, but the state of the manuscripts makes this impossible at present.

N2:

[u₄ lú kú]r im-ma-ku-nu [igi-bi]-ʳšèʼ ù-nu-ub-zu	= 23
[nam ˡta-ki-i]l-ì-lí-šu / [kù-ğál ⁱᵈabgal] ʳùʼ ⁱᵈme-ᵈen-líl	= 21
[?] ʳusuʼ-ğu₁₀ i-im-til	= 24
[bàd nu-mu-un-da-kal]-la-ge / [en-nu-(ùğ) nu-mu]-ʳda-akʼ-e	= 14
[ugnim-bi šà hur-sağ]-ʳğáʼʼ íb-tuš	= 25
[. . . .]x mu-da-ti	= 33ʼ
[. . .]-gi₄-gi₄	= 29ʼ
[. . .]-x-ʳdugudʼʼ	= 31ʼ
[. . .]-ʳmeʼ-enʼʼ	= 32ʼ
[. . .]-x	

rest of column broken

N3 i′ 1′–7′:

ʳu₄ʼʼ [lú kúr im-ma-ku-nu igi-bi-šè ù-nu-ub-zu]	= 23
nam ʳˡtaʼ-[ki-il-ì-lí-su] / kù-ğál ʳⁱᵈʼ[abgal ù ⁱᵈme-ᵈen-líl-lá]	= 21
lú kúr m[è-šè usu-ni/ğu₁₀ im-til]	= 24
ug[nim …]. =ʼ (25ʼ)	
bà[d nu-mu-un-da-kal-la-ge]	= 14
ug[nim-bi šà hur-sağ-ğá íb-tuš]	= (25ʼ)

rest of column broken

22. The interpretation of this line follows a suggestion by E. Robson.

24. The reconstruction of this line is highly uncertain; there is some confusion with line 9.

26–29. These lines are clearly intrusive and were derived from the Šu-Sin correspondence, specifically from ŠaŠu1: 17; 27–30 (18) and ŠuŠa1: 31–33 (19). The result was somewhat untidy and resulted in some confusion among teachers or students. The Nippur sources, which already differed in lines 21–25, are broken at this point. The same process is evident in the answer to this letter, ŠPu1: 20–26 (14).

27. Every manuscript has a different version of this line. The X4 includes people who are to "carry" the ᵍⁱˢdupsik (see ŠaŠu1: 16; 30, letter 18). This can be taken literally, implying that they are to carry the "corvée basket" or as an expression, probably calqued from Akkadian, that stands for "carrying our corvée labor," i.e., OB *ilqam našûm*. It is usually assumed that corvée labor—that is, military and other work for the state or for a large organization in exchange for land—is not attested before the Old Babylonian period and that the Akkadian term *ilkum* has no equivalent in Sumerian. It is now clear that corvée labor (dupsik, or "dusu"; on the reading see now M. Civil, *FS Biggs*, 13) has an earlier history; for Ur III, see M. Sigrist, *RA* 73 (1979) 103; P. Michalowski, *JNES* 45 (1986) 327; C. Wilcke, *Early Ancient Near Eastern Law*, 34 with earlier literature.

The number 7,200 is not to be taken literally; it simply means "a very large contingent." See, for example, the *Letter to the Generals* (SEpM 11) 9–10: tukum-bi ᵈutu nu-um-ta-è, šár-šár érin ugu-ba nu-ub-gub, "if the sun does not come out, not even a very large contingent of workers will prevail against it." The number occurs again, used in a similar manner, in ŠaŠu1: 29 (18): 7,200 érin mu-e-ši-in-gi₄, and in IšIb1: 8 (21) 72,000 še gur še dù-a-bi šà ì-si-inᵏⁱ-na-šè ba-an-ku₄-re-en.

28. The place-name su-da-lu-nu-tumᵏⁱ (with variants) is otherwise unattested and seems improbable; this is undoubtedly a garbled place-name that resulted from a transmission error derived from the intrusive *lú-ᵈnanna énsi zi-mu-darᵏⁱ-ra. It is also possible that at some point in the chain of transmission confusion arose under the influence of the Ur III writing LÚ.SU for Šimaški.

30. I have taken dím-ma dab₅ as a calque of the Akkadian ṭēmam ṣabātum, "to be resolved, make up one's mind." The line has many variants. Note the third-person markers in Ki1 and X4, where the idiom may have been misunderstood; translate perhaps: "his (the enemy's) mind was made up and he changed his location."

31. The idiomatic nature of this line presented difficulties for ancient students, as documented by the high level of variation in the manuscripts.

32a. Although this edition for the most part follows the Nippur text, it seems likely that this unusual line is an interpolation. The restoration of the first signs, as well as the translation, is somewhat speculative.

33. There are a number of possible interpretations of the verb in this line. Rather than interpreting the na- prefix assertively,[8] one could take it negatively ("I may not be able to finish [the work]") in concert with the parallel in *Letter to the Generals* (SEpM 11) 12: á ma-tur nu-mu-un-da-til-en, "My work force is insufficient and I cannot finish (the task)" (for other possible translations, see M. Civil, *Farmers Instructions*, 183–84). Previous editions all take the root to be ug₇; in this case, the translations would be "may I not perish!" but this is improbable. Note the clustering of variants; the non-Nippurean texts are all agreement and the Kish manuscript straddles both.

N1 has the unique fragmentary line 32a, which may perhaps have to be understood as "and has not my (previous) *letter* been ignored?"

Sources

N1 = HS 1438 (*TMH NF* 4 42)	1–14; 30–34
N2 = Ni. 9706 (*ISET* 2 112) r. iv′ 1′–23′	10–23+
N3 = Ni. 9854 (*ISET* 1 189 [131]) ii′ 1′–5′	21; 24–27+
N4 = N 3773	1–4; 29–34a

---

8. Steve Tinney suggests that this might be a calque of an Akkadian promissory oath in the negative.

Ki1 = AO 10819 (*PRAK* 2 D60)   1–34
X1 = A w/n iii 1′–20′   13–34
X2 = BM 54894 rev. i 1′–11′   4–14; 18; 15; 20
X3 = Ni. 3083 (*ISET* 2 115) i 1′–8′   25–34
X4 = YBC 4606   19–34
X5 = YBC 4654   1–18

Tablet typology: compilation tablets (Type I): N2, N3, X1, X2, X3; all others type III.

N1 collated by C. Wilcke, *Kollationen* 73, by Steve Tinney, on print photographs provided by Manfred Krebernik, and on digital photographs provided by Jerrold Cooper. X5 and X4 constitute a pair, probably written on successive days by the same scribe. Ki1 has deteriorated since I first collated it.

Bibliography: Edition: C. Wilcke, *WO* 5, 3–6. Translation: P. Michalowski, *Royal Letters*, 78.

Concordance of sigla used here (CKU) and in *RCU*:

N1	A		A	N1
N2	C		B	Ki1
N4	G		C	N2
Ki1	B		E	X5
X1	H		F	X4
X4	F		G	N4
X5	E		H	X1

Textual Matrixes

1. lugal-ğu$_{10}$-ra   ù-na-a-dug$_4$

N1	o	o	.	+	+	+	.
N4	.	.	.	+	.	o	o
Ki1	+	.	o	.	+	+	.
X5	+	+	+	.	+	+	.

2. ^{I}puzur$_4$- ^{d}šul-gi   šakkana   bàd-igi-hur-sağ-ğá

N1	oo	oo	.	+	o	.	+	+	+
N4	++	^{d}nu-m[ušda]	.	+	+	o	o	o^9	
Ki1	-.	^{d}amar.utu	.	+	+	+	.	.	⌜ke$_4$?⌝
X5	-+	..	.	.	+	+	+	+	.

3. árad-zu   na-ab-bé-a

N1	o	o	o	.	+	+
N4	+	+	+	.	o	o
Ki1	+	+	+	.	.	+
X5	.	.	+	+	-	+

9. N4: ⌜šakkana⌝ bàd-igi-[hur-sağ-ğá] / ^{I}puzur$_4$-^{d}nu-mu[š-da].

4. lugal-ǧu₁₀ kù-babbar kù-sig₁₇ diǧir-re-e-ne-ka in-ne-en-dím-dím-ma

N1 [ ] sig₁₇ ⁿᵃ⁴za-gìn diǧir-re-e-ˈneˈ-ka [in]-ˈneˈ-en-ˈdímˈ-dím-ˈmaˈ
N4 ˈlugalˈ-ǧu₁₀ ˈkù-sig₁₇ˈ [   ]
Ki1 lugal-ǧu₁₀ kù-sig₁₇ kù-babbar ˈdiǧirˈ gal-gal in-ne-ˈdím-dím-maˈ
X2 ˈlugal-ǧu₁₀ˈ kù-babbar kù-ˈsig₁₇ˈ d[iǧir]-dím-dím-ma:
X5 lugal-ǧu₁₀ ˈkù-babbar ⟨kù⟩-sig₁₇ˈ diǧir-ˈreˈ-e-ne in-dím-d[ím]

5. zi-ni-šè-àm in-nu-ù

N1 . o . + . + .
Ki1 + + + + . . .
X2 + o o o o o o
X5 + + + . + + .

6. lugal-ǧu₁₀ zi   ugnim ù kalam-ma-ni-šè

N1 .   +silim-ma .   . .   + na+ :
Ki1 .   +   +   +   + +   + . .
X2 +   +   +   .   o o   o o o
X5 +   +   .   +   + +   + + +

7. bàd gal igi-hur-saǧ-ǧá mu lú kúr hul-ǧál-šè

N1 + . . + + +/ . + + . . + :
Ki1 + + + . + + ... ˏ
X2 + + + + + + + . o o o o
X5 + + + ... + + ˏ :

8. ùǧ kalam-ma-ni-šè mu-un-dù

N1 ˏ ˏ   ˏ ˏ ˏ + + +
Ki1 + +   . . . + + . ˈaˈ
X2 Probably on same line as 7
X5 ˏ +   + + . . + +

9.   ugnim lú kúr-ra im-ma-zi

N1   . + + + + + +
Ki1   . ˏ ˏ + . + zi
X2   +   ˏ ˏ ˏ + + o
X5 ì-ne-éš . ˏ ˏ ˏ . +an+

10. diš-àm lú igi-ǧá záh-bi i-im-túm-ma

N1 . . + + + + + ++ + +:
N2 o o o o o o o oo . .
Ki1 . . . . . + + ˏ + . +:
X2 + + . + + + . oo o o
X5 xx¹⁰+ + . + . . ++ + +

10. Looks like ˈdiš zalˈ.

11. dib-dib-bé inim ma-an-dug₄-ma igi-šè ba-gin

N1	+	+	+	+	+	+	+	+	+	⌐	.	+
N2	o	o	.	.	.	.	.	.	+	.	⌜ba-an-gin⌝
Ki1	+	+	+	/+	+	+	+	o	DU igi-⌜šè⌝¹ ba-gin
X2	+	+	+	+	+	+	.	o	o o o o o
X5	.	.	.	.	+	.	.	⸗	⸗	+	+

12. ğiškim lú kúr-ra ğá-e ì-zu

N1	.	+	+	+	+	a	+ .
N2	+	+	+	+	+	+	+ .
Ki1	+	+	+	.	+	+	+ +
X2	+	+	+	+	+	.	o o
X5	.	.	.	+	.	.	+ .

13. lú kúr im-ma-til usu-ğu₁₀ ì-tur

N1	.	.	.	.	+	+	+ .
N2	+ +	+	+	.	.	.	+ +
Ki1	lú kúr mè-šè usu-ni im-til
X1	.	.	.	o	o	o	o	o o
X2	Omits or on same line as 12.
X5	o o	o o	.	.	+	al+

14. bàd nu-mu-un-da-kal-la-ge en-nu-ùğ nu-mu-da-ak-e

N1	o	o	o	o o	.	. o	o	o	o	o	o	o o o
N2	.	+	+	+	.	.	.	+	+	⸗	+	+	+ + +
Ki1	+	+	+	.	+	+	+	⌜ke₄⌝	en-nu-ùğ-da	ğá-ğá
X1	.	+	+	.	.	+	. o	o	o	o	o	o	o o o
X2	+	+	+	+	+	+	⸗	.	o	o	o	+	.	o o o
X5	o	o	o o	.	+	+ +	+	+	.	x	o	o	⌜ğá⌝-ğá

N2 additional line (?)

15. nam ˡpuzur₄-ᵈnu-muš-da énsi ul₄-lum-TUR.RAᵏⁱ

N2	.	++	++ +	+	+	+	+	+	⸗	+
Ki1	+	+⌜šu⌝	ᵈmarduk.	+	+	+	+	+
X1	.	+šu	⸗	nu-nu	+	+	+	+	+ +
X2	+	⸗šu	++ +	.	o	o	o	o	o o
X5	o	o	oo.	+	+	+	+	+	. +

16. ninnu nindan uš sağ ba-ab-gíd murub₄-ba im-ma-an-ri

N2	x	.	.	+	+ +	+ +	+ +	+ +
N3	omits or on same line as 21
Ki1	+	+	+	+	+ ⸗	+ +	+ +	da ⸗ +
X1	+	+	+	+bi	+ +	+ .	.	o o o o
X5	o	.	o	o⌜ba⌝+ ⸗	+ +	+ +	da + +

17. nam ˡlugal-me-lám šabra ⁱᵈšeg₅-šeg₅

```
N2   o    ..   +   +   +        ..    .
Ki1  +    ++   .   +   +     ì+    +
X1   +    ++   +   +   +     ++   .    tum
X5   .    ++   o   .   +     ++   +
```

18. iá nindan uš-ni ha-ni-dar-dar

```
N2   +   .        +   +   .   +   +   .
Ki1  +   +        +   ֊   +   +   +   +
X1   +   +        +   +   +   +   +   +
X2   +   +àm      +   +  ʳhu?ˀ o   o   o
X5   +   +        a   +   hé  +   +   +
```

19. nam ˡka-kù-ga-ni   énsi ma-da murub₄ᵏⁱ

```
N2   o    oo   .   .   .      +    +   +    .        .
Ki1  +    +.   .   +   +      +    +   .    .        ֊
X1   .    +šu-ᵈnu-muš-ʳdaˀ.   o   o   o            o
X4   .    ++   +   +   +      +    .   +    +        +
```

20. 35 nindan uš gaba dúr-bi ba-gul-gul

```
N2   o   o       o   .      .   +   +   +   +lu
Ki1  .   +                  ga-ba-ʳab-gul-gulˀ
X1   +   +       +   +      +   +   +   .   +
X2   .   .ʳàmˀ   .   x      o   o   o   o   o
X4   .   +       a   +      +   ba+  .   +   +
```

21. nam ˡta-ki-il-ì-lí-šu kù-ğál   ⁱᵈáb-gal ù ⁱᵈme-ᵈen-líl-lá

```
N2   o    oo o  . ++ + o  o       oo  o  .  ++  ++ + +
N3   +    ..  o  oooo +   .        .o  o  o  oo  oo o  o
Ki1  +    +++  +++ +nu-ub+         ++  +  +  ++  ++ + +
X1   .    .+  +  +++iš su /énsi    +abgal  +  ++  ++ .  ֊
X4   .    +++¹¹ +++ sú +x¹²+ /     +.  +   +  ++  ++ .  +
```

22. nimin nindan uš-ni   gúr ugu-bi-šè nu-ub-ğar

```
N2   o      o       o  x      x    .   .   .    +
Ki1  +      +       +  ֊      +    +   +   +  +   +
X1   ùšu    +       +  +      +    +  ʳbaˀ+   ù-nu-ub-zu
X4   25     .      ʳaˀ+ gul   +    +   ba ֊   +   .   +
```

23. u₄ lú kúr im-ma-ku-nu-a ugu-bi-šè ù-nu-ub-zu

```
N2   o   o   .   +   +   +   +  ֊   o    o   .  ++  ++
N3   #
Ki1  +   +   +   +   +   +   +   +       +  dúr nu-ub-ğar
X1   +   +   +   +   +   +   +   .     ʳbaˀ+  +  +   +  +
X4   +   +   .   .   +   +   +   +   .  ba  .   ֊   .   .   .
```

11. Written di.
12. Erased ğál.

24.   lú kúr mè-šè usu-ni im-til

N2   o o   o o   .   ğu₁₀ i-im-til
N3   + +   .   o o   o o o
Ki1   lú kúr ì-ku-na-a usu-ni im-til
X1   #
X4   + +   + + ⸢á⸣ a+ +   +

25.   ugnim-bi šà hur-sağ-ğá-ka íb-tuš

N2   o   o o o   o . ⸗ + +
N3   .   o o o   o o o o o
Ki1   +   + + +   + + ke₄ + +
X1   #
X3   o   o o o   o . .   .¹³
X4   +   . + +   + + +   . o

26.   tukum-bi lugal-ğá an-na-kam

N2   ?
Ki1   .   + +   + + + ka
X1   .   . +   + + + .
X3   o   o o   o . + +
X4   +   + .   . + + +

27.   7200 érin lú-kíğ-ak-ne ha-ma-ab-íl-e   ul₄-la-bi hu-mu-ši-gi₄-gi₄

N2   [   ]-gi₄-gi₄
Ki1   ⸢7200⸣ érin lú-⸢ᵍⁱˢ⸣[dupsik⸣] ⸢íl⸢⸣ kíğ-kíğ-bi ⸢ul₄⸣-[la-bi⸣] ⸢hé-em⸣-su₈-ge-eš
X1   7200 érin lú-kíğ-giˡ-giˡ   ul₄-la-bi hu-mu-ši-gi₄-gi₄
X3   [ul₄]-⸢la⸣-bi hu-mu-ši-gi₄-gi₄
X4   ⸢7200⸣ érin lú-kíğ-ak-⸢ne⸣ ᵍⁱˢdubsik-a ha-ma-ab-íl-e / ⸢ul₄⸣-la-bi
                                              hu-mu-ši-[ɪn]-gi₄-gi₄-⸢ma⸣

28.   70 àga-ús lú su-da-lu-nu-tumᵏⁱ-a

N2   traces
Ki1   .   +   + +   su-dal-tumᵏⁱ-a
X1   +   +   + +   su-da-x-⸢nu⸣-tumᵏⁱ-a
X3   o   .   . .   ⸢su-da⸣-lu-nu-tumᵏⁱ-⸢e?⸣
X4   +àm + + .   [d]a-lu-nu-t[um...]:

29.   ugu-ğu₁₀-šè hé-em-su₈-bé-eš

N2   traces
N4   .   .   o o o   o o
Ki1   ⸢ul₄-la⸣-bi ⸢hu⸣-mu-ši-in-gi₄-gi₄
X1   +   +   + ⸢hé-em-su₈⸣-bé-eš
X3   .   +   + ⸢hé⸣-em-ta-⸢dab₅⸣-bé-eš
X4   x   o   o ⸢hé⸣-en-su₈-⸢bé⸣-[]

13. It is possible that X3, like X1, omitted this line and that the traces may have to be interpreted as the end of the previous line, because the traces are somewhat ambiguous; but without
recollation, this reading must stand.

30. dím-ma-ğu₁₀ hé-dab₅   ki-tuš-bi   ga-ba-da-an-kúr

N1	o	o	o	o	. ⌐bé⌐	.	.	.	⌐ga⌐-ba-da-⌐an-kúr⌐
N4	+	+	.	o	o /		+	+	+	⌐ga⌐-[...]
Ki1	.	+	ni	⌐in⌐-dab₅		+	+	+	in-kúr
X1	+	+	+	hé-⌐en-na⌐-dab₅	+	+	+	ga-ba-ni-ib-kúr
X3	.	+	+	hé-dab₅		+	+	+	ga-ba-ni-kúr
X4	+	+	bi	[hé-en²-na²]-dab₅	+	+	+	im-ma-⌐kúr⌐

31. hé-zu   ği₆-ta   u₄ ul-lí-a-šè   nam-tag-ni dugud

N1	o	o	.	.		+	+	+	+	+	+	+	+
N4	+	+	+	.		o	o	o	o	o /	+	+	+	o
Ki1	+	+	ği₆	zu-àm	u₄-na-me			na-da		+
X1	+	+	+	da		+	+	+	-	.	o	o	o
X3	x	x	x	⌐da⌐ x	+	+	+	-		+		+	⌐bi⌐ +
X4	+	+	+	x		o	.	+	+ aš	+	.	⌐	+

32. árad ᵈšul-gi   lugal gi-na me-en

N1	o	o.	+	+ ğá	+	+	+	+
N4	.	++	+	+		.	o	o	o
Ki1	+	++	+	.		+	+	+	+
X1	.	-.	+	+		+	+	o	o
X3	o	..	+	+		+	+	+	+
X4	+	+.	.	+		+	+	+	+ :

32a. N1 [ù-na]-a-dug₄-ğu₁₀ ⌐níğ-gú-šub⌐-bu-bi in-nu-ù

33. nam-mu-da-til-en

N1	nam-mu-da-til-en
N4	nu-mu-da-til-[en]
Ki1	nam-ba-da-⌐til-àm²⌐ :
X1	⌐nam-ba-til⌐-e-dè-en :
X3	⌐nam⌐-ba-til-dè-en :
X4	nam-ba-til-e-dè-en

34. lugal-ğu₁₀ hé-en-zu

N1	+	+	+	+	+
N4	+	+	+	.	o
Ki1	.	.	.	+	+
X1	.	o	o	o	o
X3	+	+	+	+	+
X4	.	.	+	+	+

34a. N4: ⌐a⌐-ma-ru-k[am]

Colophon G (Ki1)
Colophon H (X5)
Colophon I (X4)

In X1 and X3 followed by ŠPu1 (14), in X2 by ŠuŠa1 (19).

14. Šulgi to Puzur-Šulgi 1
(ŠPu1, 3.1.08, 3.1.10, RCU 9, 10)

This letter presents unique challenges for the editor. In the past, two different redactions have been considered separate letters, but upon reflection, I have decided to edit them together. The main reason for separating them was their sequence one after the other on a single tablet (X1/X3), but this should not preclude us from considering them as different versions of the same composition.

The redactional history of the letter is undoubtedly complex, and we only have glimpses of the long history of the permutations of the text. The four earlier sources of unknown provenience can be grouped into two sets that have been edited separately here. The letter that it answers, PuŠ1 (letter 13), is known from four Nippur witnesses and one from Kish, in addition to four of undetermined origin, and it is more than probable that ŠPu1 was concocted outside of Nippur to create a pair with that epistle. One of these is X4, which may be MB; see the discussion of this tablet on pp. 56–56 above. The bilingual Susa tablet (ŠPu1MB1 = Su1S/A) with syllabic Sumerian dates to the 14th or 15th century (see pp. 42–43 above) and seems to be derived from the tradition of OB1a, with the additions of lines 9–19; the first part of this section, lines 9–14, were lifted literally from ArŠ2 (part B, letter 3). The differences between the two OB traditions appear to be concentrated at the beginning and end of the letters. Moreover, interpretation is often made difficult by the idiosyncratic Sumerian orthography of ŠPu1MB1. The scribe of this tablet uses unusual values, often indicates crasis, but also plays with different ways of writing the same word. The Akkadian version shows definite signs of post-OB composition.

Šulgi to Puzur-Šulgi OB 1a (ŠPuOB1a, 3.1.08)

Sources

X1 = A w/n iii	1–12; 1′–10′ (–7′, 8′, 9′)
X2 = BM 108870	13–23; 1′–10′

Tablet typology: compilation tablet: X1, X2 Type III (landscape).

Transliteration[1]

1. X1 ⌈puzur₄-šul-gi⌉ šak[kana bàd igi-hur-saǧ-ǧá-ra]	1
2. X1 ù-⌈na-a⌉-[dug₄]	1
3. X1 ᵈšul-gi lugal⌉-zu na-ab-⌈bé⌉-[a]	2
4. X1 ⌈u₄ bàd igi⌉-hur-⌈saǧ⌉-ǧá mu-dù-⌈a⌉	3
5. X1 kur-⌈kur⌉ ⌈uǧ⌉ daǧal-la an-né ᵈen-líl-⌈le⌉	4
6. X1 nam-en-⌈na-bi ma-an-šúm-mu-uš⌉	5
7. X1 ǧá-e x[. . .] x x x x [. . .]	
8. X1 uru¹⁷ ka[lam²-ma² ma]-da² ma²-[da-bi]	6
9. X1 ⌈un kalam daǧal-la⌉ [ú sal-la ì]-n[ú]	7
10. X1 ⌈ki níǧ daǧal-bi-a ki-tuš ne²-ha²⌉ [mu-un-tuš²]	8
11. X1 ⌈ki-tuš⌉ *traces*	
12. X1 ⌈énsi² šabra⌉ l[ú²-bi hé-eb-túm]²	23²
13. X2 uru-uru-bi ha-ra-⌈ab⌉-zi-zi-ne	23
14. X2 lú saǧ kíǧ-bi hé-⌈en⌉-dab₅	24
15. X2 ki bàd šub-ba ki-bi-šè ⌈hu⌉-mu-un-ǧar	25
16. X2 hé-en-dag ù hé-⌈en⌉-dù	26
17. X2 ⌈šà⌉ iti diš-kam á šub-ba ⌈ha-ba⌉-til	27
18. X2 kíǧ-⌈bi⌉-šè èn mu-na-⌈tar⌉-re-⌈en⌉	28
19. X2 ⌈a-da-lam⌉-ma tidnum(PIRIǦ.PIRIǦ)-e kur-bi-ta ⌈ma-ra⌉-an-⌈gur⌉	
20. X2 ⌈lú⌉-ᵈnanna énsi ma-da zi-mu-dar-⌈ra^ki-⌈ke₄⌉	29
21. X2 é[rin-na-n]i-ta im-mu-⌈e⌉-ši-⌈ri⌉	30
22. X2 [ninda kaskal-l]a-ni-ta mu-ra-⌈ǧál⌉	31
23. X2 [níǧ-á-tak]a₄ ba-ra-⌈na-ǧál⌉	32
23. X2 [u₄²] ⌈bàd²-bi²⌉ x [. . .] x x [. . .] ⌈DU²⌉	33²
1'. X1 *traces*	
2'. X1 [. . .] hé-⌈bí-ib-gi₄-gi₄⌉	
3'. X1 [. . .] al-til-la-aš	
X2 *traces*	
4'. X1 [⌈lú-ᵈnanna én]si ⌈ma-da zi⌉-mu-⌈dar⌉-ra-ke›	35
X2 ⌈⌈lú⌉-ᵈ⌈nanna⌉ [énsi ma-da] ⌈zi-mu⌉-dar-ra^ki¹³	
5'. X1 [érin-na-ni-ta] ⌈ù⌉-mu-un-šub-bu-un-zé-en	36
X2 érin-na-ni-ta ù-mu-e-šub-bu-un-⌈zé⌉-en	
6'. X1 [za-e ˡárad-mu] nam-ma-ab-lá-e-zé-en	37
X2 za-e ˡárad-mu na-ma-ab-⌈bal-le-en⌉-zé-en	
7'. X1 *	39
X2 á-áǧ-ǧá kala-ga á-zu-ne-ne-a ⌈nam-ba-e-še-bé⌉-en-zé-⌈en⌉	

---

1. The corresponding line numbers in the Middle Babylonian version (ŠPŠMB1) are indicated in the right column.

2. This is the last line of col. iii; there are at least x lines broken at the beginning of col. iv.

3. Read perhaps [ki]-⌈ka⌉.

8'. X1 *   38
   X2 ği₆ an-bar₇ kíğ ⌜hé⌝-en-dù
9'. X1 *
   X2 ği₆ an-bar₇ ù ⌜nu⌝-ku-ku-⌜un-zé⌝-en hé-zu-un-⌜zé⌝-en
10'. X1 [a-ma]-⌜ru⌝-kam   40
    X2 ⌜a⌝-ma-⌜ru⌝-kam

Colophon J (X2)

¹⁻² Speak to Puzur-Šulgi, general of Bad-Igihursağa, ³ saying (the words of) Šulgi, your king:

⁴ When I had constructed Bad-Igihursağa, ⁵⁻⁶ An and Enlil gave me to rule all the lands and far-flung peoples. ⁷ And as for me . . . ⁸ the cities of the homeland, province by province, ⁹ as well as the peoples of the far-flung homeland rested in safe pastures. ¹⁰ [*I made them dwell*] in teeming places *and peaceful habitations.* ¹¹ . . . dwelling(s) . . .

¹²⁻¹³ Have the governors and the overseers [*bring their men*] and mobilize all their cities, ¹⁴ and have someone take charge *of the beginning* of the work; ¹⁵ wherever the fortification has deteriorated, it must be restored, ¹⁶ torn down, and then rebuilt, ¹⁷ and *(the repairs to) the fallen sides (of the wall)* must be finished in the course of one month! ¹⁸ You/I will then ask him ([Aradmu⁷] for a report) about this work.

¹⁹ And now the the Tidnumites have returned to (help) me from the highlands. ²⁰ (Moreover), Lu-Nanna, governor of Zimudar province, ²¹ *is coming to you* with his worker troops. ²² He will have his own [travel provision]s for you, ²³ . . .

¹' . . . ²' . . . dispatch . . . ³' [*When the work/fortifications*] are finished,⁴' then, after Lu-Nanna, the governor of Zimudar ⁵' has left both of you with his worker troops, ⁶' you and Aradmu must not cease supervising/*alter your assignment,* ⁷' and you must not neglect the important orders *that are in your hands.* ⁸' The work must progress day and night; ⁹' neither of you is to sleep by night or day—you must both know about this! ¹⁰' It is urgent!

Commentary

The synchronization of the two OB sources is provisional at best; the reconstruction of lines 21–24 is particularly suspect, because the texts may have differed at this point.

19. This line makes little sense here and is not present in any other version; it seems to have been adopted from line 33 of a non-Nippur version of IbPu1 (24):

```
      ì-ne-éš amurrum kur-bi-ta ᵈen-líl á-dah-ğu₁₀ im-ma-zi
N1    + +  +  +         +    + + ++ +  . +    +  +  +  +
N3    + +  +  +         +    + + ++ ++ +     +  +    +  +?
Si1   [ì-n]e-éš ti-da-nu-um [. . .] / ᵈen-líl kur-bi-ta á-d[ah-ğu₁₀-šè im-ma-(an)-zi]
X1    ì-ne-éš ti-da-ma-rum amurrumᵏⁱ-a/ᵈen-líl-le kur-bi-ta á-dah-ğu₁₀-šè im-ma-an-zi
```

The difference is in the verbal root, which seems to be gur in the present text. This is probably due to the fact that Akkadian *našûm* is an equivalent of both zi and gur.

21. I take the verbal root ri as e-re, the plural perfect root of the verb du/gin, "to go." All the other versions of this line have gin.

Šulgi to Puzur-Šulgi OB 1b (ŠPu1OB1b, 3.1.10)

Sources

X3 = A w/n iv 7′–35′		1–29
X4 = Ni. 3083 (*ISET* 2 115) i 10′–16′		1–6

Tablet typology: both compilation tablets (Type I).

Transliteration[4]

1. X3	[I]ʳpuzur₄-šul-gi šakkanaꜝ bàd-igi-hur-sag̃-g̃á ʳù-naꜝ-a-dug₄	1
X4	ᴵpuzur₄-šul-gi šakkana bàd-igi-hur-⟨sag̃⟩-g̃á ù-na-dug₄	
2. X3	[ᵈšul-gi] ʳlugalꜝ-zu na-ab-bé-a	2
X4	šul-gi lugal-zu na-ab-bé-a	
3. X3	[u₄ bàd gal igi] hur-sag̃-ʳg̃áꜝ mu-dù-a	3
X3	u₄ bàd gal igi hur-sag̃-g̃á mu-un-dù-a	
4. X3	[amurrum kalam-š]è nu-è-dè-dè	
X4	ʳamurrumꜝ kalam-šè nu-è-dè-dè	
5. X3	[gú áb-gal gú] ʳⁱᵈidignaꜝ ⁱᵈburanun-na-bi-da a nu-nag̃-nag̃-dè	
X4	gú áb-gal gú ⁱᵈidigna ⁱᵈburanun-na-bi nu-nag̃-nag̃-dè	
6. X3	[ùg̃ kalam dag̃al-la ú sa]l-la nú-dè	7
X4	*traces*	
7. X3	[ki-tuš-bi-ta nu-h]uꜝ-luh-e-dè	
8. X3	[. . .]x-ni ʳtùmꜝ-ù-dè	
9. X3	[. . .]x-g̃ál ʳharꜝ-ra-ʳan kaskalꜝ-laꜝꜝ ì-DU-dè	
10. X3	[. . .]x x ʳbíꜝ-dù ʳin-nuꜝ-ù	
11. X3	[. . .]x mu-e-ʳgi₄ꜝ	
12. X3	[. . .]-šè á mu-da-an-ʳág̃ꜝ	
13. X3	[. . .]-ne-e-dù	
14. X3	[uru-uru-bi ha-(ra)-ab]-ʳzi-zi-ešꜝ	23
15. X3	[lú sag̃ kíg̃-bi] ʳhéꜝ-éb-dab₅	24
16. X3	[hé-en-dag] ʳùꜝ hé-en-dù	26
17. X3	[. . .]x-ma ha-ma-gi₄-gi₄	
18. X3	[kíg̃-bi-šè èn] ʳa?ꜝ-ra-ʳabꜝ-tar-re-en	28
19. X3	[ᴵlú-ᵈnanna énsi ma-da] ʳzi-muꜝ-dar-ra-ke₄	29
20. X3	[érin-na-ni]-ʳšèꜝ hé-mu-e-ši-gin	30

4. The corresponding line numbers in the Middle Babylonian version (ŠPŠMB1) are indicated in the right column.

21. X3 [. . .]x-en-na-a
22. X3 [. . .] ⸢ha⸣-ra-ab-tuš
23. X3 [. . .] ⸢ha-ra-ab-gi₄-gi₄⸣
24. X3 [. . .] ⸢ğál⸣-le-en
25. X3 [. . .]- ⸢e⸣ ì-zu-zu
26. X3 [éren . . . nam-b]a-e-šub-bé-⸢en⸣.   36ʾ
27. X3 [. . .] ⸢ki?⸣-ba ù-bí-tuš
28. X3 [. . .]-en-zé-en.   37/39ʾ
29. X3 [a-m]a-ru-kam   40

[1] Speak to Puzur-Šulgi, general of Bad-Igihursağa, [2] saying (the words of) Šulgi, your king:

[3] When the great fortifications of Bad-Igihursağa were being built—[4] so that the Amorites could not descend on the homeland, [5] nor water (their herds) at the banks of the Abgal as well as the Tigris and Euphrates, [6] that [the people of the far-flung homeland] rest in sa[fe pastures], [7] and not be terrori[zed in their dwellings], [8] to bring . . . [9] to go on the roads . . .[10–13] . . . [14] let them mobilize [all their villages, one by one] [15]and appoint [the man in charge of the construction]. [16] [The fortifications must be torn down], and then rebuilt. [17] . . . send me swiftly. . . .

[18] After I consult you about this undertaking,[19–20] Lu-Nanna, governor of Zimu-dar province is to come to you with his worker troops. [21–25] . . .[26] You (sing.) [should not allow the worker troops] to leave. [27] . . . [28] neither/both of you is to [. . . !] [29] It is [ur]gent!

Commentary

4–5. These lines are clearly a paraphrase of ŠaŠu1: 4–7 (18) igi-zu ma-an-ğar-ma amurrum ma-da-aš mu-un-šub-šub-bu-uš, bàd dù-ù-dè ğìri-bi ku₅-ru-dè, ⁱᵈidigna ⁱᵈburanun-na-bi-da, gú-ğìri-bi a-šà-e nam-ba-e-šú-šú á-šè mu-e-da-áğ, "and presented your views to me as follows: "The Amorites have repeat-edly raided the province." You commanded me [5] to rebuild the fortifications, to cut off their (infiltration) route, thus to prevent them from swooping down on the fields through a breach (in the defenses) between the Tigris and Euphrates." Note that these lines are absent in all other versions; moreover, they clearly contradict ŠPu1OB1a: 19 above.

Šulgi to Puzur-Šulgi MB 1 (ŠPu1MB1, ŠPŠ1, 3.1.08)

Sources

Su1S = Susa A XX/1 1962/3, Sumerian version (*MDAI* 57 pl. 1; photograph only[5])
     1–41
Su1A = Susa A XX/1 1962/3, Akkadian version (ibid.) 4–41

5. Note that the photograph of the edge in *MDAI* 57 is upside-down.

Reprise of OB 1a:
X1 = A w/n iii 1–8
X2 = BM 108870 23–41

The Susa tablet is in Tehran and was collated from photographs kindly provided by Shahrokh Razmjou and Mahboubeh Ghelichkhani with the help of Parsa Daneshmand. X2 is possibly from Sippar.

Tablet typology: compilation tablets: Su, X1. Type III: X2

Bibliography: Edition of ŠPu1MB1, D. O. Edzard, *MDAI* 57 (1974) 18–30.

In the comparative matrix, * marks an ideal reconstructed Middle Babylonian version. The reconstruction is intended only as an aid in understanding the interpretation and translation of the syllabic text, and not as a posited original version.

Comparison of Manuscripts

1. X1 ⌜puzur₄-šul-gi⌝ šak[kana bàd igi-hur-sağ-ğá-ra]
   X3 ⌜[l]puzur₄-šul-gi šakkana⌝ bàd-igi-hur-sağ-ğá ⌜ù-na⌝-a-dug₄
   X4 puzur₄-šul-gi šakkana bàd-igi-hur-⟨sağ⟩-ğá ù-na-dug₄
   * puzur₄-šul-gi šakkana bàd igi-hur-sağ-ğá-ra ù-ne-dug₄
   Su1S iii púzur-ᵈnu-muš-da-á-ra mu-un-ne-du

2. X1 ᵈ⌜šul-gi lugal⌝-zu na-ab-⌜bé⌝-[a]
   X3 [šul-gi] ⌜lugal⌝-zu na-ab-bé-a
   X4 šul-gi lugal-zu na-ab-bé-a
   * ᵈšul-gi lugal-zu na-ab-bé-a
   Su1S 2Idšul-gi lú-gal-zú na-ap-pa-a

3. X1 ⌜u₄ bàd igi⌝-hur-⌜sağ⌝-ğá mu-dù-⌜a⌝
   X3 [u₄ bàd gal igi] hur-sağ-⌜ğá⌝ mu-dù-a
   X3 u₄ bàd gal igi hur-sağ-ğá mu-un-dù-a
   * u₄ bàd igi-hur-sağ-ğá mu-dù-a
   Su1S 3up-pa-ad-ᵍⁱigiᵍⁱ-hu-ur-sağ-ga mu-un-⁴ta-a

4. X1 kur-⌜kur⌝ ⌜ùğ⌝ dağal-la an-né ᵈen-líl-⌜le⌝
   * kur-kur un dağal-la an-né ᵈen-líl-le
   Su1S kur-kur-re un di-am-ga-al-la an-ne 5dd+en-líl-le
   Su1A *mātāti nišī rapšāti Anu u Enlil*

5. X1 nam-en-⌜na-bi ma-an-šúm-mu-uš⌝
   * nam-en-na-bi ma-an-šúm-mu-uš
   Su1S mu-be mu-un-na-an-šu-um-ma-⁶ta
   Su1A *ana bēli iddinūni*

6. X1   uru¹? ka[lam?-ma? ma]-da? ma?-[da-bi]⁶
   *   uru-didli ma-da ma-da-bi
   Su1S   ⁸ʳuruʾ-di-id-di ma-da-ma-da-be
   Su1A   *ālāni mātu ina mātiša*

7. X1   ʿùĝ kalam daĝal-laʾ [ú sal-la ì]-n[ú]
   X3   [ùĝ kalam daĝal-la ú sa]l-la nú-dè
   X4   *traces*
   *   ùĝ kalam daĝal-la ú sal-la ì-nú
   Su1S   ¹⁰ùĝ kalam dam-gal-lá ú sal-lá i-nu
   Su1A   *niší mātāti rapšāti aburrī u⟨šarbiṣ⟩*

8. X1   ʿki níĝ daĝal-bi-a ki-tuš ne?-ha?ʾ [mu-un-tuš?]
   *   ki níĝ-daĝal-bi ki-tuš ne-ha mu-un-tuš
   Su1S   ¹²ki níĝ-dam-gal-be ku-tu-uš ne-ha mu-un-¹³šu-ub
   Su1A   *ina šubtišu mugallita u⟨l ušarši⟩*

9. *   nita-bi-e-ne munus-bi-e-ne
   ArŠ2   nita-bi-e-ne munus-bi-e-ne
   Su1S   ¹⁴nitaᵗᵃ-be-e-en-ne munus-e-en-ne
   Su1A   *zikarūšunu sinnišātušunu*

10. *   nita-bi ki šà-ga-na-šè ì-du
    ArŠ2   nita-bi ki šà-ga-na-šè ì-du-ne
    Su1S   ¹⁶nitaᵗᵃ-be ki šà-ga-an-ne e-du
    Su1A   *zikaršu ēmi libbišu illaka*

11. *   munus-e ᵍⁱˢbala ᵍⁱˢkirid-da ⟨har-ra-an⟩ šà-ga-na al-⟨du⟩
    ArŠ2   munus-bi ᵍⁱˢbala ᵍⁱˢkirid-da šu ḫa-e-si-ig har-ra-an šà-ga-na du-ù-ne
    Su1S   ¹⁸munus-še bala ᵍⁱˢgi-ri-iš šà-ga-an-ne al ⟨   ⟩
    Su1A   *sinništu qadu pilakkiša u kirissi⟨ša . . .⟩*

12. *   eden-na níĝ-daĝal-bi ĝá-rig₇ ù-mu-ĝar
    ArŠ2   eden níĝ-daĝal-la-ba ĝá-rig₇ mu-ni-ib-ĝar
    Su1S   ²⁰eden-na níĝ-dam-gal-be na-ri ù-mu-ĝarᵃʳ
    Su1S   *ṣēra rapša tabīnī umal⟨li⟩*

13. *   za-lam-ĝar maš-gána-bi-da ki um-ma-ni-in-ĝar-ĝar
    ArŠ2   za-lam-ĝar maš-gána-bi ki um-mi-ĝar-ĝar⁷
    Su1S   ²²za-la-am-ga-na-be-et-te ki um-ni-in-²³ĝar-ĝar
    Su1A   *kuštārīja ina pani taštanakkan*

6. The first two signs look more like ĝá-ʿeʾ.
7. TPT Var.: za-lam-ĝar maš-gána-ʿbiʾ-ta ú-sal mu-un-nú-nú.

14.   *   lú-kíǧ-ak lú-gud-apin-lá a-šà-ga u₄ mi-ni-ib-zal-zal-e-ne
    ArŠ2 lú-kíǧ-ak-bi lú-apin-lá a-šà-ga u₄ mu-un-di-ni-ib-zal-e
    Su1S ²⁵lu-ú-ki-im-ki-ik-ki lu-ú-a-pil-lá a-ša-˹gu˺-gu ú
            mi-ni-ib-²⁶za-al-za-al-˹le-en˺-ne
    Su1A *ēpiš šipri u errēšū ina eqli ušteberrū*

15.   *   énsi šabra . . .
    Su1S ²⁸im-sik šà-ab-ra-a níg-da-ra-ta-˹an-ne˺
    Su1A *iššakku u šabrû mali dūri šâtu līpušu*

16.   *   kin bàd-bi ak-ka bàd-bi nir-ǧál hé?-bí-ib-du₁₁-ge
    Su1S ³⁰ki-im ˹be˺-ed-be ak-ka-a-a ba-˹ad˺-³¹be ne-er-ga-al li-bi-ib-tu-ul-le
    Su1A *šipir dūri epēša etelliš lā aqbi*

17.   *   zi ugnim ù zi ma-da-mu-šè
    Su1S ³³zi um-ni-im ù da-šà-an-³⁴ne-et-te
    Su1A *ana napištija u napišta mātija*

18.   *   silim-ma-šè šà-kúš-šè bàd mu-na-an-dù
    Su1S ši-li-ma ³⁶šak-ku-še ša qa-al mu-un-na-an-du
    Su1A *ana šullumi aštāl amtallikma dūra šâtu ēpuš*

19.   *   ì-ne-èš ugnim im-ma-an-gin
    Su1S ³⁸e-ne-eš-še um-ni-im im-ma-an-gin
    Su1A *inanna ummānu itteḫā*

20.   *   kin bàd-ba lú kíǧ-bi hé-em-dù
    Su1S ⁴⁰ki-im bàd-be lu-ú ki-ig-be he-em-tu
    Su1A *šipir dūri ēpiš dūri lipušū*

21.   *   ì-ne-èš árad-mu mu-e-ši-in-gi₄
    Su1S ⁴²ne-e-še ur-du-um-gu ši-im-gi
    Su1A *inanna Urdumgu ubte"i*

22.   X1   ˹énsi? šabra?˺ l[ú?-bi hé-eb-túm]
    *   énsi šabra lú-bi hé-eb-túm
    Su1S ⁱⁱⁱim-sik šà-ab-ra-a lu-ú-be he-eb-du-m[u]
    Su1A *iššakku u šabrû mali dūri šâ⟨tu⟩*

23.   X2   uru-uru-bi ha-ra-˹ab˺-zi-zi-ne
    X3   [uru-uru-bi ha-(ra)-ab]-˹zi-zi-eš˺
    *   uru-uru-bi ha-ba-an-zi-zi
    Su1S ³uru-uru-be ha-pa-an-di-iz-zi-ja
    Su1S *āliš āliš udekkâkku*

24. X2   lú saĝ kíĝ-bi hé-ʿenʾ-dab₅
    X3   [lú saĝ kíĝ-bi] ʿhéʾ-éb-dab₅
    *   lú saĝ kíĝ-bi mu-un-?
    Su1S ⁵lú saĝ gi-in-ne mu-un-e
    Su1A awīlu ina qaqqad šiprišu ana bīti

25. X2   ki bàd šub-ba ki-bi-šè ʿhuʾ-mu-un-ĝar
    *   ki bàd šub-ba ki-bi-⟨šè⟩ ha-ma-gi₄-gi₄
    Su1S ⁷ki-im ga-al šub-ba ki-be ha-pa-gi-ʿgiʾ
    Su1A ašar dūru maqtu ana ašrišu litūr

26. X2   hé-en-dag ù hé-ʿenʾ-dù
    X3   [hé-en-dag] ʿùʾ hé-en-dù
    *   hé-en-dag ù hé-en-dù
    Su1S ⁹he-em-ta-ak-lu ú he-em-du
    Su1A liqqur u līpuš

27. X2   šà iti diš-kam á šub-ba ʿha-baʾ-til
    *   šà iti aš-kam bàd ha-ra-ab-til
    Su1S ¹¹šà iti aš-ka bàd ha-ra-ab-ti-il-le
    Su1A ina libbi ištēn warḫi dūru šû lū quttu

28. X2   kíĝ-ʿbiʾ-šè èn mu-na-ʿtarʾ-re-ʿenʾ
    X3   [kíĝ-bi-šè èn] ʿaʾʾ-ra-ʿabʾ-tar-re-en
    *   kíĝ-bi-šè èn nam-ta-ab-tar-re-(enʾ)
    Su1S ¹³ki-ig-be-eš-še en nam-tab-ta-re
    Su1A šipir dūri ēpiš dūri līpuš

29. X2   ʿlúʾ-ᵈʿnannaʾ énsi ma-da zi-mu-dar-ʿraʾᵏⁱ-ʿke₄ʾ
    X3   [ʿlú-ᵈnanna énsi ma-da] ʿzi-muʾ-dar-ra-ke₄
    X3   lú-ᵈnanna énsi ma-da zi-mu-dar-ra
    Su1S ¹⁵lú-ᵈnanna im-sik ma-ta zi-im-mu-¹⁶un-dar-ra
    Su1A Lu-Nanna iššiak māt Zimudar

30. X2   é[rin-na-n]i-ta im-mu-ʿeʾ-ši-ʿriʾ
    X3   [érin-na-ni]-ʿšèʾ hé-mu-e-ši-gin
    *   érin-a-ni-šè ha-ma-ši-du
    Su1S an-ne-ne-šu ha-pa-ši-im-tu
    Su1A qadu ṣabīšu aṭṭardaku

31. X2   [ninda kaskal-l]a-ni-ta mu-ra-ʿĝálʾ
    *   si-di-se hé-em-da-an-tuku
    Su1S 19zi-be-is-šè he-em-da-am-du-ku
    Su1A ṣidīssu našiku

32. X2 [níĝ-á-ta]ka₄ ba-ra-⌈na-ĝál⌉
    *   níĝ-á-taga₄ la-ba-ra-an-tuku
    Su1S ²¹níĝ-dag-ka la-ba-nam-da-at-ta
    Su1A *tēkīta lā ir4aššiku*

33. *   u₄ bàd ti-la dub-zu-ne-ne hé-bí-in-gin
    Su1A ²³up-pa-at ti-il-la du-ub-ne-en-ne-²⁴en-ne he-pi-níg-gin
    Su1A *ūmi dūru šû quttû ṭuppakunu lillika*

34. *   u₄ igi-zu-ne-ne mu-un-du₈-re-eš-a
    Su1S ²⁶ù igiᵍⁱ-zi-ne-en-ne mu-un-da-re-eš-še
    Su1A *ūmi īnkunu taštaknāni*

35. X1 [ᴵlú-ᵈnanna én]si ⌈ma-da zi⌉-mu-⌈dar⌉-ra-ke₄
    X2 ⌈ᴵlú-ᵈnanna énsi ma-da zi-mu⌉-dar-raᵏⁱ-ke₄⌉
    Su1S ²⁸lú-ᵈnanna im-⌈sik⌉ ma-⌈ta⌉ zi-im-mu-²⁹⌈un⌉-dar-⌈ra-ak-ke⌉
    Su1A *Lu-Nanna iššiak māt Zimudar*

36. X1 [érin-na-ni-ta] ⌈ù⌉-mu-un-šub-bu-un-zé-en
    X2 érin-na-ni-ta ù-mu-e-šub-bu-un-⌈zé⌉-en
    X3 [érin nam-b]a-e-šub-bé-⌈en⌉
    *   érin-na-ni-šè ha-ba-ši-in-tak₄⌉
    Su1S eri-ne-⌈eš⌉-še ha-pa-ši-im-tu
    Su1A *qadu ṣabīšu ezbāniššuma*

37. X1 [za-e ᴵárad-mu] nam-ma-ab-lá-e-zé-en
    X2 za-e ᴵárad-mu na-ma-ab-⌈bal-le-en⌉-zé-en
    *   za-e árad-mu na-ma-ab-barʔ-e
    Su1S ³²ša-e ur-du-um-gu nam-be-eb-le-e
    Su1A *atta u Urdumgu lā tuḫḫarāni*

38. X2 ĝi₆ an-bar₇ kíĝ ⌈hé⌉-en-dù (after 39)
    Su1S ³⁴ge-e ab-ra-a ki-ig-be he-em-tu
    Su1A *mūši u urri šipru linnepuš*

39. X2 á-áĝ-ĝá kala-ga á-zu-ne-ne-a ⌈nam-b/ma-e-še-bi⌉-en-zé-en
    *
    Su1S ³⁶a-ga zi kal-ka a-ga-mu-uš-ne-en-ne ³⁷⟨e-ma-ru-uk-ka⟩
    Su1A *tērtakunu lā dannat rittakunu*

40. X1 [a-ma]-⌈ru⌉-kam
    X2 ⌈a⌉-ma-⌈ru⌉-kam
    X3 [a-m]a-ru-kam
    *   e₄-ma-ru-kam
    Su1S ³⁹e-ma-ru-uk-ka
    Su1A ⟨ap⟩puttu

Translations

Sumerian

¹ Speak to Puzur-Šulgi, general of Bad-Igihursaĝa, ² saying (the words of) Šulgi, your king:

³ After I had constructed Bad-Igihursaĝa, ⁴⁻⁵ An and Enlil gave me to rule all the foreign lands and the teeming multitudes; ⁶ all the various cities, province by province, ⁷ as well as the peoples of the far-flung homeland rested in safe pastures. ⁸ I made them dwell in teeming places and peaceful habitations.

⁹ As for their men and women, ¹⁰ their man goes wherever he wishes, ¹¹ and the woman holds spindles and needles, wandering on whatever roads they wish. ¹² Having established their animal pens in the far-flung wildeness, ¹³ and pitched their tents and encampments all over, ¹⁴ the laborers and tenant farmers then spend their days (working) in the fields.

¹⁵ The farmer(s) and the overseers(s) . . . ¹⁶ Proudly I ordered the wall-work on the fortification! ¹⁷ For the well-being of my army and of my frontier territory, ¹⁸ I made inquiries, I consulted about bringing about peace, and (decided to) (re)build this fortification. ¹⁹ Now the army has arrived ²⁰ and so make the wall builders do that work!

²¹ And now I am (also) sending Aradmu to you. ²² Have the farmers and the overseers bring their people, ²³ mobilize all their cities for you, ²⁴ and have him *appoint* the man in charge of the work. ²⁵ Wherever the wall has deteriorated, it must be restored, ²⁶ torn down, and then rebuilt; ²⁷ the fortifications must be finished in one month! ²⁸ You/I will then ask (Aradmu for a report) about this work.

²⁹ Lu-Nanna, governor of Zimudar province, ³⁰ is coming to you with his worker troops. ³¹ He will have his own [travel provision]s for you, ³² and he should not complain to you. ³³ When the fortifications are finished, then and you shall both send your written report (to me). ³⁴ When both of you have inspected (the work), ³⁵ and after Lu-Nanna, governor of Zimudar ³⁶ has left you both with his worker troops, ³⁷ you and Aradmu must not *alter your assignment!* ³⁸ The work must progress day and night, ³⁹ and you must not neglect the important orders *that are in your hands!*

⁴⁰ It is urgent!

Akkadian

⟨¹ To Puzur-Šulgi, the general of Bad-Igihursaĝa, speak: ² Thus says Šulgi, your king:

³ After I had constructed Bad-Igihursaĝa,⟩ ⁴⁻⁵ An and Enlil gave me to rule all the foreign lands and the teeming multitudes; ⁶ then all the individual cities, province by province, ⁸ as well as the peoples of the far-flung lands I made rest in safe pastures, ⁹ I did not allow anyone to terrorize them in their homes.

⁹ As for their men and women, ¹⁰ their (lit., its) man goes wherever he wishes, ¹¹ and the woman with her spindle and ⟨her⟩ needles ⟨   ⟩. ¹² When she filled the far-flung wilderness with animal sheds, ¹³ she pitched tents before (them). ¹⁴ The laborers and cultivators spend their days (working) in the fields.

[15] The farmer(s) and the overseer(s) are to do all the work that is required on that fortification. [16] Proudly I ordered the wall-work on the fortification! [17] For my own well-being and well-being of my land/frontier territory, [18] I made inquiries; I consulted about bringing about peace, and (decided to) (re)build the fortification. [19] Now the army is approaching [20] and so make the wall-builders perform the task of (re)building the fortification!

[21] And now (also) I have sought out Aradmu (for you). [22–23] The farmers(s) and the overseer(s) have mobilized the villages for you on my behalf, one by one, as much as the (work on) this fortification requires. [24] May the man in charge of the work ⟨ ⟩ to the house. [25] Wherever the fortification has deteriorated, it must be restored, [26] torn down, and rebuilt; [27] that fortification must be finished in one month! [29] Make the workers perform the task of building the fortification!

[29–30] I have dispatched to you Lu-Nanna, governor of Zimudar province, together with his worker-troops, [31] He is bringing you his own travel provisions, [32] and he should not complain to you. [33] When the fortification is finished, then and you shall both send your written report to me. [34] After you have both personally inspected (the work), [35–36] then leave behind Lu-Nanna, governor of Zimudar, together with his worker troops, [37] but you and Aradmu should not tarry! [38] The work must progress day and night! [39] Your assignment is of vital importance, your . . . .. [40] It is urgent!

Commentary

1–3. As is the case with almost all bilingual letters, in MB1, the Akkadian does not render the opening formula (see p. 338 above). Here, however, unlike in the other letter on the same tablet (ŠIš1, 15), the first line of the body of the message is also not rendered into Akkadian.

1. The writing púzur(MAN) is definitely post-OB; see Aa II/4 153–54 (*MSL* 14 284), Ea II 161 (*MSL* 14 254).

4–5. Compare *Letter to Zimrilim* 14: ᵍⁱˢǧidri níǧ-si-sá šu-ni-šè ǧá kur-kur daǧa[l nam-en-na-aš mu-na-an]-šúm-uš = ᵍⁱˢgidri *ù mi-ša-ra a-na qa-ti-šu iš-ku-nu-ma ma-ta-ti* [*r*]*a-ap-ša-ti a-na be-li-im id-di-nu-šu* and ArŠ6: 3 (10): [lugal]-ǧu₁₀ ma-da daǧal-la ⸢nam-en-na⸣-aš mu-ra-an-šúm-ma-a.

4. The scribe of Su1S was inconsistent in recognizing Sumerian ǧ; e.g., saǧ-ga in line 3 but di-am-ga-al-la (daǧal) in this line. As an example of the different realizations of the same word, compare this with dam-gal in lines 7, 8, and 12.

8. The Sumerian and Akkadian do not agree here. As D. O. Edzard, *MDAI* 57 25, has noted, the Akkadian version of lines 8–9 is similar to CH xlvii 38: *nišī dadmī aburrī ušaršbiṣ mugallitam ul ušaršīšināti* "I let the inhabitants of all settlements lie in safe pastures, I did not permit anyone to terrorize them." Indeed, this may be the very source of this line, but see also the passages cited below. Interestingly, the other version of the letter seems to have had a Sumerian line corresponding more closely to the Akkadian of this version (ŠPu1 OB1b: 6–7) [uĝ kalam daĝal-la ú s]al-la nú-dè, [ki-tuš nu-h]uʾ-luh-e-dè. The hu sign may actually be dù, which would connect dù-luh, "troublemaker," with our passage. The word is rare; it is attested late with the equivalent mu-gal-[li-tu] in Antagal B 209 [MSL 17 193] but also in an unusual OB lexical text from Uṣar-Lulu (Tell Dhibāʿī): lú dù-luh-ha (AOAT 25, 3 vi 9). It must be from hu-luh (galtu) and is so documented in a similar Sumerian passage from a Hammurabi hymn (TLB 2 3: 23 [ZA 54 (1962) 52]): ˹ma-da-ĝu₁₀˺ ú-sal-la mi-ni-in-nú ùĝ-ĝá lú-hu-luh-ha nu-mu-ni-in-tuku "my country rested in safe pastures, no one terrorized it," and even more appropriately, in a royal inscription of Samsuiluna (E4.3.7.8: 61–62, D. Frayne, RIME 4 390, but see A. George, BSOAS 55 [1992] 539): ki-tuš ne-ha tuš-ù-dè lú hu-luh-ha nu-tuk-tuku-dè = šu-ba-at ne-[eḫ-tim] a-na šú-šu-b[i-im] m[u-gal-li-tam a-na la šu-ur-še-em] "that (the inhabitants) dwell in safe pastures, that no one terrorize them."

The expression ki-tuš ne-ha is characteristic of Isin, Larsa, and Babylon I royal texts and occurs also in the Nippur Lament; see S. Tinney, Nippur Lament, 183.

9–21. This passage is not in the OB version and may have been introduced in stages into the composition. Lines 9–14 were borrowed from letter ArŠ2: B3′–7′ (letter 3; for comparison, the ArŠ2 composite text is provided in the matrix). Then, the following passage is bracketed by two almost identical lines (15=22), both possibly corresponding to line 15 of ŠPuOB1a. This is a trace of a rather crude editorial process.

11 (= ArŠ2 B4′). The scribe clearly had problems with the source text; he abbreviated the Sumerian, which he clearly did not understand, and therefore did not render the end of the line into Akkadian. One should note that the writing munus-še cannot be used as evidence for the reconstruction of the final consonant of the Sumerian word for "woman," because the Susa text frequently uses various /š/ signs for /s/, and the playful orthography cannot be used as evidence for any language norms.

12 (=ArŠ2 B5′). The context makes it easy to make a guess as to the meaning of ĝá-rig₇, although the other available evidence is ambiguous; see J. Krecher, SKLy 153. A clue to the meaning of the word may be found, perhaps, in CT 15 18:37 and its unpublished duplicate CBS 145 rev. 6′ (cited by M. Civil, AfO 25 [1974–77] 65 n. 2): mu-lu ĜÁ.RIG₇-ga-na uga^mušen ba-e-dab₅ = mu-lu-mu da-ga-na uga bí-dab₅, "a man captured a raven in his dwelling." Here the syllabic text substitutes da-ga-na for ĜÁ.RIG₇. I am therefore assuming that the writing ĜÁ.RIG₇.GA.NA represents daggan^ga-na rather than ĝá-rig₇-ga-na. This is, then, another writing of da-ga-na/da-gána, "sleeping quarters." Perhaps the distinction is one of human versus animal shelter. Here the Sumerian has the otherwise incomprehensible na-ri, which may be an attempt to render /ĝarig/, and the Akkadian is tabīnu, "shelter, shed" a word that is, with two exceptions, otherwise only known from post-OB contexts; in lexical texts, it translates á-bàd, "lean-to."[8]

---

8. The only OB attestation is in two PNs; see CAD T 27. I am grateful to Martha Roth for providing me with a copy of the entry prior to publication.

It is difficult to understand how the Sumerian verbal root ǧar, usually *šakānu*, came to be translated by *mullû*; perhaps the writer recognized some resonance of the completely unrelated expression *ana ṣirî mullû*, "to fill to the brim" (*CAD* Ṣ 210).

13 (= ArŠ2 B6′). The words za-lam-ǧar and maš-gána are not common in Sumerian. Here they are used in hendiadys; note maš-gána = [a]-*ša-šum*, za-lam-ǧar = *ku-uš-ta-ru-um* (OBGT XI v 18′–19′ [*MSL* 4 117]); this must be derived from Proto-Izi I 336–37 [*MSL* 13 28]).

15=22. As things now stand, neither of these lines is securely attested in the OB version; the restoration of ŠPuOB1a: 15 is most uncertain. With the exception of the first two words, I cannot interpret the Sumerian of line 15. The word níǧ may stand for níǧ-a-na = *mala* / *mali*, but the lines are clearly corrupt.

In both 15 and 22, the Akkadian line writes the two occupations as IM.SIG and ŠÀ.AB.RA.A, using two unique logographic writings, and the same signs are used in the Sumerian version as well. The scribe of this tablet writes three signs in a similar fashion: UD, ÉRIN, and SIG, but maintains distinctions. There can be little doubt that šà-ab-ra-a (Sum.) and ŠÀ.AB.RA.A (Akk.) attempt to render šabra = *šabrû*, "overseer, chief administrator," but the word has essentially gone out of use already in the later part of the OB period (*CAD* Š/1 14), and it is probable that the MB writer did not know very much about this administrative title. It is possible that the source of this is the proximity of the words énsi and šabra in Hh II 10 and 12 (*MSL* 5 51).

16. Edzard plausibly reconstructed the end of the Sumerian line as *nir-ǧál li-bí-ib-tur-re and translated it "Cette muraille ne doit pas diminuer son prestige."

17–18. These line seem to refer to PuŠ1: 4–8 (13): lugal-ǧu₁₀ kù-sig₁₇ ⁿᵃ⁴za-gìn diǧir-re-e-ne-ka in-ne-en-dím-dím-ma, zi-ni-šè-àm in-nu-ù, lugal-ǧu₁₀ zi ugnim ù kalam-ma-ni-šè, bàd gal igi-hur-saǧ-ǧá mu lú kúr hul-ǧál-šè, uǧ kalam-ma-ni-šè mu-un-dù, "Is it not for the sake of his own well-being that my king fashions (objects) of precious metals and jewels for the gods? My king, for the well-being of the army and his country has built the great fortifications of Igihursaga against the vile enemy for the sake of his people and his country." This is the only allusion in this letter to the missive that it was designed to answer.

18. The Sumerian of this line is difficult to understand. ši-li-ma must be silim, rendered by *šullumu* in Akkadian. The sequence qa-al may be bàd, as is ga-al in line 27, and the verb must be dù. At some point in the transmission process, èn-tar was rendered by the Emesal form aš-tar.

23. Note the rare use of the D-stem of *dekû*.

24. The otherwise unattested lú saǧ kíǧ, which is already present in the OB version a, must be a back-translation from Akkadian.

The Susa text appears to be garbled. While the Sumerian can be harmonized with the OB version, the Akkadian makes little sense. Instead of a verb that corresponds to mu-un-e, the scribe wrote ÉŠ É; in the orthography used here, this should correspond to *ana bīti*, which makes little sense in this context.

27. The OB and the later text differ here, once again. The older text has á šub-ba but the SuS1 has bàd. á šub is not attested in any narrative but is found once in a lexical text: *i-du ma-aq-tum* (Proto-Izi II Bi. A iii 17′ [MSL 13 57]), which *CAD* renders as "limp arm" (M/1 255) but which must refer to the side of the wall; note á bàd = *i-di du-ri* two lines later in the same lexical text. It is possible that this is an unusual back-translation of *aḫa nadû*, "to be careless, negligent," usually gú. . .šub in Sumerian, and that the line should be rendered "the delayed work must be finished in the course of one month."

28. In this line, X2 and Su1S agree on the Sumerian verb, but the Akkadian has a completely different predicate.

29–32; 35–36. These lines are clearly derived and adapted from the Šu-Sin correspondence; see the commentary to lines 26–29 of the previous letter (PŠu1, 13).

31. The Akkadian *ṣidītu* corresponds well to the Sumerian ninda kaskal-la; see ninda kaskal-la: NINDA KASKAL.[L]A = *ṣi-di-[tum], a-ka-al ḫa-[ra-ni]* (OB Diri "Oxford" 387–88 [MSL 15 45]). The syllabic text of Su1S has zi-be-iš-šè he-em-da-an-du-ku, which seems at odds with this. Edzard suggested that this might have been a composite beginning with zì; more likely, it is a pseudo-loan in Sumerian from *ṣidītu*.

32. Edzard reconstructed the underlying text as níg kal-ka la-ba-da-TAG₄.TAG₄. The *CAD* (T 326) recognized that the first word was níg-á-taka₄, KA-taka₄ = *tēkītu*, "complaint." The Sumerian word is otherwise known only from lexical sources and from the post-OB *Examination Text A*: 52. The OB version 1a 23, although broken at the beginning, has the verbal root g̃ál and therefore seems equivalent to *tēkīta rašû*, "to complain," an idiom well attested in OB letters, which is found in the Akkadian version of the Susa text. The latter, however, has the verbal form la-ba-nam-da-at-ta, syllabic for la-ba-ra-an-tuku/taka₄.

36–37. The verbs in both lines differ from what is found in the OB versions; somewhere in the chain of transmission, misunderstandings crept in that were then resolved by somewhat convoluted means. Already in the OB manuscripts, the predicates differ: lá in X1 and bal in X2. Is one a hearing mistake for the other, or has there been a reinterpretation? In either case, it is difficult to decide which version, if any, might be primary. If lá is to be taken literally and not as a syllabic rendering, then it is probably used here similarly to Akkadian *la imaṭṭi*; see *CAD* M/1 433. It is also possible that it means "do not allow the (work) to slacken." In view of the syllabic writing on the later version, it is unclear which of the two was passed down. Most probably it is bal. The unique rendering of bal by *uḫḫuru* is possibly derived from a confusion with bal = *ḫerû*, "to dig," an explanation that is not out of line with other interpretations found in the text. The whole issue was complicated by the fact that two Akkadian verbs, *ezēbu* and *uḫḫuru*, are both associated with the same Sumerian roots in the lexical tradition (mostly Diri): tag₄ and bar (*CAD* E 416 and *CAD* U 42 sub *uḫḫuru* A (provided pre-publication, courtesy Martha Roth). This is where the combination of bar and bal resulted in the Akkadian translation.

38–39. There was clearly some transmission confusion about these lines, which are only in one of the two extant OB witnesses, albeit in reverse order from what we find in the MB version.

38. ĝi₆ an-bar₇ corresponds to Akkadian *mūšu u muṣlalu* as well as to *mūša u urra* (see the dictionaries); note the post-Ur III letter AS 22 7:3–16 *i-na mu-ši-im ù i-na mu-uṣ-la-li-im ma-ṣa-ar-tum i-na dú-ri-im la úr-ra-dam*, "The watch must not come down from the wall night and day!" It is possible that, idiomatically, this might refer to periods when work is not normally done, to the night as well as daily siesta (*muṣlalu*), as suggested to me by J. Cooper.

39. The Sumerian and Akkadian versions of the Susa text are clearly corrupt. Somewhere along the line of transmission, á-áĝ-ĝá was rendered as *têrtu*, but the rest of it was misunderstood. Somehow á became *rittu*, "hand," but then the interpretation came to a dead end, and the rest of the line seems to be incomplete. The scribe finished the line with e-ma-ru-uk-ka, then realized that this should be a separate line, inscribed the Akkadian translation, and then repeated the word, translating it defectively (⟨ap⟩-pu-tu).

Transliteration of the MB Susa Manuscript[9]

Su1S/A = Suza A XII/I i 1–ii 39 (*MDAI* 57 pl. 1)

i 1. púzur-ᵈnu-muš-da-á-ra mu-un-ne-du
2. ᵈšul-gi lú-gal-zú na-ap-pa-a
3. up-pa-ad-ᵍⁱigiᵍⁱ-hu-ur-saĝ-ga mu-un-
4. ta-a kur-kur-re un di-am-ga-al-la an-ne
5. ᵈᵈ⁺en-líl-le mu-be mu-un-na-an-šu-um-ma-
6. ta U KUR.MEŠᵗⁱ *ni-ší ra-ap-šà-ti* ANⁿᵘ
7. ù ᵈKUR.GAL ÉŠ *be-li id-di-nu-ni*

8. ʾuruʾ-di-id-di ma-da-ma-da-be
9. URU.MEŠⁿⁱ *ma-tu* TA *ma-ti-šà*
10. uĝ kalam dam-gal-lá ú sal-lá i-nu
11. *ni-ší* KUR.MEŠᵗⁱ *ra-ap-šà-ti a-bur-ri ú*

---

9. The scribe used U to separate Sumerian and Akkadian and double/triple lines to separate sections.

12. ki níǧ-dam-gal-be ku-tu-uš ne-ha mu-un-
13. šu-ub U TA *šu-ub-ti-šu mu-gal-li-ta ù*

14. nita^ta^-be-e-en-ne munus-e-en-ne
15. NITA.MEŠ-*šu-nu* MUNUS.MEŠ-*šu-nu*
16. nita^ta^-be ki šà-ga-an-ne e-du
17. NITA-*šu e-mi li-ib-bi-šu* DU^ka^
18. munus-še bala ^giš^gi-ri-iš šà-ga-an-ne al
19. MUNUS^tu^ *qa-du* ^giš^BALA-*šà ù ki-ri-is-sí*

20. eden-na níǧ-dam-gal-be na-ri ù-mu-ǧar^ár^
21. EDEN^ra^ *ra-ap-šà ta-bi-ni* ⌈*ú*⌉-*ma-al-*⟨*li*⟩
22. za-la-am-ga-na-be-et-te ki um-ni-in-
23. ǧar-ǧar U *ku-uš-ta-ri-a* TA IGI *ta-aš-*
24. *ta-*ǦAR.ǦAR^am^ U *lu-ú-ki-im-ik-ki*
25. lu-ú-a-pil-lá a-šà-⌈gu⌉ gu ú mi-ni-ib-
26. za-al-za-⌈le-en-ne⌉ U ⌈DÍM *ši*⌉*-ip ši-ip-*⟨*ri*⟩
27. *ù* ⌈*er-re*⌉-*šu* TA A.ŠÀ *uš-*⌈*te*⌉-*be-er-ru*

28. im-sik šà-ab-ra-a níǧ-da-ra-ta-⌈an-ne⌉
29. IM.SIK *ù* ŠÀ.AB.RA.A *ma-li* BÀD *šà-*⌈*tu*⌉
30. ⌈DÍM⌉ U ki-im ⌈be⌉-ed-be ak-ka-a-a ba-⌈ad⌉-
31. be ne-er-ga-al li-bi-ib-tu-ul-le
32. *ši-pir* BÀD *e-pe-šà e-te-el-li-iš lu-ú*
33. *aq-bi* U zi um-ni-im ù da-šà-an-
34. ne-et-te ši-li-ma U ÉŠ ZI-*a ù*
35. ZI KUR^ti^-*a* ÉŠ *šu-ul-lu-mi*

36. šak-ku-še ša qa-al mu-un-na-an-du
37. *aš-ta-al am-ta-li-ik-ma* BÀD *šà-tu*
38. DÍM U e-ne-eš-še um-ni-im im-ma-an-gin
39. *i-na-an-na um-ma-nu it-te-ḫa-a*

40. ki-im bàd-de lu-ú ki-ig-be he-em-tu
41. *ši-pir* BÀD DÍM DÍM BÀD DÍM
42. ne-e-še ur-du-um-gu ši-im-gi
43. *i-na-an-na ur-du-um-gu ub-te-eḫ-i*

---

ii 1. im-sik šà-ab-ra-a lu-ú-be he-eb-du-m[u]
2. IM.SIG *ù* ŠÀ.AB.RA.A *ma-li* BÀD *šà*
3. uru-uru-be ha-pa-an-di-iz-zi-ja
4. URU^iš^ URU^iš^ *ú-di-ik-ka-ak-ku*

5. lú saǧ-gi-in-ne mu-un-e
6. LÚ TA SAG^ad^ *ši-ip-ri-šu* ÉŠ É
7. ki-im-ga-al šub-ba ki-be ha-pa-gi-⌈gi⌉
8. *a-šar* BÀD ŠUB.BA ÉŠ *aš-ri-šu li-tur*

9. he-em-ta-ak-lu ú he-em-du
10. *li-iq-qú-úr ù li-pu-uš*
11. šà iti aš-ka bàd ha-ra-ab-ti-il-le
12. TA ŠÀ ITI AŠ BÀD *šu-ú lu-ú qú-ut-ˈtuˈ*

13. ki-ig-be-eš-še en nam-tab-ta-re
14. *ši-pir* BÀD DÍM BÀD DÍM*ˢᵘ*
15. lú-ᵈnanna im-sik ma-ta zi-im-mu-
16. un-dar-ra an-ne-ne šu ha-pa-ši-im-tu
17. lú-ᵈnanna IM.SIK *ma-at zi-im-*
18. *mu-un-dar qa-du* ÉRIN.MEŠ-*šu at-ta-ar-da-ak-ku*

19. zi-be-is-šè he-em-da-am-du-ku
20. *ṣi-di-is-sú na-ší-ku*
21. níg-dag-ka la-ba-nam-da-at-ta
22. *te-ki-ta la i-ra-aš-ší-ku*
23. up-pa-at ti-il-la du-ub-ne-en-ne-
24. en-ne he-pi-níg-gin
25. u₄-mi BÀD *šu-ú qu-ut-tu-ú ṭup-pa-ku-nu* DU
26. ù igiᵍⁱ-zi-ne-en-ne mu-un-da-re-eš-še
27. *u₄-mi* IGI-*ku-nu ta-aš-ta-ak-na-ni*

28. lú-ᵈnanna im-ˈsikˈ ma-ˈtaˈ zi-im-mu-
29. ˈunˈ-dar-ˈra-ak-keˈ eri-ne-ˈešˈ-še ha-pa-ši-im-tu U
30. lú-ᵈnanna IM.SIK *ma-at* ˈzi-imˈ-mu-
31. un-dar qa-du ÉRIN.MEŠ-*šu ez-ba-ni-iš-šu-ma*
32. ša-e ur-du-um-gu nam-be-eb-le-e
33. *at-ta ù ur-du-um-gu la tu-ḫa-ra-ni*

34. ge-e ab-ra-a ki-ig-be he-em-tu
35. *mu-ši ù ur-ri ši-ip-rum* DÍM*ᵘˢ*
36. a-ga zi kal-ka a-ga-mu-uš-ne-en-ne
37. e-ma-ru-uk-ka *te-er-ta-ku-nu*

38. lu-ú da-an-at *ri-it-ta-ku-nu*
39. e-ma-ru-uk-ka ⟨ap⟩-pu-tu

15. Šulgi to Išbi-Erra 1

(ŠIš1, 3.1.13.2, RCU 15)

Su1 = Susa XII/I ii 40–iv 37 (*MDAI* 57 pl. 1 [photographs only]). New photographs kindly provided by Dr. Shahrokh Razmjou and Ms. Mahboubeh Ghelichkhani.

Tablet: compilation tablet (Type I).

Bibliography: Edition: D. O. Edzard, *MDAI* 57 20–23.

Text Transliteration[1]

ii 40. ⸢iš-be-ᵈèr-ra-á-ra mu-un-ne-du

iii 1. ᵈšul-gi lú-gal-zú na-ap-pa-a

  2. inim me-e-ga-na ú-ud-ki-im me-e-hu-le

  3. *a-na a-wa-at ta-aš-pu-ra da-an-ni-iš aḫ-⟨du⟩* U

  4. ⸢e⸣-me-du di-ik-ki-nam mi-in-na na-

  5. ar-ra a-ba ma²-an-šu U ÁRAD *šà ki-ma ka-⟨ta⟩*

  6. *ta-ak-lu ja-a-ší ma-an-nu i-na-an-di-na*

  7. a-am-ga lu-ga-al-be šu zi-im-ga-ra a-ba

  8. ab-tu-ku-e-še U *le-e-a šà a-na be-li-*

  9. *šu šu-ud-mu-qú ma-an-nu i-šu-uš*

  10. ne-e-še ⸢níg₉⸣-ga-⸢na⸣ ⸢mu⸣-ši-iq-an-gu

  11. *i-na-an-na mi-im-ma šà ta-aš-pu-ra*

  12. ĝiš-ki-im li-gi-in-ne ú-gu-ze-eš-še

  13. me-e-ra-am-gi U *ù-ul e-gi* ÉŠ EDEN-*ka*

  14. *aṭ-ṭa-ar-da* U ba-ba-tu pi-šà-⸢du⸣-ba-

  15. ar-ra at-ta-at-ta e-eg-la-am-gu

  16. ⸢ba-ba-ti *šà-an-da-ba-ak-ki* U *li-be-ra*

  17. ad-ki-ki ad-ki-ki mu-un-da-a

  18. *la-be-ra mu-un-ta-al-ka šà mi-it-*

  19. *lu-ú-ka i-du-ú*

    1. The scribe used U to separate Sumerian and Akkadiandand double/triple lines to separate sections.

    2. Written as ba.

20. un ge-eš-tu ku₇²-bábbar un ge-eš-tu ku-us-
21. ke-eš še mu-ra-ad-ka
22. *ne-er* GÚ.UN MA.NA KÙ.BABBAR 60 GÚ.UN MA.NA KÙ.SIG₁₇
23. *uš-te-bi-la-ak-ku*
24. mu mu-nu-ut-ku-we eğer mi-na-an-gu
25. *aš-šu mu-nu-ut-ke-e šà* EĞER *um-ma-ni-ja*
26. šu mu-un-te-em-ga im-ma-ši-im-gi
27. *il-qa-am-ma it-ta-al-ka-ak-ku*
28. ú-mu-uš eri-na-ak-ke ú-gu-uz-ze-
29. eš-še me-e-ra-am-gi U *ţe-mi um-ma-*
30. *ni-ja* ÉŠ *şe-ri-ka tu-úr-ku*
31. e-ne-er-ra šu mu-un-na ni-ig-
32. na-ma-an-ne ak-ka-a U *a-na šà-šu*
33. *i-di-iš-šu-um-ma šà qa-be-šu* DÍM*ᵘˢ*
34. e-ma-ru-uk-ka *šà-ap-pi hu-un-na-*
35. an-gi-ga U *ap-pu-tu* ŠÀ-*šu la i-ma-*
36. *ra-aş-ku* U ú za-e kù-sik-⌜ki²⌝ kub-bábbar
37. zu-un-ne-et-ta šu-ú zi-ba-ab
38. *ù at-ta* KÙ.BABBAR *ù* KÙ.SIG₁₇ *šà* ŠU-*šu*
39. *le-qé-ma* U šakanka zú-e da-da-
40. be-e šà-a-šà-a-ma-an-ne
41. [KI].LAM*ᵃᵗ* Ì.ĞÁL*ˢᵘ⁻ᵘ́* ŠE.AM
iv 1. *ší-ta-ʾa-a-ma* U šu du-uz-zu
2. ni-ig-nam na-an-nu-le U TA ŠU-*ka*
3. *li-ib-qur-ma mi-im-ma la ta-ar-ru-úr*
4. ú-da-da dumu*ᵐᵘ šà-az-zu-ga-am-*⌜gu²⌝-
5. ú de-mi-in U *uš-tu u₄-mi an-ni-i*
6. DUMU*ⁿᵃᵐ mu-ţi-ib li-ib-bi-ja at-ta*
7. iri-du kur MAR.TU é-nam du-a-be mu-ra-ga
8. me-e-ek-ke-na-mi du-gu-ut-ta
9. ÉŠ IGI *a-mur-ri-i ù* NIM*ᵗⁱ ka-li-šu*
10. ĞAR*ⁿᵃ⁻ᵗᵃ! ki-ma ja-a-ti* TUŠ*ⁱᵇ*
11. ku-uz-zi barag ku-uz-zi igi*ᵍⁱ*-ne-en-ne
12. eš-še tu-uš-šà AH BI IR
13. TA *ku-us-sí* BÁRA KÙ.SIG₁₇ ÉŠ IGI-*šu-nu* TUŠ-*ma²*
14. za-na lu-ú ki-im-ga-ne-en-ne
15. he-li-ib-za-za-an-ne
16. ÉŠ *ka-šu* DUMU.MEŠ *ši-ip-ri-šu-nu*
17. *li-iš-ke-nu-ni-ik-ku*
18. du-ru-be-šu uz-zu hu-ur-mi ni-ig-na-me
19. na-an-tu-uk-ku U *e-li-šu-nu ú-te-el-*
20. *li mi-im-ma la te-ne-eḫ-a*
21. im-sik zi-ga im-sik zi-im-ga-ra-a

22. IM.SIG ZI.GA IM.SIG ĜAR^{un}
23. saĝ-gin ga-ra nu-bànda ĝiš-ki-im ku-ra
24. *šà-ak-ka-na-ak-ka* ĜAR^{un} NU.BÀNDA *wu-ud-di*
25. lu-ú na-an-ga lu-ú-uk-ka igi^{gi} lu-ú-uk-
26. ka hu-la-a U *be-el an-ni a-šu-úr*
27. *uz-ni* LÚ *qu-ul-li-il*
28. ú-ku-uš i-gi-du-uq-qa im-ma-an-sig₅-ga₅
29. *re-e-da-a šà* TA IGI-*ka id-dam-qú-ma*
30. é nam-šul-zu e-ne-er-ra du-mu-
31. un-na šu-um-ĝar-zu ma-ha
32. É^{ti} *eṭ-lu-ti* ÉŠ *šà-šu* DÍM-*ma gi-mil-*
33. *la-ka li-ti-ir*
34. ne-e-še níĝ-ga-na mu-ši-iq-qa-an-gu
35. *i-na-an-na mi-im-ma šà ta-aš-pu-ra*
36. e-ma-ru-uk-ka-az-zu na-ap-pa-le-e
37. *ap-pu-tu pi-ka la te-en-na-a*

Colophon K

Analytical Reconstruction of Text in Standard Sumerian Orthography and Akkadian Transcription

1. ᴵiš-bi-ᵈèr-ra-ra ù-ne-dug₄
   ⁱⁱ⁴⁰ ᴵiš-be-ᵈèr-ra-á-ra mu-un-ne-du
2. ᵈšul-gi lugal-zu na-ab-bé-a
   ⁱⁱⁱ¹ᵈšul-gi lú-gal-zú na-ap-pa-a
3. inim mu-e-gi₄-a-za usu-gin₇ mu-e-húl-le-en
   ²inim me-e-ga-na ú-ud-ki-im me-e-hu-le
   ana awat tašpura danniš aḫdu
4. émedu za-e-gin₇ nir-ĝál ĝá-ra a-ba ma-an-šúm
   ⁴ʳeˀ-me-du di-ik-ki nam-mi-in-na na-⁵ar-ra a-ba ma-an-šu
   warda ša kīma kâta taklu jâši mannu inandina
5. á-ĝál lugal-bi šu zi ĝar-ra a-ba ab-tuk-uš
   ⁷a-am-ga lu-ga-al-be šu zi-im-ga-ra a-ba ⁸ab-tu-ku-e-še
   lē'â ša ana bēlišu šudmuqu mannu īšuš
6. ì-ne-šè níĝ a-na mu-e-ši-gi₄-a-ĝu₁₀
   ¹⁰ne-e-še ˹níĝ₉˺-ga-˹na˺ ˹mu˺-ši-iq-an-gu
   inanna mimma ša tašpura
7. ĝiškim li-bí-ne ugu-zu-šè mu-e-ra-gi₄
   ¹²ĝiš-ki-im li-gi-in-ne ú-gu-ze-eš-še ¹³me-e-ra-am-gi
   ul ēgi ana ṣērika aṭṭarda

8. ba-ba-ti pisaǧ-dub-ba ad-ad-da ì-ǧál-la-ǧu$_{10}$
   ^{14}ba-ba-tu pi-šà-⌈du⌉-ba-^{15}ar-ra at-ta-at-ta e-eg-la-am-gu
   Babati šandabakki

9. libir ad-gi$_4$-gi$_4$ ad-gi$_4$-gi$_4$ mu-un-zu-a
   ^{16}li-be-ra ^{17}ad-ki-ki ad-ki-ki mu-un-da-a
   labīra muntalka ša mitluka idū

10. gú-un ǧéš kù-bábbar gú-un ǧéš kù-sig$_{17}$ sá mu-ra-du$_{11}$-ga-(àm)
    ^{20}un ge-eš-tu ku$_7$⌐-bábbar un ge-eš-tu ku-us-^{21}ke-eš še mu-ra-ad-ka
    nēr bilat kaspa šūši bilat ḫurāṣa uštēbilakku

11. mu mu nu-tuku eǧer ugnim-ma-ǧu$_{10}$
    ^{24}mu mu-nu-ut-ku-we eǧer mi-na-an-gu
    aššu munūte ša warkat ummānija

12. šu mu-un-te-ǧá im-ma-ši-gin
    ^{26}šu mu-un-te-em-ga im-ma-ši-im-gi
    ilqâmma ittalkakku

13. umuš érin-na ugu-zu-šè mu-(e)-ra-gi$_4$
    ^{28}ú-mu-uš eri-na-ak-ke ú-gu-uz-zè-^{29}eš-še me-e-ra-am-gi
    ṭēmi ummanija ana ṣērika tūrku

14. e-ne-ra šúm-mu-na níǧ-nam-ma-ni ak-a
    ^{31}e-ne-er-ra šu mu-un-na ni-ig-^{32}na-ma-an-ne ak-ka-a
    ana šâšu idiššuma ša qabêšu epuš

15. e$_4$-ma-ru-kam šà-ga-ni hul na-gig
    ^{34}e-ma-ru-uk-ka šà-ap-pi hu-un-na-^{35}an-gi-ga
    apputtu libbašu lā imarraṣku

16. ù za-e kù-sig$_{17}$ kù-bábbar šu-ni-ta šu ti-ba-ab
    ^{36}ú za-e kù-sik-⌈ki⌉ kub-bábbar ^{37}zu-un-ne-et-ta šu-ú zi-ba-ab
    u atta kaspa u ḫurāṣa ša qātišu leqema

17. šakanka za-e dab$_5$-bé še sa$_{10}$-sa$_{10}$-ma-né
    ^{39}šakanka zú-e da-da-^{40}be-e šà-a-šà-a-ma-an-ne
    maḫīrat ibbaššû ū'a šita"mā

18. šu-du$_8$-a-zu níǧ-nam na-an-ul/r$_4$-en
    ^{iv1}šu du-uz-zu ^{2}ni-ig-nam na-an-nu-le
    ina qātika libqurma mimma la tarrur

19. u$_4$-da-ta dumu šà du$_{10}$-ga-mu za-e-me-en
    ^{4}ú-da-da dumu^{mu} šà-az-zu-ga-am-⌈gu⌉ ^{5}ú de-mi-in
    uštu ūmi annī māru muṭīb libbija atta

20. igi-du kur amurru^{ki} elam^{ki} dù-a-bi mu-ra-ǧar ǧá-e-gin$_7$-nam tuš-a
    ^{7}iri-du kur amurru é-nam du-a-be mu-ra-ga ^{8}me-e-ek-ke-na-mi du-gu-ut-ta
    ana pani Amurrī u Elamti kalīšu šaknāta kīma jâti šib

21. ^{ǧiš}gu-za barag kù-sig$_{17}$-ga igi-ne-ne-šè tuš-a x x x
    ^{11}ku-uz-zi barag ku-uz-zi igi^{gi}-ne-en-ne-^{12}eš-še tu-uš-šà AH BI IR
    ina kussī parak ḫurāṣi ana panišunu tuššabma

22. za-ra lú kíǧ-gi₄-a-ne-ne ki hé-ri-ib-za-za-ne
     ¹⁴za-na lu-ú ki-im-ga-ne-en-ne ¹⁵he-li-ib-za-za-an-ne
     ana kâšu mārū šiprišunu liškēnunikku

23. ugu-bi-šè e₁₁-dè ur₅-gin₇ níǧ-na-me na-an-tu-lu
     ¹⁸du-ru-be-šu uz-zu hu-ur-mi ni-ig-na-me ¹⁹na-an-tu-uk-ku
     elīšunu utelli mimma la tene"a

24. énsi zi-ga énsi ǧar-ra
     ²¹im-sik zi-ga im-sik zi-im-ga-ra-a
     iššakka usuḫ iššakka šukun

25. šakkana ǧar-ra nu-bànda ǧiškim du₁₁-ga
     ²³saǧ-gin ga-ra nu-bànda ǧiš-ki-im ku-ra
     šakkanakka šukun laputtâ wuddi

26. lú nam-tag-ga lú-ka igi lú hul-a
     ²⁵lu-ú na-an-ga lu-ú-uk-ka igiᵍⁱ lu-ú-uk-²⁶ka hu-la-a
     bēl anni ašur uznī awīli gullil

27. àga-ús igi-zu-ka im-ma-sig₅-ga
     ²⁸ú-ku-uš i-gi-du-uq-qa im-ma-an-sig₅-ga₅
     rīdā ša ina īnika iddamquma

28. é nam-šul-zu e-ne-ra dù-mu-na šu-ǧar-zu mah-a
     ³⁰é nam-šul-zu e-ne-er-ra du-mu-³¹un-na šu-um-ǧar-zu ma-ha
     bīti eṭlūti ana šâšu epušma gimillaka litīr

29. ì-ne-šè níǧ a-na mu-e-ši-gi₄-a-mu
     ³⁴ne-e-še níǧ-ga-na mu-ši-iq-qa-an-gu
     inanna mimma ša tašpura

30. e₄-ma-ru-kam ka-zu na-ab-bal-en
     ³⁶e-ma-ru-uk-ka-az-zu na-ap-pa-le-e
     apputtu pīka la tennâ

Translation

Sumerian

[1] Speak to Išbi-Erra, [2] saying (the words of) Šulgi, your king:

[3] You make me very happy with the news that you sent me. [4] Who could give me a house-born slave as reliable as you? [5] Who has someone so able entrusted to his lord? [6] Now, concerning all that you have written to me, [7] I am sending you a tablet with the secret instructions.[3]

[8] The high commissioner Babati, who is (like) a grandfather to me, [9] the judicious elder, skilled in councel, [10] has now arrived before you (with) six hundred talents of silver and six hundred talents of gold. [11-12] . . . [13] I have (also) sent you news about the troops: forward them to him [14] and (do) whatever he asks. [15] Please be careful that his heart does not turn (against you)! [16] And as for you, take the gold and silver from

---

3. Or: passwords.

his care, [17] and buy all the grain at the prevailing market rate. [18] *Once it is all in your possession, you do not have to hurry.*

[19] From this day on you are the son who gladdens my heart. [20] You are established (as the guardian) against all of Amurru and Elam; sit as my representative! [21] Sit before them on a throne (set up on) a gold (encrusted) dais, [22] so that you will be the one before whom their envoys prostrate themselves. [23] Elevate yourself over them, never turn back! [24] Depose governors, appoint governors, [25] appoint generals, assign lieutenants, [26] *punish the guilty by blinding.*

[27] As for a soldier who finds favor with you, [28] build for him his (first) adult house—your favor will be great. [29] Now, concerning all that I have written to you, [30] it is urgent, you must not change your allegiance!

Akkadian

[1] ⟨Speak to Išbi-Erra: [2] thus says Šulgi, your king:⟩

[3] I greatly rejoiced at the news that you sent me. [4] Who could give me a servant who is as reliable as you? [5] Who has one so able who is so exceedingly pleasing to his lord? [6] Now, concerning all that you have written to me, [7] I respond to you without delay.

[8-10] I have now sent to you the high commissioner Babati, [9] the judicious elder, who is skilled in councel, (together with) six hundred talents of silver and sixty talents of gold; [11-12] *he has come to you in the matter of the credit balance left over from what the troops have already received.* [13] News of my troops have been sent to you: [14] forward them to him and do whatever he asks. [15] Please be careful that his heart does not turn against you!

[16-17] And as for you, take the gold and silver from his hand and buy up the all grain at the prevailing market rate, [18] and should anyone claim it from you, you should pay it no mind.

[19] From this day on, you are the son who gladdens my heart. [20] You are established (as the guardian) against all of Amurru and Elam; sit as my representative! [21] You sit before them on a throne (set up on) a gold (encrusted) dais, [22] so that you will be the one before whom their envoys prostrate themselves. [23] Elevate yourself over them, so that you never turn back! [24] Depose governors, appoint governors, [25] appoint generals, assign lieutenants! [26] Keep a check on transgressors, *rip off* the ears of (guilty) people!

[27] As for a soldier who finds favor with you, [28] build for him his (first) adult house so that he will return your favor. [29] Now, concerning all that you have written to me, [30] it is urgent, do not change your allegiance!

Commentary

One must keep in mind that this letter is undoubtedly a late Old or Middle Babylonian pastiche of the Šulgi correspondence and that the one existing manuscript is post-OB; we have no idea of when and where it was written or whether the Susa characteristics are primary or secondary. The transliteration follows closely the edition of D. O. Edzard but has been collated on photographs. The line numbers in the commentary refer to the analytical reconstruction.

1. As is usually the case with bilingual letters, the Akkadian does not render the opening formula; see p. 338 above.

3. The form usu-gin₇ is an awkward attempt to render the adverbial form *danniš*; this suggests that the author either composed the text in Akkadian, and then translated it into Sumerian, or that he was thinking in terms of Akkadian when he concocted the letter. Note that adverbials in *-iš* are more characteristic of later stages of Standard Babylonian (e.g., W. Meyer, *OrNS* 64 [1995] 161–86]); only five such occurrences are known from OB literary texts (N. Wasserman, *Style and Form*, 132–33). Nevertheless, this expression harks back to the use of *danniš* with the verb *ṣiāhum* in OAkk letters (B. Kienast and K. Volk, *FAOS* 19, 256).

5. Confusions abound here. The Akkadian has the rare *šudmuqu*, which was clearly intended as elative; the Sumerian has šu zi . . . ĝar, normally *šutlumu*. The Akkadian *išuš* is presumably from *išû* and would correspond to tuku in Sumerian, but it is possible that the scribe confused *išû* with *ašāšu*. The ending -e-še on the Sumerian verb cannot be the quotative, nor should it be a plural ending, and therefore it is most likely a mistake, driven by the -*š(u)* ending of the Akkadian verb.

6. Here, once again there are problems with the translation of the verb gi₄. The Sumerian has "I have written to you," whereas the Akkadian has "you have written to me." The same is true of line 29. In both cases, logic requires that one prefer the Sumerian version.

7. The sign sequence ĝiš-ki-im li-gi-in-ne cannot be reconciled with the Akkadian *ul ēgi*. Once again, someone was translating back from Akkadian, albeit imperfectly. The scribe may have confused Akkadian *egû* with *idû*, a mistake conditioned by the rendering of Sumerian /d/ by /g/ in this text, and then understood the Sumerian as a form of ĝiškim . . . dug₄, that is, Akkadian *uddû*, as in line 25. The word li-gi-in-ne clearly has nothing to do with ⁽ⁱᵐ⁾li-gi₄-in = *liginnu*, "exercise tablet."

8. The Sumerian has the suspicious ad-ad-da ì-ĝál-la-mu, which is entirely missing in the Akkadian. In historical terms, Babati was the brother of Abi-simti, who was the mother of Šu-Sin, and therefore he was possibly the brother-in-law of Šulgi. Later scribes, if they knew anything about the Ur III royal family, undoubtedly believed the incorrect tradition already established in the OB version of the *Sumerian King List*, which automatically registered each ruler as the son of his predecessor. Anything is possible in this text, but this is probably a metaphorical expression of respect for his age; it is unlikely that the author knew that Babati was šeš ereš, "queen's brother," and incorrectly deduced this grandfather-like relationship in strict kinship terms.

9. Here the composer used two rare Akkadian words that are otherwise known only from late sources: *muntalku* and the relatively rare *mitluku*. Not having a handy Sumerian correspondence for either, he drew upon ad-gi₄-gi₄ = *malāku*; hence the awkward repetition of the same word in the Sumerian version. The use of ad-gi₄-gi₄ for *muntalku* is attested in two other late bilinguals but not in any lexical text; see *CAD* M/II 206. In epistolary literature, see *Letter of Inim-Enlila* 3: alan sukud-da dím-ma ad-gi₄-gi₄ in-tuku.

10. The Sumerian un ge-eš-tu must stand for gun ĝéš-u, but the measure should not precede the number. Edzard has already commented on the absurd nature of the numbers. Note the different verbs in the two versions, as well as the Assyrian/SB form *uštēbilakku*; the Sumerian apparently has sá . . . dug₄, which normally corresponds to *kašādu*, not *šūbulu*.

11. The Sumerian is a garbled back-translation from Akkadian. Someone mistook *munûtu*, "accounting," for *munutukû*, "without heir," a rare learned loanword from Sumerian.

15. Note the very Akkadian use of *apputtu* that is transferred to Sumerian a-ma-ru-kam, which is otherwise never used in this manner but is only attested in letter closure formulas. The writing e-ma-ru-uk-ka, here and in line 30, suggests that the scribe thought that the word for "water" in Sumerian was /e/ and not /a/, as is traditionally transliterated today, and he may have been correct; how he analyzed the etymology of the a-ma-ru-kam is another matter.

17–18. I do not understand either version very well. The Sumerian šakanka za-e dab₅-bé (or dab₅-dab₅-bé; šakanka zú-e da-da-be-e), if properly reconstructed, does not correspond to Akkadian *maḫīrāt ibbaššû*; one expects something on the order of šakanka al-ĝál-la. Since this scribe uses -zú for the second-person bound pronoun, it is also possible that he misinterpreted *maḫīrāt* as a stative.

In the following line šu-du₈-a-zu (or perhaps simply šu-zu-a-šè) does not in any way render Akkadian *ina qātika libqurma*. It is possible that the author confused *b/paqāru* with *paqādu* and interpreted the latter as šu . . . du₈. Most probably, the whole line was garbled as a result of a mix-up between *arāru* ("to fear") and *arāḫu* ("to hurry") as well as their Sumerian equivalents ur₄ and ul₄. For the Sumerian, see *Lipit-Eštar Hymn* A 85: níg-nam-e nu-ul₄-en eĝer-bi kin-kin-me-en, "I never rush (with my decisions) but search out the background."

The signs KI.LAM (line 17) are usually read as ganba, although the evidence for this has never been clear. The lexical lists agree on the Akkadian equivalent *maḫiru* but not on the reading. According to MB Diri, the reading should be šaka(n)ka (ša-ka-an-ka, Diri Ugarit III 178 [*MSL* 15 82]). The later version offers two readings: x-ka-ka and x-x-ba (Diri IV 297–98 [*MSL* 15 162], see also the gloss [š]a-ka-k[a?] in *MSL* SS 1 101. The only evidence for ganba is from *ana ittišu* II 17a′ (*MSL* 1 26): KI[gán!(ĜÁ)-ba]LAM. See now P. Attinger, *NABU* 2008/4: 104.

20. IRI.DU is problematical. Edzard suggested a connection with Eridu, but that does not recommend itself. A more probable explanation is that IRI.DU is a writing for igi-du, i.e., palil, which would correspond to *ana pani*. The use of /r/ for /g/ is found often in this tablet.

21. I have no explanation for the sign sequence AH BI IR between the Sumerian and Akkadian versions.

24–26. These lines clearly echo ŠAr1: 20–23 (2): énsi nam-énsi-ta, lú ǧárza ǧárza-ta, ní-te-ní-te-a li-bí-ib-ǧar ù nu-ub-ta-gub-bu, lú nu-un-gaz igi nu-un-hul, "... had not by his very own authority appointed and removed governors from the office of governor, office holders from official positions, had not (punished anyone) by death or blinding..."

25. The writing sag-gin for KIŠ.NÍTA has been discussed by Edzard in his commentary; I am more reluctant to use this text as evidence for the reading of the Sumerian word for "general." The matter is complex, but it is more likely that the proper reading was šak(k)an(a); see the unique gloss ša-ak-an to in KIŠ.NÍTA in *RIIA* 47:3, an OB school text (possibly earlier).

The verbal form ǧiš-ki-im ku-ra cannot be rendered as ǧiškim ku_4-ra (Edzard, followed by P. Attinger, *Eléments*, 549). In this tablet k = d and r = g; hence, this is simply a writing for ǧiškim . . . dug_4, that is, Akkadian *uddû*, "to mark, inform, reveal, assign, etc."

26. Something is very wrong with both the Sumerian and the Akkadian here. Edzard struggled with the passage; using some of the same facts, I propose a slightly different interpretation. It seems that whatever the "original" may have contained, some misinterpretation came from a form that had syllabic Sumerian, and the Akkadian version was either composed after the corruption or was altered to match the new reading. The model for this line must be sought in the royal prerogative for execution and blinding that is expressed in two other letters: ŠAr1: 23 (2): lú nu-un-gaz igi nu-un-hul, and ŠuŠa1: 25 X1 (19): lú gaz-dè lú igi hul-hul-da, X2: lú [g]az-dè hul-hul-le-dè (see p. 280, above). One can assume that the "original" text had a syllabic version of *lú gaz-a igi lú hul-a, "execute people, blind them." Everything went wrong; someone reinterpreted the first part of the line as na-an-gaz and produced a syllabic writing na-an-ga, which was interpreted as a standing for lú nam-tag-ga, which the lexical texts render as *bēl ar/nni*, "transgressor, guilty person." The original translation of igi lú hul-a was misread so that *i-ni* became *uz-ni*. Sum. hul was rendered by Akk. *qullulu* on the basis of lexical equivalencies with Akk. *g/qullulu*, a verb, or verbs, that still present some interpretive difficulties (see the dictionaries); e.g., al-hul-h[ul] = *gu-u[l-lu-ul]*, ba-hul-hul = *ig-[da-li-li]* (OBGT XI iv 10′–12′ [MSL 4 116]), and hul-hul = *gu-u[l-lu-lu-um]* (Antagal G 131 [MSL 17 224]). Whatever the line of errors, one can be fairly sure that at one point the meaning of the line was "You are permitted to execute and blind people." This series of distortions may have also been affected by the association of *q/qullulu* with *gillatu,* "crime," and its Sumerian lexical counterpart lúg (lu-ú-uk-ka²).

28. The otherwise unattested é nam-šul = *bīt eṭlūti* is problematic. The Akkadian *eṭlātu* is usually rendered by Sumerian nam-ĝuruš; nam-šul is usually *meṭlūtu,* "manliness, maturity," and it is probable that this is what the author had in mind. The -zu on the Sumerian word is superfluous.

30. The final verbal phrase probably results from a misinterpretation of the Akkadian use of *pû* + *nabalkutu,* equivalent to Sumerian ka bal but equating the latter with *enû.* The idiom means "to change allegiance/mood" and is similar in meaning to dím-ma ma-da kúr = *ṭēm māti šanû,* for which see p. 401 below.

16. Amar-Sin to Šulgi 1

(AmŠ1, 3.1.12)

Composite Text

1. lugal-ǧu₁₀-ra ù-na-a-dug₄
2. ᴵamar-ᵈen.zu-na árad-zu na-ab-bé-a
3. a-šà níǧ lugal-ǧu₁₀ ma-an-dug₄
4. uru ǧá-ǧá-tum ǧá DUB²-ra mu-un-tur
5. árad lugal-ǧu₁₀ ǧá-e al-me-en-na-ta saǧ-ki lugal-ǧu₁₀ igi mu-du₈-a-gin₇ ᵍⁱˢtukul-ǧu₁₀ ba-šub
6. a-šà šà ma-da-ka šu mu-ni-tak₄²
7. ᵍⁱˢhur peš₁₀ a-šà² nu-x saǧ [ma-an-si-ga]¹
8. a-šà-bi gú íd-da-šè limmu₅ dana-bi nu-tehe
9. pa₅ a du₁₁-ga hur-saǧ nu-níǧin²²
10. a-ša-an-gàr-ra nu-me-e inim lugal-ǧá-ke₄ ab-bé-e
11. a-šà-bi nu-mu-un-da-zàh²
12. níǧ lugal-ǧu₁₀ ab-bé-en-a lugal-ǧu₁₀ hé-en-zu

¹ Speak to my king, ² saying (the words) of Amar-Sin, your servant: ³ In the matter of the field that my liege spoke to me about: ⁴ . . . diminished. ⁵ Because I am my king's servant, *as soon as I saw his majesty's face, I dropped my weapons (to deal with the issue).* ⁶ I (?) dispatched (someone) to the field in the territory. ⁷ *In the plans, the riverbank did not . . . the field; it's side seems much too short for me.* ⁸ That field does not (even) come close to the river by forty (fifty) km. ⁹ The irrigation ditch does not wind around the Hursag. ¹⁰ There is no deceit here; (I am obedient) to the orders that my liege has given. ¹¹ That field cannot be lost (to cultivation)! ¹² Whatever you, my king order me to do, (I will do). . . . Now my king knows (all this)!

Commentary

Two texts of unknown origin form the basis of the reconstruction, and both are unreliable. X1 is idiosyncratic, difficult to read, and is broken on the right edge. X2

1. Var.: ᵍⁱˢapin a-šà x x saǧ ma-an-si-ga.
2. Var.: x x šušana² dana-bi min-àm a-šà engar nu-ǧál.

is known only from a hand-copy made years ago by T. G. Pinches that was found by Irving Finkel, who was kind enough to make it available to me. The "Relph Collection," which belonged to Arthur E. Relph, was first studied by Pinches, who published some Old Babylonian documents from this group in a three-part article in *PSBA* 39 (1917). Subsequently, many or all of these tablets came into the hands of A. O. Haldar, and after his death some of them entered the Danish National Museum, while others became part of a private collection in Uppsala. For the history of these tablets, see J. Anderrson, *Orientalia Suecana* 57 (2008) 5–7. All of my attempts to locate Relph 16 have been fruitless.[3] Until the tablet can be found, or new manuscripts surface, this provisional edition will have to suffice.

4. These lines are preserved only in the old copy by Pinches, and it is not at all certain that he drew the signs correctly.

7. The signs KI.A can be read as $peš_{10}$, "(river) bank," or as $ki-duru_5$, "wet place." The admittedly speculative interpretation of saĝ . . . si-ig is based on K. Maekawa's discussion of the use of saĝ si-ig-ga in Ur III land texts (*ASJ* 14 [1992] 188–89).

8. This line, with a discussion of the verb tehe, "to draw near," had been cited in M. Civil, *Jacobsen Memorial*, 70.

9. It is always possible that hur-saĝ refers here to a mountain range/ridge or valley, so that the line might have to be translated: "the irrigation ditch does not wind around the ridge/valley." The current rendition is based on the notion that this is a reference to a specific topographical feature in the vicinity of Apiak, the one that gave us the fortification name bàd-igi-hur-saĝ-ĝá; see Appendix C, pp. 231–232 above.

10. I have assumed that the first word is the rare a-ša-an-gàr-ra = *tašgertu*, "deception."

Sources

N1 = N 2901	= 6–12
X1 = Ni. 3083 ii 2′–9′ (*ISET* 2 115)	= 1–12
X2 = Relph 16 (copy T. G. Pinches)[4]	= 1–9, +

Tablet typology: compilation tablet: X1. The rest are all Type III. X2 is in landscape format.

---

3. I must thank Jakob Andersson (Uppsala) and John Lund (Copenhagen) for their help in this search.

4. There is a note on the side of the copy that reads: "Relph, no. 16. 59 mm. high, 79 mm. long."

Textual Matrix

1. lugal-ğu₁₀-ra ù-na-a-dug₄

X1 .   +   +   + + + +   :
X2 +   ğá   -   + + + +

2. ⌈amar-ᵈen.zu-na árad-zu na-ab-bé-a

X1 oo   oo o o   o   o o o o o
X2 ++   ++ + +   +   + + + + +

3. a-šà níğ lugal-ğu₁₀ ma-an-dug₄

X1 + + +   +   +   + + +:
X2 + + -   +   +   mu-un-gi

4. uru ğá-ğá-tum ğá DUBʔ-ra mu-un-tur

X1 .   x x x   o o   o o o o
X2 +   + + +   + +   + + + +

5. árad lugal-ğu₁₀ ğá-e al-me-en-na-ta sağ-ki lugal-ğu₁₀ igi mu-du₈-a-gin₇ ᵍⁱˢtukul-ğu₁₀ ba-šub

X1 +   +   +   + + - + + + - + + x   + x o + -.   oo   o o o
X2 +   +   +   + + ++ + + +   .⁵ + + +   +   + +x⁶ + + +   + +   + + .

6. a-šà šà ma-da-ka   šu mu-ni-takʔ

N1 . . .   o   o o   o ⌈maʔ⌉ o o
X1 + + +   +   + +   +ʔ bíʔ - +ʔ :
X2 + + +   +   + ke₄-eš + +   + +ʔ

7. ᵍⁱˢhur peš₁₀ a-šàʔ nu-x sağ [ma-an-si-ga]

N1 +   +   +o o o o   .ʔ o o o
X1 +   +   + + . + o   o   o o o
X2 ᵍⁱˢapin a-šà-geⁱʔ x sağ ma-an-si-ga

8. a-šà-bi gú íd-da-šè limmu₅ dana-bi   nu-tehe

N1 + + + .   o o o +   .   o   o o
X1 + + + +   + + + limmuʔ +   +   + +
X2 + + + +   + + + +   +   +   + te-eh

9. pa₅ a du₁₁-ga hur-sağ nu-níğinʔ

N1 + +. o o o . o
X1 + + + + + + + +:
X2 x x šušanaʔ dana-bi min-àm a-šà engar nu-ğál

10. a-ša-an-gàr-ra   nu-me-e inim lugal-ğá-ke₄ ab-bé-e

N1 + + + + -   . o o +   +   + o o o o
X1 + + - + +   + + + /+ +   ğu₁₀ + + + +

5. Or: bi.
6. Possibly ⌈e⌉.

11. a-šà-bi nu-mu-un-da-záh?

N1 + + + .   o   o   o   o
X1 + + + +   +   +   +   + :

12. níg lugal-ğu$_{10}$ ab-bé-en-a lugal-ğu$_{10}$ hé-en-zu

N1 +   +   .   o   o   o   o   o   o   o   o
X1 +   +   +   + + + +   +   +   + .

N1 catchline: ᴵamar-ᵈe[n.zu-na-ra] ù-n[a-(a)-dug$_4$] (ŠAm1, 17)
X1 followed by ŠAm1 (17).

The reverse of X2 has traces of three lines after line 9, followed by a double line and then:

  [. . .]-x-dab$_5$-bé ʳhaꞌ-mu-un-da-dag-ʳgeꞌꞌ
  [. . .]x lugal-ğu$_{10}$ kìri šu ʳgálꞌ nam?-baꞌ-dab$_5$-bé

It is not certain that this is still part of the same text, although imgidas of this type usually only have one composition.

17. Šulgi to Amar-Sin 1

(ŠAm1, 3.1.13, RCU 13)

This letter not fully edited here. It is unclear how many lines it had, but it was undoubtedly short. In X1, it covers 11 lines, and there does not seem to be any room for more text, because the last four lines are written on the lower edge and the next column (iii in my reconstruction) starts with the first line of ŠaŠu1 (18).[1] The landscape format Isin practice tablet, which probably had the whole text, is very poorly preserved; the obverse has the remains of eight lines, and the reverse seems to have had only a colophon. It was read from a hand-copy and photograph kindly provided by Claus Wilcke.

I can only offer a preliminary edition of the first half of the text to assist in future identification of duplicates:

Sources

Is1 = IB 733 (IM 78644)
X1 = Ni. 3083 ii 10′–20′ (*ISET* 2 115)
Tablet typology: compilation tablet (Type I): X1. Ib1 is Type III in landscape
    format.

Textual Matrix

1. ˡamar-ᵈen.zu-   na-ra ù-na-a-dug₄
Is1   ++   ++ +   + + + + + +
X1   ++   +suʾenₓ(30) + +   + +   + +

2. ᵈšul-gi lugal-zu na-ab-bé-a
Is1   ++ + +   + + + + +
X1   -+ + +   + + + + +

---

1. On the reconstruction of X1, see above, p. 56. Even if one were to interpret the obverse and reverse differently, the letter would only have eleven lines, because this would be the end of the last column of the tablet.

3.   aša₅ KA nam² lugal ù-na-a-dug₄-ba šu mu-ni-tak₄²-a

Is1 +   +   +   +   + +² + +   +   +   +   + +   +

X1 +   +   x   x   + + + +   +   +² - - +   x

4.   šà gi-na-zu-ta numun nam-lugal za-e-me-en

Is1 + + + + + +   +   +   + + + +

X1 ne-šè ù-na-a-dug₄-ĝu₁₀ ...²

5.   a-na-aš-àm ka-aš-bar a-šà-ga x nu-mu-e-ši-in-šub

Is1 ++ ++ + x x + . + x + + - + . o

X1 ++ ++ + + + ++ + x + + + + + +

[1] Speak to Amar-Sin, [2] saying (the words) of Šulgi, your king:

[3] In the matter of the . . . field, concerning which that letter was dispatched: By your righteous birth you are of royal seed! Why have you not . . . the decisions concerning the field? . . . .

The rest of the text cannot be reconstructed at the present time.

Inasmuch as I cannot do more with this composition, it is necessary to comment on line 4, which seems to indicate that Amar-Sin was Šulgi's son and was recognized as crown prince in his father's lifetime. The line is present only in Is1 and not in X1. The expression numun nam-lugal is otherwise unattested in Old Babylonian Sumerian and is surely spurious here, calqued from Old Babylonian Akkadian; this may reflect *zēr šarrūtim, zērum dārium ša šarrūtim*, first documented from the time of Hammurabi (*CH* ii 13, v 1).

2. ù-na written as na-ù.

18. Šarrum-bani to Šu-Sin 1

(ŠaŠu1, 3.1.15, RCU 17)

Composite Text

1. ^{d}šu-^{d}en.zu lugal-ǧu$_{10}$-ra ù-na-a-dug$_4$
2. šar-ru-um-ba-ni gal-zu unken-na árad-zu na-ab-bé-a
3. bàd gal mu-ri-iq-tidnim-e dím-me-dè kíǧ-gi$_4$-a-aš mu-e-gi$_4$
4. igi-zu ma-an-ǧar-ma amurrum ma-da-aš mu-un-šub-šub-bu-uš
5. bàd dù-ù-dè ǧìri-bi ku$_5$-ru-dè
6. ^{íd}idigna ^{íd}buranun-na-bi-da
7. gú-ǧìri-bi a-šà-e nam-ba-e-šú-šú á-šè mu-e-da-áǧ
8. zi-zi-da-ǧu$_{10}$-ne
9. gú ^{íd}áb-gal-ta en-na ma-da zi-mu-dar^{ki}-ra-šè
10. éren$^?$-bi ì-zi-dè
11. bàd-bi 26 dana-kam dím-e-da-ǧu$_{10}$-ne
12. dal-ba-na hur-saǧ min-a-bi-ka sá di-da-ǧu$_{10}$-ne
13. dím-me-ǧu$_{10}$-šè amurrum šà$^?$ hur-saǧ-ǧá-ka íb-tuš-a ǧéštu mu-ši-in-ak
14. si-mu-ur$_4$^{ki} nam-tab-ba-ni-šè im-ma-da-gin$^?$
15. dal-ba-na hur-saǧ ebih^{ki}-ke$_4$ ^{ǧiš}tukul sìg-ge-dè im-ma-ši-gin
16. ù ǧá-e érin ^{ǧiš}dubsik ì-íl-íl-eš-àm x ⌜nu⌝-um-mi-du$_8$
17. ^{ǧiš}tukul sìg-ge-dè gaba-ri-ni-šè ba-gen-en
18. tukum-bi lugal-ǧá an-na-kam
19. érin kíǧ-ak-ne ha-ma-ab-dah-e á ha-ma-ǧá-ǧá
20. u$_{18}$-ru ma-da sá nu-ub-da-du$_{11}$-ga inim-bi x x
21. ma-da murub$_4$^{ki}-šè lú-kíǧ-gi$_4$-a mu-ni-gi$_4$
22. ma-da dím-ma-bi ba-da-kúr
23. bàd dù-ù-dè nu-šub-bé-en ì-dù-en ù ^{ǧiš}tukul ì-sìg-ge-en
24. gal-zu unken-na im-ri-a gu-la-àm hé-em-ma-da-ri
25. dím-ma ma-da nu-ub-da-kúr-ra-aš sá hu-mu-un-e
26. u$_4$ lú-kíǧ-gi$_4$-a-ǧu$_{10}$ igi-zu-šè mu-e-ši-gi$_4$-a-ǧu$_{10}$
27. eǧir-ra-ni-ta lú-^{d}nanna énsi ma-da zi-mu-dar-ra^{ki}-šè
28. lú-kíǧ-gi$_4$-a mu-ni-gi$_4$
29. 7200 érin mu-e-ši-in-gi$_4$

30. lú ᵍⁱdubsik íb-si lú ᵍⁱˢtukul sìg-ge bí-ib-tur
31. tukum-bi lugal-ǧu₁₀ érin kíǧ-ak-ne duh-ù-bé ab-bé
32. ù-šub ᵍⁱˢtukul ga-àm-da-sìg
33. lú gal-gal ma-da-za lú in-ne-ši-in-gi₄
34. igi-ne-ne ma-an-ǧar-re-eš-ma
35. me-en-dè uru-uru en-nu-ùǧ nu-mu-da-ak-en-dè-en
36. a-na-gin₇-nam ugnim a-ra-ab-šúm-mu
37. lú-kíǧ-gi₄-a-ǧu₁₀ mu-na-ni-in-ge₄-eš
38. u₄ lugal-ǧu₁₀ á mu-e-da-áǧ-ta
39. u₄-te ǧi₆-ba kíǧ im-mi-íb-gi₄-gi₄-in ù ᵍⁱˢtukul ì-sìg-ge-en
40. mu inim lugal-ǧá-ke₄ ì-gub-bé-en ù ᵍⁱˢtukul íb-lah₅-lah₅-e
41. usu nu-um-ǧar ᵍⁱˢtukul-ta nu-silig-ge-en
42. lugal-ǧu₁₀ hé-en-zu[1]

[1] Speak to Šu-Sin, my king: [2] saying (the words of) the prefect Šarrum-bani, your servant:

[3] You commissioned me to carry out construction on the great fortifications of Muriq-Tidnim [4] and presented your views to me as follows: "The Amorites have repeatedly raided the frontier territory." [7] You commanded me [5] to rebuild the fortifications, to cut off their access, [6–7] and thus to prevent them from repeatedly overwhelming the fields through a breach (in the defenses) between the Tigris and Euphrates.

[8] As I was leaving (for the assignment), [9] from the banks of the Abgal canal up to the territory of Zimudar, [10] I levied workers there.

[11] When I had been working on the fortifications that then measured 26 dana (269 km.), [12] after having reached (the area) between the two mountain ranges, [13] the Amorite camped in the mountains turned his attention to my building activities. [14] (The leader of) Simurum came to his aid, and [15] he went out against me between the mountain ranges of Ebih to do battle. [16] And therefore I, even though I could not *spare* corvée workers (for fighting), [17] went out to confront him in battle.

[18] If my king is agreeable, [19] he will reinforce my laborers *so that I can get to work.* [20] Although I have not been able to reach *the (main) fortification tower* of the frontier territory, [as soon as I received] information, [21] I sent an envoy *to the interior.* [22] But the territory has changed its allegiance, [23] and so I have not neglected to build the fortifications—(to the contrary), I have been building and fighting (at the same time). [24–25] *Even if (another) prefect were to be selected from the grandest of (military) units, he would still not be able to attain the goal of preventing the frontier territory from changing its allegiance.*

[26] After I dispatched my envoy to you, [27–28] right behind him I dispatched (another) envoy to Lu-Nanna, the governor of Zimudar, and [29] he sent me a very large contingent (namely, 7,200) of workers. [30] There are enough corvée laborers but not

---

1. Var.: u₄ kur-kur-ra hé-en-dul.

enough fighting men! [31] Once my king gives the orders to release the workers (for military duty), [32] then when (the enemy) raids, I shall be able to fight him!

[33] He (Lu-Nanna?) dispatched the (same) man to the nobles of your frontier territory [34] and they presented their case to me as follows: [35] "We cannot even guard all the cities by ourselves, [36] how can (we) give you (more) troops?" [37] They then sent my messenger back (to me) through him.

[38] Ever since my king commanded me, [39]day and night I have been diligently doing the assigned work as well as fighting (the enemy). [40] Because I am obedient to my king's command (to build the fortifications) and I continue to *battle again and again*, [41] even though the requisite force has not been assigned to me, I will not cease fighting. [42] Now my king is informed (about all of this)![2]

Commentary

At the present time, this letter is only attested in sources from Ur and from tablets of uncertain provenience, but it was also known to the compiler of the *Uruk Letter Catalog*, which includes the entry: 4′ ⌈šu-ᵈen.zu šar-ru-um-ba-ni⌉ [. . .] (followed by the incipit of the response).

3–7. The verb igi . . . ğar is used in such contexts to introduce direct speech, as in PuIb1 (23), although the sources differ on the person who is speaking. In X1, it is the messenger (igi-ni ⌈ma-an⌉-ğar-ma), in X3 it is the king (igi-zu mu-e-ğar-ma), and Ur1 has a hybrid form (igi-zu ma-an-ğar-ma). On the other hand, the parallel use of á . . . áğ (line 7) in ArŠ1: 8 (1) suggests that we are dealing with indirect speech. The variants in all manuscripts compound the problem.

Apparently, kíğ-gi₄-a-aš . . . gi₄ is used here in the sense of "send work orders"; X1 must have had kíğ mu-[e-da-gi₄], "sent me an order." The subordinate temporal clauses in line 5 require a main clause, and if this is á . . . áğ, then only the first sentence is a direct quotation and the rest is a summary of the instructions.

7. The reconstructed text follows Ur1. The scribe of X2 either missed two signs or understood the text differently: "so that from a breach in the Tigris and Euphrates waters should not overwhelm (the land/fields)." Note that a-šà is far from certain, because the second sign looks more like ba than šà.

8/10. The verb in both lines must be zi(g), "to rise (transitive and intransitive), levy, etc." For the form in line 8, compare *Ur-Ninurta Hymn A* 49: [(im)-u₁₈]-lu-gin₇ zi-zi-da-zu-ne, "when you arise like the south wind." The meaning here probably reflects the Akkadian use of *tebû*, in the meaning "to set out, depart, leave" (*CAD* T 311). In line 10, it reflects the more common Sumerian usage, meaning "to levy," (*dekû*). This conforms to what Ur III sources tell us about Šarrum-bani. Presumably

---

2. Var: May the storm (of my king) cover the land!

he was stationed at Apiak, on the Abgal, when he received his order from the king and he apparently levied workers as he made his way to Zimudar.

11–12. In Ur III, as in later times, the dana was equivalent to ca. 10 ⅔ km.; see, most recently, R. Englund, *JESHO* 31 (1988) 168 n. 40. Therefore, according to this text, the fortifications at this point measured ca. 269 km. in length. Note the writing dana (KASKAL.BU), which is standard in OB but in Ur III is used only at Nippur; it is regularly written da-na (or te-na) in all other archives of that time. On these lines, see P. Attinger, *Eléments* 639 n. 1839; he considers min-a-bi-kam/àm as mistake (for a-ba), but it is more likely that this is an example of a morpho-phonemic writing.

16. The reading of the first signs of the final verb is uncertain. I have read ⸢x nu-⸣, because the remains of x do not resemble the expected igi. One could translate: "and as for me, as soon as I had released . . . the corvée workers."

For dupsik, "corvée," see the comments on PuŠ1: 27 (13) above. Such workers, like éren, could do both labor and military duties.

19. The second verb in the line is difficult. Normally, á . . . ĝar is interpreted as "to win, oppress, defeat" (F. Karahashi, *Sumerian Compound Verbs*, 76–77), and this would result in a translation "he will reinforce my laborers *so that he will assure my victory.*" While I would not rule this out, with some reservations, I suggest that á . . . ĝá-ĝá is idiomatically equivalent to Akkadian *aham šakānum*, "to initiate work" (*CAD Š* /1 136). Although at present this meaning for the Akkadian is attested only in NA, see already á ĝá-ĝá = *a-ḫu-[um . . .*] (OBGT XI iii 12). Perhaps this means simply "to provide wages" and the line should be translated: "he will reinforce my laborers and provide me with the (appropriate) wages."

20. The word u₁₈-ru has been discussed numerous times, without a final consensus as to its meaning; see, most recently, J. Klein, *FS Hallo*, 126. It appears that two different words have to be posited, an adjective that has been translated "valiant," "mighty," or as a noun. The latter has been rendered "tower" by Klein and others, but this is a guess only.

21. On ma-da murub₄ki, see p. 142 above.

22. dím-ma ma-da kúr, "to alter the allegiance/state of the frontier/territory," which is not attested in Sumerian outside of CKU, is a calque from Akkadian *ṭēm mātim šanûm*; on the Akkadian expression, which is limited to omen texts, see J. Bot-téro, in A. Finet, ed., *La voix d'opposition*, 146–49. *Ur Lament* 230 and *Udug-hul* vi 560 have dím-ma kalam-ma, "the state of the homeland."

24. In the lexical tradition, the word im-ri-a is generally rendered by *kimtum*, *šalātum*, and *nišātum*; see the dictionaries and Å. Sjöberg, *HSAO* 1 202–9. Prior to Ur III, it is written as im-ru-a; this is still the case in Gudea and in the common Ur III PN lugal-im-ru-a, at Girsu, Drehem, Ur, Nippur, and in the Turam-ili archive.

In Ur III, im-ri-a is attested only in single occurrence of the PN lugal-im-ri-a (*AUCT* 1 300:5) from Drehem and twice in a summary of an Umma legal proceeding, *NSGU* 201 (*TCL* 5 6059). While generally translated "family, kin-group," or the like, the exact meaning of im-ri-a in early texts is difficult to determine. The Gudea Cylinders include mention of the im-ri-a of Ningirsu, Nanše, and Inana (*Cyl.* A xvi 18–27); these seem to be corporate groups, not necessarily related by kinship ties, that have labor and possibly military obligations to the state. Something similar seems to be the case in *Šulgi Hymn* B 98–99: ⁱˢⁱˢkak-pana-ta zú-kéš-ğá na-me, im-ri-a diš-àm lú na-ma-ta-éd-e, "And as for (shooting) arrows, not one man from any *unit* among my regiments could outdo me!" Here there can be no doubt that im-ri-a is a military unit of some kind; it might be kin-based but this cannot be established at present.

In this line, the term is qualified by the adjective gu-la, which is usually found in geographical names and in cultic texts but is rare in main-dialect Sumerian school compositions. The meaning of the word is still open to debate; it is usually viewed as a phonetic variant of gal but it is more likely that it is a superlative, as in ur-gu-la, which, like ur-mah, is one of the various words for "lion" in Sumerian (see my forthcoming study of this feline terminology). Note, in epistolary literature, *Letter of Inim-Enlila* 8–9: nam-tag-ğu₁₀ nu-zu nam-tag-ğá ğéštu la-ba-ši-ğál, nam-im-ri-a šár-ré⁷ i-si-iš-bi íb-gu₇-en, which I would translate, with all due caution, "I have no idea of my transgression, I have not been told of (the true nature of my) transgression; because (of the shame that this has brought) on (my) numerous family, I am consumed with sorrow." It is therefore possible that the present line also refers to a kin group rather than a military unit.

24–25. The verb in line 25 and the syntax of both lines are problematical. The form sá hu-mu-un-e is third-person, and although the non-perfect form normally has the agent suffixed, this particular verb (dug₄/e) is used with a prefixed agent with the non-perfect root in OB Sumerian literary texts.

30. The verb si is used here in the sense of Akkadian *maṭû*, "to be sufficient for," a usage that is probably derived from Akkadian—almost always in the form (i)-íb-si—and found mainly in logographic usage in mathematical school texts; e.g., *PBS* and *SET* 38:3 (see E. Robson, *Mesopotamian Mathematics*, 105 for a different interpretation).

The use of tur as a verbal rather than adjectival root is likewise an Akkadism; it is based on the use of *maṭû* (normally rendered in lexical and bilingual texts by lal). Compare, for example, the Old Babylonian letter *AbB* 14 167:16–18: ù dam.gàr maš-gán-šabraᵏⁱ 16 érin.hi.a *i-sí-ḫu-nim-ma* iá kaskal.meš *ma-ṭi-a-nim*, "And while the traders of Maškan-šapir have assigned me 16 workers, I still have five *work gangs* too little." Indeed, the phraseology of this line brings to mind the logographic hé.diri (hé).ba.lal, that is, *litir limṭi*, "let it be more or less," in Old Babylonian documents (*CAD* A/II 488).

31. The verb duh is the opposite of kešd; it is used when releasing people from work or obligations. See *Schooldays* 8: u_4 é-dub-ba-a duh-ù-dè é-šè ì-du-dè, "when school was let out, I would go home."

33–37. The shifters seem confusing, but it appears that Šarrum-bani sent a messenger to Lu-Nanna asking for troops. The latter, in turn, addressed the nobles of his land, who replied that they could not spare any soldiers, addressing Šarrum-bani as well as Lu-Nanna. It may be that the Lu-Nanna and Šarrum-bani letter (LuŠa1, 20) contains that response. The lú of line 33 must be the same messenger as the one in lines 28 and 37; it appears that, after hearing out Šarrum-bani's envoy, Lu-Nanna sent him on to the nobles, and they, in turn, had him return directly to Šarrum-bani.

38–39. Alternative translation: "Once my king (issues me new) orders, night and day I will do the assigned work and fight (the enemy)."

39. See the Ur III letter-order *TCS* 1 56: 9: ú-la-bi u_4-te-ta $\tilde{g}i_6$-ba-šè and OBGT I 811 (*MSL* 4 59): $\tilde{g}i_6$-bi-ta u_4-te-en-šè = *mu-ša-am a-di ur-ri-im.*

The interpretation of the verb kíĝ . . . gi_4 is based on *TCS* 1 326:7 [k]i-ĝu_{10}-šè ʿhaʾ-àm-ʿgi_4ʾ-gi_4; see the comments of E. Sollberger.

40. I know of only one other occurrence of ᵍⁱˢtukul(. . .)lah₅-lah₅, in *Amurrum Hymn A* 50: eškiri zi-ʿdaʾ-[na ᵍⁱˢ]tukul šár lah₅-lah₅ šà-ga-na lá-a-ni, "when he is armed with his righteous staff and with his beloved weapon *that mows down multitudes.*"

41. X2 has nu-silig-ge-en but X3 reads silig-ge-[en]. The finite verbal form (in the meaning "to cease") occurs almost exclusively with the negative prefix; hence, the latter variant is preferred. For examples, see Å. Sjöberg, *TCS* 3 64. It is possible that the author of X3 interpreted the verb as *šugašpūru*, "to be mighty." The translation of this line is uncertain; alternatively, one could also propose a rendition "*even though I have inadequate forces at my disposal, I will not be finished off by force.*"

Sources

Ur1 = U. 16885 (*UET* 6/2 183, No. 1 Broad St.)[3]	= 1–16; 18–23
X1 = Ni. 3083 (*ISET* 2 115) iii 1–4	= 1–5
X2 = YBC 4672	= 22–42
X3 = YBC 7149 i 1–ii 20	= 1–42

Tablet typology: compilation tablets: X1, X3, rest Type III (X2 landscape).
Bibliography: Translation: P. Michalowski, Royal Letters, 79.

---

3. The tablet has deteriorated since it was copied.

Textual Matrix

1. ^{d}šu-^{d}en.zu   lugal-ğu$_{10}$-ra   ù-na-a-dug$_4$

```
Ur1  -ʔ.  . . .    o    o    .    + . . .
X1   -+  -  sin +    +    +  + + + +   :
X3   .+  +  + +.     ⌈ğá⌉ -  + + + +
```

2. šar-ru-um-ba-ni   gal-zu unken-na   árad-zu   na-ab-bé-a

```
Ur1  + + +  . .    + + +     +   +   +   .  + + +
X1   + . . .  .    + + +     +   +   +   + +  . .
X3   + + + + +     + + +     +   +   +   + + + -
```

3. bàd   gal   mu-ri-iq-tidnim-e   dím-me-dè   kíğ-gi$_4$-a-aš   mu-e-gi$_4$

```
Ur1  +    +    +   + + PIRIĜ.PIRIĜ-e +   +   +    +  + + + bí - +
X1   +    +    +   - - PIRIĜ.PIRIĜ-e .   + ⌈da⌉.  - - - .  . o
X3   +    +    +   + + PIRIĜ-e          +   e +    +  + + +  + + +
```

4. igi-zu   ma-an-ğar-ma   amurrum   ma-da-aš   mu-un-šub-šub-bu-uš

```
Ur1  + + + + + +   +        + + +   +  + + + + +
X1   . ni . .  + +  .        o o o  .  . . o o o
X3   + + mu e +  +/  +        + + + +  . + + + -
```

5. bàd   dù-ù-dè   ğìri-bi   ku$_5$-ru-dè

```
Ur1  +   + + + + +    + -  .
X1   o   o . . o o    o o o
X3   +   + + + + +    + + .
```

6. ^{íd}idigna ^{íd}buranuna-na-bi-da

```
Ur1  ++     ++        + . .
X3   .+     ++        + + ta
```

7. gú-ğìri-bi   a-šà-e   nam-ba-e-šú-šú   á-šè   mu-e-da-áğ

```
Ur1  + +  +  + +⁴+ +   + + + .  + + +  + .⌈na⌉.
X3   . +  +  + - - +   bí ib+ + + +  +  . . +
```

8. zi-zi-da-ğu$_{10}$-ne

```
Ur1  + + + +    .
X3   + + + +    .
```

9. gú ^{íd}áb-gal-ta   en-na   ma-da   zi-mu-dar^{ki}-ra-šè

```
Ur1  + +abgal + . .   o o¹. . .   o  o  o:
X3   + + + + + + +   + . . + da+ +  +
```

10. éren$^{?}$-bi   ì-zi-dè

```
Ur1  o    o o o o
X3   .    + + +. +
```

4. The sign looks more like ba.

11. bàd-bi 26 dana-kam dím-e-da-ğu₁₀-ne

Ur1	.	.	+	+	⸢àm⸣	o	o o	o	o
X3	.	.	+	+	+	.	+ +	+	+

12. dal-ba-na hur-sağ min-a-bi-ka sá di-da-ğu₁₀-ne

Ur1	+	+	+	+	+	+	+. o	o	o o	o	o
X3	+	+	+	.	.	+	+ + +	+	+ +	+	+

13. dím-me-ğu₁₀-šè amurrum šà? hur-sağ-ğá-ka íb-tuš-a ğeštu mu-ši-in-ak

Ur1	+	+	+	+	+		x	o	o	o o i	+ +	-	+	.	o	o o
X3	.	.	.	.	.		.	+	+	. +	+ +	+	.	.	.	. .

14. si-mu-ur₄^ki nam-tab-ba-ni-šè im-ma-da-gin?

Ur1	+ +	+ + +		+	+	.	o	o	o	o	o
X3	. .	o .⁵	+	+	+	+ +	+	+	.	.?	

15. dal-ba-na hur-sağ ebih^ki-ke₄ ^ğiš tukul sìg-ge-dè im-ma-ši-gin

Ur1	+	. .	+	+	.	o o	o o		o o	o	.?	.?	ni	o
X3	.	o o	.	+	.	+ +	+ +		+ +	.	.	+	+	+

16. ù ğá-e éren ^gi dubsik ì-íl-íl-eš-àm hu?-mu?-um-mi-du₈

Ur1	traces												
X3	.	+ + +	. .		+ .	+ + +	.?	.?	.	+	+		

17. ^ğiš tukul sìg-ge-dè gaba-ri-ni-šè ba-gin-en

X3	+ +	. .	+	.	. +	+	+ +	.		

18. tukum-bi lugal-ğá an-na-kam

Ur1	.	o o	o	o o o				
X3	.	. +	.	+ + +				

19. éren kíğ-ak-ne ha-ma-ab-dah-e á ha-ma-ğá-ğá

Ur1	.	.	o o	o o o o o	.	o	o o						
X3	.	+	+ +	+ +	. .	.	+ +	+	+				

20. u₁₈-ru ma-da sá nu-ub-da-du₁₁-ga inim-bi x x

Ur1	+	+	.	.	o o	o o o	o o		o	o o				
X3	DAR-a	+	+	+	+ +	+ .	. .		+	x x				

21. ma-da murub₄^ki-šè lú-kíğ-gi₄-a mu-ni-gi₄

Ur1	+	+	.	. .	.	o o	o o	o o			
X3	.	.	.	+ +	+ +	+ +	+ .	.			

22. ma-da dím-ma-bi ba-da-kúr

Ur1	.	.	+	+	+	o o	o	
X2	+	+	+	.	.	+ +	+	
X3	.	+	+	+	+	+ +		

5. The spacing suggests that this text had si-m[u-ur₍₄₎-ru-um^k]^i.

23. bàd dù-ù-dè   nu-šub-bé-en ì-dù-en   ù   ^{giš}tukul ì-sìg-ge-en
Ur1 .[dí]m-ʳmeʾ-dè + .   o o o. ʳeʾ + oo   o o o o
X2   +   + . .   + + + + ++ + +.   + + . +
X3   +   + + +   + + . + ++ e. + ++   + . + +

24. gal-zu unken-na im-ri-a gu-la-àm hé-em-ma-da-ri
X2   + + +   +   + ++ + + +   + -   + + +
X3   + + +   +   + +. . +.   + +   + + +

25. dím-ma ma-da nu-ub-da-kúr-ra-aš sá hu-mu-un-e
X2   +   +   .   .   + + ++ + -   .   +⁶ + + +
X3   +   +   +   + + + ++   + +   + + + +

26. u₄ lú-kíǧ-gi₄-a-_u₁₀ igi-zu-šè mu-e-ši-gi₄-a-ǧu₁₀
X2   + . + + + +   + + + +   ++ + ++
X3   + + .   + + +   + + - +   + + gi - +

27. egir-ra-ni-ta lú-ᵈnanna énsi ma-da zi-mu-dar-ra^{ki}-šè
X2   . . . + + +.   +   + + /. .   + + + +
X3   .   + + +   + +en-ki +   +   + + + + + + +

28. lú-kíǧ-gi₄-a mu-ni-gi₄
X2   + . . + + + +
X3   + + + ++ + +

29. 7200⁷ éren mu-e-ši-in-gi₄
X2   +   +   + + + + +
X3   +   +   + + + + +

30. lú ^{gi}dubsik íb-si lú ^{giš}tukul sìg-ge bí-ib-tur
X2   + +.   + + + ++   + + + + +⁸
X3   + + +   + + + ++   + + + . +

31. tukum-bi lugal-ǧu₁₀ éren kíǧ-ak-ne duh-ù-bé ab-bé
X2   +   + +   .   +   + + + + ++ + +
X3   +   + +   +   +   + + + + +. . .

32. ù-šub ^{giš}tukul ga-àm-da-sìg
X2   . .   ++   + + + +:
X3   + +   ++   + an + +

33. lú gal-gal ma-da-za lú in-ne-ši-in-gi₄
X2   o . +   + + + + + + ++ +
X3   + + +   + + + + + + +- ʳgiʾ

6. Written ri.
7. Written ŠÁR.ŠÁR in both manuscripts.
8. 10 mark on left margin.

34. igi-ne-ne   ma-an-ğar-re-eš-ma

X2 o . .   + + + + + +
X3 + + +   + + + + + +

35. me-en-dè   uru-uru   en-nu-ùğ nu-mu-da-ak-en-dè-en

X2 o . + en + . me + + + + + + + + + +
X3 + + +   + +   + + + + + + . . .

36. a-na-gin$_7$-nam ugnim a-ra-ab-šúm-mu

X2 #
X3 + + +   +   +   + + . . .

37. lú kíğ-gi$_4$-a-ğu$_{10}$ mu-na-ni-in-ge$_4$-eš

X2 . + + + +   + + + + +
X3 . . + + +   + + + - ge .

38. u$_4$ lugal-ğu$_{10}$ á   mu-e-da-áğ-ta

X2 o . +   + + + + + +
X3 + . .   + + + + + .

39. u$_4$-te ği$_6$-ba kíğ im-mi-íb-gi$_4$-gi$_4$-in ù ^{giš}tukul ì-sìg-ge-en

X2 . + _e$_{17}$ + +   + + + + + + + + +   + + . +
X3 + + + + ... o + + +   + + o^9 .

40. mu inim lugal-ğá-ke$_4$ ì-gub-bé-en ù ^{giš}tukul íb-lah$_5$-lah$_5$-e

X2 + +   +   . +   + + + + + ++   . + . +
X3 + .   +   + +   + + + + + oo   o o o   o

41. usu nu-um-ğar ^{giš}tukul-ta nu-silig-ge-en

X2 + + + +   + +   + + +^{10} + +:
X3 + + + +   + +   + - +   . o

42. lugal-ğu$_{10}$ hé-en-zu

X2 u$_4$ ˹kur˺-kur hé-en-˹dul˺
X3 + +   + + .

In X3 followed by ŠuŠa1 (19).
Colophon L (X2)

9. A piece of clay has been glued in the break, possibly in the place of ge.
10. It seems that the scribe had problems with this sign and wrote silig(URU×IGI) as
URU×IGI+IGI.

19. Šu-Sin to Šarrum-bani 1

(ŠuŠa1, 3.1.16, RCU 18)

Sources

X1 = BM 54327 iii 1′–12′	8–24
X2 = YBC 7149 ii 21–iv 12	1–45

Tablet typology: both are compilation tablets (Type I).
Translation: P. Michalowski, Royal Letters 79–80.

Text Transliteration

1. X2 ^{I}šar-ru-um-ba-ni-ra ù-na-a-d[ug$_4$]
2. X2 ^{d}šu-⟨^{d}en.zu⟩ lugal-zu na-ab-bé-a
3. X2 lú-kíǧ-gi$_4$-a mu-e-ši-gi-a-ǧu$_{10}$ dirig šà-šè x[. . .]
4. X2 ^{r}u$_4$-è^{1} á-ág-gá-ǧu$_{10}$ ǧá-a-gin$_7$-nam ma-[. . .] li^1-bí-íb-diri-g[e-(en)]
5. X2 u$_4$ ^{r}è-da-zu^{1}-ne igi-ǧu$_{10}$ ^{r}i^{1}-x[. . .]
6. X2 ǧá-e a-na ma-ab-en-^{r}na^{1} x[. . .]
7. X2 šà ma-da-ka gin-a-zu-^{r}ne^{1}
8. X1 ma-^{r}da^{1} [   ]
   X2 ma-da-a ba-e-te ǧi$_6$ sá na-[. . .]
9. X1 lú gal-gal-bi-^{r}e^{1}-n[e . . .]
   X2 lú gal-gal-bi-ne KA ù-[. . .]
10. X1 tukum-bi nam-^{r}te^{1}-n[a$^?$ . . .]
    X2 tukum-bi ní-te-na-ǧá SU [. . .]
11. X1 #, or on line 10.
    X2 umuš-ne-ne SU-a-ni [. . .]
12. X1 lú gal-gal-bi-e-ne ^{r}šubtum^{1} (KASKAL.^{r}LAGAB×U^{1})
    $^{LAGAB×U}$
    hé-mu-^{r}e-da-su$_8$^{1}-[ge-eš]
    X2 lú gal-gal-bi-ne KASKAL.TÚG.MU[L ...]
13. X1 tur-ne-ne ub-ta-ri :
    X2 tur-tur-ne-ne ub-ta-^{r}ri^{1}

1. Preceded by an erased sign (hé$^?$).

14. X1 e-ne-ne-gin₇-nam ma-⌈da⌉ x [. . .]
    X2 e-ne-ne-gin₇-nam ma¹²-da x[. . .]
15. X1 tukum-bi u₁₈³-lú ğárza-bi-e-ne :
    X2 tukum-bi ù-⌈lú⌉ [. . .]
16. X1 umuš-bi aša-⌈àm⌉
    X2 umuš-bi-⌈ne⌉ aša-[. . .]
17. X1 bùru-da-ne-ne nu-e-da-sì-ke :
    X2 bùru-da-ne-ne-a nu-mu-ud-x[. . .]
18. X1 lú kúr-ra ğar-ğar-bi-⌈da⌉
    X2 lú kúr-ra ğar-ğar-bi-[. . .]
19. X1 uru-bi zag ù-bí-⌈dib⌉
    X2 uru-bi zag-bi ù-b[í²-. . .]
20. X1 en-na íb-ta-ab-e₁₁-ne na-ab-ta-⌈bal⌉-e-ne
    X2 en-na bàd-bi ab-ta-⌈è⌉-[ne] na-ab-ta-bal-e-[ne]
21. X1 nita-bi ù-gaz
    X2 ⌈nita⌉-bi ù-g[az]
22. X1 érin-bi uru ma-da-ka-zu-šè dab₅-àm la-ab⁴-x-x :
    X2 munus-bi uru ⟨ma⟩-da-ka-zu-šè ab-dab₅-e(-)x[. . .]
23. X1 á-ša mu-e-da-áğ
    X2 á-šè mu-e-da-áğ-x²
24. X1 a-na-aš-àm ğá-a-gin₇-nam nu-ak
    X2 a-na-aš-àm ğá-a-gin₇-nam nu-⌈ak⌉
25. X1 ⌈lú⌉ gaz-dè lú igi hul-⌈hul-da⌉
    X2 lú ⌈gaz⌉-dè igi hul-hul-le-⌈dè⌉
26. X2 ⌈uru gul⌉-gul-dè šu-zu-šè nu-ğar-ra
27. X2 ⌈nam-nir⌉-ğál mu-ra-šúm
28. X2 u₄ ⌈bàd⌉ igi-ša¹-⌈da⌉-hur ᵈšul-gi ad-da-⟨ğu₁₀⟩ mu-un-dù-a
29. X2 za-e-⌈en⌉-zé-en in-nu
30. X2 ᵍⁱˢgu-za-⌈ğá⌉ ᵍⁱˢgu-⌈za⌉ ᵈšul-gi-ra-ka in-nu
31. X2 ¹⟨lú⟩-ᵈen-ki ⌈énsi⌉ ma-da zi-mu-dar-ra¹ᵏⁱ-šè
32. X2 hé-mu-e-ši-DU
33. X2 ğéš ugnim-ma-⌈ka⌉ hé-de₆
34. X2 [érin-na-ni]-⌈ta⌉ hé-mi-ib-gi₄-gi₄
35. X2 [¹ba-b]a-ti ⌈pisağ-dub⌉-ba NE-i-e-da-áğ-ta
36. X2 [m]u-na-an-⌈šúm-ma-ta⌉ bàd-bi hé-dù-a
37. X2 ⌈ù²⌉ za-e érin šu-zu-ta ì-ğál-la
38. X2 [h]i-ri-tumᵏⁱ ba-al-lá
39. X2 [m]a-da dím-⌈ma-bi⌉ nu-ku₅-ru-dè
40. X2 [n]am-ba-šúm-mu-⌈un-zé⌉-en

2. Written dím¹.
3. Written URU rather than ĞIŠGAL.
4. Preceded by an erased ba.

41. X2 [e]n-na ma-da mu-un-gi¹(nam)-na-ta
42. X2 ⌜érin⌝ nam-mu-un-du₈-re-zé-en
43. X2 lú-⌜kíĝ⌝-gi₄-a-e-ne á-áĝ-ĝá ma-da
44. X2 ᵈutu-è-da-bi ha-ma-túm
45. X2 a-ma-ru-kam

¹ Speak to Šarrum-bani: ² saying (the words of) Šu-Sin, your king:
³ The envoy whom I sent to you, . . . above and beyond. . . . ⁴ At daybreak my orders that I had provided, to me . . . you were not to exceed. ⁵ After you went away, before . . . ⁶ As for me, whatever (you) say to me . . . ⁷ After you set out for to the center of the frontier territory, ⁸ you approached the territory and after spending the night . . . ⁹ Its nobles . . . ¹⁰ If by yourself . . . ¹¹ their understanding . . . his. . . . ¹² Their nobles then staged an ambush against you. ¹³ When their *people had been expelled,* ¹⁴ like them the frontier territory. . . . ¹⁵ If their officer . . . ¹⁶ are of one mind, ¹⁷ you will not be able to root them out from their hiding places. ¹⁸ The enemy all gathered together. . . . ¹⁹ When their cities have been handed over, ²⁰ until they come out from these fortifications, let no one get through. ²¹ Once their (fighting) men had been killed, ²² their women/workers of the citi(es) of your territory, who had been captured, were not to be [harmed?]. ²³ Thus did I command you. ²⁴ Why did you not act in accordance with my instructions?
²⁵⁻²⁶ But although it was not (normally) in your power to execute and blind people, nor to destroy cities, ²⁷ I gave you (that) authority. ²⁸ When earlier ⟨my⟩ father Šulgi had built *Bad-igihursaga,* ²⁹ none of you were there. ³⁰ The throne is mine, it not the throne of Šulgi! ³¹ Lu-Nanna,⁵ the governor of Zimudar ³² is to come to you and ³³ he will bring 60 *soldiers.* ³⁴ He is to send them [from among his own conscripts]. ³⁵ Babati, the high commissioner, *in accordance with orders* ³⁶ that I have already given to him, is to build the fortifications. ³⁷⁻³⁸ But you, with the workers that have been entrusted to you—dig the moat! ⁴⁰ You were both enjoined ³⁹ to do nothing that would alter the allegiance of the frontier territory; ⁴¹ until (that) territory is secured, ⁴² neither you can demobilize the troops! ⁴³⁻⁴⁴ Then, have envoys bring news of the territory to me each morning! ⁴⁵ It is urgent!

Commentary

The only two sources for this letter are of unknown origin and both contain mistakes, omissions, and unorthodox writings, and therefore all precise grammatical analysis must be taken with a grain of salt. Needless to say, the interpretation of this letter is highly conjectural. The text of this letter was also known to the compiler of the *Uruk Letter Catalog,* according to line 5′: šar-ru-um-ba-⌜ni-ra⌝.

8. The scribe of X2 may have written e for u₄, and the passage may have read u₄-te gi₆ sá.

5. Written as ¹⟨lú⟩-ᵈen-ki.

12. The reading šubtum of KASKAL.$^{\text{LAGAB×U}}_{\text{LAGAB×U}}$ is documented in lexical texts (the variant KASKAL.TÚG.MU[L . . .] in X2 is inexplicable to me); see *CAD* Š/3 172 sub *šubtu*. The Akkadian word means both "dwelling" and "ambush, military post," but the Sumerian loan only encompasses the latter meaning. See, for example, *Letter of Sin-tillati to Iddin-Dagan* (SEpM 2) 5: amurrum ^giš^tukul-bi-da šubtum-ta im-ma-zi, "the Amorites sprung an armed ambush against me."

19–20. These lines were translated differently in *PSD* B 53a: "its cities, it borders, and finally right up to its walls—they climbed up, indeed they got over." Because of the fragmentary nature of this passage it is not clear just where the previous royal instructions begin. My translation is based on the understanding that Šu-Sin had ordered Šarrum-bani to concentrate on building rather than on fighting, because the province had already been pacified, and for the time being the conquered hostiles could not break through into Babylonia.

25–27. The nuances of the words nir-ğál and nam-nir-ğál require a full treatment; the meanings cover the conceptual range from "trust" to "authority." It is possible that this passage, should be understood as "Although you were not permitted to execute and blind people nor to destroy cities, (other than that) I gave you (full) authority." Compare *Šulgi Hymn* G 22: é-kur-ta nam-nir-ğál šúm-ma lugal ⌜uri₅⌝[ki]-ma, "One Given Authority/Trust by Enlil, King of Ur" (part of a long name bestowed on the monarch by Enlil).

28. bàd IGI.TA/ŠA.⌜DA.HUR⌝ makes no sense, and the one text that preserves this line is clearly corrupt. The scribe had problems both with the content and the layout of the text and had to squeeze it into the line, which may also account for the omission of the pronoun on ad-da. One may suggest two emendations. The first possibility is that this is a confused writing of bàd-igi-hur-saḡ-ğá, the name used in other CKU letters for the fortifications built by Šulgi. The scribe who wrote X2 regularly abbreviated proper names (šu for Šu-Sin, ^d^en-ki for lú-^d^nanna). He wrote bàd-igi, then began Akkadian *ša-da*, followed by hur, and left it at that. The grammatical case of the Akkadian word is a problem, nevertheless. Note that this is the only direct evidence that Šu-Sin was Šulgi's son (but see D. I. Owen, *NABU* 15 [2001] 19–20). One should also consider another possibility: that the confusion stemmed from the name of another player in the CKU, namely Puzur-Šulgi. Faced with a badly written original, the scribe may have assumed that this was the name of Šarrum-bani's father and may have understood this all as *u₄ bàd igi-ta puzur₄-^d^šul-gi ad-da-⟨zu⟩ mu-un-dù-a, "when earlier Puzur-Šulgi, your father, had worked on the wall. . . ." In view of what follows, I have chosen the first interpretation.

29. The plural pronominal form za-e-en-zé-en, "y'all," is rare; the proper form seems to be za-e-me-en-zé-en (OBGT I 377–78 [MSL 4 50], *Inanna's Descent* 240/267). In the last example, the referent is dual. The only other example of za-e-en-zé-en known to me refers to more than two: ilimmu za-e-en-zé-en diš-àm šu te-ba-ab-zé-en, ğá-e dili-ğu₁₀-ne ilimmu šu ga-ba-ab-ti, "(the fox said:) 'you

all are nine, take one (sheep); I as I am alone, let me take nine!'" (*SP Coll 5* Vers. B
74:5–6). It is possible that Sumerian at one time distinguished between "y'all" and
"you two," but that distinction, if it existed, would probably have been lost on the
OB scribe of this text. Whatever the case, the referent remains elusive, since up to
this point the words of the king were directed to one person, Šarrum-bani.

The only source for this passage has in-nu in 29 and 30; in light of the many irregu-
larities of this text, it is possible that it stands for in-nu-ù and that other versions
may turn up that have it as "Is my throne not the throne of Šulgi?"

30. The form ^{giš}gu-za-˹ĝá˺ may be simply a mistake for ^{giš}gu-za-ĝu$_{10}$. The translation is based on the assumption that it stands for guza.ĝu.am. It is also possible that
this is to be interpreted as "it is my throne" and the previous line as "none of you
were there."

33. The word ugnim does not usually refer to individuals, and therefore it is possible that the DIŠ sign is to be read diš and that the translation should be: "he will
bring one army regiment." The rendition here is based on the analogy with the only
other use of a number before ugnim that I am aware of, in the *Letter from Nanna-
ki'aĝa to Lipit-Eštar* (SEpM 4) 5–6: ša é-dana^{ki}-šè àš me-at ugnim gu-un-gu-nu-
um, ˡat-ta-ma-an-nu-um ba-ni-in-ku$_4$, "Attamanum brought (a contingent of)
six hundred soldiers of Gungunum into Edana."

I cannot explain the double genitive or genitive and locative in this line.

35. NE-i-e-da-áĝ-ta makes absolutely no sense; I have provisionally understood
this as a garbled form of *á mu-e-da-(a)-áĝ-ta. Steve Tinney suggests to me that
this may be a visual error from a badly written original: á misread as NE and mu
misread as i-i. See also line 41.

39–45. These lines are addressed to both Šarrum-bani and Babati (or perhaps Lu-
Nanna), like the end of ŠAr1 (2), which is directed at both Aradmu and Apilaša.

38. ba-al-lá must be an imperative form of ba-al, "to dig." Despite the place-name
classifier, hi-ri-tum = ḫirītum must mean "moat" here. The classifier ki is a mistake brought about by the association with hi-ri-tum^{ki}, for which see *RGTC* 3 98.
For a moat associated with fortifications, see, e.g., *Samsu-iluna Inscription* 8: 66–71
(D. Frayne, *RIME* 4 E4.3.7.8): ša iti min-kam-ma-ka-àm, gú ^{ˡd}dur-ùl-ka-ta,
bàd-*sa-am-su-i-lu-na-a*, bí-in-dù, ^{ˡd}hi-ri-tum-bi, im-mi-in-ba-al, "in the course
of two months he constructed Dur-Samsu-iluna ('Fort Samsu-iluna') on the bank of
the Diyala and dug its moat."

39. The writing ku$_5$-ru-dè is undoubtedly a syllabic rendering of kúr-ru-dè, and is
only attested in X2, which is hardly surprising.

41. The verbal root nam makes no sense, and the context strongly suggests that this
is a visual mistake for gi.

43–44. Compare *Letter of Šamaš-ṭab to Ilak-niʾid* (SEpM 17) 18: u₄-da-ta á-áǧ-ǧá-zu hé-em-tùm, "from now on bring me your news (continuously)."

20. Šu-Sin to Lu-Nanna and Šarrum-bani 1

(ŠuLuŠa1, 3.3.31)

N1 = Ni. 4164 (*ISET* 2 117) "obv." ii′ 5′–11′.
Compilation tablet (Type I).

I had the occasion to collate this tablet briefly, but it is badly preserved and requires prolonged concentrated analysis that would undoubtedly result in better readings.

This is a fragment of a multi-column tablet that also contains official letters and related texts. There are four such compositions in the preserved parts, and the tablet undoubtedly contained more. The remains of the "obverse" col. ii′ preserve the remains of three lines that end with [a]-ma-ru-[kam], that is, the end of a letter from an official or a king, but I cannot identify this text. It is difficult to reconstruct what follows; at first glance, it appears to be a letter from Šarrum-bani to Lu-Nanna, but the narrow columns make it difficult to fit in all that is required in an opening letter formula. It is therefore more likely that this was a letter addressed to both officials by King Šu-Sin, or possibly even by the "nobles" (lú-gal-gal) of the territory of Zimudar (see ŠaŠu1: 33–37 [18]). It may also be a one-off invention by someone who knew that composition. Whatever the case may be, this text provides the only evidence we have for the knowledge of the Šu-Sin correspondence in Nippur, if my analysis of the source distribution is correct (see p. 57). The tablet is important because it documents, albeit fragmentarily, at least four otherwise unknown literary letters.

Instinct propels one to reconstruct first two lines as follows:

1. ⌈l⌉lú-ᵈnanna pisaĝ-du[b-ba]
2. [é]nsi ma-da ⌈zi⌉-[mu-darᵏⁱ-ra ù-na-(a)-dug₄]
3. ⌈l⌉šar⌉-ru-um-ba-ni x x [x]
4. ⌈gal²-zu²-unken²-na²⌉

etc.

$^{1-2}$ Speak to Lu-Nanna, high commissioner, governor of the territory of Zimudar, $^{3-4}$ saying (the words of) Šarrum-bani, the x, the prefect: . . .

However, there is no room for such a restoration of line 2; rather, I propose to reconstruct the opening section as:

1. ⌜¹⌝lú-ᵈnanna pisaĝ-du[b-ba]
2. [é]nsi ma-da ⌜zi⌝-[mu-darᵏⁱ-ra]
3. ⌜šar⌝-ru-um-ba-ni x x [x]
4. [x] x ⌜gal?⌝-⟨zu?⟩ ⌜unken?-na?⌝
5. [x] x x ⌜ù-na-dug₄⌝
6. [⁽ᵈ⁾šu-ᵈen.zu lugal-zu] ⌜na-ab-bé⌝-[a]

remnants of six lines, rest of column broken

⁵Speak to ¹⁻²Lu-Nanna, high commissioner, governor of the territory of Zimudar, ³⁻⁴and to Šarrum-bani, the x, the prefect, x x x, ⁶saying (the words of) [Šu-Sin, your king] . . .

The readings of lines 4–6 are highly uncertain. Note that in this text Lu-Nanna, uniquely, carries the title "high commissioner," as well as his customary "governor of the territory of Zimudar." There may be confusion here between Lu-Nanna and Šarrum-bani's successor in charge of Muriq-Tidnim, Babati, who was identified by the former title in Ur III texts as well as in CKU. Note also the entry in the *Uruk Letter Catalog* 12 ⌜pisaĝ-dub-ba⌝ x x [. . .]. It is possible that this refers to a variant recension of this letter (see p. 26 with n. 23, above).

The one preserved column of the "reverse" has the last ten lines of a letter, possibly to Šu-Sin, and the remains of the first line of another letter:

1′. [. . .]x x ⌜mu⌝ x x [. . .]
2′. min li-mu-um saĝ-DU [. . .] hu-mu-ni-i[n-. . .]
3′. x-x-bi-ne-ne x x [. . .] hé-im-mi-í[l?. . .]
4′. [ug]nim dugud h[é?- . . .]
5′. [x n]am-nun/zil-ba/zu mu-da-a[n?- . . .]
6′. [x] mu ⌜mah⌝ x [. . .]
7′. [tu]kum-bi ⌜lugal?⌝-[ĝá an-na-kam] x-bi x [. . .]
8′. [t]ukum-bi x [x] x x [. . .]
9′. ⌜eĝer?⌝-bi šu-ĝu₁₀ x x[. . .] x x x [. . .]
10′. [lugal?]-⌜ĝu₁₀?⌝ hé-en-⌜zu?⌝
11′. *traces*

Line 11′ must contain the opening line of a letter salutation. Read perhaps [Ilú-ᵈnanna pisaĝ]-⌜dub-ba-ra⌝?

None of this resembles anything that we know at present. The tablet may have contained a collection of otherwise unattested letters between various officials, perhaps including the letter of King Šu-Sin concerning the construction of Muriq-Tidnim. On the other hand, the mention of "two thousand (men)" may link this missive to the Aba-indasa affair; see ArŠ3: 8 (7).

21. Išbi-Erra to Ibbi-Sin 1

(IšIb1, 3.1.17, RCU 19)

Composite Text

Version A (Short Version)

1. ^{I}i-bi-^{d}en.zu lugal-ğu$_{10}$-ra ù-na-a-dug$_{4}$
2. ^{I}iš-bi-èr-ra árad-zu na-ab-bé-a
3. kaskal ì-si-in^{ki} ka-zal-lu^{ki}-šè
4. še sa$_{10}$-sa$_{10}$-dè á-šè mu-e-da-a-áğ
5. šakanka aš gur-ta-àm še sá ba-an-dug$_{4}$
6. 20 gun kù-babbar še sa$_{10}$ RI-dè ba-an-ğar
7. inim amurrum lú kúr-ra šà ma-da-zu ku$_{4}$-ra ğiš ì-tuk-àm
8. 72,000 še gur še dù-a-bi šà ì-si-in^{ki}-na-šè ba-an-ku$_{4}$-re-en
9. a-da-al-la-bi amurrum dù-dù-a-bi šà kalam-ma-šè ba-an-ku$_{4}$-ku$_{4}$
10. erim$_{3}$ gal-gal-didli-bi im-mi-in-dab$_{5}$-dab$_{5}$
11. mu amurrum še ba-sìg-ge nu-mu-e-da-šúm-mu[1]
12. ugu-ğu$_{10}$ mu-ta-ni-kalag ba-dúr-en
13. lugal-ğu$_{10}$ ğéš-u ^{ğiš}má-gur$_{8}$ 120 gur-ta-àm hé-em-duh-e
14. ^{ğiš}má 12 kal-ga 20 ^{ğiš}za-am-ru-tum 30 ^{ğiš}illar
15. 30 ĞIŠ.ĞIŠ 5 ^{ğiš}ig má ugu má$^{?}$-e hé-ğá-ğá ù ^{ğiš}má dù-a-bi hé-x
16. íd-da íd(-)kur-ra íd(-)pa-li-iš-tum-ta
17. zar$^{?}$sal-la-šè hé-em-ta-ab-è-dè-eš
18. ù ğá-e igi-ni-šè ga-àm-ta-è
19. ki ^{ğiš}má kar-bi ugu-ğá ì-tuku
20. 72,000 gur še dù-a-bi hé-ğá-ğá hé-e-silim
21. tukum-bi še-àm ba-ab-tur-re
22. ğá-e še ga-ra-ab-ku$_{4}$-e[2]
23. lugal-ğu$_{10}$ elam^{ki}-ma šen-šen-na zi ba-an-ir
24. še-ba-ni ul$_{4}$-la-bi al-til-la
25. lirum lirum na-an-duh-en

1. Followed by two fragmentary lines in X1.
2. Var. (21–22): tukum-bi še ba-an-tur-re-en / ğá-e še-bi mu-ra-ku$_{4}$.

416

26. nam-árad-da-ni-šè saĝ-zu na-an-šúm-mu-un
27. ù eĝir-ra-ni-šè na-an-du-un
28. še mu udila-ta-àm šà-gal é-gal-zu ù un dù-a-bi šà uru^{ki}-ĝu₁₀-ta-àm ì-ĝál³
29. uru ì-si-in^{ki} ù nibru^{ki}-ke₄ en-nu-ùĝ ak-dè ugu-ĝá hé-tuku⁴
30. lugal-ĝu₁₀ hé-en-zu

Version B (Long Version)

31. lugal-ĝu₁₀ ní nu-te ní nu-gíd-i šà-ba ĝá-e nu-te-BU
32. diĝir-didli-bi šà hé-ni-íb-kíĝ-kíĝ-e ki-bi hé-kíĝ-kíĝ
33. ùĝ daĝal-bi nam-lú-ùlu-bi mah
34. hé-silim-me-eš numun zi-da hé-en-kal-le-eš
35. uri₅^{ki} uru kù-zu an-ki-da mú-a
36. nun gal išib-e dù-a-bi saĝ-ki-bi kal-la
37. me šúm-mu ús ĝiš-hur ge-en-ge-né kur sig igi-nim-ma
38. šu-ta hé-kar-re inim-bi hé-éb-bé
39. é-kiš-nu-ĝál èš an-ki šú-šú gaba-ri nu-tuku
40. elam^{ki} ur idim lú níĝ-ha-lam-ma-ke₄
41. šu pe-el nu-ma-ak-e ^dlama-bi nu-si-il
42. lugal-ĝu₁₀ gù-šúm-šúm gal-gal dùb-tuku mu-si-il-a
43. ¹i-bi-^den.zu šà-ta è-a-ni diĝir ki-áĝ-me-eš
44. an ^den-líl ^den-ki igi zi hu-mu-un-ši-bar-re-e-ne
45. [. . .] x x x x x x hé-en-ĝar igi-bi hé-éb-gi
46. ^[ĝiš]ig abul uri₅^{ki}-ma ĝál-tak₄-tak₄-da-a-a
47. (x) x i-ni-ib-bé a-ba-àm lugal-ĝu₁₀ e-še
48. lugal ^den-líl-le gaba-ri nu-tuku-me-en
49. x nu x x x x šà-zu na-an-gig-ge
50. x šu mu-un-gi suhuš-bi mu-ri-in-ge-en
51. [. . .]-x šu² nu-du₇-a šà-zu hé-en-du₁₀-ge
52. en-na lugal-ĝu₁₀ al-ti-la nam-lugal uri₅^{ki} mu-un-ak-e
53. níĝ-na-me lugal-ĝu₁₀ kíĝ mu-na-ni-íb-gi₄
54. a-ma-ru-kam nam-ba-e-šub-dè-en-zé-en
55. igi ^dutu-kam ka-ĝu₁₀ nu-bal-e

Part A

¹ Speak to Ibbi-Sin, my king, ² saying (the words of) Išbi-Erra, your servant:

³⁻⁴ You gave me orders concerning an expedition from Isin to Kazallu to purchase grain. ⁵ As the market price of grain was equivalent to (one shekel) per kor, ⁶ twenty talents of silver was invested in the purchase of grain. ⁷ Word having reached me that hostile Amorites had entered your frontier territory, ⁸ I proceeded to deliver all the

---

3. Var. ù uru dù-a-zu/bi šu-mu-ta ì-ĝál.
4. Var. nibru^{ki} isin^{ki} en-nu-ùĝ ha-ra-ab-ak-e (lugal-ĝu₁₀) ugu-ĝá hé-(en)-tuku.

grain—72,000 kor—into (the city of) Isin. [9] But now all the Amorites have entered the homeland, [10] and have captured all the great storehouses, one by one. [11] Because of (these) Amorites I cannot hand over the grain for threshing;[5] [12] they are too strong for me, and I am made to stay put. [13] Therefore, my king should (order) the caulking of 600 barges of 120 kor capacity, [14] *escorted by 12 armed ships*, and load each with 20 *swords*, 30 *bows*, [15] load each ship with 30 *beams* and five (additional) hatches, and have all the boats . . . [16-17] so that they can be brought down by water, through the Idkura and the Palištum canals so they can pile up (the grain) in stacks (for drying), [18] and I will myself go out to meet him (i.e., Ibbi-Sin).

[19] I shall take responsibility for the place where the boat(s) moor, [20] so that the 72,000 kor of grain—that is all of the grain—will be placed (there), and be safe. [21-22] Should there be a shortage of grain, I will be the one who brings you grain.[6]

[23] My king is troubled by the war with the Elamite, [24] but his own grain rations are rapidly being depleted, [25] so do not release your grip on power, [26] do not rush to become his servant, [27] and to follow him! [28] There is (enough) grain in my city to provision your palace and all the people for fifteen years,[7] [29] so let the responsibility of guarding the cities of Isin and Nippur be mine![8] [30] Now my king is informed (about all of this)!

Part B

[31] My king, I am neither afraid, nor worried, and (if I were you) I would certainly not be *worried* in there (i.e., Ur). [32] Seek out the intentions of the various gods and attend to them [33-34] so that its teeming people and its expansive populace will be safe and it's fertile offspring[9] be cherished!

[35] Ur, city of wisdom, linking the upper and lower regions; [36] having been built by Great Prince (Enki), the exorcist, (it is a city) whose façade is precious (to the people), [37] one endowed with cosmic rites, whose foundations and ground plans are secure (among all the) lands, south to north, [38] *it will surely be spared and its (favorable divine) decision announced!*

[39] (Temple) Ekišnuǧal, shrine that envelops the upper and lower regions, without rival—[40] the Elamite, an evil[10] vicious beast, [41] will not defile it, nor render asunder its guardian deities! [42] My king, *the loudest noisemakers haveong run away*,[43] Ibbi-Sin, beloved by the gods as he came out of the womb—[44] An, Enlil, and Enki looked so favorably upon him! [45] Established . . . so that its front be secure, [46] are ordering that the doors of the gate of Ur be opened, [47] saying "Who is really king?" [48] But it is you

5. Followed by two fragmentary lines in X1.
6. Var.: Should you lack grain, I will bring you that grain.
7. Var.: I have at my disposal (enough) grain (to provision) your palace and all of its/your cities for fifteen years.
8. Var.: Please let me guard Isin and Nippur for you, let me have (that) responsibility (O my king)!
9. Alt. transl.: seed.
10. Alt. transl.: destructive.

who are the king to whom Enlil gave no rival! [49] So do not. . . , so be of good spirits! [50] (He/they) has/have taken revenge, and secured its foundations for you. [51] Not being . . . may your spirit be happy! [52] As long as my king is alive, he will exercise kingship over Ur, [53] and (I will do) for him whatever my king might command me to do! [54] Please, I will not neglect (your orders)! [55] By Utu, I will not change my allegiance!

Commentary

All well-conserved sources from outside of Nippur have the longer version. The long version omits the salutation in line 31. Source X5, which has only six lines preserved, could have had either version but has space for the longer one. However, it omits two lines within the preserved section, and therefore it is possible that it originally contained a shorter version of Version B. X4 has the first 29 lines, followed by a double line—that is, the short version but without the final salutation. One suspects that it was the first of two tablets with the long version.

The manuscript history of this letter is complex and difficult to trace at present. There seem to be at least two different traditions of the long version, with X1 often at odds with X2 and X3, with some lines quite different and others omitted altogether. The reconstruction presented here is an eclectic text, and it could be constructed differently due to the wide range of variants; wherever possible, in section A it follows the Nippur manuscripts. There is a long section between lines 15 and 34 where no Nippur text is currently available. Ideally, all eight manuscripts of this composition should be transliterated and translated separately but this is hardly a practical solution here.

5. For the reading šakanka of KI.LAM, see the commentary to ŠIš1:17 (15).

Two Nippur manuscripts, as well as one of unknown origin, have the non-finite form sá-di, but a Nippur source (N1), as well as an unprovenienced one (X4), have the finite, albeit somewhat ungrammatical, predicate sá ba-an-dug$_4$; in these texts, lines 5–6 should read, in translation: "The market price of grain was equivalent to (one shekel) per kor; twenty talents of silver was invested in the purchase of grain." The expression used here is unique and is probably a calque from Akkadian. The word šakanka occurs only once in the Ur III documentation (*Nik* 2 447:9, é šakanka PN), and the verb sá. . .dug$_4$ is used in the same sense as Akkadian kašādum, so that the phrase can either be rendered as "equivalent to," or "having reached" (*CAD* K 275).

6. The otherwise unattested sa$_{10}$(-)RI-dè requires comment. It is present in two of the Nippur sources (N2 and N3), while N1 and probably X1 have the more obvious sa$_{10}$-sa$_{10}$-dè. It is probable that the form is a calque from the use of *ana šīmi leqû*, "to buy," although the latter is attested only in Old Assyrian and at Alalakh (*CAD* Š/3 30). However, when it is equivalent to *leqûm*, RI is to read de$_5$-(g), and one would expect the writing de$_5$-ge-dè. More remotely, one may consider d/ri(g), "to collect," for which see C. Wilcke, *BBVO* 18 (1999) 321–22 n. 10 but most examples are re-duplicated and likewise would require an ending in /g/. In this case, perhaps the line means "twenty talents of silver was invested in collecting the purchased of grain."

8. E. Robson, "More than Metrology. . ." 351, already observed that this letter reads suspiciously like an OB mathematical exercise applied in a semi-realistic context. In view of this, it is particularly troublesome that some of the scribes had problems with the numbers in this text and in the answer IbIš1 (22). The number and the capacity of the barges in line 13 and the recapitulation of the full amount of grain in line 20 indicate that 72,000 kor are at stake, but different parts of the letter are reconstructed on the basis of different manuscripts, and this complicates matters somewhat.[11] The scribe of N3 wrote ŠÁR×30, that is, he wrote one inscribed "10" too many. N2 is par-tially broken at this point; one can see ⌈ŠÁR×20⌉ but there may have been another "10" inscribed here as well. The students are using the "non-mathematical" notation with inscribed ŠÁR signs instead of the "mathematical" writing of multiples of ŠÁR, which is what we find in X4 in line 20.

I am at a loss to explain the mathematical difficulties of the scribes who copied the Išbi-Erra letters; they should have mastered metrological lists at an earlier stage of their education. For such lists, see, for example, E. Robson, *SCIAMVS* 5 (2004) 30–37. But, as she observes on p. 35, students had problems with such lists as well.

9. The only full surviving form of the verb among the Nippur texts is ba-an-ku$_4$-re-en (N3). This is clearly incorrect, with the first-person ending most likely dit-tography from the line above.

11. Note the use of še sìg to designate threshing of grain. M. Civil, *Farmer's Instruc-tions*, 95, has discussed the various terms used in Ur III for this activity; this expres-sion occurs only once in texts from this period (*UET* 3 1346).

The syntax and meaning of this line are uncertain. Only one Nippur source has the verb šúm (N3), which is broken in the other witnesses from that city. The X sources have a different verb—AK—but also do not have the first part of the line preserved and may have had a different text. N1 has ⌈sìg⌉-ge-⌈dè⌉, which seems the bet-ter text (*še sìg-ge-dè nu-mu-e-da-šúm-mu), but N2 and N3 have ba-sìg-ge, which may have to be translated differently. This line is crucial for the understanding of the text; see p.189 above.

12. I know of no similar usages of the two Sumerian verbs in this line. The transla-tion cautiously offered here is based on the idiomatic use of *dunnunu* with preposi-tions such as *eli* and *muḫḫi* in Akkadian, "to be too strong/much," although this attested only in later periods (see *CAD* D 84 for examples). Note the rare sequence of prefixes -ta-ni-.

---

11. The Sumerian capacity measure gur, "kor," was roughly equivalent to 300 liters.

C. Wilcke, *WO* 5 (1969) 12, read the final verb as dab$_5$. T. Jacobsen, *JCS* 7 (1953) 39, read it as bu$_7$ and translated "I shall winnow(?) it." The reading dúr in N3 is based on [mu$^?$-t]a-ni-dúr-ù-dè-en in X1.

13. Three Nippur witnesses have ^{ĝiš}má-gur$_8$ and X1 and X4 have ^{ĝiš}má. The former usually refers to a ceremonial barge or boat, and it is not clear if the Nippur usage reflects OB literary usage, because such watercraft are well attested in Sumerian poetry, or if there is some irony involved. The non-Nippur texts are more consonant with Ur III texts, which include boats (^{ĝiš}má) of 120 gur capacity. The outfitting of such a boat is detailed in *TCL* 5 5672 (from Umma), which begins (lines 1–4): 1 má 120 gun ésir hád-bi 204 gun ésir gul-gul-bi 12 gun ésir é-a-bi 2.2.0 gur. If this text is any guide, it took more than 324 talents of bitumen to make such a boat. This means that it would have required more than 194,400 talents to caulk 600 such vessels: that is, 5,832,000 kg. of bitumen! OB references for expenditures of bitumen for boats are collected in D. T. Potts, *Mesopotamian Civilization*, 131–32. I should note that M. Civil, *ARES* 4 129, has proposed that the word má-gur$_8$ can be a ceremonial barge but also refers to large rafts made of reed bundles, sometimes supported by inflated skins.

The verb duh is a technical term that refers to the caulking of boats with bitumen, but it can also be used in a more general sense for the repair and maintenance of watercraft. This is the case in, for example, *CT* 7 31 (BM 18390), where various wood parts are listed for the duh of a boat, together with bitumen.

14–15. The state of preservation of these lines, as well as redactional differences, makes it difficult to provide a credible interpretation. Assuming that the 600 boats/barges/rafts of 120 gur capacity of line 13 are all that is required to transport 72,000 gur of grain, the boats mentioned in these lines are military escort vessels.

15. The word ĜIŠ.ĜIŠ does not appear in any Sumerian narrative known to me. In Hh 5 104 and 105 (*MSL* 6 14), it is equated with *nīru* and *epinnu*, that is, with the "yoke/crossbeam" and the "plough," so perhaps the former is what is meant here. The interpretation cautiously suggested here relates it to am-ra = ĜIŠ.ĜIŠ.MÁ.RA = *am-ru-um* (Diri Nippur 2213, *MSL* 15 20; see also p. 62, line 7′), that is, *amrû* "beam."

14. The word written $^{⌜ĝiš⌝}$za-am-ru-tum in X1 and ^{ĝiš}za-we-$^{⌜}$ru$^?$-tum$^{?⌝}$ in X4 is otherwise attested in Sumerian contexts only in OB HAR-ra I 549 and in HAR-ra VI–VII OB Forerunner A 124 (*MSL* 6 152), known in a variety of different writings (za-am-ru-tum, za-mir-tum, za-mi-ru-tum, za-am-ri-tum, ša-am-ri-tum, etc.). *CAD* A 120 lists it under Akkadian *samrūtu*, with the translation "a rivet or nail." In light of the following ^{ĝiš}illar, it is tempting to think of za-am-ru-tum as a weapon as well, an interpretation that is supported by the listing in OB HAR-ra within a section on martial implements; note also the two in EA 22 i 42 (Tušratta, cited *CAD* T 415). N. Veldhuis, *Elementary Education*, 164 renders it "lance" and derives it, more properly, from Akkadian *zamirītum* (p. 183).[12] In Ur III, the word is written zà-mi-rí-tum; these are clearly martial implements made of wood and copper or bronze, sometimes encrusted with silver.[13] In one case, the wood is specified as hašhur, "apple" (*UET* 3 547:1). The bronze or copper parts were "blades," eme (*BIN* 10 124:1), but they also had an a-lá saĝ-è, that is, possibly a knob or sharp end (*UET* 3 575: 2–3). The more precious ones are given as gifts: e.g., *TIM* 6 34:6–7: 1 zà-mi-rí-tum zabar ĝiš-bi kù-babbar šub-ba, aḫ-ba-bu amurrum, "One bronze ẓ., its wooden part plated in silver, for Aḫbabu, the 'Amorite.'" This individual served the general Abuni, and the context is decidedly military. This suggests that ẓ. was a sword rather than a lance.

The meaning of ^{ĝiš}illar = *tilpānu* has been a matter of some debate; for the translation "bow" rather than "throw-stick," see *CAD* T 416, although the matter is far from settled.

16. It is impossible to identify these watercourses. The íd-kur-ra occurs in some literary texts, but it is not always certain if this is the name of a canal or its description. The same term is documented in the nineteenth year-name of Gungunum of Larsa, and here the meaning is likewise ambiguous, although one suspects that it is indeed a proper name: mu inim an ^{d}en-líl ^{d}nanna-ta ma-al-gi₄-a ^{ĝiš}tukul ba-ab-sìg ù é-dana bí-in-gi-na ù íd-kur-ra ka-bi ba-an-dib, "Year: By command of En, Enlil, and Nanna, Malgium was defeated in war and Edana was established, and the opening of the Idkura was crossed." If this year-name can be interpreted in a manner that associates the watercourse with the vicinity of Edana, it may provide a rough geographical location, in Old Babylonian times at least, for Idkura, because the town was probably located east of Isin, on the Iturungal, just upstream of Adab (D. Frayne, *Early Dynastic List*, 33–37).

The Palištum canal is known only from an Emar version of Hh XXII, Msk74198b iv 12'–13': íd-kur-ra, íd-pa-li-iš-tum (D. Arnaud, *Emar* VI.2 484 = VI.4 152). None of the OB forerunners, or the later standard recension, have this sequence, and it is possible that these entries are in fact quotations from this letter. It is possible that the translations should read: "so that they can be brought down by water, by a mountain river, through the narrows, so they can pile up (the grain) in stacks (for drying)."

17. The reading zar(LAGAB×ZÀR) is uncertain; the sign is preserved in X4, which is unavailable for study and known only from J. van Dijk's hand-copy, in which the inside of the grapheme is shaded. In *RCU*, the sign was read as su₇. If the reading is correct, then we have here zar . . . sal, the literary means of describing the spreading/piling up of stacks of grain to dry them for threshing (M. Civil, *Farmer's Instructions* 91).

---

12. I. J. Gelb, *MAD* 3 182, followed by T. J. H. Krispijn, *Akkadica* 70 (1990) 8, proposed that it was a musical instrument, with the name a compound of two instrument names: **zami mirītum*.
13. See also zà-bí-rí-tum (*MVN* 22 199 11) in an account of weapons (^{ĝiš}gíd-da, ^{ĝiš}ban).

The verb è(d) is undoubtedly the equivalent of Ur III e_{11}(d), which is regularly used for movement of goods up and down watercourses, especially of grain to and from threshing floors; see M. Civil, *Farmer's Instructions*, 92–93, and also the comparable use of Akkadian *elû*.

19. The difficult ugu tuku is a calque from Akkadian *eli/ina muḫḫi* + *rašûm*, for which see *CAD* R 203. See also line 29.

21–22. These lines are only preserved in X1 and X4 and are omitted in X5.

23. There is some question regarding the proper understanding of the syntax of the first half of the line. An alternative interpretation would be: "My king, the Elamite (ruler) has become tired of war. . . ."

25. The sequence lirum lirum is unique. The first is probably "power," but the second one must be interpreted as *kirimmum*, "hold." The only possible parallels for this line that I know are in *Ur Lament* 229–30: di_4-di_4-la úr ama-ba-ka nú-a ku_6-gin_7 a ba-ab-de_6, emeda^da lirum kala-ga-bi lirum ba-an-da-duh, "Infants lying in their mother's laps were swept off like fish (borne by) waters, their nursemaids, (although) holding them strongly, lost their grip (on children)" (also in later bilingual parallels, for which see *CAD* K 406, *kirimmu*), as well as in two OB incantations: *YOS* 11 86 33–34: emeda^da lirum kala-ga-bi, gal-gal-bi duh-a, "The nursemaid's strong grip (on her charge), released with great force," and *TCL* 16 89 10: emeda^da dumu-da mu-na-te lirum-bi mu-e-duh, "It draws near to the nursemaid with a child in her care and releases her grip (on her charge)."

26–27. The Nippur manuscript N3, which is broken from line 15 on, picks up here and may have had a somewhat different from the long version. The traces at the beginning of both lines differ, as do the predicates. Perhaps the lines read: *árad-da-ni ba-ra-ab-šúm-mu-un x eğer-ra-ni na-an-du-ù-un (note ù), "don't even think of putting yourself in his service, certainly, you could not become one of his followers!"

36. The reading išib follows a suggestion by Steve Tinney.

40. The Elamites are described here as lú níğ-ha-lam-ma, which may be interpreted in two interrelated ways. The translation offered here is based on a lexical entry in Nigga Bil. B 84 (*MSL* 13 117), where it is rendered in Akkadian as *ša le-mu-ut-tim*. However, some OB scribes would undoubtedly have been aware of the omens in which Ibbi-Sin is associated with just one word, *šaḫluqtum*, "disaster, catastrophe," which also translates níğ-ha-lam-ma in some lexical and bilingual texts (e.g., *CAD* Š /1 98).

42. The final verbal forms, preserved only in fragmentary form in X2 and X3, are uncertain. The signs KA.ŠÚM.ŠÚM can be interpreted as gù . . . sì, "to roar," as gù . . . šúm, "to echo," (for both, see F. Karahashi, *Sumerian Compound Verbs*, 111–12), or as inim . . . sì, "to express an idea" (M. Civil, *Mélanges Birot*, 75). The second half of the line is equally enigmatic. The tentative translation is based on dùb-tuku, "runner" (*bēl birkim*) and si-il (if that is indeed the proper reading)= *nesûm*, "to be distant." This should properly be the end of a paragraph, but the final -a requires that the narrative continue here.

43. The sign sequence šà-ta a in X2 and X3 is possibly to be understood as šà-ta-a; the scribe of X1, who often reinterprets difficult passages, wrote è-a-ni. This leads to the question of whether the final a is to be interpreted as a variant writing of è or if we are dealing with different traditions here.

47. The expression a-ba-àm lugal-g̃u$_{10}$ is a fascinating allusion to the passage toward the end of the Sargonic section of the *Sumerian King List* (line 284) that reads a-ba-àm lugal a-ba-àm nu lugal (with variants), "who was king, who was not king?" The Ur III and some of the OB Nippur versions have this passage in Akkadian, but sources from other places, like the texts of the letter, offer the Sumerian-language version (P. Steinkeller, *FS Wilcke* 279).

54. The line has been lifted from IbPu1: 36 (24), without taking care to change the second-person plural suffix into the first-person singular, as the new context requires. This error is found in both X2 and X3; the savvy scribe of X1 does not include this line or the one preceding it. The verbal root šub followed by dè is a writing for še-bé-da = *egû*, "to be negligent." The expression used here and at the conclusion of the following letter is a calque from the Akkadian *apputtum la teggi*, "please, do not be negligent," often encountered at the end of Old Babylonian letters (*CAD* A/2 191).

Sources

Version A (Short version)

N1 = 3 N-T 306 (A 30207)	= 1–14
N2 = CBS 2272 (PBS 13 9)	= 1–14
N3 = Ni. 3045 + 4093 + 4489 (*ISET* 2 121)	= 1–15; 23–30

Version B (Long version)

X1 = A 7475 i 3–44	= 3–54 (–8, 9, 38, 42, 46–51, 53, 54)[14]
X2 = AN1922-167 (*OECT* 5 29)[15]	= 29; 31–55
X3 = AN1930-581 (*OECT* 5 28)[16]	= 29; 31–55
X4 = IM 44134 (*Sumer* 15 pl. 6; *TIM* 9 40)	= 1–29
X5 = Ni. 3083 (*ISET* 2 115) iv 1–6	= 17–25 (–21, 22)

---

14. X1 has two additional fragmentary lines after 11.

15. Formerly Ash. 1922-167.

16. Formerly Ash. 1930-581. The tablet has deteriorated somewhat since it was copied by O. Gurney and since I first collated it.

X3 "said to be from Warka,"[17] X4 collated by Jeremy Black.[18]

Tablet typology: compilation tablets (Type I): X1, X5; all others type III.

Concordance of sigla used here (*CKU*) and in *RCU*:

N1	C		A	N2
N2	A		B	N3
N3	B		C	N1
X1	F		E	X4
X3	H		F	X1
X4	E		H	X3

Textual Matrix

Part A

1. ^{l}i-bi-^{d}en.zu lugal-ğu$_{10}$-ra ù-na-a-dug$_4$

N1	oo o o.	+	+		+	.	+	+	+	+	
N2	++.	++	+	.		o	o	o	o	o	.
N3	+++	++	+	+		+		+	+	+	- .
X4	xx o o.	.	.		o		o	+	+	+	+

2. ^{l}iš-bi-èr-ra árad-zu na-ab-bé-a

N1	o.	+	+	+	+		+	+	+	+	+
N2	+++	+	+	.		o	o	o	o	o	
N3	.^{d}+ -	+	+	+		+	+	+	+	.	
X4	oo o o o	x		o	o	.	+	+		

3. kaskal ì-si-in^{ki} ka-zal-lu^{ki}-šè

N1	o		o	+	+ +	+	+	+ + +	
N2	+		+ +	+ +na	.	.	o o o		
N3	+		+ +	+ +	+	+	+ + +		
X1	o		o o o o	.	o	o o o			
X4	o		o o o o	o	o	o. +			

4. še sa$_{10}$-sa$_{10}$-dè á-šè   mu-e-da-a-áğ

N1	o	.	+	+^{19}	+^{20}+	+	+	+	+	+	
N2	+	+	.	+	.^{r}še^1	.	o	o	o	.	
N3	+	+	+	+	+ +	+	+	+	+	+	
X1	o	o	o	o	o o	o	o	o	an.		
X4	o	o	o	o	o o	o	o	o.	.	+	

17. OECT 5 p. 45.

18. "Most of the surface is (now) in a worse condition than is implied by the copy and I can't really make any specific improvements."

19. In all Nippur sources, sa$_{10}$ is consistently written NÍNDA×ŠE. X1 uses NÍNDA×ŠE. ÀM.

20. Preceded by erased á.

5.   šakanka aš gur-ta-àm še sá ba-an-dug₄

	šakanka	aš	gur-ta-àm		še	sá	ba-an-dug₄			
N1	.	+ še +	+	+	+	+	+	+	+	
N2	+		+	+	+ +	+	+	-	-	di
N3	+		+	+	+ +	+	+	-	-	di
X1	o		o	o	o o	o	.	-	-	di
X4	o		o	o	o o	o	o	.	+	+

6.   20 gun kù-babbar še sa₁₀ RI-dè ba-an-ĝar

	20	gun	kù-babbar	še	sa₁₀	RI-dè	ba-an-ĝar				
N1	o	o	.	.		.	⌜sa₁₀⌝-sa₁₀-dè ba-ĝar-ra				
N2	+	.	+	+	+	+	+	+	+	-	+
N3	+	+	+	+	+	.	+	+	+	+	+
X1	o	o	o	o	o	.	-	+	.	.	+
X4	o	o	o	o	o	o	o	.	.	.	+

7.   inim amurrum lú kúr-ra šà ma-da-zu ku₄-ra   ĝiš ì-tuk-àm

	inim	amurrum	lú	kúr-ra	šà	ma-da-zu	ku₄-ra		ĝiš	ì-tuk-àm		
N1	o	.		-	-	-	.	+	+ za	+ +	+	. . .
N2	.	.		.	+	.	+	+	+ +	+ +	+	+ + +
N3	+	+		-	+	.	+	+	+ +	+ +	+	- + .
X1	o	o		o	o	o	o	o	.	+	ku₄-ku₄-dè [ ]-⌜an⌝-tuk-⌜e⌝
X4	o	o		o	o	o	o	o	.	. ⌜še⌝ kur-ra	ĝiš bí-⌜tuku⌝

8.   72,000   še   gur še dù-a-bi šà ì-si-in^ki-na-šè ba-an-ku₄-re-en

	72,000		še	gur	še	dù-a-bi	šà	ì-si-in^ki-na-šè	ba-an-ku₄-re-en			
N1	o		o	o	o	+	. .	+	+ + + o	o o	o	. + + .
N2	⌜ŠÁR×20⌝	-	+	.	+	+ +	+	+ + + + +	+	.	+ +	. . .
N3	ŠÁR×20	+	+	+	+	o	.	. . . . +	+	+	. . + .
X1	#											
X4	o		o	o	o o	o o o	o	o o o .	+	.	o o o o	o x

9.   a-da-al-la-bi amurrum dù-dù-a-bi šà kalam-ma-šè ba-an-ku₄-ku₄

	a-da-al-la-bi	amurrum	dù-dù-a-bi	šà	kalam-ma-šè		ba-an-ku₄-ku₄			
N1	o o . . -	.	+ + . o²¹	.	.	. .	+ ni o	o		
N2	+ + + + +	.	. . o o	+	+	+ +	+ .	.	o	
N3	. . . . o	.	+ + + +	.	.	. .	+ + +	re-en		
X1	#									
X4	. o o o o	o	o o o o	o	o	o o	. .	+	+	

10.   erim₃ gal-gal-didli-bi im-mi-in-dab₅-dab₅

	erim₃	gal-gal-didli-bi				im-mi-in-dab₅-dab₅			
N1	o	o o o	.	.	+	.	o	o	
N2	+	+ + +	+	+	.	o	o	o	
N3	o	o . o	+	+	+	+ +	+		
X1	o	o o o	o	o x	.	+	+		
X4	.	. o o	o	o o	o o	o			

21. There may be more missing at the end of the line. If not, then the scribe ended half the line two-thirds into the line and then either started a new or indented line.

11. mu amurrum še ba-sìg-ge nu-mu-e-da-šúm-mu

N1	o	.		.	-	.	.	⌜dè⌝o	o	o	o o	o	o

N1 o   .   . - . .⌜dè⌝o o o o o   o
N2 +   +   + + + +   + .   o o o   o
N3 o   o   . + + .   + + + + +   +
X1 o   o   o o o o ⌜nu⌝-mu-un-da-ak-e
X4 .   o   o o o o   nu-mu]-un-da-ak-e

11a. X1 [. . .]x in-sá-dug₄-⌜ne?⌝

11b. X1 [. . .]-e ì-in-ku₄²²

12. ugu-ĝu₁₀ mu-ta-ni-kalag ba-dúr-en

N1 o   o   o   . + +   . o o
N2 +   +   +   + + .   o o o
N3 o   o   o   . + +   + + +
X1 o   o   o   o o .   ì-dúr-ù-dè-⌜en⌝
X4 +   .   .   + . .   + . o

13. lugal-ĝu₁₀ ĝéš-u ᵍⁱˢmá-gur₈ 120 gur-ta-àm hé-em-duh-e

N1 o   o   o   o   o. +   .   o o o   o o o   o
N2 +   +   +   +   ++ +   +   . o o   . . .   o
N3 o   o   o   o   o. +   .   - + + ⌜ha?⌝x o   o
X1 o   o   o   o   o+ -   +   + + +   + + +   +
X4 .   .   .   .   -+ -   +   + + .   o x +   +

14. ᵍⁱˢmá 12 kal-ga 20 ᵍⁱˢza-am-ru-tum 30 ᵍⁱˢillar

N1 [. . .] ⌜12 kal?⌝ [. . .]
N2 má-⌜gur₈⌝ x[. . .]
N3 [x x x] ⌜má⌝ [x+] ⌜2 kal⌝ x[. . .]
X1 [   ]⌜ᵍⁱˢ⌝za-am-ru-tum   30-àm ᵍⁱˢillar
X4 ᵍⁱˢmá 60+12 kal-ga 20 ᵍⁱˢza-we-⌜ru?⌝-tum?⌝ 30 ᵍⁱˢillar

15. 30 ĜIŠ.ĜIŠ 5 ᵍⁱˢig má ugu ⌜má?⌝-e hé-⌜ĝá-ĝá⌝ ù ᵍⁱˢmá dù-a-bi hé-x

N3 traces
X1 [. . .]-⌜mu-àm⌝ ĜIŠ.ĜIŠ ù 5 ᵍⁱˢ⌜ig má?⌝-a / [. . .-à]m? hé-em-ĝá-ĝá /[ù ᵍⁱˢmá dù]-⌜a⌝-bi hi?-
    x-nam (má=mè?)
X4 50 ĜIŠ.ĜIŠ 5 ᵍⁱˢig má ugu ⌜má?⌝-e hé-⌜ĝá-ĝá⌝ ù ᵍⁱˢmá dù-a-bi hé-x

16. íd-da íd(-)kur-ra íd(-)pa-li-iš-tum-ta

X1 o o o   o o   .   + + eš+   ⌜šè⌝
X4 + + +   + +   +   + + + +   +

17. zar? sal-la-šè hé-em-ta-ab-è-dè-eš

X1 o   o   o o   o b]í-ib-è-⌜dè⌝
X4 .   +   . .   + + + - + + +
X5 o   .   + +   + + + + + + .

---

22. It is not clear if this is a separate line or the indented continuation of the previous one.

18. ù ğá-e   igi-ni-šè ga-àm-ta-è

X1 o o o   o   . . + +ma ši .
X4 + + +   +   + + + +   . .
X5 . + +   + ne ne + + +   + +

19. ki ^{ğiš}má kar-bi ugu-ğá ì-tuku

X1 o o o   . . +   ğu₁₀-šè hé-en-tuku
X4 + + +   . + +   + ⌈e⌉ +
X5 . + +   + + a +   + + +

20. 72,000   gur še dù-a-bi hé-ğá-gá hé-e-silim

X1 o   o o o o o ⌈ga-àm⌉-ma-⌈an⌉⌉-silim ga-àm-ma-⌈an⌉-kíğ⌉⌉
X4 ŠÁR.ŠÁR -   + + + + + + + + .
X5 ⌈ŠÁR×20⌉ + + + + + + gar-ra ga-àm-kíğ⌉

21. tukum-bi še-àm   ba-ab-tur-re

X1 o   . . .⌉ . . + +
X4 +   + + - ba-an-tur-re-en
X5 #

22. ğá-e še   ga-ra-ab-ku₄-e

X1 o o +   + + . . .
X4 + + + bi mu-ra-ku₄
X5 #

23. lugal-ğu₁₀ elam^{ki}-ma   šen-šen-na zi ba-an-ir

N3 o o   o o o   . . o o o o o :
X1 o o   . +²³ + + + - + . . .
X4 + +   + ma ki + + + + + + .
X5 o o   . . . . . - . + - +

24. še-ba-ni ul₄-la-bi al-til-la

N3 o o o o o o o o
X1 o o o + + + + + aš
X4 + + + + + + + +
X5 traces²⁴

25. lirum lirum na-an-duh-en

N3 o .   . .⌉ .⌉ o
X1 o .   nu-⌈mu-e⌉-da-duh-⌈e⌉
X4 + +   + + + +
X5 traces

23. Followed by an erased sign (ki?).
24. Lines 24 and 25 probably on one line.

26.   nam-árad-da-ni-šè   saǧ-zu   na-an-šúm-mu-un

N3   ⌜árad²-da²-ni¹⌝-šè ba-ra¹-ab-šúm-⌜mu-un⌝

X1   o   o   .   + +   .   +   na-an-na-šúm

X4   +   +   + + +   .   + + + +   +   +

27.   ù   eǧir-ra-ni-šè   na-an-du-un

N3   .   +   + + -   .   +   +ù .

X1   o   .   . + + + + + +

X4   +   +   + + + + + +

28.   še   mu udilia-ta-àm   šà-gal   é-gal-zu   ù   un   dù-a-bi   šà   uru^{ki}-ǧu$_{10}$-ta-àm   ì-ǧál

N3   + + +   + -   +   .   + +   + +   .   ++ / .²   . .   .   .

X1   o   o   .   + .   + +   ++   + + uru + +zu šu-ǧu$_{10}$-ta   ⌜ì-ni/in¹-ǧál

X4   + + +   + +   + +   ++   +/ + uru +   ++ šu-ǧu$_{10}$-ta   ì-ǧál

29.   uru ì-si-in^{ki} ù   nibru^{ki}-ke$_4$ en-nu-uǧ   ak-dè   ugu-ǧá hé-tuku

N3   +   ++ +.   .   +   + + /+ + +   +   .   +   +   +   +

X1   -   [nibru]^{ki} i-⌜si¹-in^{ki} -   +   + -   +   +   +   ⌜ha¹-[ra]-⌜ab¹-ak-e -   -   -   -

X2   -   ++ +.   -   o   o .²   +   +   +   ha-ra-ab-ak-e   o   +   +

X3   -   ++ ++   -   +   + a   +   +   +   ha-ra-ab-ak-e   +   +   +en+

X4   -   ++ ++   -   +   + +   +   +   +   +/ lugal-ǧu$_{10}$ +   +   e   +

30.   lugal-ǧu$_{10}$ hé-en-zu

N3   +   +   .   .   +

X1   #

X2   #

X3   #

X4   #

Part B

31.   lugal-ǧu$_{10}$ ní   nu-te ní nu-gíd-i šà-ba ǧá-e nu-te-BU

X1   [x x x]x   ní[x]-la na-an-te ⌜šà¹ x x x ⌜bí¹⌝-te

X2   +   +   +   +   .   .   .   o   .   +   + ...

X3   +   .   +   +   + + +   +   ++   +   + +   .   .

32.   diǧir-didli-bi   šà   hé-ni-íb-kíǧ-kíǧ-e   ki-bi   hé-kíǧ-kíǧ

X1   x x-zu x-bi hé-íl-íl-i ⌜ki²⌝-ba mu-e-⌜kíǧ²-kíǧ²⌝

X2   +   +   +.   .   .   o   o   x   .   +   .   .   +

X3   .   +   .   .   .   +.   +   + + + + -   +   .

33.   uǧ daǧal-bi nam-lú-ùlu-bi mah

X1   [x h]ul-la ⌜nam-lú-ùlu¹-ba mah-⌜àm¹[25]

X2   + +   +   .   .   .   + +

X3   . .   + +   + +   .   .

25. Preceded by erased a.

34. hé-silim-meš numun zi-da hé-en-kal-le-eš
X1   [ ]x   a-ʳriʾ numun zi-bi ʳhéʾ-i-i
X2   + +   +   .   . o o o . + +
X3   + +   .   .   .   + +   + . ʳgalʾ . .

35.   uri₅ᵏⁱ uru kù-zu an-ki-da mú-a
X1   [   ]   nam +   +²⁶ + ...
X2   ʳuruʾ + .   .   o o o o   .   . +
X3   + + .   .   + + + .   .   +

36. nun gal išib-e dù-a-bi saĝ-ki-bi kal-la
X1   o   o   o   o o . + + . + . +
X2   x   +   +   + . o o o o . + +
X3   +   +   +   + + o o + + + . .

37. me šúm-mu ús ĝiš-hur ge-en-ge-né kur sig igi-nim-ma
X1   o   o   o   o   . + + + ʳenʾ+ + + + +
X2   o   .   .   .   o o o o o   o   . . . .
X3   +   +   +   +   + . . + + + -   + . . .

38. šu-ta hé-kar-re inim-bi hé-éb-bé
X1   #
X2   o x + . o o   o + + +
X3   + + + + + .   . + . +

39. é-kiš-nu-ĝál èš an-ki šú-šú sukud-rá nu-tuk-a
X1   [x] x [. . .] ʳuri₅ʾᵏⁱ ʳanʾ-šà-a-ga sukud-ra nu-tuk-a
X2   o o o o o o o o o o   x + + .
X3   + + + + + + + + + x   o . . o

40. elamᵏⁱ ur idim lú níĝ-ha-lam-ma-ke₄
X1   o o . +   . . + la . +²⁷
X2   o o o o   o o . .   + +
X3   + + + +   + + + +   + .

41. šu pe-el nu-ma-ak-e ᵈlama-bi nu-si-il
X1   o o x o o   . . ++ + xˀ ʳsagˀ-kalˀʾ
X2   o o o o o   o o ++ . + + .
X3   + + + + +   + + ++ + + . .ˀ

42. lugal-ĝu₁₀ gù-šúm-šúm gal-gal dùb-tuku mu-siˀ-ilˀ-a
X1   #
X2   o o   o o o   o o o x   + ʳáĝʾʾ
X3   + +   + + +   + + + +   . + + +

26. Written su.
27. The space at the beginning of the line, including a fragment of a sign, suggest that there may have been more here than in X3.

43. ⌈i⌉-bi-ᵈen.zu šà-ta è-a-ni diĝir ki-áĝ-meš

X1 oo o o. . . + +++ + . o ⌜e?⌝
X2 oo o oo o o . . . . +
X3 +++ ++ + ˌ ˌ ++ ˌ + + . .

44. an ᵈen-líl ᵈen-ki igi zi hu-mu-un-ši-bar-re-e-ne

X1 . oo o o. + + . . + ˌ ++ . oo
X2 o oo o oo . + .x + . + . . o oo
X3 + ++ + ++ + + + + + + ++ +++

45. [...] x x x x x hé-en-ĝar igi-bi hé-éb-gi

X1 [...] x hé-⌜mu-un-gi?⌝ hé⌝-[...] ⌜hé⌝-em-d[ug₄?]
X2 [...] + + + ++ + + + + ++ . ⌜eb?⌝ +
X3 o o o o o o o . + . oo . . .

46. ᵍⁱˢig abul uri₅ᵏⁱ-ma ĝál-tak₄-tak₄-da-a-a

X1 #
X2 o . + + ++ + + + + ++
X3 o o o . + ˌ + + + + +.

47. (x) x i-ni-ib-bé a-ba-àm lugal-ĝu₁₀ e-še

X1 #
X2 o + ++ + + ++ + + + +.
X3 o o o oo o oo . + + ++

48. lugal ᵈen-líl-le gaba-ri nu-tuku-me-en

X1 #
X2 . ++ . . + . + . o o
X3 o oo . ˌ . + + + + .

49. x nu x x x x šà-zu na-an-gig-ge

X1 #
X2 x + x x x x + + + + . .
X3 oo o oo o + + + + + x ⌜en?⌝

50. x šu mu-un-gi suhuš-bi mu-ri-in-ge-en

X1 #
X2 x . + . + + + + + ++ +
X3 o o o o . + + + + . . o

51. [x]x šu? nu-du₇-a šà-zu hé-en-du₁₀-ge

X1 #
X2 [x]x + + ++ + o . + + +
X3 [] x . o . ++ + . + +

52. en-na lugal-ĝu₁₀ al-ti-la nam-lugal uri₅ᵏⁱ mu-un-ak-e

X1 o o o o oo. . . . o o o + x
X2 o . + + +++ . . . + + + ++
X3 . o . + + . .a . + . + + +++

53. níg̃-na-me lugal-g̃u₁₀ kíg̃ mu-na-ni-íb-gi₄

X1   #
X2   o . + +   +   + + + + +
X3   + + + ...   + + + gi

54. a-ma-ru-kam   nam-ba-e-šub-dè-en-zé-en

X1   #
X2   o + + +   +   + ++   + + + +
X3   ++ + +   +   . ++   + + . .

55. igi ᵈutu-kam ka-g̃u₁₀ nu-bal-e

X1   [igi ᵈutu-kam ka-g̃u₁₀ nu-ba]l-e ⌈lugal⌉-e hé-en-⌈zu⌉
X2   .   ++ +   + + + + +
X3   .   .+ .   + + + + .

In X1 followed by IbIš (22).

Colophon M (X2)
Colophon N (X4)
Colophon O (X1)

22. Ibbi-Sin to Išbi-Erra

(IbIš1, 3.1.18, RCU 20)

Sources

X1 = A 7475 i 44 – ii 1–24 = IbIš1A
X2 = AN1922-165 (OECT 5 27) = IbIš1B[1]
Tablet typology: compilation tablet (Type I): X1; Type III: X2.
Bibliography: X2 edited by S. N. Kramer, OECT 5 15–16.

Text Transliterations

IbIš1A = source X1

1. [ˡiš-bi-èr-ra-r]a ⸢ù-na-a-dug₄⸣
2. [ᵈi-bí-ᵈen.zu lugal-zu] ⸢na-ab⸣-[bé]-⸢a⸣
   Two or three lines broken
1′. x ᵈen-líl-lá íb ba-an-ak [. . .]
2′. ⸢ki-šà⸣-bi nu-me-a lú kúr mu-un-zi-ma ⸢kur-kur⸣ i[m-sùh-sùh]
3′. ⸢u₄⸣ ᵈen-líl-le dumu-ni ᵈen.zu-ra im-m[i-gur]
4′. za-e inim-zu ĝiškim bí-in-tuk-à[m]
5′. niš gú-un kù-babbar še sa₁₀-sa₁₀²-dè šu bí-⸢in-ti⸣
6′. min₆ še gur-ta-àm aš gín-⸢àm⸣ bí-ib-sa₁₀-s[a₁₀ (. . .)]
7′. ĝá-ra-aš še gur-ta³-àm gi₄-ĝu₁₀-da
8′. amurrum lú kúr-ra ⸢šà⸣ ma-da-ka ì-gub-ba
9′. usu kalam-ma-ĝu₁₀ érin-bi-ta mu-un-zu-a
10′. a-gin₇ ma-da-ĝu₁₀ saĝ ba-e-šúm-ma bàd gal-ĝu₁₀ mu-e-⸢dab₅-dab₅⸣
11′. ˡpuzur₄-ᵈʳmarduk šakkana⸣ bàd-igi-hur-saĝ-ĝá
12′. a-gin₇ amurrum an-⸢ta⸣ nam-mu-un-gi₄-gi₄
13′. u₄ na-me-ka ᵍᶦštukul kala-ga-zu li-bí-in-túm-⸢ma⸣
14′. nir-ĝál-zu-ta x⁴ ᵘᵍᵘugu₄-bi kur-bi-ta im-ta-x-x-x

1. Formerly Ashm. 1922-165. The tablet has deteriorated in parts since O. Gurney copied it and since I first collated it many years ago.
2. In this text, sa₁₀ is written NÍNDA×ŠE.ÀM.
3. The scribe began to write àm and then wrote ta over it.
4. Possibly an erased ugu.

15′. á-še ⌈180⌉-àm ᵍⁱˢmá gu-la ᵍⁱˢmá 120 gur-⌈ta-àm⌉ im-ma-an-duh-e
16′. ù ĝéš-u-àm ᵍⁱˢmá ĝéš <gur>-ta-àm im-⌈ma⌉-an-⌈duh⌉-[e]
17′. ⌈šu-ᵈen-⌈líl⌉ énsi ⌈kiši^{ki}-àm⌉
18′. ⌈nu-úr-é-a énsi èš-nun-na^{⌈ki⌉}-[àm]
19′. ⌈puzur₄-tu-tu énsi bàd-zi-ab-ba[^{ki}-àm]
20′. ⌈ŠÁR×20[?]⌉ še gur še šu-zu-ta bí-íb-si-ge-eš
21′. kù šu-zu-ta ⌈ù sá[?]⌉-dug₄ mah[?]-⌈di[?]⌉
22′. ŠÁR×20 še sa₁₀-⌈sa₁₀-dè⌉ saĝ-ĝá hé-en-⌈ĝál⌉
23′. en-na mu-e-ši-in-gi₄ nam-ma-ši-du-un
24′. ⌈nibru^{⌈ki⌉} ⌈ì-si-in^{ki}⌉ en-nu-ùĝ aka-dè ugu-zu-⌈šè⌉ ⌈e⌉-tuku a-ma-ru-kam

Followed by PuIb1 (23).

(Colophon O)

IbIš1B = source X2

1. ⌈ᵈ⌉iš-bi-èr-ra-ra ⌈ù-na⌉-a-dug₄
2. ᵈi-bí-ᵈen.⌈zu lugal-zu na-ab⌉-bé-⌈a⌉
3. en-na ᵈen-líl ⌈lugal-ĝu₁₀⌉ me-šè i-im-du-dè-en
4. za-e ur₅-gin₇ ka ì-bal-e
5. u₄-da ᵈen-líl-le ĝá-a-ra hul ba-an-gig
6. dumu-ni ᵈen.zu-na-ra hul ba-an-gig
7. uri₅^{ki} lú kúr-ra bí-in-šúm-mu
8. ki ⌈šà[?]⌉-ba nu-me-a lú kúr im-zi-ge kur-kur im-sùh-sùh
9. u₄ ᵈen-líl-le dumu-ni ᵈen.zu-na-ra im-me-gur
10. za-e inim-zu ĝiškim im-ma-an-⌈tuku⌉
11. niš gun kù·babbar še sa₁₀⁵-e-dè ⌈šu⌉ ba-e-ti
12. min₆ še gur-ta-àm kù-babbar aš gín-e bí-in-⌈sa₁₀-sa₁₀-e⌉
13. ĝá-a-ra aš še gur-ta-àm za-e mu-un-gi
14. puzur₄-ᵈnu-muš-da šakkana bàd-igi-hur-⌈saĝ⌉-ĝá
15. amurrum lú kúr-ra šà kalam-ma-ĝu₁₀-šè a-gin₇ im-da-an-ku₄-re-en
16. en-na ᵍⁱˢtukul sìg-ge-dè nam-mu-e-ši-in-gi
17. lú saĝ-du nu-tuku kalam-ma ì-ĝál-la
18. a-gin₇ amurrum-e an-ta nam-mu-ši-in-gi

Translations

IbIš1A

¹Speak to [Išbi-Erra], ²s[aying (the words of) Ibbi-Sin, your king]:
(ca. 5 lines missing)
^{1′}(Now) Enlil's heart(?) is angry. . . .

5. In this text sa₁₀ is written NÍNDA×ŠE.ÀM.

²′ The enemy, although not. . . , has mustered (his army), and has [brought disorder] in all the foreign lands. ⁴′ But then you, according to your statement, had an omen ³′ (telling you that) now Enlil [has returned] to the side of his son Sin.

⁵′ You (text: he) received twenty talents of silver to purchase grain. ⁶′ You (text: he) purchased grain at the price of two kor per shekel, ⁷′ only to return it to me⁶ as if (you had purchased it) at one kor (per shekel)!

⁸′ The hostile Amorite, having stationed himself in the frontier territory, ⁹′ having come to know the strength of my homeland and its troops—¹⁰′how could you let him sweep into my frontier zone and capture all my large fortresses? ¹¹′–¹²′ Why has Puzur-Marduk, general of Badigihursağa, not confronted the Amorite(s)? ¹³′ Your powerful forces were never brought into play, ¹⁴′ it is because of your self-confidence the monkey has [*been allowed to come down*] from its mountain!

¹⁵′ Now I am overhauling 180 great barges, each (vessel) with a capacity of 120 kor, as well as overhauling 600 barges with a capacity of 60 kor each. ¹⁷′ Šu-Enlil, governor of Kish, ¹⁸′ Nur-Ea (i.e., Nur-aḫum), governor of Ešnunna, ¹⁹′(and) Puzur-Tutu, governor of Borsippa ²⁰′ have handed over 72,000 kor of grain to you, ²¹′–²²′ and therefore you should measure out the silver that you have as well *as what (was set aside for even) the most exalted allotments* to pay for the 72,000 (kor) of grain. ²³′ Do not dare to come back here until you have dispatched (the grain) to me! ²⁴′ Guarding Nippur and Isin is your responsibility. It is urgent!

IbIš1B

¹ Speak to Išbi-Erra, ² saying (the words of) Ibbi-Sin, your king:

⁴ You tell me so: ³ "as long as Enlil is my master, where else (in the world but with you) would I go?" ⁵ Right now Enlil is angry with me, ⁶ angry with his son Sin, ⁷ and is handing over Ur to the enemy. ⁸ The enemy, although not (yet) within it, has mustered (his army), and created disorder in all the foreign lands. ¹⁰ But you, according to your statement, had an omen ⁹ that Enlil has reconciled with his son Sin.

¹¹ You received twenty talents of silver to purchase grain. ¹² You purchased grain at the price of two kor per shekel, ¹³ but you then returned it to me (as if you had purchased it) at one kor (per shekel).

¹⁴ How could you, together with Puzur-Numušda, general of Bad-Igihursaĝa, ¹⁵ allow the enemy Amorite(s) to enter into my homeland? ¹⁶ Until he returns to you to fight (them) ¹⁷ there will be idiots (running around) in the homeland—¹⁸ why has he not confronted the Amorite(s)?

Commentary

This letter is attested in two different versions. Both accounts are defective and appear to be variant Old Babylonian concoctions that mix together information from IšIb1 (21) and the Puzur-Numušda correspondence (23–24).

6. Alt. transl.: return it to me.

Both manuscripts are of unknown origin, even if it is possible that X1 comes from Sippar, but they share certain features, most noticeably a shaky command of Sumerian verbal morphology. It appears that the authors of these texts used the third-person animate agreement prefix /n/ indiscriminately, so that forms with this element often have to be interpreted as first- or second-person verbs, and forms with /e/ are clearly intended as first- or third-person. The texts make little sense in the context of the CKU, and we are at a loss to discern if this is a function of scribal ineptitude or if there are ironies here that escape us.

A 4′. The idea that an ominous sign presages the victory of Ibbi-Sin is derived from the Puzur-Numušda correspondence but is turned around, because here it is Išbi-Erra, not the king, who has received an omen.

A 6′–7′ = B 12–13. These lines are important because they are the source of the commonly repeated notion that Išbi-Erra blackmailed Ibbi-Sin, asking him to pay him double for grain he had already received funds to buy in the first place. Although the grammar of these lines is characteristically flimsy, there can be no doubt that according to both sources the issue is not blackmail at all; the king of Ur is desperate and offers to take it at double the original price. It is unclear if the writer of A intended the verbal form in line 7′ as the participial gi.ĝu.ed.am or as an imperative gi.mu.da.

A 13′. The Sumerian u_4 na-me-ka (for u_4 na-me-kam) is used here in the same sense as Akkadian *matima* with a negated verb ("never").

A 14′. The signs used for writing /ugubi/, "monkey," are partially destroyed and difficult to read. From what I can discern, it is either ⌈DUL⌉.A⌉.SAG.GU₅ or possibly ⌈UGU.UGU⌉.GU₅.

A 15′–16′. As in the previous letter, the numbers in these lines do not add up properly. According to line 20′, we are dealing here with 72,000 kor of grain; that is all that Išbi-Erra wants to send back at the rate of two gur per shekel, because he is obviously keeping either half the silver he received or half of the grain that he purchased. 180 boats of 120 kor capacity would carry 21,600 kor. According to line 16′, there were 600 (géš-u) vessels, each of 60 kor capacity, and therefore the tonnage would be 36,000 kor. Thus, the combined carrying capacity of all the boats would be 57,600 kor. The only way that I can make some sense of this is to assume that the scribe made a mistake that involved confusion between the decimal and sexigesimal systems: he wrote 3×ĜÉŠ—that is, 180—but was thinking of 3×100 (i.e., 3 ⟨me⟩) = 300, and thus the total in line 16′ would also be 36,000. If this were indeed the case, both lines would add up to 72,000 kor. Alternatively, we are dealing with a scribal error; the correct number would be 5×ĜÉŠ—that is, 300.

A 17′–19′. This passage is clearly derived from PuIb1 36–38 (23). Note that here, as in the source letter, X1 writes ͪnu-úr-é-a for Nur-aḫum of Ešnunna.

A 20′. The idiom šu-PRO-ta ǧál (šu-zu-ta bí-ib-sì-ge-eš) must be a calque from Akkadian *ana qātim mullûm*, "to hand over," (*CAD* M/1 187) with -ta functioning as a locative, as it often does in Larsa and late OB Sumerian texts. Unfortunately, the translation "they have handed over to you" makes little sense in the context. The present translation assumes that this is a mistake and that the intention here was to use a Sumerian equivalent of the Akkadian use of *mullûm* in the technical sense of "to load a boat" (*CAD* M/1 185).

A 21′. The reading and translation of the second half of this line are most uncertain.

B 3. There is some ambiguity in the reading of the verbal root. There are two possible idioms that could come into play here: me-šè de$_6$ and me-šè gin; see the information in *CAD* A/1 233 sub *ajiš*, "whereto, whither; where," and M. Civil, *AfO* 25 (1974–77) 71. For a very different interpretation of lines B 3–4, see C. Wilcke, Politik im Spiegel der Literatur, 64: "Bis dahin—(bei) mein(em) Konig Enlil!—wirst du gehen, wirst du derart die Worte verdrehen?"

B 4. The verb ka . . . bal provides a direct link to the previous letter, from Išbi-Erra to the king, which ends with the line (55): igi ^{d}utu-kam ka-ǧu$_{10}$ nu-bal-e.

B 15. The verbal im-da-an-ku$_4$-re-en is formally first or second person, but this is most probably a mistake for third person. Alternatively, it is possible that the scribe intended "how could you allow PN. . . ."

B 17. lú saǧ-du nu-tuku is translated as *la išānu*, "weakling, poor person," in the late lexical entry in SIG$_7$.ALAN IV 23 (MSL 16 77); in *Instructions of Šuruppak*, 115, it seems to designate an idiot; see, most recently, B. Alster, *Wisdom of Ancient Sumer* 141. Note the use of gi for gi$_4$ here and in the next line; the form ì-ǧál-la must stand for i.ǧal.am.

Comparison of the Common Part of Versions A and B (X1 1–2; 1′–7′ and X2 1–13)

1. X1:1   [r]a ⌜ù-na-a-dug$_4$⌝
   X2:1 ^{d}iš-bi-èr-ra-ra ⌜ù⌝-na-a-dug$_4$

2. X1:2   [   ]-a
   X2:2 ^{d}i-bí-^{d}en.⌜zu lugal-zu na-ab⌝-bé-a

3. X2:3   en-na ^{d}en-líl ⌜lugal⌝-ǧu$_{10}$ me-šè i-im-du-dè-en

4. X2:4   za-e ur$_5$-gin$_7$ ka ì-bal-e

5. X2:5   u$_4$-da ^{d}en-líl-le ǧá-a-ra hul ba-an-gig

6. X2:6   dumu-ni ^{d}en.zu-na-ra hul ba-an-gig

7. X1:1′ x ᵈen-líl-lá íb ba-an-ak [. . .]
    X2:7 uri₅ᵏⁱ lú kúr-ra bí-in-šúm-mu

8. X1:2′ ⸢ki šà⸣-bi nu-me-a lú kúr mu-un-zi-ma ⸢kur-kur⸣ i[m-sùh-sùh]
    X2:8 ki ⸢šà⸣-ba nu-me-a lú kúr im-zi-ge   kur-kur im-sùh-sùh

9. X1:3′ ⸢u₄⸣ ᵈen-líl-le dumu-ni ᵈen.zu-ra   im-m[i-gur]
    X2:9 u₄ ᵈen-líl-le   dumu-ni ᵈen.zu-na-ra im-me-gur

10. X1:4′ za-e inim-zu ĝiškim bí-in-tuk-à[m]
    X2:10 za-e inim-zu ĝiškim im-ma-an-tuku

11. X1:5′ 20 gú-un kù-babbar še sa₁₀-sa₁₀-dè šu bí-⸢in-ti⸣
    X2:11 20 gun kù-babbar   še sa₁₀-e-dè   šu ba-e-ti

12. X1:6′ min₆ še gur-ta-⸢àm⸣   aš gín-⸢àm⸣ bí-ib-sa₁₀-s[a₁₀]
    X2:12 min₆ še gur-ta-àm kù-babbar aš gín-e   bí-in-⸢sa₁₀-sa₁₀-e⸣

13. X1:7′ ĝá-ra   aš še gur-ta-àm   gi₄-mu-da
    X2:13 ĝá-a-ra aš še gur-ta-àm za-e mu-un-gi

23. Puzur-Numušda to Ibbi-Sin 1

(PuIb1, 3.1.19, A3, RCU 21)

Composite Text

1. ^{d}i-bí-^{d}en.zu lugal-ğu$_{10}$-ra ù-na-a-dug$_4$
2. ^{I}puzur$_4$-^{d}nu-muš-da énsi ka-zal-lu^{ki} árad-zu na-ab-bé-a
3. lú-kíğ-gi$_4$-a ^{d}iš-bi-èr-ra ugu-ğu$_{10}$-šè ì-gin
4. ^{d}iš-bi-èr-ra lugal-ğu$_{10}$ ugu-zu-šè kin-gi$_4$-a im-mi-in-gi$_4$
5. igi-ni ma-an-ğar-ma
6. ^{d}en-líl lugal-ğu$_{10}$ nam-sipa kalam-ma ka-ka-ni ma-an-šúm
7. gú ^{íd}idigna gú ^{íd}buranun-na gú ^{íd}abgal ù gú ^{íd}me-^{d}en-líl-lá
8. uru^{ki}-bi-ne diğir-bi-ne ù ugnim-bi-ne
9. ma-da ha-ma-zi^{ki}-ta en-na a-ab-ba má-gan-na^{ki}-šè
10. igi ^{d}nin-in-si-na-ka-šè ku$_4$-ku$_4$-dè
11. ì-si-in^{ki} nam-ğá-nun ^{d}en-líl-lá-šè ğá-ğá-da mu tuk-tuk-da
12. nam-ra-ak-ne-ne uru-uru-bi durun-ù-dè
13. ^{d}en-líl-le ğá-a-ra ma-an-dug$_4$
14. a-na-aš-àm gú mu-da-ak
15. mu ^{d}da-gan diğir-ğá ì-pàd[1]
16. ka-zal-lu^{ki} šu-ğu$_{10}$ sá hé-eb-bé
17. uru ma-da ^{d}en-líl-le ma-an-du$_{11}$-ga-àm
18. šà ì-si-in^{ki}-na-ka zag-gu-la-ne-ne ga-bí-ib-dù-dù
19. èš-èš-a-ne-ne-a ga-àm-ak
20. alam-mu šu-nir-ğu$_{10}$ en lú-mah ereš-diğir-ğu$_{10}$-ne
21. ği$_6$-par$_4$-ra-ne-ne-a ga-bí-ib-durun$_x$[2]
22. igi ^{d}en-líl-lá šà é-kur-ra-šè
23. igi ^{d}nanna šà é-kiš-nu-ğál-šè
24. tur-tur-ğu$_{10}$ sízkur-bi hé-eb-bé
25. ù za-e lú ğiškim-ti-zu-um
26. ma-da-ni-ta ga-àm-ta-an-gub-bu

---

1. Var.: mu ^{d}en-líl lugal-ğu$_{10}$ ù ^{d}da-gan diğir-ğá ì-pàd.
2. KU.KU.

27. ì-si-in^{ki}-na bàd-bi ga-àm-dù
28. i-di-il-pa-šu-nu mu-šè ga-an-sa$_4$
29. bí-in-du$_{11}$-ga-gin$_7$-nam
30. ì-si-in^{ki}-na bàd-bi ba-an-dù
31. i-di-il-pa-šu-nu mu-šè ba-an-sa$_4$
32. nibru^{ki} ba-an-dab$_5$ en-nu-ùg-gá-ni ba-an-gar
33. ù ^{I}níg-du$_{11}$-ga-ni saga nibru^{ki} ba-an-dab$_5$
34. ^{I}zi-in-nu-um énsi su-bir$_4$^{ki}-a šaga i-ni-in-dab$_5$
35. ha-ma-zi^{ki} nam-ra-aš im-mi-in-ak
36. ^{I}nu-úr-a-hi énsi èš-nun-na^{ki}
37. ^{I}šu-^{d}en-líl énsi kiši^{ki}-a
38. ù ^{I}puzur$_4$-^{d}tu-tu énsi bàd-zi-ab-ba^{ki}
39. ki-ni-šè ba-an-gur-ru-uš
40. za-pa-áǧ-ǧá-ni^3 ma-da gi-sig-gin$_7$ ì-bur$_{10}$-e
41. ^{d}iš-bi-èr-ra igi érin-na-šè ì-gin-gin
42. bí-in-du$_{11}$-ga-gin$_7$-nam
43. gú ^{íd}idigna gú ^{íd}buranun-na gú ^{íd}abgal ù gú ^{íd}me-^{d}en-líl-lá ba-an-dab$_5$
44. ^{I}i-di mà-al-gi$_4$^{ki}-a ba-ni-in-ku$_4$
45. ^{I}gir-bu-bu énsi ǧír-kal^{ki}-ke$_4$
46. gú im-da-bar-re-ma ^{kuš}guru$_{21}$-ni ba-an-ku$_5$ ù e-ne ba-an-dab$_5$
47. za-pa-áǧ-ǧá-ni im-ma-dugud
48. ugu-ǧu$_{10}$-uš igi-ni ma-an-ǧar
49. lú tab-ba nu-tuku lú nu-mu-un-da-sá-e
50. šu-ni sá nu-mu-un-da-ab-du$_{11}$-ga-ta
51. ù-mu-un-šub ga-àm-ma-gin lugal-ǧu$_{10}$ hé-en-zu

^{1} Speak to Ibbi-Sin, my king, ^{2} saying (the words of) Puzur-Numušda, governor of Kazallu, your servant:

^{3} The envoy of Išbi-Erra came before me (and said): ^{4} "My king Išbi-Erra, has sent me to you to you with a message." ^{5} He presented the matter as follows: ^{6} "My master Enlil has promised me stewardship of the homeland. ^{13} Yes, it was me that Enlil ordered ^{10} to deliver to Ninisina ^{7} the banks of the Tigris and Euphrates, the Abgal and Me-Enlila canals, ^{8} their cities, their (city) gods and their armies, ^{9} from the territory of Hamazi to the Magan Sea, ^{11} and having made Isin the storehouse of Enlil, made it famous,^{4} ^{12} to (then) settle their war captives in all those cities.

^{14} Why do you oppose me? ^{15} I have sworn by my personal god Dagan^5 ^{16} that I shall conquer Kazallu! ^{17} Because Enlil has promised me the cities of the frontier,^{6} ^{18} I

---

3. Var. za-pa-áǧ-ǧá-ni-ta.

4. Alt. transl.: Isin, which has to be made the storehouse of Enlil and which has to be made famous.

5. Var.: I have sworn by the name of Enlil, my lord, and of Dagan, my personal god.

6. Alt. transl.: territory/land.

shall build all their (i.e. the city gods) shrines in Isin, [19] I shall celebrate their regular festivals; [20-21] I shall set up my own statues, my own emblems, (choose by omen) my own high priests, chief priests, and high priestesses in their special abodes, [24] so that my subjects may offer their prayers, [22] before Enlil in the Ekur (in Nippur) [23] and before Nanna in the Ekišnuĝal (in Ur). [25-26] And as for you, I shall chase out the person you depend on (Ibbi-Sin) from his territory! [27] Isin's wall I shall rebuild [28] (and) name it Idil-pašunu."

[29] It was just as he had predicted: [30] He rebuilt Isin's wall [31] (and) named it Idil-pašunu; [32] he took over Nippur, appointed his own guard over it, [33] and arrested Niĝdugani, the chief temple administrator of Nippur. [34] (His ally), the ruler/governor Zinnum, took prisoners in Subir [35] (and) plundered Hamazi.[7] [36] Nur-aḫum, the governor of Ešnunna, [37] Šu-Enlil, the governor of Kish, [38] and Puzur-Tutu, the governor of Borsippa [39] *came over to his side*. [40] His clamor shakes the frontier territory like a reed fence,[8] [41] as Išbi-Erra goes everywhere at the head of the troops.

[42] It was just as he had predicted: [43] he captured the banks of the Tigris, the banks of the Euphrates, as well as the banks of the Abgal and Me-Enlila. [44] He installed Iddi in Malgium,[9] [45-46] and when Girbubu, governor of Girkal, resisted him and cut off his (Iddi's) shield, he (Išbi-Erra) took him prisoner. [47] His clamor has become louder, [48] (and now) he has turned his attention in my direction. [49] I have no ally, no one who can match him! [50] Although he has not yet been able to defeat me, [51] when he finally strikes, I will have to flee! Now my king is informed (about all of this)!

Commentary

Although this letter is fairly well documented, there are many variants, and it is clear that some students did not understand certain lines and attempted to make their own sense of the text. There are eight Nippur manuscripts, and these are relatively consistent. The clusters of variants between the Ur and Sippar exemplars and those from unknown sites may be of significance. Of the five unprovenienced texts, X1 is in almost total harmony with the Sippar tablet Si1, and X3 agrees in almost all cases with Ur2. See p. 46 above. Note that the composition was also known at Uruk. The *Uruk Letter Catalog* contains the following two entries:

6'. i-bi-^{d}en.zu lugal-^{r}ĝu$_{10}$$^{\rceil}$ [. . .]
7'. i-bi-rden.zu$^{\rceil}$ [x x] x x [. . .]

Perhaps the compiler of this catalog was aware of two diverse recensions of this epistle; it is also possible that he had access to a completely different letter to the last king of Ur, one that has not yet been recovered.

7. Var.: . . . captured Niĝdugani, the chief temple administrator of Nippur, and plundered Hamazi. (His ally), the ruler/governor Zinnum, took prisoners in Subir.
8. Var.: The frontier territory trembles like a reed fence from his clamor.
9. Alt. transl.: He installed Iddin-Malgium.

4–5. The order of these lines consistently differs in Nippur manuscripts and in all other sources. It is clear that some scribes understood the awkward nature of the Nippur order and modified it, moving line 5 after line 3 and including it in the initial statement of Puzur-Numušda. X1 even added a clarifying line after line 5: "Thus speaks my king Išbi-Erra:" It seems that outside of Nippur the letter began:

> [1] Speak to Ibbi-Sin, my king, [2] saying (the words of) Puzur-Numušda, governor of Kazallu, your servant:
> [3] The envoy of Išbi-Erra came before me [5] (and) presented the matter as follows:
> [4] "My king Išbi-Erra has sent me to you to you with a message. Thus speaks my king Išbi-Erra: [6] 'My master Enlil has promised to make me shepherd of the land. . .'."

7/43. Note the distribution of variants in the writing of the name of the Euphrates in these lines. This is not apparent in line 7 because of the state of preservation of the witnesses, but in line 43 the Nippur texts have buranun(UD.KIB.NUN)-na, while all the other sources with the exeption of X1 write buranuna(UD.KIB.NUN)^{ki}. On the use of na and ki in this name, see, in general, C. Woods, ZA 95 (2005) 26.

9/35. On the possible location of Hamazi south of the Lower Zab, see Appendix D.

11. The present translation takes into account the use of /-da/ in the predicates of this line in the Nippur sources, as opposed to /-de/ of the surrounding lines. This distinction between adjunct nonfinite clauses (da) and purpose infinitive clauses (de) has been elucidated by Fumi Karahashi and is followed here.[10] This subtle morphological and syntactic distinction was unknown, or was ignored, by the author of Ur2; in X1 the first verb has /-da/, while the second has /-de/ (in all other sources, the verbs are broken). Therefore, in Ur2, and perhaps in other manuscripts, this line should be translated "to make Isin the storehouse of Enlil, and make it famous."

13. The translation "Yes, . . ." attempts to render into English the emphatic force of the independent pronoun ĝá-a-ra.

14. The interpretation of the rare gú . . . ak as "to be hostile, aggressive" follows M. Jaques, *Le vocabulaire des sentiments*, 153 n. 345. It is possibly the opposite of gú . . . ĝál = kanāšum, "to submit," and therefore the line may have to be translated "why are you unsubmissive to me?"

15. In all the Nippur sources and the Sippar manuscript (N5 is very worn at this point and somewhat uncertain), Išbi-Erra invokes his personal god, Dagan. This is undoubtedly meant to underline his foreign origins. The texts Ur2 and X3, which are so often in harmony, add the figure of the main god of Sumer, Enlil, as his master. All discussions of this line cite the fuller version. Note the passage in the royal

---

10. "Nonfinite Relative Clauses in Gudea Cylinder B, Revisited," paper presented at the 55th Rencontre Assyriologique Internationale, Paris, July 8, 2009. I am grateful to Fumi Karahashi for providing me with a copy of her presentation.

inscription Iddin-Dagan 3:36–37 (*RIME* E.4.1.3.3, in curse formula): lú-ba ᵈen-líl lugal-ǧu₁₀ ᵈnin-líl ereš-ǧu₁₀, ᵈda-gan diǧir-ǧá nam ha-ba-an-da-ku₅-ru-ne, "May Enlil, my king, Ninlil, my queen, and Dagan, my personal god, curse him." It may be that the tradition of Ur2 and X3 was corrupted by the memory of some Išme-Dagan text, perhaps reinforced by contamination from line 6 above.

16. Tablets N1 and S1 write the bound pronoun on the direct object as ǧu₁₀. The oblique -ǧá, found in texts from other sites (Ur2, X1, X3), is probably more correct. The idiomatic predicate šu sá . . . dug₄ here and in line 50 is a calque from Akkadian *qātam kašādum*, "to conquer." It is otherwise attested, as far as I know, only in Larsa and Babylon I royal inscriptions (Kudur-mabuk 2 13 [E4.2.13]; Rim-Sin 37 ii 9′ [E4.2.14.14]; Rim-Sin 12 28 [E4.2.14.5]; Samsu-iluna D 33 [E4.3.7.8]); see also IBPu1: 31 (24).

17. The only complete version of this line is in text Ur2; manuscript X3 was similar. Note that X1 has an additional emphatic personal pronoun, ǧá-ra, "to me," while the Nippur witness N5 apparently had the epithet lugal, "king," following the name of the god Enlil.

My comprehension of this paragraph hinges on the notion of mada as "frontier," in this case referring to the area around Kazallu, which is the main issue of the letter. However, it is probable that even if this were the case at some moments of transmission, many Old Babylonian students and teachers would have understood it simply as "land."

18. The term zag-gu/gú-la/lá has been translated in a variety of ways. S. N. Kramer, *JAOS* 69 (1949) 214, rendered it "a kind of chair," Å. Sjöberg, *Nanna-Suen*, 63 n. 3, translated it *"Ehrenplatz,"* i.e., "place of honor," followed by W. Sallaberger, *Kultische Kalender*, 176 n. 820, while G. Selz, *FAOS* 15/2, 556; *SEL* 13 (1996) 7, proposes *"Gerätekammer,"* an "equipment room." Literary use of this term is rare; I know only *UET* 6/1 67: 23 (*Nanna Hymn E*) zag-gu-lá šà hi-li mah si-a i[m-mi-niʾ]-in-dúr-uš, *SLTNi* 35 iii 13 (*Dumuzi-Inana C1*), "(Nanna) has seated (the gods) in places of honor that fill the heart with sublime pleasure," where Dumuzi addresses Inana: zag-gu-la diǧir-ǧá-ka ᵈinin mu-un-da-tuš-ù-dè-en,[11] "Inana, I will seat you in a chair of honor," and *Schooldays*, 53: é-a ù-mu-ni-in-ku₄ zag-gu-la bí-in-tuš, "after (the teacher) entered the house, he was seated in a chair of honor." Clearly, zag-gu-la is a sacred seat of some kind. In ED and Ur III economic texts, it is written zag-gú-lá, e.g., *PDT* 1200: 5, *CT* 32 27 ii 6, *TrDr* 5521:6, *YOS* 4 226:10, *AUCT* 3 413:25, all in Ur III cultic contexts (Drehem, Umma, Garšana); for OB references to ᵍⁱˢbanšur zag-gu-la, see D. Charpin, *Archives*, 37–38. Note also Erimhuš VI 188 (*MSL* 17 86) zag-gu-la = sa-a-gu—that is, *sagû*, "shrine, holy room in a temple," (*CAD* S 26). While it seems that in literary texts one "sits" or "occupies" a zag-gu-la, Ur III economic texts tend to support the interpretation of

11. There are illegible signs underneath the verb, most probably an Akkadian gloss.

the late Erimhuš, providing evidence that they were located in palaces and temples. Thus in *AnOr* 7 87: it is šà ⌜é⌝-gal, in *Princeton* 1 123:7 šà é-gal uru an-na, in *SET* 66:3 šà é [. . .], in *AUCT* 3 413:25–26 in the house of one Arbitum (undoubtedly the wife of the important general Hun-Habur). It seems that rhetorically the future king intends to follow Ur III customs and impose royal control over cultic activities from the highest religious offices to the smallest house and temple shrines.

The plural pronouns in this and the following line are somewhat problematical. They cannot refer to Dagan and Enlil, because the plural shifters are present in manuscripts that only mention the former.

20. The en, lú-mah, and ereš-digir are the highest cultic officials of the land, distinct from the administrative temple organization functionaries such as saga and šabra (on the lú-mah, in many cases the highest priest of a deity, of the same rank as en, and possibly higher than the ereš-digir, see P. Steinkeller, *FS Kienast*, 632–37). Most importantly, these were royal appointees, chosen by the gods by means of omens, and Išbi-Erra is thus claiming divine sanction for his rule. The reading ereš rather than nin follows Steinkeller.

24. The reading and meaning of TUR.TUR is uncertain in this context; one can read tur-tur or di₄-di₄. Note that in N1 and possibly in X4 this is followed by -ma, but I am not aware of any other evidence pointing in this direction. On the difference between tur-tur and di₄-di₄-lá, see M. Civil, *OrNS* 42 (1973) 32. One could entertain a translation "even my poorest citizens will celebrate their festivals." Note that a technical use of the term is encountered in an Ur III letter-order (W. W. Hallo, *BiOr* 26 [1969] 173:1–5): ¹ba-na-na, ù-na-a-dug₄, 3 (gur) 230 (sìla) še gur, še-ba TUR.TUR-ne, hé-na-ab-šúm-mu. In such contexts, the word simply means "servants," which may be the usage followed in this letter.

26. Two of the Nippur texts (N1 and N2) use the verb gub (with -ta-) in the sense of *nasāḫum*, "to remove from office," as in ŠAr1: 22 (2; note that in this text X1 shows the same variant). Apparently, this meaning created problems for some scribes (at least N4, X1, X3, X3), who simplified the verb (gub-bu) to bu, with a similar but more forceful meaning. It is, of course, equally possible that this is free variation and that one cannot assume the primacy of either version of the verb.

34–35. All previous translations have rendered these lines "He captured Zinnum, the ruler/governor of Subir, and plundered Hamazi." Although the traditional interpretation should not be completely ruled out, the present rendition is based on the verbal morphology of these and the preceding lines. In lines 30–33, the verbs all begin with the negative-focus prefix ba-, which signifies that the agent of the action (Išbi-Erra) is not mentioned in the clause. In lines 34–35, the verbal prefix changes to i- (or immi-), and one must assume that Zinnum is the agent of these lines. One would expect an ergative ending on the agent, but that is not always necessary with proper names; the author of X1, who seems to try to make sense of things that are unclear to him, provides Zinnum with an ergative marker. The unreliable scribe of N1 may have understood the line in the same manner as most modern renditions. Note that su-bir^{ki}-a has to be interpreted as a locative (missing only in N1) and not as a possessive form, hence "in Subir"; this is supported by the locative prefix ni- in the predicate. See p. 194 above.

The noun written LÚ×GÁNA-*tenû*(.A) has been read in a variety of ways; the presently attested readings are šaĝa, še₂₉, and heš₅ (for the first two, see P. Steinkeller, *FS Civil*, 231; the sign is also glossed he-eš in Diri 6 B:47 [*MSL* 15 190]). There is ample evidence for both šaĝa and heš₅. In the first reading, the second consonant is /ĝ/, as evidenced by the gloss ša-ĝá (Proto-Ea 628 [*MSL* 14 56], OB Lu A 496 [*MSL* 12 172]; see also *Šulgi Hymn X* 145: ša-ĝá-aš-šè), indicating the reading šaĝa. Though in lexical texts the word is usually written LÚ×GÁNA-*tenû*, in literary texts and in royal inscriptions it is encountered as LÚ×GÁNA-*tenû*.A (i.e. šaĝaᵃ); e.g., LÚ×GÁNA-*tenû*.A ha-ni-dab₅ (Šulgi 36 [E3/2.1.2.36] x 6′–7′); see, moreover, *Ur-Ninurta Hymn A* 51; *Gilgameš and Aka* 81, 99; Samsuiluna 8 46 (E.4.3.7.8). It is clear that the final A is not a grammatical ending but is originally a gloss that became part of the logogram. On the other hand, syllabic writings indicate that LÚ×GÁNA-*tenû* can also be read heš₅ (S. Tinney, *Nippur Lament*, 180–81); in such instances, it is often followed by the gloss šè. The difference in meaning is possibly that of "captive, prisoner" (šaĝa) vs. "captivity" (heš₅).

The three Nippur manuscripts that preserve the last sign have dab₅ (N1, N3, N7) as the verb; this is attested only once, in the inscription of Šulgi cited above, and seems to be the earlier usage. The tradition represented by X1 and X3 bears witness to a hypercorrection based on the common OB literary use of šaĝa . . .ak (but dab₅ in the royal inscriptions of Šulgi and Samsuiluna). The ever resourceful scribe of X1 then changed the verb ak of the next line to lah₅ to avoid repetition of the same word, in accordance with the standard aesthetics of Sumerian literature.

Some students, or teachers, had difficulties with these lines and apparently did not know if Hamazi was a place (GN) or a personal name (PN). Three of the four Nippur manuscripts treat it as a PN (N3, N5, N7) and omit the postfixed place-name classifier /ki/, using instead the prefixed PN classifier (broken in N7); one should therefore really translate the Nippur "version" as "he took Mr. Hamazi prisoner." The undependable writer of N1 solved the problem by omitting the line altogether. Since Hamazi is mentioned as a GN in line 9, it seems to indicate a lack of attention on the part of the students. The Sippar, Ur, and unprovenianced sources treat it as a GN. Ur2 and X3, which are often in agreement with each other in opposition to most other sources of this letter, have the line after 33, with the result that this event is ascribed by them to Išbi-Erra rather than to Zinnum.

36. Note the variant Nur-Ea (Si1, X1) for Nur-aḫi—properly Nur-aḫum—the historically attested ruler of Ešnunna. This may suggest that the name Ea was still thought to begin with /ḫ/ or/h/ by some in this period, but it could also be a clue as to the place in which these manuscripts were written. The form *nu-úr-a-ḫi* is now documented in the Ur III text *TCCP* 2 35:7 (Nippur, ŠS5.-.-).

39. ki-ni-šè gur is otherwise unattested. It has always been rendered "he returned to their places," but if this were the case, one might expect ki-ne-ne-šè (is this a calque from Akkadian *ana ašrišu/ašriš utîršunūti?*). Note also that the third-person marker on the verb, which is consistent in all manuscripts, should refer to the various governors as subjects, not objects. It is quite possible that for some this was the understanding, but students obviously had problems with the long span of text back to the referent, Išbi-Erra. The scribe of X1 used gúr, "to bow down in obeisance," possibly trying to make sense of all this.

40. The metaphor used here, and its echo in line 47, recalls *Inninšagura* 11–12: za-pa-áǧ dugud-da-ni-šè diǧir kalam-ma-ke₄ ní àm-ma-ur₄-ru-ne, ur₅-ša₄-a-ni ᵈa-nun-na gi dili-gin₇ saǧ mu-da-sìg-sìg-ge-ne, "Her loud clamor makes the gods of the country tremble, her scream makes the Anuna quiver like a single reed." This is the only other occurrence of zapaǧ + dugud in Sumerian; in Akkadian, compare Enlil's words in *Atraḫasis* II 7 (Lambert and Millard, *Atra-ḫasīs*, 72): *iktabta rigim awīlūti*, "the 'noise' of humanity had become oppressive to me."

41. There are no variants to gin-gin. F. Ali, *SL* 44, read gub and translated "Išbierra stood at the head of his army," as did S. N. Kramer, *The Sumerians*, 334. The reduplication of the intransitive root with a singular subject implies habitual action.

44–46. There is more confusion and deviation in these lines than in any other passage in this letter, suggesting interpretive confusion in antiquity.

44. The personal name at the beginning of the line is problematical, compounded by the fact that the city of Malgium is not attested prior to OB times. All previous renditions interpret it as Iddin-Malgium or the like, a name that would be highly improbable in an Ur III context. The matter is further complicated by the wide variety of writings of the name of the city attested in the Old Babylonian period. One scribe, who wrote N4, put Iddi and Malgium on separate lines; it may be that others interpreted it as the personal name Iddin-Malgium, although this was clearly not well understood by some of scribes (X1 solved it with a hypocoristic Iddiluma). The verbal form ba-ni-in-ku₄ must be transitive here (see the discussion of Ur III ba-ni-ku₄ by C. Wilcke, *ZA* 78 [1988] 27) and includes the locative prefix ni-; if the name is Iddin-Malgium, then the verb has no direct object and the locative has no referent. Malgium, of course, is unattested in Ur III documents; see p. 199 above.

46. The verb gú . . . bar is otherwise encountered only in martial contexts in the inscriptions of Hammurabi and Samsuiluna and in one Inana hymn (M. Jaques, *Le vocabulaire des sentiments*, 147) and is usually translated "to hate" (Akkadian *zêrum*) but here, as in the inscriptions, it is used in the sense "to resist, rebel"; see, e.g., Samsuiluna 8:36 [E4.3.7.8] and Samsuiluna YD 14. The non-Nippur texts X1 and X2 as well as N4 have the quasi-synonym gú . . . ak (see note to line 1 above), with the meaning "opposed him."

There is some question as to the subject of the three verbs in the sentence. I take Girbubu to be the agent of gú . . . bar but Išbi-Erra as the agent of dab₅, with the switch of reference indicated by the independent pronoun ene. More problematical is the matter of the agents in these lines, an issue that obviously also caused problems for ancient students, as exemplified by the erroneous first- or second-person ending in N1 ("I/you resisted"); indeed, all nine witnesses to this line have completely different forms of the initial predicate.

It is usually assumed that Išbi-Erra was the one who instigated the action symbolized by the "cutting" of Girbubu's shield. The grammar, such as it is, suggests that Girbubu did the cutting to symbolize his resistence to the man imposed by Išbi-Erra and that the independent pronoun marks the switch of reference to the latter, who imposed his vengence. However, in the reply, Ibbi-Sin demands action of both Puzur-Numušda and Girbubu.

For the reading as well as the meaning of gur(u)₂₁, "shield," see M. Civil, JCS 55 (2003) 52. Note the variant guru₇ in N4; most likely, it is a clever phonetic variant, similar to those discussed by M. Civil, JAOS 92 (1972) 271. The scribe then substituted sù for ku₄ and reinterpreted the phrase as "he emptied his grain stores."

48–49. F. Ali, *SL* 52, translated these lines: "He has fixed his eyes upon me, I have no ally (and) no one to go with." The translation of the last verb was based on a reading di rather than sá; the verb is undoubtedly sá, with the prefix -da-, "to be equal to, to compare with, to vie with."

This use of igi . . . ĝar with the meaning "turn attention to" is also encountered in *Curse of Agade*, 222–24: mìn-kam-ma-šè ᵈsuʾen ᵈen-ki ᵈinana ᵈnin-urta ᵈiškur ᵈutu ᵈnuska ᵈnidaba diĝir hé-em-me-eš, uruᵏⁱ-šè igi-ne-ne i-im-ĝá-ĝá-ne, a-ga-dèᵏⁱ áš hul-a im-ma-ab-bal-e-ne, "Then again Sin, Enki, Inana, Ninurta, Iškur, Utu, Nuska, Nidaba, the gods who were (there), turned their attention to the city, and cursed Agade." Note that lines 48–49 are quoted in the answer from Ibbi-Sin to Puzur-Numušda (IbP1: 8–9, Letter 24).

50. As G. Gragg (*JNES* 32 [1973] 126) has observed, this is one of only two attestations of a negative verbal form in subordinate clauses of the type S-a+ta. He notes the incongruence of negation and a temporal clause and suggests the causative meaning "since."

Sources

N1 = 3 N-T 311 (IM 58418) (*SL* xxii–xxiii; *Sumer* 26 171–72) iii–iv   1–51
N2 = 3 N-T 919, 459[12] (*SL* xliii; *Sumer* 26 178; *SLFN* 22)   23–31; 45–51
N3 = CBS 6895 + 6896 + 6906 + 7663 (first three *SL* xxxv; *Sumer* 26 173)   29–51
N4 = CBS 6987 + N 3603 + N 4154 + Ni. 9463 (*ISET* 1 228[170])[13]   4–16;24–28;
                                                                          30–34; 41–49
N5 = CBS 7787 + N1200 + N1203 + N1204 + N1208 + N1210-27a +
        N1210-27b + N1210-27d + N1210-27e + N1212 + N1214 +
        N1218 (+?) Ni. 4061 + Ni. 4188 (*ISET* 2 118) ii 6'–13'   1–6, 11–21; 28–51
N6 = Ni. 4165 (*ISET* 1 136[78][14])   4–9; 31–34
N7 = Ni. 13180 (*ISET* 2 117[15])   33–36; 40–43
N8 = N 1447 (*SL* xxxiv; *Sumer* 26 176) + N 3102   1–7; 20–22
N9 = HS 2394   1–23
Ur1 = U. 16853 (*UET* 6/2 174) + *UET* 6/3 557 (*532) obv. iii' 2'–19';
        rev. i' 1'–17'   1–9; 17–29
Ur2 = *UET* 6/3 558 (*264)[16]   1–36
Si1 = Si. 524 (Copy F. Geers)   6–16; 35–46
Su1 = *MDP* 27 212   8–10
X1 = A 7475 ii 27-52, iii 1–22   1–51
X2 = BM 54327 iv 1'–16'   21–29; 43–46; 31–34
X3 = IM 13347 (*TIM* 9 38)   1–33; 44; 35; 34; 36; 38–48; 50–51
X4 = Cornell 63   19–44
X5 = NYPLC 334[17]   17

N1 collated from a photograph. Su1 could not be located. X3 collated by P. Steinkeller.

X1 possibly from Sippar; X3 possibly from Ur. X4 was identified by Alhena Gadotti, who kindly transliterated it and arranged for photographs (by Lisa Kinney-Bajwa), just as this book was being finished. I was not able to study the tablet in person. The tablet is extremely worn. N9 was also identified at the last minute by Manfred Kre-bernik, who kindly provided a transliteration and digital photo.

---

12. In *SL* labeled as 3N-T 919, 959 (in list of sources as 3N-T 919), in RCU as 3N-T919, 486.

13. CBS 6987 also *STVC* 98, N 3603 also *SL* xliii; *Sumer* 26 175.

14. Obverse and reverse to be reversed.

15. Obverse and reverse to be reversed.

16. The surface of this tablet is very worn in parts and extremely difficult to read. The inter-pretations offered here are the result of multiple collations.

17. Small rectangular tablet with two lines on obverse; reverse uninscribed. This unpro-venienced piece from the collections of the New York Public Library was published in photo on CDLI as P342755 when this book was already in press and kindly brought to my attention by Nike Veldhuis. I have not had the opportunity to collate it (http://cdli.ucla.edu/cdlisearch/search/index.php?SearchMode=Text&txtID_Txt=P342755).

Tablet typology: compilation tablets (Type I): N1, N5, Ur1, X1, X2. All the rest are Type III, except Su1, which is a Type IV round practice tablet.

Bibliography: Editions: F. Ali, *SL* 42–52; F. Ali, *Sumer* 26 (1970) 160–69; Yuhong, *A Political History*, 8–10. Translation: S. N. Kramer, *The Sumerians*, 333–34; P. Michalowski, *Royal Letters*, 80.

Concordance of sigla used here (*CKU*) and by F. Ali in *SL* and in *Sumer* 26, with additions in *RCU*:

N1	A		A	N1
N2	G		B	X3
N3	H		C	Ur1
N4	E		D	N8
N5	I+F		E	N4
N6	M		F	N5
N7	J		G	N2
N8	D		H	N3
Ur1	C		I	N5
Ur2	O		J	N7
Si1	K		K	Si1
X1	L		L	X1
X2	N		M	N6
X3	B		N	X2

Textual Matrix

1. ^{d}i-bí-^{d}en.zu lugal-ğu$_{10}$-ra ù-na-a-dug$_4$

N1	ooo	..	.	.		+	o	o	o	o	o	
N5	ᵀ..	o.	+	.		.	+	+	+	˗	+	
N8	..	+	++	+	+		.	o	/o.	+	.	
N9	.+	+	++	+	.		+	.	/++	+	+	
Ur1	.+	+	++	+	+		+	+	/. a	na	+	
Ur2	oo.	..	.	o		o	o	o	o	o	o	
X1	..	.	+..	+		+	.	+	+	.	+	
X3	ᴵ.	o	oo	o	o		o	o	o	o	o	o

2. ^{I}puzur$_4$-^{d}nu-muš-da énsi ka-zal-lu^{ki} árad-zu na-ab-bé-a

N1	..		.	o	o	o	o		o	o	oo	+	.	.	. o	o
N5	+.		+	+	+	+	+		+	+	+ -/	+	.	+	. +	+
N8	oo		o	.	.	+	.		o	o	oo	o	o	.	. o	o
N9	˗.		+	+	+	+	+		+	+	+ +/	+	+	+	+ +	+
Ur1	+.		.	⌜šul⌝-gi		+		+	+	+ +/	+	+	.	+ +	+
Ur2	o.		+	šul-⌜gi⌝		o		o	o	o o/	o	.	.	. .	o
X1	+.		.	⌜šul-gi⌝		.		+	+	+.	.	.	+	+ +	+
X3	+.		o	o	o	o	o		o	o	oo	o	o	o	o o	o

3. lú-kíğ-gi$_4$-a ^{d}iš-bi-èr-ra   ugu-ğu$_{10}$-šè ì-gin

N1	+	+	+	+	+++	.	o		o	o	o	o o					
N5	+	.	.	.	..	.	.		o	o	o	o o					
N8	o	o	o	o	o	oo o o o			.	.	o	o o					
N9	+	+	+	+	+++	.	.		+	+	+	+ +					
Ur1	+	+	.	+	+++	+	+ /		.	.	⌜im$^?$-mi$^?$-in$^?$-gin-en⌝						
Ur2	.	.	.	+	-+	.	o o	⌜ke$_4$⌝	.	o	o	o o					
X1	+	.	.	.	.o o	+ +			+	.	-	+im +					
X3	.	.	o	o	oo o o o				o	o	o	o o					

4. ^{d}iš-bi-èr-ra lugal-ğu$_{10}$ ugu-zu-šè kíğ-gi$_4$-a im-mi-in-gi$_4$

N1	^{I}++	.	+	.	+	.	o o	.	+	.	+	. o					
N4	oo	.	o o	o	o	o	o o	o	o	o	o	o o					
N5	..	o	. +	-	-	+	+ -	+	.	o	o	o o					
N6	oo o	.	.	.	o	o	o o	o	o	o	o	o o					
N8	++ +	.	. o	o	.	+ +	.	o	o	o	o	o o					
N9	++ + +	+	.	+	+	.	+ +	.	.	+	+ -	.					
Ur1	++ + + +	+	+	.	. uš	+	.	-	.	o o	.						
Ur2	..	.	.	.	.	.	+/	.	.	.	.	+ .[18]					
X1	.+ + +	.	.	+	+	.	-	.	+	+	. -	.					
X3	# (or on same line with 3)																

5. igi-ni ma-an-ğar-ma

N1	+	+	+	.	o	o
N4	.	+	.	o	o	o
N5	.	o	+	+	+	.
N6	o	.	.	o	o	o
N8	.	+	+	o	o	o
N9	+	+	+	+ +	+	
Ur1	.	.	+	+ .	.	(after 3)
Ur2	.	+	.	. .	+	(after 3)
X1	+	+	+	+ +	-	(after 3)
X3	.	.	o	o o	o	(after 3)

6. ^{d}en-líl lugal-ğu$_{10}$ nam-sipa kalam-ma ka-ka-ni ma-an-šúm

N1	++ +	+	+	.	+	.	o	+	+	+	ba	.	o
N4	.+ .	o	o /	.	+	.	o/	.	+	+	.	o	o
N5	oo .	+	+	+	+	.	.	.	.	.	.	o	o
N6	..	.	+	.	.	o	o	o	o o	o	o	o o	
N8	.+ +	+	.	o	o	o	o	+	+ o	o	o	o o	
N9	++ +	+	+	+	+	+	+	+	+ .	+	+	+	
Ur1	++ +	+	+	+	.	+	./	+	.	.	⌜ba⌝	.	.
Ur2	..	.	.	.	.	.	.	.	o	o	ba	+	+
Si1	o.	+	+	+	.	o	o	o	.	.	o	o o	
X1	.+ +	.	.	.	.	.	.	+	+	+	+	+	.
X3	..	.	.	.	o	.	o	o	o o	o	o	o o	

18. Followed by a unique line: ⌜^{I}iš-bi-èr-ra lugal-ğu$_{10}$ na-ab⌝-bé-[a].

7.

	gú ídidigna	gú ídburanun-na	gú ídabgal	ù gú ídme-den-líl-lá
N1	+ ++	- +.	o + +.	. o oo oo o o
N4	. ..	/. .o	o/ + +o	/+ + +. oo o o
N6	o ..	o oo	o o oo	o . oo oo o o
N8	o .+	. oo	o/ o ..	o o oo oo o o
N9	+ +.	+ ++	+ + -+	+ - ++ ++ + +
Si1	. +.	. .o	o + .⌈áb⌉-gal	. o oo oo o o
Ur1	. .+	. ..	o/ . +⌈áb⌉abgal-bi⌉	/+ +. ++ + . .
Ur2	o ..	. ..	. o .o o	/. . .o .. . o
X1	. ..	. ..	. .áb-gal	. - .. .. . +
X3	. ++	. +.	-[19] - +.	o o oo oo o o

8.

	uruki-bi-ne	diğir-bi-ne	ù ugnim-bi-ne
N1	+ + + +	+ + .	- o o
N4	+ + + +	. o o	/+ + . o
N6	o o o o	o . o	o o o o
N9	+ - + e +	+ +e+	+ + + e +
Ur1	. + .⌈ne⌉.	. . o	/. + x o
Ur2	+ . .⌈e⌉.	o . o	/. . . o
Si1	. - + +	+ . o	+ . o o
Su1	+ + + e +/	+ +e+	- .[20] . e +
X1	. - + .	. . .	. . + .
X3	. - + e +	+ +⌈e⌉.	o o o o

9.

	ma-da	ha-ma-ziki-ta	en-na	a-ab-ba	má-ganki-na-še
N1	+ .	+ + . + +	+ -	+ + o	o o o o o
N4	+ +	+ + . o o/	+ +	+ + +	+ . o o .
N6	o o	o o . o o	o o	o o o	o o o o o
N9	+ +ki	+ + + + +	+ +	+ + +	+ + + + +
Ur1	. .	+ + ⌈zí⌉oo/	. .	. ⌈a?⌉ o/	ù + . o o o[21]
Ur2	. .	. . ⌈zí⌉..	. .	o o o	o o o o o
Si1	+ +	+ + .. +	+ .	o o o	o o o o o :
Su1	. +ki	+ + zí- ./	- -	. a -	+ +an naki ta
X1	+ +	+ + . . .	. +	+. +	. . naki +
X3	. +	⌈+ + + + +	o o	o o o	o o o o o

19. Although this source utilizes the writing with final na in line 43, there does not seem to be enough space here for this sign (UD.⌈KIB.NUN⌉).

20. Written: SU.LU.ÚB.⌈ĞAR⌉.

21. Ur1 must have had more after ⌈a-a?⌉-[ab-ba], perhaps Dilmun.

10.   igi ^dnin-in-si-na-ka-šè   ku₄-ku₄-dè

N1	+	++	ì	+	.^{ki}	+	+	+	.	o	o
N4	.	++	+	+	+	.	.	+	+	.	
N9	.	++	+	+	IN^{ki}	+	+	+	+	+	
Ur2	.	++	ì	+	+	+	x	(-)	o	.	.
Si1	.	++	.	o	.	+	+	.	o	o	
Su1	.	++	ì	+	+^{ki}	ˎ	ˎ	+	+	ta	
X1	+	+.	+	+	.	ˎ	ˎ	.	+	+	
X3	.	++	+	+	+	ˎ	ˎ	+	+	o	

11.   ì-si-in^{ki}   nam-ğá-nun ^den-líl-lá-šè   ğá-ğá-da mu   tuk-tuk-da

N1	+	+	+	+	+		+	+	++	+	o	o	+	+	+	+
N4	+	+	+	+	+		.	o/	++	+	+	+	+	+	o/	o
N5	o	o	o	o	o		o	+	++	o	o	o	o	o	o	+
N9	.	+	+	+	+		+	+	++	.	.	+	+	+	+	+
Ur2	+	+	+	.	+		.	.	..	+	ˎ	ˎ	+	.ʼdèʼ/	+	šu
Si1	.	+	+	+	+		+	.	++	+	.	o	o	o	o	+
X1	+	+	.	.	+		+	.	.+	+	.	.	+	+	.	+
X3	.	+	+	+	+		+	.	..	o	o	o	o	o	o	.

(continued columns for line 11): + + . (N1) | + o o o (N4) | + + x²² (N5) | + + . (N9) | . + dè (Ur2) | . + o (Si1) | + + dè (X1) | + + o (X3)

12.   nam-ra-ak-ne-ne   uru-uru-bi   durun-ù-dè

N1	+	+	+	+	+a ak-dè	+ki	.ʼkiʼo	+		+	.
N4	.	+	+	+	+/	+ki	+ki	+	+	+	+
N5	o		o	o	o	o		o	o	+	+	.
N9	+	+	+	+	+ ak-dè	+	+	+	.	ˎ	+
Ur2	+	+	ka	+	.	.	+	ba	+	ˎ	+
Si1	+	+	.	.	+	+	.	+	+²³	. o:	
X1	.	.	.	.	.	.ʼ	.	ʼbaʼ	.	+	+
X3	.	.	ka	.	o	+	+	+	+	o	o

13.   ^den-líl-le   ğá-a-ra   ma-an-dug₄

N1	++	+	.		.	.	+	ʼbaʼ	.	.
N4	++	+	+		+	++	+	+	+	
N5	o+	+	-ğáʼ-eʼ-daʼ	+	++					
N9	++	+	+		+	e	+	+	+	+
Ur2	.+	+	.		o	o	o	o	.	.
Si1	..	.	+		.	o	.	.	.	o
X1	..	.	.		.	ˎ	.	.	.	.
X3	.+	+	+		o	o	.	+	+	o

22. The surface of N5 is extremely worn at this point (lines 11–21). To simplify matters, whenever a sign can be even vaguely identified, it is marked as +; only non-broken signs at the ends of lines are notated as . or x.

23. Written as dib.

14. a-na-aš-àm gú mu-da-ak

N1	o .	+ +	+	+	+ +
N4	+ +	+ +	+	+	+ +
N5	+ +	+ +	+	+	+ + e
N9					
Ur2	o .	. .	.	.	.ab+
Si1	o o	o +	.	o	. .
X1	o o	o o	.	+	+ .e
X3	+ +	+ +	+	+	+ o

15. mu ^{d}da-gan diĝir-ĝá ì-pàd

N1	.		. + .	+	+ +
N4	.		. . +	+	+ +
N5	+		+ + .	o	o o o
N9	+		+ + +	+	ĝu$_{10}$ in-ši-pàd
Ur2	o $^{[d]r}$en-líl lugal-ĝu$_{10}$^{7}	. + +	+$^{!24}$ +	in .
Si1	o		o . .	+	+ .:
X1	o		o o o	+	+ .
X3	. ^{d}en-líl ^{r}lugal-ĝu$_{10}$^{7} ù	+ + .	o o	o o

16. ka-zal-lu^{ki} šu-ĝu$_{10}$ sá hé-eb-bé

N1	.	o + +	+ +	+	+ +
N4	traces			
N5	+	+ + +	. o	o o o o
N9	+	+ + +	+ +	+ + +
Ur2	o	+ + +	+ ^{r}ĝá^7	+^{25} + bí di
Si1	+	. o o	o .	. . . o
X1	o	o o o	+ ĝá	+ . + ^{r}dug$_4$^{7}
X3	+	+ + +	+ ĝá	+ o o o

17. uru ma-da ^{d}en-líl-le   ma-an-du$_{11}$-ga-àm

N1	.	.	+	++ + +	. .	. + o
N5	+	+	+	+. o o	o o	o o o
N9	+	+	+ki++	+ +	+ +	+ + +
Ur1	x	x	o oo	o o	o o	o o o^{26}
Ur2	.	+	+	.. . +	.	. + +
X1	o	o	o	o. . + ĝá-ra	. +	. . .
X3	.	.	+	++ . ^{r}lá^7	+ +	. o o
X5	+ki	+	+/ .	. . +	+ +	+ + -

24. Written as MU!

25. Possibly, the student began to write hé and then continued with sá.

26. The remnants of two signs at the beginning of the line cannot be deciphered; it is impossible to determine if the line was split over two lines or not.

18.   šà ì-si-in^{ki}-na-ka   zag-gu-la-ne-ne   ga-bí-ib-dù-dù

N1	+	++	+++	+	.	.	.	.	o	+	+	+	.	.	
N5	+	++	+++	+	.	o	o	o	o	o	o	o	o	o	
N9	+	++	++-	-	+	+	+^{27}	.		+ a+	+	+	durun-uš		
Ur1	.	. . .	-.	o/^{giš}.	+	lá+	./	+	+	+	+	.			
Ur2	.	. +	+-+	+⌈^{giš}⌉.	.	++	+	+	.	⌈íb⌉	. +				
X1	o	o ooo.	+	o	+	.	.	.⌈a⌉	.	.	. +	+			
X3	.	. +	++.	.	.	. -$^?$	lá+	o	+	.	+	ğaro			

19.   èš-èš-a-ne-ne-a   ga-àm-ak

N1	.	+++	++	+	.	.	.			
N5	+	+++	+-	.	o	o				
N9	+	+++	++	++	+					
Ur1	x	la++	+-	+⌈an⌉	.					
Ur2	.	.. +	+.	. .	nígin^{28}					
X1	o	oo o .	+	+.ma	+					
X3	+	+++	+.	+ +ma	x					
X4	o	o..	.o	oo	o					

20.   alam-ğu$_{10}$ šu-nir-ğu$_{10}$ en   lú-mah ereš-diğir-ğu$_{10}$-ne

N1	.	+	^{giš} .	++	.		. .	+	+	+	o
N5	+	+	+	++	.		o o	o	o	o	o
N8	o	o	o o	.	o		o o	.	+	.	o
N9	+	+	+	++	+		+ +	+	+	+	+^{29}
Ur1	+	+ne ^{giš}	+	.	./	+	ğu$_{10}$-ne -	-	+	+	.	o
Ur2	.	+	+	++	.		o	./	.	.	. +:
X1	o	o	o o	.	.		.	+	.	.	.
X3	.	+	+	+ .	.		. .	o	o	o	o
X4	.	.	⌈^{giš}⌉.	+	+		. .	.	.	+	

21.   ği$_6$-par-ra-ne-ne-a   ga-bí-ib-durun$_x$(KU.KU)

N1	.	+	. .	.	+	.	+	+	dúr ru dúr	
N5	o	+	+ .	.	o	o	o	o	o	
N8	o	o	.	+	++	+	.	.	o	
N9	+	+	+	+	+	.	+	+	+ .	
Ur1	+	.	+	+	+	+	.	o	o o	
Ur2	+	.	. .	+	-	+	.	o	.	
X1	o	o	o	. .	+	+	+	+	+	
X2	o	o	o	o o	o	o	o	o	.	
X3	+	+	+	+ +	+	+	+	.	.	
X4	.	.	. .	.	+	+	⌈ba⌉-	.		

27. Misshapen; looks more like um.
28. Possibly tuš.
29. Preceded by an erased ne.

```
22.  igi ᵈen-líl-lá        šà  é-kur-ra-šè

N1   .   .. . -            .  . . . +
N8   o   oo . +            +  + + + +
N9   +   ++ + +            -  + + + .
Ur1  +   ++ + + šè         +  + + . o
Ur2  o   oo o o            o  . o . -
X1   o   oo o o ʿšèʾ       .  + . + -
X2   o   oo o o            o  o . . -
X3   +   ++ . + ʿšèʾ       -  + + + -
X4   .   .. . . ʿšèʾ       -  + o . -
```

```
23.  igi ᵈnanna        šà  é-kiš-nu-ğál-šè

N1   . ʿen.zuʾ         .  o . . +x[30]+
N2   o oo              o  o o o . .
N9   + ++      na +    +  + . + ???
Ur1  + ..      šè +    +  . o o o
Ur2  o oo              o  . o o . ta
X1   o oo              .  . . . . ʿtaʾ
X2   o oo              o  . . + + ta
X3   + ++              o  + + . . o
X4   + ..              -  . . . ta
```

```
24.  tur-tur-ğu₁₀ sízkur-bi hé-eb-bé

N1   . .ma ğá .        .  + + +
N2   o o o o           .  . + +
N4   o o o o           o  . . .
Ur1  . + + .           +  + ʿíbʾo
Ur2  o o o o           .  . b[í-ib]-ʿdugʾ
X1   . . . .           o  . . ʿdugʾ
X2   o o o o           o  . + +
X3   + + ni .[31]      +  + . x
X4   + + x x           +  + . + +
```

```
25.  ù za-e lú ğiškim-ti-zu-um

N1   . + + + +      . + +
N2   o o o o .      + + +
N4   o . . + +      + + o
Ur1  + + + + .      . o o
Ur2  . o o o o      o o o
X1   o o o o .      . o o
X2   o o o o o      o o o :
X3   + + + . o      + me-en :
X4   . . . . .      + -? -? :
```

30. Probably an erased sign; it appears that the student began to write la.
31. It is possible that there was a sign between ni and sízkur.

26.   ma-da-ni-ta   ga-àm-ta-an-gub-bu

```
N1     .  +  +  +  +  .  .  ⌐  .  +
N2     o  o  o  o  o  o  +  +  +  +
N4     +  +ki +  + / +  +  +  +  ⌐  +
Ur1  ša +  +  .  .  .  o  o  o  o  o
Ur2    +  .  .  .  .  +  o  o  o  o
X1     o  o  o  o  o  o  o  +  ⌐  .
X2     .  .  +  +  o [a]b+ +  ⌐  +
X3     +  +  .  o  o  x  +  ⌐  ⌐  +
X4     o  o  .  x  +  .  .?  o  o  o
```

27.   ì-si-in^ki-na   bàd-bi   ga-àm-dù

```
N1     + + + + +   +   +   + + +
N2     o o o o o   .   +   + + +
N4     + + + + + / .   +   + + +
Ur1    + + + ⌐ +   .   .   o o o
Ur2    . . .na ki  +   .   . o o
X1     o o o o o   o   x   + + +
X2     o o o o o   .   +   + + +
X3     + + + o o   +   +a  + . o
X4     . . . . .   .   +   + . `
```

28.   i-di-il-pa- šu-nu mu-šè   ga-an-sa$_4$

```
N1     ⌐.+  + ⌐KA⌐ +  +  +   sa₄-àm ga-sa₄
N2     oo  o o    .  +  o  o  .   .   .
N4     o.  + +    +  +  o  o  o   o   .?
N5     oo  o o    .  .  .  o  o   o   o
Ur1    o.  . ⌐KA⌐. o  x  x  +   ⌐bí⌐o
Ur2    ì + + +    +  +  +  +  ꟾ  bí  .
X1     oo  o o    o  o  o  .   .  ⌐àm⌐.
X2     oo  o o    o  o  +  +  +   +   +
X3     ++  + +    o  o  +  +   +  ⌐àm⌐.
X4     .   . .    .  .  .  .   .   x  o
```

29.   bí-in-du$_{11}$-ga-gin$_7$-nam

```
N1     + + +   + +   +
N2     o o o   o o   o
N3     . + +   o o   o
N5     . o o   . +   o
Ur1    o . .   . .   o
Ur2    . + +   + +   +
X1     . . .   . +   .
X2     o o o   o +   +
X3     + + +   o +   o
X4     + + +   . .   .
```

30. ì-si-in^{ki}-na   bàd-bi   ba-an-dù

N1	+	+	+	+	.	.	.	+	+
N2	o	o	o	o	o	o	.	o o	.
N3	+	+	+	+	+	+	.	o o	x
N4	traces			/	o	.	+	+	.
N5	.	.	.	+	+	.	x	o	o
Ur2	.	.	.	⸢na^{ki}⸣	o	o	.⸢àm⸣	+
X1	+	+	+	+	+	+	+	+	+
X2	#
X3	.	+	+	+	+	.	+	⸢im⸣ ma .
X4	+	+	+	+	+	.	.	.	o

31. i-di-il-pa-šu-nu   mu-šè   ba-an-sa₄

N1	⸢+⸣+	+	KA+	+		+	sa₄-a	ba-sa₄-a
N2	o o	o	o o	o		o	o	o o	.
N3	+ +	el	KA+	+		+	.	.	+	.
N4	o .	+	+	.	+/	o	o	.	+	.
N5	⸢e-de³²-⸢el⸣-KA-šu-nu mu-šè ì-i[m⸣...]
N6	o o	.	⸢KA⸣o o		o	o	o o o
Ur2	ì +	+	. o	o		.	+	+	àm.
X1	+ +	+	+ +	+		+	+	+ +
X2	o o	o	o o	o		o	.	. + +
X3	o .	+	+ .	.		.	.	⸢ga àm⸣o
X4	++	.	. .	.		.	+	+ . o

32. nibru^{ki} ba-an-dab₅   en-nu-ùĝ-ĝá-ni   ba-an-ĝar

N1	+	+	+	.	.	.	.	+	+	+³³	+	+	+
N3	+	+	+	+	+	+	.	+	+	-	+	+	.
N4	o	.	+	.	+/	o	o	.	.	+	+	+	+
N5	+	+	+	.	.	+	+	+	+	.	o	o	o
N6	.	+	+	+	.	.	o	o	o	o	o	o	o
Ur2	.	.	.	.	.	+	+	-	+	+	.	.	.
X1	+	+	+	+	+	+	+	+	+	+	+	+	+
X2	o	o	o	o	o	o	o	o	x	+	+	+	+
X3	.	.	.	.	+	+	+	.	+	+	o	o	o
X4	.	.	+	+	+	+	+	+	.	o	o	o	o

32. It may be that the student began to write te and then decided to use di.
33. The sign looks more like lú.

33. ù ^{I}níĝ-du$_{11}$-ga-ni saĝa nibru^{ki} ba-an-dab$_5$

N1	+	++	+	+	+	+	+	+	+	+	+
N3	+	-+	+	+	+	+	.		+	+	+	+
N4	o	oo	o	.	+	+/	o	o	.	+	+
N5	+	-+	+	.	+	+	+	+	.	o	o
N6	o	o.	+	+	+	+	.		o	o	o	o
N7	o	oo	o	o	o	.		.	o	o	o	o
Ur2	o	oo	.	+	+	.		.	+	.	o	o
X1	-	++	+	+	+	+	+	+	+	+	+
X2	o	oo	o	o	o	o	o	o	+	+	+
X3	+	-+	+	+	+	+	+	+^{r}a^1+	.	o
X4	.	-.	.	.	.	.		.	o	o	o

34. ^{I}zi-in-nu-um énsi su-bir$_4$^{ki}-a   šaĝa^a i-ni-in-dab$_5$

N1	o.	.	+	+	+		+	+	+	-	.	^{r}ba^1-	-	.
N3	-+	+	+	+	+		+	+	+	+	+	+	+-	+
N4	oo	o	o	o	./		o	o	o	o	o	o	oo	o
N5	++	+	+	+	+		+	.	o	o	+	+	+.	o
N6	oo	o	.	.	.		.	.	o	o	o	o	oo	o
N7	oo	o	.	+	+		.	.	-^{34}-	.	+	++	+
Ur2	omits, or had after line 35											
X1	++	-	+	+e	+		+	+	+	+	+	+	++	ak
X2	oo	o	o	o	o		.	.	.	.	.	.	.	^{r}ak^1
X3	++	+	+	+		kiši^{ki}	o	o	o	o	o	o(after 35)
X4	o.	-	.	.		.	.	o	o	o	o	oo	o

35. ha-ma-zi^{ki} nam-ra-aš   im-mi-in-ak

N1	#									
N3	^{l}+	+	+-	+	^{r}ma^1+	+	+	+	+
N5	^{l}+	+	+-	+	+	+	.	o	o	o
N7	o	o	.	-	+	+	+	+	+	+
Si1	+	+	.	.	.	o	o	o	o	o	o
Ur2	o	o	o+	+	+^{r}a^1.	+ ma^{r}an$^?$^{1} o (after 33)
X1	+	+	++	+	+	+	+	+	an-lah$_5$
X3	^{l}.	+	^{r}zi^1.	.	+	.	.	ma-^{r}an-ak$^?$^{1} (after 33,44)
X4	.	.	.	.	.	.	x	x	o	o

---

34. There does not seem to be room for ki; note that the scribe omits the ki in the next line as well but writes it in line 36.

36. ᴵnu-úr-a-hi   énsi   èš-nun-naᵏⁱ

N1	oo	.	+	+	+	+	.	+	+
N3	++	+	+	+	+	+	+	‑	+
N5	++	+	+	+	+	+	.	o	o
N7	oo	o	o	o	.	+	.	ᵏⁱ na	
Si1	++	+	é-a	.		o	o	o	o (after 37)
Ur2	traces								
X1	++	+	é-a	+		+	+	.	‑ (after 37)
X3	++	+	+	.i	.	o	o	o	o
X4	o.	.	.	.	.		.	o	o o

37. ᴵšu-ᵈen-líl   énsi   kišiᵏⁱ-a

N1	..	++	+	+	+	+	‑	
N3	++	++	+	.	+	+	+	
N5	++	++	+	+	.	.	o	
Si1	++	++	+	.	o	o	o (after 35)	
X1	++	++	+	+	+	+	+ (after 35)	
X3	#	(see l. 35)						
X4	#							

38. ù   ᴵpuzur₄-ᵈtu-tu   énsi   bàd-zi-ab-baᵏⁱ

N1	.	‑+		.+	+	+		.	.	.	+ +
N3	+	‑+		++	.	+	+	.	+	+	+
N5	+	‑+		..	.	+	+	+	+	+	+
Si1	‑	++		‑+	+	.	.	+	+	.	o :
X1	‑	++		‑+	+	+	+	+	+	+	.
X3	‑	+.		.+	+	o	o	o	o	o	o
X4	‑	o.		.+	.	o	o	o	x	o	o :

39. ki-ni-šè   ba-an-gur-ru-uš

N1	.	+	+	+	+	+	+	+
N3	o	.	.	.	.	+	+	.
N5	+	.	+	+	+	+	+	+
Si1	+	+	+	+	ʳeˀ	+	+	+
X1	+	+	+	+	e	gúr ‑		+
X3	.	+	.	bí-i[n]	o	o	o	
X4	.	.	.	+	.	.	.	.

40. za-pa-áǧ-ǧá-ni   ma-da   gi-sig-gin₇   ì-bur₁₀-e

N1	#												
N3	o	.	+	+	+		.	.	.	.	o	+ .	.
N5	+	.	+	+	+		+	+ki	.	.	ge en	. .	o
N7	o	o	o	o	o	o	o	o	o .	+	+ .	ʳreˀ	
Si1	+	+	+	+	+	ta	+	+	+ +	+	+ +	+	
X1	+	+	+	+	+	ta	+	+	+ +	+	íb+	re	
X3	.	+	.	+	+	ta	+	+	. o	o	ì .	o	
X4	o	o	.	+	+	ta	+	+	. .	+	. +	+	

41.　ᵈiš-bi-èr-ra　igi érin-na-šè　ì-gin-gin

N1	#										
N3	.	+	+	+	.	+	+	+	+	+ +	.
N4	o o o o o	/ o	.		o	o o o	o				
N5	˻ +	+	ᵈ+ +		+	+	˼	+	+ +	.	
N7	o o o o o		o	o	.	+	+ +	+			
Si1	+ + + + +		+	.		+	+	+ +	.		
X1	+ + + + +		+	+		+	+	+ +	+		
X3	. . . . .		+	+		+	+	+ .	o		
X4	o o o ˹ᵈ˺ . .		+	+		.	+	+ +	.		

42.　bí-in-du₁₁-ga-gin₇-nam

N1	+	+ +	+ +	+
N3	.	+ +	. +	+
N4	.	+ .	. .	o
N5	+	+ +	+ +	.
N7	o	o .	o .	+
Si1	+	+ +	+ .	.
X1	+	+ +	+ +	+
X3	# or on previous line
X4	o	o o	o o	o :

43.　gú ᶦᵈidigna gú ᶦᵈburanun-na gú ᶦᵈabgal ù gú ᶦᵈme-ᵈen-líl-lá ba-an-dab₅

N1	+ ++	˻ .+	+ ˼	+ +	+ ˼	++	++ + +	+ +	+
N3	o ++	+ .+	+ / o	+ +	+ ˼	++	++ + +	+ .	.
N4	. ++	/. +.	+ / .	+ + /	. +	++	++ + +	+ +	+
N5	+ ++	+ ++⁺³⁵	+ .	. o	+ ˼	++	++ + +	+ .	o
N7	o oo	. ..	+ / o	o o	. ˼	++	++ + +	+ +	+
Si1	+ +.	+ +.	ki +	.˹áb˺-gal + ˼	..	++ +.	o o	o
X1	+ ++	+ .+	+ +	+áb-gal + ˼	++	++ + +	+ .	o
X2	o oo	o o.	ki +	+áb-gal .	+	++	++ + +	+ +	+
X3	+ .+	+ ++	ki ˼	˼ ˼	˼ ˼	˼˼ ˼˼ ˼ ˼	+ +	.
X4	. .+	. ..	ki /	o o	o o	o o o o o + ˼	+ +	+

44.　ˡi-di　mà-al-gi₄ᵏᶦ-a　ba-ni-in-ku₄

N1	+++	. .	+ . +	+ + + .
N3	oo .	+	+ + . +	+ + . .
N4	o.o/	o	.gu₇ a˹ᵏᶦ˺/	. + + .
N5	++ dì	+	+ + aᵏᶦ	+ . o o
Si1	o.+	+	+ + aᵏᶦ	o o o o
X1	ˡid-di-lum-a		+ . . +
X2	oo o o	o o o o	+ + + +
X3	++ + .	+˹gu₇ a˼ᵏᶦ	+ + + . (after 33)
X4	oo o o	o o o o	o . . .

35. Written UD.NUN.

45. ᴵgir-bu-bu   énsi   ğír-kalᵏⁱ-ke₄

N1	++ +	.	+		+	+ +	-		
N2	oo o	o	.		.	o o	o		
N3	oo ʳᵈ¹++	.			+	. o	o		
N4	++ +	+	.		+	+ +	o		
N5	.. +	+	+		.	. o	o		
Si1	oo .	.	.		o	. o	o		
X1	++ +	+	+		+	+ +	+ :		
X2	oo o	o	o		o	o o	. :		
X3	+. .	.	+		+	+ +	- :		

46. gú   im-da-bar-re-ma   ᵏᵘˢguru₂₁-ni   ba-an-ku₅   ù   e-ne   ba-an-dab₅

N1	+	in	.	+	eno	+ +		+	+ +	+	+ + +	+	+			
N2	o	o o	o o	o o		o .		.	. . .	-	- - -	-	₋³⁶			
N3	.	. .	. .	. .		+ +		.	ib -	. /	+ + +	.	+ +			
N4	+	in	+	ak	à[m]	/ -guru₇	+	+	+ sù /	+ +	+ +	.				
N5	+	+	+	+	ʳra¹o	. o		o	o o o	+ +	. o	o	o			
Si1	traces															
X1	+	in-da-ʳan-ak¹-e				+ +		+	+ + +	+ +	+ +	+	+			
X2	.	in-da-ak-e	/			o o		o	o o o	o .	+ +	+	+			
X3	.	i[n]o	o	o		/-x		x	. . .	. +	+ +	+	.			

47. za-pa-áğ-ğá-ni   im-ma-dugud

N1	+ +	+ +	+	+	+	+	
N2	o o	o o	o	.	+	+	
N3	+ +	+ +	+	.	+ an	+	
N4	+ +	+ +	.	+	+	.	
N5	+ +	+ .	o	o	o	o	
X1	+ +	+ +	+	+	+ an	+	
X3	+ x	x x	x	.	+	.	

48. ugu-ğu₁₀-uš   igi-ni   ma-an-ğar

N1	+	+	+ +	+	+	+	.
N2	o	o	o o	o	+	+	+
N3	+	+	šè +	.	[i]m-ma-ni-in-ğar		
N4	+	+	+ +	+	[m-ma]-ni-in-[ğar]		
N5	.	.	. .	o	o	o	o
X1	+	+	šè +	+	+	+	.
X3	.	x	x .	x	x	x	x

36. Perhaps the end of the line continued around the edge.

49. lú tab-ba nu-tuku lú nu-mu-un-da-sá-e

N1	.	+	+	+	+		+	+	+	+	+	+	.
N2	o	o	o	o	o		o	.	+	+	+	+	
N3	+	+	+	+	+		.	.	e	-	+	+	.
N4	.	+	.	o	o /		-	+	.	o	o	o	o
N5	.	+	+	+	o		o	o	o	o	o	o	o
X1	+	+	+	+	+		+	+	+	+	+	⊦	+
X3	#												

50. šu-ni sá nu-mu-un-da-ab-du$_{11}$-ga-ta

N1	.	+	+	+	+	+	+	+	.	+	+
N2	o	o	o	o	o	o	⌈na?⌉-ab-ta-ta				
N3	+	+	+	+	+	-	.^{37} o	.	+⌈a⌉+		
N5	.	+	+	.	o	o	o	u]b?	+	.	o
X1	+	+	+	nu-ub-du$_{11}$-ga :							
X3	⌈šu-[ ] sá mu-un-ib-ib⌉-du$_{11}$-ga-a-⌈ta⌉^{138}										

51. ù-mu-un-šub ga-àm-ma-gin lugal-ğu$_{10}$ hé-en-zu

N1	+	+	-	+^{ub}	+	.	.	.	.	+	.	.	o
N2	o	o	o	o	o	o	.	+	o	o	.	+	+
N3	+	+	+	+	.	.	+	. /	+	+	.	.	.
N5	.	.	.	o	o	o	+	+	+	+	.	.	.
X1	+	+	.	.	.	+	-	+	.	.	.	o	o [a]-ma-ru-kam
X3	.	.	.	.	.	.	. /	.	.	+	+	+

Catchline N3: [$^{(I)}$puz]ur$_4$-^{d}nu-mu[š-da...] (IbPu1 [24])

In N5 and X1 followed by IbPu1 (24)

Colophon O (X1)

37. Sign looks more like the beginning of da rather than of un. There is no room for both.
38. Reading of line uncertain.

24. Ibbi-Sin to Puzur-Numušda 1
(IbPu1, 3.1.20, RCU 22)

Composite Text

Version A (Short Version)

1. ᴵpuzur₄-ᵈnu-muš-da énsi ka-zal-luᵏⁱ
2. ù-na-a-dug₄
3. ᵈi-bí-ᵈen.zu lugal-zu na-ab-bé-a
4. u₄ érin-ta mu-ra-suh-a-gin₇ nam-énsi ka-zal-luᵏⁱ-šè mu-ra-ğál
5. ğá-e-gin₇-nam érin-zu dugud-da-zu in-nu-ù
6. a-na-aš-àm ur₅-gin₇ lú mu-e-ši-gi₄
7. ᴵiš-bi-èr-ra ugu-ğu₁₀-šè igi-ni im-ma-ši-in-ğar
8. ù ğá-e ù-mu-un-šub ga-àm-gin
9. en-na iš-bi-èr-ra kur šu-ni bí-in-gi₄-a a-gin₇ nu-e-zuˡ
10. za-e gir-bu-bu énsi ğír-kalᵏⁱ-a-ke₄
12. a-na-aš-àm érin šu-zu-šè ì-ğál-la igi-ni-šè la-ba-an-su₈-ge-za-na
13. kur ki-bi gi₄-gi₄-da a-gin₇ mi-ni-ib-šúm-mu-za-na
13. u₄ na-me ᵈen-líl-le ki-en-gi hul mu-un-gi₄
14. ᵘᵍᵘugu₄-bi kur-bi-ta è-dè nam-sipa kalam-ma-šè mu-un-íl
15. ì-ne-éš ᵈen-líl-le lú im-sa₁₀-sa₁₀ nu-luh-haˢᵃʳ
16. ᴵiš-bi-èr-ra numun ki-en-gi-ra nu-me-a nam-lugal-la mu-na-an-šúm
17. ga-nam pu-úh-rumᵏⁱ dingir-re-e-ne ki-en-gi ság ba-ab-dug₄
18. a-a ᵈen-líl du₁₁-ga-du₁₁-ga-ni dab₅-bé-da
19. en-na uri₅ᵏⁱ-ma lú érim-ša mu-un-ri-a
20. iš-bi-èr-ra lú má-ríᵏⁱ-ke₄ suhuš-bi ba-bu-re
21. ki-en-gi hé-áğ-e ur₅-gin₇-nam bí-in-dug₄
22. ù tukum-bi énsi uru-didli ì-ğar-ğar-re-en-zé-en
23. inim ᵈen-líl-lá-ta iš-bi-èr-ra ì-bal-e-eš-àm
24. lú tab-ba-gin₇ uru érim-ra ba-šúm-mu-na-ta
25. ù za-e árad gi-na-ğu₁₀-gin₇ iš-bi-èr-ra nu-mu-un-zu-a
26. ì-ne-éš inim du₁₀-ga gi₄-gi₄-dè
27. lul du₈-du₈-ù-da hé-ni-ib-túm-túm-mu
28. un-zu buru₁₄-ba hé-ak-e-ne

1. Var.: en-na iš-bi-ᵈèr-ra kur-šè bí-in-gi₄-a a-gin₇ nu-e-zu.

29. za-e na-an-gur$_{10}$-un ugu-ğu$_{10}$-šè nam-ma-ši-du-un
30. šu-ni uru^{ki}-a nam-bí-ib-sá-di
31. lú má-rí^{ki}-ke$_4$ ğalga ur-re nam-en na-an-ak-e
32. ì-ne-éš amurrum kur-bi-ta ^{d}en-líl á-dah-ğu$_{10}$ im-ma-zi
33. elam^{ki} zag mu-un-tag-ge ù ^{d}iš-bi-èr-ra mu-un-dab$_5$-bé
34. kalam ki-bi gi$_4$-gi$_4$-dè nam-kala-ga kur-kur-ra hé-zu-zu
35. a-ma-ru-kam za-e nam-ba-e-še-ba-e-dè-en-zé-en

Translation (A)

[1-2] Speak to Puzur-Numušda, governor of Kazallu, [3] saying (the words of) Ibbi-Sin, your king:

[4] Ever since I selected you out of the ranks and made you the governor of Kazallu, [5] have you not been honored among the troops as my representative? [6] How could you send someone to me (with a letter beginning) thus: [7] "Išbi-Erra has presented his matter before me," [8] (and ending with) "and as far as I am concerned, when he finally strikes, I will have to flee!" [9] *How is it that you do not know when Išbi-Erra will take back control over his enemy country?*[2] [10-11] Why did you and Girbubu, governor of Girkal, not confront him with the troops that are under your authority (while you still had the chance)? [12] To restore the lands to their previous condition—that was the assignment you were both given!

[13] At some time in the past, Enlil had already come to hate Sumer, [14] and had elevated a monkey descending from his mountain (home) to the stewardship of the homeland. [15-16] But now Enlil has given the kingship to a (*mere*) *peddler of exotic spices*, to Išbi-Erra, who is not even of Sumerian seed. [17] Moreover, the assembly of the gods has scattered Sumer. [18] Father Enlil conveyed his decisions: [19] "As long as an enemy is installed in Ur, [20] Išbi-Erra, the man of Mari, will continue to rip out its foundations, [21] and so Sumer will be measured out (like grain)"—thus he spoke! [22] But if you both gather together the governors of all the individual cities, [23] it is by the (very) command of Enlil that they will overthrow Išbi-Erra! [24-25] But even if you should hand over the city to the enemy as an ally, do you think that Išbi-Erra would not recognize that you are my trusty servant?

[26] Now, to return to reconciliation [27] *and bring an end to all treason,* . . . [28] and have your men work on their harvest. [29] But neither of you should do the reaping yourself nor run away to me; [30] I assure you that he will not conquer (your) city; [31] the man from Mari, with the mind of a beast,[3] will not exercise legitimate power! [32] For even now Enlil has roused up the Amorites from the highlands to aid me. [33] They will repulse the Elamite (forces) and capture Išbi-Erra [34] to restore the homeland, so that all the lands will know the power! [35] Please, you both must not neglect (my orders)!

2. Var.: How is it that you do not know when Išbi-Erra will return (back) to (his) enemy country?

3. Alt. tr.: with hostile intentions.

Sources

Version A (short version)

N1 = CBS 7772 (*MBI* 9)		= 18–35
N2 = CBS 14224 (*PBS* 13 3)		= 1–18
N3 = CBS 14230 (*PBS* 13 6) + N 2964 + N 3003		= 3–35

N4 = CBS 7787 + N1200 + N1203+N1204 + N1208 +
    N1210-27a + N1210-27b + N1210-27d + N1210-27e +
    N1212 + N1214 + N1218 (+?) Ni. 4061 +
    Ni. 4188 (*ISET* 2 118-19) iii–iv   = 1–2; 5–13, 14–33, 34–35

Ki1 = AO 10630 (*PRAK* II C10)	= 10–11; 14–16
Si1 = Si. 557 (Copy F. Geers)[4]	= 4–12; 30–35

Version B (long version)

X1 = A 7475 iii 24–iv 34	= 1–61 (A 1–35)
X2 = MM 1039 (M. Molina and B. Böck, *AuOr* 15 [1997] 36)	= 13–36; 39–45
(A 8–17, 19–25)	

X2 collated on photographs provided by Miguel Civil and Manuel Molina.
X1 possibly from Sippar, X2 reportedly from Babylon. N1 and N2 were
    written by the same scribe.

Tablet typology: Compilation tablets (Type 1): N4, X1; all others type III.

Textual Matrixes

Version A (short version)

1. ᴵpuzur₄-ᵈnu-muš-da énsi ka-zal-luᵏⁱ

N2	++	++ +	+	.		+	+ ++
N4	o o	oo o	x	+		.	+ . .
X1	++	+šul-ᶦgi-raᴵ	-		-	- - -	:

2. ù-na-a-dug₄

N2	+ +	+ +
N4	o .	- .
X1	. .	. .

3. ᵈi-bí-ᵈen.zu lugal-zu na-ab-bé-a

N2	+. +++ +	+	+ / .	+ + +
N3	oo o oo o	o	o o o . o	
X1	++ +++ +	.	o .	+ . o

---

4. This text has a double line after line 35 and therefore definitely had the short version.

4. u₄ érin-ta mu-ra-suh-a-gin₇ nam-énsi ka-zal-luᵏⁱ-šè mu-ra-ğál

N2	.	+	+	+	+ +	+ +	+	+	+ +	+ + +	+	+ +
N3	o	o	o	o	o o	o o	o	o	. .	. . ꜥkaꜥ	o	o +
Si1	o	.	.	.	o .	o o	o	+	. o	o o o	o	o o
X1	+	+	+	+	+ +	+ .	.	.	. +	+ . o	o-ꜥeꜥ-ğar-ra	

5. ğá-e-gin₇-nam érin-zu dugud-da-zu in-nu-ù

N2	+	. +	+	+	+	+	+ +	+ + +
N3	o	o o	o	o	o	.	. +	+ + +
N4	.	o o	o	o	o	o	o o	o o o
Si1	o	o .	.	kalam-ma	.	o o	o o o	
X1	+	+ +	+	kalam-ma	.	o o	. +	.

6. a-na-aš-àm ur₅-gin₇ lú mu-e-ši-in-gi₄

N2	+ +	+ +	. .	+	+	+ + +	.
N3	o o	o o	o o	o	.	+ . .	+
N4	. o	o o	o o	o	o	o o o o	
Si1	. .	+ +	+ .	o	o	o o o o	
X1	za-e ğá-ꜥraꜥ	ur₅ꜥ-gin₇	lú	mu-e-ši-in-[gi₄ (...)]			

7. ⁱiš-bi-ᵈèr-ra ugu-ğu₁₀-šè igi-ni im-ma-ši-in-ğar

N2	+++ ++ +	+	+	+	+	+	+	+	+ + +
N3	oo o oo o	o	.	+	.	.	.	+	+ + +
N4	+. o oo +	.	.	.	.	.	.	.	. . o
Si1	ᵈ+ + ꜥ-+ + ğu₁₀ +	.	o	o	o	o	o	o o o	
X1	ᵈ+ + -ꜥ. .e	+	+	+	+	+	ma-ꜥan-ğarꜥ		

8. ù ğá-e ù-mu-un-šub ga-àm-gin

N2	+	+	+	+ +	+ +	+	+	+
N3	o	o	o	o o	o o	.	.	.
N4	+	.	o	o .	. -	+	+	. DU.DU
Si1	-	+	+	- +	- .	+	àm-m[a]	
X1	+	+	.	. +	. .	+	ꜥgaꜥ-àm-ma-ši-ꜥginꜥ	
X2	o	o	o	o o	o o	o	o x	+

9. en-na iš-bi-ᵈèr-ra kur-šè bí-in-gi₄-a a-gin₇ nu-e-zu

N2	.	.	+ + ++ +	+	.	+ + + +	+ +	+ + +
N3	o	o	o o oo o	.	– šu-ꜥniꜥ.	+ +	. -	- - - -⁵
N4	+	.	o o o. +	+	- ꜥšu-niꜥ+ +	.	+ .	. + + +
Si1	+	+	ᵈ. + -+ .	o	o o	o o o o	o o	o o o
X1	+	+	ᵈ+ + -+ +	kur ki-bi-šè ğá-ğá-a a-gin₇ nu-e-zu				
X2	o	o	o o oo .	kur ki-bi-ꜥšè gi₄ꜥ-a a-gin₇ nu-e-zu				

5. It is possible that the last two words were either wrapped around and broken, or may have been at the beginning of line 10.

10. za-e gir-bu-bu énsi ğír-kal^(ki)-a-ke₄

N2	+	+	.	.	+	+		+	+	+-	+
N3	o	o	o	o	o	.		+	.	.	+	+
N4	+	.	.	.	.	.		.	+	+	o
Ki1	o	o	o	o	o	o		.	.	--	.
Si1	+	+	+	+	.	o		o	o	o	o	o
X1	+	+	+	+	+	.		+	+	+-	+
X2	o	o	o	o	o	.		+	+	+	+

11. a-na-aš-àm éren šu-zu-šè ì-ğál-la igi-ni-šè la-ba-an-su₈-ge-za-na

N2	+	+	.	.		.	.	+	+	.	+	.	.	+	+	+	+	+	+	+	.
N3	o	o	o	o		o	o	o	o	o.	.	.	.	o	.	.	.	o	o	o	o
N4	o	o	o	.		+	+	+	-	+.	+àmo	.	+	+	+	ši	.	+en	+	+
Ki1	o	o	o	o		o	o	o	o	oo	o	o	o	x	.	.	+	+	.	.	+
Si	+	+	+	+		+	+.	o	oo	o	o	o	o	+.	o	o	o	o	o
X1	+	+	+	+		+	+	+	-	+	+	+	+	+	+-	+	+	+	o
X2	o	o	o	o		o	o	in-ğál-le-eš	+	+	+	+	+	su₈-su₈-ge-eš

12. kur ki-bi gi₄-gi₄-da a-gin₇ mi-ni-ib-šúm-mu-za-na

N2	x	.	.	+	+	+	.	.	.	.	+	+	-	+	+
N3	o	o	o	o	o	o	o.	.	.	.ʼíbʼ⁻	o	o	o	o
N4	.	.	o	+	+	+	.	o	x	x	.	.	.	.	.
Si1	.	.	.	o	o	o	oo	o	o	o	o	o	o	o
X1	+	.	+	še	+	+	dè	+	+	+	+	+	.	ʼunʼ
X2	o	o	o	gur]-ʼruʼ-uš	+	+	+	+	íb	+	+	+	+

13. u₄ na-me ^(d)en-líl-le ki-en-gi hul mu-un-gi₄

N2	.	.	+		..	.	+	+	+	+	+	+	.	+
N3	o	o	o		oo	o	o	o	+	+	+	.	.	o
N	o	o	o		oo	o	x	.	o	o	o	o	o	o
X1	+	na-an-ʼga-ma	++	+	+	+	+	+	+	ba-an-ʼgigʼ
X2	o	o	o		oo	o	o	o	o	x	+	ba-an-gig

14. ^(úgu)ugu₄-bi kur-bi-ta è-dè nam-sipa kalam-ma-šè mu-un-íl

N2	+	+	+	+	.	.	.	./	+	+		+		+	+	.	.	.
N3	o	o	o	o	o	.	+	+	+	+		.		o	o	o	o	o
N4	+⁶+	+	.	+	+	o	o	+	+		+		+	o	o	o	o
Ki1	o	o	o	o	o	o	o	o	+	+		.		+	+	+	.	o
X1	+	+	+	+	+	+	+	+	+	+		+		+	.	ʼba-eʼ-gub-bu-dè
X2	o	o	o	o	o	o	.ʼ .ʼ	.	+	+		+	ke₄	x	x	x

6. Written A.UGU.

15. ì-ne-éš ^{d}en-líl-le   lú   im-sa$_{10}$-sa$_{10}$ nu-luh-ha^{sar}

N2	+.	+	++	+	+	+	+	+	+	+	+	+
N3	oo	o	oo	o	+	+	+	+	+	o	o	o o
N4	++	+	++	+	-	.	o	o	o	+	+	. o
Ki1	oo	o	oo	o	o	o	o	.	.	+	ha la	+

X1   a-da-lam ^{d}en-líl-le nu-luh-ha$^{r sar 1}$ sa$_{10}$-sa$_{10}$-^{r}dè lú$^{?1}$ tumu nígin

X2   oo   o   oo   o   o   o   o   o   o   nu   ha ra

16. ^{d}iš-bi-^{d}èr-ra   numun   ki-en-gi-ra   nu-me-a   nam-lugal-la   mu-na-an-šúm

N2	^{1}+	+	+	++	+	+		+	+	+	+	+	+	+	+	+	.	.	+	+
N3	-.	o	oo	o	.		+	+	++	+	+	+	.	o	o	o	.	+	.
N4	+++	++	.	o		o	o	oo	o	o	o	.	+	.	o	o	o	o ^{r}ma$^{?1}$
Ki1	oo	o	oo	o	o		o	o	oo	.	.	.	.	.	o	o	o	o
X1	+++	-	+	+	+		+	+	++	+	+	+	+	+	-	[im$^{?}$-m]a$^{?}$-an-šúm
X2	oo	o	oo	o	o		o	o	oo	o	+	+	+	+	+	.$^{?}$	-	.

17. ga-nam   pu-úh-rum^{ki} diğir-re-e-ne   ki-en-gi   ság   ba-ab-dug$_{4}$

N2	+	+	+	+	+	+	.	.	++	+	+	+	+	+	+	+
N3	+	.	.	.	+	+	+	+	++	+	.	o	.	+	.	+
N4	+	+	.	.	o	o	o	o	o.	.	.	o	o	o	.	+
X1	+	+	+	+	+	-	+	+	++	+	+	+	bir-bir-re ba-[...du]g$_{4}$
X2	o	o	o	o	o	o	o	o	oo	o	o	x	.	ù-bí-in-^{r}dug$_{4}$^{1}

18. a-a ^{d}en-líl   du$_{11}$-ga-du$_{11}$-ga-ni   dab$_{5}$-bé-da

N1	+	+	++	+	.	+	+	+	+	dib	+	+
N2	+	+	++	+	+	+	+	+	+	+	+
N3	+	+	++	+	.	.	.	.	.	.	+	.	^{r}aš^{1}
N4	+	+	++	+	.	.	o	o	o	dib	+	+	aš
X1	+	+	++	+	+	+	+	+	+	+	+	+	aš ka[lam] ^{r}ì$^{?1}$-[b]al-e

19. en-na   uri$_{5}$^{ki}-ma   lú   érim-ša   mu-un-ri-a

N1	+	+	+	+.	+	+	+	+^{7}	+	+ +
N3	+	+	.	o o	o	.	.	+	+	+ +
N4	+	+	+	+ +	.	+	+	+	.	+ +
X1	+	+	+	+ +šè	+	+	ra	+	+	. o aš
X2	traces

20. iš-bi-èr-ra   lú   má-rí^{ki}-ke$_{4}$ suhuš-bi   ba-bu-re

N1	+	+	+	+	+	+	++	+	+	+	+	.	+
N3	+	+	+	.	o	o	oo	o	o	o	.	+	+
N4	^{d}+	+	^{d}.	.	+	++	+	+	.	.	+	+ en
X1	^{d}+	+	+	+	+	+	++	.	+	+	ba-ab-^{r}bu-re^{1}
X2	o	o	o	o	o	o	oo	.$^{?}$	.$^{?}$	o	o o	.

7. Proceeded by an erased árad.

21. ki-en-gi   hé-áǧ-e   ur₅-gin₇-nam   bí-in-dug₄

N1   + + +   + + + + +   +   + + +
N3   + + +   .   o o o o   o   o . +
N4   + + +   .   o o .   +   +   + . +
X1   . . .   .   + + + +   +   + ᵣíbᵔ +
X2   o o o   o o o o o   o   . . .

22. ù tukum-bi énsi uru-didli ì-ǧar-ǧar-re-en-zé-en

N1   + +   + +   + +   + + + + + +
N3   + .   o o   o o   o o o o + + +
N4   + .   o o   . +   + + + + + . +
X1   o .   + .   .ᵣuruᵔ+   - . x o o o o
X2   o o   o o   .ᵣuruᵔ.ᵎ   - . . . ᵣneᵔ

23. inim ᵈen-líl-lá-ta iš-bi-èr-ra ì-bal-e-eš-àm

N1   +   .+ + + +   + + + +   + + + + a
N3   +   .. . + .   o o o o   + + + + e
N4   +   .. o o o   + + ᵈ+ +   o . + + +
X1   o   oo o o o   . . . .   oo o o o
X2   o   oo o o o   o . . .   ᵣhéᵔⁿ-ni-bal-e

24. lú tab-ba-gin₇ uru érim-ra ba-šúm-mu-na-ta

N1   +   +   +⁸ +   +   +   + + +   + + +
N3   +   +   + +   +   .   o o .   + + +
N4   +   .   o .   +   +   +a. o   .un-ne-ta
X1   o   o   o .   .   +   šè ba-ra-mu-un-ᵣšúm-ma-taᵔ
X2   o   o   o o   o   .   ma ba-ra-an-šúm-ma-a

25. ù za-e árad gi-na-ǧu₁₀-gin₇ iš-bi-èr-ra nu-mu-un-zu-a

N1   + + + +   + + +   +   + + + +   + +   + + +
N3   + + + +   + + .   o   . . + +   + +   + + +
N4   + + o o   . + +   +   o o . +   + +   + + .
X1   ù ᵈiš-bi-èr-ra za-e árad gi-na-ǧu₁₀-gin₇ ní-ba mi-ni-ib-zu-a-ta
X2   o o o o   o o o   o   o o . +   ní-bi   mu-un-zu-a

26. ì-ne-éš inim du₁₀-ga gi₄-gi₄-dè

N1   ++ +   +   +   +   + +
N3   . + +   +   +   +   + +
N4   +o o   +   +   +   + +
X1   en-na u₄-bi-da-ke₄ inim du₁₀ gi₄-bí-ib / gin-na ì-ne-éš inim du₁₀ gi₄-ib :

27. lul du₈-du₈-ù-da hé-ni-ib-túm-túm-mu

N1   +   + +   + + +   + + +   + +
N3   o   . +   + + +   + + +   + +
N4   .   o o   o o o   . + +   + +
X1   lul du₁₀-ud-ak-da mi-ni-in-túm-túm-mu

8. Written as su.

28. ùĝ-zu   buru₁₄-ba   hé-ak-e-ne

N1	+	ba	+		+	+	+	+ +
N3	o	o	.		+	+	+	+ .
N4	o	o	o		o	o	+	+ -
X1	+	+	+		+	+	+	- +

29. za-e   na-an-gur₁₀-un   ugu-ĝu₁₀-šè   nam-ma-ši-du-un

N1	.	+	+	+ +	+	+	+	+	+	+ + +
N3	o	o	.	+ gur₄ ru	+	+	+	+	+	+ + .
N4	o	o	o	o o	o	o	.	+	+	+ + .
X1	+	+	nam-ba-da-ĝír-e	+	+	+	+	+	- +	-

30. šu-ni   uru^(ki)-a   nam-bí-ib-sá-di

N1	+	+	+	+ +	+	+ + + +
N3	.	.	+	+ +	+	+ + + +
N4	o	o	o	o o	o	o + + + x
Si1	o	.	.	o o	o	o o o o
X1	+	+	+	- ni	sá	nu-ub-du₁₁-ga

31. lú   má-rí^(ki)-ke₄   ĝalga   ur-re   nam-en   na-an-na-ak-e

N1	+	+	+ + +	+		+	+	+		+		+	+	+	+ +
N3	+	+	+ + +	+		+	+	+		+		+	+	+	+ .
N4	o	o	o o o	o		.	+	-		+ na		.	.	.	. .
Si1	o	+	+ + x	o		o	o	o		o		o	o	o	o o
X1	+	+	+ + +	+		+	+	+		+ bi		+	+	-	+ +

32. ì-ne-éš   amurrum   kur-bi-ta   ᵈen-líl   á-dah-ĝu₁₀   im-ma-zi

N1	+ +	+	+		+	+ +	+ +	+ .	+	+		+	+	+
N3	+ +	+	+		+	+ +	+ +	+ +	+	+		+	+	+
N4	o .	.	+		+	+ .	o o	. .	+			.	.	o
Si1	⌈ì-ne⌉-éš ti-da-nu-um [...] / ᵈen-líl kur-bi-ta á-d[ah-ĝu₁₀-šè im-ma-(an)-zi]
X1	ì-ne-éš ti-da-ma-rum amurrum^(ki)-a/ᵈen-líl-le kur-bi-ta á-dah-ĝu₁₀-šè im-ma-an-zi

33. elam^(ki)   zag   mu-un-tag-ge   ù   ᵈiš-bi-èr-ra   mu-un-dab₅-bé

N1	+	+ki+	+	+	+	+	+	++ -	+	+	+	+	+	+
N3	+	+ +	+	+	+	+	+	++ + +	+	+	+	+
N4	o	o o	o	x	+	.	o	o o o o o	o	o	o	o
Si1	+	+ +	.	+	+	o	o	o o o o o	+	o	o	o
X1	+	+ +	+	+	+	ga/	+	++ + +	+	ba	ab	+	+

34. kalam   ki-bi   gi₄-gi₄-dè   nam-kala-ga   kur-kur-ra   hé-zu-zu

N1	+		+	+	+	+ +	+		+		+	+	+	+ +
N3	+		+	+	+	+ +	+		+		+	+	+	+ +
N4	o		o	o	o	o o	.		.		.	o	o	o . . .
Si1	+		+	+	+	da o	o		o		o	o	o	o o o :
X1	kalam ki-bi-šè bí-íb-gi₄-gi₄ / kala-ga-ĝu₁₀ kur-re bí-ib-zu-zu

35.	a-ma-ru-kam	za-e	nam-ba-e-še-ba-e-dè-en-zé-en													
N1	+ +	+ +	+ + +	+	-	+	-	-	+	-	-	+				
N3	+ +	+ +	+ + +	+	+	+	+	+	+	+	+	+				
N4	. +	+ +	+ + .	.	+	.	.	+	+	.	.	+				
Si1	- -	- -	- -^{9} nam-ba-še-bé-d[è]													
X1	. .	+ +	+ + nam-ba-še-bé-dè-ne													

Version B (long version)

X1 with variants from X2 (equivalent lines in A in right-hand column)^{10}

1.	^{I}puzur -^{d}šul-^{r}gi-ra ù-na-a-dug ^{1}	1–2
2.	^{d}i-bi-^{d}en.zu luga[l-zu n]a-ab-^{r}bé^1-[a]	3
3.	u$_4$ érin-ta mu-ra-suh-a-g[in$_7$ na]m-^{r}énsi^1 ^{r}ka^1-zal-lu^{rki1}-[šè mu]-^{r}e^1-ğar-^{r}ra^1	4
4.	ğá-e-gin$_7$-nam kalam-ma d[ugud-da-zu i]n-nu-^{r}ù^1	5
5.	ka-zal-lu^{ki} lú-ùlu [. . .]$^{rki?1}$-šè$^{?1}$ b[í-. . .]	
6.	lú al-m e-a-gin$_7$ ^{r}ù$^{?1}$ x [. . .] a [. . .]	
7.	ma-da-zu-ta ^{d}en-líl-^{r}le nu-mu^1-ra-ab-tuk[u . . .]	
8.	diri lú za-e-gin$_7$-nam nam ^{r}uru^1 tur$^{?1}$-ra-^{r}ta$^{?1}$ x[. . .]	
9.	a-na-aš-àm ní šà-zu-šè ì-bu-^{r}bu^1	
10.	ní ul$_4$-^{r}la^1 mu-e-te igi tur-^{r}zu^1 mu-^{r}e-gíd^1-[i . . .]	
11.	za-e ğá-^{r}ra ur$_5$^{1}-gin$_7$ lú mu-e-ši-in-[gi$_4$ (. . .)]	6
12.	^{d}iš-bi-^{r}èr-ra^1-e ugu-ğu$_{10}$-šè igi-ni ma-^{r}an-ğar^1	7
13.	ù ğá-^{r}e ù^1-mu-^{r}un^1-šub ^{r}ga^1-àm-ma-ši-^{r}gin^1	8
	X2 [ ]-x-gin$^{?11}$	
13a. *		
	X2 [ ]x-e-NE [ ] ^{r}en^1 e su$_8$-^{r}dè$^{?1}$-eš	
14.	en-na ^{d}iš-bi-èr-ra kur ki-bi-šè ğá-ğá-a a-gin$_7$ nu-e-zu	9
	X2 [r]a kur ki-bi-^{r}šè gi$_4$^{1}-a a-gin$_7$ nu-e-zu	
15.	za-e gir-bu-bu ^{r}énsi^1 ğír-kal^{ki}-ke$_4$	10
	X2 [éns]i ğír-kal^{ki}-a-ke$_4$	
16.	a-na-aš-àm érin šu-zu-šè ğál-la igi-ni-šè la-ba-su$_8$-ge-za-[na]	11
	X2 [ ] in-ğál-le-eš igi-ni-šè la-ba-an-su$_8$-su$_8$-ge-eš	
17.	kur ^{r}ki^1-bi-šè gi$_4$-gi$_4$-dè a-gin$_7$ mi-ni-ib-šúm-^{r}mu-un^1	12
	X2 [gur]-^{r}ru^1-uš a-gin$_7$ mi-ni-íb-šúm-mu-za-na	
18.	u$_4$ na-an-ga-ma ^{d}en-líl-le ki-en-gi hul ba-an-^{r}gig^1	13
	X2 [ ]x hul ba-an-gig	

9. The equivalents of the beginning parts of the line may have been on line 34.

10. X1 has deteriorated somewhat since I first began to study it.

11. There seem to be remnants of the last sign of at least three lines before this, as well as the additional line that does not appear to match X1. Unfortunately, I have not been able to inspect this tablet in person.

19.　　^{ugu}ugu$_4$-bi kur-bi-ta è-dè　　nam-sipa kalam-ma-ʿšèʾ ba-eʾ-gub-bu-dè　　14
　　X2 [　　　　　　　　　] ʿèʾ-dèʾ ʿnamʾ-sipa kalam-ma-ke$_4$ x x x
20.　　a-da-lam ^{d}en-líl-le nu-luh-ha^{ʿsarʾ} sa$_{10}$-sa$_{10}$-ʿdè lúʾ tumu nígin　　15
　　X2 [　　　　　　] nu-ha-ra
21.　　^{d}iš-bi-èr-ra numun ki-en-gi-ra nu-me-a nam-lugal　　[imʾ-m]aʾ-an-šúm　　16
　　X2 [　　　　　　　　　　　nu]-me-a nam-lugal-la mu-ʿnaʾ-šúmʾ
22.　　ga-nam pu-úh-rum dingir-re-e-ne ki-en-gi bir-bir-re ba-[... d]ug$_4$　　17
　　X2 [.　　　　　　　　　　　]x ʿságʾ ù-bí-in-ʿdug$_4$ʾ
23.　　a-a ^{d}en-líl du$_{11}$-ga-du$_{11}$-ga-ni dab$_5$-bé-da-aš ka[lam] ʿìʾ-[b]al-e　　18
24.　　en-na uri$_5$^{ki}-ma-šè lú érim-ra mu-un-ʿriʾ-[. . .]-aš　　19
　　X2 traces
25.　　^{d}iš-bi-èr-ra lú má-rí^{ki}-ʿke$_4$ʾ suhuš-bi ba-ab-ʿbu-reʾ　　20
　　X2 [　　　　　] -ke$_4$ʾ suhušʾ [　　　　-r]e
26.　　ʿki-en-gi héʾ-áǧ-e ur$_5$-gin$_7$-nam ʿbí-íb-dug$_4$ʾ　　21
　　X2 [　　　　　　　　] ʿbí-in-dug$_4$ʾ
27.　　[ù tu]kum-bi ʿénsi uru-uruʾ-didli ʿǧarʾ x [　　]　　22
　　X2 [　　　　　] ʿuru-uru-didliʾ ǧar-ǧar-e-neʾ
28.　　[inim ^{d}en-líl-lá-ta ^{d}]ʿiš-bi-èr-raʾ [　　　　　]　　23
　　X2 [　　　　iš]-ʿbi-èr-raʾ ʿhéʾ-ni-bal-e
29.　　[lú tab-ba]-ʿgin$_7$ uruʾ érim-šè ba-ra-mu-un-ʿšúm-ma-taʾ　　24
　　X2 [　　　　　ér]im-ma ba-ra-an-šúm-ma-a
30.　　ù ^{d}iš-bi-èr-ra za-e árad gi-na-ǧu$_{10}$-gin$_7$ ní-ba mi-ni-ib-zu-a-ta　　25
　　X2 [ù $^{(d)}$iš-bi]-ʿèrʾ-ra　　　　　　ní-bi mu-un-zu-a
30a. X2 [ ] hé-me-en
　　(X1: *)
31.　　mu-e-du$_{11}$-ga-zu níǧ-na-me nam-ba-e-hul
　　X2 [ ]-e-ši-hul
32.　　mu-e-zu-zu diǧir-ra ǧá-a-kam
　　X2 [　　　　　] ʿǧáʾ-a-kam
33.　　a-a ^{d}en-líl du$_{11}$-ga-du$_{11}$-ga-ni dib-bé-da-aš kalam　　ì-bal-e-eš
　　X2 [　　　　　　　　　] x.NE.A kalam-ma ì-bal-e
34.　　gin ì-ne-éš ma-ra ma-ab-gi$_4$-gi$_4$
　　X2 [　　　　　]-ʿabʾ-gi$_4$-gi$_4$
35.　　i-^{d}utu kiri$_3$ šu-ta ba-ǧál
　　X2 [　　] kiri$_3$ šu ǧál-la-ǧá
36.　　en gal ^{d}en-líl-le ǧéštu-bi mu-un-ǧar
　　X2 [　　^{d}]ʿen-líl-láʾ ǧéštu-bi mu-ri
37.　　igi níg-sa$_6$-ʿgaʾ-ni ǧá-ra mu-un-ši-in-bar
　　X2 *
38.　　šà-ne-ša$_4$-ǧu$_{10}$ šà kù-bi-šè mu-un-ǧar
　　X2 *
39.　　kíǧ-gi$_4$-a-ǧu$_{10}$ uzu silim-ma-ke$_4$ ma-an-ǧar
　　X2 [kíǧ-gi$_4$-a]-ʿǧáʾ uzu silim-ma　　im-ma-an-ǧar

40.   uzu zi-da-na uzu gùb-⌜ba?-ĝá?⌝ á-diri ù-ni-ak
    X2 [z]i-da   á-gùb-bu-ba   á-diri ù-mu-ni-ak

41.   ĝištukul á zi-da-ĝá gú-bi zi-da ul gùr-ru mi-ni-šúm
    X2 *

42.   ĝištukul gùb-bu-na gu-da lá-lá gú-ri-bi ĝar-ra
    X2 *

43.   lú hul-ĝál-ĝu₁₀ šu-ĝá ì-ĝá-ĝá   saĝ ĝiš bí-ra
    X2 [   ]-⌜ĝál⌝-e šu-ĝá ba-ni-in-ĝál saĝ ĝiš bi-ra-ra

44.   un kúkku-ga-ke₄ zalag-šè è-dè dúr silim-⌜ma⌝ nú-dè
    X2 [   ]-⌜ga⌝-ke₄ zalag-šè è-⌜dè⌝ dúr silim⌝-ma nú-dè

45.   ᵈutu en ka-aš-bar an-ki-ke₄ á-áĝ-ĝá im-ma-an-ĝar
    X2 traces

46.   en-na u₄-bi-da-ke₄ inim du₁₀ gi₄-bí-ib

47.   gin-na ì-ne-éš inim du₁₀ gi₄-ib lul du₁₀-ud ak-da mi-ni-in-túm-túm-mu

                                                  26–27

48.   ùĝ-zu ebur-ba hé-ak-ne   28

49.   za-e nam-ba-da-ĝír-e ugu-ĝu₁₀-šè nam-ma-du   29

50.   šu-ni uru-ni sá nu-ub-du₁₁-ga   30

51.   lú má-ríki-ke₄ ĝalga ur-re nam-en-bi na-an-ak-e   31

52.   ì-ne-éš ti-da-ma-rum amurrumki-a   }32

53.   ᵈen-líl-le kur-bi-ta á-dah-ĝu₁₀-šè im-ma-an-zi

54.   u₄-ne-a an ᵈen-líl ᵈen-ki-bi-ke₄

55.   ⌜uri₅⌝ki-ma sá mu-ub-du₁₁-ga an-ta-bi aka-dè

56.   elamki zag mu-un-tag-ga   }33

57.   ù ᵈiš-bi-èr-ra ba-ab-dab₅-bé

58.   kalam ki-bi-šè bí-íb-gi₄-gi₄   }34

59.   kala-ga-ĝu₁₀ kur-re bí-ib-zu-zu

60.   ⌜u₄⌝-na-me inim za-e mu-sa₆-ga-zu

61.   ⌜a-ma⌝-ru-kam za-e nam-ba-še-bé-dè-ne   35

Colophon O (X1)

Translation (B)

¹⁻²Speak to Puzur-Šulgi, governor of Kazallu, ⁴saying (the words of) ³Ibbi-Sin, your king:

³Ever since I selected you out of the ranks and made you the governor of Kazallu, ⁴have you not been honored throughout the homeland as my representative? ⁵Kazallu . . . ⁶A man who is . . . ⁷Enlil has not . . . from your frontier area. ⁸Someone excellent, a man who is like you . . . the responsibilities over the smaller cities . . . ⁹Why is it that all valor has been torn from your heart, ¹⁰why are you so panicked and full of contempt? ¹¹You even sent someone to me (saying) thus:¹² ¹²"Išbi-Erra

12. Var.: But you sent me someone with the following message.

has presented his matter before me, [13] and as far as I am concerned, when he finally strikes, I will have to flee!" [14] How is it that you do not know *when Išbi-Erra will restore his own enemy country?* [15-16] Why did you and Girbubu, governor of Girkal, not stand up against him with the troops that are under your authority (while you still had the chance)? [17] To restore the lands to their previous condition—that was the assignment you were both given!

[18] Enlil had earlier already come to hate Sumer, [19] appointing a monkey descending from its mountain (home) to the stewardship of the homeland. [20-21] But now Enlil has handed kingship to a *(mere) peddler of exotic spices*, one who chases the wind, to Išbi-Erra, who is not even of Sumerian descent. [22] Moreover, once the assembly of the gods (decided) to scatter the (inhabitants of the) Sumer, [23] Father Enlil, having conveyed his commands, proceeded to overthrow the homeland. [24] "As long as Ur *is imbued with evildoers,* [25] Išbi-Erra, the man of Mari, will tear out its foundations, [26] and Sumer will be measured out," thus he spoke! [27] And if the governors of the individual cities should gather together, [28] by Enlil's command Išbi-Erra will fall.

[29] But even supposing that he is not (betrayed) as if being handed over to an enemy city by a comrade, [30] and you, although acting as if you were my trusted servant, recognize Išbi-Erra by yourself/out of fear, [31] your statements would do nothing to upset me, [32] for you know very well that I am (a favorite) of the gods.

[33] Father Enlil, by means of his angry commands, has overthrown the homeland. [34] Come now, he has returned to my side! [35] My *complaints were submitted by humble prayer,* [36] and Great Lord Enlil heard me out; [37] he cast his favorable glance upon me, [38] set his holy heart on mercy, [39] and established for me my favorable omen. [40] And after I had the follow-up reading made concerning his *pars familiaris* and my *pars hostilis,*[13] [41] the weapon-mark on my right side, its trunk is straight, and that (good news) gave me joy; [42] on the weapon-mark on his (i.e., Išbi-Erra's) left side a filament is suspended,[14] it is placed (against) the other side. [43] (The message was:) "My enemy shall fall into my hands, he shall be killed, [44] the people, having come out of darkness into the light, will lie in peaceful habitations." [45] Utu, lord who makes the decisions of the heavens and the earth, has provided (this) omen.

[46] Return to reconciliation *as before,* [47] come now, (you too) must return to reconciliation, *so that all treachery is undone,* [48] so that your can people can work on their harvest. [49] You must not hurry to come to me; [50] (I assure you that) he will not conquer the city that he (wants), [51] the man of Mari, with the mind of a beast, will not exercise sovereignty there! [52-53] Now Enlil has mustered the Tidnumite(s) in (the land of) Amurrum as my helper(s). [54-55] . . . [56] The Elamite (forces) will be repulsed, [52] Išbi-Erra will be captured, and [58] the homeland will be restored (to me). [59] The foreign land(s) will learn of my strength! [60] From now on you. . . . [61] It is urgent, you must make sure that everyone must not neglect (my orders)!

13. So X1; X2 omits 41 and 42: After I had the follow-up reading made concerning the left and right sides, (the message was): . . .

14. Alt. tr.: is attached.

Commentary

This letter is known in two versions, a shorter one (A) from Nippur, Kish, and Sippar, and a longer one (B) attested in two manuscripts of unknown provenience. As noted above, there are clues that suggest that X1 may come from Sippar and X2 from Babylon, but the evidence is hardly conclusive. Version B adds six lines between lines 5 and 6, fourteen or fifteen lines between 25 and 26, and two lines between 32 and 33. The short version appears to be fairly stable, with few substantive variants, but the two sources of B clearly represent different redactional traditions. X1 is dated to the 27th year of Samsu-iluna, providing a historical context for one manuscript the long version. Moreover, the text was known to the compiler of the *Uruk Letter Catalog*, as documented by the entry in line 8: puzur₄-ᵈšul-g[i P]A.TE.⟨SI⟩ k[a-zal-luᵏⁱ].

The differences between the two versions are not only in length. A has many difficult passages, and some of them seem to have been as puzzling to some ancients as they are to many of us. Redactors of what became "B"—itself not uniform—attempted to make sense of some version of "A" that was at their disposal, reinterpreting some of the grammar and vocabulary to fit a specific understanding of the text.

B10. This difficult line, which is not in the short version, contains words that are otherwise rare in Sumerian. The noun ní-ul₄, "fear, terror," occurs, to my knowledge only once in another text, in *Ininšagura* 161 (see Å. Sjöberg, ZA 65 [1975] 161): ní-àm ur₄-re ní ⌈ul₄⌉ ní-⌈ri⌉-ti-la ní gal me-lám-ma, which consists of a series of synonyms and quasi-synonyms for "fear," "terror." Here ul₄ seems to qualify the noun in the compound verb ní ... te, "to fear"; it could either be construed as ul₄ = *piqittu*, "terror," or as the adverb "greatly" (*magal*); see now M. Jaques, *Le vocabulaire des sentiments*, 189.

The verb must be igi-tur ... gíd-i, "to hold in contempt, despise," which is otherwise only attested in *SP Coll. 2* 16 and in bilingual and lexical texts (= *šēṭūtam leqûm*).

A6 = B11. Note that ur₅-gin₇ is used, like its Akkadian equivalent *kīam*, to introduce direct speech. In line 22, it follows the quotation and the form is ur₅-gin₇-nam, which corresponds to *kīamma*, which is likewise used to introduce quoted statements.

The verbal form in A is, technically speaking, in the third person—"he sent a man to you"—but this is clearly incorrect. A redactor of B attempted to clarify this with the superfluous za-e ǧá-ra, "you to me."

A7–8 = B12–13. These are the incipit and last lines of the previous letter; this is a unique example of the way in which one could refer to previous correspondence in Sumerian.

A9 = B14. The syntax of this line is difficult. The first part, governed by a temporal adverb (en-na = *adi*), must be dependent on the main clause, which is introduced by an interrogative preposition (a-gin$_7$ = kî). Redactors of the long version recognized the problem and attempted to resolve it by changing the predicate of the dependent clause but only managed to introduce more confusion. The tentative interpretation of šu . . . gi$_4$ as "to take charge of" is inspired by the comments of W. Sallaberger, *Klein AV* 250.

A13–15 = B18–20. The proper understanding of this passage relies on the first word, which is u$_4$ na-me in one manuscript of A but clarified as u$_4$ na-an-ga-ma in B.[15] The scribe of X1 has taken pains to interpret a difficult passage, since in all other cases u$_4$ na-me occurs with negative verbal forms (*matima*, "never"; see commentary to IbIš1A 13′ [22]); here it must be a temporal adverb. These lines have to be compared to *Lugalbanda II* 74–77 (C. Wilcke, *JNES* 27 [1968] 241, and idem, *Das Lugalbandaepos* 98–100 with commentary on p. 159; H. Vanstiphout, *Epics of Sumerian Kings*, 140–41):

u$_4$ na-an-ga-ma mušen-e gùd-bi-šè šid$_{17}$ un-gi$_4$
amar-bi gùd-bi-ta gù ba-ni-ib-gi$_4$-gi$_4$
ì-ne-éš mušen-e gùd-bi-šè
amar-bi gùd-bi-ta gù nu-um-ma-ni-ib-gi$_4$-gi$_4$

Earlier, whenever the bird screeched at its nest,
Its young answered it from its nest,
But now, when the bird screeched at its nest,
Its young did not answer it from its nest.

Thus, the phrases governed by the adverbs u$_4$-na-me . . . ì-ne-éš (A) and u$_4$ na-an-ga-ma . . . a-da-lam (B) are structurally identical, contrasting earlier and later events. This is extremely important; we now realize that the word "monkey" does not refer to Išbi-Erra, as has always been thought, but must be a characterization of someone else, undoubtedly "Elamites." Is it possible that this refers to events that provided the enigmatic name of Ibbi-Sin's 23rd and penultimate, year: mu ^{d}i-bí-^{d}en.zu lugal uri$_5^{ki}$-ma-ra ^{ugu}ugu$_4$-bi dugud kur-bi mu-na-e-ra, "The year: The *dumb/formidable* monkey *struck out* from its mountain against Ibbi-Sin, king of Ur." Note that the Gutians are described as having the form of monkeys (uludin$_2$ ugu$_4$-bi) in the *Curse of Agade*, 156, and the same expression is used to characterize Amorites in the *Marriage of Amurru* (line 127). This may be a reference to some other highlanders here, Elamites, or perhaps the Amorites, according to IbIš1A: 14′ (22), although the latter is definitely untrustworthy. More importantly, if this holds true, it would date the Puzur-Numušda correspondence to the very end of Ibbi-Sin's reign. See p. 201 above.

A13 = B18. The verb hul . . . gig(gi$_4$) is usually translated as "to hate." The sense here is more precise: Enlil has broken his bond with Sumer, and thus the verb is used

---

15. Note that u$_4$ na-an-ga-ma, "earlier," is derived from na-an-ga-ma, "moreover, furthermore."

here in the "judicial" sense of scorn or repudiation discussed in M. Jaques, *Le vocabulaire des sentiments*, 156–58.

A15 = B20. The expression lú im-sa$_{10}$-sa$_{10}$ nu-luh-ha^{sar}, which is attested in at least five manuscripts of the short version, is grammatically and lexically difficult. The term nu-luh-ha^{sar}, Akkadian *nuḫurtu* or *tījatu*, has been rendered "asafoedita," ever since it was thus defined in R. C. Thompson, *DAB*, 354–58; see B. Landsberger, *FS Baumgartner*, 179 n. 1, with earlier references to our passage. As far as I can gather, there is not a single other example of this word in any Sumerian text outside of the lexical tradition (documented in the dictionaries). It is listed in an OB school coefficient list of unknown origin, followed by še-lú^{sar}, presumably "coriander," (E. Robson, *Mesopotamian Mathematics*, 193:15–16). The presumption has been that asafoedita is a foul-smelling spice, and thus peddlers of such a substance would have been tainted by its odor. But there is no evidence to support this identification, etymology aside ("unclean"), because the extant documentation provides no evidence on the nature of this plant.[16] Moreover, asafoedita, as anyone who has cooked northern Indian food knows, "is virtually odorless until it is powdered, when it releases its strong characteristic smell" (J. Sahni, *Classic Indian Cooking*, 9). It was a foreign plant, at least in Assyria, since it was listed as such by Assurnaṣirpal in his "Banquet Stela" (*Iraq* 14 33 [1952]: 48 = *RIMA* 2 A.0.101.30).[17] Perhaps this is the clue to the metaphor: Išbi-Erra is a mere peddler of exotic foreign substances, once again stressing his foreign origins.

The two versions have different forms of the line:

A   ì-ne-éš ^{d}en-líl-le lú im-sa$_{10}$-sa$_{10}$ nu-luh-ha^{sar}
B   a-da-lam ^{d}en-líl-le nu-luh-ha$^{⌈sar⌉}$ sa$_{10}$-sa$_{10}$-⌈dè lú⌉ tumu nígin
     (At present the end of the line in X1 reads: sa$_{10}$-sa$_{10}$-d[è lú] tumu-x)

The text was in better condition when it was cited by B. Landsberger, *FS Baumgartner*, 179 n. 1. X2 has the idiosyncratic syllabic writing nu-ha-ra. The end of the line may have to be read lú$^?$ im-nígin.

A16 = B21. The phrase numun ki-en-gi-ra nu-me-a is unique. Compare, perhaps, the invective raised against Šamši-Addu by Puzur-Sin of Assur: *la šīr aššur*, "not of the flesh of the city of Assur" (A. K. Grayson, *ARRIM* 3 [1985] 12 lines 12–13 and 25; see already J. Cooper, *Curse of Agade*, 35 n. 42).

A17 = B22. ga-nam seems to be used in two different ways, either as an adverb meaning "moreover" (Akk. *appūna*) or as a particle introducing irrealis (*piqa, tušama,*

---

16. See now *CAD* T 400: "The identification with asafoedita in Thompson, *DAB* 358 is not supported by the botanical evidence."

17. D. T. Potts, *Mesopotamian Civilization*, 66, claims that asafoedita was grown in the gardens of Merodach-Baladan (*CT* 14 50:65) but the plant in question is *ṣurbu*, a different, albeit unidentified plant. The identification of the plant as asafoedita was already questioned by A. Kilmer, *OrNS* 29 (1960) 297 n. 1.

etc.; see C. Wilcke, *JNES* 27 [1968] 240–42). Note that the irrealis occurrences, as well as all Akkadian translations, are post-OB and have no relevance for this passage.

The writer of X1 reinterpretedság ... dug$_4$ = *sapāḫum*, "to scatter," with a synonym bir-bir but in a sense combined the two, apparently creating a neologism, a compound verb bir-bir ... dug$_4$.

A18 = B23. In A, the idiom du$_{11}$-ga-du$_{11}$-ga dab$_5$ is a calque from Akkadian *awatam ṣabātum*, "to convey a message" (*CAD* Ṣ 25). It may not have been properly understood by the author of B.

A19 = B24. The final sign in lú-NE.RU-ša (only in A; B: -ra) presents a problem. This passage was discussed by Å. Sjöberg, *ZA* 83 (1993) 18–19. Most of the evidence points to a reading érim of NE.RU, but this clearly demonstrates that some scribes read the signs NE.RU.DU as ne-ru-ša$_4$.

A24–25 = B29–30. The interpretation of A offered here is hardly secure, because the line has no known parallels and the syntax is difficult to analyze. These problems may have already vexed the ancients; somewhere along the line of transmission, someone either did not understand the passage correctly or wanted to amend it to reflect better a particular understanding of the lines. This may have been a multi-step process. In A25, the verbal form ba-šúm-mu-na-ta is positive, but in B29 the two sources differ. X1 has the negative ba-ra-mu-un-šúm-ma-ta, but X2 has ba-ra-an-šúm-ma-a, which may be either negative or positive second-person. This change is echoed in the verb in the next line, where the negative prefix nu- has been reinterpreted as ní, "fear," or as the reflexive particle, and the verbal form changed to positive. The new interpretation may have then led to the insertion of the two new lines that follow in B but were not in A.

From a syntactic point of view, these lines are difficult to analyze; at first glance, we have two subordinate clauses with no main sentence. With some reservations, I take nu-mu-un-zu-a not as a subordinated verbal form but as a question, although one would expect *nu-mu-un-zu-ù. The basic meaning of the passage is: even if you were to surrender to him, do you think he would really believe that you were no longer loyal to me?

A29=B49. The first verb is different in all manuscripts. The composite text follows N1 (gur$_{10}$); N2 has a phonetic variant gur$_4$. The tradition of X1 (B) once again follows a track of reinterpretation. The root /gur/ was found wanting and was understood as ul$_4$ (i.e., gír-*gunû*) = *ḫamāṭum*, "to hurry"; under Akkadian influence, the two verbs in the line were taken as hendiadys.

A30 = B50. The predicate is šu + sá . . . dug, a calque of *qātam kašādum*, "to conquer," discussed in the commentary to PuIb1: 16 (23). Indeed, this line undoubtedly alludes to that particular line in the letter that this one answers. The use of the unseparated sá-di, used in all three Nippur sources, is characteristic of Larsa Sumerian but is unique in this letter, in which compound verbs are otherwise are properly used correctly. Note that the author of X1 insisted on a correct form (sá nu-ub-du₁₁-ga).

A33 = B56. The complex ideological games that are being played here are echoed in the OB omen tradition, which preserves a very different version of these events, using very similar language, albeit in Akkadian (YOS 10 46 v 4–6): *šumma*(diš) *kakkum*(ĝiš.tukul) *ra-bu-um i-na i-mi-tim ša-ki-im-ma, e-li mar-tim ra-ki-ib kakkum* (ĝiš.tukul) ˡ*iš-bi-èr-ra, ša e-la-am-tam is-ki-pu,* "If there is a large Weapon-mark present in the pars familiaris and it straddles the gall-bladder, it is the Weapon-mark of Išbi-Erra, who repulsed the Elamite (forces)." Note that Akkadian *sakāpum* is the lexical equivalent of Sumerian zag ... tag, "to push away, to repulse." In both versions of the letter, the promise is that it will be Ibbi-Sin who will repulse Elam and capture Išbi-Erra.

B36. Note the use of the uncommon géštu ... ri in X2, while X1 has ĝéštu ... ĝar. For examples of the former, which is often misinterpreted, see F. Karahashi, *Sumerian Compund Verbs*, 86. Both mean, "to listen, pay attention."

B37. The normal Sumerian version of this expression does not have níĝ; e.g., *Nippur Lament*, 229: an-né ᵈen-líl-le igi sa₆-ga-ne-ne im-ši-in-bar-re-eš-àm, "An and Enlil looked favorably at them (i.e., Girsu and Lagaš)." The only other example known to me that is similar to the one found here is found in an OB incantation VAS 17 14:17–18 ᵈutu agrun-na-ta [è-a-niʔ], igi níĝ-sa₆-ga-ni h[é-em-kù-ge], "May Utu [purify it] upon coming out of his lower region abode." The difference between ADJ and níĝ-ADJ in Sumerian is not clear to me.

B39–43. This is the only actual omen in Sumerian and therefore requires a full discussion. The technical vocabulary is unique; it must be compared to the Akkadian language of extispicy, since there are no second-millennium omens in Sumerian. The passage in question is attested only in non-Nippurean manuscripts and was clearly invented by some northern scribe, who cleverly invented a Sumerian technical vocabulary for extispicy. The observations in Michalowski, *FS Leichty*, 247–58 must now be adjusted accordingly. Nevertheless, the new rendition of these lines remains hypothetical, at best.

B39. This line contains two technical terms: kíĝ-gi₄-a and uzu silim-ma. The former is undoubtedly *tērtum* or *amutum*; see D. Foxvog, *FS Sjöberg*, 172–73. Sumerian uzu is sometimes used as synonym for *tērtum*, but here it probably has a more limited meaning; the phrase is a back-translation from Akkadian *šīrum šalmum*, "favorable ominous part." As such, uzu probably reflects the more generalized technical use of *šīrum* to designate various sorts of ominous phenomena, as discussed by J.-P. Durand, ARM 26, 15–19.

B40. In X1, the two sides of the liver are here described as uzu zi-da and uzu gùb-bu; the *pars familiaris* and *pars hostilis*, for which see I. Starr, *Rituals of the Diviner*, 15–29. In X2, there are only the two sides, without uzu; this scribe also omits lines 41 and 42—that is, the laborious Sumerian description of the exta. Without additional duplicates, it is impossible to decide if X2 actually omits these lines or if they were added by the scribe of X1.

The reading á-diri, or perhaps better, á-SI.A, if correct, presents multiple difficulties. *PSD* A/II 51 renders á-diri as "superior strength," and this is clearly not at issue here. There remains the administrative term á diri, "additional work (assignment)," listed in the dictionary on the following page, and one might consider the usage in the letter to be related to the latter. I see three possibilities. Either the author used it here in an adverbial sense, and the hence the translation should be "*additionally, furthermore*," or this is another attempt to create a Sumerian extispicy term in Sumerian. The two texts differ substantially here, but note that the technically incorrect ascription of the right side to Išbi-Erra and the left to Ibbi-Sin in X1 in line 40 seems to be reversed in 41 and 42. Therefore, with all due caution, I suggest that á-diri is an attempt to render Akkadian *aḫītum*, "follow-up." As I understand it, Ibbi-Sin implies, according to the Old Babylonian author, that he had omens performed, and the follow-up was favorable to him, as he relates here.

B41–42. The expressions ^{giš}tukul á zi-da and ^{giš}tukul gùb-bu are renditions of Akkadian *kak imittim* and *kak šumēlim*, "Weapon of the right/left (side of a permanent feature); for the Akkadian, see U. Jeyes, *OBE* 82. The *kakkum* has no parts in Akkadian extispicy; Ulla Koch suggests to me that gú may therefore refer to something else, perhaps a part of the gall bladder.

In Akkadian divination texts, gu = *qûm*, "filament," is another negative mark; see U. Jeyes, *OBE*, 91–92, and U. Koch-Westenholz, *BLO* 63, with previous literature. As Jeyes observed, this feature connotes restraint or obstruction, which in this case must pertain to Išbi-Erra. The verb lá renders Akkadian *šuqallulum*, "to be suspended, dangle," or perhaps even *kamûm*, "to attach" (suggested to me by R. D. Biggs), both of which are commonly used in conjunction with the "filament."

B43. Note that the apodosis of this omen contains a Sumerian calque of an Akkadian expression that is found in omen and dream reports from Mari; šu . . . ĝar here used in the sense of *ana qāti mullû*, "to deliver to someone." Note *ARMT* X 8 = *AEM* I/1 214 12–14: *na-ak-ri-ka a-na qa-ti-ka ú-ma-al-la*, "I will deliver your enemies to you," (quotation from the speech of a woman who fell into a trance in the temple of Annunitum). Similar phrases are found in the highly formalized letters of Dam-ḫuraṣim to Zimri-Lim, *ARMT* X 62 and 63.

B44. The motif of turning darkness into light, or the reverse, a metaphor for the reversal of fortune, is well attested in Sumerian literature; see, e.g., *Eridu Lament* 1:22–24 uru-a u$_4$ zalag-ga è-a u$_4$ ba-da-ku$_{10}$-ku$_{10}$, eridu^{ki}-ga u$_4$ zalag-ga è-a u$_4$ ba-da-ku$_{10}$-ku$_{10}$, ^{d}utu an-úr-ra šú-a-gin$_7$ an-usan-šè ba-dù, "In the city where bright sunlight used to shine forth, the day darkened. In Eridu, where bright sunlight used to shine forth, the day darkened. As if the sun had set below the horizon, it turned into twilight"; see also *Letter of Sin-iddinam to Utu* 7, or *Letter of Sin-šamuḫ to Enki* 48. Sumerian za lag was "read" as *nūrum* already in Ur III; note the playful writing hu-ùh-ZALAG^{ki} for the place name Huhnuri in B. Lafont, *Documents* 79:13. More to the point is the similarity with expressions found in OB "historical" omens pertaining to Sargon and the otherwise unknown TE-Enlila: *amūt Šarrukên ša eklētam illikuma/iḫbutma nūram/nūrum īmuru/ūṣiaššum*, "Omen of Sargon who went through/made an incursion into the darkness and then saw/had appear light to him;" *amūt* TE-Enlil *ša nūrum ūṣiaššum*, "omen of TE-Enlil for whom the light appeared;" for references, see A. Goetze, JCS 1 (1947) 256–57, 263, and also J. S. Cooper, *Death in Mesopotamia*, 102.

The end of the line is grammatically difficult. One could read è d/nú-ne rather than è/nú-dè.

A27 = B46. The two versions have very different interpretations of this line; inim du$_{10}$ is here equivalent to *salīmum*, "peace, reconciliation," known only from bilingual texts and as a logogram in Akkadian, rather than the more common "favorable pronouncement."

The temporal adverb u$_4$-bi-da-(k) in B is very rare; it is found only in inscriptions of Warad-Sin and Rim-Sin in the expression diri u$_4$-bi-da-šè/ka, which seems to mean "more than previously/before."

A28 = B47. The expression lul du$_8$-du$_8$-ù-da hé-ni-ib-túm-túm-mu is unique; it must be compared with the line in *Father and Son* 63: du$_{10}$-ak-a$_5$-dè lul-da mi-ni-in-túm-túm-mu nu-mu-e-ši-in-še, translated by Å. Sjöberg as "Bitte ich kann nicht zulassen, dass du immer wieder unzuverlässig und falsch bist" (JCS 25 [1973] 116, with commentary on p. 124). My interpretation is based on du$_8$-du$_8$ as *puḫḫuru*, "to undo." The author of B had trouble with this line and may have interpreted du$_8$-du$_8$-ù-da as du$_{10}$-ud-ak = *tespītum*, "prayer," possibly influenced by the *Father and Son* line cited above.

A31 = B51. The translation of this line has been taken for granted but it is not without problems. Were it not for similar sentiments found in other texts, one would interpret ğalga ur-re, the form found in all the Nippur manuscripts, as "of hostile intentions," rather than as "the mind of a dog/beast." For ur in the sense of Akkadian *nakru*, see, e.g., *Uruk Lament* 4.11 gu-ti-um ur-re ba-e-ʾbalʾ [. . .], "Gutium, the enemy, overturned. . . ." "Mind of a beast" would be ğalga ur-ra or ğalga ur-ra-ke$_4$, and, indeed, the former is what X1 writes. The most instructive parallel is in *Curse of Agade* 156, where Gutium is described as: dím-ma lú-ùlu ğalga/arhuš ur-ra/a/e uludin$_2$ ^{ugu}ugu$_4$-bi, "With human instinct but the mind of a dog/beast, and monkey's looks" (see J. Cooper, *Curse of Agade*, 31, 353 n. 46, with parallels). It is probable that the Nippur scribes understood this passage as referring to "hostile intentions" but that the ever-vigilant author of X1 hypercorrected it to conform to the usage he knew from other texts.

A32–33 = B52–53. From the purely formal grammatical point of view, the Amorites are referred to in singular third person of the animate class. The tradition represented by X1 (B) indicates that someone recognized this and attempted to take it literally, hence the otherwise inexplicable writing ti-da-ma-rum, which I take to be a clumsy attempt at a Sumerian *nisbe*, hence the reading -rum rather than -aš. Note that only manuscript Si1 among the A version texts has ti-da-nu-um.

A35 = B61. Following the singular second-person pronoun za-e, most manuscripts have a different form of the final verb: two have second-person plural (N2, N3), one has first/second-singular (N1 but this might be simply abbreviation of the plural form), one has third-plural (X1, probably also Si1). Most probably, the confusion derives from the contrast between the singular independent pronoun, addressed to Puzur-Numušda, and the plural verb form that references both him and Girbubu, governor of nearby Girkal. Compare *Letter of Nanna-ki'aĝa to Lipit-Eštar* (SEpM 4) 18: lugal-ĝu$_{10}$ nam-ba-e-še-ba-e-ne, "my king, (the troops) will not neglect (your orders)."

Bibliography

Abdi, Kamyar
    2003   The Early Development of Pastoralism in the Central Zagros Mountains. *JWP* 17: 395–448.

Abusch, I. Tzvi
    1987   Alaktu and Halakhah: Oracular Decision, Divine Revelation. *HTR* 80: 15–42.

Adams, Robert McC.
    1981   *Heartland of Cities: Surveys of Ancient Settlement and Land Use on the Central Floodplain of the Euphrates.* Chicago: University of Chicago Press.
    1988   Contexts of Civilizational Collapse: A Mesopotamian View. Pp. 20–43 in *The Collapse of Ancient States and Civilizations*, ed. Norman Yoffee and George L. Cowgill. Tucson: University of Arizona Press.
    1974   The Mesopotamian Social Landscape: A View from the Frontier. Pp. 1–20 in *Reconstructing Complex Societies*, ed. Charlotte B. Moore. Bulletin of American Schools of Oriental Research Supplement 20. Cambridge, MA: ASOR.
    2006   Shepherds at Umma in the Third Dynasty of Ur: Interlocutors with a World beyond the Scribal Field of Ordered Vision. *JESHO* 49: 133–69.
    2009   Old Babylonian Networks of Urban Notables. *CDLJ* 2009, 7: 1–14.

Al-Fouadi, Abdul-Hadi A.
    1969   *Enki's Journey to Nippur: The Journeys of the Gods.* Ph.D. Dissertation, University of Pennsylvania.

Al-Rawi, F. N. H.
    1990   Tablets from the Sippar Library, I. The "Weidner Chronicle": A Supposititious Royal Letter Concerning a Vision. *Iraq* 52: 1–13.
    1994   Texts from Tell Haddad and Elsewhere. *Iraq* 56: 35–43.

Al-Rawi, F. N. H., and George, A. R.
    1994   Tablets from the Sippar Library. III. Two Royal Counterfeits. *Iraq* 56: 135–48.

Ali, Fadhil Abdulwahid
    1964   *Sumerian Letters: Two Collections from the Old Babylonian Schools.* Ph.D. Dissertation, University of Pennsylvania.

Allred, Lance
    2006   *Cooks and Kitchens: Centralized Food Production in Late Third Millennium Mesopotamia.* Ph.D. Dissertation, The Johns Hopkins University.

Altman, Janet Gurkin
    1982   *Epistolarity: Approaches to a Form.* Columbus, OH: Ohio State University Press.

Alster, Bendt
    1991–93   The Sumerian Folktale of the Three Ox-Drivers from Adab. *JCS* 43/45: 27–38.
    1997   *Proverbs of Ancient Sumer: The World's Earliest Proverb Collections.* Bethesda, MD: CDL.
    2005   *Wisdom of Ancient Sumer.* Bethesda, MD: CDL.

Alster, Bendt, and Vanstiphout, Herman L. J.
    1987   Lahar and Ashnan: Presentation and Analysis of a Sumerian Disputation. *ASJ* 9: 1–43.
Andersson, Jakob
    2008   Some Cuneiform Texts from the Haldar Collection: Two Old Babylonian Contracts. *Orientalia Suecana* 57: 5–22.
André, Béatrice, and Salvini, Mirjo
    1989   Réflexions sur Puzur-Inšušinak. *Iranica Antiqua* 24: 53–72.
Aqrawi, A. A. M.
    2001   Stratigraphic Signatures of Climatic Change during the Holocene Evolution of the Tigris-Euphrates Delta, Lower Mesopotamia. *Global and Planetary Change* 28: 267–83.
Archi, Alfonso
    1985   Mardu in the Ebla Texts. *OrNS* 54: 7–13.
Arkhipov, I. S.
    2002   Toponim "Subir/Subartu" v mesopotamii III—pervoi poloviny II tyc. do n.e. (The Toponym Subir/Subartu during the III Mill. and the 1st Half of the II Mill B.C.) *VDI* 243: 76–97.
Astour, Michael
    1987   Semites and Hurrians in Northern Transtigris. Pp. 3–68 in *Studies on the Civilization and Culture of Nuzi and the Hurrians 2: General Studies and Excavations at Nuzi 9/1*, ed. Martha A. Morrison and David I. Owen. Winona Lake, IN: Eisenbrauns.
Attinger, Pascal
    1984   Enki et Ninḫursaĝa. *ZA* 74: 1–52.
    1993   *Eléments de linguistique sumérienne: La construction de du₁₁/e/di "dire."* Göttingen: Vandenhoeck & Ruprecht.
    1995   Review of Å.W. Sjöberg et al., eds., *The Sumerian Dictionary of the University Museum of the University of Pennsylvania, Vol. 1: A Part I. ZA* 85: 127–41.
    1998   Inanna et Ebiḫ. *ZA* 88: 164–95.
    2007   Tableau grammatical du sumérien (problèmes choisis): Text of lectures presented at the École pratique des hautes études, Paris, February–May, 2007. Online: htp://www.arch.unibe.ch/content/e8254/e8254/e8548/e8549/index_ger.html.
    2008   À propos de quelques lectures. *NABU* 2008/4: 103–4.
    2010   La légende de Sargon. Manuscript posted on the Internet.
Balke, Thomas E.
    2010   The Sumerian Ternery Numeral System. *JCS* 62: 45–52.
Baqir, Taha
    1948   Date-List of Ishbi-Irra. *Sumer* 4: 103–14.
Barnett, R. D.
    1963   Xenophon and the Wall of Media. *JHS* 83: 1–26.
Barker, Rodney
    2001   *Legitimating Identities: The Self-Representation of Rulers and Subjects.* Cambridge: Cambridge University Press.
Barthes, Roland
    1968   L'effet de réel. *Communications* 11: 84–89.
Bauer, Theo
    1926   *Die Ostkanaanäer: Eine philologisch-historische untersuchung über die wanderschicht der sogennanten "Amoriter" in Babylonien.* Leipzig: Asia Major.
    1929   Eine Überprüfung der "Amoriter"-Frage. *ZA* 38: 145–70.
Bauer, Josef
    1993   Review of Jacob Marzahn, *Altsumerische Verwaltungstexte aus Girsu/Lagaš, Textedition.* Vorderasiatische Schriftdenkmäler, Neue Folge 10. *BiOr* 50: 173–79.

1995 Review of Å. W. Sjöberg, et al., ed., *The Sumerian Dictionary of the University Museum of the University of Pennsylvania, Vol. 1: A Part I. JAOS* 115: 293–97.

Beale, Thomas W.
1973 Early Trade in Highland Iran: A View from a Source Area. *World Archaeology* 5: 133–48.

Becker, Andrea
1985 Neusumerische Renaissance? Wissenschaftsgeschichtliche Untersuchungen zur Philologie und Archäologie. *BaM* 16: 229–316.

Begemann, F. and Schmitt-Strecker, S.
2009 Uber das frühe Kupfer Mesopotamiens. *Iranica Antiqua* 44: 1–45.

Behrens, Hermann
1988 Eine Axt für Nergal. Pp. 27–32 in *A Scientific Humanist: Studies in Memory of Abraham Sachs*, ed. Erle Leichty et al. Occasional Publications of the Samuel Noah Kramer Fund, 9. Philadelphia: The Samuel Noah Kramer Fund/University Museum.

Bellwood, Peter
2001 Early Agriculturalist Population Diasporas? Farming, Languages, and Genes. *ARA* 30: 181–207.

Benstock, Shari
1985 From Letters to Literature: *La Carte Postale* in the Epistolary Genre. *Genre* 18: 257–95.

Berlin, Adele
1979 *Enmerkar and Ensuḫkešdanna: A Sumerian Narrative Poem.* Occasional Publications of the Babylonian Fund 2. Philadelphia: The University Museum.

Biggs, Robert D.
1967 More Babylonian "Prophecies." *Iraq* 29: 117–32.
1985 The Babylonian Prophecies and the Astrological Traditions of Mesopotamia. *JCS* 37: 86–90.
1997 Šulgi in Simurrum. Pp. 169–78 in *Crossing Boundaries and Linking Horizons: Studies in Honor of Michael C. Astour on His 80th Birthday*, ed. G. Young, M. Chavalas and R. Averbeck. Bethesda, MD: CDL.

Biggs, Robert D., and Stolper, Matthew W.
1983 A Babylonian Omen Text from Susiana. *RA* 77: 155–62.

Boeder, Winfried
1991 A Note on Synonymic Parallelism and Bilingualism. *Studia Linguistica* 45: 97–126.

Bonechi, Marco
1991 Onomastica dei testi di Ebla: nome propri come fossili-guida? *SEL* 8: 59–79.

Bonechi, Marco, and Durand, Jean-Marie
1992 Oniromancie et magie à Mari à l'époque d'Ébla. Pp. 152–61 in *Literature and Literary Language at Ebla*, ed. Pelio Fronzaroli. Florence: Università di Firenze.

Borger, Rykle
1971 Gott Marduk und Gott-König Šulgi als Propheten. Zwei prophetische Texte. *BiOr* 28: 3–24.
1991 *Ein Brief Sîn-idinnams von Larsa an den Sonnengott sowie Bemerkungen über "Joins" und das "Joinen."* Nachrichten der Akademie der Wissenschaften in Göttingen I. Philologisch-historische Klasse, Jahrgang 1991, Nr. 2. Göttingen: Vanderhoeck & Ruprecht.

Borges, Jorge Luis
1964 *Other Inquisitions.* Austin: University of Texas Press.

Bottéro, Jean
1973 Le pouvoir royal et ses limitations d'après les texts divinatoires Pp. 119–65 in *La voix d'opposition en Mésopotamie ancienne*, ed. A. Finet. Brussels: Institut des Hautes Études de Belgique.

Bowersock, G. W.
1991 Review of *The Collapse of Complex Societies*, by Joseph A. Tainter (1988). *JFA* 18: 119–21.

Brant, C.
2000   The Epistolary Novel. Pp. 377–80 in *History of European Literature*, ed. A. Benoit-Dusausoy and G. Fontaine. London: Routledge.

Brinker, Christopher
2010   The Meaning and Significance of the Old Assyrian *sikkātum*. *AoF* 37: 49–62.

Brisch, Nicole Maria
2007   *Tradition and the Poetics of Innovation: Sumerian Court Literature of the Larsa Dynasty (c. 2003–1763 BCE)*. AOAT 339. Münster: Ugarit-Verlag.

Brusasco, P.
1999–2000 Family Archives and the Social Use of Space in Old Babylonian Houses at Ur. *Mesopotamia* 34/35: 3–174.

Buccellati, Giorgio
1966   *The Amorites of the Ur III Period*. Naples: Istituto Orientale di Napoli.
1972   On the Use of the Akkadian Infinitive after "ša" or Construct State. *JSS* 17: 1–29.
1990   "River Bank," "High Country," and "Pasture Land": The Growth of Nomadism on the Middle Euphrates and the Khabur. Pp. 87–117 in *Tell al-Hamidiyah 2*, ed. S. Eichler, M. Wäfler, and D. Warburton. Göttingen: Vandenhoek & Ruprecht.
2004   Il secondo millennio a.C. nella memoria epica di Giuda e Israele. *La Rivista Teologica di Lugano* 9: 521–43.
2008   The Origin of the Tribe and of "Industrial" Agropastoralism in Syro-Mesopotamia. Pp. 141–59 in *The Archaeology of Mobility: Old World and New World Nomadism*, ed. H. Barnard and Willemina Wendrich. Cotsen Advanced Seminars Series 4. Los Angeles: Cotsen Institute of Archaeology.

Campbell, Lyle
2006   Languages and Genes in Collaboration: Some Practical Matters. Paper presented at the Languages and Genes conference, University of California, Santa Barbara, Sept. 8–10, 2006.

Canby, Jeanny Vorys
2001   *The Ur-Nammu Stela*. University Museum Monograph 110. Philadelphia: The University Museum

Carroué, François
1991   Etudes de géographie et de topographie sumériennes II. A la recherche de l'Euphrate au IIIe Millénaire. *ASJ* 13: 111–56.

Carter, Elisabeth
1979   Elamite Pottery, ca. 2000–1000 B.C. *JNES* 38: 111–28.
1985   Notes on Archaeology and the Social and Economic History of Susiana. *Paléorient* 11: 43–48.

Carter, Elisabeth, and Stolper, Matthew W.
1984   *Elam: Surveys of Political History and Archaeology*. Berkeley: University of California Press.

Cavigneaux, Antoine
1987   Notes sumérologiques. *ASJ* 9: 45–66.
1996   *Uruk: Albabylonische Texte aus dem Planquadrat Pe XVI–4/5 nach Kopien von Adam Falkenstein*. Mainz: von Zabern.

Cavigneaux, Antoine, and Al-Rawi, Farouk N. H.
2000a   La fin de Gilgameš, Enkidu et les Enfers d'après des manuscrits d'Ur et de Meturan (Textes de Tell Haddad VIII). *Iraq* 62: 1–19.
2000b   *Gilgames et la mort. Textes de Tell Haddad VI*. CM 19. Groningen: STYX.

Cavigneaux, Antoine, and d'Istria, Laurent Colonna
2009   Les découverts épigraphiques des fouilles récentes de Mari. État des recherches en janvier 2009. *Studia Orontica* 6: 51–68.

Charpin, Dominique
1980   *Archives familiales et propriété privée en Babylonie ancienne: étude des documents de "Tell Sifr."* Geneva: Librairie Droz.
1986   *Le clergé d'Ur au siècle d'Hammurabi (XIXᵉ–XVIIIᵉ siècles av. J.-C.).* Geneva: Librairie Droz.
1992   Les malheurs d'un scribe ou de l'inutilité du sumérien loin de Nippur. Pp. 7–27 in *Nippur at the Centennial*, ed. M. deJ. Ellis. Philadelphia: The University Museum.
1999   Hagalum, šakkanakkum de Râpiqum et ses serviteurs. Pp. 95–108 in *Munuscula Mesopotamica: Festschrift für Johannes Renger*, ed. Barbara Böck, Eva Cancik-Kirschbaum, and Thomas Richter. AOAT 267. Münster: Ugarit-Verlag.
2003a   La 'toponymie en miroir' dans le Proche-Orient amorrite. *RA* 97: 3–34.
2003b   *Hammu-rabi de Babylone.* Paris: Presses universitaires de France.
2004a   Histoire politique du Proche-Orient amoritte (2002–1595). Pp. 25–480 in *Mesopotamien: Die altbabylonische Zeit*, by Dominique Charpin, D. O. Edzard, and Marten Stol. OBO 160/4. Friburg: Academic Press / Göttingen: Vandenhoeck & Ruprecht.
2004b   La circulation des commerçants, des nomades et des messagers dans le Proche-Orient amorrite (XVIIIe siècle av. J.-C.). Pp. 51–69 in *La mobilité des personnes en Méditerranée de l'Antiquité à l'époque moderne: Procédures de contrôle et documents d'identification*, ed. Claudia Moatti. Collection de l'Ecole française de Rome 341. Rome: Ecole français de Rome.
2007   Chroniques bibliographiques, 10: Économie, société et institutions paléo-babylonienne: nouvelles sources, nouvelles approches. *RA* 101: 147–82.
2008   *Lire et écrire à Babylone.* Paris: Presses Universitaires de France.
Charpin, Dominique, and Ziegler, Nele
2003   *Mari et le Proche-Orient à l'époque amorrite: Essai d'histoire politique.* Florilegium marianum V: Mémoires de N.A.B.U. 6. Paris: SEPOA.
2007   Amurritisch lernen. *WZKM* 97: 55–77.
Cherewatuk, Karen
1993   Ragemund and Epistolary Tradition. Pp. 20–45 in *Dear Sister: Medieval Women and the Epistolary Genre*, ed. Karen Cherewatuk and Ulrike Wiethaus. Philadelphia: University of Pennsylvania Press.
Cherewatuk, Karen, and Wiethaus, Ulrike, eds.
1993   *Dear Sister: Medieval Women and the Epistolary Genre.* Philadelphia: University of Pennsylvania Press.
Cherniack, Susan
1994   Book Culture and Textual Transmission in Sung China. *HJAS* 54: 5–125.
Chew, Sing C.
2001   *World Ecological Degradation: Accumulation, Urbanization, and Deforestation, 3000 B.C.–A.D. 2000.* Walnut Creek, CA: AltaMira.
Çığ Muazzez, and Kramer, Samuel Noah
1976   The Ideal Mother: A Sumerian Portrait. *Belleten* 40: 413–21.
Civil, Miguel
1962   Un nouveau synchronisme Mari–IIIᵉ dynastie d'Ur. *RA* 56: 213–14.
1964a   The "Message of Lú-dingir-ra to His Mother" and a Group of Akkado-Hittite "Proverbs." *JNES* 23: 1–11.
1964b   A Hymn to the Beer Goddess and a Drinking Song. Pp. 67–89 in *Studies Presented to A. Leo Oppenheim, June 7, 1964*. Chicago: The Oriental Institute.
1969   The Sumerian Flood Story. Pp. 138–45 in *Atra-ḫasīs: The Babylonian Story of the Flood*, by W. G. Lambert and A. R. Millard. Oxford: Clarendon; repr., Winona Lake, IN: Eisenbrauns, 1999.
1972   The Anzu Bird and Scribal Whimsies. *JAOS* 92: 271.
1973   The Sumerian Writing System: Some Problems. *OrNS* 42: 21–34.
1974–77 Enlil and Namzitarra. *AfO* 25: 65–71.

1976   Lexicography. Pp. 123–57 in *Sumerological Studies in Honor of Thorkild Jacobsen on His Seventieth Birthday June 7, 1974*, ed. Stephen J. Lieberman. AS 20. Chicago: The Oriental Institute.

1979a   *Ea A = naqû, Aa A = naqû, with Their Forerunners and Related Texts*. MSL 14. Rome: Pontifical Biblical Institute.

1979b   Sur l'inscription de Lugalannemundu. *RA* 73: 93.

1985   Sur les "livres d'ecolier" à l'époque paléo-babylonienne. Pp. 67–78 in *Miscellanea Babylonica: Melanges offerts a Maurice Birot*, ed. J.-M. Durand and J.-R. Kupper. Paris: Éditions Recherche sur les civilizations.

1990   The Verb šu-tak₄ "to send." *AuOr* 8: 109–11.

1993   On Mesopotamian Jails and their Lady Wardens. Pp. in 72–78 in *The Tablet and the Scroll: Near Eastern Studies in Honor of William W. Hallo*, ed. Mark E. Cohen, Daniel C. Snell, and David B. Weisberg. Bethesda, MD: CDL.

1994   *The Farmer's Instructions: A Sumerian Agricultural Manual*. Sabadell: AUSA.

2000   From the Epistolary of the Edubba. Pp. 105–18 in *Wisdom, Gods and Literature: Studies in Assyriology in Honour of W. G. Lambert*, ed. A. R. George and I. L. Finkel. Winona Lake, IN: Eisenbrauns.

2002   The Forerunners of *Marû* and *Ḫamṭu* in Old Babylonian. Pp. 63–71 in *Riches Hidden in Secret Places: Ancient Near Eastern Studies in Memory of Thorkild Jacobsen*, ed. T. Abusch. Winona Lake, IN: Eisenbrauns.

2003   Of Bows and Arrows. *JCS* 55: 49–54.

2005   The Unveiling of the *parakku*. Paper presented at the 51st RAI, July 21, 2005, Chicago, IL.

2007   Early Semitic Loanwords in Sumerian. Pp. 11–34 in *Studies Presented to Robert D. Biggs, June 4, 2000*, ed. Martha T. Roth, Walter Farber, Matthew W. Stolper, and Paula von Bechtolsheim. Chicago: The Oriental Institute of the University of Chicago.

2008a   A Sumerian Connective Particle and Its Possible Semitic Counterparts. *AuOr* 26: 7–15.

2008b   *The Early Dynastic Practical Vocabulary A (Archaic HAR-ra A)*. ARES 4. With copies by Alfonso Archi. Rome: Missione Archeologica in Siria.

2010   Sumerian Compound Verbs: Class II. Pp. 523–33 in *Language in the Ancient Near East: Proceedings of the 53e Rencontre Assyriologique Internationale*, Vol 1, Part 2, ed. Leonid Kogan et al. Bible und Bibel 4/2. Winona Lake, IN: Eisenbrauns.

forthcoming   The Code of Ur-Namma.

Civil, Miguel, and Sjöberg, Åke W.
1979   Introduction. P. vii in Jane W. Heimerdinger, *Sumerian Literary Fragments from Nippur*. Occasional Publications of the Babylonian Fund 4. Philadelphia: The University Museum.

Clay, Albert Tobias
1919   *The Empire of the Amorites*. YOSR 6. New Haven: Yale University Press.

Cohen, Mark
1976   Literary Texts from the Andrews University Archaeological Museum. *RA* 70: 129–44.

Cohen, Phillip
1996   Is There a Text in This Discipline? Textual Scholarship and American Literary Studies. *American Literary History* 8: 728–44.

Cole, Donald P.
2003   Where Have the Bedouin Gone? *Anthropological Quarterly* 76: 235–67.

Cole, Stephen W.
1994   Marsh Formation in the Borsippa Region and the Course of the Lower Euphrates. *JNES* 53: 81–109.

Cole, Steven W., and Gasche, Hermann
1998   Second- and First-Millennium BC Rivers in Northern Babylonia. Pp. 1–64 in *Changing Watercourses in Babylonia: Towards a Reconstruction of the Ancient Environment in Lower*

Mesopotamia. Mesopotamian History and Environment, Memoirs-5/1, ed. Hermann Gasche and Michel Tanret. Ghent: University of Ghent / Chicago: The Oriental Institute of the University of Chicago.

Collingwood, R. G.
1921   Hadrian's Wall: A History of the Problem. *The Journal of Roman Studies* 11: 37–66.

Cooper, Jerrold S.
1980   Apodotic Death and the Historicity of "Historical" Omens. Pp. 99–105 in *Death in Mesopotamia*, ed. Bendt Alster. Mesopotamia 8. Copenhagen: Akademisk Forlag.
1983   *The Curse of Agade*. Baltimore: The Johns Hopkins University Press.
1999   Sumerian and Semitic Writing in Most Ancient Syro-Mesopotamia. Pp. 61–77 in *Languages and Cultures in Contact: At the Crossroads of Civilizations in the Syro-Mesopotamian Realm. Proceedings of the 42th RAI*, ed. K. Van Lerberghe and G. Voet. Orientalia Lovaniensia Analecta 96. Leuven: Peeters & Departement Oosterse Studies.
2006   Genre, Gender, and the Sumerian Lamentation. JCS 58: 39–47.

Cooper, Jerrold. S., and Heimpel, Wolfgang
1983   The Sumerian Sargon Legend. *JAOS* 103: 67–82.

Cullen, H. M., et al.
2000   Climate Change and the Collapse of the Akkadian Empire: Evidence from the Deep Sea. *Geology* 28: 379–82.

Dahl, Jacob L.
2007   *The Ruling Family of Umma: A Prosopographical Analysis of an Elite Family in Southern Iraq 4000 Years Ago*. Leiden: Nederlands Instituut voor het Nabije Ooosten.

Dalley, Stephanie
2009   *Babylonian Tablets from the First Sealand Dynasty in the Schøyen Collection*. CUSAS 9. Bethesda, MD: CDL.

Dällenbach, Lucien
1977   *Le récit spéctaculaire: Essai sur la mise en abyme*. Paris: Seuil.
1980   Reflexivity and Reading. *New Literary History* 11: 435–49.

Daneshmand, Parsa
2004   An Extispicy Text from Haft-Tappe. JCS 56: 13–17.

Dankbaar, Ben
1984   Alternative Defense Policies and the Peace Movement. *Journal of Peace Research* 21: 141–55.

De Graef, Karen
2005   *Les archives d'Igibuni. Les documents Ur III du Chantier B à Suse*. MDAI 54. Ghent: University of Ghent.
2006   *De la dynastie Simaški au Sukkalmaḫat: Les documents fin PE IIb—début PE III du Chantier B à Suse*. MDAI 55. Ghent: University of Ghent.
2008   Annus Simaškensis. L'usage des nomes d'année pendant la période simaškéenne (ca. 1930–1880 av. notre ère) à Suse. *Iranica Antiqua* 43: 67–87.

Delnero, Paul
2006   *Variation in Sumerian Literary Compositions: A Case Study Based on the Decad*. Ph.D. Dissertation, University of Pennsylvania.

Derrida, Jacques
1980   *La Carte Postale: de Socrate à Freud at au-delà*. Paris: Flammarion.

Diakonoff, Igor Mikhailovich
1939   Amorei. *VDI* 9: 60–69.
1969   The Rise of the Despotic State in Ancient Mesopotamia. Pp. 173–203 in *Ancient Mesopotamia*, ed. I. M. Diakonoff. Moscow: Nauka.
1990   *Lyudi Goroda Ura* [The People of the City of Ur]. Moscow: Nauka.

Diamond, Jarred
2005   Collapse: How Societies Choose to Fail or Succeed. New York: Viking.
Dijk, J. J. A. van
1959   Textes divers du Musée de Baghdad, III. Sumer 15: 5–13.
1960   Sumerische Götterlieder II. Heidelberg: Winter.
1978   Išbi'erra, Kindattu, l'homme d'Elam, et la chute de la ville d'Ur. Fragments d'une hymne
         d'Išbi'erra. JCS 30: 189–208.
1983   Lugal ud me-lám-bi nir-gál: La récit épique et didactique des Travaux de Ninurta du Déluge et de
         la nouvelle Création. Texte, traduction et introduction. 2 vols. Leiden: Brill.
1989   Ein spätbabylonischer Katalog einer Sammlung sumerischer Briefe. OrNS 58: 441–52.
Driel, Gus van
1989   The British Museum "Sippar" Collection: Babylonia 1882–1893. ZA 79: 102–17.
1995   Nippur and the Inanna Temple during the Ur III Period. JESHO 38: 393–406.
Donbaz, Veysel, and Foster, Benjamin R.
1982   Sargonic Texts from Telloh in the Istanbul Archaeological Museum. OPBF 5. Philadelphia: The
         University Museum.
Dossin, Georges
1927   Autres textes sumériens et accadiens. MDP 18. Paris: Ernest Leroux.
Driel, Gus van
1989   The British Museum "Sippar" Collection: Babylonia 1882–1983. ZA 79: 102–17.
1995   Nippur and the Inanna Temple during the Ur III Period. JESHO 38: 393–406.
Durand, Jean-Marie
1988   Archives épistolaires de Mari. ARM 26 I/1. Paris: Éditions Recherche sur les Civilisations.
1997   Les documents épistolaires du palais de Mari, tome I. LAPO 16. Paris: Cerf.
1998   Les documents éépistolaires du palais de Mari, tome II. LAPO 17. Paris: Cerf.
2004   Peuplement et sociétes à l'époque amorrite (1): Les clans bensim'alites. Pp. 111–98 in
         Nomades et sédentaires dans le Proche-Orient ancien. Compe rendu de la XLVIe Rencontre
         Assyriologique Internationale (Paris, 10–13 juillet 2000), ed. Christophe Nicole. Amurru 3.
         Paris: Éditions Recherche sur les Civilisations.
Dyckhoff, Christian
1998   Balamunamḫe von Larsa: Eine altbabylonische Existenz zwischen Ökonomie, Kultus und
         Wissenschaft. Pp. 117–24 in Intellectual Life of the Ancient Near East: Papers Presented at the
         43rd Rencontre Assyriologique Internationale, Prague, July 1–5, 1996, ed. J. Prosecký. Prague:
         Oriental Institute.
1999   Das Haushaltsbuch des Balamunamḫe, Bd. 1: Darstellung, Bd. 2: Belegmaterial. Inaugural-
         Dissertation, Ludwig-Maximilian-Universität, Munich.
Edzard, Dietz Otto
1957   Die zweite Zwischenzeit Babyloniens. Wiesbaden: Harrassowitz.
1972   Hamazi. RLA 4: 70–71.
1990   Gilgamesh und Huwawa A. I. Teil. ZA 80: 165–203
1997   Gudea and His Dynasty. Royal Inscriptions of Mesopotamia, Early Periods 3/1. Toronto:
         University of Toronto Press.
2003   Sumerian Grammar. HdO 1/71. Leiden: Brill.
2004   Altbabylonische Literatur und Religion. Pp. 483–640 in Mesopotamien: Die altbabylonische
         Zeit, by Dominique Charpin, D. O. Edzard, and Marten Stol. OBO 160/4. Friburg: Aca-
         demic Press / Göttingen: Vandenhoeck & Ruprecht.
Edzard, Dietz Otto, and Farber, Gertrud
1974   Die Ors- und Gewässername der Zeit der 3. Dynastie von Ur. RGTC 2. Wiesbaden: Reichert.
Edzard, Dietz Otto, Farber, Gertrud, and Sollberger, Edmond
1977   Die Ors- und Gewässername präsargonischen und sargonischen Zeit. RGTC 2. Wiesbaden:
         Reichert.

Edzard, Dietz Otto, and Röllig, Wolfram
  1980   Kimaš. *RLA* 5: 593.
Ellis, Maria deJong
  1975   An Old Babylonian Adoption Contract from Tell Harmal. *JCS* 27: 130–51.
  1987   The Goddess Kititum Speaks to King Ibalpiel: Oracle Texts from Ishchali. *M.A.R.I.* 5: 235–66.
  1989   Observations on Mesopotamian Oracles and Prophetic Texts: Literary and Historiographical Considerations. *JCS* 41: 127–86.
Emberling, Geoff
  1997   Ethnicity in Complex Societies: Archaeological Perspectives. *JAR* 5: 295–344.
Emberling, Geoff, and Yoffee, Norman
  1999   Thinking About Ethnicity in Mesopotamian Archaeology and History. Pp. 272–81 in *Fluchtpunk Uruk. Archäologische Einheit aus methodischer Vielhaft: Schriften für Hans Jörg Nissen*, ed. H. Kühne, R. Bernbeck, and K. Bartl. Rahden: Leidorf.
Englund, Robert K.
  1988   Administrative Timekeeping in Ancient Mesopotamia. *JESHO* 31: 121–85.
  1990   *Organisation und Verwaltung der Ur III-Fischerei.* BBVO 10. Berlin: Dietrich Reimer.
Fagan, Brian
  2004   *The Long Summer: How Climate Changed Civilization.* New York: Basic Books.
Falkenstein, Adam
  1949   Ibbisîn—Ishbiʾerra. *ZA* 49: 59–79.
  1953   Die babylonische Schule. *Saeculum* 4: 125–37.
  1956   *Die Neusumerische Gerichtsurkunden II.* Bayerische Akademie der Wissenschaften (München) Kommission zur Erschliessung von Keilschrifttexten, Bayerische Akademie der Wissenschaften (München) Philosophisch-Historische Klasse. Munich: Bayerische Akademie der Wissenschaften.
  1959   *Sumerische Götterlieder*, I. Abhandlungen der Heidelberger Akademie der Wissenschaften, Phil.-hist. Kl., Jahrgang 1959, 1. Abh. Heidelberg: Carl Winter Universitätsverlag.
  1963   Zu den Inschriftenfunden der Grabung in Uruk-Warka 1960–1961. *BaM* 2: 1–82.
Faivre, Xavier
  1995   Le recyclage des tablettes cunéiformes. *RA* 89: 57–66.
Finkel, Irving L.
  1980   Bilingual Chronicle Fragments. *JCS* 32: 65–80.
Finkelstein, Jacob J.
  1966   The Genealogy of the Hammurapi Dynasty. *JCS* 20: 95–118.
  1972   *Late Old Babylonian Documents and Letters.* Yale Oriental Series 13. New Haven: Yale University Press.
Fish, Thomas
  1932   *Catalogue of Sumerian Tablets in the John Rylands Library.* Manchester: The Manchester University Press, and the Librarian, the John Rylands Library.
Fitzgerald, Madelaine André
  2002   *The Rulers of Larsa.* Ph.D. Dissertation. Yale University.
Flückiger-Hawker, Esther
  1999   *Ur-Namma of Ur in Sumerian Literary Tradition.* OBO 166. Fribourg: University Press.
Foster, Benjamin R.
  1982a   A Postscript to the "Letter of Gilgamesh." *AnSt* 32: 43–44.
  1982b   Education of a Sargonic Bureaucrat in Sargonic Sumer. *ArOr* 50: 238–41.
  2005   *Before the Muses: An Anthology of Akkadian Literature.* Bethesda, MD: CDL.
Foxvog, Daniel A.
  1976   Texts and Fragments 101–106. *JCS* 28: 101–6.

1989   A Manual of Sacrificial Procedure. Pp. 167–76 in *DUMU E₂-DUB-BA-A: Studies in Honor of Åke W. Sjöberg*, ed. Hermann Behrens, Darlene Loding, and Martha T. Roth. Occasional Publications of the Samuel Noah Kramer Fund, 11. Philadelphia: The Samuel Noah Kramer Fund, University Museum.

Frahm, Eckhardt
2005   On Some Recently Published Late Babylonian Copies of Royal Letters. *N.A.B.U.* 2005: 43–46.
2006   Šulgi Sieger über Assur und die Skythen? *N.A.B.U.* 2006: 21–24.
2009   Assurbanipal in Der. Pp. 51–64 in *Of God(s), Trees, Kings, and Scholars: Neo-Assyrian and Related Studies in Honour of Simo Parpola*, ed. Mikko Luukko, Saana Svärd, and Raija Mattila. Studia Orientalia 106. Helsinki: The Finnish Oriental Society.

Frangipane, Marcella
2009   Rise and Collapse of the Late Uruk Centres in Upper Mesopotamia and Eastern Anatolia. *Science dell'Antichità* 15: 15–31.

Frayne, Douglas R.
1982   New Light on the Reign of Išbi-Erra. Pp. 25–32 in *Vorträge gehalten auf der 28. Rencontre Assyriologique Internationale in Wien 6.–10. Juli 1981*, ed. H. Hirsch and H. Hunger. AfO Beiheft 19. Horn, Austria: Ferdinand Berger.
1990   *The Old Babylonian Period (2003–1595 BC)*. The Royal Inscriptions of Mesopotamia, Early Periods 4. Toronto: University of Toronto Press.
1992   *The Early Dynastic List of Geographical Names*. AOS 74. New Haven: American Oriental Society
1997   *Ur III Period (2112–2004 BC)*. Royal Inscriptions of Mesopotamia, Early Periods 3/2. Toronto: University of Toronto Press.

Friberg, Jöran
2007   *A Remarkable Collection of Babylonian Mathematical Texts: Manuscripts in the Schøyen Collection Cuneiform Texts*. New York: Springer.

Fronzaroli, Pelio
2003   *Testi di cancelleria: I rapporti con le città: (archivio L. 2769)*. Archivi reali di Ebla, Testi 13. Roma: Missione Archeologica Italiana in Siria.

Gadotti, Alhena
2005   *Gilgameš, Enkidu and the Netherworld and the Sumerian Gilgameš Cycle*. Ph.D. Dissertation, The Johns Hopkins University.

Garfinkle, Steven J.
2008   Was the Ur III State Bureaucratic? Patrimonialism and Bureaucracy in the Ur III Period. Pp. 55–61 in *The Growth of an Early State in Mesopotamia: Studies in Ur III Administration*, ed. Steven J. Garfinkle and J. Cale Johnson. BPOA 5. Madrid: Consejo Superior de Investigaciones Cientifícas.

Gasche, Hermann
1973   *La poterie élamite du douxième millénaire a.C.* Leiden: Brill.

Gasche, Hermann, et al.
2002   Fleuves du temps et de la vie. Permanences et instabilité du réseau fluviatile babylonien entre 2500 et 1500 avant notre ère. *Annales* 57: 531–44.

Gelb, I. J.
1938   Studies in the Topography of Western Asia. *AJSL 55*: 66–85.
1961   The Early History of the West Semitic Peoples. *JCS* 15: 27–47.
1965   The Ancient Mesopotamian Ration System. *JNES* 24: 230–43.
1982   Terms for Slaves in Ancient Mesopotamia. Pp. 81–98 in *Societies and Languages of the Ancient Near East: Studies in Honour of I. M. Diakonoff*, ed. M. A. Dandamayev et al. Warminster: Aris & Phillips.

Genouillac, Henri de
   1924   *Premières recherches archéologiques à Kich (Fouilles françaises d'El-'Akhymer, mission d'Henri de Genouillac, 1911–1912)*. Paris: Champion.
Gentili, Paulo
   2006   Where is Diniktum? Remarks on the Situation and a Supposition. *RSO* 79: 231–38.
George, Andrew R.
   1992   Review of Frayne 1990. *BSOAS* 55: 358–40.
   2005   In Search of the é.dub.ba.a: The Ancient Mesopotamian School in Literature and Reality. Pp. 127–37 in *An Experienced Scribe Who Neglects Nothing: Ancient Near Eastern Studies in Honor of Jacob Klein*, ed. Y. Sefati. Bethesda, MD: CDL.
   2009   *Babylonian Literary Texts in the Schøyen Collection*. CUSAS 10. Bethesda, MD: CDL.
Geyer, Bertrand
   2009   Die syrische Mauer: Eine 4000 Jahre Alte "Grenze" in der syrischen Steppe," Pp. 36–45 in A. Nunn, *Mauern als Grenzen*. Mainz am Rhein: Philipp von Zabern.
Geyer, Bertrand, et al.
   2007   The Arid Margins of Northern Syria: Occupation of the Land and Modes of Exploitation in the Bronze Age. Pp. 269–81 in *Urban and Natural Landscapes of an Ancient Syrian Capital: Settlement and Environment at Tell Mishrifeh/Qatna and in Central-Western Syria*, ed. Danielle Morandi Bonacossi. Studi Archeologici su Qatna, 1. Udine: Forum.
Gibson, McGuire
1998–99   Nippur and Umm Al-Hafriyat. *Oriental Institute Annual Report 1998–99*. Online: http://oi.uchicago.edu/research/pubs/ar/98-99/nippur.html.
Glassner, Jean-Jacques
   1997   L'historien mésopotamien et l'événement. *Mètis* 12: 97–117.
   2004   *Mesopotamian Chronicles*. SBLWAW 19. Atlanta: Society of Biblical Literature.
   2005   L'aruspicine paléo-babylonienne et le témoignage des sources de Mari. *ZA* 95: 276–300.
   2009   Écrire des livres à l'époque paléo-babylonienne: le traité d'extispicine. *ZA* 99: 1–81.
Goddeeris, Anne
   2002   *Economy and Society in Northern Babylonia in the Early Old Babylonian Period (ca. 2000–1800 BC)*. Leuven: Peeters.
Goetze, Albrecht
   1947   Historical Allusions in Old Babylonian Omen Texts. *JCS* 1: 253–65.
   1950   Sin-iddinam of Larsa: New Tablets from his Reign. *JCS* 4: 83–118.
   1963   The Šakkanakku's of the Ur III Empire. *JCS* 17: 1–31.
   1964   Remarks on the Old Babylonian Itinerary. *JCS* 18: 114–19.
Goldstein, Ronnie
   2010   Late Babylonian Letters on Collecting Tablets and Their Hellenistic Background: A Suggestion. *JNES* 69: 199–207.
Gomi, Tohru
   1980   On Dairy Productivity in the Late Ur III Period. *JESHO* 23: 1–42.
   1984   On the Critical Situation at Ur Early in the Reign of Ibbisin. *JCS* 36: 211–42.
Gragg, Gene B.
   1972   Observations on Grammatical Variations in Sumerian Literary Texts. *JAOS* 92: 204–13.
   1973   A Class of "When" Clauses in Sumerian. *JNES* 32: 124–34.
Grayson, A. K.
   1966   Divination and the Babylonian Chronicles: A Study of the Rôle which Divination Plays in Ancient Mesopotamian Chronography. Pp. 69–76 in *La divination en Mésopotamie ancienne et dans les régions voisines. XIV Rencontre Assyriologique Internationale*. Paris: Presses universitaires de France.
   1975   *Assyrian and Babylonian Chronicles*. TCS 5. Locust Valley, N.Y.: Augustin; repr., Winona Lake, IN: Eisenbrauns, 2000.

1985   Rivalry over Rulership at Aššur: The Puzur-Sîn Inscription. *ARRIM* 3: 9–14.
Grayson, A. K., and Lambert, W. G.
1964   Akkadian Prophecies. *JCS* 18: 7–30.
Green, Margaret W.
1978   The Eridu Lament. *JCS* 30: 127–67.
1984   The Uruk Lament. *JAOS* 104: 253–79.
Grégoire, J.-P.
1996   *Archives administratives et inscriptions cunéiformes: Ashmolean Museum, Bodleian Collection,
           Oxford.* Paris: Paul Geuthner.
Guichard, M.
1997   Copie de la supplique bilingue suméro-akkadienne "Les malheurs d'un scribe" (texte no
           6). Pp. 79–82 in *Florilegium marianum III: Recueil d'études à la mémoire de Marie-Thérèse
           Barrelet,* ed. D. Charpin and J.-M. Durand. Memoires de NABU 4. Paris: SEPOA.
Guillén, Claudio
1986   Notes Toward the Study of the Renaissance Letter. Pp. 70–104 in *Renaissance Genres:
           Essays on Theory, History, and Interpretation,* ed. Barbara Kiefer Lewalski. Harvard English
           Studies 14. Cambridge, MA: Harvard University Press.
Gurney, Oliver R.
1957   The Sultantepe Tablets (Continued). VI. A Letter of Gilgamesh. *AnSt* 7: 127–36.
Gurney, Oliver R., and Kramer, Samuel Noah
1976   *Sumerian Literary Texts in the Ashmolean Museum.* OECT 5. Oxford: Clarendon.
Güterbock, Hans
1934   Die historische Tradition und ihre literarische Gestaltung bei Babyloniern und Hethitern
           bis 1200. *ZA* 42: 1–91.
Hallo, W. W.
1953   *The Ensis of the Ur III Dynasty.* MA thesis, University of Chicago.
1960   A Sumerian Amphictyony. *JCS* 14: 88–114.
1963a   On the Antiquity of Sumerian Literature. *JAOS* 83: 167–76.
1963b   Royal Hymns and Mesopotamian Unity. *JCS* 17: 112–18.
1968   Individual Prayer in Sumerian: The Continuity of a Tradition. *JAOS* 88: 71–89.
1969   The Neo-Sumerian Letter-Orders. *BiOr* 26: 171–76.
1972   The House of Ur-Meme. *JNES* 31: 87–95.
1977   Seals Lost and Found. *BibMes* 6: 55–60.
1981   Letters, Prayers, and Letter-Prayers. Pp. 17–27 in *Proceedings of the Seventh World Congress
           of Jewish Studies: Studies in the Bible and the Ancient Near East.* Jerusalem: Magnes.
1982   The Royal Correspondence of Larsa, II: The Appeal to Utu. Pp. 95–109 in *zikir šumim:
           Assyriological Studies Presented to F. R. Kraus on the Occasion of His Seventieth Birthday,* ed.
           G. van Driel et al. Leiden: Brill.
1985   Back to the Big House: Colloquial Sumerian, Continued. *OrNS* 54: 56–64.
1998   Two Letter-Prayers to Amurru. Pp. 397–410 in *Boundaries of the Ancient Near Eastern
           World: A Tribute to Cyrus H. Gordon,* ed. Meir Lubetski, Claire Gottlieb, and Sharon
           Keller. Sheffield: Sheffield Academic Press.
2006   A Sumerian Apocryphon? The Royal Correspondence of Ur Revisited. Pp. 85–104 in
           Approaches to Sumerian Literature: Studies in Honor of Stip (H. L. J. Vanstiphout), ed. Piotr
           Michalowski and Niek Veldhuis. CM 35. Leiden: Brill.
2008   Day Dates in Texts from Drehem. Pp. 99–118 in *The Growth of an Early State in Mesopo-
           tamia: Studies in Ur III Administration,* ed. Steven J. Garfinkel and J. Cale Johnson. BPOA
           5. Madrid: Consejo Superior de Investigaciones Científicas.
Halstead, Paul
1990   Quantifying Sumerian Agriculture: Some Seeds of Doubt and Hope. *BSA* 5: 187–95.

Hattori, Atsuko
   2006   The Return of the Governor. Pp. 197–208 in *If a Man Builds a Joyful House: Assyriological Studies in Honor of Erle Verdun Leichty*, ed. Ann K. Guinan et al. CM 31. Leiden: Brill.
Heimpel, Wolfgang
   1974–77   Sumerische und akkadische Personennamen in Sumer und Akkad. *AfO* 25: 171–74.
   1990   Ein Zweiter Schritt zur Rehabilitierung der Rolle des Tigris in Sumer. *ZA* 80: 204–13.
   1994   ne-sağ. *NABU* 1994/4: 72–73.
   1995   Plow Animal Inspection Records from Ur III Girsu and Umma. *BSA* 8: 71–171.
   1998   The Industrial Park of Girsu in the Year 2042 B.C.: Interpretation of an Archive Assembled by P. Mander. *JAOS* 118: 387–99.
   2003   *Letters to the King of Mari: A New Translation, with Historical Introduction, Notes, and Commentary.* MC 12. Winona Lake, IN: Eisenbrauns.
   2009a   Blind Workers in Ur III Texts. *KASKAL* 6: 43–48.
   2009b   The Location of Madga. *JCS* 61: 25–61.
   2009c   *Workers and Construction Work at Garšana.* CUSAS 5. Bethesda, MD: CDL.
Helman, Sarit
   1989   The Javanese Concept of Order and its Relationship to Millenarian Motif and Imagery. Pp. 126–38 in *Order and Transcendence: The Role of Utopias and the Dynamics of Civilization*, ed. A. B. Seligman. International Studies in Sociology and Social Anthropology 50. Leiden: Brill.
Hilgert, Markus
   2002   *Akkadisch in der Ur III-Zeit.* Münster: Rhema.
Hinüber, Oskar von
   2010   Did Hellenistic Kings Send Letters to Aśoka? *JAOS* 130: 261–66.
Hirsch, E. D.
   1967   *Validity in Interpretation.* New Haven: Yale University Press.
House, J. W.
   1980   The Frontier Zone: A Conceptual Problem. *International Political Science Review* 1: 456–77.
Huber, Fabienne
   2001   La Correspondance Royale d'Ur: un corpus apocryphe. *ZA* 91: 169–206.
Huffmon, H. B.
   1965   *Amorite Personal Names in the Mari Texts. A Structural and Lexical Study.* Baltimore: The Johns Hopkins University Press.
Hunger, Hermann, and Pingree, David
   1989   *MUL.APIN: An Astronomical Compendium in Cuneiform.* Archiv für Orientforschung, Beiheft 24. Horn, Austria: F. Berger & Söhne.
Hussein, Ayad Mohamed, et al.
   2010   Tell Abu Sheeja /Ancient Pashime: Report on the First Season of Excavations, 2007. *Akkadica* 131: 47–104.
Jacobsen, Thorkild
   1939   *The Sumerian King List.* AS11. Chicago: University of Chicago Press.
   1940   Historical Data. Pp. 116–200 in Henri Frankfort, Seton Lloyd, and Thorkild Jacobsen, *The Gimilsin Temple and the Palace of the Rulers at Tell Asmar.* OIP 43. Chicago: The University of Chicago Press.
   1941   Review of *Lamentation over the Destruction of Ur* by Samuel N. Kramer. *AJSL* 58: 219–24.
   1953   The Reign of Ibbī-Suen. *JCS* 7: 36–47.
   1960   The Waters of Ur. *Iraq* 22: 174–85.
   1963   Ancient Mesopotamian Religion: The Central Concerns. *PAPS* 107: 473–84.
   1997   *The Harps that Once…: Sumerian Poetry in Translation.* New Haven: Yale University Press.

Jahn, Brit
2007 The Migration and Sedentarization of the Amorites from the Point of View of the Settled Babylonian Population. Pp. 193–209 in *Representations of Political Power: Case Histories from Times of Change and Dissolving Order in the Ancient Near East*, ed. Marlies Heinz and Marian H. Feldman. Winona Lake, IN: Eisenbrauns.

Janssen, Caroline
1991 Samsu-iluna and the Hungry Naditus. Pp. 3–39 in *Northern Akkad Project Reports 5*, ed. L. de Meyer and H. Gasche. Ghent: University of Ghent.

Jaques, Margaret
2006 *Le vocabulaire des sentiments dans les texts sumériens: Recherche sur le lexique sumérien et akkadien*. AOAT 332. Münster: Ugarit-Verlag.

Javitch, Daniel
1998 The Emergence of Poetic Genre Theory in the Sixteenth Century. *Modern Language Quarterly* 59: 139–69.

Jean, Joan de
1989 *Fictions of Sappho, 1546–1937*. Chicago: University of Chicago Press.

Jeyes, Ulla
1989 *Old Babylonian Extispicy: Omen Texts in the British Museum*. Leiden: Nederlands Instituut voor het Nabije Oosten.

Joannès, Francois
1996 Routes et voies de communication dans les archives de Mari. Pp. 323–61 in *Mari, Ebla et les Hourrites dix ans de travaux: Première partie*, ed. Jean-Marie Durand. Amurru 1. Paris: Editions Recherche sur les Civilisations.

Kagan, Kimberly
2006 Redefining Roman Grand Strategy. *The Journal of Military History* 70: 333–62.

Kamp, Kathryn A., and Yoffee, Norman
1980 Ethnicity in Ancient Western Asia during the Early Second Millennium B.C.: Archaeological Assessments and Ethnoarchaeological Prospectives. *BASOR* 237: 85–104.

Keetman, Jan
2010 Zwei Stellen aus Enmerkara und der Herr von Aratta. *NABU* 2010/3: 72–73.

Kapp, A.
1955 Ein Lied auf Enlilbani von Isin. *ZA* 51: 76–87.

Karahashi, Fumi.
2000 *Sumerian Compound Verbs with Body-Part Terms*. Ph.D. dissertation, University of Chicago.

Katz, Dina
1993 *Gilgamesh and Akka*. Groningen: STYX.
2007 Sumerian Death Rituals in Context. Pp. 167–88 in *Performing Death: Social Analyses of Funerary Traditions in the Ancient Near East and Mediterranean*, ed. Nicola Laneri. OIS 3. Chicago: The Oriental Institute of the University of Chicago.

Khazanov, A. M.
1984 *Nomads and the Outside World*. Cambridge: Cambridge University Press.

Kienast, Burkhart, and Volk, Konrad
1995 *Die sumerischen und akkadischen Briefe des III. Jahrtausends aus der Zeit vor der III. Dynastie von Ur*. FAOS 19. Stuttgart: Steiner.

Kiernan, V. G.
1957 Foreign Mercenaries and Absolute Monarchy. *Past & Present* 11: 66–86.

Kilmer, A. D.
1960 Two New Lists of Key Numbers for Mathematical Operations. *Or NS* 29: 273–308.

Kiser, Edgar, and Cai, Yong
2003 War and Bureaucratization in Qin China: Exploring an Anomalous Case. *American Sociological Review* 68: 511–39.

Klein, Jacob
  1981   *Three Šulgi Hymns: Sumerian Royal Hymns Glorifying King Šulgi of Ur*. Ramat Gan: Bar Ilan University Press.
  1991   The Coronation and Consecration of Šulgi in the Ekur (Šulgi G). Pp. 292–313 in *Ah, Assyria: Studies in Assyrian History and Ancient Near Eastern Historiography Presented to Hayim Tadmor*, ed. M. Cogan and I. Eph'al. Scripta Hierosolymitana 33. Jerusalem: Magnes.
  1993   A Self-Laudatory Šulgi Hymn Fragment from Nippur. Pp. 124–31 in *The Tablet and the Scroll: Near Eastern Studies in Honor of William W. Hallo*, ed. Mark E. Cohen, Daniel C. Snell, and David B. Weisberg. Bethesda, MD: CDL.
  1996   *The Marriage of Martu*. The Urbanization of "Barbaric" Nomads." Pp. 83–96 in *Mutual Influences of Peoples and Cultures in the Ancient Near East*, ed. Meir Malul. Michmanim 9. Haifa: Reuben and Edith Hecht Museum / University of Haifa.
  1997   The God Martu in Sumerian Literature. Pp. 99–116 in *Sumerian Gods and Their Representations*, ed. I. L. Finkel and M. J. Geller. CM 7. Groningen: STYX.
Klein, Jacob, and Abraham, Kathleen
  2000   Problems of Geography in the Gilgameš Epics: The Journey to the "Cedar Forest." Pp. 63–73 in *Landscapes, Territories, Frontiers and Horizons in the Ancient Near East 3*, ed. L. Milano et al. HANES III/3. Padova: Sargon.
Kleinerman, Alexandra
  2009   *Education in Early 2nd Millennium BC Mesopotamia: The Sumerian Epistolary Miscellany*. Ph.D. Dissertation, The Johns Hopkins University.
  2011   *Education in Early 2nd Millennium BC Babylonia: The Sumerian Epistolary Miscellany*. Cuneiform Monographs 42. Leiden: Brill.
Koch-Westenholz, Ulla
  1995   *Mesopotamian Astrology: An Introduction to Babylonian and Assyrian Celestial Divination*. Copenhagen: Museum Tusculanum Press.
  2000   *Babylonian Liver Omens: The Chapters Manzāzu, Padānu and Pān Tākalti of the Babylonian Extispicy Series Mainly from Assurbanipal's Library*. Copenhagen: Museum Tusculanum Press.
Koskenniemi, Heikki
  1956   *Studien zur Idee und Phraseologie des griechischen Briefes bis 400 n. Chr.* Helsinki: Finnischen Akademie der Wissenschaften.
Kramer, Samuel Noah
  1942   The Oldest Literary Catalogue. A Sumerian List of Literary Compositions Compiled about 2000 B.C. BASOR 88: 10–19.
  1949   Schooldays: A Sumerian Composition Relating to the Education of a Scribe. JAOS 69: 199–215.
  1963   *The Sumerians: Their History, Culture, and Character*. Chicago: University of Chicago Press.
  1976   *Sumerian Literary Texts in the Ashmolean Museum*, by Oliver R. Gurney and Samuel Noah Kramer. OECT 5. Oxford: Clarendon.
Kraus, F. R.
  1955   Provinzen des neusumerischen der Reiches von Ur. ZA 51: 45–75.
  1980   Der Brief des Gilgameš. AnSt 30: 109–21.
  1983   Eine neue Probe akkadischer Literatur. Brief eines Bittstellers an eine Gottheit. JAOS 103: 205–9.
Krebernik, Manfred
  2006   Philologische Aspekte elamisch-mesopotamischer Beziehungen im Überblick. Pp. 59–99 in *Babel und Bibel 3: Annual of Ancient Near Eastern, Old Testament and Semitic Studies*, ed. L. Kogan et al. Winona Lake, IN: Eisenbrauns.

Krecher, Joachim
 1965   Zur sumerischen Grammatik. ZA 57: 12–30.
 1966   *Sumerische Kultlyrik*. Wiesbaden: Harrassowitz.
 1969   Schreiberschulung in Ugarit: Die Tradition von Listen und sumerischen Texten. *UF* 1: 131–58.
 1976–80   Kataloge, literarische. *RLA* 5 478–85.
 1987   /ur/ "Mann", /cmc/ "Frau" und die sumerische Herkunft des Wortes urdu(-d). *WO* 18: 7–19.

Krispijn, T. J. H.
 1990   Beiträge zur altorientalischen Musikforschung. Šulgi und die Musik. *Akkadica* 70: 1–27.

Kupper, J. R.
 1961   *L'iconographie du dieu Amurru dans la glyptique de la Ire dynastie babylonienne*. Brussells: Palais des Académies.

Kutscher, Raphael
 1968–69   Apillaša, Governor of Kazallu. *JCS* 22: 63–65.
 1982   Review of *Sumerian Literary Texts in the Ashmolean Museum*, by Oliver Gurney and Samuel Noah Kramer. Oxford: Clarendon, 1976. *BiOr* 39: 583–90.
 1989   *The Brockmon Tablets at the University of Haifa: Royal Inscriptions*. Haifa: Haifa University Press.

Kutscher, Raphael, and Wilcke, Claus
 1978   Eine Ziegel-Inschrift des Königs Takil-ilissu von Malgium, gefunden in Isin und Yale. *ZA* 68: 95–128.

Labat, René, and Edzard, D. O.
 1974   *Textes littéraire de Suse*. MDAI 57. Paris: Geuthner.

Lafont, Bertrand
 1985   *Documents administratifs sumériens provenant du site de Tello et conservés au Musée du Louvre*. Paris: Éditions Recherche sur les civilisations.
 1994   L'Avènement de Šu-Sin. *RA* 88: 97–119.
 1995   La chute des rois d'Ur et la fin des archives dans les grands centres administratifs de leur empire. *RA* 89: 3–13.
 1996   L'extraction du minerai de cuivre en Iran à la fin du IIIe millénaire. Pp. 87–93 in *Tablettes et images au pays de Sumer et d'Akkad: Mélanges offerts à Professeur Henri Limet*, ed. Ö. Tunca and D. Deheselle. Liège: Université de Liège.
 2009a   The Army of the Kings of Ur: The Textual Evidence. *CDLJ* 2009 no. 5.
 2009b   Eau, pouvoir et société dans l'Orient ancien: approches théoriques, travaux de terrain et documentation écrite. Pp. 11–23 in *Stratégies d'acquisition de l'eau et société au Moyen-Orient depuis l'Antiquité*, ed. Mohamed Al-Dbiyat and Michel Mouton. Bibliothèque archéologique et historique, 186. Beirut: Presses de l'Ifpo.
 2010   Sur quelques dossiers des archives de Girsu. Pp. 167–79 in *Why Should Someone Who Knows Something Conceal It? Cuneiform Studies in Honor of David I. Owen on His 70th Birthday*, ed. Alexandra Kleinerman and Jack M. Sasson. Bethesda, MD: CDL.

Lambert, Maurice
 1974   Les villes du Sud-mésopotamien et l'Iran au temps de Naramsin. *OrAn* 13: 1–24.
 1979   Le prince des Suse Ilish-mani et l'Elam de Naramsin à Ibisîn. *JA* 267: 11–40.

Lambert, W. G.
 1974   DINGIR.ŠÀ.DIB.BA Incantations. *JNES* 33: 267–322.

Lambert, W. G., and Millard, A. R.
 1969   *Atra-ḫasīs: The Babylonian Story of the Flood*. Oxford: Clarendon; repr., Winona Lake, IN: Eisenbrauns, 1999.

Landsberger, Benno
1967   Akkadische–Hebraïsche Wortgleichungen. Pp. 176–204 in *Hebräische Wortforschung: Festschrift zum 80. Geburtstag von Walter Baumgartner*, ed. B. Hartmann. Leiden: Brill.
Latham, J. D.
1983   The Beginnings of Arabic Prose Literature: The Epistolary Genre. Pp. 154–79 in *Arabic Literature to the End of the Umayyad Period*, ed. A. F. L Beeston et al. Cambridge: Cambridge University Press.
Lattimore, Owen
1940   *Inner Asian Frontiers of China.* New York: American Geographical Society.
Leemans, W. F.
1968   King Hammurabi as Judge. Pp. 110–20 in *Symbolae Iuridicae et Historicae Martino David Dedicatae*, ed. J. A. Ankum, R. Feenstra, and W. F. Leemans. Leiden: Brill.
1989   A propos du livre de Dominique Charpin, *Le Clergé d'Ur au siècle d'Hammurabi*: La fonction de *šandabakku*. *JESHO* 32: 229–36.
Leichty, Erle
1970   *The Omen Series Šumma Izbu.* TCS 4. Locust Valley, NY: Augustin.
Levine, Louis D.
1973   Geographical Studies in the Neo-Assyrian Zagros I. *Iran* 11: 1–28.
1974   Geographical Studies in the Neo-Assyrian Zagros II. *Iran* 12: 99–122.
Lieberman, Stephen J.
1968–69   An Ur III Text from Drēhem Recording "Booty from the Land of Mardu." *JCS* 22: 53–62.
Lightfoot, Kent G., and Martinez, Antoinette
1995   Frontiers and Boundariès in Archaeological Perspective. *ARA* 24: 471–92.
Limet, Henri
1972   L'étranger dans la société sumérienne. Pp. 123–38 in *Gesellschaftsklassen im Alten Zweistromland und in den angrenzenden Gebieten: XVIII Rencontre assyriologique internationale, München, 29. Juni 1970*, ed. D. O. Edzard. Munich: Bayerische Akademie der Wissenschaften.
1978   Étude sémantique de ma-da, kur, kalam. *RA* 72: 1–12.
Lindner, Rudi Paul
1982   What Was a Nomadic Tribe? *Comparative Studies in Society and History* 24: 689–711.
Lion, Brigitte
2009   Les femmes scribes de Sippar. Pp. 289–303 in *Femmes, cultures et sociétés dans les civilisations méditerranéennes et proches-orientales de l'Antiquité*, ed. F. Briquel-Chatonnet et al. Topoi Supplément 10. Paris: De Boccard.
Lion, Brigitte, and Robson, Eleanor
2005   Quelques textes scolaires paléo-babyloniens rédigés pare des femmes. *JCS* 57: 37–54.
Liverani, Mario
1995   The Medes at Esarhaddon's Court. *JCS* 47: 57–62.
1997   Lower Mesopotamian Fields: South vs. North. Pp 219–27 in *Ana šadî Labnāni lū allik: Beiträge zur altorientalischen und mittelmeerischen Kulturen: Festschrift für Wolfgang Röllig*, ed. Beate Pongratz-Leisten, Hartmut Kühne, and Paolo Xella. Kevelaer: Butzon und Bercker/ Neukirchen-Vluyn: Neukirchener Verlag.
2001   The Fall of the Assyrian Empire: Ancient and Modern Interpretations. Pp. 374–91 in *Empires: Perspectives from Archaeology and History*, ed. Susan E. Alcock, et al. Cambridge: Cambridge University.
Liverani, Mario, ed.
1993   *Akkad, the First World Empire: Structure, Ideology, Traditions.* HANES 5. Padova: Sargon.

Llop, Jaume, and George, A. R.
2003   Die babylonisch-assyrischen Beziehungen und die innere Lage Assyriens in der Zeit der Auseinandersetzung zwischen Ninurta-tukulti-Aššur und Mutakkil-Nusku nach neuen keilschriftlichen Quellen. *AfO* 48–49: 1–23.

Luciani, Marta
1999   Zur Lage Terqas in schriftlichen Quellen. *ZA* 89: 1–23.

Ludwig, Marie-Christine
1990   *Untersuchungen zu den Hymnen des Išme-Dagan von Isin.* SANTAG 2. Wiesbaden: Harrassowitz.
2009   *Literarische Texte aus Ur: Kollationen und Kommentare zu UET 6/1–2.* Berlin: de Gruyter.

Luttwak, Edward N.
1976   *The Grand Strategy of The Roman Empire from the First Century* A.D. *to the Third.* Baltimore: Johns Hopkins University Press.

Lyonnet, Bertile
1998   Le peuplement de la Djéziré occidentale au début du 3e millénaire, villes circulaires et pastoralisme: questions et hypothèses. Pp. 179–93 in *About Subartu: Studies Devoted to Upper Mesopotamia,* vol. 1, ed. Marc Lebeau. Subartu 4. Turnhout: Brepols.
2001   L'occupation des marges arides de la Djéziré: pastralisme et nomadisme aux débuts de 3e et du 2e millénaire. Pp. 15–26 in *Conquête de la steppe et appropriation des terres sur les marges arides du croissant fertile,* ed. Bernard Geyer. Travaux de la Maison de l'Orient méditerranéen 36. Lyon: Maison de l'Orient Méditerranéen-Jen Pouilloux.
2004   Le nomadisme et l'archéologie: problèmes d'identification. Le cas de la partie Occidentale de la Djéziré aux 3ème et début du 2ème millénaire avant notre ère. Pp. 25–49 in *Nomades et sédentaires dans le Proche-Orient ancien. Compte rendu de la XLVIᵉ Rencontre Assyriologique Internationale (Paris, 10–13 juillet 2000).* Amurru 3. Paris: Editions Recherche sur les Civilisations.
2008   Who Lived in the Third-Millennium "Round Cities" of Northern Syria? Pp. 199–223 in *Nomads, Tribes, and the State in the Ancient Near East: Cross-Disciplinary Perspectives,* ed. Jeffrey Szuchman. OIS 5. Chicago: The Oriental Institute of the University of Chicago.

Lyonnet, Bertille, and Kohl, Philip L.
2008   By Land and by Sea: The Circulation of Materials and Peoples, ca. 3500–1800 B.C. Pp. 29–52 in *Intercultural Relations between South and Southwest Asia: Studies in Commemoration of E. C. L. During Caspers (1934–1996),* ed. Eric Olijdam and Richard H. Spoor. BAR International Series 1826. Oxford: Archaeopress.

McAnany, Patricia A., and Yoffee, Norman
2010   Why We Question Collapse and Study Human Resilience, Ecological Vulnerability, and the Aftermath of Empire. Pp. 1–17 in *Questioning Collapse: Human Resilience, Ecological Vulnerability, and the Aftermath of Empire,* ed. Patricia A. McAnany and Norman Yoffee. Cambridge: Cambridge University Press.

McCown, Donald E., and Haines, Richard C.
1967   *Nippur 1: Temple of Enlil, Scribal Quarter, and Soundings.* OIP 78. Chicago: The Oriental Institute of the University of Chicago.

McEwan, Gilbert
1980   Review of *MSL* 11. *WO* 11: 158–64.

McGann, Jerome J.
1983   *A Critique of Modern Textual Criticism.* Chicago: University of Chicago Press.

MacGinnis, John
1995   *Letter Orders from Sippar and the Administration of the Ebabbara in the Late-Babylonian Period.* Poznań: Bonami.

Maeda, Tohru
1992   The Defense Zone during the Rule of the Ur III Dynasty. *ASJ* 14: 135–72.

Maekawa, K.
1989   Rations, Wages and Economic Trends in the Ur III period. *AoF* 16: 42–50.
1996   Confiscation of Private Properties in the Ur III Period: A Study of the é-dul-la and níg-GA. *ASJ* 18: 103–68.

Manak, Joseph M.
2004   The Law of Written Description in Pharmaceutical and Biotechnology Patents. *Biotechnology Law Report* 23: 30–47.

Mann, C. J.
1979   Force and the Frontiers of the Empire. *Journal of Roman Studies* 69: 175–83.

Marchesi, Gianni
2001   Alleged SIG_7 = $agar_4$ and Related Matters. *OrNS* 70: 313–17.
2006   *LUMMA in the Onomasticon and Literature of Ancient Mesopotamia History of the Ancient Near East Studies.* Padua: Sargon.

Maul, Stefan M.
1988   *Herzberuhigungsklagen: Die sumerisch-akkadischen Eršaḫunga-Gebete.* Wiesbaden: Harrassowitz.
1997   Zwischen Sparmassnahme und Revolte. . . : Die Aktivitäten des Iasīm-Sūmû, des šandabakkum von Mari. *MARI* 8: 755–74.

Maaijer, Remco de
1998   Land Tenure in Ur III Lagash. Pp. 50–73 in *Landless and Hungry: Access to Land in Early and Traditional Societies. Proceedings of a Seminar held in Leiden, 20 and 21 June, 1996,* ed. B. Haring and R. de Maaijer. CNWS Publications 67. Leiden: Research School CNWS, Leiden University.

Maaijer, Remco de, and Jagersma, Bram
2003/4   Review of PSD A/3. *AfO* 50: 351–55.

Mayr, Rudolf H., and Owen, David I.
2004   The Royal Gift Seal in the Ur III Period. Pp. 145–74 in *Von Sumer nach Ebla und zurück: Festschrift für Giovanni Pettinato zum 27. September 1999 gewidmet von Freunden, Kollegen und Schülern,* ed. H. Waetzoldt. Heidelberg: Heidelberger Orientverlag.

McAnany, Patricia A. and Norman Yoffee
2010   Why We Question Collapse and Study Human Resilience, Ecological Vulnerability, and the Aftermath of Empire. Pp. 1–17 in *Questioning Collapse: Human Resilience, Ecological Vulnerability, and the Aftermath of Empire,* ed. Patricia A. McAnany and Norman Yoffee. Cambridge: Cambridge University Press.

Meijer, Diederik J. W.
forthcoming   Nomadism, Pastoralism and Town and Country: About the Roaming Elements in the Syrian Middle Bronze Age. In *Proceedings of the Third International Congress on the Archaeology of the Ancient Near East (Paris, April 14th–19th, 2002),* ed. Jean-Claude Margueron, Pierre de Miroschedji, and Jean-Paul Thalmann. Winona Lake, IN: Eisenbrauns.

Michalowski, Piotr
1975   The Bride of Simanum. *JAOS* 95: 716–19.
1976   *The Royal Correspondence of Ur.* Ph.D. Dissertation, Yale University.
1977   The Neo-Sumerian Silver Ring Texts. *Syro-Mesopotamian Studies* 2/3: 43–58
1978a   Foreign Tribute to Sumer in Ur III Times. *ZA* 68: 34–49.
1978b   Two Sumerian Literary Letters. *JCS* 30 114–20.
1981   Königsbriefe. *RLA* V: 51–59.
1983a   Review of L. Cagni, *Briefe aus der Iraq Museum* (Leiden, 1980). *JCS* 35: 221–28.
1983b   History as Charter: Some Observations on the Sumerian King List. *JAOS* 103: 237–48.
1983c   Review of *A = nâqu, Aa A = nâqu, with Their Forerunners and Related Texts,* by Miguel Civil. *JNES* 42: 151–53.

1986a   Mental Maps and Ideology: Reflections on Subartu. Pp. 129–56 in *The Origins of Cities in Dry-Farming Syria and Mesopotamia in the Third Millennium* B.C., ed. Harvey Weiss. Guilford, CT: Four Quarters.

1986b   Review of *Neo-Sumerian Archival Texts Primarily from Nippur in the University Museum, the Oriental Institute and the Iraq Museum*, by David I. Owen. *JNES* 45: 326–28.

1987   On the Early History of the Ershahunga Prayer. *JCS* 39: 37–48.

1989   *The Lamentation over the Destruction of Sumer and Ur.* MC 1. Winona Lake, IN: Eisenbrauns.

1991   Incantation Incipits, *N.A.B.U.* 1991: 48.

1993   *Letters from Early Mesopotamia.* SBLWAW 3. Atlanta: Scholars Press.

1996   Ancient Poetics. Pp. 141–53 in *Mesopotamian Poetic Language: Sumerian and Akkadian*, ed. M. E. Vogelzang and H. L. J. Vanstiphout. CM 6. Groningen: STYX.

1999a   Commemoration, Writing, and Genre in Ancient Mesopotamia. Pp. 69–90 in *The Limits of Historiography: Genre and Narrative in Ancient Historical Texts*, ed. Christina Shuttleworth Kraus. Mnemosyme Supplementum 191. Leiden: Brill.

1999b   Sumer Dreams of Subir: Politics and the Geographical Imagination. Pp. 305–16 in *Languages and Cultures in Contact: At the Crossroads of Civilizations in the Syro-Mesopotamian Realm*, ed. K. van Lerberghe and G. Voet. Leuven: Peeters.

2004   The Ideological Foundations of the Ur III State. Pp. 219–35 in *2000 v. Chr. Politische, wirtschaftliche und kulturelle Entwicklung im Zeichen einer Jahrtausendwende. 3. Internationales Colloquium der Deutschen Orient-Gesellschaft 4.–7. April 2000 in Frankfurt/Main und Marburg/Lahn*, ed. W. Meyer and W. Sommerfeld. Saarbrücken: Saarbrücken Druckerei.

2005a   Iddin-Dagan and his Family. *ZA* 95: 65–76.

2005b   Literary Works from the Court of King Ishbi-Erra of Isin. Pp. 199–212 in *An Experienced Scribe Who Neglects Nothing: Ancient Near Eastern Studies in Honor of Jacob Klein*, ed. Yitschak Sefati, et al. Bethesda, MD: CDL.

2006a   How to Read the Liver? In Sumerian. Pp. 247–57 in *If a Man Builds a Joyful House: Assyriological Studies in Honor of Erle Verdun Leichty*, ed. Ann K. Guinan, et al. CM 31. Leiden: Brill.

2006b   Love or Death? Observations on the Role of the Gala in Ur III Ceremonial Life. *JCS* 58: 49–61.

2006c   The Lives of the Sumerian Language. Pp. 159–84 in *Margins of Writing, Origins of Culture*, ed. Seth Sanders. Oriental Institute Seminars 2. Chicago: The Oriental Institute of the University of Chicago.

2006d   The Strange History of Tumal. Pp. 145–65 in *Approaches to Sumerian Literature: Studies in Honour of Stip (H. L. J. Vanstiphout)*, ed. P. Michalowski and N. Veldhuis. CM 35. Leiden: Brill.

2006e   Royal Letters of the Ur III Kings. Pp. 75–81 in *The Ancient Near East*, ed. Mark W. Chavalas. Blackwell's Sourcebooks in Ancient History. Oxford: Blackwell.

2006f   The Scribe(s) of MDAI 57 Susa Omens? *N.A.B.U.* 41: 39–41.

2008   Observations on "Elamites" and "Elam" in Ur III Times. Pp. 109–23 in *On the Third Dynasty of Ur: Studies in Honor of Marcel Sigrist*, ed. Piotr Michalowski. JCSSup 1. Boston: American Schools of Oriental Research.

2009a   Aššur During the Ur III Period. Pp. 149–56 in *Here and There Across the Ancient Near East: Studies in Honour of Professor Krystyna Łyczkowska*, ed. Olga Drewnowska-Rymarz. Warsaw: Agade.

2009b   The Ur III Literary Footprint and the Historian. Paper presented at *Antico Oriente: Nonsolostoria: International Conference in Honour of Mario Liverani*, Rome, April 21, 2009.

2010   Literacy, Schooling, and the Transmission of Knowledge in Early Mesopotamian Culture, in *Theory and Practice of Knowledge Transfer*, ed. W. S. van Egmond and W. H. van Soldt. PIHANS 117. Leiden/Istanbul: Nederlands Instituut voor het Nabije Oosten.

2011   On Early Mesopotamian Epistolary Pragmatics. In *LEGGO! Studies presented to Prof. Frederick Mario Fales on the Occasion of His 65th Birthday*, ed. G. B. Lanfranchi, D. Morandi Bonacossi, C. Pappi, and S. Ponchia. Leipziger Altorientalische Studien 2. Wiesbaden: Harrassowitz.

Michalowski, Piotr, and Daneshmand, Parsa
2005   An Ur III Tablet from Iran. *JCS* 57:31–36.

Michalowski, Piotr, and Wright, Henry T.
2010   The Mid-Late Third Millennium on the Deh Luran Plain. Pp. 106–9 in *Elamite and Achaemenid Settlement on the Deh Luran Plain: Towns and Villages of the Early Empires in Southwestern Iran*, ed. Henry T. Wright and James A. Neely. Memoirs of the Museum of Anthropology, 47. Ann Arbor: Museum of Anthropology, University of Michigan.

Millar, Fergus
1982   Emperors, Frontiers and Foreign Relations, 31 B.C. to A.D. 378. *Britannia* 13: 1–23.

Miller, Naomi F.
1985   Paleoethnobotanical Evidence for Deforestation in Ancient Iran: A Case Study of Urban Malyan." *Journal of Ethnobiology* 5 (1985) 1–19.

Mittermayer, Catherine
2006   *Altbabylonische Zeichenliste der sumerisch-literarischen Texte.* OBO Sonderband. Fribourg: Academic Press / Göttingen: Vandenhoeck & Ruprecht.

2009   *Enmerkar und der Herr von Aratta: ein ungleicher Wettstreit.* OBO 239. Fribourg: Academic Press / Göttingen: Vandenhoeck & Ruprecht.

Molina, Manuel
2000   Lexical and Other School Tablets in the Montserrat Museum. Pp. 751–64 in *Studi sul Vicino Oriente Antico dedicati alla memoria di Luigi Cagni* II, ed. Simonetta Graziani, Maria C. Casaburi, and Giancarlo Lacerenza. Naples: Istituto Universitario Orientale, Napoli.

2008   The Corpus of Neo-Sumerian Tablets: An Overview. Pp. 19–53 in *The Growth of an Early State in Mesopotamia: Studies in Ur III Administration*, ed. S. J. Garfinkel and J. Cale Johnson. BPOA 5. Madrid: Consejo Superior de Investigaciones Científicas.

Molina, Manuel, and Böck, Barbara
1997   *Textos y fragmentos literarios sumerios AuOr* 15: 33–41.

Morozova, Galina S.
2005   A Review of Holocene Avulsions of the Tigris and Euphrates Rivers and Possible Effects on the Evolution of Civilizations in Lower Mesopotamia. *Geoarchaeology* 20: 401–23.

de Morgan, Jacques, and Scheil, Vincent
1893   Les deux stèles de Zohâb. *RT* 14: 100–106.

Muhamed, Ahmad Kamel
1992   *Old Babylonian Cuneiform Texts from the Hamrin Basin: Tell Hadad.* Edubba 1. London: NABU.

Müller-Karpe, Michael
2002   Die Toten von Awal. Reiche Gräber des 3. und 2. Jahrttausends v. Chr. vom Tell Suleima, Iraq. *Jahrbuch des Römisch-Germanischen Zentralmuseums Mainz* 49: 410–12.

2003   The Shu-Sin Bowl: A New Royal Inscription from the IIIrd Dynasty of Ur. Paper presented at the Rencontre Assyriologique Internationale, London.

Nashef, Khaled
1982a   *Die Orts- und Gewässernamen der mittelbabylonischen und mittelassyrischen Zeit.* RGTC 5. Wiesbaden: Reichert.

1982b   Der Ṭaban Fluss. *BaM* 13: 117–41.

Nasidze, Ivane, and Stoneking, Mark
2001   *Mitochondrial DNA Variation and Language Replacements in the Caucasus. Proceedings of the Royal Society: Biological Sciences* 268 (no. 1472): 1197–206.

Nasrabadi, Behzad Mofidi
  2005   Eine Steininschrift des Amar-Suena aus Tappeh Bormi (Iran). ZA 95: 161–71.
Neumann, Hans
  1992a   Ein Brief an König Šulgi in einer späten Abschrift. *AoF* 19: 29–39.
  1992b   Nochmals zum Kaufmann in neusumerischer Zeit: die Geschäfte des Ur-DUN und anderer
            Kaufleute aus Nippur. Pp. 83–94 in *La circulation des biens, des personnes et des idées dans
            le Proche-Orient ancien: Actes de la XXXVIIIᵉ Rencontre Assyriologique Internationale, 38
            (Paris, 8–10 juillet 1991)*, ed. D. Charpin and F. Joannès. Paris: Éditions Recherche sur les
            Civilisations.
  2006   Sumerische und akkadische Briefe des 3. Jt. v. Chr. Pp. 1–20 in *Briefe*, ed. Michael Lich-
            tenstein. TUAT, Neue Folge, 3. Gütersloh: Gütersloher Verlagshaus.
Nichols, Johanna
  1997   Modeling Ancient Population Structures and Movement in Linguistics. *ARA* 26: 359–84.
Nokandeh, Jebrael, et al.
  2006   Linear Barriers of Northern Iran: The Great Wall of Gorgan and the Wall of Tammishe.
            Iran 44: 121–73.
Nougayrol, Jean
  1945   Note sur la place des "présages historiques" dans l'extispicine babylonienne. *Annuaire
            d'École Pratique des Hautes Études, Section des Sciences Religieuses 1944–1945*: 5–41.
Ohgama, Naoko, and Robson, Eleanor
  2010   Scribal Schooling in Old Babylonian Kish. Pp. 207–36 in *Your Praise is Sweet: A Memo-
            rial Volume for Jeremy Black from Students, Colleagues and Friends*, ed. Heather D. Baker,
            Eleanor Robson, and Gábor G. Zólyomi. London: British Institute for the Study of Iraq.
Olmstead, A. T.
  1918   The Calculated Frightfulness of Ashur Nasir Apal. *JAOS* 38: 209–63.
Owen, David I.
  1972   A Unique Letter-Order in the University of North Carolina. *JCS* 24: 133–34.
  1973   Miscellanea Neo-Sumerica I–III. Pp. 131–37 in *Orient and Occident: Essays Presented to
            Cyrus H. Gordon on the Occasion of his Sixty-fifth Birthday*, ed. H. A. Hoffner. AOAT 22.
            Kevelaer: Butzon & Bercker Neukirchen-Vluyn: Neukirchener Verlag.
  1980   A Sumerian Letter from an Angry Housewife? Pp. 189–202 in *The Bible World: Studies in
            Honor of Cyrus H. Gordon*, ed. G. Rendsburg, et al. New York: Ktav.
  1981   Review of *Die Ors- und Gewässername der Zeit der 3. Dynastie von Ur*, by Dietz Otto Edzard
            and Gertrud Farber. Wiesbaden: Reichert, 1974. *JCS* 33: 244–69.
  1988   Random Notes on a Recent Ur III Volume. *JAOS* 108: 111–22.
  1992   Syrians in Sumerian Sources from the Ur III Period. Pp. 107–75 in *New Horizons in the
            Study of Ancient Syria*, ed. Mark W. Chavalas and John L. Hayes. BibMes 25. Malibu:
            Undena.
  1993   Some New Evidence on Yamḫadiu = Aḫlamû. Pp. 181–84 in *The Tablet and the Scroll:
            Near Eastern Studies in Honor of William W. Hallo*, ed. M. E. Cohen, et al. Bethesda, MD:
            CDL.
  1997   Ur III Geographical and Prosopographical Notes. Pp. 367–98 in *Crossing Boundaries and
            Linking Horizons: Studies in Honor of Michael C. Astour on His 80th Birthday*, ed. G. Young,
            M. Chavalas, and R. Averbeck. Bethesda, MD: CDL.
  2001a   On the Patronymy of Šu-Suen. *NABU* 15/1: 19–20.
  2001b   The Royal Gift Seal of Ṣilluš-Dagan, Governor of Simurrum. Pp. 829–89 in *Studi sul Vi-
            cino Oriente antico dedicati alla memoria di Luigi Cagni*, vol. 2, ed. S. Graziani. Naples: IUO,
            Dipartimento di Studi Asiatici.
Owen, David I., and Mayr, Rudolf H.
  2007   *The Garshana Archives*. CUSAS 3. Bethesda, MD: CDL.

Owen, David I., and Veenker, Ron
    1987   MeGum, the First Ur III Ensi of Ebla. Pp. 263–91 in *Ebla 1975–1985: Diecianni di studi linguistici e filologici. Atti del convegno internazionale (Napoli, 9–11 ottobre 1985)*, ed. Luigi Cagni. Napoli: Istituto Universitario Orientale di Napoli.
Pardee, Dennis, and Whiting, Robert M.
    1987   Aspects of Epistolary Verbal Usage in Ugaritic and Akkadian. BSOAS 50: 1–31.
Parpola, Simo
    1987   The Forlorn Scholar. Pp. 257–78 in *Language, Literature, and History: Philological and Historical Studies Presented to Erica Reiner*, ed. F. Rochberg-Halton. New Haven: American Oriental Society.
Peters, John Punnett
    1897   *Nippur or Explorations and Adventures on the Euphrates: The Narrative of the University of Pennsylvania Expedition to Babylonia in the Years 1888–1890*. New York: Putnam's Sons.
Pientka-Hinz, Rosel
    2006   Der *rabi sikkatum* in altbabylonischer Zeit. Pp. 53–70 in *Recht gestern und heute: Festschrift zum 85. Geburtstag von Richard Haase*, ed. Joachim von Hengstl and Ulrich Sick. Wiesbaden: Harrassowitz.
Pinches, Theophilus G.
    1917   Some Texts of the Relph Collection, with Notes on Babylonian Chronology and Genesis XIV. PSBA 39: 4–15, 55–72, 89–98.
Postgate, J. N., and Mattila, R.
    2004   Il-Yada's and Sargon's Southeast Frontier. Pp. 235–54 in *From the Upper Sea to the Lower Sea: Studies on the History of Assyria and Babylonia in Honour of A. K. Grayson*, ed. G. Frame. PIHANS 101. Istanbul: Nederlands Instituut voor het Nabije Oosten.
Porter, Anne
    2002   The Dynamics of Death. Ancestors, Pastoralism and the Origins of a Third Millennium City in Syria. BASOR 325: 1–36.
    2004   The Urban Nomad: Countering the Old Cliches. Pp. 69–74 in *Nomades et sédentaires dans le Proche-Orient ancien: Compe rendu de la XLVIᵉ Rencontre Assyriologique Internationale (Paris, 10-13 juillet 2000)*, ed. Christophe Nicole. Amurru 3. Paris: Éditions Recherche sur les Civilisations.
    2009   Beyond Dimorphism: Ideologies and Materialities of Kinship as Time-space Distanciation. Pp. 199–223 in *Nomads, Tribes, and the State in the Ancient Near East: Cross-Disciplinary Perspectives*, ed. Jeffrey Szuchman. OIS 5. Chicago: The Oriental Institute of the University of Chicago.
Potts, Daniel T.
    1997   *Mesopotamian Civilization: The Material Foundations*. Ithaca, NY: Cornell University Press.
    1999   *The Archaeology of Elam: Formation and Transformation of an Ancient Iranian State*. Cambridge: Cambridge University Press.
    2008   Puzur-Inšušinak and the Oxus Civilization (BMAC): Reflections on Šimaški and the Geopolitical Landscape of Iran and Central Asia in the Ur III period. ZA 98: 165–94.
Potts, Timothy F.
    1994   *Mesopotamia and the East: An Archaeological and Historical Study of Foreign Relations 3400–2000 B.C.* Oxford: Oxford University Committee for Archaeology.
Powell, Marvin
    1985   Salt, Silt, and Yields in Sumerian Agriculture: A Critique of the Theory of Progressive Salinization. ZA 75: 7–38.
Rasheed, Fawzi
    1981   *The Ancient Inscriptions in Himrin Area*. Himrin 4. Baghdad.
Rashid, Fawzi
    1984   Akkadian Texts from Tell Sleima. *Sumer* 40: 55–56.

Reade, Julian E.
   1972   The Neo-Assyrian Court and Army: Evidence from the Sculptures. *Iraq* 34: 87–112.
Reichel, Clemens D.
   2001a   *Political Changes and Cultural Continuity at the Palace of the Rulers in Eshnunna (Tell Asmar) from the Ur III Period to the Isin-Larsa Period (ca. 2070–1850 B.C.)*. Ph.D. Dissertation: University of Chicago.
   2001b   Seals and Sealings at Tell Asmar: A New Look at an Ur III to Isin/Larsa Palace. Pp. 101–31 in vol. 2 of *Seals and Seal Impressions: Proceedings of the XLVᵉ Rencontre Assyriologique Internationale*, ed. W. W. Hallo and I. J. Winter. Bethesda, MD: CDL.
Reiner, Erica
   1956   Lipšur Litanies. *JNES* 15: 129–49.
   1974   New Light on Some Historical Omens. Pp. 257–61 in *Anatolian Studies Presented to Hans Gustav Güterbock on the Occasion of His 65th Birthday*, ed. K. Bittel, P. H. J. Houwink Ten Cate and E. Reiner. Leiden: Nederlands Historisch-Archaeologisch Instituut in het Nabije Oosten.
   1995   *Astral Magic in Babylonia*. TAPS 85/4. Philadelphia: The American Philosophical Society.
Rekavandi, H. O., Sauer, E., and Wilkinson, T.
   2007   An Imperial Frontier of the Sassanian Empire: Further Fieldwork at the Great Wall of Gorgan. *Iran* 45: 95–136.
Rekavandi, H. O., et al.
   2008   The Enigma of the "Red Snake:" Revealing One of the World's Greatest Frontier Walls. *Current World Archaeology* 27: 12–22.
Renfrew, Colin
   1992   Archaeology, Genetics and Linguistic Diversity. *Man* 27: 445–78.
Richardson, Seth
   2008   Ningirsu Returns to His Plow: Lagash and Girsu Take Leave of Ur. Pp. 153–57 in *On the Third Dynasty of Ur: Studies in Honor of Marcel Sigrist*, ed. Piotr Michalowski. JCSSup 1. Boston: American Schools of Oriental Research.
Riehl, Simone
   2008   Climate and Agriculture in the Ancient Near East: A Synthesis of the Archaeobotanical and Stable Carbon Isotope Evidence. *Vegetation History and Archaeobotany* 17: 43–51.
   2009   Archaeobotanical Evidence for the Interrelationship of Agricultural Decision-Making and Climate Change in the Ancient Near East. *Quaternary International* 197: 93–114.
Riehl, Simone, Bryson, Reid, and Pustovoytov, Konstantin
   2008   Changing Growing Conditions for Crops During the Near Eastern Bronze Age (3000–1200 BC): The Stable Carbon Isotope Evidence. *Journal of Archaeological Science* 35: 1011–22.
Robson, Eleanor
   1999   *Mesopotamian Mathematics, 2100–1600 BC: Technological Constants in Bureaucracy and Education*. Oxford: Clarendon.
   2001   The Tablet House: A Scribal School in Old Babylonian Nippur. *RA* 95: 39–67.
   2002   More than Metrology: Mathematics Education in an Babylonian Scribal School. Pp. 325–65 in *Under One Sky: Astronomy and Mathematics in the Ancient Near East*, ed. John M. Steele and Annette Imhausen. Münster: Ugarit-Verlag.
   2004   Mathematical Cuneiform Tablets in the Ashmolean Museum, Oxford. *SCIAMVS* 5: 3–65.
Röllig, W.
   1972–75   *Heirat, politische*. RLA 4: 282–87.
Römer, Willem H. P.
   1965   *Sumerische 'Königshymnen' der Isin-Zeit*. Leiden: Brill.
   1980   *Das sumerische Kurzepos "Gilgamesh and Akka."* AOAT 290. Neukirchen-Vluyn: Neukirchener Verlag.

Ron, Moshe
1987   The Restricted Abyss: Nine Problems in the Theory of *Mise en Abyme*. *Poetics Today* 8: 417–38.
Rosenmeyer, Patricia A.
2001   *Ancient Epistolary Fictions: The Letter in Greek Literature*. Cambridge: Cambridge University Press.
Roth, Martha T.
1983   The Slave and the Scoundrel: CBS 10467, a Sumerian Morality Tale? *JAOS* 103: 275–82.
1995   *Law Collections from Mesopotamia and Asia Minor*. SBLWAW 6. Atlanta: Scholars Press.
Rothenberg, Jerome
1981   Total Translation: An Experiment in the Translation of American Indian Poetry. Pp. 76–92 in Jerome Rothenberg, *Pre-Faces and Other Writings*. New York: New Directions.
1992   "We Explain Nothing, We Believe Nothing." American Indian Poetry and the Problematics of Translation. Pp. 64–79 in *On the Translation of Native American Literatures*, ed. Broan Swann. Washington: Smithsonian Institution.
Rouda, Robert R.
1992   Livestock Production in Southern Lebanon. *Rangelands* 14: 115–18.
Rowton, M. M.
1969   Watercourses and Water Rights in the Growth of Mesopotamian Civilization. *JCS* 21: 267–74.
1982   Sumer's Strategic Periphery in Topological Perspective. Pp. 318–25 in *Zikir Šumim: Assyriological Studies Presented to F.R. Kraus on the Occasion of his Seventieth Birthday*, ed. G van Driel, Th. J. Kripijn, M. Stol and K. R. Veenhof. Leiden: Brill.
Rubio, Gonzalo
2006   Šulgi and the Death of Sumerian. Pp. 167–79 in *Approaches to Sumerian Literature: Studies in Honor of Stip (H. L. J. Vanstiphout)*, ed. Piotr Michalowski and Niek Veldhuis. CM 35. Leiden: Brill.
in press   *Sumerian Literary Texts from the Ur III Period*. MC 17. Winona Lake, IN: Eisenbrauns.
Rutten, M.
1938   Trente-deux modèles de foies en argile provenant de Tell Hariri (Mari). *RA* 35: 36–70.
Rutz, Matthew T.
2006   Textual Transmission between Babylonia and Susa: A New Solar Omen Compendium. *JCS* 58: 63–96.
Sallaberger, Walther
1993   *Der kultische Kalender der Ur III–Zeit*. Berlin: de Gruyter.
1999   Ur III-Zeit. Pp. 119–414 in *Mesopotamien: Akkade-Zeit u. Ur III-Zeit*, ed. Pascal Attinger and Markus Wäfler. OBO 160/3. Freiburg: Universitätsverlag / Göttingen: Vandenhoeck & Ruprecht.
2003   Nachrichten an den Palast von Ebla: Eine Deutung von níg-mul-(an). Pp. 600–25 in *Semitic and Assyriological Studies Presented to Pelio Fronzaroli by Pupils and Colleagues*, ed. Paolo Marrassini. Wiesbaden: Harrassowitz.
2003–4   Schlachtvieh aus Puzriš-Dagān: Zur Bedeutung dieses königlichen Archivs. *JEOL* 38: 45–62.
2007   From Urban Culture to Nomadism: A History of Upper Mesopotamia in the Late Third Millennium. Pp. 417–56 in *Sociétés humaines et changement climatique à la fin du troisième Millénaire: Une crise a-t-elle eu lieu en Haute Mésopotamie? Actes du Colloque de Lyon, 5–8 décembre 2005*, ed. C. Kuzucuoğlu and C. Marro. Paris: de Boccard.
2009   Die Amurriter-mauer. Pp. 27–37 in A. Nunn, *Mauern als Grenzen*. Mainz am Rhein: Philipp von Zabern.

Salzman, Philip Carl
2002   Pastoral Nomads: Some General Observations Based on Research in Iran. *JAR* 58: 245–64.
Samet, Nili
2009   *The Lamentation Over the Destruction of Ur: A Revised Edition.* Ph.D. Dissertation, Bar-Ilan University.
Saporetti, Claudio
2002   *La rivale di Babilonia: Storia di Ešnunna ai tempi di Ḫammurapi.* Rome: Newton & Compton.
Sauer, Eberhard, et al.
2009   Die sasanidischen Mauern. Pp. 127–43 in A. Nunn, *Mauern als Grenzen.* Mainz am Rhein: Philipp von Zabern.
Sauvage, Martin
1998   La Construction des ziggurats sous la troisième dynastie d'Ur. *Iraq* 60: 45–63.
Scharaschenidzė, M.
1976   Die sukkal-mah des alten Zweistromlandes in der Zeit der III. Dynastie von Ur. Pp. 103–12 in *Wirtschaft und Geselslschaft im Alten Vorderasien,* ed. J. Harmatta and G. Komoróczy. Budapest: Akadémiai Kiado.
Schwartz, Glenn
1995   Pastoral Nomadism in Ancient Western Asia. Pp. 249–58 in *Civilizations of the Ancient Near East,* ed. Jack Sasson. New York: Scribner's.
Sharlach, Tonia M.
2002   Foreign Influences on the Religion of the Ur III Court. Pp. 91–114 in *General Studies and Excavations at Nuzi,* 10/3, ed. David. I. Owen and Gernot Wilhelm. Bethesda, MD: CDL.
2005   Diplomacy and the Rituals of Politics at the Ur III Court. *JCS* 57: 17–29.
Scheil, Vincent
1902   *Une saison de fouilles à Sippar.* Cairo: Imprimerie de l'Institut français d'archéologie orientale.
Sefati, Yitschak
1998   *Love Songs in Sumerian Literature: Critical Edition of the Dumuzi-Inanna Songs.* Bar-Ilan Studies in Near Eastern Languages and Culture. Publications of the Samuel N. Kramer Institute of Assyriology. Ramat-Gan: Bar-Ilan University Press.
Selz, Gebhard J.
1989   *Altsumerische Verwaltungstexte aus Lagas, Teil 2: Die altsumerischen Wirtschaftsurkunden der Eritage zu Leningrad.* FAOS 15/1. Stuttgart: Steiner.
1992   *Altsumerische Verwaltungstexte aus Lagas, Teil 2: Die altsumerischen Wirtschaftsurkunden aus amerikanischen Sammlungen.* 2. FAOS 15/2. Stuttgart: Steiner.
2005   *Sumerer und Akkader. Geschichte—Gesellschaft— Kultur.* Munich: Beck.
Seri, Andrea
2005   *Local Power in Old Babylonian Mesopotamia.* London: Equinox.
Sigrist, Marcel
1979   ERÍN—UN-íl. *RA* 73: 101–20.
1989   Le deuil pour Šu-Sin. Pp. 499–505 in *DUMU-E₂-DUB-BA-A: Studies in Honor of Åke W. Sjöberg,* ed. Hermann Behrens, Darlene Loding, and Martha T. Roth. Occasional Publications of the Samuel Noah Kramer Fund 11. Philadelphia: The Samuel Noah Kramer Fund, The University Museum.
1992   *Drehem.* Bethesda, MD: CDL.
1995   *The Administration at Drehem.* Neo-Sumerian Texts from the Royal Ontario Museum 1. Bethesda, MD: CDL Press
Sinopoli, Carla
1994   The Archaeology of Empires. *ARA* 23: 159–80.

Sjöberg, Åke W.

1960   *Der Mondgott Nanna-Suen in der sumerischen Überlieferung.* Stockholm: Almquist & Wiksell.

1967   Zu einigen Verwandtschaftsbezeichnungen im Sumerischen. Pp. 201–32 in *Heidelberger Studien zum Alten Orient: Adam Falkenstein zum (60. Geburtstag) 17. Sept. 1966,* ed. Dietz Otto Edzard. HSAO 1. Wiesbaden: Harrassowitz.

1972   Hymns to Meslamtaea, Lugalgirra and Nanna-Suen in Honour of King Ibbīsuen (Ibbīsîn) of Ur. *Orientalia Suecana* 19–20 (1970–1971): 140–78.

1973a   Der Vater und sein missratener Sohn. *JCS* 25: 105–69.

1973b   Miscellaneous Sumerian Hymns. *ZA* 63: 1–55.

1975a   The Old Babylonian Eduba. Pp. 159–79 in *Sumerological Studies in Honor of Thorkild Jacobsen on His Seventieth Birthday, June 7 1974,* ed. Stephen J. Lieberman. AS 20. Chicago: University of Chicago Press.

1975b   in-nin ša-gur₄-ra: A Hymn to the Goddess Inanna by the en-Priestess Enḫeduanna. *ZA* 65: 161–253.

1977   A Blessing of King Urninurta. Pp. 189–95 in *Essays on the Ancient Near East in Memory of Jacob Joel Finkelstein,* ed. Maria deJong Ellis. Memoirs of the Connecticut Academy of Arts & Sciences 19. Hamden: Archon.

1993a   The Ape from the Mountain Who Became the King of Isin. Pp. 211–20 in *The Tablet and the Scroll: Near Eastern Studies in Honor of William W. Hallo,* ed. Mark. E. Cohen, Daniel C. Snell, and David B. Weisberg. Bethesda, MD: CDL.

1993b   CBS 11319+. An Old Babylonian Schooltext from Nippur. *ZA* 83: 1–21.

1996   UET 7 no. 93. A Lexical Text or a Commentary? *ZA* 86: 220–37.

Sjöberg, Åke W., and Bergmann, E.

1969   *The Collection of the Sumerian Temple Hymns.* TCS 3. Locust Valley, NY: Augustin.

Small, Ian

1999   Identifying Text and Postmodernist Editorial Projects. *The Yearbook of English Studies* 29, *The Text as Evidence: Revising Editorial Principles*: 43–56.

Sollberger, Edmond

1953   Remarks on Ibbīsîn's Reign. *JCS* 7: 48–50.

1954   New Lists of the Kings of Ur and Isin. *JCS* 8: 135–36.

1954–56   Sur la chronologie des rois d'Ur et quelques problèmes connexes. *AfO* 17: 10–48.

1965   A Three-Column Silbenvokabular A. Pp. 21–28 in *Studies in Honor of Benno Landsberger on His Seventy-Fifth Birthday, April 25, 1965.* AS 16. Chicago: The Oriental Institute.

1966   *The Business and Correspondence under the Kings of Ur.* TCS 1. Locust Valley, NY: Augustin.

1968   Two Kassite Votive Inscriptions. *JAOS* 88: 191–97.

1980   Ibbi-Sin. *RLA* 5: 1–8.

Sommerfeld, Walther

1999   *Die Texte der Akkad-Zeit, 1: Das Dijala-Gebiet: Tutub.* IMGULA 3/1. Münster: Rhema.

Sørbø, Gunnar M.

2003   Pastoral Ecosystems and the Issue of Scale. *Ambio* 32: 113–17.

Spooner, Brian

1971   Towards a Generative Model of Nomadism. *Anthropological Quarterly* 44: 198–210.

1986   Review of *Nomads and the Outside World,* by A. M. Khazanov. *American Ethnologist* 13: 183–84.

Starr, Ivan

1983   *The Rituals of the Diviner.* BibMes 12. Malibu: Undena.

Steiner, Peter
  1982   The Semiotics of Literary Reception. Pp. 503–20 in *The Structure of the Literary Process: Studies Dedicated to the Memory of Felix Vodička*, ed. Peter Steiner, Miroslac Červenka, and Ronald Vroon. Amsterdam: Benjamins.
Steinkeller, Piotr
  1980   On the Reading and Location of the Toponyms ÚR×Ú and A.ḪA.KI. JCS 32: 23–33.
  1981   Early History of the Hamrin Basin in the Light of Textual Evidence. Pp. 163–68 in *Uch Tepe 1: Tell Razuk, Tell Ahmed al-Mughir, Tell Ajam*, ed. McGuire Gibson. Chicago: The Oriental Institute and the Institute of Assyriology.
  1981   The Renting of Fields in Early Mesopotamia and the Development of the Concept of "Interest" in Sumerian. JESHO 24: 113–45.
  1981   The Signs ŠEN and ALAL. OrAn 20: 243–49.
  1982a   The Mesopotamian God Kakka. JNES 41: 289–94.
  1982b   On Editing Ur III Economic Texts. JAOS 102: 639–44.
  1986   Seal of Išma-ilum, Son of the Governor of Matar. VO 6: 27–40.
  1987   The Administrative and Economic Organization of the Ur III State: The Core and the Periphery. Pp. 19–41 in *The Organization of Power: Aspects of Bureaucracy in the Ancient Near East*, ed. McGuire Gibson and Robert D. Biggs. SAOC 46. Chicago: Oriental Institute of the University of Chicago.
  1988   On the Identification of the Toponym LÚ.SU(.A). JAOS 108: 197–202.
  1989   *Sale Documents of the Ur III Period.* FAOS 17. Stuttgart: Steiner.
  1991   The Reforms of UruKAgina and an Early Sumerian Term for "Prison." Pp. 227–33 in *Velles Paraules: Ancient Near Eastern Studies in Honor of Miguel Civil on the Occasion of his Sixty-fifth Birthday*, ed. P. Michalowski, et al. Barcelona: Editorial AUSA.
  1993   Early Political Development in Mesopotamia and the Origins of the Sargonic Empire. Pp. 107–29 in *Akkad: The First World Empire: Structure, Ideology, Traditions*, ed. Mario Liverani. HANES 5. Padova: Sargon.
  1995   Sheep and Goat Terminology in Ur III Sources from Drehem. BSA 8: 49–70.
  1998   The Historical Background of Urkeš and the Hurrian Beginnings in Northern Mesopotamia. Pp. 75–98 in *Urkesh and The Hurrians: A Volume in Honor of Lloyd Cotsen*, ed. Giorgio Buccellati and Marilyn Kelly-Buccellati. BibMes 26. Malibu: Undena.
  2001   New Light on the Hydrology and Topography of Southern Babylonian in the Third Millennium. ZA 91: 22–84.
  2003a   An Ur III Manuscript of the Sumerian King List. Pp. 267–92 in *Literatur, Politik und Recht in Mesopotamien: Festschrift für Claus Wilcke*, ed. Walther Sallaberger, Konrad Volk, and Annette Zgoll. OBC 14. Wiesbaden: Harrassowitz.
  2003b   The Question of Lugalzagesi's Origins. Pp. p 621–37 in *Festschrift für Burkhart Kienast zu seinem 70. Geburtstage dargebracht von Freunden, Schülern und Kollegen*, ed. Gebhard J. Selz. AOAT 274. Münster : Ugarit-Verlag.
  2004   A History of Mashkan-shapir and Its Role in the Kingdom of Larsa. Pp. 26–42 in *The Anatomy of a Mesopotamian City: Survey and Soundings at Mashkan-shapir*, ed. Elizabeth C. Stone and Paul Zimansky. Winona Lake, IN: Eisenbrauns.
  2006   New Light on Marhaši and Its Contacts with Makkan and Babylonia. JMS 1: 1–17.
  2007a   New Light on Šimaški and Its Rulers. ZA 97: 215–32.
  2007b   On Sand Dunes, Mountain Ranges, and Mountain Peaks. Pp. 219–32 in *Studies Presented to Robert D. Biggs, June 4, 2004*, ed. Martha T. Roth, et al. Chicago: The Oriental Institute of the University of Chicago.
  2007c   Tiš-atal's Visit to Nippur. N.A.B.U. 2007/1: 14–16.
  2007d   City and Countryside in Third-Millennium Southern Mesopotamia. Pp. 185–211 in *Settlement and Society: Essays Dedicated to Robert McCormick Adams*, ed. Elizabeth C. Stone. Los Angeles: Cotsen Institute of Archaeology.

2008   On Birbirrum, the Alleged Earliest-Documented *rabiānum* Official, and on the End of Ibbi-Suen's reign. *NABU* 2008/1: 3–5.

2010   On the Location of the Towns of Ur-Zababa and Dimat-Enlil and on the Course of the Arahtum. Pp. 369–82 in *Festschrift für Gernot Wilhelm anläßlich seines 64 Geburtstages am 28. Januar 2010*, ed. Jeanette C. Finke. Dresden: ISLET.

forthcoming   The Gutian Period in Chronological Perspective. In *Chronology of the Third Millennium: History and Philology*, ed. Walther Sallaberger and Ingo Schrakamp. Turnout: AR-CANE Publications.

Steve, M.-J, Gasche, H. and de Mayer, L.

1980   La Susiane au deuxiéme millènaire à propos d'une interprétation des fouilles de Suse. *Iranica Antiqua* 15: 49–154.

Stol, Marten

1982   A Cadastral Innovation by Hammurabi. Pp. 351–58 in *Zikir Šumim: Assyriological Studies Presented to F. R. Kraus*, ed. G. van Driel, et al. Leiden: Brill.

1991   Old Babylonian Personal Names. *SEL* 8: 191–212.

1995   Old Babylonian Corvée (*tupšikkum*). Pp. 293–309 in *Ancient Near Eastern Studies Presented to Philo H. J. Houwink ten Cate on the Occasion of His 65th Birthday*, ed. Theo P. J. van den Hout and Johan de Roos. PIHANS 74. Leiden: Nederlands Instituut voor het Nabije Oosten.

2004   Wirtschaft und Gesselschaft in Altbabylonischer Zeit. Pp. 643–975 in *Mesopotamien: Die altbabylonische Zeit*, by Dominique Charpin, D. O. Edzard, and Marten Stol. OBO 160/4. Friburg: Academic Press / Göttingen: Vandenhoeck & Ruprecht.

Stolper, Matthew W.

1982   On the Dynasty of Šimaški and the Early Sukkalmahs. *ZA* 72: 42–67.

Stone, Elizabeth C.

1987   *Nippur Neighborhoods*. SAOC 44. Chicago: The Oriental Institute of the University of Chicago.

2002   The Ur III–Old Babylonian Transition: An Archaeological Perspective. *Iraq* 64: 79–84.

Streck, Michael P.

2000   *Das amurritische Onomastikon der altbabylonischen Zeit*. Münster: Ugarit-Verlag.

Sullivan, Brian Barry

1979   *Sumerian and Akkadian Sentence Structure in Old Babylonian Literary Bilingual Texts*. Ph.D. Dissertation, Hebrew Union College–Jewish Institute of Religion, Cincinnati.

Szuchman, Jeffrey, ed.

2009   *Nomads, Tribes, and the State in the Ancient Near East: Cross-Disciplinary Perspectives*. OIS 3. Chicago: The Oriental Institute of the University of Chicago.

Tainter, Joseph A.

1988   *The Collapse of Complex Societies*. Cambridge: Cambridge University Press.

2006   The Archaeology of Overshoot and Collapse. *ARA* 35: 59–74.

Thureau-Dangin, François

1910   *Lettres et contrats de l'èpoque de la première dynastie babylonienne*. TCL 1. Paris: Geuthner.

Tinney, Steve

1995   On the Poetry for King Išme-Dagan. *OLZ* 90: 5–26.

1996   *The Nippur Lament: Royal Rhetoric and Divine Legitimation in the Reign of Išme-Dagan of Isin (1953–1935 B.C.)*. Occasional Publications of the Samuel Noah Kramer Fund 16. Philadelphia: The Samuel Noah Kramer Fund.

1998   Texts, Tablets, and Teaching: Scribal Education in Nippur and Ur. *Expedition* 40: 40–50.

1999   On the Curricular Setting of Sumerian Literature. *Iraq* 61: 159–72.

Toorn, K. van der

1985   *ARM XIV* 78 (= *TCM I* 78). *RA* 79: 189–90.

1996　　　*Family Religion in Babylonia, Syria, and Israel: Continuity and Change in the Forms of Religious Life.* Leiden: Brill.

Trigger, Bruce G.
1989　　　Review of *The Collapse of Complex Societies*, by Joseph A. Tainter. Cambridge: Cambridge University Press, 1988. *Man* 24: 374–75.

Tynianov, Yuri
1981　　　*The Problem of Verse Language*, ed. and trans. Michael Sosa and Brent Harvey. Ann Arbor, MI: Ardis.

Vallat, François
1993　　　*Les noms géographiques des sources suso-élamites.* RGTC 11. Wiesbaden: Reichert.
1994　　　Succession royale en Elam au IIème millenaire. Pp. 1–14 in *Cinquante-deux réflexions sur le Proche-Orient ancien offertes à Léon De Meyer*, ed. H. Gasche, et al. Mesopotamian History and Environment, Occasional Publications 2. Leuven: Peeters.

Van de Mieroop, Marc
1987　　　*Crafts in the Early Isin Period: Study of the Isin Craft Archive from the Reigns of Ishbi-Erra and Shu-Ilishu.* Leuven: Departement Orientalistiek.
2004　　　*A History of the Ancient Near East, ca. 3000–323 BC.* Malden: Blackwell.
2005　　　*King Hammurabi of Babylon: A Biography.* Oxford: Blackwell.

Vanstiphout, Hermann
1978　　　Lipit-Eštar's Praise in the Edubba. *JCS* 30: 33–61.
1979　　　How Did They Learn Sumerian? *JCS* 31: 118–26.
1983　　　Problems in the "The Matter of Aratta." *Iraq* 45: 35–42.
1985　　　Some Thoughts on Genre in Mesopotamian Literature. Pp. 1–11 in *Keischriftliche Literaturen, XXXII RAI*, ed. K. Hecker and W. Sommerfeld. Berlin: Reimer.
1989　　　Enmerkar's Invention of Writing Revisited. Pp. 515–24 in *DUMU-E_2-DUB-BA-A: Studies in Honor of Åke W. Sjöberg*, ed. Hermann Behrens, Darlene Loding, and Martha T. Roth. Occasional Publications of the Samuel Noah Kramer Fund, 11. The Samuel Noah Kramer Fund.
1989–90　The Man from Elam: A Reconsideration of Ishbi-Erra "Hymn B." *JEOL* 31: 53–62.
2003　　　*Epics of Sumerian Kings: The Matter of Aratta.* SBLWAW 20. Atlanta: Society of Biblical Literature.

Veldhuis, Niek
1996　　　The Cuneiform Tablet as an Educational Tool. *Dutch Studies on Near Eastern Languages and Literature* 2: 11–26.
1997　　　*Elementary Education at Nippur.* Ph.D. Dissertation. University of Groningen.
2000　　　Kassite Exercises: Literary and Lexical Extracts. *JCS* 52: 67–94.
2003　　　Entering the Netherworld. *CDLB* 2003/6: 1–4.

Vincente, Claudine-Adrienne
1995　　　The Tall Leilan Recension of the Sumerian King List. *ZA* 85: 234–70.

Volk, Konrad
1995　　　*Inanna und Šukaletuda: Zur historisch-politischen Literaturwerkes.* SANTAG 3. Wiesbaden: Harrassowitz.
1996　　　Methoden altmesopotamischer Erziehung nach Quellen der altbabylonischen Zeit. *Saeculum* 47: 178–216.
2000　　　Edubba'a und Edubba'a-Literatur: Rätsel und Lösungen. *ZA* 90: 1–30.
2004　　　Altorientalische Tontafel, Keilschrift, ca. 2048 v. Chr. Pp. 29–31 in *Gratianustiftung: Sammlungskatalog 1*. Reutlingen: G. Lachnemaier.

Wagensonner, Klaus
2008　　　Nin-Isina(s)s Journey to Nippur: A Bilingual Divine Journey. *WZKM* 98: 277–94.

Waldron, Arthur
1992　　　*The Great Wall of China: From History to Myth.* Cambridge: Cambridge University Press.

Walker, C. B. F.
  1983   Another Babati Inscription. *JCS* 35: 91–96.
Wall-Romana, Christophe
  1990   An Areal Location of Agade. *JNES* 49: 205–45.
Wasserman, Nathan
  2003   *Style and Form in Old Babylonian Literary Texts.* Cuneiform Monographs 27. Leiden: Styx.
Weeks, Noel
  1985   The Old Babylonian Amorites: Nomads or Mercenaries? *OLP* 16: 49–57.
Weidner, Ernst F.
  1929   Historisches Material in der babylonischen Omina-Literatur. *MAOG* 4: 226–40.
Weiss, Harvey
  2000   Beyond the Younger Dryas: Collapse as Adaptation to Abrupt Climate Change in Ancient
          West Asia and the Eastern Mediterranean. Pp. 75–98 in *Environmental Disaster and the
          Archaeology of Human Response*, ed. Garth Bawden and Richard Martin Reycraft. Maxwell
          Museum of Anthropology, Anthropological Papers, No. 7. Albuquerque: University of
          New Mexico Press.
Westbrook, Raymond
  2005   Patronage in the Ancient Near East. *JESHO* 48: 210–33.
Westenholz, Aage
  1999   The Old Akkadian Period: History and Culture. Pp. 17–117 in *Mesopotamien: Akkade-Zeit
          u. Ur III-Zeit*, ed. Pascal Attinger and Markus Wafler. OBO 160/3. Freiburg: Universitäts-
          verlag / Göttingen: Vandenhoeck & Ruprecht.
Westenholz, Joan Goodnick
  1997   *Legends of the Kings of Akkade.* MC 7. Winona Lake, IN: Eisenbrauns.
  2008   The Memory of Sargonic Kings under the Third Dynasty of Ur. Pp. 251–60 in *On the Third
          Dynasty of Ur: Studies in Honor of Marcel Sigrist*, ed. Piotr Michalowski. JCSSup 1. Boston:
          American Schools of Oriental Research.
Westenholz, Joan Goodnick, and Westenholz, Aage
  2006   *Cuneiform Inscriptions in the Collection of the Bible Lands Museum Jerusalem: The Old Baby-
          lonian Inscriptions.* CM 33. Leiden: Brill.
Whiting, Robert M.
  1976   Tiš-atal of Nineveh and Babati, Uncle of Šu-Sin. *JCS* 28: 173–82.
  1987   *Old Babylonian Letters from Tell Asmar.* AS 22. Chicago: The Oriental Institute of the
          University of Chicago.
  1995   Amorite Tribes and Nations of Second-Millennium Western Asia. Pp. 1231–42 in *Civili-
          zations of the Ancient Near East 2*, ed. Jack Sasson. New York: Scribners.
Widell, Magnus
  2003   *The Administrative and Economic Ur III Texts from the City of Ur.* Piscataway, NJ: Gorgias.
Wilcke, Claus
  1968   Das modale Adverb i-gi₄-in-zu-in-zu im Sumerischen. *JNES* 27: 229–42.
  1969a   *Das Lugalbandaepos.* Wiesbaden: Harrassowitz.
  1969b   Zur Geschichte der Amurriter in der Ur-III Zeit. *WO* 5: 1–33.
  1970   Drei Phasen des Niedergangs des Reiches von Ur III. *ZA* 60: 54–69.
  1974–77 Die Keilschrift-Texte der Sammlung Böllinger. *AfO* 25: 84–94.
  1976   *Kollationen zu den sumerischen literarischen Texten aus Nippur in der Hilprecht-Sammlung Jena.*
          Berlin: Akademie Verlag.
  1988   Anmerkungen zum 'Konjugationspräfix' /i/- und zur These vom "silbischen Charakter der
          sumerischen Morpheme" anhand neusumerischer Verbalformen beginnend mit ì-íb-, ì-im-
          und ì-in-. *ZA* 78: 1–49.
  1990   Zur Rekonstruktion der Šū-Sîn Inschriften-Sammlung B. N.A.B.U. 1990/33: 25–26.
  1991   Die Lesung vos ÁŠ-da = kiššātum. *N.A.B.U.* 1991: 16.

1993   Politik im Spiegel der Literatur, Literatur als Mittel der Politik im älteren Babylonien. Pp. 29–75 in *Anfänge des politischen Denkens in der Antike*, ed. Kurt Raaflaub. Schriften des Historischen Kollegs, Kolloquien 24. Munich: Oldenburg.

1998   Zu "Gilgamesh und Akka." Überlegungen zur Zeit von Entstehung und Niedershrift, wie auch zum Text des Epos mit einem Exkurs zur Überliefung von "Šulgi A" und "Lugalbanda II." Pp. 457–85 in *dubsar anta-men: Studien zur Altorientalistik: Festschrift für Willem H. Ph. Römer zur Vollendung seines 70. Lebensjahres mit Beiträgen von Freunden, Schülern und Kollegen*, ed. Manfred Dietrich and Oswald Loretz. AOAT 253. Münster: Ugarit-Verlag.

1999   Flurschäden, verursacht durch Hochwasser, Unwetter, Militär, Tiere und schuldhaftes Verhalten zur Zeit der 3. Dynastie von Ur. Pp. 301–39 in *Landwirtschaft im Alten Orient. Ausgewählte Vorträge der XLI. Rencontre Assyriologique Internationale Berlin, 4.—8. 7. 1994*, ed. H. Klengel and J. Renger. Berliner Beiträge zum Vorderen Orient 18. Berlin: Reimer.

2000   *Wer las und schrieb in Babylonien und Assyrie. Überlegungen zur Literalität im Alten Zweistromland.* Sitzungsberichte der Bayerischen Akademie der Wissenschaften, Philosophisch-Historische Klasse Jahrgang 2000, Heft 6. Munich: Bayerische Akademie der Wissenschaften.

2002   Der Kodex Urnamma (CU): Versuch einer Rekonstruktion. Pp. 291–333 in *Riches Hidden in Secret Places: Ancient Near Eastern Studies in Memory of Thorkild Jacobsen*, ed. T. Abusch. Winona Lake, IN: Eisenbrauns.

2007   *Early Ancient Near Eastern Law: A History of Its Beginnings. The Early Dynastic and Sargonic Periods.* 2nd ed. Winona Lake, IN: Eisenbrauns.

Wilson, Mark

2008   *Education in the Earliest Schools: Cuneiform Manuscripts in the Cotsen Collection.* Los Angeles: Cotsen Occasional Press.

Wiseman, D. J., and Black, J. A.

1996   *Literary Texts from the Temple of Nabû.* Cuneiform Texts from Nimrud, 4. London: British School of Archaeology in Iraq.

Woods, Christopher

2003   The Element -re and the Organization of Erim-ḫuš. Paper presented at the 213th annual meeting of the American Oriental Society, April 4th, 2003 in Nashville, TN.

2005   On the Euphrates. ZA 95: 7–45.

2006   Bilingualism, Scribal Learning, and the Death of Sumerian. Pp. 91–120 in *Margins of Writing, Origins of Culture: New Approaches to Writing and Reading in the Ancient Near East. Papers from the Symposium Held February 25–26, 2005*, ed. Seth Sanders. OIS 2. Chicago: The Oriental Institute of the University of Chicago.

Wu, Yuhong

1994   *A Political History of Eshnunna, Mari and Assyria during the Early Old Babylonian Period (From the End of Ur III to the Death of Šamši-Adad).* Changchun: Institute of History of Ancient Civilizations, Northeast Normal University.

1998a   Review of Lamia al-Gailani Werr, *Old Babylonian Cylinder Seals from the Hamrin.* JAOS 118: 577–8.

1998b   Review of Ahmad Kamel Muhamed, *Old Babylonian Cuneiform Texts from the Hamrin Basin: Tell Hadad.* JAOS 118: 578–80.

Yıldız, Fatma, and Gomi, Tohru

1988   *Die Puzriš-Dagan Texte der Istanbuler Archäologischen Museen, Teil 2, Nr. 726–1379.* FAOS 16. Stuttgart: Steiner.

Yoffee, Norman

1977   *The Economic Role of the Crown in the Old Babylonian Period.* Malibu: Undena.

1978   On Studying Old Babylonian History: A Review Article. JCS 30: 18–32.

1988   Context and Authority in Early Mesopotamian Law. Pp. 95–114 in *State Formation and Political Legitimacy*, ed. Ronald Cohen and Judith Drick Toland. Edison, NJ: Transaction.

1995   Political Economy in Early Mesopotamian States. ARA 24: 281–311.

2005   *Myths of the Archaic State.* Cambridge: Cambridge University Press.

2010   Collapse in Ancient Mesopotamia: What Happened, What Didn't. Pp. 176–203 in *Questioning Collapse: Human Resilience, Ecological Vulnerability, and the Aftermath of Empire*, ed. Patricia A. McAnany and Norman Yoffee. Cambridge: Cambridge University Press.

Yoffee, Norman, and Cowgill, George L., eds.

1988   *The Collapse of Ancient States and Civilizations.* Tucson: University of Arizona Press.

Zadok, Rsn

2006   The Geography of the Borsippa Region. Pp. 389–454 in *Essays on Ancient Israel in Its Near Eastern Context: A Tribute to Nadav Na'aman*, ed. Yairah Amit, et al. Winona Lake, IN: Eisenbrauns.

Zarins, Juris

2008   Magan Shipbuilders at the Ur III Lagash State Dockyards. Pp. 209–29 in *Intercultural Relations between South and Southwest Asia: Studies in Commemoration of E.C.L. During Caspers (1934–1996)*, ed. Eric Olijdam and Richard H. Spoor. Society for Arabian Studies Monographs 7. BAR International Series 1826. Oxford: Archaeopress.

Zettler, Richard L.

1984   The Genealogy of the House of Ur-Meme: A Second Look. *AfO* 31: 1–9.

1992   *The Ur III Temple of Inanna at Nippur: The Operation and Organization of Urban Religious Institutions in Mesopotamia in the Late Third Millennium B.C.* Berlin: Reimer.

2006   Tišatal and Nineveh at the End of the 3rd Millennium BCE. Pp. 503–14 in *If a Man Builds a Joyful House: Assyriological Studies in Honor of Erle Verdun Leichty*, ed. Ann K. Guinan et al. Leiden: Brill.

Zhi, Yang

1989   *Sargonic Inscriptions from Adab.* Changchun: Institute for the Study of Ancient Civilizations, Northeast Normal University..

List of
Sumerian Literary Texts Cited

Amurrum Hymn A	Falkenstein 1959: 120–40
An Axe for Nergal (SEpM 10)	Behrens 1988, Kleinerman 2011
Announcement of a Lost Seal (SEpM 14)	Kleinerman 2011
Code of Ur-Namma	mss. M. Civil
Curse of Agade	Cooper 1983
Enki and Ninhursanga	Attinger 1984
Enki and the World Order	mss. J.S. Cooper
Enki's Journey to Nippur	Al-Fouadi 1969
Enlil-bani Hymn A	Kapp 1955, mss. S. Tinney
Enmerkar and Ensuhgirana	Berlin 1979
Enmerkar and the Lord of Aratta	Mittermayer 2009
Eridu Lament	Green 1978
Farmer's Instructions	Civil 1994
Father and Son	Sjöberg 1973a
Flood Story	Civil 1969
Gilgameš and Aga	Römer 1980, Katz 1993
Gilgameš and Huwawa A	Edzard 1990
Gilgameš, Enkidu, and the Netherworld	Gadotti 2005
Gudea Cyl. A & B	Edzard 1997: 68–101
Gudea St. B	Edzard 1997: 30–8
Iddin-Dagan Hymn B	Römer 1965: 209–35
Išbi-Erra Hymn A	Sjöberg 1993a
Išbi-Erra Hymn B	van Dijk 1978
Išme-Dagan Hymn A + V	Ludwig 1990: 161–225
Inana and Ebih	Attinger 1998, Mss. B. Eichler
Inana and Šukaletuda	Volk 1995
Ininšagura	Sjöberg 1975b
Instructions of Šuruppak	Alster 2005: 56–102
Lamentation Over the Destruction of Sumer and Ur	Michalowski 1989
Letter of Etel-pi-Damu to Amurrum	Hallo 1998: 405–9
Letter of Gudea to his God	Kleinerman 2011
Letter of Iddatum to Sumutara	Kleinerman 2011
Letter of Iddin-Dagan to Sin-illati (SEpM 3)	Kleinerman 2011
Letter of Inim-Enlila	UET 6/2 173 i 5–14; ii
Letter of Inim-Inina to Lugal-ibila (SEpM 22)	Kleinerman 2011
Letter of Ininka to Nintinuga (SEpM 19)	Kleinerman 2011
Letter of Lipit-Eštar to Nanna-kiağa (SEpM 5)	Kleinerman 2011

Letter of Monkey to Mother(SEpM 16)	Kleinerman 2011
Letter of Nanna-ki'aǧa to Lipit-Eštar (SEpM 4)	Kleinerman 2011
Letter of Ninšatapada to Rim-Sin	Brisch 2007: 245–61
Letter of Sin-iddinam to Nininsina	Brisch 2007: 142–56
Letter of Sin-iddinam to Utu	Brisch 2007: 158–78
Letter of Sin-šamuḫ to Enki	Hallo 1968: 82–88
Letter of Sin-tillati to Iddin-Dagan (SEpM 2)	Kleinerman 2011
Letter of Šamaš-ṭab to Ilad-ni'id (SEpM 17)	Kleinerman 2011
Letter of Ursaga to a King (SEpM 6)	Kleinerman 2011
Letter to the Generals (SEpM 11)	Kleinerman 2011
Letter to Zimri-Lim	Charpin 1992, mss. P. Michalowski
Lipit-Eštar Hymn A	Vanstiphout 1978
Lugalanemundu Inscription	Güterbock 1934: 40–47; mss. P. Michalowski
Lugalbanda II	Wilcke 1969
Lugale	van Dijk 1983
Marriage of Amurrum	Klein 1996
Message of Ludiǧira	Çığ and Kramer 1976, mss. P. Michalowski
Nidaba Hymn C	mss. P. Michalowski
Ningišzida Hymn A	van Dijk 1960: 81–107
Nippur Lament	Tinney 1996
Rim-Sin Hymn B	Brisch 2007: 186–98
Rim-Sin Hymn E	Brisch 2007: 212–26
Sargon and Ur-Zababa	Heimpel and Cooper 1983, Attinger 2010
Schooldays	Kramer 1949, Edzard 2004: 531–9
Sheep and Grain	Alster and Vanstiphout 1987
SP Coll. 2	Alster 1997: 40–75
SP Coll. 5	Alster 1997: 119–43
SP Coll 13	Alster 1997: 206–15
Sumerian King List	Jacobsen 1939
Summer and Winter	mss. M. Civil
Supervisor and Scribe	mss. M. Civil
Šulgi Hymn A	Klein 1981: 182–217, Edzard 2004: 500–9
Šulgi Hymn B	Castellino 1972: 27–242, mss. G. Haayer
Šulgi Hymn C	Castellino 1972: 247–94
Šulgi Hymn D	Klein 1981: 70–123
Šulgi Hymn G	Klein 1991
Šu-Sin Hymn B	Sefati 1985: 400–6
Tale of the Three Ox-drivers of Adab	Alster 2005: 377–81
Tree and Reed	mss. M. Civil
Tumal Inscription (SEpM 9)	Kleinerman 2011
Two Scribes	mss. M. Civil
Ur Lament	Samet 2009
Ur-Namma Hymn A	Flückiger-Hawker 1999
Ur-Namma Hymn B	Flückiger-Hawker 1999
Ur-Namma Hymn C	Flückiger-Hawker 1999
Ur-Ninurta Hymn A	Sjöberg 1977
Uruk Lament	Green 1984

List of CKU Tablets

Tablet	Place	Type	Comp	Sigla
3 N-T 306 (A 30207)	Nippur	III	21	N1
3 N-T 309 (A 30231) (*SL* liii)	Nippur	III	4	N2
3 N-T 311 (IM 58418) (*SL* xxii–xxiii, *Sumer* 26 171–72)	Nippur	I (M)	1, 2, 23	N1(1), N1(2), N1(23)
3 N-T 8 (IM 58335) (*SL* xxxvii)	Nippur	III	4	N1
3 N-T 80 (30135) (*SL* xxxi)	Nippur	III	7	N1
3 N-T 900,25 (*SLF* 21)	Nippur	III	1	N2
3 N-T 903,102 (*SL* xxxiv, *Sumer* 26 176)	Nippur	III	2	N2
3 N-T 918,440 (*SLF* 22) + 3 NT 919,486 (*Sumer* 26 174)	Nippur	III	1	N3
3 N-T 919,459 (*Sumer* 26 178; *SLF* 22)	Nippur	III	23	N2
3 N-T 927,516 (*SLF* 21 and *Sumer* 26 174)	Nippur	III	1	N4
A 7475	X (Sippar?)	I (M)	21, 22, 23, 24	X1 (21), X1 (22), X1(23), X1(24)
A w/n	X	I (M)	1, 2, 3, 13, 14	X1(1), X1 (2), X1(3), X1(13), X1, X3(14)
AO 10630 (*PRAK* II C10)	Kish	III	24	Ki1
AO 10819 (*PRAK* II D60)	Kish	III	13	Ki1
AN1922-163 (*OECT* 5 26)	X	III	6	X1
AN1922-165 (*OECT* 5 27)	X	III	22	X2
AN1922-167 (*OECT* 5 29)	X	III	21	X2
AN1930-581 (*OECT* 5 28)	X ("Warka"?)	III	21	X3
BM 108869	X (Sippar?)	III	3	X2
BM 108870	X (Sippar?)	III	14	X2
BM 16897+22617	X (Sippar?)	III	1	X3

Tablet	Place	Type	Comp	Sigla
BM 54327	X (Sippar?)	I	1, 2, 13, 19, 23	X2(1), X2(2), X2(13), X1(19), X2(23)
BM 54894	X (Sippar?)	I	13	X2
CBS 10069	Nippur	III	4	N10
CBS 14224 (*PBS* 13 3)	Nippur	III	24	N2
CBS 14230 (*PBS* 13 6) + N2964 + N 3003	Nippur	III	24	N3
CBS 2272 (*PBS* 13 9)	Nippur	III	21	N2
CBS 346 (*PBS* 10/4 8)	Sippar?	III	9	Si1
CBS 6513 + N 3096 (*SL* xxxiii, *Sumer* 26 177)	Nippur	III	2	N3
CBS 6895 + 6896 + 6906+ 7663	Nippur	III	23	N3
CBS 6987+N 3603+N 4154+Ni. 9463 (*ISET* 1 228[170)	Nippur	III?	23	N4
CBS 7096	Nippur	III?	1	N5
CBS 7772 (*MBI* 9)	Nippur	III	24	N1
CBS 7787 +	Nippur	I (M)	3, 23, 24	N1(3), N5(23), N4(24)
CBS 7848+7856 (*SL* xxxviii)	Nippur	I (P)	5, 7	N1(5), N2(7)
CBS 8007 (*STVC* 110) +Ni. 4592 (*ISET* 2 21)	Nippur	III	4	N3
CBS 8385 + N 3290	Nippur	III	3	N2
CBS 8875 (*Sumer* 26 175) + N 6672	Nippur	III	1	N6
Cornell 63	X	III	23	X4
Cotsen 40832 (Wilson, *Education* 159 [p. 251])	X	III	4	X3
Cotsen 521157 (Wilson, *Education* 158 [p. 250])	X	III	1	X8
Crozer 206	X	I	4	X1
HMA 9-1815 (*JCS* 28 102)	X ("Tutub")	III	1	X6
HMA 9-1820 (*JCS* 28 103)	X ("Tutub")	III	2	X4
HS 1438 (*TMHnf* 4 42)	Nippur	III	13	N1
HS 1456 (*TMHnf* 4 43)	Nippur	III	4	N4
HS 2394	Nippur	III	23	N9
IM 13347 (*TIM* 9 38)	X	III	23	X3
IM 13712 (*Sumer* 15 pl. 6; *TIM* 9 39)	X	III	10	X1
IM 44134 (*Sumer* 15 pl. 6; *TIM* 9 40)	X	III	21	X4
IM 78644 (*IB* 733)	Isin	III	17	Is1
LB 2543 (*TLB* 3 172)	X	oval	1, 2	X4(1), X3(2)

Tablet	Place	Type	Comp	Sigla
MDP 18 51	Susa	IV	4	Su1
MDP 27 207	Susa	IV	4	Su2
MDP 27 212	Susa	IV	23	Su1
MDP 27 87	Susa	IV	2	Su1
MDP 27 88	Susa	IV	2	Su2
MM 1039	X ("Babylon"?)	III	21	X2
MS 2199/1	X	III	1a	X1 [Z(1), Z(2)]
MS 2199/2	X	III	8	X1
MS 3275	X	III	1	X5
N 1447 (*SL* xxiv, *Sumer* 26 176) + N 3102	Nippur	III	23	N8
N 1555	Nippur	III	4	N8
N 2884	Nippur	III	3	N3
N 2901	Nippur	III	16	Ni1
N 3264 + 3266 + 3294 + 3301 + 3303 + 3308 + 3310 +Ni. 9701 (*ISET* 2 114) + UM 29-16-139 (*SL* xxiv-xxv)	Nippur	I	4	N6
N 3461	Nippur	III	4	N9
N 3773	Nippur	III	13	N4
Ni. 13180 (*ISET* 2 117)	Nippur	III?	23	N7
Ni. 2191 (*ISET* 1 64[122] = BE 31 54)	Nippur	III	3	N4
Ni. 2317 (*SLTN* 126)	Nippur	III	2	N4
Ni. 2723 (*SLTN* 136)	Nippur	III	2	N5
Ni. 2786 (*ISET* 2 120)	Nippur	III	7	N4
Ni. 3045 + 3093 + 4489 (*ISET* 2 121)	Nippur	III	21	N3
Ni. 3083 (*ISET* 2 115)	X	I (M)	13, 14,16, 17, 18, 23	X3(13), X4(14), X1(16), X1(17), X1(18), X5(21)
Ni. 4149 (*ISET* 2 122)	Nippur	I (M)	1, 2	N7(1), N6(2)
Ni. 4164 (*ISET* 2 117)	Nippur	I (M)	20	N1
Ni. 4165 (*ISET* 1 136[78])	Nippur	III?	23	N6
Ni. 4389 (*ISET* 1 144[86])	Nippur	III?	2	N7
Ni. 4490 (*ISET* 2 122)	Nippur	III	1	N8
Ni. 4586	Nippur	III	7	N4
Ni. 9702 (*ISET* 2 122)	Nippur	I (P)	6, 7	N1(6), N5(7)
Ni. 9703 (*ISET* 2 122)	Nippur	I (P)	5	N1
Ni. 9706 (*ISET* 2 112)	Nippur	I (M)	1, 2, 3, 13	N9(1), N8(2), N5(3), N2(13)
Ni. 9709 (*ISET* 1 180[122])	Nippur	III	2	N9

Tablet	Place	Type	Comp	Sigla
Ni. 9711 (*ISET* 1 63[121])	Nippur	III	3	N6
Ni. 9854 (*ISET* 1 189[131])	Nippur	I	2, 13	N10(2), N3(13)
Ni. 9866 (*ISET* 1 133[191])	Nippur	III	3	N7
NYPL 334	X	X	23	X5
Relph 16	X	III	16	X2
Si. 420 (*USFS* 134)	Sippar	IV	3	Si1
Si. 524	Sippar	III	23	Si1
Si. 557	Sippar	III	24	Si1
Susa A XX/1 1962/3 (*MDAI* 57 1)	Susa	I (M)	14, 15	Su1A&B (14), Su1(15)
U. 16853 (*UET* 6/2 174) + *UET* 6/3 557 (*532)	Ur	I (M)	1, 2, 23	Ur1(1), Ur1(2), Ur1(23)
U. 16857 (*UET* 6/2 178)	Ur	III	4	Ur2
U. 16885 (*UET* 6/2 183)	Ur	III	18	Ur1
U. 16894B (*UET* 6/2 179)	Ur	III	4	Ur3
U. 17900v (*UET* 6/2 181)	Ur	III	2	Ur2
U. 7741 (*UET* 6 173)	Ur	I	4	Ur1
UET 6/3 558 (*264)	Ur	III	23	Ur2
UET 6/3 561 (*187)	Ur	III	(11?), 12	(Ur1[11]?), Ur1(12)
UM 29-13-20 + 29-13-24 (both *SL* liii)	Nippur	I (M)	4	N5
UM 29-13-330 (*Sumer* 26 176)	Nippur	III	2	N11
UM 29-15-535	Nippur	III	4	N7
UM 29-15-555 (*SL* xxxvii, *Sumer* 26 177)	Nippur	III	1	N10
W 16743 gb (Cavigneaux, *Uruk* 143)	Uruk	I (M)	1	Uk1
YBC 4185	X	III	2	X5
YBC 4596	X	III	1, 2	X7(1), X6(2)
YBC 4606	X	III	13	X4
YBC 4654	X	III	13	X5
YBC 4672	X	III	18	X2
YBC 5011	X	III	11	Ur1
YBC 6458	X	III	4	X2
YBC 7149	X	I (M)	18, 19	X3(18), X2(19)

List of Joined Elements

BM 22617; see BM 16897
CBS 6896; see CBS 6895
CBS 6906; see CBS 6895
CBS 7663; see CBS 6895
CBS 7856; see CBS 7848
N 2964; see CBS 14230
N 3003; see CBS 14230
N 3096; see CBS 6513
N 3102; see N 1447
N 3266; see N 3264
N 3290; see CBS 8385
N 3294; see N 3264
N 3301; see N 3264
N 3303; see N 3264
N 3308; see N 3264
N 3310; see N 3264
N 3603; see CBS 6987
N 4154; see CBS 6987
N 6672; see CBS 8875
N1200; see CBS 7787

N1203; see CBS 7787
N1204; see CBS 7787
N1208; see CBS 7787
N1210-27a; see CBS 7787
N1210-27b; see CBS 7787
N1210-27d; see CBS 7787
N1210-27e; see CBS 7787
N1212; see CBS 7787
N1214; see CBS 7787
N1218; see CBS 7787
Ni. 3093; see Ni. 3045
Ni. 4061; see CBS 7787
Ni. 4188; see CBS 7787
Ni. 4489; see Ni. 3045
Ni. 4592; see CBS 8007
Ni. 9463; see CBS 6987
Ni. 9701; see N 3264
UET 6/3 557; see U. 16853
UM 29-13-24; see UM 29-13-20
UM 29-16-139; see N 3264

Index of Passages Cited
from Sumerian Literary Texts
and Royal Inscriptions

In the following indexes, the references are either to the commentaries on individual letters in Part 2 or to page numbers of Part 1.

Indexes to the Text Editions

In the following indexes the first number refers to the composition, the second to the line number in the commentary or in the text itself.

Index of Words Discussed

Sumerian

7200	13:27	bala	3:5′
á . . . áĝ	18:3–7	bar inim-ma	7:4
á-áĝ-ĝá	2:31, 14:39	barag	1:18
a-ba-àm lugal-ĝu₁₀	21:47	bir-bir(. . . dug₄)	24:A17 = B22
á-bàd	14:12	buranuna	23:7/23
a bal	3:18–19	dab₅	3:9&12, 15:17–18,
a ĝar	3:8 & 15	21:12	
á-bi-šè gin	3:9′	daĝal	14:4
á . . . dar	11:18	/dana/ (dan₂/₃/₄/₆)	4:20
á-diri	24:B40	dana	18:11
á . . . ĝá-ĝá	18:19	de₅-(g)	21:6
á . . . ĝar	18:19	di₄-di₄	23:24
á-gàr	3:8/15	dím-ma dab₅	13:30
á-ĝi₆-ba	3:9′	dím-ma ma-da kúr	18:24–25
a-ma-ru-kam	15:15	diri u₄-bi-da-šè/ka	24:A27 = B46
a-na-aš-àm	2:5	d/ri(g)	21:6
á u₄-da	1:8	dugud(-)RI	6:5
a-ša-an-gàr-ra	16:10	duh	18:31, 21:12
á-še	1:8	dù-luh	14:8
á šub	14:27	du₁₁-ga-du₁₁-ga dab₅	24:A18 = B23
ad-gi₄-gi₄	15:9	du₁₀-ud-ak	24:A27 = B47
àga-ús saĝ-ĝá	1:21	⁽ᵍⁱˢ⁾dupsik	13:27, 18:16
agrig šu-dim₄-ma	3:10′	dúr . . . ĝar	1:11
alal	1:35	dúr(. . .)zi	1:11
al-me-a	3:11′	dusu	13:27
an-ga-àm	2:5	e₁₁/è(d)	21:17
a-rá zu	1:5	é-gal	1:9
ba-al	19:38	é kaskal-(la)	1:14
bal	14:36–37	eme₅-gal	12:17

525

Akkadian (cited without mimation)

rabi sikkatu/i	8:5	*šubtu*	19:12
sakāpu	24:A34 = B56	*šudmuqu*	15:5
samūrtu	21:14	*šutlumu*	15:5
sīrum	24:B39	*tēkīta rašû*	14:32
ṣidītu	14:31	*tērtum*	24:B39
šaḫluqtu	21:40	*tījatu*	24:A15=B20
šēpa parāsu	9:6	*uddû*	15:7, 15:25
šertu	5:5, 8	*zamirītu*	21:14
šīru šalmu	24:B39		

Index of Personal Names

s = sender
s= recipient
v = variant

Aba-indasa
  s: 4
  5:3, 6:3, 7:3, 7:7, 8: 14 (a-ba-an-da-sá), 9:11

Amar-Sin, future ruler of Ur
  s: 16
  r: 17

Apilaša, prefect
  1:6, 1a:11, 2:14, 3B: 14′, 8:14, 11:8

Aradmu, (grand vizier)
  r: 2, 5, 6
  s: 1, 1a, 3, 7, 8, 9, 10, 12′
  11:12, 14 1a: 6′, 14 MB1:37

Babati, high commissioner
  11:12, 15:8, 19:35

Girbubu, governor/ruler of Girkal
  23:45, 24A:11, 24B:15

Ibbi-Sin, king of Ur
  r: 22, 24
  s: 21, 23
  21:43

Iddi of Malgium
  23:44 (v: Iddiluma [X1])

Išbi-Erra, in royal service/king of Isin
  r: 15, 22
  s: 21
  23:4, 24A:8, 24A:10, 24A:17, 24A:21, 24B12,
      24B:14, 24B30

Kakugani, governor of the inland territory
  13:19 (v. Šu-Numušda [X1])

Kunši-matum
  9:10 (Sum.: Kurgamabi)

Kurgamabi
  9:10 (Akk.: Kunši-matum)

Lugal-melam, the overseer of the
      Šeššektum canal
  13:17

Lu-Nanna, governor of Zimudar
  r: 20
  14 OB1a:20, 14 OB1a: 4′, 14 OB1b: 19, 14
      MB1:29, MB1:35, 18:27 (v. Lu-Enki [X3]),
      119:31 (written ᵈen-ki [X2])

Niĝdugani, temple administrator of Nippur
  23:33

Nur-aḫi (=Nur-aḫum), governor of Ešnunna
  22A:18′(written ᴵnu-úr-é-a), 23:36 (v: Nur-Ea
      [Si1, X1])

Puzur-Numušda 1, governor of Kazallu
  r: 24 (v Puzur-Šulgi [X1])
  s: 23 (v Puzur-Šulgi [Ur1, Ur2, X1])
  22B:14

Puzur-Numušda 2, governor of Ullum-ṣeḫrum
  13:15(v: Šu-Marduk [Ki1], Šu-Nunu [X1])

Puzur-Šulgi, general of Bad-Igihursaĝa
  r: 14 (v: Puzur-Numušda [N4], Puzur-Marduk
      [Ki1])
  s: 13

Puzur-Tutu, governor/ruler of Bad-ziaba
  22A:19′, 23:38

Šarrum-bani, prefect
  r: 19, 20?
  s: 18

Šu-Enlil, governor/ruler of Kish
  22A:17′, 23:37

Šulgi, king of Ur
  r: 1, 1a, 3, 4, 7, 8, 9, 10, 11, 12?, 13, 15, 16
  s: 2, 5, 6, 14, 17
  3:8′, 4:28, 13:32, 19:28, 19:30

Šulgi-x-x-x
  8:18

Šu-Sin, king of Ur
  r: 18
  s: 19 (written ᵈšu), 20?

Takil-ilišu, Canal Inspector of the Abgal and
     Me-Enlila Waterways
     19:21
Ur-dun, commerscial agent
     s: 11
     12:8, 12:9, 12:14, 12:19

Ur-Namma, king of Ur
     6:10
Zinnum
     23:34

Index of Geographical Names

Includes cities, territories, "peoples," constructions, as well as watercourses.

A'aba Magana
     23:9
Abgal
     13:21, 14 1b:5, 18:9, 23:7, 23:43
Amurrum
     9:9, 14 1b:4, 15:20, 18:13, 21:7, 21:9, 21:11,
          22A:8', 22A:12', 22B:15, 24:33
Bad-Igihursağa
     22A:11', 22B:14
Bad-ziaba (Borsippa?)
     22A:19', 23:38
Buranun
     10:8, 14 1a:5, 18:6, 23:7, 23:43
Ebih
     18:15
Ekišnuğal
     21:39, 23:23
Ekur
     23:22
Elam
     15:20, 21:23, 21:40, 24:34
Ešnunna
     22A:18'., 23:36
Girkal
     23:45, 24:11
Gutium
     10:5'
Hamazi
     23:9, 23:35
Hursağ
     16:9
Idigna
     10:8, 10:9, 14 1a:5, 18:6, 23:7, 23:43
Idil-pašunu
     23:31

Isin
     21:3, 21:29, 22A:24', 23:11, 23:18, 23:27, 23:30
Kish
     22A:17', 23:37
Kazallu
     21:3, 23:2, 23:16, 24:1, 24:5
Mada murub
     13:19, 18:21
Malgium
     23:44
Mari
     10:6', 24:21, 24:32
Me-Enlila
     13:21, 23:7, 23:43
Muriq-Tidnim
     18:3
Nippur
     21:29, 22A:24', 23:32, 23:33
Rapiqum
     10:6'
Simurru
     18:14
Subir
     1:3, 1a:3, 23:34
Sudalunutum
     13:28
Šegšeg (Šeššektum canal)
     13:17
Ullum-seḫrum
     13:15
Ur
     21:35, 21:46, 21:35, 22B:7, 24:20
Zimudar
     7:5, 11:13, 14 1a:19, 14 MB:29, 14 MB:35, 18:9,
          19:31